Introduction to Management 13E

International Student Version

John R. Schermerhorn, Jr.
Ohio University

Daniel G. Bachrach
University of Alabama

WILEY

Founded in 1807, John Wiley & Sons, Inc. has been a valued source of knowledge and understanding for more than 200 years, helping people around the world meet their needs and fulfill their aspirations. Our company is built on a foundation of principles that include responsibility to the communities we serve and where we live and work. In 2008, we launched a Corporate Citizenship Initiative, a global effort to address the environmental, social, economic, and ethical challenges we face in our business. Among the issues we are addressing are carbon impact, paper specifications and procurement, ethical conduct within our business and among our vendors, and community and charitable support. For more information, please visit our website: www.wiley.com/go/citizenship.

ISBN: 978-1-118-95118-7

Printed in Asia

10 9 8 7 6 5 4 3 2 1

ABOUT THE AUTHORS

Ohio University named Dr. Schermerhorn a University Professor, the university's highest campus-wide honor for excellence in undergraduate teaching.

Dr. John R. Schermerhorn, Jr., is the Charles G. O'Bleness Professor of Management Emeritus in the College of Business at Ohio University, where he teaches graduate courses in management and organizational behavior. Dr. Schermerhorn earned a PhD in organizational behavior from Northwestern University, an MBA (with distinction) in management and international business from New York University, and a BS in business administration from the State University of New York at Buffalo. He previously taught at Tulane University, the University of Vermont, and Southern Illinois University at Carbondale, where he also served as head of the Department of Management and associate dean of the College of Business Administration.

International experience adds a unique global dimension to Dr. Schermerhorn's teaching and writing. He holds an honorary doctorate from the University of Pécs in Hungary. He was a visiting professor of management at the Chinese University of Hong Kong, on-site coordinator of the Ohio University MBA and Executive MBA programs in Malaysia, and Kohei Miura visiting professor at Chubu University in Japan. He has served as adjunct professor at the National University of Ireland at Galway and advisor to the Lao-American College in Vientiane, Laos. He presently teaches an MBA course at Università Politecnica Delle Marche in Ancona, Italy, and PhD seminars in the Knowledge and Innovation Management doctoral program at Bangkok University, Thailand. At Ohio University, he has twice been Director of the Center for Southeast Asian Studies.

A member of the Academy of Management, Dr. Schermerhorn was chairperson of the Management Education and Development Division. Management educators and students alike know him as author of *Exploring Management* 4e (Wiley, 2014), *Management* 12e (Wiley, 2013), and co-author of *Organizational Behavior* 13e (Wiley, 2014). Dr. Schermerhorn has also published numerous articles, including ones in the *Academy of Management Journal, Academy of Management Review, Academy of Management Executive, Organizational Dynamics, Asia-Pacific Journal of Management,* the *Journal of Management Development,* and the *Journal of Management Education.*

Ohio University named Dr. Schermerhorn a University Professor, the university's highest campus-wide honor for excellence in undergraduate teaching. He is a popular guest speaker at colleges and universities. He is available for student lectures and classroom visits, as well as for faculty workshops on scholarly manuscript development, textbook writing, high engagement teaching, and instructional and curriculum innovations.

Dr. Bachrach serves on the editorial boards of the *Journal of Applied Psychology* and *Organizational Behavior and Human Decision Processes.*

Dr. Daniel G. Bachrach (Dan) is the Robert C. and Rosa P. Morrow Faculty Excellence Fellow and Professor of Management in the Culverhouse College of Commerce and Business Administration at the University of Alabama, where he teaches graduate and undergraduate courses in management. Dr. Bachrach earned a PhD in organizational behavior and human resource management—with a minor emphasis in strategic management—from Indiana University's Kelley School of Business, an MS in industrial/organizational psychology from the University of Wisconsin-Oshkosh, and a BA in psychology from Bates College in Lewiston, Maine.

A member of the Academy of Management and the Society for Industrial and Organizational Psychology, Dr. Bachrach serves on the editorial boards of the *Journal of Applied Psychology and Organizational Behavior and Human Decision Processes.* He is co-editor of the *Handbook of Behavioral Operations Management: Social and Psychological Dynamics in Production and Service Settings* (Oxford University Press, 2014), co-author of *Transformative Selling: Becoming a Resource Manager and a Knowledge Broker* (Axcess Capon, 2014), and senior co-author of *10 Don'ts on your Digital Devices: The Non-Techie's Survival Guide to Digital Security and Privacy* (Apress, 2014). Dr. Bachrach also has published extensively in a number of academic journals including *Organization Science, Journal of Applied Psychology, Strategic Management Journal, Organizational Behavior and Human Decision Processes, Personnel Psychology, Journal of Management, Leadership Quarterly, Production and Operations Management, Journal of Operations Management, Journal of Supply Chain Management,* and *the Journal of Personal Selling and Sales Management.*

PREFACE

From the beautiful cover of this book to the realities of organizations today, great accomplishments are much like inspired works of art. Whether one is talking about arranging objects or bringing together people, technology, and other resources in organizational systems, it is a balancing act. But the results are spectacular when goals and talent combine to create a lasting and positive impact.

Just as artists find inspiration in all the senses that bring our world to life, managers find inspiration in daily experiences, from the insights of scholars, through relationships with other people, and among the goals that guide organizations in an ever more demanding society. And like artists, managers must master many challenges as they strive to create the future from the opportunities of the present.

A well-managed organization—for profit or nonprofit, large or small—can build, mix, and integrate all the beauties of human talent to achieve great things. This capacity for positive impact through people is the goal bound into the pages of *Introduction to Management 13e*. It is an opportunity to gain knowledge, find inspiration, and learn practices that can help build the organizations we need to forge a better world.

New to *Introduction to Management 13e*

Introduction to Management 13e has been revised and updated with a focus on real-world anchors for timely content, student engagement in critical thinking about real-world and personal career issues, and instructor opportunities for enriched classroom activities and assignments.

Timely content—All chapters have been updated. Examples of new and expanded coverage include triple bottom line and shared value view (Chapter 3), disruptive innovation and human sustainability (Chapter 4), reshoring and tax inversions (Chapter 5), social entrepreneurship and crowdfunding (Chapter 6), data mining and analytics (Chapter 7), goal management and goal downsides (Chapter 8 and Chapter 16), employment issues and controversies (Chapter 13), followership and leadership (Chapter 14), technology personality and mood contagion (Chapter 15), and team virtuousness (Chapter 17).

Student engagement features—Student engagement is an embedded theme in *Introduction to Management 13e*. Look for these chapter features that bring life to disciplinary content: *Analysis*—Make Data your Friend, *Ethics*—Know Right from Wrong, *Insight*—Learn About Yourself, and *Wisdom*—Learn from Role Models. Each feature is designed and visually presented to attract student attention and engage them in reflection and critical thinking.

Enriched Classroom Opportunities—The active and enriched classroom is also an embedded theme in *Introduction to Management 13e*. Look for these end-of-chapter opportunities that make it easy to bring text content to life in discussions, activities, and individual and team assignments: Evaluate Career Situations, Reflect on the Self-Assessment, Contribute to the Class Exercise, Manage a Critical Incident, Collaborate on the Team Activity, and Analyze the

Case Study. These instructional enrichments are introduced in the chapter opening page as part of the: *Skills Make You Valuable* lists.

Introduction to Management 13e Philosophy

Today's students are tomorrow's leaders and managers. They are our hope for the future during this time of social transformation. New values and management approaches are appearing; organizations are changing forms and practices; jobs are being redefined and relocated; the age of information is a major force in our lives; and, the intricacies of globalization are presenting major organizational and economic challenges.

Introduction to Management 13e and its rich selection of timely examples and thought provoking features for analysis and reflection is designed for this new world of work. It is crafted to help students understand that management is real and that is an everyday part of their lives. By engaging with *Introduction to Management 13e,* students explore the essentials of management while also discovering their true potential for developing useful career skills. The content, pedagogy, and features of this edition were carefully blended to support management educators who want their students to:

Introduction to Management 13e is designed to help students discover their true potential and accept personal responsibilities for developing career skills.

- grow in career readiness,
- become attractive internship and job candidates,
- gain confidence in critical thinking,
- identify timely social and organizational issues,
- embrace lifelong learning for career success.

Introduction to Management 13e Pedagogy

The pedagogical foundations of *Introduction to Management 13e* are based on four constructive balances that are essential to higher education for business and management.

- *The balance of research insights with formative education.* As educators we must be willing to make choices when bringing the theories and concepts of our discipline to the attention of the introductory student. We cannot do everything in one course. The goal should be to make good content choices that set the best possible foundations for lifelong learning.

Our goal as educators should be to make good content and pedagogical choices that set the best possible foundations for lifelong learning.

- *The balance of management theory with management practice.* As educators we must understand the compelling needs of students to learn and appreciate the applications of the material they are reading and thinking about. We must continually bring to their attention interesting and relevant examples.

- *The balance of present understandings with future possibilities.* As educators we must continually search for the directions in which the real world of management is heading. We must select and present materials that can both point students in the right directions and help them develop the confidence and self-respect needed to best pursue them.

- **_The balance of what "can" be done with what is, purely and simply, the "right" thing to do._** As educators we are role models; we set the examples. We must be willing to take stands on issues such as managerial ethics and social responsibility. We must be careful not to let the concept of "contingency" betray the need for positive "action" and "accountability" in managerial practice.

Our students have pressing needs for direction as well as suggestion. They have needs for application as well as information. They have needs for integration as well as presentation. And they have needs for confidence that comes from solid understanding. Our goal is to put into your hands and into those of your students a learning resource that can help meet these needs.

Introduction to Management 13e Highlights

Introduction to Management 13e introduces the essentials of management as they apply to organizations and careers in a complex global society. The subject matter is carefully chosen to meet AACSB accreditation guidelines, while still allowing extensive flexibility to fit various course designs, class sizes, and delivery formats.

The timely chapter content offers flexibility in meeting a wide variety of course objectives and instructor preferences. The chapters are organized in five logical parts—Management, Environment, Planning and Controlling, Organizing, and Leading. The parts and individual chapters can be used in any order and combination. All chapters have been updated and enriched with new features and examples from the latest current events.

Learning Model

The _Introduction to Management 13e_ learning model makes it easy for students to read, study, reflect, and use critical thinking. Their attention is focused on building management skills and competencies through active learning, and on discovering that management issues and themes permeate current events that affect everyday living.

Each chapter opens with a list of _Key Takeaways_ and _Skills Make You Valuable_—with features on Evaluate, Reflect, Contribute, Manage, Collaborate, and Analyze. Major _Figures_ within chapters provide visual support for student comprehension as concepts, theories, and terms are introduced. Where appropriate, _Small Boxed Figures_ and _Content Summaries_ are embedded in the text to help clarify major points. The _Management Learning Review_ section at the end of each chapter helps students prepare for quizzes and exams by completing a _Takeaway Question Summary_ and _Chapter Self-Test_.

Self-Reflection, Active Learning, and Critical Thinking

The chapter-opening learning dashboards in _Introduction to Management 13e_ provide students with a road map to the skills they will be learning in each chapter and provides them with important opportunities for self-reflection, active learning, and critical thinking. Within each chapter, real world examples present current events, timely issues, and real people and situations to build awareness and stimulate personal reflection. Examples include:

analysis > MAKE DATA YOUR FRIEND
Multiple Generations Meet and Greet in the Workplace

choices > THINK BEFORE YOU ACT
Want Vacation? No Problem, Take as Much as You Want

ethics > KNOW RIGHT FROM WRONG
Social Media Searches Linked with Discrimination in Hiring

insight > LEARN ABOUT YOURSELF
Self-Awareness and the Johari Window

wisdom > LEARN FROM ROLE MODELS
Ursula Burns Moves from Student Intern to *Fortune* 500 CEO

At the end of each chapter, *Skills Make You Valuable* features provide a variety of opportunities to build management skills through individual and team learning activities. Examples include:

SKILLS MAKE YOU **VALUABLE**

- **EVALUATE** *Career Situations:*
  What Would You Do?

- **REFLECT** *On the Self-Assessment:*
  Career Readiness "Big 20"

- **CONTRIBUTE** *To the Class Exercise:*
  My Best Manager

- **MANAGE** *A Critical Incident:*
  Team Leader Faces Test

- **COLLABORATE** *On the Team Activity:*
  The Amazing Great Job Race

- **ANALYZE** *The Case Study:*
  McDonald's: Grilling Up an Empire

Introduction to Management 13e Teaching and Learning Resources

Instructor's Resource Manual. The Instructor's Resource Manual offers helpful teaching ideas. It has advice on course development, sample assignments, and recommended activities. It also offers chapter-by-chapter text highlights, learning objectives, lecture outlines, class exercises, lecture notes, answers to end-of-chapter material, and tips on using cases.

Test Bank. This comprehensive Test Bank (available on the instructor portion of the *Introduction to Management 13e* website) has more than 175 questions per chapter. The true/false, multiple-choice, and short-essay questions vary in degree of difficulty. All questions are tagged with learning objectives, Bloom's Taxonomy categories, and AACSB Standards. The *Computerized Test Bank* allows instructors to modify and add questions to the master bank and to customize their exams.

PowerPoint Presentation Slides. This robust set of slides can be accessed on the instructor portion of the *Introduction to Management 13e* website. Lecture notes accompany each slide.

Pre- and Post-Lecture Quizzes. Included in WileyPLUS Learning Space, the Pre- and Post-Lecture Quizzes focus on the key terms and concepts. They can be used as stand-alone quizzes, or in combination with evaluate students' progress before and after lectures.

Lecture Launcher Videos. Short video clips developed from CBS News source materials provide an excellent starting point for lectures or for general class discussion. Teaching Notes are available and include video summaries and quiz and discussion questions.

Movies and Music. The *Art Imitates Life* supplement, prepared by Robert L. Holbrook of Ohio University, offers tips for those interested in integrating popular culture and the humanities into their courses. It provides innovative teaching ideas and scripts for using movies and music to enrich day-to-day classroom activities. It is widely praised for increasing student involvement and enthusiasm for learning. The *Art Imitates Life* supplement offers tips for those interested in integrating popular culture and the humanities into their courses. This is available separately.

Practice Quizzes. An online study guide with quizzes of varying levels of difficulty helps students evaluate their progress through a chapter. It is available on the student portion of the *Introduction to Management 13e* website.

Student Portfolio Builder. This special guide to building a student portfolio is complete with professional résumé and competency documentation templates. It is on the student portion of the *Introduction to Management 13e* website.

Companion Website. The *Introduction to Management 13e* website at www.wiley.com/college/schermerhorn contains a myriad of tools and links to aid both teaching and learning, including resources described earlier.

WileyPlus Learning Space

What is *WileyPLUS Learning Space*? It's a place where students can learn, collaborate, and grow. Through a personalized experience, students create their own study guide while they interact with course content and work on learning activities.

WileyPLUS Learning Space combines adaptive learning functionality with a dynamic new e-textbook for your course—giving you tools to quickly organize learning activities, manage student collaboration, and customize your course so that you have full control over content as well as the amount of interactivity between students.

You can:

- Assign activities and add your own materials
- Guide students through what's important in the e-textbook by easily assigning specific content
- Set up and monitor collaborative learning groups
- Assess student engagement
- Benefit from a sophisticated set of reporting and diagnostic tools that give greater insight into class activity

Learn more at www.wileypluslearningspace.com. If you have questions, please contact your Wiley representative.

ACKNOWLEDGMENTS

Introduction to Management 13e was initiated and completed with the support of our dedicated and helpful Project Editor, Jennifer Manias; Executive Editor, Lisé Johnson, who again rallied the expertise of a great Wiley team; and Susan McLaughlin, a talented and dedicated "Jack of all trades." We all have benefitted from the special support of George Hoffman (Publisher), Yana Mermel (Editorial Operations Manager), Tom Nery (designer), Mary Ann Price (photo research), Suzie Chapman (production), and Kelly Simmons and Amy Scholz (marketing). We also thank the numerous colleagues—too many to list here—whose help with this book at various stages of its life added to our understanding of management and management education.

As always, John works with the support and encouragement of his wife Ann. She perseveres even when "the book" overwhelms many of life's opportunities. Dan is grateful for the love, support, and guidance of his wife Julie, and the opportunity to work with John.

BRIEF CONTENTS

CONTENTS

3   Ethical Behavior and Social Responsibility   45

Part Two Environment

4   External Environment and Organizational Culture   67

Part Three Planning and Controlling

Part Four Organizing

Part Five Leading

14 Essentials of Leadership 283

15 Foundations of Individual Behavior 305

Management Cases for Critical Thinking

THE MANAGEMENT PROCESS

KEY TAKEAWAYS

- Recognize the challenges of working in the new economy.

- Describe the nature of organizations as work settings.

- Discuss what it means to be a manager.

- Explain the functions, roles, and activities of managers.

- Identify essential managerial skills and discuss how they are learned.

SKILLS MAKE YOU **VALUABLE**

- **EVALUATE** *Career Situations:*
  What Would You Do?

- **REFLECT** *On the Self-Assessment:*
  Career Readiness "Big 20"

- **CONTRIBUTE** *To the Class Exercise:*
  My Best Manager

- **MANAGE** *A Critical Incident:*
  Team Leader Faces Test

- **COLLABORATE** *On the Team Activity:*
  The Amazing Great Job Race

- **ANALYZE** *The Case Study:*
  McDonald's: Grilling Up an Empire

Management is part of our everyday lives. We manage ourselves, we manage relationships, we manage families, and we manage teams and co-workers. Now is a good time to study the fundamentals of management, learn more about your capabilities, and start building skills for career and life success.

Welcome to *Introduction to Management 13/e* and its theme of personal development for career success. We live and work in a very complex world. Unemployment and job scarcities, ethical miscues by business and government leaders, financial turmoil and uncertainties, environmental challenges, and complex global economics and politics are regularly in the news. Today's organizations are fast changing, as is the nature of work itself. Talent and technology reign supreme in the most desired jobs. Learning, performance, and flexibility are in as individual attributes; habit, complacency, and free-riding are out. Employers expect the best from us, and the best employers provide us with inspiring leadership and supportive work environments full of respect, involvement, teamwork, and rewards.[1]

Working Today

TAKEAWAY 1   What are the challenges of working in the new economy?

LEARN MORE ABOUT | Talent • Technology • Globalization • Ethics • Diversity
Careers and Connections

In her book *The Shift: The Future of Work Is Already Here,* scholar Lynda Gratton describes why things are changing so quickly today and how young people can navigate their careers through these changes. "Technology shrinks the world but consumes all of our time," Gratton says. "Globalization means we can work anywhere, but must compete with people from everywhere."[2] What does the changing nature of work mean as you plan for career entry and advancement? You can't expect a guarantee of long-term employment in today's workplace. More and more jobs have to be continually earned and re-earned through everyday performance and accomplishments. And in times of continuous change, you have to accept that your career will be defined by "flexibility," "free agency," "skill portfolios," and "entrepreneurship." There is also no escaping the fact that your career success will require a lot of initiative, self-awareness, and continuous learning. The question is: Are you ready?

Talent

A study by management scholars Charles O'Reilly and Jeffrey Pfeffer found that high-performing companies are better than their competitors at getting extraordinary results from employees. "These companies have won the war for talent," they argue, "not just by being great places to work—although they are that—but by figuring out how to get the best out of all of their people, every day."[3]

People and their talents—what they know, what they learn, and what they achieve—are the crucial foundations for organizational performance. They represent what managers call **intellectual capital**, which is the combined brainpower and shared knowledge of an organization's employees.[4] Intellectual capital is a strategic asset that organizations can use to transform human creativity, insight, and decision making into performance. Intellectual capital also is a personal asset, one to be nurtured and continually updated. It is the package of intellect, skills, and capabilities that sets us apart, and that makes us valuable to potential employers.

> **Intellectual capital** is the collective brainpower or shared knowledge of a workforce.

> **Competency** represents your personal talents or job-related capabilities.

> **Commitment** represents how hard you work to apply your talents and capabilities to important tasks.

> A **knowledge worker** is someone whose mind is a critical asset to employers.

Think about the personal implications of this *intellectual capital equation*: Intellectual Capital = Competency × Commitment.[5] What does it suggest in terms of developing your talents for career success? **Competency** represents your personal talents or job-related capabilities. Although extremely important, by itself competency won't guarantee success. You have to be committed. **Commitment** represents how hard you work to apply your talents and capabilities to important tasks. Both are essential. Having one without the other won't allow you to achieve important career goals or to meet even basic performance requirements. It takes both competency and commitment to generate intellectual capital.

Workplace talents in today's age of information, technology, and change are dominated by **knowledge workers** whose minds—their creativity and insight—are critical assets.[6] Futurist Daniel Pink says we will soon enter a *conceptual age* where the premium will be on "whole mind" competencies. Those who have them will be both "high concept"—creative and good with ideas—and "high touch"—joyful and good with relationships.[7] Management scholar and consultant Gary Hamel talks about a *creative economy* "where even knowledge itself is becoming a commodity" and "the most important differentiator will be how fast you can create something new."[8] Mastering these intellectual challenges requires ongoing development of multiple skill sets that always keep your personal competencies aligned with—and at the forefront of—emerging job trends.

analysis > MAKE DATA YOUR FRIEND

> *72% of college students want "a job where I can make an impact."*

Multiple Generations Meet and Greet in the New World of Work

Is the notion of a "9 to 5" job about to become a relic? What happens as younger workers advance into management? How can baby boomers and millennials work well with each other? The changing mix of ages and attitudes in the workplace is putting the pressure on traditional employment practices. Here's some survey data to consider.

- 60% of millennials change their first jobs after three years and employers spend $15,000 to $25,000 recruiting replacements.

- The best predictor of job loyalty for millennials is "a good culture fit."

- 45% of millennials rate workplace flexibility higher than pay and 71% hope co-workers will become a "second family."

- 68% of millennials get high scores for being enthusiastic about work, 45% for being team players, and 39% for being hardworking.

- 73% of boomer managers get high scores for being hard-working, 55% for being team players, 21% for flexibility, and 16% for inclusive leadership.

- 72% of college students say they want "a job where I can make an impact."

WHAT ARE THE IMPLICATIONS?

How do these findings compare with your own career preferences or what you hear from people you know? How might this evidence influence your approach to seeking a job? What characteristics and practices define your ideal employer? What can employers do to attract and retain talented millennials while keeping older generations happy? Is what's good for millennials necessarily good for everyone? How can managers effectively integrate people with varying needs and interests so employees from different generations work together with respect and pride?

Technology

Technology continuously tests our talents and intrudes into every aspect of our lives. Think Skype, Twitter, Instagram, Facebook, and more. We are continuously bombarded with advertisements for the latest developments—from smartphones to smart apparel to smart cars to smart homes, and from tablets to mini-tablets to e-readers. We struggle to keep up with our social media involvements, stay connected with messaging, and deal with inboxes full of e-mail and voice mail. It is likely that, right now, you are reading this "book" on your favorite tablet or smartphone rather than in its traditional form. Given what has already happened with how we use technology, what will things look like tomorrow?

It is critical to build and to maintain a high **Tech IQ**—the ability to use current technologies at work and in your personal life, combined with the commitment to keep yourself updated as technology continues to evolve. Whether you're checking inventory, making a sale, ordering supplies, sourcing customers, prioritizing accounts, handling payrolls, recruiting new hires, or analyzing customer preferences, Tech IQ is indispensable. More and more people spend at least part of their workday "telecommuting" or "working from home" or in "mobile offices." Workplaces are full of "virtual teams" with members who meet, access common databases, share information and files, make plans and decisions, solve problems together, and complete tasks without ever meeting face to face. Tech IQ is a baseline foundation for succeeding in this fast-changing world of technological innovation.

Even finding work and succeeding in the job selection process today involves skilled use of technology. Poor communication, sloppy approaches, and under-researched attempts do not work in the world of electronic job search. Filling in your online profile with the right key words

Tech IQ is the ability to use technology and to stay updated as technology continues to evolve.

does work. Many employers use sophisticated software to scan online profiles for indicators of real job skills and experiences that fit their needs. Most recruiters today also check social media for negative indicators about applicants.

Globalization

You can't function National boundaries hardly count anymore in the world of business.[9] Over 5 million Americans work in the United States for foreign employers.[10] We buy cars like Toyota, Nissan, BMW, and Mercedes that are assembled in America. We buy appliances from the Chinese firm Haier and Eight O'Clock coffee from India's Tata Group. Top managers at Starbucks, IBM, Sony, Ford, and other global companies have little need for the words "overseas" or "international" in their vocabulary. They operate as global businesses serving customers around the globe. They source materials and talent wherever in the world it can be found at the lowest cost.

Globalization is the worldwide interdependence of resource flows, product markets, and business competition.

These are among the many consequences of **globalization**, which is the worldwide interdependence of resource flows, product markets, and business competition.[11] Under its influence, government leaders worry about the competitiveness of nations, just as corporate leaders worry about business competitiveness.[12] Countries and people are interconnected through labor markets, employment patterns, and financial systems. We are hardly surprised anymore to find that our customer service call is answered in Ghana, CT scans are read by a radiologist in India, and business records maintained by accountants in the Philippines.

Job migration occurs when firms shift jobs from a home country to foreign ones.

One controversial consequence of globalization is **job migration**, which is the shifting of jobs from one country to another. While the United States has been a net loser to job migration, countries like China, India, and the Philippines have been net gainers. Politicians and policymakers regularly debate the costs of job migration as local jobs are lost and communities lose economic vitality. One side looks for new government policies to stop job migration and protect U.S. jobs. The other side calls for patience, arguing that the national economy will grow jobs in the long run as the global economy readjusts.

Reshoring occurs when firms move jobs back home from foreign locations.

The flip side of job migration is **reshoring**, which is the shift of manufacturing and jobs back home from overseas. As global manufacturing and transportation costs rise along with worries about intellectual property protection in countries like China, manufacturing firms including Caterpillar, Ford, and General Electric are doing more reshoring.[13] When Intel announced an expansion of its semiconductor plant in Arizona, an industry analyst said: "The huge advantage of keeping manufacturing in the U.S. is you don't have to worry about your intellectual property walking out the door every evening."[14]

Ethics

It's old news now that Bernard Madoff was sentenced to 150 years in jail for a Ponzi scheme costing investors billions of dollars. But the message is still timely and crystal clear: Commit white-collar crime and you will be punished.[15] Madoff's crime did terrible harm to numerous individuals who lost their life savings, charitable foundations that lost millions in charitable gifts, and employees who lost their jobs. Our society also paid a large price as investors' faith in the business system was damaged by the scandal. Although very high profile, the Madoff scandal was by no means a unique or isolated case of bad behavior by a lone executive. Fresh scandals regularly make the news.

Ethics set moral standards of what is "good" and "right" in one's behavior.

The issues here move beyond criminal behavior and into the broader notion of **ethics**—a code of moral principles that sets standards for conduct that is "good" and "right" versus "bad" and "wrong."[16] At the end of the day we depend on individuals, working at all organizational levels, to conduct themselves in ethical ways. And even though ethics failures get most of the publicity, you'll find many examples of managers who demonstrate moral leadership and integrity. Believing that most CEOs are overpaid, the former CEO of Dial Corporation, Herb Baum, once gave his annual bonus to the firm's lowest-paid workers.[17] In his book *The Transparent Leader,* he argues that integrity is a key to leadership success and that the responsibility for setting an organization's ethical tone begins at the top.

One indicator of ethics in organizations is the emphasis given to social responsibility and sustainability practices. Patagonia, for example, states its commitment to a *responsible economy* "that allows healthy communities, creates meaningful work, and takes from the earth only what it can replenish."[18] Another ethics indicator is the strength of **corporate governance**. Think of it as the active oversight of top management decisions, corporate strategy, and financial reporting by a company's board of directors.

> **Corporate governance** is the active oversight of management decisions and performance by a company's board of directors.

wisdom > LEARN FROM ROLE MODELS

> *"I'm in this job because I believe I earned it through hard work and high performance."*

Ursula Burns Moves from Student Intern to Fortune 500 CEO

Ramin Talale/Bloomberg/Getty Images

"Frankness," "sharp humor," "willingness to take risks," "deep industry knowledge," and "technical prowess." These are all phrases used to describe Ursula Burns, CEO of Xerox Corporation.

She started as a mechanical engineering intern and moved up to become the first African American woman to head a Fortune 500 firm. Her experience and leadership skills were well matched to the job's many challenges.

In her prior role as president, Burns made tough decisions to downsize the firm, close manufacturing operations, and change the product mix. She also knew how to work well with the firm's board. Director Robert A. McDonald of Procter & Gamble says: "She understands the technology and can communicate it in a way that a director can understand it."

A working mother and spouse, Burns was raised in a low-income environment by a single mom in New York City public housing. She says her mom "did everything you could imagine" and was "amazing." The advice she passed along included: "Don't get confused when you are rich and famous." Burns studied hard, earned a master's degree in mechanical engineering from Columbia University, and from there started the internship with Xerox. The rest is corporate history.

Pride in her achievements comes across loud and clear when Burns talks about her work. "I'm in this job because I believe I earned it through hard work and high performance," she says. "Did I get some opportunities early in my career because of my race and gender? Probably . . . I imagine race and gender got the hiring guys' attention. And the rest was really up to me."

FIND INSPIRATION

Ursula Burns's trajectory from student intern to CEO of a Fortune 500 firm is impressive. What career lessons are here for others to follow? Which special skills and personal characteristics may have helped Burns grow into her corporate leadership role? She's an African American woman who grew up poor. How can her success in the male-dominated corporate environment serve as a role model for others?

Diversity

Workforce diversity
describes workers'
differences in terms
of gender, race, age,
ethnicity, religion,
sexual orientation, and
able-bodiedness.

The term **workforce diversity** describes the composition of a workforce in terms of gender, age, race, ethnicity, religion, sexual orientation, and able-bodiedness.[19] The changing demographics in society are well recognized. Members of minority groups now constitute more than one-third of the U.S. population, and women may soon outnumber men in the U.S. workforce.[20] By the year 2050, African Americans, Native Americans, Asians, and Hispanics will be the new majority, and by 2050, the U.S. Census Bureau also expects that more than 20% of the population will be at least 65 years old.

Despite these changes, the way we deal with diversity in the workplace remains complicated. Women now lead global companies like IBM, PepsiCo, Xerox, and Kraft, but they hold only just 4% of all top jobs in American firms and 5% in large firms worldwide.[21] The proportion of women at the top is growing, but female CEOs are also getting fired at a higher rate than their male counterparts.[22] People of color hold just 11% of executive jobs in the Fortune 500, and among the CEOs, there are six African Americans, eight Asians, and eight Hispanics.[23]

Why aren't there more women and people of color leading organizations? To what extent does diversity bias still influence recruitment and selection decisions? Researchers have found that résumés with white-sounding first names, such as Brett, receive 50% more responses from employers than equivalent résumés with black-sounding first names, such as Kareem.[24] Researchers also note that white leaders are viewed as more successful than minority leaders, and that white leaders are expected to succeed because of competence while non-white leaders are expected to succeed despite incompetence.[25]

Prejudice is the
display of negative,
irrational attitudes
toward members of
diverse populations.

The stage for diversity bias is set by **prejudice**—which is the display of negative, irrational opinions and attitudes regarding members of diverse populations. An example of bias is the lingering prejudice against working mothers. The nonprofit Families and Work Institute reported that in 1977, 49% of men and 71% of women believed that mothers can be good employees; by 2008, the figures had risen to 67% and 80%.[26] Don't you wonder why there isn't 100% support for working mothers? And, how do you account for a study that sent faux résumés to recruiters and found that the least desirable candidates were women with children?[27]

Discrimination
actively denies minority
members the full
benefits of organiza-
tional membership.

**The glass ceiling
effect** is an invisible
barrier limiting career
advancement of women
and minorities.

Prejudice becomes active **discrimination** when minority members are unfairly treated and denied the full benefits of organizational membership. One example of discrimination is a manager inventing reasons not to interview a minority job candidate. Another example is a supervisor who refuses to promote a working mother for fear that parenting responsibilities will make it hard for her to do a good job. This thinking shows a subtle form of discrimination called the **glass ceiling effect**, an invisible barrier or ceiling that prevents women and minorities from rising to top jobs.

Scholar Judith Rosener warns that discrimination of any sort leads to "undervalued and underutilized human capital."[28] To avoid this problem, the position of chief diversity officer, or CDO, is gaining stature in organizations. Its presence recognizes that diversity is not only a moral issue but an opportunity for real performance gains. The job of CDO is to make sure the work environment allows women and minorities to flourish, and fully utilizes their talents.[29]

Careers and Connections

When the economy is down and employment markets are tight, the task of finding a career entry point can be daunting. It always pays to remember the importance of online résumés and job searches, and the power of social networking with established professionals. In addition, job seekers should consider internships as pathways to first-job placements. But everything still depends on the mix of skills you can offer a potential employer and how well you communicate those skills. Picture yourself in a job interview. The recruiter asks this question: "What can you do for us?" How do you reply? Your answer can set the stage for your career success . . . or something less.

British scholar and consultant Charles Handy uses the analogy of the **shamrock organization** to highlight the challenges of developing skill portfolios that fit the new workplace.[30] The first leaf in the shamrock is a core group of permanent, full-time employees who follow standard career paths. The number of people in this first leaf is shrinking.[31] They are being replaced by a second leaf of "freelancers" and "independent contractors" who offer specialized skills and talents on a contract basis, then change employers when projects are completed.[32] Full-time employees are also being replaced by a third leaf of temporary part-timers. They often work without benefits and are the first to lose their jobs when an employer runs into economic difficulties.

> ## Early Career Survival Skills
>
> *Mastery:* You need to be good at something; you need to be able to contribute real value to your employer.
>
> *Networking:* You need to know people and get connected; networking with others within and outside the organization is essential.
>
> *Entrepreneurship:* You must act as if you are running your own business, spotting ideas and opportunities and pursuing them.
>
> *Technology:* You have to embrace technology; you have to stay up to date and fully utilize all that is available.
>
> *Marketing:* You need to communicate your successes and progress—both yours personally and those of your work team.
>
> *Renewal:* You need to learn and change continuously, always improving yourself for the future.

The fact is that you will have to succeed in a **free-agent economy**, one where people change jobs more often and work on flexible contracts with a shifting mix of employers over time. Skills like those in the nearby box must be kept up to date and portable.[33] They can't be gained once and then forgotten. They must be carefully maintained and upgraded all the time. All this places a premium on your capacity for **self-management**—being able to assess yourself realistically, recognize strengths and weaknesses, make constructive changes, and manage your personal development.

Connections count highly in the free-agent economy. They open doors to opportunities and resources that otherwise wouldn't be available. People with connections gain access to valuable information about potential jobs and often score more interviews and better jobs than those without connections. While in the past the best connections may have been limited to people who had gone to the "right" kinds of schools or came from the "right" kinds of families, this is no longer the case. **Social networking** tools—such as LinkedIn, Facebook, Google+, and Reddit—that connect users with similar interests have become the great equalizer. They make the process of connecting much easier and more democratic than ever before. Importantly, they are readily available ways for you to make connections that can help with job searches and career advancement.

A **shamrock organization** operates with a core group of full-time long-term workers supported by others who work on contracts and part-time.

In a **free-agent economy** people change jobs more often, and many work on independent contracts with a shifting mix of employers.

Self-management is the ability to understand oneself, exercise initiative, accept responsibility, and learn from experience.

Social networking is the use of dedicated websites and applications to connect people having similar interests.

Learning Check 1

TAKEAWAYQUESTION 1 **What are the challenges of working in the new economy?**

BE SURE YOU CAN • describe how intellectual capital, ethics, diversity, globalization, technology, and the changing nature of careers influence working in the new economy • define *intellectual capital, workforce diversity,* and *globalization* • explain how prejudice, discrimination, and the glass ceiling can hurt people at work

Organizations

TAKEAWAY 2   What are organizations like as work settings?

LEARN MORE | Organizational purpose • Organizations as systems
ABOUT | Organizational performance • Changing nature of organizations

As pointed out earlier, what happens from this point forward in your career is largely up to you. So, let's start with organizations. In order to make good employment choices and perform well in a career, you need to understand the nature of organizations and recognize how they work as complex systems.

Organizational Purpose

An organization is a collection of people working together to achieve a common purpose.

An **organization** is a collection of people working together to achieve a common purpose. It is a unique social phenomenon that enables its members to perform tasks far beyond the reach of individual accomplishment. This description applies to organizations of all sizes and types that make up the life of any community, from large corporations to small businesses, as well as such nonprofit organizations as schools, government agencies, and community hospitals.

The broad purpose of any organization is to provide goods or services of value to customers and clients. A clear sense of purpose tied to "quality products and services," "customer satisfaction," and "social responsibility" can be an important source of organizational strength and performance advantage. IBM's former CEO, Samuel Palmisano, once said: "One simple way to assess the impact of any organization is to ask the question: How is the world different because it existed?"[34] Whole Foods founder John Mackey answers by saying: "I think that business has a noble purpose. It means that businesses serve society. They produce goods and services that make people's lives better." On the Whole Foods website, this is stated as a commitment to "Whole Foods—Whole People—Whole Planet."[35]

Organizations as Systems

An open system transforms resource inputs from the environment into product outputs.

All organizations are **open systems** that interact with their environments. They do so in a continual process of obtaining resource inputs—people, information, resources, and capital—and transforming them into outputs in the form of finished goods and services for customers.[36]

As shown in Figure 1.1, feedback from the environment indicates how well an organization is doing. When Starbucks started a customer blog, for example, requests for speedier service popped up. The company quickly made changes that eliminated required signatures on credit card charges less than $25. Salesforce.com is another company that thrives on feedback. It set up a website called Idea Exchange to get customer suggestions, even asking them at one point to vote on a

FIGURE 1.1
Organizations as open systems interacting with their environments.

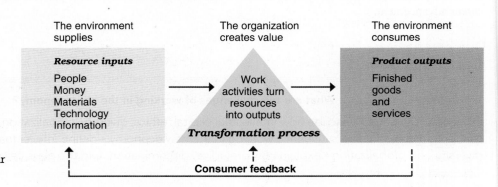

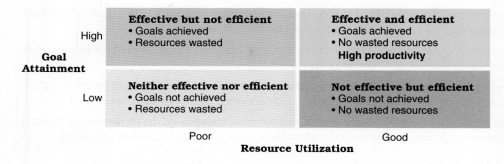

	Poor ← Resource Utilization → Good
High Goal Attainment	**Effective but not efficient** • Goals achieved • Resources wasted	**Effective and efficient** • Goals achieved • No wasted resources **High productivity**
Low	**Neither effective nor efficient** • Goals not achieved • Resources wasted	**Not effective but efficient** • Goals not achieved • No wasted resources

FIGURE 1.2
Productivity and the dimensions of organizational performance.

possible name change—the response was "No!"[37] Gathering and listening to customer feedback is important; without loyal customers, a business can't survive. When you hear or read about bankruptcies, they are stark testimonies to this fact of the marketplace.

Organizational Performance

Organizations create value when they use resources well to produce good products and take care of their customers. When operations add value to the original cost of resource inputs, then a business organization can earn a profit—selling a product for more than the costs of making it, and a nonprofit organization can add wealth to society—providing a public service like fire protection that is worth more than its cost.

One of the most common ways to assess performance by and within organizations is **productivity**. It measures the quantity and quality of outputs relative to the cost of inputs. And as Figure 1.2 shows, productivity involves both performance effectiveness and performance efficiency.

Performance effectiveness is an output measure of task or goal accomplishment. If you are working as a software engineer for a computer game developer, performance effectiveness may mean that you meet a daily production target in terms of the quantity and quality of lines of code written. This productivity helps the company meet customer demands for timely delivery of high-quality gaming products.

Performance efficiency is an input measure of the resource costs associated with goal accomplishment. Returning to the gaming example, the most efficient software production is accomplished at a minimum cost in materials and labor. If you are producing fewer lines of code in a day than you are capable of, this amounts to inefficiency; if you make lots of mistakes that require extensive rewrites, this is also inefficient work. All such inefficiencies drive up costs and reduce productivity.

Productivity is the quantity and quality of work performance, with resource utilization considered.

Performance effectiveness is an output measure of task or goal accomplishment.

Performance efficiency is an input measure of resource cost associated with goal accomplishment.

Changing Nature of Organizations

Change is a continuing theme in our society, and organizations are no exception. The following list shows some organizational trends and transitions relevant to the study of management.[38]

- *Focus on valuing human capital:* The premium is on high-involvement work settings that rally the knowledge, experience, and commitment of all members.

- *Demise of "command-and-control":* Traditional top-down "do as I say" bosses are giving way to participatory bosses who treat people with respect.

- *Emphasis on teamwork:* Organizations are becoming less hierarchical and more driven by teamwork that pools talents for creative problem solving.

▶ Management trends and transitions ·

- *Preeminence of technology:* Developments in computer and information technology keep changing the way organizations operate and how people work.

- *Importance of networking:* Organizations and their members are networked for intense, real-time communication and coordination.

- *New workforce expectations:* A new generation of workers is less tolerant of hierarchy, attentive to performance merit, more informal, and concerned for work–life balance.

- *Concern for sustainability:* Social values call for more attention on the preservation of natural resources for future generations and understanding how work affects human well-being.

Learning Check 2

TAKEAWAYQUESTION **2 What are organizations like as work settings?**

BE SURE YOU CAN • describe how organizations operate as open systems • explain productivity as a measure of organizational performance • distinguish between performance effectiveness and performance efficiency • list several ways in which organizations are changing today

Managers

TAKEAWAY 3   What does it mean to be a manager?

LEARN MORE ABOUT | Importance of managers • Levels of managers • Types of managers
Managerial performance • Changing nature of managerial work

In an article titled "Putting People First for Organizational Success," Jeffrey Pfeffer and John F. Veiga argue forcefully that organizations perform better when they treat their members better.[39] Managers in these high-performing organizations don't treat people as costs to be controlled; they treat them as valuable strategic assets to be carefully nurtured and developed. So, who are today's managers and just what do they do?

What Is a Manager?

A **manager** is a person who supports, activates, and is responsible for the work of others.

You find them in all organizations and with a wide variety of job titles—team leader, department head, supervisor, project manager, president, administrator, and more. We call them **managers**, people in organizations who directly support, supervise, and help activate the work efforts and performance accomplishments of others. Whether they are called direct reports, team members, work associates, or subordinates, these "other people" are the essential human resources whose contributions represent the real work of the organization. And as pointed out by management scholar Henry Mintzberg, being a manager remains an important and socially responsible job. "No job is more vital to our society than that of the manager," he says. "It is the manager who determines whether our social institutions serve us well or whether they squander our talents and resources."[40]

Levels of Managers

Members of a **board of directors** or board of trustees are supposed to make sure an organization is well run and managed in a lawful and ethical manner.

At the highest levels of business organizations, as shown in Figure 1.3, we find a **board of directors** whose members are elected by stockholders to represent their ownership interests. In nonprofit organizations such as a hospital or university, this level is often called a *board of trustees,* and it may be elected by local citizens, appointed by government bodies, or invited by existing members. The basic responsibilities of board members are the same in both business and the public sector—to make sure that the organization is always being well run and managed in a lawful and ethical manner.[41]

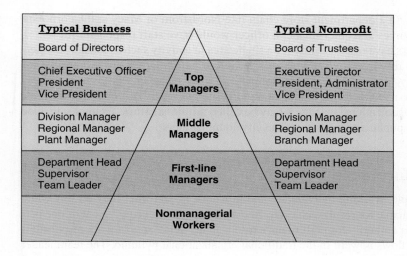

Typical Business		Typical Nonprofit
Board of Directors		Board of Trustees
Chief Executive Officer President Vice President	**Top Managers**	Executive Director President, Administrator Vice President
Division Manager Regional Manager Plant Manager	**Middle Managers**	Division Manager Regional Manager Branch Manager
Department Head Supervisor Team Leader	**First-line Managers**	Department Head Supervisor Team Leader
	Nonmanagerial Workers	

FIGURE 1.3
Management levels in typical business and nonprofit organizations.

Common job titles just below the board level are chief executive officer (CEO), chief operating officer (COO), chief financial officer (CFO), chief information officer (CIO), chief diversity officer (CDO), president, and vice president. These **top managers** constitute an executive team that reports to the board and is responsible for the performance of an organization as a whole or for one of its larger parts. It is common to find the members of an organization's top management team referred to as part of the *C-suite*.

Top managers are supposed to set strategy and lead the organization consistent with its purpose and mission. They should pay special attention to the external environment and be alert to potential long-run problems and opportunities. The best top managers are strategic thinkers able to make good decisions under highly competitive and even uncertain conditions. A CEO at Procter & Gamble once said the job of top managers is to "link the external world with the internal organization . . . make sure the voice of the consumer is heard . . . shape values and standards."[42]

Reporting to top managers are the **middle managers**, who are in charge of relatively large departments or divisions consisting of several smaller work units. Examples include clinic directors in hospitals; deans in universities; and division managers, plant managers, and regional sales managers in businesses. Job descriptions for middle managers may include working with top managers, coordinating with peers, and supporting lower–level team members to develop and pursue action plans that implement organizational strategies to accomplish key objectives.

A first job in management typically involves serving as a **team leader** or supervisor—someone in charge of a small work group composed of non-managerial workers.[43] Typical job titles for these first-line managers include department head, team leader, and supervisor. The leader of an auditing team, for example, is considered a first-line manager, as is the head of an academic department in a university. Even though most people enter the workforce as technical specialists such as engineer, market researcher, or systems analyst, at some point they probably advance to positions of initial managerial responsibility.

Types of Managers

Many types of managers comprise an organization. **Line managers** are responsible for work that makes a direct contribution to the organization's outputs. For example, the president, retail manager, and department supervisors of a local department store all have line responsibilities. Their jobs in one way or another are directly related to the sales operations of the store. **Staff managers**, by contrast, use special technical expertise to advise and support the

Top managers guide the performance of the organization as a whole or of one of its major parts.

Middle managers oversee the work of large departments or divisions.

Team leaders report to middle managers and supervise non-managerial workers.

Line managers directly contribute to producing the organization's goods or services.

Staff managers use special technical expertise to advise and support line workers.

Functional managers are responsible for one area, such as finance, marketing, production, personnel, accounting, or sales.

General managers are responsible for complex, multifunctional units.

An **administrator** is a manager in a public or nonprofit organization.

Accountability is the requirement to show performance results to a supervisor.

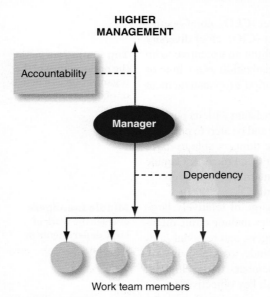

Work team members

An **effective manager** helps others achieve high performance and satisfaction at work.

Quality of work life is the overall quality of human experiences in the workplace.

The **upside-down pyramid** view of organizations shows customers at the top being served by workers who are supported by managers.

efforts of line workers. In a department store chain like Nordstrom or Macy's, the corporate director of human resources and chief financial officer would have staff responsibilities.

Functional managers have responsibility for a single area of activity such as finance, marketing, production, human resources, accounting, or sales. **General managers** are responsible for activities covering many functional areas. An example is a plant manager who oversees everything from purchasing to manufacturing to human resources to finance and accounting functions. In public or nonprofit organizations, managers may be called **administrators**. Examples include hospital administrators, public administrators, and city administrators.

Managerial Performance

All managers help people, working individually and in teams, to perform. They do this while being personally accountable for results achieved. **Accountability** is the requirement of one person to answer to a higher authority for performance results in his or her area of work responsibility. This accountability flows upward in the traditional organizational pyramid. The team leader is accountable to a middle manager, the middle manager is accountable to a top manager, and even the top manager is accountable through corporate governance to a board of directors or board of trustees.

But what, you might ask, constitutes excellence in managerial performance? When is a manager "effective"? A good answer is that **effective managers** successfully help others achieve both high performance and satisfaction in their work. This dual concern for performance and satisfaction introduces **quality of work life** (QWL) as an indicator of the overall quality of human experiences at work. A "high-QWL" workplace offers such things as respect, fair pay, safe conditions, opportunities to learn and use new skills, room to grow and progress in a career, and protection of individual rights and wellness.

Scholar Jeffrey Pfeffer considers QWL a high-priority issue of human sustainability. Why, he asks, don't we give more attention to human sustainability and "organizational effects on employee health and mortality"?[44] What do you think? Should managers be held accountable not just for performance accomplishments of their teams and work units, but also for the human sustainability of those who work with and for them? In other words, shouldn't productivity and quality of working life go hand in hand?

Changing Nature of Managerial Work

Cindy Zollinger, president and CEO of Cornerstone Research, directly supervises more than 20 people. But, she says: "I don't really manage them in a typical way; they largely run themselves. I help them in dealing with obstacles they face, or in making the most of opportunities they find."[45] These comments describe a workplace where the best managers are known more for "helping" and "supporting" than for "directing" and "order giving." The words *coordinator, coach,* and *team leader* are heard as often as *supervisor* or *boss.*

The concept of the **upside-down pyramid** shown in Figure 1.4 fits well with the changing mind-set of managerial work today. Notice that the operating and frontline workers are at the top of the upside-down pyramid, just below the customers and clients they serve. They are supported in their work efforts by managers below them. These managers aren't just order-givers; they are there to mobilize and deliver the support others need to do their jobs best and

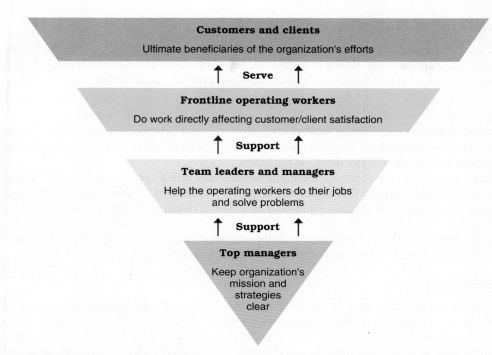

FIGURE 1.4
The organization viewed as an upside-down pyramid.

serve customer needs. Sitting at the bottom are top managers and C-suite executives; their jobs are to support everyone and everything above them. The upside-down pyramid view leaves no doubt that the entire organization is devoted to serving customers and that the job of managers is to support the workers who make this possible.

Learning Check 3

TAKEAWAY QUESTION 3 **What does it mean to be a manager?**

BE SURE YOU CAN • describe the various types and levels of managers • define *accountability* and *quality of work life*, and explain their importance to managerial performance • discuss how managerial work is changing today • explain the role of managers in the upside-down pyramid view of organizations

The Management Process

TAKEAWAY 4   What are the functions, roles, and activities of managers?

LEARN MORE | Functions of management • Managerial roles and activities
ABOUT | Managerial agendas and networks

The ultimate "bottom line" in every manager's job is to help an organization achieve high performance by best utilizing its human and material resources. This is accomplished through the four functions of management in what is called the **management process** of planning, organizing, leading, and controlling.

The **management process** is planning, organizing, leading, and controlling the use of resources to accomplish performance goals.

Functions of Management

All managers, regardless of title, level, type, and organizational setting, are responsible for the four management functions shown in Figure 1.5. These functions are continually engaged as a manager moves from task to task and opportunity to opportunity in his or her work.

Planning

Planning is the process of setting goals and objectives and making plans to accomplish them.

Planning is the process of setting performance objectives and determining what actions should be taken to accomplish them. Through planning, a manager identifies desired results—goals and objectives, and ways to achieve them—action plans.

There was a time, for example, when top management at EY (previously Ernst & Young) became concerned about the firm's retention of female professionals.[46] Then-chairman Philip A. Laskawy launched a Diversity Task Force with the planning objective to reduce turnover rates for women. When the task force began its work, this turnover was running some 22% per year, and it cost the firm about 150% of a departing employee's annual salary to hire and train each replacement. Laskawy considered this performance unacceptable and put plans in place to improve it.

Organizing

Organizing is the process of defining and assigning tasks, allocating resources, and providing resource support.

Once plans are set, they must be implemented. This begins with **organizing**, the process of assigning tasks, allocating resources, and coordinating the activities of individuals and groups to accomplish plans. Organizing is how managers put plans into action by defining jobs and tasks, assigning them to responsible persons, and then providing support such as technology, time, and other resources.

At EY, Laskawy organized and chaired a Diversity Task Force to meet his planning objective. He also established a new Office of Retention and hired Deborah K. Holmes, now serving as global director of corporate responsibility, to head it. Holmes's office was responsible for identifying retention problems in various parts of the firm, creating special task forces to tackle them, and recommending location-specific solutions to the Diversity Task Force.

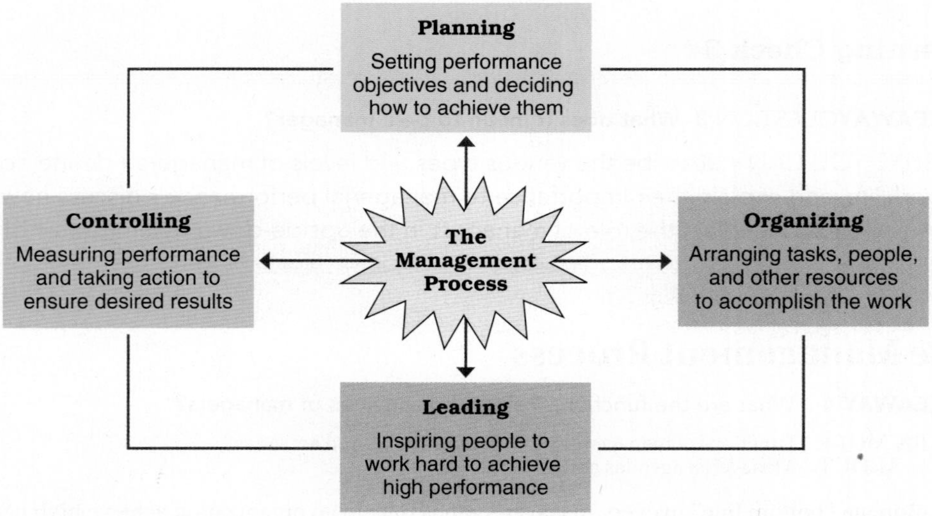

FIGURE 1.5
Four functions of management—planning, organizing, leading, and controlling.

Leading

Leading is the process of arousing people's enthusiasm and inspiring their efforts to work hard to fulfill plans and accomplish objectives. Managers lead by building commitments to a common vision, encouraging activities that support goals, and influencing others to do their best work on the organization's behalf.

Leading is the process of arousing enthusiasm and inspiring efforts to achieve goals.

Deborah K. Holmes actively pursued her leadership responsibilities at EY. She noticed that, in addition to stress caused by intense work at the firm, women often faced more stress because their spouses also worked. She became a champion for improved work–life balance and pursued it vigorously. She started "call-free holidays" where professionals did not check voice mail or e-mail on weekends and holidays. She started a "travel sanity" program that limited staffers' travel to four days a week so they could be home for weekends. And, she started a Woman's Access Program to provide mentoring and career development.

Research Brief

Worldwide Study Identifies Success Factors in Global Leadership

Robert J. House and colleagues developed a network of 170 researchers to study leadership around the world. Over a 10-year period they investigated cultural frameworks, cultural differences, and their leadership implications as part of Project GLOBE. The results are summarized in the book *Culture, Leadership and Organizations: The GLOBE Study of 62 Societies.*

Data from over 17,000 managers working in 62 national cultures were collected and analyzed. The researchers found that the world's cultures do have some differences in what constitutes leadership effectiveness. But they also share some universal facilitators to leadership success—such as leaders being honest and trustworthy, and impediments—such as leaders being self-protective and dictatorial.

In terms of leadership development, the GLOBE researchers concluded that global mindsets, tolerance for ambiguity, cultural adaptability, and flexibility are essential as leaders seek to influence persons whose cultural backgrounds are different from their own. Personal aspects that seemed most culturally sensitive in terms of leadership effectiveness were being individualistic, being status conscious, and being open to risk.

YOU BE THE RESEARCHER

Take a survey of workers at your university, your place of employment, or a local organization. Ask them to describe their best and worst leaders. Use the results to answer the question: How closely do local views of leadership match with findings of the GLOBE study? Don't you agree that we still have a lot more to learn about how leadership success is viewed in the many cultures of the world? The links between culture and leadership seem particularly important, not only in a business context, but also as governments try to work together both bilaterally and multilaterally in forums such as the United Nations.

Universal facilitators of leadership effectiveness

- Trustworthy, honest, just
- Having foresight, ability to plan ahead
- Positive, dynamic, encouraging, motivating
- Communicative, informed, integrating

Universal impediments to leadership effectiveness

- Loner, asocial, self-protective
- Noncooperative, irritable
- Dictatorial, autocratic

Controlling

The management function of **controlling** is the process of measuring work performance, comparing results to objectives, and taking corrective action as needed. Managers exercise control by staying in active contact with people as they work, gathering and interpreting performance measurements, and using this information to make constructive changes. Control is indispensable in the management process. Things don't always go as anticipated, and plans must often be modified and redefined to fit new circumstances.

At EY, Laskawy and Holmes documented what the firm's retention rates for women were when they started the new programs. This gave them a clear baseline against which they were able to track progress. They regularly measured retention rates for women and compared them to the baseline. They were able to identify successes and pinpoint where they needed to further improve their work–life balance programs. Over time, collected data showed that turnover rates for women were reduced at all levels.

Controlling is the process of measuring performance and taking action to ensure desired results.

Managerial Roles and Activities

The management process and its responsibilities for planning, organizing, leading, and controlling are more complicated than they appear at first glance. They must be successfully accomplished during a workday that can be very challenging. In a classic book, *The Nature of Managerial Work*, Henry Mintzberg describes the daily work of corporate chief executives as follows: "There was no break in the pace of activity during office hours. The mail . . . telephone calls . . . and meetings . . . accounted for almost every minute from the moment these executives entered their offices in the morning until they departed in the evenings."[47] Today, we might add to Mintzberg's list of executive preoccupations relentless "work anytime and anywhere" demands of smartphones, ever-full e-mail and voice mail in-boxes, chat and instant message streams, and social media alerts.

Managerial Roles

In trying to better understand the complex nature of managerial work, Mintzberg identified a set of roles commonly filled by managers.[48] Shown in the nearby figure, they describe how managers must be prepared to succeed in in a variety of interpersonal, informational, and decisional responsibilities.

Interpersonal roles	Informational roles	Decisional roles
How a manager interacts with other people • Figurehead • Leader • Liaison	How a manager exchanges and processes information • Monitor • Disseminator • Spokesperson	How a manager uses information in decision making • Entrepreneur • Disturbance handler • Resource allocator • Negotiator

A manager's interpersonal roles involve interactions with people inside and outside the work unit. A manager fulfilling these roles will be a *figurehead*, modeling and setting forth key principles and policies; a *leader*, providing direction and instilling enthusiasm; and a *liaison*, coordinating with others. A manager's informational roles involve the giving, receiving, and analyzing of information. A manager fulfilling these roles will be a *monitor*, scanning for information; a *disseminator*, sharing information; and a *spokesperson*, acting as official communicator. The decisional roles involve using information to make decisions to solve problems or address opportunities. A manager fulfilling these roles will be a *disturbance handler*, dealing with problems and conflicts; a *resource allocator*, handling budgets and distributing resources; a *negotiator*, making deals and forging agreements; and an *entrepreneur*, developing new initiatives.

Managerial Activities

Managers must not only master key roles, they must implement them in intense and complex work settings. Their work is busy, demanding, and stressful at all levels of responsibility. The managers Mintzberg studied had little free time to themselves. In fact, unexpected problems and continuing requests for meetings consumed almost all available time. The small box shows their workdays were hectic; the pressure for continuously improving performance was all-encompassing.[49] Mintzberg summarized his observations this way: "The manager can never be free to forget the job, and never has the pleasure of knowing, even temporarily, that there is nothing else to do. . . . Managers always carry the nagging suspicion that they might be able to contribute just a little bit more. Hence they assume an unrelenting pace in their work."[50]

> ### A Manager's Workday
> - long hours
> - intense pace
> - fragmented and varied tasks
> - many communication media
> - filled with interpersonal relationships

Managerial Agendas and Networks

Scene: On the way to a meeting, a general manager bumped into a colleague from another department. In a two-minute conversation she used this opportunity to (a) ask two questions and receive the information she had been needing; (b) reinforce their good relationship by sincerely complimenting the colleague on something he had recently done; and (c) get a commitment for the colleague to do something else that the general manager needed done. *Analysis:* This brief incident provides a glimpse of an effective general manager in action. It also portrays two activities that consultant and scholar John Kotter considers critical to a manager's success—agenda setting and networking.[51]

Through **agenda setting**, good managers develop action priorities that include goals and plans spanning long and short time frames. These agendas are usually incomplete and loosely connected in the beginning, but they become more specific as the manager utilizes information continually gleaned from many different sources. The agendas are always present in the manager's mind and are played out or pushed ahead whenever an opportunity arises, as in the preceding example.

Good managers implement their agendas by **networking**, the process of building and maintaining positive relationships with people whose help may be needed to implement one's agendas. Such networking creates **social capital**—a capacity to attract support and help from others in order to get things done. In the earlier example, the general manager received help from a colleague who did not report directly to her. The manager's networks and social capital would also include relationships she cultivates with other peers, higher-level executives, subordinates and members of their work teams, as well as with external customers, suppliers, and community representatives.

Agenda setting develops action priorities for accomplishing goals and plans.

Networking is the process of creating positive relationships with people who can help advance agendas.

Social capital is a capacity to get things done with the support and help of others.

Learning Check 4

TAKEAWAYQUESTION 4 **What are the functions, roles, and activities of managers?**

BE SURE YOU CAN • define and give examples of each of the management functions—*planning, organizing, leading,* and *controlling* • explain Mintzberg's view of what managers do, including the 10 key managerial roles • explain Kotter's points on how managers use agendas and networks to fulfill their work responsibilities

Learning How to Manage

TAKEAWAY 5   What are the essential managerial skills and how do we learn them?

LEARN MORE | Learning and lifelong learning • Technical skills • Human and interpersonal skills
ABOUT | Conceptual and critical-thinking skills

A survey of corporate CEOs of major employers like Accenture, Unilever, and Liberty Mutual Insurance revealed dissatisfaction with what they are seeing in business school students. Top criticisms were a lack of self-awareness, poor teamwork and critical thinking skills, and an absence of creativity.[52] There's no doubt that career success in today's turbulent times depends greatly on **learning**—changing behavior through experience. But, learning begins with self-awareness—a real, unbiased, understanding of your strengths and weaknesses. And when it comes to self-awareness in a management context, the learning focus in is on skills and competencies that help you to confidently deal with the complexities of human behavior and problem solving in organizations.

As you read the various chapters and special features in this book and participate in course discussions and activities, be sure to self-assess in regard to your career readiness and the learning that might advance that success immediately and in the longer term. And don't forget, it's not just formal learning in the classroom that counts. The events of everyday life—from full-time and part-time jobs to teamwork in school, sports, and leisure activities to customer interactions—are rich in learning opportunities . . . if you take advantage of them. There's a lot to be gained from making a sincere commitment to **lifelong learning**—the process of continuous learning from all of our daily experiences and opportunities.

A **skill** is the ability to translate knowledge into action that results in desired performance.[53] Harvard scholar Robert L. Katz described the essential, or baseline, skills of managers in three categories: technical, human, and conceptual.[54] He suggests that all three sets of skills are necessary for management success, and that their relative importance varies by level of managerial responsibility as shown in Figure 1.6.

Learning is a change in behavior that results from experience.

Lifelong learning is continuous learning from daily experiences.

A **skill** is the ability to translate knowledge into action that results in desired performance.

Technical Skills

A **technical skill** is the ability to use a special proficiency or expertise to perform particular tasks. This is what someone can do that brings value to an employer. Accountants, engineers, market researchers, financial planners, and systems analysts, for example, possess technical skills within their areas of expertise. Knowing how to write a business plan with a cash flow projection, use statistics to analyze data from a market survey, update software on a computer network, and deliver a persuasive oral presentation are also technical skills. Although initially acquired through formal education, technical skills can become quickly outdated in today's world. It is important to nurture and develop them through ongoing learning that takes full advantage of training and job experiences.

A **technical skill** is the ability to use expertise to perform a task with proficiency.

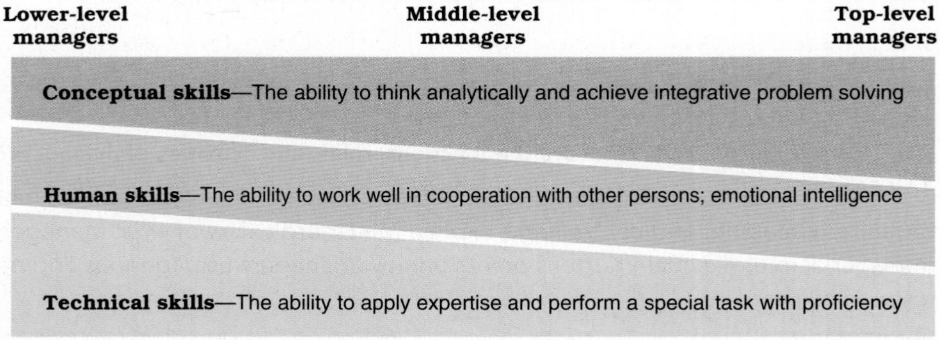

Lower-level managers	Middle-level managers	Top-level managers
Conceptual skills—The ability to think analytically and achieve integrative problem solving		
Human skills—The ability to work well in cooperation with other persons; emotional intelligence		
Technical skills—The ability to apply expertise and perform a special task with proficiency		

FIGURE 1.6
Katz's essential managerial skills—technical, human, and conceptual.

Figure 1.6 shows that technical skills are very important at job entry and early career levels. As you look at this figure, take a quick inventory of your technical skills. They are things you must be able to tell a prospective employer when interviewing for a new job. Get prepared by asking this all-important self-assessment question: "What, exactly, can I do for a prospective employer?"

Human and Interpersonal Skills

Recruiters today put a lot of emphasis on a job candidate's "soft" skills—things like ability to communicate, collaborate, and network, to lead and contribute to teams, and to engage others with a spirit of trust, enthusiasm, and positive impact.[55] These are all part of what Katz called the ability to work well in cooperation with other persons, or **human skill**. As pointed out in Figure 1.6, the interpersonal nature of managerial work makes human skills consistently important across all levels of managerial responsibility.

A manager with good human skills will have a high degree of **emotional intelligence**, defined by scholar and consultant Daniel Goleman as the "ability to manage ourselves and our relationships effectively."[56] Strength or weakness in emotional intelligence shows up as the ability to recognize, understand, and manage feelings while interacting and dealing with others. Someone high in emotional intelligence will know when her or his emotions are about to become disruptive, and act to control them. This same person will sense when another person's emotions are negatively influencing a relationship, and act to understand and better deal with them.[57] Check your interpersonal skills and emotional intelligence by asking and answering this self-assessment question: "Just how well do I relate with and work with others in team and interpersonal situations?"

> A **human skill** or interpersonal skill is the ability to work well in cooperation with other people.
>
> **Emotional intelligence** is the ability to manage ourselves and our relationships effectively.

Conceptual and Critical-Thinking Skills

The ability to think analytically is a **conceptual skill**. It involves the capacity to break problems into smaller parts, see the relations between the parts, and recognize the implications of any one problem for others. We call this a critical-thinking skill, and it is a top priority when recruiters screen candidates for sought-after jobs.[58] Annmarie Neal, Vice President, Cisco Center for Collaborative Leadership within Human Resources, describes it as an ability to "approach problems as a learner as opposed to a knower" and "taking issues and situations and problems and going to root components . . . looking at it [a problem] from a systematic perspective and not accepting things at face value . . . being curious about why things are the way they are and being able to think about why something is important."[59]

> A **conceptual skill** is the ability to think analytically to diagnose and solve complex problems.

Figure 1.6 shows that conceptual skills gain in importance as one moves up from lower to higher levels of management. This is because the problems faced at higher levels of responsibility are often ambiguous and unstructured, full of complications and interconnections, and pose longer-term consequences. The end-of-chapter features—*Manage a Critical Incident* and *Analyze the Case Study*—are ways to further develop your conceptual skills in management. And, the relevant self-assessment question to ask and honestly answer is: "Am I developing the strong critical-thinking and problem-solving capabilities I will need for long-term career success?"

Learning Check 5

TAKEAWAYQUESTION 5 **What are the essential managerial skills and how do we learn them?**

BE SURE YOU CAN • discuss the career importance of learning and lifelong learning • define three essential managerial skills—*technical, human,* and *conceptual skills* • explain how these skills vary in importance across management levels • define *emotional intelligence* as an important human skill

Management Learning Review
Get Prepared for **Quizzes and Exams**

SUMMARY

TAKEAWAYQUESTION **1**

What are the challenges of working in the new economy?

- Work in the new economy is increasingly knowledge based, and intellectual capital is the foundation of organizational performance.
- Organizations must value the talents of a workforce whose members are increasingly diverse with respect to gender, age, race and ethnicity, able-bodiedness, and lifestyles.
- The forces of globalization are bringing increased interdependencies among nations and economies, as customer markets and resource flows create intense business competition.
- Ever-present developments in information technology are reshaping organizations, changing the nature of work, and increasing the value of knowledge workers.
- Society has high expectations for organizations and their members to perform with commitment to high ethical standards and in socially responsible ways.
- Careers in the new economy require great personal initiative to build and maintain skill "portfolios" that are always up to date and valuable in a free agent economy.

FOR DISCUSSION What career risks and opportunities is globalization creating for today's college graduates?

TAKEAWAYQUESTION **2**

What are organizations like as work settings?

- Organizations are collections of people working together to achieve a common purpose.
- As open systems, organizations interact with their environments in the process of transforming resource inputs into product and service outputs.
- Productivity is a measure of the quantity and quality of work performance, with resource costs taken into account.
- High-performing organizations achieve both performance effectiveness in terms of goal accomplishment, and performance efficiency in terms of resource utilization.

FOR DISCUSSION When is it acceptable to sacrifice performance efficiency for performance effectiveness?

TAKEAWAYQUESTION **3**

What does it mean to be a manager?

- Managers directly support and facilitate the work efforts of other people in organizations.
- Top managers scan the environment, create strategies, and emphasize long-term goals; middle managers coordinate activities in large departments or divisions; team leaders and supervisors support performance of frontline workers at the team or work-unit level.

- Functional managers work in specific areas such as finance or marketing; general managers are responsible for larger multifunctional units; administrators are managers in public or non-profit organizations.
- The upside-down pyramid view of organizations shows operating workers at the top, serving customer needs while being supported from below by various levels of management.
- The changing nature of managerial work emphasizes being good at "coaching" and "supporting" others, rather than simply "directing" and "giving orders."

FOR DISCUSSION In what ways should the work of a top manager to differ from that of a team leader?

TAKEAWAYQUESTION **4**

What are the functions, roles, and activities of managers?

- The management process consists of the four functions of planning, organizing, leading, and controlling.
- Planning sets the direction; organizing assembles the human and material resources; leading provides the enthusiasm and direction; controlling ensures results.
- Managers implement the four functions in daily work that is often intense and stressful, involving long hours and continuous performance pressures.
- Managerial success requires the ability to perform well in interpersonal, informational, and decision-making roles.
- Managerial success also requires the ability to build interpersonal networks and use them to accomplish well-selected task agendas.

FOR DISCUSSION How might the upside-down pyramid view of organizations affect a manager's approach to planning, organizing, leading, and controlling?

TAKEAWAYQUESTION **5**

What are the essential managerial skills and how do we learn them?

- Careers in the new economy demand continual attention to lifelong learning from all aspects of daily experience and job opportunities.
- Skills considered essential for managers are broadly described as technical—ability to use expertise; human—ability to work well with other people, including emotional intelligence; and conceptual—ability to analyze and solve complex problems with critical thinking.
- Human skills are equally important for all management levels, whereas conceptual skills gain importance at higher levels and technical skills gain importance at lower levels.

FOR DISCUSSION Which management skills and competencies do you consider the most difficult to develop, and why?

SELF-TEST 1

Multiple-Choice Questions

1. The process of management involves the functions of planning, _____, leading, and controlling.
   (a) accounting
   (b) creating
   (c) innovating
   (d) organizing

2. An effective manager achieves both high-performance results and high levels of _____ among people doing the required work.
   (a) turnover
   (b) effectiveness
   (c) satisfaction
   (d) stress

3. Performance efficiency is a measure of the _____ associated with task accomplishment.
   (a) resource costs
   (b) goal specificity
   (c) product quality
   (d) product quantity

4. The requirement that a manager answer to a higher-level boss for performance results achieved by a work team is called _____.
   (a) dependency
   (b) accountability
   (c) authority
   (d) empowerment

5. Productivity is a measure of the quantity and _____ of work produced, relative to the cost of inputs.
   (a) quality   (c) timeliness
   (b) cost   (d) value

6. _____ managers pay special attention to the external environment, looking for problems and opportunities and finding ways for the organization to best deal with them.
   (a) Top   (c) Lower
   (b) Middle   (d) First-line

7. The accounting manager for a local newspaper would be considered a _____ manager, whereas the editorial director for sports would be considered a _____ manager.
   (a) general, functional
   (b) middle, top
   (c) staff, line
   (d) senior, junior

8. When a team leader clarifies desired work targets and deadlines for members of a work team, he or she is fulfilling the management function of _____.
   (a) planning
   (b) delegating
   (c) controlling
   (d) supervising

9. The process of building and maintaining good relationships with others who may help implement a manager's work agendas is called _____.
   (a) governance
   (b) networking
   (c) authority
   (d) entrepreneurship

10. In Katz's framework, top managers tend to rely more on their _____ skills than do first-line managers.
    (a) human
    (b) conceptual
    (c) decision-making
    (d) technical

11. The research of Mintzberg and others concludes that managers _____.
    (a) work at a leisurely pace
    (b) have blocks of private time for planning
    (c) are never free from the pressures of performance responsibility
    (d) have the advantages of flexible work hours

12. When someone holds a negative attitude toward minorities, this is an example of _____. When a team leader with a negative attitude toward minorities makes a decision to deny advancement opportunities to a Hispanic team member, this is an example of _____.
    (a) discrimination, prejudice
    (b) emotional intelligence, social capital
    (c) performance efficiency, performance effectiveness
    (d) prejudice, discrimination

13. Trends in the new workplace include which of the following?
    (a) More emphasis by managers on giving orders.
    (b) More attention by organizations to valuing people as human assets.
    (c) Less teamwork.
    (d) Less concern for work–life balance among the new generation of workers.

14. The manager's role in the "upside-down pyramid" view of organizations is best described as providing _____ so that workers can directly serve _____.
    (a) direction, top management
    (b) leadership, organizational goals
    (c) support, customers
    (d) agendas, networking

15. The management function of _____ is being performed when a retail manager measures daily sales in the women's apparel department and compares them with daily sales targets.
    (a) planning
    (b) agenda setting
    (c) controlling
    (d) delegating

Short-Response Questions

16. Discuss the importance of ethics in the relationship between managers and the people they supervise.

17. Explain how "accountability" operates in the relationship between (a) a team leader and her team members, and (b) the same team leader and her boss.

18. Explain how the "glass ceiling effect" may disadvantage newly hired African American college graduates in a large corporation.

19. What is globalization, and what are its implications for working in the new economy?

EssayQuestion

20. You have just been hired as the new head of an audit team for a national accounting firm. With four years of experience, you feel technically well prepared for the assignment. However, this is your first formal appointment as a "manager." Things are complicated at the moment. The team has 12 members of diverse demographic and cultural backgrounds, as well as work experience. There is an intense workload and lots of performance pressure. How will this situation challenge you to develop and use essential managerial skills and related competencies to manage the team successfully to high levels of auditing performance?

ManagementSkills& Competencies Make yourself **valuable!**

Evaluate Career Situations for New Managers

What Would You Do?

1. Opportunity with Foreign Employer

One of the plus sides of globalization is new jobs created by foreign employers setting up operations in local communities. How about you: Does it make any difference if you receive a job offer from a foreign employer such as Honda or a domestic one such as Ford? Assume you just had an offer from Honda for a great job in Marysville, Ohio. Prepare a Job Hunter's Balance Sheet. On the left, list the "pluses" and on the right, the "minuses" of working at home for a foreign employer.

2. Interviewing for Dream Job

It's time to take your first interview for a "dream" job. The interviewer is sitting across the table from you. She smiles, looks you in the eye, and says: "You have a very nice academic record and we're impressed with your extracurricular activities." But she then says: "Now tell me, just what can you do for us that will add value to the organization right from day one?" You're on the spot. How will you answer? What can you add to the conversation that clearly shows you have strong human and conceptual skills, not just technical ones?

3. Supervising Old Friends

When people are promoted into management, they sometimes end up supervising friends and colleagues they previously worked with. This could happen to you. When it does, how can you best deal with this situation right from the start? What will you do to earn the respect of everyone under your supervision and set the foundations for what will become a well-regarded and high-performing work team?

Reflect on the Self-Assessment

Career Readiness "Big 20"

Instructions

Use this scale to rate yourself on the following "Big 20" personal characteristics for management and career success.[60]

(S) Strong, I am very confident with this one.

(G) Good, but I still have room to grow.

(W) Weak, I really need work on this one.

(U) Unsure, I just don't know.

Big 20 Personal Characteristics

1. *Inner work standards*: The ability to personally set and work to high performance standards.

2. *Initiative*: The ability to actively tackle problems and take advantage of opportunities.

3. *Analytical thinking*: The ability to think systematically and identify cause–effect patterns in data and events.

4. *Creative thinking*: The ability to generate novel responses to problems and opportunities.

5. *Reflective thinking*: The ability to understand yourself and your actions in the context of society.

6. *Social objectivity*: The ability to act free of racial, ethnic, gender, and other prejudices or biases.

7. *Social intelligence*: The ability to understand another person's needs and feelings.

8. *Emotional intelligence*: The ability to recognize and manage emotions.

9. *Cultural intelligence*: The ability to respect other cultures and work well in diverse cultural settings.

10. *Interpersonal relations*: The ability to work well with others and in teams.

11. *Self-confidence*: The ability to be consistently decisive and willing to take action.

12. *Self-objectivity*: The ability to evaluate realistically personal strengths, weaknesses, motives, and skills.

13. *Tolerance for uncertainty*: The ability to work in ambiguous and uncertain conditions.

14. *Adaptability*: The ability to be flexible and adapt to changes.

15. *Stress management*: The ability to get work done under stressful conditions.

16. *Stamina*: The ability to sustain long work hours.

17. *Communication*: The ability to communicate well orally and in writing.

18. *Impression management*: The ability to create and sustain a positive impression in the eyes of others.

19. *Introspection*: The ability to learn from experience, awareness, and self-study.

20. *Application*: The ability to apply learning and use knowledge to accomplish things.

Self-Assessment Scoring

Give yourself 1 point for each S, and 1/2 point for each G. Do not give yourself points for W and U responses. Total your points and enter the result here [_____].

Interpretation

This assessment is a good starting point for considering where and how you can further develop useful managerial skills and competencies. It offers a self-described profile of your personal management foundations—things that establish strong career readiness. The higher you score the better. Are you a perfect 10, or something less? There shouldn't be too many 10s around. Ask someone you know to assess you on this instrument as well. You may be surprised at the differences between your score and the one they come up with.

Contribute to the Class Exercise

My Best Manager
Preparation

Working alone, make a list of the *behavioral attributes* that describe the "best" manager you have ever had. This could be someone you worked for in a full-time or part-time job, summer job, volunteer job, student organization, or elsewhere. If you have trouble identifying an actual manager, make a list of behavioral attributes of the manager you would most like to work for in your next job.

1. Make of list of the behavioral attributes that describe the "worst" manager you have ever had.

2. Write a short synopsis of things that this bad manager actually did or said that would qualify for "Believe it or not, it's really true!" status.

3. If you also made a list of attributes for your "best" manager, write a quick summary of the most important differences that quickly sort out your best from your worst.

Activity

Form into groups as assigned by your instructor, or work with a nearby classmate. Share your list of attributes and listen to the lists of others. Be sure to ask questions and make comments on items of special interest.

Work together in the group to create a master list that combines the unique attributes of the "best" and/or "worst" managers experienced by members. Have a spokesperson share that list with the rest of the class for further discussion. Share the "Believe it or not!" stories provided by group members.

Manage a Critical Incident

Team Leader Faces Test

It's happened again for the second time in a week. Charles walked into your cubicle and started a rant about his not getting enough support from you as his team leader. Before you could say anything, he accused you of playing favorites in assigning projects and not giving him the respect he deserved for his seniority and expertise. Then he gave you an angry look, turned around, and stomped off. You let it go the last time he exploded like this. And after cooling down, he came by later to apologize and give you a fist-bump of reconciliation. You've since learned, however, that the other team members have been on the receiving end of his outbursts and are starting to complain to one another about him. Charles is your top software engineer and has a lot of technical expertise to offer the team and you. He's a valuable talent, but his behavior has become intolerable. It's time for action.

Questions

How do you handle Charles and the full team in these circumstances? Does this call for direct confrontation between you and him? If so, how do you handle it? If not, how do you handle it? Is this something that the team as a whole needs to get involved with? If so, how do you proceed as team leader? How can you use each of the management functions to best deal with this situation? How can essential managerial skills help you succeed in this and similar situations?

Collaborate on the Team Activity

The Amazing Great Job Race

The fantastic variety of jobs out there for the well-prepared candidate is almost unimaginable. But our lives have gotten busy—really complicated! We spend time with work, school work, meetings, friends, family, video games, listening to music, watching television, surfing the Internet, going to concerts, social engagements, and so on! It seems like our calendars are always full with activities, leaving less time available to figure out what we really want from a first "real" job and a career.

You might say or hear: "I haven't got time for that—I need a job now . . . !" It's easy to overestimate how much you can get done at the last minute. There may also be lots of uncertainty as to what kind of job you really want. Thinking about likes and dislikes, talents and areas of deficit, goals, aspirations, wants, needs, understanding yourself and what makes you happy—all takes time. It also takes time spent in the right ways.

A job that looks really great to you might require a series of classes that you haven't taken, an internship that you haven't done, software that you don't know, or a foreign language you don't speak. If you spend time thinking about what you want, searching for what's out there, and figuring out now what you'll need in order to be prepared when you graduate, you just might find yourself running and winning the Amazing Great Job Race.

Instructions

1. *Reflect*: What classes have you enjoyed the most? What did you like most about them? How was your thinking challenged in these courses? What work experiences have been most satisfying for you? Why?

2. *Share*: Listen without criticism to how others in the group answered these reflection questions. Share your answers and listen to the comments of others. Turn group discussion into a brainstorming session about the kinds of jobs each member might like to do and the careers they might pursue.

3. *Debate*: Push each other to identify baseline requirements for jobs that might be good fits for them. Ask: What classes would you need to take to be in a position to compete for these jobs? What kinds of internships would you need to participate in order to gain experience and access? What tests and certifications might be necessary? How much time would these preparations take so that you are ready to compete for your best job with other candidates who might want it also?

Analyze THE CaseStudy : MCDONALD'S Grilling Up an Empire

Go to *Management Cases for Critical Thinking* at the end of the book to find this case.

HISTORY OF MANAGEMENT THOUGHT

2

KEY TAKEAWAYS

- Identify what can be learned from the classical management approaches.
- Identify what can be learned from the behavioral management approaches.
- Identify what can be learned from the modern management approaches.

SKILLS MAKE YOU **VALUABLE**

- **EVALUATE** *Career Situations:*
  What Would You Do?

- **REFLECT** *On the Self-Assessment:*
  Managerial Assumptions

- **CONTRIBUTE** *To the Class Exercise:*
  Evidence-Based Management Quiz

- **MANAGE** *A Critical Incident:*
  Theory X versus Theory Y

- **COLLABORATE** *On the Team Activity:*
  Management in Popular Culture

- **ANALYZE** *The Case Study:*
  Zara International: Fashion at the Speed of Light

Ancestry.com is a hugely popular website. It helps people learn more about their roots—and by extension, themselves. The history of management thought offers similar insights. In order to manage successfully today, and into the ever-changing future, it is critical to understand the insights and lessons of the past. Knowing where you're going requires knowledge of where you've been. That is our focus in this chapter.

In his book *The Evolution of Management Thought*, Daniel Wren traces management as far back as 5000 BC, when the ancient Sumerians used written records to improve government and business activities.[1] Management was crucial in the construction of the Egyptian pyramids, the spread of the Roman Empire across the globe, and the renowned commercial success of 14th-century Venice. By the time of the start of the Industrial Revolution in the late 1700s, great social changes helped stimulate major manufacturing advances in basic products and consumer goods. Adam Smith's revolutionary (at the time) concepts of division of labor and task specialization accelerated industrial development. With the turn of the 20th century, Henry Ford had made mass production a core aspect of the emerging economy. Since then, both the science and practice of management have been on the fast track toward continued development.[2]

Many crucial insights can be taken from the history of management thought. Rather than assuming that our generation invented current management practice out of thin air, it is important to understand the historical roots of what we think of today as modern ideas, and also to admit that we are still trying to perfect these ideas and approaches to best match current business reality.

Classical Management Approaches

TAKEAWAY 1   What can we learn from classical management thinking?

LEARN MORE | Scientific management • Administrative principles • Bureaucratic organization
ABOUT

Our study of management begins with a focus on the three major classical approaches: (1) scientific management, (2) administrative principles, and (3) bureaucratic organization.[3] Figure 2.1 ties each of these classical approaches to a prominent historical figure—Taylor, Fayol, and Weber. What can be seen here is that the classical approaches share a common assumption: People rationally consider their opportunities and do whatever is necessary to achieve the greatest personal and monetary gain.[4]

Scientific Management

In 1911, Frederick W. Taylor published *The Principles of Scientific Management*, where he stated: "The principal object of management should be to secure maximum prosperity for the employer, coupled with the maximum prosperity for the employee."[5] Taylor, often called the "father of scientific management," noticed that workers often did their jobs with wasted motions and without a consistent approach. This resulted in inefficiency and low performance. He believed that this problem could be fixed if workers were taught to do their jobs in the best ways and then were helped and guided by supervisors to always work this way.

Taylor's goal was to improve workers' productivity. He used the concept of "time study" to analyze the motions and tasks required to do a job, and to develop the most efficient ways to perform that job. He then linked these job requirements to both worker training and support from supervisors in the form of precise direction, work assistance, and monetary incentives. Taylor's approach, known as **scientific management**, includes four guiding principles.

Scientific management emphasizes careful alignment of worker training, incentives, and supervisory support with job requirements.

1. Develop a "science" that includes rules of motion, standardized work implements, and proper working conditions for every job.

2. Carefully select workers with the right abilities for the job.

3. Carefully train workers to do the job and give them incentives to cooperate with the job "science."

4. Support workers by carefully planning their work and by smoothing the way as they do their work.

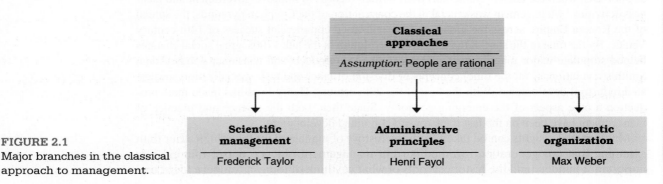

FIGURE 2.1
Major branches in the classical approach to management.

Although Taylor called his approach "scientific" management, contemporary scholars have questioned his truthfulness in reporting and the scientific rigor of his studies.[6] But Taylor's ideas still influence management thinking.[7] A contemporary example is the United Parcel Service (UPS). UPS workers are guided by carefully calibrated productivity standards. Sorters at regional hubs are timed according to strict task requirements and are expected to load vans at a set number of packages-per-hour. A GPS is used to plot the shortest delivery routes; delivery stops are registered in on-board computers that are studied to identify wasted time. Industrial engineers design explicit procedures for drivers—with 340 delivery and pickup rules like avoid left turns in traffic, unbuckle seat belt with left hand, and walk at a "brisk" pace. Consistent with scientific management principles, efficiency is a top priority at UPS; saving a few seconds at each stop adds up to significant increases in productivity.[8]

> ## Practical Insights from Scientific Management
>
> - Make results-based compensation a performance incentive.
> - Carefully design jobs with efficient work methods.
> - Carefully select workers with the abilities to do these jobs.
> - Train workers to perform jobs to the best of their abilities.
> - Train supervisors to support workers so they can perform to the best of their abilities.

One of the most enduring legacies of scientific management grew from Taylor's interest in **motion study**, the science of reducing a job or a task to its most basic physical aspects. Two of his contemporaries, Frank and Lillian Gilbreth, pioneered the use of motion studies as a management tool.[9] In one famous case, the Gilbreths cut down the number of motions used by bricklayers and tripled their productivity!

Motion study is the science of reducing a task to its basic physical motions.

Insights from scientific management have led to advances in job design, work standards, and incentive wage plans—all of which are techniques organizations use today. The next time you pass by a Taco Bell, think of the number 164, which is the average number of seconds it takes from the point of order to taco-in-hand. Taco Bell measures performance based on both time and accuracy, which are linked to standardized systems for order taking, money handling, food preparation, and order delivery. Workers' actions are carefully designed in assembly-line style, where each worker learns the script for his or her station and then delivers it over and over again. The whole process is supported by training, and rewards are given to employees for doing things the Taco Bell way.[10]

Administrative Principles

In 1916, after a career in French industry, Henri Fayol published *Administration Industrielle et Générale*[11] in which he outlines his views on the management of organizations and workers. Fayol identifies five "rules" or "duties" of management, which support the four functions of management—planning, organizing, leading, and controlling—that we talk about today:

1. *Foresight*—to complete a plan of action for the future.

2. *Organization*—to provide and mobilize resources to implement the plan.

3. *Command*—to lead, select, and evaluate workers to get the best work toward the plan.

4. *Coordination*—to fit diverse efforts together and to ensure information is shared and problems solved.

5. *Control*—to make sure things happen according to plan and to take necessary corrective action.

Fayol believed that management could be taught. He wanted to improve the quality of management and defined a number of "principles" to help managers. A number of these principles still guide managers today. They include the *scalar chain principle*—there should be a clear and unbroken line of communication from the top to the bottom of the organization; the *unity of command principle*—each person should receive orders from only one boss; and the *unity of direction principle*—one person should be in charge of all activities that have the same performance objective.

Bureaucratic Organization

Max Weber was a late-19th-century German political economist who had a major impact in the fields of management and sociology. His ideas developed after noticing that organizations often performed poorly. Among other things, Weber noticed that employees often held positions of authority not because of their capabilities, but because of their "privileged" social status in German society. At the heart of Weber's thinking was an ideal; an intentionally rational, and very efficient form of organization called a **bureaucracy**.[12] It was founded on principles of logic, order, and legitimate authority. The defining characteristics of Weber's bureaucratic organization are:

> **A bureaucracy** is a rational and efficient form of organization founded on logic, order, and legitimate authority.

> Characteristics of ► Weber's bureaucracy

- *Clear division of labor:* Jobs are well defined, and workers are highly skilled at performing them.

- *Clear hierarchy of authority:* Authority and responsibility are well defined for each position, and each position reports to a higher level.

- *Formal rules and procedures:* Written guidelines direct behavior and decisions in jobs, and written files are kept for historical record.

- *Impersonality:* Rules and procedures are impartially and uniformly applied, with no one receiving preferential treatment.

- *Careers based on merit:* Workers are selected and promoted on ability, competency, and performance, and managers are career employees of the organizations.

Weber believed that organizations structured as bureaucracies would use resources more efficiently and treat employees more fairly than other systems. He wrote:[13]

> The purely bureaucratic type of administrative organization . . . is, from a purely technical point of view, capable of attaining the highest degree of efficiency. . . . It is superior to any other form in precision, in stability, in the stringency of its discipline, and in its reliability. It thus makes possible a particularly high degree of calculability of results for the heads of the organization and for those acting in relation to it.

Today we recognize that bureaucracy works well sometimes, but not all of the time. In fact it's common to hear the terms *bureaucracy* and *bureaucrat* used with negative connotations. We picture bureaucracies as bogged down in excessive paperwork or "red tape," slow in handling problems, rigid in the face of shifting customer needs, and high in resistance to change and employee apathy.[14] These are disadvantages for organizations that have to be flexible and adaptive to the changing circumstances that are common today. A major management challenge is to know when bureaucratic features work well and what are the best alternatives when they don't. Later in the chapter we'll call this *contingency thinking*.

The United States Postal Service (USPS) is perhaps the most current, large-scale example of the problems bureaucracies face in meeting customers' constantly evolving needs. As more and more business is conducted online and through web-based services, a Government

The Classic Bureaucracy

Fair
Impersonal
Career managers
Clear division of labor
Promotion based on merit
Formal hierarchy of authority
Written rules and standard procedures

Accountability Office (GAO) report stated that the "USPS's business model is not viable."[15] This conclusion is not surprising in light of continuing, annual losses of billions of dollars. What is clear is that if Weber's bureaucratic principles are to retain practical viability in the USPS and other organizations, they need to be modified to best handle the constraints of the modern marketplace—more flexibility and creativity, and a better customer focus. Would you agree that bureaucracies like the USPS can be retrofitted to today's challenges, or is it time to put in place all-new organizational designs?

Learning Check 1

TAKEAWAYQUESTION **1 What can we learn from classical management thinking?**

BE SURE YOU CAN • state the underlying assumption of the classical management approaches • list the principles of Taylor's scientific management • identify three of Fayol's principles for guiding managerial action • list the key characteristics of bureaucracy and explain why Weber considered it an ideal form of organization • identify the possible disadvantages of bureaucracy in today's environment

Behavioral Management Approaches

TAKEAWAY 2 What insights come from the behavioral management approaches?

LEARN MORE ABOUT | Follett's organizations as communities • The Hawthorne studies
Maslow's hierarchy of needs • McGregor's Theory X and Theory Y
Argyris's personality and organization

During the 1920s, an emphasis on the human side of the workplace began to influence management thinking. Major branches in the behavioral—or human resource—approaches to management are shown in Figure 2.2. These include Follett's ideas about organizations as communities, the Hawthorne studies, Maslow's theory of human needs, and related ideas of Douglas McGregor and Chris Argyris. The behavioral approaches assume that people enjoy social relationships, respond to group pressures, and search for personal fulfillment. These historical foundations set the stage for what is now known as the field of **organizational behavior**, the study of individuals and groups in organizations.

Organizational behavior is the study of individuals and groups in organizations.

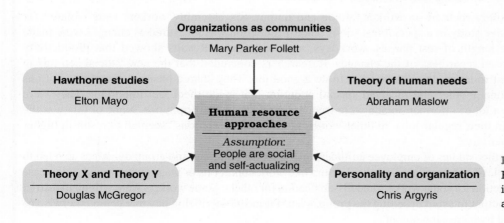

FIGURE 2.2
Foundations in the behavioral or human resource approaches to management.

Follett's Organizations as Communities

The work of Mary Parker Follett was part of an important transition from classical thinking into behavioral management. The book *Mary Parker Follett—Prophet of Management: A Celebration of Writings from the 1920s* offers an important reminder of the wisdom that can come from an understanding of history. Although Follett wrote at a different time in history, her ideas are rich with foresight. She taught respect for workers' experience and knowledge, warned against the dangers of too much hierarchy, and called for visionary leadership. Follett was eulogized upon her death in 1933 as "one of the most important women America has yet produced in the fields of civics and sociology."[16]

Follett thought of organizations as "communities" where managers and workers should labor in harmony without one party dominating the other, and with the freedom to talk over and truly reconcile conflicts and differences. For her, groups were a way for individuals to combine their talents toward a greater good. She believed it was the job of managers to help workers cooperate with one another and to integrate their goals and interests.

Follett's emphasis on groups and her commitment to human cooperation are highly relevant themes today.[17] She believed that making every employee an owner in a business would create feelings of collective responsibility. Today, we address the same issues under such labels as *employee ownership, profit sharing*, and *gain-sharing plans*. She believed that business problems involve a wide variety of factors that must be considered in relationship to one another. Today, we talk about "systems" and "contingency thinking." Follett also believed that businesses were service organizations and that private profits should always be considered vis-à-vis the public good. Today, we pursue the same issues under the labels *managerial ethics* and *corporate social responsibility*. Follett was, in many ways, a woman ahead of her time, and whose insights and philosophy bear on organizational practice today.

The Hawthorne Studies

The shift toward behavioral thinking in management gained momentum in 1924 when the Western Electric Company commissioned a research program to study worker productivity at the Hawthorne Works of the firm's Chicago plant.[18] A team led by Harvard's Elton Mayo set out to learn how economic incentives and workplace conditions affected workers' output. But they concluded that unforeseen "psychological factors" somehow interfered with their experiments.

Social Setting and Human Relations

One study focused on worker fatigue and output. Six assembly workers were isolated for intensive study in a special test room. Their production was measured as changes were made to the length of rest pauses, workdays, and workweeks. Results showed that productivity increased regardless of the changes. Researchers concluded that the new "social setting" in the test room made workers want to do a good job. They shared pleasant social interactions with one another and received special attention that made them feel important. They were given a lot of information and were frequently asked for their opinions. None of this was the case in their regular jobs. In other words, good "human relations" seemed to result in higher productivity.

Further studies of employee attitudes, interpersonal relations, and group dynamics also led to "complex" and "baffling" results. Factors like work conditions or wages were found to increase satisfaction for some workers and dissatisfaction for others. Some workers were willing to restrict their output to avoid upsetting the group, even if it meant sacrificing pay that could otherwise be earned by increasing output.

ethics > KNOW RIGHT FROM WRONG

> *"If our drivers have to veer off, they call and say we are taking a little personal time. It is changing their behavior in a positive way."*

Tracking Technology Monitors Worker Behavior

If you put technology together with scientific management, what do you get? For many in the trucking industry, the answer is GPS tracking technology that monitors drivers to make sure they follow their engineered routes and aren't wasting—or even stealing—company time. How far should this tracking technology go and what ground rules should be followed?

At a small pest control company, the general manager secretly installed GPS software on company-issued smartphones. This allowed him to track drivers. After noticing that one was stopping regularly at a single address, the manager confronted the driver and learned he was seeing a woman. The driver was fired. That was the first anyone knew the manager was using the tracking technology. Now, the manager says: "If our drivers have to veer off, they call and say we are taking a little personal time. It is changing their behavior in a positive way."

The founder of the National Workrights Institute, Lewis Maltby, champions worker privacy. But he also says the issue is not "whether employers should monitor" but "a question of how." The institute's position is that employees have the right to know they are being monitored and also what the procedures are for handling alleged violations. The landscaping firm Plants, Inc., follows that advice, and all 16 employees know their company phones have mobile monitoring turned on. Still, some employees complain that their privacy rights are being violated.

Employees who don't like tracking technology have little legal recourse. Employment law professor Matt Finkin from the University of Illinois says that this is an area where "technology is ahead of the law by about a generation." Unions are taking issue with the practice in some cases and negotiating rules of use, including disciplinary procedures. But for now electronic monitoring has gained a strong foothold both inside and outside the office.

WHAT DO YOU THINK?

Should the use of tracking technology to monitor employee behavior be regulated by law? Or, is it a practice that employers have the rights to use at their discretion? Would you be comfortable being monitored when making outside sales calls, for example, or when using your company phone for private browsing and conversations? What message does the use of electronic monitoring communicate to employees? What are the limits to using technology this way, and who has the rights to what in this case? How would you feel if your phone or computer had a tracking device on it that informed your parents what sites you'd visited, or what people you'd called? Would it matter if they were paying for these devices? Why or why not?

Lessons of the Hawthorne Studies

Scholars now criticize the Hawthorne studies for poor research design and weak empirical support for the conclusions drawn.[19] Yet, despite these problems, the studies shifted managers' and researchers' attention toward social and human factors as drivers of productivity. They brought visibility to the idea that workers' feelings, attitudes, and relationships with co-workers affected their work, and that groups have important influences on individuals. They also identified the **Hawthorne effect**—the tendency of workers singled out for special attention to perform as good—or better than anticipated—because of expectations created by the situation.

Maslow's Theory of Human Needs

The work of psychologist Abraham Maslow, in the area of human "needs," also has had a major impact on the behavioral approach to management.[20] Maslow described a **need** as a physiological

The **Hawthorne effect** is the tendency of persons singled out for special attention to perform as expected.

A **need** is a physiological or psychological deficiency that a person feels compelled to satisfy.

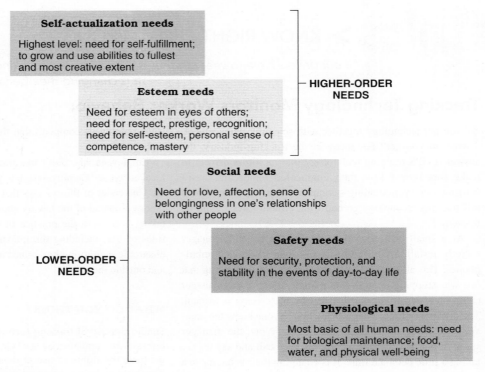

FIGURE 2.3
Maslow's hierachy of human needs.

or psychological deficiency a person feels compelled to satisfy. Importantly, needs create tensions that can influence workers' attitudes and behaviors. Maslow placed needs into the hierarchy shown in Figure 2.3. From lowest to highest in order, they are physiological, safety, social, esteem, and self-actualization needs.

Maslow's theory is based on two underlying principles—the **deficit principle** and the **progression principle**. The deficit principle is a satisfied need that does not motivate behavior. People try to satisfy "deprived" needs or those for which there is a "deficit" (i.e., when I'm hungry, I seek to satisfy my hunger by eating—when I'm done eating, hunger doesn't motivate me anymore). The progression principle is the five needs that exist in a hierarchy of "prepotency." A need at any level becomes active only when the next-lower-level need is satisfied (i.e., I'm thirsty and lonely—but I won't be motivated to chat with my friends until I've had something to drink). Maslow argued that people try to satisfy these five needs in sequence. They progress, step by step, from the lowest level in the hierarchy up to the highest. Along the way, a deprived need dominates attention and determines behavior until it is satisfied. Then, the next-higher-level need is activated. At the level of self-actualization, the deficit and progression principles cease to operate. The more this need is satisfied, the stronger it grows.

Consistent with human relations thinking, Maslow's theory implies that managers who understand and help workers to satisfy their important needs at work will get more productivity out of their employees. Although scholars now recognize things are more complicated than this, Maslow's ideas are still relevant. Consider the case of volunteer workers at the local Red Cross, animal shelter, or other community organizations. What can be done to motivate workers who aren't paid? Maslow's ideas suggest linking volunteer work with opportunities to satisfy higher-order needs like esteem and self-actualization.

According to the **deficit principle** a satisfied need does not motivate behavior.

According to the **progression principle** a need is activated only when the next-lower-level need is satisfied.

McGregor's Theory X and Theory Y

Douglas McGregor was heavily influenced by both the Hawthorne studies and Abraham Maslow. In his classic book, *The Human Side of Enterprise*, McGregor argued that managers should give more attention to workers' social and self-actualizing needs.[21] He called on managers to shift their view of human nature away from a set of assumptions he called Theory X and toward ones he called Theory Y. You can check your own managerial assumptions by completing the self-assessment at the end of the chapter.

According to McGregor, managers with **Theory X** assumptions believe that employees generally dislike work, have little ambition, are irresponsible, resistant to change, and prefer to be led rather than to lead. In contrast, managers with **Theory Y** assumptions believe employees are willing to work hard, accept responsibility, are capable of self-control and self-direction, and are imaginative and creative.

One important point regarding Theory X and Theory Y is that McGregor believed these assumptions create **self-fulfilling prophecies**. When managers behave consistent with the assumptions, he said, they end up encouraging employees to act in ways that confirm managers' original expectations.[22]

Managers with Theory X assumptions tend to act in a very directive, command-and-control, top-down way that gives employees little say over their work. These behaviors create passive, dependent, reluctant subordinates, who tend to do only what they are told to do or required to do, reinforcing the original Theory X viewpoint. In contrast, managers with Theory Y assumptions tend to behave in ways that engage workers, giving them more job involvement, freedom, and responsibility. This creates opportunities for employees to satisfy esteem and self-actualization needs, and they respond by performing with initiative and high performance, creating a positive self-fulfilling prophecy.[23]

Theory Y thinking is reflected in a lot of the ideas and developments discussed in this book, such as valuing diversity, employee engagement, self-managing teams, empowerment, and leadership. You need to ponder your Theory X and Y assumptions and think through their implications for how you behave as a manager and team leader. You also must be prepared to meet and work with others holding different assumptions.

Theory X assumes people dislike work, lack ambition, act irresponsibly, and prefer to be led.

Theory Y assumes people are willing to work, like responsibility, and are self-directed and creative.

A **self-fulfilling prophecy** occurs when a person acts in ways that confirm another's expectations.

Argyris's Theory of Adult Personality

The ideas of Maslow and McGregor inspired the well-regarded scholar and business consultant Chris Argyris. In his book *Personality and Organization*, Argyris contrasts management practices found in traditional, bureaucratic organizations with the needs and capabilities of mature adults.[24] Argyris believed that common problems, such as absenteeism, turnover, apathy, alienation, and low morale may be signs of a mismatch. He also argued that managers who treat employees as responsible adults will achieve the highest productivity. It's the self-fulfilling prophecy notion again: If you treat people as grown-ups, that's the way they'll behave.

Consider these examples of how Argyris's thinking differs from that of earlier management thinking. In scientific management, the principle of specialization assumes that people will work more efficiently as tasks become simpler and better defined. Argyris believed that this principle limits opportunities for self-actualization. In Weber's bureaucracy, people work in a clear hierarchy of authority, with higher levels directing and controlling lower levels. Argyris worried that this creates dependent, passive workers who feel they have little control over their work environments. In Fayol's administrative principles, the concept of unity of direction assumes that efficiency increases when work is planned and directed by supervisors. Argyris argued that this may create conditions for psychological failure; conversely, psychological success is more likely when employees are allowed to define their own goals.

wisdom > LEARN FROM ROLE MODELS

> His life changed and its "second chapter" started after a trekking holiday in Nepal.

Former Microsoft Executive Fights Illiteracy and Gains Fulfillment

AFP Photo/Room To Read/NewsCom

There are many ways to help build a better society. John Wood's choice is social entrepreneurship that promotes literacy for children in the developing world. During a successful career as a Microsoft executive, his life changed after he went on a trekking vacation to the Himalayas of Nepal. While there, Wood was shocked at the lack of schools and limited access to educational materials. He pledged to collect books for a Nepalese school that he visited on his trip, and he returned a year later with 3,000 to give to the students. But the impact on his future didn't end there. Wood was inspired to leverage his years of executive experience to accomplish more through nonprofit work.

Wood quit his Microsoft job to found Room to Read. It builds libraries and schools in poor nations like Nepal, Cambodia, Vietnam, and Laos, and publishes local language books to help fill them. Now in what he calls the "second chapter" in his life, Wood's passion is to provide the lifelong benefits of education to poor children. His organization's website describes the vision this way: "We envision a world in which all children can pursue a quality education that enables them to reach their full potential and contribute to their community and the world."

Picture this scene in Laos, one of the world's poorest nations. Children sit happily in a small library filled with books reading a story with their teacher. It's a Room to Read project. So far the organization has put in place over 700 libraries and built 140 schools in this small land-locked Southeast Asian country. Laos has just over 8,000 primary schools nationwide and the majority offer only incomplete educational experiences.

The Room to Read model is so efficient that it can build schools for as little as $6,000 and is now setting up five or six new libraries each day. Over 10,000 libraries are already in place in Asia and Sub-Saharan Africa. *Time* magazine called Wood and his team "Asian Heroes." *Fast Company* magazine gave Room to Read its Social Capitalist Award. Noting that one-seventh of the global population can't read or write, Wood says: "I don't see how we are going to solve the world's problems without literacy."

FIND THE INSPIRATION

Room to Read builds one school or library at a time, but the results add up quickly—almost 10 million children have benefited from Room to Read's programs to date. Is the success of Room to Read due in part to Wood's prior business and management experience? How can such experience help nonprofit organizations? Can you identify a social problem in your community that might be addressed using John Wood and his work with Room to Read as a role model? How do you see yourself fulfilling higher order needs in the future? Will earning good money at work be enough, or will your self-actualization require something more?

Learning Check 2

TAKEAWAYQUESTION **2 What insights come from the behavioral management approaches?**

BE SURE YOU CAN • explain Follett's concept of organizations as communities • define the *Hawthorne effect* • explain how the Hawthorne findings influenced the development of management thought • explain how Maslow's hierarchy of needs operates in the workplace • distinguish between Theory X and Theory Y assumptions, and explain why McGregor favored Theory Y • explain Argyris's criticism that traditional organizational practices are inconsistent with mature adult personalities

Modern Management Foundations

TAKEAWAY 3   What are the foundations of modern management thinking?

LEARN MORE ABOUT | Quantitative analysis and tools • Organizations as systems
Contingency thinking • Quality management • Evidence-based management

The concepts, models, and ideas discussed so far helped set the stage for continuing developments in management thought. They ushered in modern management approaches that include the use of quantitative analysis and tools, a systems view of organizations, contingency thinking, commitment to quality management, and the importance of evidence-based management.

Quantitative Analysis and Tools

The typical quantitative approach to management works like this: a problem is encountered, it is systematically analyzed, appropriate mathematical techniques are applied, and an optimum solution is identified. The following examples show this in action.

Problem: An oil exploration company is worried about future petroleum reserves in various parts of the world. *Quantitative approach—Mathematical forecasting* makes future projections for reserve sizes and depletion rates that are used in the planning process and oil prospecting strategies.

Problem: A "big box" retailer is trying to deal with decreasing profit margins by minimizing inventory costs, but must also avoid being "out of stock" for customers. *Quantitative approach—Inventory analysis* helps control inventories by mathematically determining how much inventory to automatically order and when to order it.

Problem: A grocery store is getting complaints from customers that wait times are too long for checkouts during certain times of the day. *Quantitative approach—Queuing theory* allocates service personnel and workstations based on alternative workload demands in a way that minimizes both customer wait time and personnel costs.

Problem: A manufacturer wants to maximize profits on the production of three different products on three different machines, each of which can be only be used at distinct periods of times and for runs at different costs. *Quantitative approach—Linear programming* calculates how best to allocate production across the three machines.

Problem: A real estate developer wants to control costs and finish building an apartment complex on schedule. *Quantitative approach—Network models* break large tasks into smaller components and diagram them in step-by-step sequences. This allows project managers to analyze, plan, and control timetables for the completion of activity sub-sets.

Analytics is the systematic analysis of large databases to solve problems and make informed decisions.

Although quantitative analysis has always been useful in management, the availability of inexpensive, convenient, affordable computing is dramatically expanding its power. With the collection, storage, and analysis of data now easier than ever before, an area known as **analytics** is becoming indispensable to organizations of all types. Think of analytics as the systematic analysis of large databases—often called "big data"—to solve problems and make informed decisions.[25] Here are two examples.

Problem—Sales were flat and inventories were high at the Schwan Food Company. Delivery drivers were using six-week-old lists of customers' prior orders to decide who to visit and what to offer them. *Solution*—The situation improved substantially after Schwan installed a new analytics program. It churns vast amounts of historical data to predict customer preferences and sends daily sales recommendations directly to each driver's tablet.

Problem—Software engineering talent is in short supply for Google and other high-tech companies. Competition for new hires is intense and retention is difficult as experienced engineers become poaching targets for rival firms. *Solution*—Google has an analytics tool that pools information from performance reviews, surveys, and pay and promotion histories, and uses a math formula (algorithm) to identify engineers who might be open to offers from other firms. Managers use this information to develop plans for retaining these talented engineers and reduce the likelihood that they will find competing offers attractive.[26]

Organizations as Systems

A system is a collection of interrelated parts working together for a purpose.

A subsystem is a smaller component of a larger system.

An open system interacts with its environment and transforms resource inputs into outputs.

Organizations have long been described as cooperative systems that achieve great things by focusing resources and the contributions of many individuals toward a common purpose. In reality, cooperation among people and different moving parts is imperfect and can be improved. That is why it's critical to understand the full complexity of organizations as a **system** of interrelated parts or **subsystems** that work together to achieve common goals.[27]

Organizations function as **open systems** that interact with their environment in a continual process of transforming inputs—people, technology, information, money, and supplies—into outputs—goods and services. Figure 2.4 shows how an organization functions as an interacting network of subsystems. The activities of these subsystems individually and collectively support the larger system to make things happen. The operations and service management subsystems anchor the transformation process, while linking with other subsystems such as purchasing, accounting, and sales. Organizations can only perform well when each subsystem both performs its tasks well and cooperates with other subsystems.

FIGURE 2.4
Organizations as complex networks of interacting subsystems.

Contingency Thinking

Successful managers identify and implement practices that best fit with the unique demands of different situations. This requires **contingency thinking** that matches actions with problems and opportunities specific to different people and settings. From a contingency perspective, there is no "one best way" to manage in all circumstances. The challenge is to understand situational differences and respond to them in ways that fit with their unique characteristics.[28] Can you think of situations at work or at school where you need to adjust your interpersonal behavior, for example, to succeed?

Contingency thinking is an important theme in this book, and its implications extend to all of the management functions—from planning and controlling for diverse environmental conditions, to organizing for different strategies, to leading in different performance situations. A good illustration takes us back once again to the concept of bureaucracy, which Weber offered as an ideal form of organization. But from a contingency perspective, bureaucracy is only one possible way of organizing. What turns out to be the "best" structure in any given situation will depend on a range of factors, including environmental uncertainty, an organization's primary technology, and the strategy being pursued. A tight bureaucracy works best when the environment is relatively stable and operations are predictable and uncomplicated. In complex and changing situations, more flexible structures are needed.[29]

Contingency thinking tries to match management practices with situational demands.

Quality Management

The work of W. Edwards Deming is a cornerstone of the quality movement in management.[30] His story began in 1951, when he was invited to Japan to explain quality control techniques that had been developed in the United States. "When Deming spoke," we might say, "the Japanese listened." The principles he taught the Japanese were straightforward and they worked: Tally defects, analyze and trace them to the source, make corrections, and keep a record of what happens afterward. Deming's approach emphasizes the use of statistical tools, commitment to quality assurance training, and constant innovation.[31]

insight > LEARN ABOUT YOURSELF

> *There's no right or wrong when it comes to learning styles. But we should recognize and understand them.*

Make Learning Style Work for You

In light of all the complexities associated with modern management practice, it is important to know your own personal **learning style**. Think of learning style as how you like to learn through receiving, processing, and recalling new information.

Each of us tends to learn in slightly different ways. Look how some students do well in lecture classes, while others do not. But these others might excel in case study or project classes that emphasize discussion and problem solving rather than digesting information.

There's no right or wrong learning style; however, it is critical to recognize and understand some underlying differences. Some people learn by watching. They observe others and model what they see. Others learn by doing. They act and experiment, learning as they go. Some people are feelers, for whom emotions and values are very important. Others are thinkers who emphasize reason and analysis.

It's a personal challenge to learn something new every day, and it's a managerial challenge to consistently help employees learn as well. One of our most significant challenges is to always embrace experiences at school, at work, and in everyday living and try our best to learn from these experiences. Every employee is unique, most problem situations are complex, and key performance factors are constantly changing. Professional success is much more likely for managers who are excited to learn, and also are excited to help others to learn.

GET TO KNOW YOURSELF BETTER

Look at the diagram of learning styles and think about your own preferences. Shade in each circle to show the degree to which that description best fits with your preferences. This snapshot of your personal learning style is good food for thought. Ask: (1) "What are the implications of my learning style for how I perform academically and how well I perform at work? (2) "How does my learning style influence my relationships with others in study groups and work teams?" (3) "How does my learning style influence the kinds of information I pay the most attention to and the kind of information I tend to overlook?"

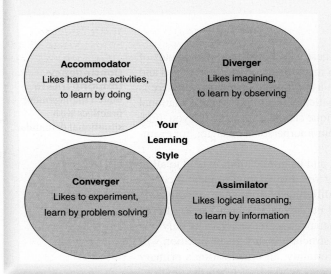

Accommodator
Likes hands-on activities, to learn by doing

Diverger
Likes imagining, to learn by observing

Your Learning Style

Converger
Likes to experiment, learn by problem solving

Assimilator
Likes logical reasoning, to learn by information

Total quality management is an organization-wide commitment to continuous improvement, product quality, and customer needs.

Continuous improvement involves always searching for new ways to improve work quality and performance.

These ideas contributed to the emergence of **total quality management**, or TQM, which incorporates quality principles in organizations' strategic objectives. TQM principles are applied to all aspects of operations with a focus on meeting customers' needs by doing things right the first time. Most TQM approaches begin with buy-in on a total quality commitment. This applies to all employees and every organizational subsystem—from resource acquisition and supply chain management, through production and into physical distribution of finished goods and services, and ultimately to customer relationships. The search for and commitment to quality reflects an emphasis on **continuous improvement**—always looking for new ways to improve on current practices. The key takeaway is that it is critical to never be satisfied; something always can and should be improved—whether it is machines, people, processes, or relationships.

ISO certification by the International Standards Organization in Geneva, Switzerland, has become a global stamp of approval for quality management. Businesses and nonprofits that strive to be "world-class" are increasingly expected to have ISO certification. To obtain it, they undergo a rigorous assessment by independent auditors to determine whether ISO's strict quality requirements have been met.

ISO certification indicates conformance with a rigorous set of international quality standards.

Evidence-Based Management

Managers are always searching for practical answers to questions dealing with day-to-day dilemmas and situations.[32] What is the best performance appraisal method? What selection method works best for high-performance teams? How should a merit pay system be designed and implemented? When does directive leadership work best? How do you structure organizations for innovation? Given the importance of the answers to such questions, it is critical to be cautious and a bit skeptical when separating fads from facts and assumptions from informed insight based on empirical data and analysis.

In light of the complexity of work and organizations today, a critical concern of management scholars is that we may be too quick to accept the results of studies based on poor science or questionable evidence. And if research may be flawed or preliminary in terms of drawing firm conclusions, extra care needs to be taken when interpreting and applying results to management practice.[33]

Scholars Jeffrey Pfeffer and Robert Sutton make the case for **evidence-based management** where management decisions are made based on "hard facts"—that is, about what really works—rather than on "dangerous half-truths"—things that sound good but lack solid evidence.[34] Pfeffer and Sutton want managers to be well informed and knowledgeable when making decisions. Evidence-based management is about managers "making decisions through the conscientious, explicit, and judicious use of four sources of information: practitioner expertise and judgment, evidence from the local context, a critical evaluation of the best available research evidence, and the perspectives of those people who might be affected by the decision."[35] You may recognize incidents in your personal affairs where you make decisions based on less-than-complete information, or even hearsay. When you do, are you prepared to learn from experience and rely more on evidence-based decision making in the future?

Evidence-based management involves making decisions based on hard facts about what really works.

Management scholars support and inform evidence-based management by conducting solid and meaningful research using scientific methods, and by rigorously examining and reporting case studies and insights from managers' experiences.[36] Some research carves out new and innovative territory while other research refines and extends knowledge that has come down in building-block fashion over time. You'll notice that management research involves data collection and analysis in one form or another. But just because a research study uses data, doesn't make it solid and scientific. The following criteria are useful as a first step to determine whether or not good scientific methods have been used.

- A research question or problem is clearly identified.

◄ Criteria for evaluating scientific methods

- One or more hypotheses is stated to describe possible explanations.

- The research design provides a good test of the hypotheses.

- Data are rigorously gathered, analyzed, and interpreted.

- Hypotheses are accepted or rejected and conclusions made based on the evidence.

When research satisfies the scientific methods test, managers can be more confident accepting and applying results in actual practice. Gathering data from a sample of some 1,000 firms, for example, Pfeffer and a colleague studied the link between human resource management and organizational performance.[37] They found that firms using a mix of positive human resource management practices had more sales-per-employee and higher profits-per-employee than firms that did not. These positive practices included employment security, selective hiring, self-managed teams, high wages based on performance merit, training and skill development, minimal status differences, and shared information.[38]

Learning Check 3

TAKEAWAYQUESTION 3 **What are the foundations of modern management thinking?**

BE SURE YOU CAN • define *system, subsystem,* and *open system* • apply these concepts to describe the operations of an organization in your community • define *contingency thinking* and give examples of how it is used by managers • describe evidence-based management and its link with scientific methods

Management Learning Review
Get Prepared for **Quizzes and Exams**

SUMMARY

TAKEAWAYQUESTION 1

What can we learn from classical management thinking?

- Frederick Taylor's four principles of scientific management focused on the need to carefully select, train, and support workers for individual task performance.
- Henri Fayol suggested that managers should learn what are now known as the management functions of planning, organizing, leading, and controlling.
- Max Weber described bureaucracy with its clear hierarchy, formal rules, and well-defined jobs as an ideal form of organization.

FOR DISCUSSION Should Weber's notion of the ideal bureaucracy be scrapped altogether, or is it still relevant today?

TAKEAWAYQUESTION 2

What insights come from the behavioral management approaches?

- The behavioral approaches shifted management attention toward the human factor as a key element in organizational performance.
- Mary Parker Follett described organizations as communities within which members combine talents to work for a greater good.
- The Hawthorne studies suggested that work behavior is influenced by social and psychological forces and that work performance may be improved by better "human relations."
- Abraham Maslow's hierarchy of human needs introduced the concept of self-actualization and the potential for people to experience self-fulfillment in their work.
- Douglas McGregor urged managers to shift away from Theory X and toward Theory Y thinking, which views people as independent, responsible, and capable of self-direction in their work.
- Chris Argyris pointed out that adults may react negatively when constrained by strict management practices and rigid organizational structures.

FOR DISCUSSION How can a manager benefit by using insights from Maslow's hierarchy of needs theory?

TAKEAWAYQUESTION 3

What are the foundations of modern management thinking?

- Analytics that use advanced quantitative analysis techniques in decision sciences and operations management can help managers solve complex problems.
- Organizations are open systems that interact with their external environments, while consisting of many internal subsystems that must work together in a coordinated way to support the organization's overall success.
- Contingency thinking avoids "one best way" arguments, instead recognizing the need to understand situational differences and respond appropriately to them.
- Quality management focuses on making a total commitment to product and service quality throughout an organization, maintaining continuous improvement and meeting worldwide quality standards such as ISO certification.
- Evidence-based management uses findings from rigorous scientific research to identify management practices for high performance.

FOR DISCUSSION Can system and subsystem dynamics help describe and explain performance problems for an organization in your community?

SELF-TEST 2

Multiple-Choice Questions

1. The assumption that people are complex with widely varying needs is most associated with the _____ management approaches.
   (a) classical
   (b) neoclassical
   (c) behavioral
   (d) modern

2. The father of scientific management is _____.
   (a) Weber
   (b) Taylor
   (c) Mintzberg
   (d) Katz

3. When the registrar of a university deals with students by an identification number rather than a name, which characteristic of bureaucracy is being displayed and what is its intended benefit?
   (a) division of labor, competency
   (b) merit-based careers, productivity
   (c) rules and procedures, efficiency
   (d) impersonality, fairness

4. If an organization was performing poorly and Henri Fayol was called in as a consultant, what would he most likely suggest to improve things?
   (a) Teach managers to better plan and control.
   (b) Teach workers more efficient job methods.
   (c) Promote to management only the most competent workers.
   (d) Find ways to increase corporate social responsibility.

5. One example of how scientific management principles are applied in organizations today would be:
   (a) conducting studies to increase efficiencies in job performance.
   (b) finding alternatives to a bureaucratic structure.
   (c) training managers to better understand worker attitudes.
   (d) focusing managers on teamwork rather than individual jobs.

6. The Hawthorne studies raised awareness of how _____ can be important influences on productivity.
   (a) structures
   (b) human factors
   (c) physical work conditions
   (d) pay and rewards

7. Advice to study a job, carefully train workers to do that job, and link financial incentives to job performance would most likely come from _____.
   (a) scientific management
   (b) contingency management
   (c) Henri Fayol
   (d) Abraham Maslow

8. The highest level in Maslow's hierarchy includes _____ needs.
   (a) safety
   (b) esteem
   (c) self-actualization
   (d) physiological

9. Which management theorist would most agree with the statement "If you treat people as grownups, they will perform that way"?
   (a) Argyris
   (b) Deming
   (c) Weber
   (d) Fuller

10. When people perform in a situation as they are expected to, this is sometimes called the _____ effect.
    (a) Hawthorne
    (b) systems
    (c) contingency
    (d) open-systems

11. Resource acquisition and customer satisfaction are important when an organization is viewed as a/an _____.
    (a) bureaucracy
    (b) closed system
    (c) open system
    (d) pyramid

12. The loan-processing department would be considered a _____ of your local bank or credit union.
    (a) subsystem
    (b) closed system
    (c) resource input
    (d) cost center

13. When a manager notices that Sheryl has strong social needs and assigns her a job in customer relations and gives Kwabena lots of praise because of his strong ego needs, the manager is displaying _____.
    (a) systems thinking
    (b) Theory X
    (c) motion study
    (d) contingency thinking

14. Which is the correct match?
    (a) Follet–analytics
    (b) McGregor–motion study
    (c) Deming–quality management
    (d) Maslow–Theory X and Y

15. When managers try to avoid hearsay and make decisions based on solid facts and information, this is known as _____.
    (a) continuous improvement
    (b) evidence-based management
    (c) TQM
    (d) Theory X management

Short-Response Questions

16. Explain how McGregor's Theory Y assumptions can create self-fulfilling prophecies consistent with the current emphasis on participation and involvement in the workplace.

17. How do the deficit and progression principles operate in Maslow's hierarchy-of-needs theory?

18. Define contingency thinking and give an example of how it might apply to management.

19. Explain why the external environment is so important in the open-systems view of organizations.

Essay Question

20. Enrique Temoltzin has just been appointed the new manager of your local college bookstore. Enrique would like to make sure the store operates according to Weber's bureaucracy. Describe the characteristics of bureaucracy and answer this question: Is the bureaucracy a good management approach for Enrique to follow? Discuss the possible limitations of bureaucracy and the implications for managing people as key assets of the store.

Management Skills & Competencies Make yourself **valuable!**

Evaluate Career Situations

What Would You Do?

1. **Paying a Summer Worker**

   It's summer job time and you've found something that just might work—handling technical support inquiries at a local Internet provider. The regular full-time employees are paid by the hour. Summer hires like you fill in when they go on vacation. However, you will be paid by the call for each customer that you handle. How will this pay plan affect your work behavior as a customer service representative? Is this summer pay plan a good choice by the management of the Internet provider?

2. **Good Performance but No Pay Raises**

   As a manager in a small local firm, you've been told that because of the poor economy, workers can't be given any pay raises this year. You have some really hardworking and high-performing people on your team whom you were counting on giving solid raises to. Now what can you do? How can you use insights from Maslow's hierarchy of needs to solve this dilemma of finding suitable rewards for high performance?

3. **I've Got This Great Idea**

   You've just come up with a great idea for improving productivity and morale in a shop that silk-screens T-shirts. You want to allow workers to work four 10-hour days if they want instead of the normal five-day/40-hour week. With the added time off, you reason, they'll be happier and more productive while working. But your boss isn't so sure. "Show me some evidence," she says. Can you design a research study that can be done in the shop to show whether your proposal is a good one?

Reflect on the Self-Assessment

Managerial Assumptions

Instructions

Read the following statements. Use the space in the margins to write "Yes" if you agree with the statement, or "No" if you disagree with it. Force yourself to take a Yes or No position.

1. Are good pay and a secure job enough to satisfy most workers?

2. Should a manager help and coach subordinates in their work?

3. Do most people like real responsibility in their jobs?

4. Are most people afraid to learn new things in their jobs?

5. Should managers let subordinates control the quality of their work?

6. Do most people dislike work?

7. Are most people creative?

8. Should a manager closely supervise and direct the work of subordinates?

9. Do most people tend to resist change?

10. Do most people work only as hard as they have to?

11. Should workers be allowed to set their own job goals?

12. Are most people happiest off the job?

13. Do most workers really care about the organization they work for?

14. Should a manager help subordinates advance and grow in their jobs?

Scoring

Count the number of Yes responses to items 1, 4, 6, 8, 9, 10, 12.
Write that number here as [X = _____].
Count the number of Yes responses to items 2, 3, 5, 7, 11, 13, 14.
Write that score here as [Y = _____].

Interpretation

This assessment provides insight into your orientation toward Douglas McGregor's Theory X (your "X" score) and Theory Y (your "Y" score) assumptions as discussed earlier in the chapter. You should review the discussion of McGregor's thinking in this chapter and consider the ways you are likely to behave toward other people at work. Think, in particular, about the types of "self-fulfilling prophecies" your managerial assumptions are likely to create.

Contribute to the Class Exercise

Evidence-Based Management Quiz

Instructions

1. For each of the following questions, answer "T" (true) if you believe the statement is backed by solid research evidence, or "F" (false) if you do not believe it is an evidence-based statement.[39]

   T F 1. Intelligence is a better predictor of job performance than having a conscientious personality.

   T F 2. Job candidates screened for values perform better than those screened for intelligence.

   T F 3. A highly intelligent person will have a hard time performing well in a low-skill job.

   T F 4. "Integrity tests" are good predictors of whether employees will steal, be absent, or take advantage of their employers in other ways.

   T F 5. Goal setting is more likely to result in improved performance than is participation in decision making.

   T F 6. Errors in performance appraisals can be reduced through proper training.

   T F 7. People behave in ways that show pay is more important to them than what they indicate on surveys.

   T F 8. People hired through employee referrals have better retention rates than those hired from other recruiting sources.

   T F 9. Workers who get training and development opportunities at work tend to have lower desires to change employers.

   T F 10. Being "realistic" in job interviews and telling prospective employees about both negative and positive job aspects improves employee retention.

2. Share your answers with others in your assigned group. Discuss the reasons members chose the answers they did; arrive at a final answer to each question for the group as a whole.

3. Compare your results with these answers "from the evidence."

4. Engage in a class discussion of how commonsense answers can sometimes differ from answers provided by evidence. Ask: What are the implications of this discussion for management practice?

Manage a Critical Incident

Theory X versus Theory Y

You've been at Magnetar Logistics Solutions for nine years and earned a reputation for leading a team that gets done what you say it will get done when you say it will be done. Now your sales team is close to landing a new 10-figure contract with an established client, Peterson Warehousing, Inc. You brought Peterson on board six years ago and have since grown and nurtured the relationship, and gotten to know this client in depth. One of the reasons you've achieved so much over the years is that you've always trusted your team members and given them the room and support they need to operate in their own way. They've repaid you by coming through time and time again with top quality solutions that always matched clients' needs. But Peterson is a different case—at least it seems that way to you—it's your baby and it's a big account. You know Peterson better than anyone else, and now you're facing a very hard deadline in only weeks, which will determine whether or not you get the new contract. At this point, you're doing a lot of close supervision on this project and not giving team members very much space to operate. There are many complexities with Peterson that you're worried the team will overlook, but which you are on top of. The team as a whole is starting to feel the impact of your switch in management style.

Questions

(1) What are the consequences of your shifting management style midstream during this project (a) on success with the client, (b) on your team, and (c) on your reputation as a successful manager? (2) Is a hands-on Theory X approach the best way to go here, or have you made a miscalculation? (3) Should you back off and return to the Theory Y assumptions that worked well in the past? (4) Is it too late to revert to your normal approach? (5) How can you infuse your Peterson expertise into the project while still keeping team members motivated and satisfied with your leadership?

Collaborate on the Team Activity

Management in Popular Culture

Movies, television shows, and music display a lot about our popular culture. Many deal with work situations and themes—

things like leadership, team dynamics, attitudes, personalities—that are topics of the management course. Management learning is readily available in popular culture. We just have to look for it.

Team Task

Choose one or more topics from this or a prior chapter and discuss popular culture examples that offer insights into them. Select one to share with the class at large in a multimedia presentation. Be sure to include a strong justification for your choice.

Suggestions

- Listen to music. Pick out themes that reflect important management concepts and theories. Identify what their messages say about management and working today.
- Watch movies, YouTube videos, and television episodes and advertisements. Look for the workplace issues and management themes.
- Read the comics. Compare and contrast management and working themes in two or three popular comic strips.
- Create your own alternative to the above suggestions.

Analyze THE **CaseStudy** | **ZARA INTERNATIONAL**
Fashion at the Speed of Light

Go to *Management Cases for Critical Thinking* at the end of the book to find this case.

ETHICAL BEHAVIOR AND SOCIAL RESPONSIBILITY

3

From the classroom to the meeting room to the boardroom and on into the family room, we often find ourselves confronting complex and debatable issues. We live in a world of great transparency where information flows freely and actions are closely scrutinized. It's easy to get caught up in dilemmas that put values and ethics to the test. And it's not going to get any easier in the days ahead. This chapter is an opportunity to think about ethics in our personal lives and at work, as well as in the responsibilities organizations have to society.

Who doesn't want high ethics, social responsibility, and principled leadership in business, government, and all of the organizations of our society? But isn't it easy to become cynical when the news reports yet another scandal and shows photos of some financial figure, corporate executive, or government official doing the "perp walk" into the police station? Why do some people and organizations fall prey to avarice and greed, while others are positive role models for ethical practices and admirable behavior? In business, think of the good examples set by Ben and Jerry's, Burt's Bees, Patagonia, Tom's of Maine, and Whole Foods Markets. Surely there are others right in your local community.

The actions of organizations are ultimately driven by the people who run them. Principled—or ethical—behavior by people at the top and at all levels is the real differentiator between organizations that do good things and those that don't. When criticizing Toyota Motor Corporation for misleading consumers about vehicle safety issues, for example, U.S. District Court Judge William H. Pauley declared that corporate misconduct is driven by people. He urged prosecutors "to hold those individuals responsible for making these decisions accountable."[1] There's no doubt that managers hold special ethical responsibilities in this regard. Consider this reminder from Desmond Tutu, archbishop of Capetown, South Africa, and winner of the Nobel Peace Prize.

You are powerful people. You can make this world a better place where business decisions and methods take account of right and wrong as well as profitability. . . . You must take a stand on important issues: the environment and ecology, affirmative action, sexual harassment, racism and sexism, the arms race, poverty, the obligations of the affluent West to its less-well-off sisters and brothers elsewhere.[2]

Ethics

TAKEAWAY 1   What is ethical behavior?

LEARN MORE | Laws and values as influences on ethical behavior • Alternative views of ethics
ABOUT | Cultural issues and ethical behavior

How many times a day do you ask this question: What should I do? How often do you consider "ethics" when formulating your answer? **Ethics** is defined as the moral code of principles that sets standards of good or bad, or right or wrong, in one's conduct.[3] An individual's moral code is influenced by a variety of sources including family, friends, local culture, religion, educational institutions, and individual experiences.[4] Importantly, ethics guide and help people make moral choices. They give us confidence when taking action in difficult situations. They encourage **ethical behavior** that is accepted as "good" and "right" in the context of the governing moral code.

Ethics establish standards of good or bad, or right or wrong, in one's conduct.

Ethical behavior is "good" or "right" in the context of a governing moral code.

Laws and Values as Influences on Ethical Behavior

Individuals often assume that anything that is legal should be considered ethical. Slavery was once legal in the United States, and laws once permitted only men to vote.[5] But that doesn't mean these practices were ethical. Sometimes legislation lags behind changes in a society's moral position. The delay makes it possible for something to be legal during a time when most people think it should be illegal.[6] On the flip side, some actions or activities may be illegal when many or most people think they should be legal. High-profile examples include gay marriage—legal in an increasing number of states but banned in others, and marijuana use—legal for medical use in more than 20 states and legalized for recreational use in two. Although the "law" serves as a broad-stroke benchmark, social complexity and change may call for a more nuanced approach to determine whether behavior is ethical or not.

By the same token, just because an action is not strictly illegal doesn't make it ethical.[7] Matching up behavior to the "letter of the law" doesn't guarantee that one's actions are ethical. Is it truly ethical, for example, for an employee to take longer than necessary to do a job? . . . to call in sick in order to take a day off work for leisure? . . . to fail to report rule violations or antisocial behavior by a co-worker? Although none of these acts is strictly illegal, many would consider them to be unethical.

Most ethical problems in the workplace arise when people are asked to do, or find they are about to do, something that violates their personal beliefs. For some, if the act is legal, they proceed without worrying about it. For others, the ethical test goes beyond legality and into the domain of personal **values**—the underlying beliefs and attitudes that help influence individual behavior.

The psychologist Milton Rokeach distinguishes between "terminal" and "instrumental" values.[8] **Terminal values** are preferences about desired ends, such as the goals one strives to achieve in life. Examples of terminal values include self-respect, family security, freedom, and happiness.

Values are broad beliefs about what is appropriate behavior.

Terminal values are preferences about desired end states.

Instrumental values are preferences regarding the means for accomplishing these ends. Among the instrumental values are honesty, ambition, imagination, and self-discipline.

Although value patterns for individuals tend to be very enduring, values also vary significantly from person to person. This can result in different interpretations of what behavior is ethical or unethical, even in what might be thought of as a clear-cut situation like taking an exam. After encountering cheating problems, an ethics professor once told business school students they were emphasizing means over ends: "The academic values of integrity and honesty in your work can seem to be less relevant than the instrumental goal of getting a good job."[9] And when about 10% of an MBA class was caught cheating on a take-home final, some argued the behavior should be expected from students taught to value collaboration, teamwork, and mobile communications. Others argued that the instrumental values driving such behavior were totally unacceptable—it was an individual exam, the students cheated, and they should be penalized.[10]

Instrumental values are preferences regarding the means to desired ends.

Alternative Views of Ethics

Figure 3.1 shows four views of ethical behavior—the utilitarian, individualism, moral rights, and justice views.[11] Each view offers a slightly different way to assess whether a behavior in a given situation is ethical or unethical, and each has its drawbacks. Examining issues through all four viewpoints provides a more complete picture of the ethicality of a decision than reliance on a single point of view alone.

Utilitarian View

The **utilitarian view** considers ethical behavior to be that which delivers the greatest good to the greatest number of people. Based on the work of 19th-century philosopher John Stuart Mill, this results-oriented view assesses the moral implications of actions in terms of their consequences. Managers, for example, are inclined to use profits, efficiency, and other performance criteria to judge what is best for the most people. An executive leading a firm facing hard financial times may decide to cut 30% of the workforce to keep the company profitable and save the jobs of remaining workers. She could justify this decision based on a utilitarian sense of business ethics. But she can't know for sure if the economy will get better or worse, nor can she accurately measure the social and economic consequences for those losing their jobs.

*In the **utilitarian view**, ethical behavior delivers the greatest good to the most people.*

Individualism View

The **individualism view** of ethical behavior is based on the belief that one's primary commitment should be to advance long-term self-interests. The basic idea is that society will be best off if everyone acts in ways that maximize their own utility or happiness. The assumption is that people are self-regulating in the quest for long-term individual advantage. For example, lying and cheating for short-term gain should not be tolerated, because if everyone behaves this way, then no one's long-term interests are served. The individualism view is supposed to

*In the **individualism view**, ethical behavior advances long-term self-interests.*

Individualism view
Does a decision or behavior promote one's long-term self-interests?

Moral rights view
Does a decision or behavior maintain the fundamental rights of all human beings?

Utilitarian view
Does a decision or behavior do the greatest good for the most people?

Justice view
Does a decision or behavior show fairness and impartiality?

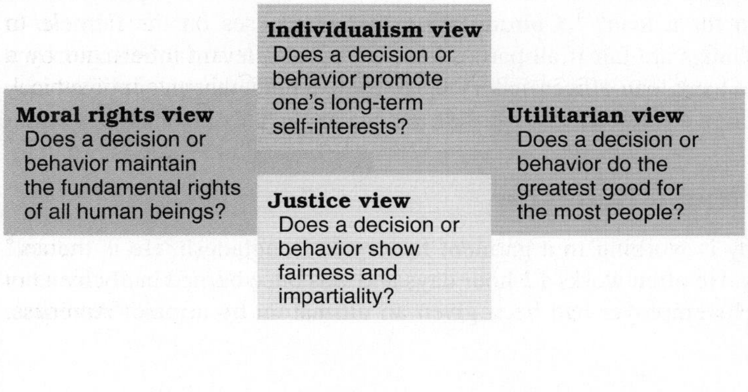

FIGURE 3.1
Four views of ethical behavior.

> ## Selections from the Universal Declaration of Human Rights
>
> - All human beings are born free and equal in dignity and rights.
> - Everyone has the right to life, liberty, and security of person.
> - No one shall be held in slavery or servitude.
> - No one shall be subjected to torture or to cruel, inhuman, or degrading treatment or punishment.
> - All are equal before the law and are entitled without any discrimination to equal protection of the law.

promote honesty and integrity. But not everyone has the same capacity or desire to self-control. If only a few individuals driven by greed take advantage of the freedom allowed by this approach, trust in the system dissolves. One executive described this as the tendency to "push the law to its outer limits" and "run roughshod over other individuals to achieve one's objectives."[12]

Moral Rights View

In the moral rights view, ethical behavior respects and protects fundamental rights.

Behavior is ethical under a **moral rights view** when it respects and protects the fundamental rights of people. The teachings of John Locke and Thomas Jefferson uphold the rights of all people to life, liberty, and fair treatment under the law as sacred. In organizations today, the moral rights view bears on employees' right to privacy, due process, free speech, health, safety, and freedom of conscience. It is evidenced at the global level by the Universal Declaration of Human Rights, passed by the United Nations General Assembly in 1948 and highlighted in the above box.[13] Although the moral rights view emphasizes individual rights, it does not address whether the outcomes associated with protecting those rights are beneficial to the majority of society. What happens, for example, when someone's right to free speech makes the workplace uncomfortable for others or offends a key customer or stakeholder of the organization?

Justice View

In the justice view, ethical behavior treats people impartially and fairly.

The **justice view** maintains that behavior is ethical when people are treated impartially, according to legal rules and standards. This approach defines the ethics of a decision based on whether it is "equitable" for everyone affected.[14] Justice issues in organizations often focus on four dimensions—procedural, distributive, interactional, and commutative justice.[15]

Procedural justice is concerned that policies and rules are fairly applied.

Procedural justice involves the degree to which policies and rules are fairly applied to all individuals. For example, does a sexual harassment charge levied against a senior executive receive the same full hearing as one made against a first-level supervisor? **Distributive justice** involves the degree to which outcomes (i.e., rewards, vacation time, etc.) are allocated fairly across employees without respect to individual characteristics such as ethnicity, race, gender, age, or other individual characteristics. For example, are women and minorities treated fairly when pay raises and promotions are made? Do universities allocate a proportionate share of athletic scholarships to male and female students?

Distributive justice focuses on whether or not outcomes are distributed fairly.

Interactional justice is the degree to which others are treated with dignity and respect.

Interactional justice involves the degree to which people treat one another with dignity and respect. For example, does a bank loan officer take the time to fully explain to an applicant why he or she was turned down for a loan?[16] **Commutative justice** focuses on the fairness of exchanges or transactions. Things are fair if all parties have access to relevant information and obtain some benefit.[17] Does a bank loan officer make it clear, for example, that an applicant may have difficulty repaying the loan if interest rates increase and the applicant's income does not?

Commutative justice is the degree to which an exchange or a transaction is fair to all parties.

Cultural Issues in Ethical Behavior

Situation: A 12-year-old boy is working in a garment factory in Bangladesh. He is the sole income earner for his family. He often works 12-hour days and was once burned badly by a hot iron. One day he is fired. His employer had been given an ultimatum by a major American

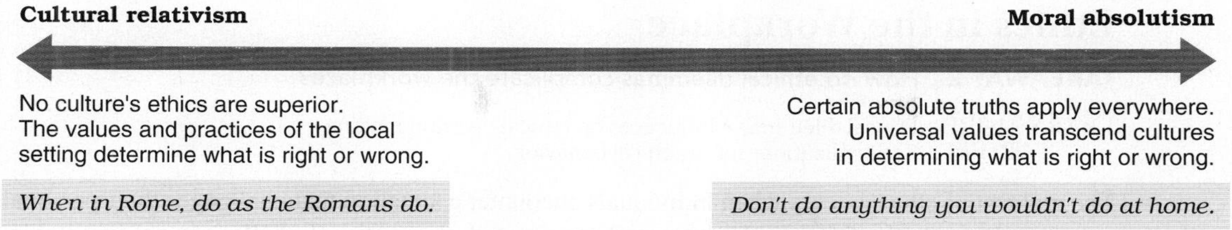

Cultural relativism   **Moral absolutism**

←——————————————————————————————————————→

No culture's ethics are superior.   Certain absolute truths apply everywhere.
The values and practices of the local   Universal values transcend cultures
setting determine what is right or wrong.   in determining what is right or wrong.

| *When in Rome, do as the Romans do.* | *Don't do anything you wouldn't do at home.* |

FIGURE 3.2
Cultural relativism and universalism in international business ethics.

Source: Developed from Thomas Donaldson, "Values in Tension: Ethics Away from
Home," *Harvard Business Review*, vol. 74 (September–October 1996), pp. 48–62.

customer: "No child workers if you want to keep our contracts." The boy says, "I don't understand. I could do my job very well. My family and I need the money." *Question*: Should the boy
be allowed to work?

   This difficult and perplexing situation is one example of the many ethics challenges faced in
international business. Former Levi Strauss CEO Robert Haas once said that an ethical problem
"becomes even more difficult when you overlay the complexities of different cultures and values
systems that exist throughout the world."[18] Those who believe that behavior in foreign settings
should be guided by the classic rule of "when in Rome, do as the Romans do" reflect an ethical
position known as **cultural relativism**.[19] This is the belief that there is no one right way to behave
and that ethical behavior is always determined by its cultural context. An American business
executive guided by rules of cultural relativism, for example, would argue that the use of child
labor is acceptable in another country as long as it is consistent with local laws and customs.

   Figure 3.2 contrasts cultural relativism with **moral absolutism**. This is the belief that if a
behavior or practice is not ethical in one's home environment, it is not acceptable anywhere else.
Moral absolutism holds that ethical standards are universal and should apply absolutely across
cultures and national boundaries. In the former example, the American executive would not do
business in a setting where child labor was used since it is unacceptable at home. Critics of the
absolutist approach maintain it is a form of **ethical imperialism**, an attempt to impose one's
ethical standards on others.

   Business ethicist Thomas Donaldson finds fault with both cultural relativism and ethical imperialism. He argues instead that certain fundamental rights and ethical standards can be preserved
at the same time that values and traditions of a given culture are respected.[20] Core values or
"hyper-norms" that should transcend cultural boundaries include respect for human dignity, basic
rights, and good citizenship. Donaldson believes international business practices can be tailored
to local and regional cultural contexts while upholding these core values. In the case of child
labor, the American executive might take steps so that children working in a factory under contract to his or her business are provided daily scheduled schooling, as well as employment.[21]

Cultural relativism suggests there is no one right way to behave; ethical behavior is determined by its cultural context.

Moral absolutism suggests ethical standards apply universally across all cultures.

Ethical imperialism is an attempt to impose one's ethical standards on other cultures.

Learning Check 1

TAKEAWAY QUESTION 1 **What is ethical behavior?**

BE SURE YOU CAN • define *ethics* • explain why obeying the law is not necessarily the same as behaving
ethically • explain the difference between terminal and instrumental values • identify the four alternative
views of ethics • contrast cultural relativism with moral relativism

Ethics in the Workplace

TAKEAWAY 2   How do ethical dilemmas complicate the workplace?

LEARN MORE | Ethical dilemmas • Influences on ethical decision making
ABOUT | Rationalizations for unethical behavior

The real test of ethics occurs when individuals encounter a situation that challenges their personal values and standards. Often ambiguous and unexpected, these ethical challenges are inevitable. Everyone has to be prepared to deal with them, even students. A college student gets a job offer and accepts it, only to get a better offer two weeks later. Is it right for her to reject the first job to accept the second? A student knows that his roommate submitted a term paper purchased on the Internet. Is it right for the student not to tell the instructor? One student confides to another that a faculty member promised her a high final grade in return for sexual favors. Is it right for the confidant to inform the instructor's department head?

Ethical Dilemmas

An **ethical dilemma** is a situation that offers potential benefit or gain and that may also be considered unethical.

An **ethical dilemma** is a situation that requires a choice regarding possible courses of action that, although offering the potential for personal or organizational benefit, or both, may be unethical. It is often a situation in which action must be taken but for which there is no clear consensus on "right" and "wrong." An engineering manager speaking from experience sums it up this way: "I define an unethical situation as one in which I have to do something I don't feel good about."[22] Here are some common examples of situations that present ethical dilemmas.[23]

- *Discrimination*—Your boss suggests that it would be a mistake to hire a qualified job candidate because she wears a headscarf for religious purposes. The boss believes your traditional customers might be uncomfortable with her appearance.

- *Sexual harassment*—A female subordinate asks you to discipline a co-worker whom she claims is making her feel uncomfortable with inappropriate sexual remarks. The co-worker, your friend, says that he was just kidding around and asks you not to take any action that would harm his career.

- *Conflicts of interest*—You are working in another country and are offered an expensive gift in return for making a decision favorable to the gift giver. You know that such exchanges are common practice in this culture and that several of your colleagues have accepted similar gifts in the past.

- *Product safety*—Your company is struggling financially and can make one of its major products more cheaply by purchasing lower-quality materials, although doing so would slightly increase the risk of consumer injury.

- *Use of organizational resources*—You bring an office laptop computer home so you can work after hours. Your wife likes the computer better than hers and asks if she can use it for her online business during the weekends.

It is almost too easy to confront ethical dilemmas from the safety of a textbook or a classroom discussion. In reality it is a lot harder to consistently choose ethical courses of action. We end up facing ethical dilemmas at unexpected and inconvenient times, in situations where events and facts are ambiguous, and when pressures to perform seem unforgiving and intense. Is it any surprise, then, that 56% of U.S. workers in one survey reported feeling pressured to act unethically in their jobs? Or that 48% said they had committed questionable acts within the past year?[24]

Look at the box with a six-step checklist for dealing with an ethical dilemma.[25] The checklist is a way to double-check the ethics of decisions before taking action. Step 5 highlights a key test: the risk of public disclosure. Asking and answering the recommended *spotlight questions* is a powerful way to test whether a decision is consistent with your personal ethical standards. Use them the next time you're making an uncomfortable decision. *Question*: "How will I feel if my family finds out, or if this gets reported in the local newspaper or posted on the Internet?" If the answer is "embarrassed," "mortified," or "anxious,"

> ## Quick Check for Dealing with Ethical Dilemmas
>
> **Step 1.** Recognize the ethical dilemma.
>
> **Step 2.** Get the facts and identify your options.
>
> **Step 3.** Test each option: Is it legal? Is it right? Whom does it affect? Who benefits? Who gets hurt?
>
> **Step 4.** Decide which option to follow.
>
> **Step 5.** Double-check your ethics by asking these *spotlight questions:*
>
> > *"How will I feel if my family finds out about my decision?"*
> >
> > *"How will I feel about this if my decision is reported in the local newspaper or posted on the Internet?"*
> >
> > *"What would the person I admire most for their character and ethical judgment say about my decision?"*
>
> **Step 6.** Take action.

the decision is probably not the one you should be making. *Question*: "What would the person I admire most for their character and ethical judgment say about my decision?" If the answer is "bad choice" or "I don't agree," the decision is probably not the one you should be making.

Influences on Ethical Decision Making

Standing up for what you believe is not always easy, especially in social situations full of contradictory or just plain bad advice. Consider these words from a commencement address delivered some years ago at a well-known school of business administration. "Greed is all right," the speaker said. "Greed is healthy. You can be greedy and still feel good about yourself." How would this speech be received today? Students at the time greeted the remarks with laughter and applause. The speaker was Ivan Boesky, once considered the "king of the arbitragers."[26] Not long after his commencement speech, however, Boesky was arrested, tried, convicted, and sentenced to prison for trading on inside information.

*An **ethical framework** is a personal rule or strategy for making ethical decisions.*

Personal Influences on Ethics

Values, family, religion, and personal needs all help determine a person's ethics. Managers without a strong, clear set of personal ethics will find their decisions varying from situation to situation. Those with a solid **ethical framework**, which is a set of personal rules or strategies for ethical decision making, will act more consistently and confidently. These frameworks serve as moral anchors that support ethical decision making even in difficult circumstances. Their foundations rest on individual character and personal values that emphasize virtues such as courage, honesty, fairness, integrity, and self-respect.

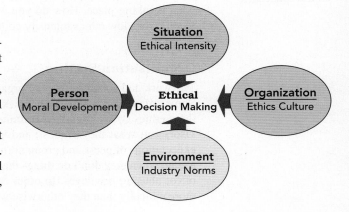

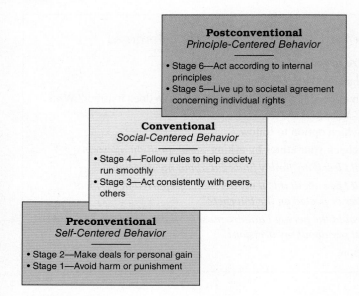

FIGURE 3.3
Kohlberg's levels
of individual moral
development.

Stages of Moral Development

Lawrence Kohlberg identified the three levels of moral development, shown in Figure 3.3—preconventional, conventional, and postconventional.[27] People at the different levels have different ethical approaches to situations. Very few of us consistently act at the postconventional level, and most operate at the preconventional or conventional levels.

People are self-centered at the *preconventional level* of moral development. Moral thinking is largely limited to issues of punishment, obedience, and self-interest. Decisions are focused on personal gain or avoiding punishment, and following the rules. Behavior at the *conventional level* of moral development is more social-centered. Decisions are likely to follow social norms, to meet the expectations of group memberships, and to live up to agreed-on role obligations.

Moral development at the *postconventional level* is principle-centered and a strong ethics framework is evident. Individuals at this level are willing to break with norms and conventions, even laws, to make decisions consistent with universal principles. An example might be the student who doesn't cheat on a take-home examination because he or she believes it's wrong. This belief holds even though other students will cheat, there is almost no chance of getting caught, and the consequence of not cheating is likely to be a lower grade on the test.

Situational Context and Ethics Intensity

Ethical dilemmas sometimes catch us off guard and we struggle to respond morally. Other times, we might fail to see that an issue or a situation has an ethics component. This may happen with cheating, for example, when it becomes so commonplace that it results in an accepted standard of behavior. Scholars discuss this as an issue of **ethics intensity** or **issue intensity**, the extent to which situations are perceived to pose important ethics challenges.[28]

The greater the ethics intensity of the situation, the more attention decision makers give to ethics issues and the more likely it is that their behavior will be ethical. Ethics intensity rises when the potential harm is perceived as great, likely, and imminent, when the potential victims are visible and close by, and when there is more social agreement on what is good or bad about what is taking place. How do you assess the ethics intensity of pirated music or movie downloads? Does low ethics intensity contribute to the likelihood of pirating?

Ethics intensity or issue intensity indicates the degree to which an issue or a situation is recognized to pose important ethical challenges.

Organization Setting

The work and social settings of organizations have a strong influence on the ethics of members. Some organizations set a high ethics bar by issuing formal policy statements and guidelines. But these ethics codes often have a limited impact. The way top managers, team leaders, and supervisors act; what they request; and what they reward or punish have strong impacts, as do the expectations of peers and group norms.[29] In some cases, members find themselves shunned from a team when they don't do things that outsiders would consider unethical—for example, slacking off or abusing privileges. In other cases, high ethics standards may push employees to behave more ethically than they otherwise would.

insight > LEARN ABOUT YOURSELF

> *It's the character of the people making key decisions that determines whether our organizations act in socially responsible or irresponsible ways.*

Individual Character Is a Confidence Builder

There is no doubt that **individual character** is evident in all we do. Persons with high character act consistently and confidently due to the self-respect it provides, even in difficult situations. Those with less character are more insecure. They act inconsistently and suffer in self-esteem and in the esteem of others.

Ethics and social responsibility issues facing organizations today can put individual character to a very stiff test. We need to know ourselves well enough to make principled decisions that we can be proud of and that others will respect. After all, it's the character of the people making key decisions that determines whether our organizations act in socially responsible or irresponsible ways.

Personal integrity is a foundation for individual character. It provides an ethical anchor shaping how we behave at work and in life. Think of it as demonstrated honesty, civility, caring, and sense of fair play. Your integrity and character should be more than occasional concerns. They deserve constant attention. Ethical dilemmas can arise unexpectedly. Expediency pressures—meeting deadlines, for example, can cause action without having thought through the consequences. To deal with these situations, we have to know ourselves well enough to make principled decisions we can be proud of and that others will respect.

One trait that can undermine individual character is hyper-competitiveness. You see it in people who think that winning— or getting ahead—is the only thing that matters. They hate to lose. These types judge themselves more on their outcomes achieved than the methods used to get there. Moreover, they may be quick to put aside virtues to succeed in competitive situations, including those in the workplace.

Self-Check for Signs of Hyper-Competitiveness

Y or N Winning makes me feel powerful

Y or N Winning increases my sense of self-worth

Y or N I hate to lose an argument

Y or N I turn everything into a contest

Y or N I am not satisfied unless I win a competition

Y or N If it helps me win, I am willing to obstruct my opponent

---

GET TO KNOW YOURSELF BETTER

Do a personal integrity and individual character self-check. Make notes on two situations that presented you with some ethical test. From the perspectives of a parent, loved one, or good friend, write a critique of how you handled each incident and what this shows about your individual character. Did you act with high integrity, or not? Watch yourself for signs of hyper-competitiveness in school and work situations. Ask: What are the ethical implications of my behavior?

External Environment, Government Regulation, and Industry Norms

Government laws and regulations can describe and encourage ethical behavior, but they can't guarantee ethical conduct. Laws reflect social values and define appropriate behavior for the members of organizations; regulations help governments monitor these behaviors and keep them within acceptable limits. After a number of high-profile corporate scandals hit the news, for example, the U.S. Congress passed the Sarbanes-Oxley Act of 2002 to make it easier for corporate executives to be tried and sent to prison for financial misconduct.

The climate of competition in an industry also sets standards for what may be considered ethical or unethical behavior. Former American Airlines president Robert Crandall once telephoned Howard Putnam, then president of the now-defunct Braniff Airlines. Both companies were suffering from money-losing competition on routes from their home base of Dallas. A portion of their conversation follows.[30]

PUTNAM: Do you have a suggestion for me?

CRANDALL: Yes . . . Raise your fares 20 percent. I'll raise mine the next morning.

PUTNAM: Robert, we—

CRANDALL: You'll make more money and I will, too.

PUTNAM: We can't talk about pricing.

CRANDALL: Oh, Howard. We can talk about anything we want to talk about.

The U.S. Justice Department strongly disagreed with Crandall. It alleged that his suggestion of a coordinated fare increase amounted to an illegal attempt to monopolize airline routes.

Rationalizations for Unethical Behavior

Picture this: A college professor sends students an e-mail containing both the school's honor code and a link to answers from the prior year's final exam. The link is clicked by 41% of

analysis > MAKE DATA YOUR FRIEND

> *The most common unethical acts by managers involve verbal, sexual, and racial harassment.*

Manager Behavior Key to Ethical Workplace

Masterfile

There's no question that managers strongly influence ethical behavior at work. Whether you call them bosses, team leaders, supervisors, or higher-ups, people in management positions make decisions every day that set an ethics-tone affecting their co-workers. A survey conducted for Deloitte & Touche USA found the following.

- Most common unethical acts by managers and supervisors include verbal, sexual, and racial harassment, misuse of company property, and giving preferential treatment.

- 91% of workers are more likely to behave ethically when they have work–life balance; 30% say they suffer from poor work–life balance.

- Top reasons for unethical behavior are low personal integrity (80%) and poor job satisfaction (60%).

- Most workers consider it unacceptable to steal from an employer, cheat on expense reports, take credit for another's accomplishments, and lie on time sheets.

- Most workers consider it acceptable to ask a work colleague for a personal favor, take sick days when not ill, or use company technology for personal affairs.

WHAT DOES THIS MEAN?

Are there any surprises in these data? Is this emphasis on manager and direct supervisor behavior justified as the key to an ethical workplace? What is your reaction to what the workers in this survey reported as acceptable and unacceptable work behaviors? Based on your experiences, what would you add to the list of unacceptable behaviors? Have you seen these kinds of behaviors where you work? What would your supervisor say if you reported these behaviors? Would you feel safe doing so? Why or why not?

students. Why? *How about this?* An internal audit by Avon revealed that executives in its China operation made illegal payments to obtain local direct sales licenses for the firm.[31] Why?

The fact is that people often rationalize ethical transgressions with after-the-fact justifications like *"It's not really illegal."*[32] This expresses a mistaken belief that one's behavior is acceptable in shady or borderline situations. When you are having trouble precisely determining right from wrong, the advice is quite simple: Don't do it. *"It's in everyone's best interests."* This excuse involves the mistaken belief that because someone can be found who benefits from the behavior, the behavior is also good for everyone. Overcoming this rationalization depends on the ability to look beyond short-term results to address longer-term implications, and to examine the way in which results are obtained. The best answer to the question "How far can I push it to accomplish this goal?" is probably "Don't try to find out."

Sometimes rationalizers tell themselves that *"no one will ever know about it."* They mistakenly believe that questionable behavior is safe from discovery and will never be made public. And if no one knows, the argument goes, no crime was actually committed. Lack of accountability, unrealistic pressures to perform, and a supervisor who prefers "not to know" can reinforce this kind of wrongful thinking. The best deterrent is for everyone to understand that unethical behavior will be punished whenever it is discovered. Finally, rationalizers may mistakenly believe that *"the organization will stand behind me."* This is misperceived loyalty. Believing that the organization benefits from their actions, the individual expects to be protected from harm. However, showing loyalty to the organization is not an acceptable excuse for misconduct. It shouldn't stand above the law and social morality.

Learning Check 2

TAKEAWAYQUESTION **2 How do ethical dilemmas complicate the workplace?**

BE SURE YOU CAN • define *ethical dilemma* and give workplace examples • identify Kohlberg's stages of moral development • explain how ethics intensity influences ethical decision making • explain how ethics decisions are influenced by an organization's culture and the external environment • list four common rationalizations for unethical behavior

Maintaining High Ethical Standards

TAKEAWAY 3   How can high ethical standards be maintained?

LEARN MORE | Moral management • Ethics training • Codes of ethical conduct
ABOUT | Whistleblower protection

Item: Bernard Madoff sentenced to 150 years in prison for masterminding the largest fraud in history by swindling billions of dollars from thousands of investors. *Item:* HP pays $108 million to settle a bribery case for corruption in Russia, Mexico and Poland. *Item:* U.S. safety regulators demand that General Motors answer 107 questions regarding the firm's handling of faulty ignition switches that resulted in 13 deaths.[33] There is no shortage of this kind of bad news from the financial, corporate, and government worlds. You just have to follow the headlines. The stories behind the headlines reveal that there is no substitute for making sure organizations are staffed with honest people and principled leaders who set positive examples and always act as ethical role models.

Moral Management

An **immoral manager** chooses to behave unethically.

An **amoral manager** fails to consider the ethics of her or his behavior.

A **moral manager** makes ethical behavior a personal goal.

Management scholar Archie Carroll distinguishes among immoral, amoral, and moral managers.[34] **Immoral managers** choose to behave unethically. They make choices purely for personal gain and knowingly disregard the ethics of their choice or the situation. **Amoral managers** also disregard the ethics of their choices and decisions, but do so unintentionally or unknowingly. These managers do not consider the ethical consequences of their actions, and they typically use the law as a behavioral guideline. **Moral managers** pursue ethical behavior as a personal goal. They make decisions and choices in full consideration of ethical issues.[35]

Chooses to behave unethically	Fails to consider ethics	Makes ethical behavior a personal goal
↑	↑	↑
Immoral manager	Amoral manager	Moral manager

It may surprise you that Carroll believes that most managers act amorally. Although well intentioned, they remain mostly uninformed or undisciplined regarding the ethical aspects of their behavior. They don't make unethical choices on purpose. They just don't think through the ethics issues associated with their decisions. Moral managers, by contrast, always have ethics on their mind. They champion ethical behavior and serve as an ethics role model for their co-workers.

Ethics Training

Ethics training seeks to help people understand the ethical aspects of decision making and to incorporate high ethical standards into their daily behavior.

Ethics training is one way to try to instill ethical behavior in an organization. It takes the form of structured programs to help members understand the ethical aspects of decision making and better integrate high ethical standards into their everyday behaviors. Look back to the six-step quick check for dealing with ethical dilemmas that was introduced earlier. It is a sample from an ethics training session designed to provide participants with a simple but powerful framework for double-checking the ethics of their decisions. Other common ethics training topics include ways to deal with conflicts of interest, gifts, client relationships, and bribery.

Colleges and universities are strengthening ethics coverage in academic curricula. But, do you think that you and your classmates benefit from these initiatives? Are coursework and discussions of ethics conducted in ways that keep cynicism from diminishing their potential positive impact? Regardless of when, where, or how ethics training is conducted, it is important to recognize the limits: It is no guarantee of ethical behavior. A banking executive once summed things up this way: "We aren't teaching people right from wrong—we assume they know that. We aren't giving people moral courage to do what is right—they should be able to do that anyhow. We focus on dilemmas."[36]

Codes of Ethical Conduct

A **code of ethics** is a formal statement of values and ethical standards.

It is now common for most organizations to have **codes of ethics**. In fact, you may be asked to sign one as a condition of employment. These codes are formal statements of an organization's values and ethical principles that set expectations for behavior. Ethics codes typically address organizational citizenship, illegal or improper acts, and relationships with co-workers and customers. Specific guidelines are often set for bribes and kickbacks, political contributions, records-keeping honesty, and confidentiality of corporate information.

Ethics codes are very common in the increasingly complicated world of International Business. For example, global manufacturing at Gap, Inc., is governed by a Code of Vendor Conduct.[37] The document addresses several issues, including:

Discrimination—"Factories shall employ workers on the basis of their ability to do the job, not on the basis of their personal characteristics or beliefs."

Forced labor—"Factories shall not use any prison, indentured or forced labor."

Working conditions—"Factories must treat all workers with respect and dignity and provide them with a safe and healthy environment."

Freedom of association—"Factories must not interfere with workers who wish to lawfully and peacefully associate, organize or bargain collectively."

But even as global firms like the Gap have ethics codes in place, it is hard for them to police practices when they have many, potentially hundreds, of suppliers from different parts of the world. In international business, as elsewhere, ethics codes are good at describing ethical expectations, but they cannot always guarantee ethical conduct.

Whistleblower Protection

- Agnes Connolly pressed her employer to report two toxic chemical accidents.
- Dave Jones reported that his company used unqualified suppliers in the construction of a nuclear power plant.
- Margaret Newsham revealed that her firm allowed workers to do personal business while on government contracts.
- Herman Cohen charged that the ASPCA in New York was mistreating animals.
- Barry Adams complained that his hospital followed unsafe practices.[38]

These five people come from different work settings and are linked to different issues. However, they share two important things in common. First, each was a **whistleblower** who exposed misconduct in and by their organizations while hoping to preserve ethical standards and protect against further wasteful, harmful, or illegal acts.[39] Second, each of these individuals was fired from their job.

A **whistleblower** exposes the misdeeds of others in organizations.

At the same time that we can admire whistleblowers for taking ethical stances, there is no doubt they risk impaired career progress and other forms of organizational retaliation, up to and including termination. Although laws such as the Whistleblower Protection Act of 1989 offer some defense against "retaliatory discharge," legal protections for whistleblowers are continually being tested in court and many consider them inadequate.[40] Laws vary from state to state, and federal laws primarily protect government workers.

Research on whistleblowing that reports violations within organizations indicates that even though 20% of workers notice ethical violations by co-workers, only half of them report the wrongdoing.[41] Top reasons why people fail to report such misdeeds include lack of ethical leadership, unethical peers, lack of confidence that corrective action will be taken, and fear of public disclosure as the whistleblower.[42] Typical barriers to whistleblowing within an organization include a strict chain of command that makes it hard to bypass immediate supervisors, strong work group identities that encourage loyalty and self-censorship, and ambiguous priorities that make it hard to distinguish right from wrong.[43]

Learning Check 3

TAKEAWAYQUESTION 3 **How can high ethical standards be maintained?**

BE SURE YOU CAN • compare and contrast ethics training and codes of ethical conduct as methods for encouraging ethical behavior in organizations • differentiate between amoral, immoral, and moral management • define *whistleblower* • identify common barriers to whistleblowing and the factors to consider when determining whether whistleblowing is appropriate

Social Responsibility

TAKEAWAY 4   What is an organization's social responsibility?

LEARN MORE ABOUT Stakeholders and stakeholder management • Social responsibility, sustainability, and the triple bottom line • Perspectives on corporate social responsibility • Evaluating corporate social performance • Corporate governance

Stakeholders are the persons, groups, and other organizations that are directly affected by the behavior of the organization and that hold a stake in its performance.

Stakeholder power refers to the capacity of the stakeholder to positively or negatively affect the operations of the organization.

Demand legitimacy indicates the validity and legitimacy of a stakeholder's interest in the organization.

Issue urgency indicates the extent to which a stakeholder's concerns need immediate attention.

Corporate social responsibility is the obligation of an organization to serve the interests of multiple stakeholders, including society at large.

All organizations have **stakeholders**, the persons, groups, and other organizations directly affected by the behavior of the organization and that hold a stake in its performance.[44] Figure 3.4 shows a typical stakeholder network that includes owners or shareholders, employees, customers, suppliers, business partners, government representatives and regulators, community members, and future generations.

An organization's stakeholders can have different and conflicting interests that make it hard for all of them to be satisfied all the time. Customers typically want value prices and quality products; owners want profits and a strong return on their investment; suppliers want long-term business relationships; communities want good corporate citizenship and support for public services; employees want good wages, benefits, security, and satisfaction in their work; and future generations want a clean environment that isn't polluted by manufacturing by-products and industrial waste. When stakeholders' interests clash, an organization's leadership can face difficult challenges and controversial decisions.[45]

One way to deal with conflicting stakeholder interests is to assess the power of the stakeholder, the legitimacy of the demand, and the urgency of the issue.[46] **Stakeholder power** refers to the capacity of the stakeholder to positively or negatively affect the operations of the organization. **Demand legitimacy** reflects the extent to which the stakeholder's demand is perceived as valid and the extent to which the demand comes from a party with a legitimate stake in the organization. **Issue urgency** deals with the extent to which the issues require immediate attention or action.

Social Responsibility, Sustainability, and the Triple Bottom Line

The way organizations behave in relation to their stakeholders is a good indication of their underlying ethics cultures and moral characters. When we talk about the "good" and the "bad" in business and society relationships, **corporate social responsibility**, or CSR, is center stage. It is defined as the obligation of an organization to act in ways that serve the interests of multiple stakeholders, including society at large.

The good and the bad in CSR come to life in day-to-day practice as a result of decisions made and actions taken by people in organizations. When hazardous waste finds its way into landfills, it does so because of human decision making. When an automaker fails to recall vehicles known to have dangerous defects, it does so because of human decision making. You have to "deter bad individual conduct" in order to keep organizations from doing bad things.[47] And in order to get organizations to do the right things, their members—especially managers and leaders—must continually exercise good

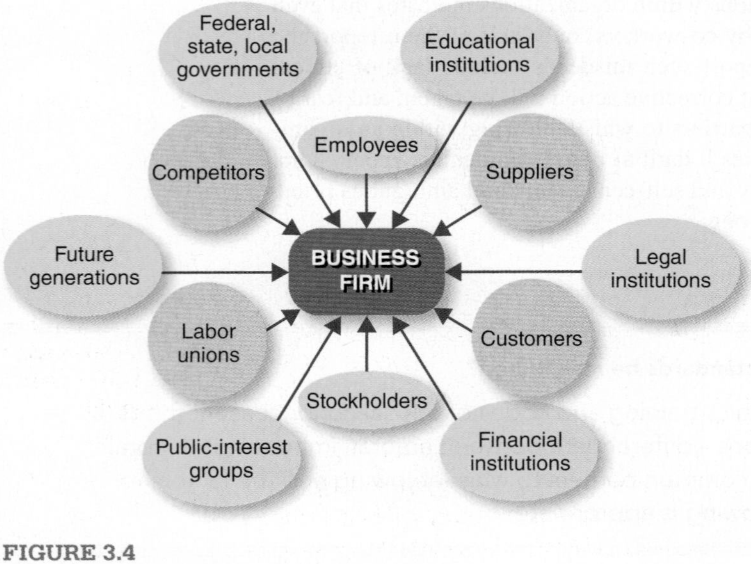

FIGURE 3.4
The many stakeholders of organizations.

stewardship. This means taking personal responsibility to act in ways that always respect and protect the interests of the full range of organizational stakeholders.

Sustainability is one of the pillars of stewardship. Procter & Gamble defines it as acting in ways that help ensure "a better quality of life for everyone now and for generations to come".[48] Good stewardship and sustainability opportunities are evident when organizations invest in things like clean energy, recycling, water conservation, and waste avoidance. Bad stewardship and sustainability problems can be seen when questionable decisions cause organizations to create preventable disasters like massive oil spills or to pollute soil with harmful waste that ends up finding its way into the food stream.

The tendency in the past was to define stewardship rather narrowly and focus its attention on what accountants call the "bottom line" of business profitability. Today's notion of stewardship is broader and more attention is being given to the **triple bottom line** of economic, social, and environmental performance.[49] Many call this the **3 P's of organizational performance**—profit, people, and planet.[50] Triple bottom line outcomes can be assessed by asking questions like these: Profit—Is the decision economically sound? People—Does the decision treat people with respect and dignity? Planet—Is the decision good for the environment?

Perspectives on Corporate Social Responsibility

Chances are you'd like your employer to value social responsibility. Surveys report that 70% of students believe "a company's reputation and ethics" is "very important" when deciding whether or not to accept a job offer; and that 79% of 13–25-year-olds "want to work for a company that cares about how it affects or contributes to society."[51] "Students nowadays want to work for companies that help enhance the quality of life in their surrounding community," says one recruiter.[52] So, would it surprise you to learn that CSR as a business priority has been a subject of considerable debate?[53]

Classical View

The **classical view of CSR** holds that management's only responsibility is to maximize profits. In other words, "the business of business is business" and the principal obligation of management is to owners and shareholders. This narrow stakeholder perspective is linked to the respected economist and Nobel Laureate, Milton Friedman, who once said: "Few trends could so thoroughly undermine the very foundations of our free society as the acceptance by corporate officials of social responsibility other than to make as much money for their stockholders as possible."[54]

Although not explicitly against CSR in its own right, proponents of the classical view maintain that society's interests are served in the long run by executives focused on maximizing profits. They believe that society gains when business competition makes things like healthier foods and energy-efficient products attractive to produce because they are profitable.[55] They fear that pursuit of CSR as a separate business goal will reduce profits, raise costs, reduce competitiveness with foreign firms, and give business too much social power with too little accountability to the public.

Socioeconomic View

The **socioeconomic view of CSR** holds that managers should explicitly focus on the organization's effect on the broader social welfare and not just with corporate profits. This broad stakeholder perspective puts the focus on the triple bottom line that emphasizes not just financial performance but also social and environmental performance as well. In its support, another distinguished economist and Nobel Laureate, Paul Samuelson, has said: "A large corporation these days not only may engage in social responsibility, it had damn well better try to do so."[56]

Proponents of the socioeconomic view argue that the pursuit of CSR will enhance long-run profits, improve public image, make organizations more attractive places to work, and help avoid government regulation. They also believe that businesses should act responsibly because society provides them with the infrastructure they need to operate.

Stewardship means taking personal responsibility to always respect and protect the interests of organizational stakeholders, including society at large.

Sustainability means acting in ways that support a high quality of life for present and future generations.

The **triple bottom line** evaluates organizational performance on economic, social, and environmental criteria.

The **3 P's of organizational performance** are profit, people, and planet.

The **classical view of CSR** is that business should focus on profits.

The **socioeconomic view of CSR** is that business should focus on broader social welfare as well as profits.

ethics > KNOW RIGHT FROM WRONG

> *"A job listed on a resume wouldn't impress me just because it was a paid position. What matters is the experience you get from a job."*

Interns Are Suing Their Employers for Back Pay

Alex Brandon/AP Photo

I t's true. Two interns sued Fox Searchlight Pictures claiming they did work that would otherwise have been done by paid employees . . . and they wanted to be paid for it. A federal judge in New York agreed and turned the notion of the unpaid internship upside down. In the Fox case, there wasn't a lot of money at stake, about $8 an hour. But there is a lot at stake in the controversy created by the legal ruling. Fox's lead attorney Juno Turner says: "I think it would be the very rare internship that would meet the criteria set forth in this decision."

The U.S. Fair Labor Standards Act allows businesses to hire unpaid interns but sets forth rules that must be followed. For example, interns can't "displace regular employees" and

employers can't receive "immediate advantage from the activities of the intern." A strict interpretation of these guidelines seems to push employers in the direction of offering only paid internships. Turner claims it would be "rare" for an unpaid internship to meet the legal criteria applied in the Fox case. The exception is in the public sector where the law allows nonprofits to employee interns as volunteers.

Internships are a well-established source of valuable experience for students and a job entry point for many. Heather Huhman, author of *Lies, Damned Lies & Internships*, says: "A job listed on a resume wouldn't impress me just because it was a paid position. What matters is the experience you get from a job." Data show that 37% of unpaid interns and 60% of paid interns get job offers.

So, who benefits from the Fox case? Are we about to see the demise of the student internship?

WHAT DO YOU THINK?

Is it right for interns to demand pay in return for valuable work experience and a possible job entry point? Are employers taking advantage of interns by not paying them for doing real work? What's the dividing line between fairness and exploitation in an internship contract? Who benefits from the Fox case? Are we about to see a decline in the number of available student internships? What's your internship experience? Did you engage in tasks that had an immediate positive benefit for the firm you were working for? Did it seem wrong to you that you weren't being paid?

The shared value view of CSR sees economic progress for a firm and social progress for society as fundamentally interconnected.

The virtuous circle occurs when socially responsible behavior improves financial performance, which leads to more responsible behavior in the future.

Shared Value View

Mark Kramer and Michael Porter advocate a **shared value view of CSR** where economic progress for the firm and social progress for the broader community are fundamentally interconnected.[57] They believe that "the purpose of a corporation must be redefined as creating shared value, not just profit per se."[58] This creates a win-win situation for both business and society. It eliminates the tendency to pit the interests of shareholders and owners against one another, and it moves CSR priorities from serving mainly reputational and branding goals for the organization up to the level of being strategic components of the core business model.

Organizations pursuing a shared value approach try to align their strategies and practices with social issues like aging, illiteracy, nutrition, resource conservation, and poverty. This ideally creates a **virtuous circle** in which investments in CSR lead to improved financial performance, which, in turn, leads to more socially responsible actions in the future.[59] Len Sauers, Procter &

Gamble's Vice President of Global Sustainability, says that the firm's priority on reducing waste "almost always results in cost savings." Nestlé's support for local sourcing and rural businesses near its factories helps build communities while reducing distribution costs for the firm and ensuring its supplies of high-quality products. Carpet manufacturer Desso's CEO Stef Kranendijk says that investments in a green supply chain and cradle-to-grave manufacturing have paid off in more innovation.[60]

Evaluating Corporate Social Performance

If we are to get serious about social responsibility and shared value, we need to get rigorous about measuring social performance and holding organizational leaders accountable for the results. It is increasingly common for organizations to take **social responsibility audits** at regular intervals and issue formal reports on their social performance. And, research finds that mandatory social reporting of this nature improves socially responsible behavior.[61] In other words, the more we measure CSR, the better it gets.

When social responsibility audits are taken, the performance of firms can be scored on behaviors that range from *compliance*—acting to avoid adverse consequences—to *conviction*—acting to create positive impact.[62] Compliance behaviors focus on being profitable and obeying the law, while conviction behaviors focus on doing what is right and contributing to the broader community. Figure 3.5 shows how different emphases on compliance and conviction result in alternative social responsibility strategies, ones you may recognize in news reports and current events.[63]

On the compliance side, an **obstructionist strategy** ("Fight social demands") focuses mainly on economic priorities. Social demands lying outside the organization's perceived self-interests are resisted. Cigarette manufacturers, for example, tried to minimize the negative health effects of smoking for decades until indisputable evidence became available. A **defensive strategy** ("Do minimum legally required") focuses on protecting the organization by meeting minimum legal requirements and responding to competitive market forces, perhaps even activist pressures. Mortgage lenders are required to provide certain information to customers concerning loans they may be receiving. But whereas some take time to carefully review everything with customers, others may rush the conversation in hopes the customer won't question details.

On the conviction side, an **accommodative strategy** ("Do minimum ethically required") focuses on satisfying society's ethics expectations. An oil firm may engage in appropriate cleanup activities following a spill and provide compensation to communities harmed by the spill. But the firm may be slow to invest in new technologies to prevent future spills. Following a more **proactive strategy** ("Take leadership in social initiatives"), the firm would invest in these technologies, and in the search for alternative energy sources, taking discretionary steps toward making things better in the future.

Corporate Governance

The term **corporate governance** refers to the active oversight of management decisions and company actions by boards of directors.[64] Businesses are required by law to have boards of directors elected by shareholders to represent their interests.

A **social responsibility audit** measures an organization's performance in various areas of social responsibility.

An **obstructionist strategy** tries to avoid and resist pressures for social responsibility.

A **defensive strategy** does the minimum legally required to display social responsibility.

An **accommodative strategy** accepts social responsibility and tries to satisfy society's basic ethical expectations.

A **proactive strategy** actively pursues social responsibility by taking discretionary actions to make things better in the future.

Corporate governance is the oversight of top management by a board of directors.

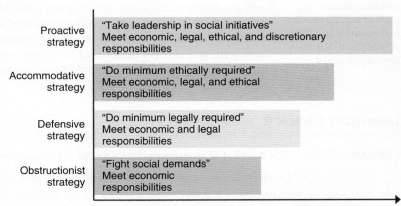

FIGURE 3.5
Four strategies of corporate social responsibility—from obstructionist to proactive behavior.

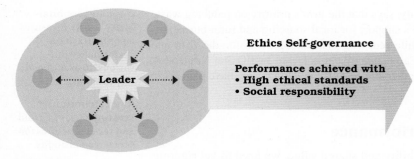

Ethics Self-governance

Performance achieved with
- **High ethical standards**
- **Social responsibility**

FIGURE 3.6
Ethics self-governance in leadership and the managerial role.

Most public organizations, like state universities, have boards of trustees whose elected and appointed members serve the same purpose. The governance exercised by boards involves hiring, firing, and compensating the executives in the C-suite—CEO, CFO, CIO, and other members of top management. It also involves verifying financial records and assessing strategies, including CSR.

The expectation is that board members will hold management accountable for high-performance leadership that is always ethical and socially responsible. Ethics failures and CSR controversies by organizations are often blamed on weak governance. And, you will sometimes see government stepping in to take actions designed to reduce the likelihood of future failures. Hearings are held, bills are proposed and laws passed, and government agencies are directed or created to better control business practices.

The **Sarbanes-Oxley Act of 2002**, for example, was passed by Congress in response to loud public outcries over major ethics and business scandals. The goal of Sarbanes-Oxley, or SOX, is to protect investors and the public by making sure that top managers properly oversee and are held accountable for the financial conduct of the organizations they lead. Here are some SOX facts to remember from executive briefings on the the law. 1) Saying "I didn't know" doesn't count—SOX "removes the defense of 'I wasn't aware of financial issues' from CEOs and CFOs, holding them accountable for the accuracy of financial statements." 2) Violators can expect to be punished and penalties are tough—under SOX, a "CEO or CFO who submits a wrong certification is subject to a fine up to $1 million and imprisonment for up to ten years. If the wrong certification was submitted 'willfully', the fine can be increased up to $5 million and the prison term can be increased up to twenty years." 3) Whistleblowers are protected—SOX prohibits employers "from retaliating against employees who raise various protected concerns or provide protected information to the employer or the government."[65]

While the behavior and examples set by top-level or C-suite executives have the longest reach, it is critical to recognize that all managers have personal responsibility for good stewardship of the organization and doing the "right" things in their day-to-day work. Figure 3.6 highlights **ethics self-governance** and points out that it isn't enough to fulfill daily task responsibilities; they must be performed in an ethical, socially responsible way. Managers shoulder the full weight of this responsibility, and it holds in every organizational setting, from small to large, from private to nonprofit, and at every managerial level from top to bottom. There is no escaping the ultimate reality—every manager is a steward of stakeholder interests, and being a manager is an extremely socially responsible job!

The **Sarbanes-Oxley Act of 2002**, SOX, is designed to hold top managers accountable for the financial conduct of the organizations they lead.

Ethics self-governance is making sure day-to-day performance is achieved ethically and in socially responsible ways.

Learning Check 4

TAKEAWAYQUESTION 4 **What is an organization's social responsibility?**

BE SURE YOU CAN • identify key organizational stakeholders and discuss stakeholder management • define *corporate social responsibility* • summarize arguments for and against CSR • define *shared value* and describe how it links business and society • explain the difference between compliance and commitment in social responsibility • identify four possible social responsibility strategies • define *corporate governance* and ethics self-governance, and discuss their importance to managers at all organizational levels

Management Learning Review
Get Prepared for **Quizzes and Exams**

SUMMARY

TAKEAWAY QUESTION 1
What is ethical behavior?

* Ethical behavior is behavior accepted as "good" or "right" as opposed to "bad" or "wrong."
* Because an action is not illegal does not necessarily make it ethical.
* Because values vary, the question "What is ethical behavior?" may be answered differently by different people.
* The utilitarian, individualism, moral-rights, and justice views offer alternative ways of thinking about ethical behavior.
* Cultural relativism argues that no culture is ethically superior to any other; universalism argues that certain ethical standards apply everywhere.

FOR DISCUSSION Is there ever a justification for cultural relativism in international business ethics?

TAKEAWAY QUESTION 2
How do ethical dilemmas complicate the workplace?

* An ethical dilemma occurs when someone must decide whether to pursue a course of action that, although offering the potential for personal or organizational benefit or both, may be unethical.
* Managers report that ethical dilemmas often involve conflicts with superiors, customers, and subordinates over issues such as dishonesty in advertising and communication, as well as pressure from supervisors to do unethical things.
* Common rationalizations for unethical behavior include believing the behavior is not illegal, is in everyone's best interests, will never be noticed, or will be supported by the organization.

FOR DISCUSSION Are ethical dilemmas always problems, or can they also be opportunities?

TAKEAWAY QUESTION 3
How can high ethical standards be maintained?

* Ethics training can help people better deal with ethical dilemmas in the workplace.

* Written codes of ethical conduct formally state what an organization expects of its employees regarding ethical behavior at work.
* Immoral managers intentionally choose to behave unethically; amoral managers do not really pay attention to or think through the ethics of their actions or decisions; moral managers consider ethical behavior a personal goal.
* Whistleblowers expose the unethical acts of others in organizations, even while facing career risks for doing so.

FOR DISCUSSION Is it right for organizations to require employees to sign codes of conduct and undergo ethics training?

TAKEAWAY QUESTION 4
What is an organization's social responsibility?

* Social responsibility is an organizational obligation to act in ways that serve both its own interests and the interests of its stakeholders.
* The triple bottom line for assessing organizational performance reflects how well organizations achieve economic, social, and environmental performance outcomes.
* The argument against corporate social responsibility holds that businesses should focus on profit; the argument for corporate social responsibility holds that businesses should serve broader social concerns.
* The shared value concept links business and social goals with the idea that businesses can find economic value by pursuing opportunities and practices that advance societal well being.
* An organization's social performance can be evaluated based on how well it meets economic, legal, ethical, and discretionary responsibilities.
* Corporate strategies in response to demands for socially responsible behavior include obstruction, defense, accommodation, and proactivity.
* Corporate governance is the responsibility of a board of directors to oversee the performance of C-suite executives.

FOR DISCUSSION What questions would you include on a social audit for an organization in your community?

SELF-TEST 3

Multiple-Choice Questions

1. Values are personal beliefs that help determine whether a behavior is considered ethical or unethical. An example of a terminal value is _____.
   (a) ambition   **(c)** courage
   (b) self-respect   **(d)** imagination

2. Under the _____ view of ethical behavior, a business owner would be considered ethical if she reduced a plant's workforce by 10% in order to cut costs to keep the business from failing and thus save jobs for the other 90%.
   (a) utilitarian   **(c)** justice
   (b) individualism   **(d)** moral rights

3. A manager's failure to enforce a late-to-work policy the same way for employees on the day and night shifts is an ethical violation of _____ justice.
   - **(a)** ethical
   - **(b)** moral
   - **(c)** distributive
   - **(d)** procedural

4. The Sarbanes-Oxley Act of 2002 makes it easier for corporate executives to _____.
   - **(a)** protect themselves from shareholder lawsuits
   - **(b)** sue employees who commit illegal acts
   - **(c)** be tried and sentenced to jail for financial misconduct
   - **(d)** shift blame for wrongdoing to boards of directors

5. Two "spotlight" questions for conducting the ethics double-check of a decision are (a) "How would I feel if my family found out about this?" and (b) "How would I feel if _____?"
   - **(a)** my boss found out about this
   - **(b)** my subordinates found out about this
   - **(c)** this was published in the local newspaper
   - **(d)** this went into my personnel file

6. Research on ethical dilemmas indicates that _____ is/are often the cause of unethical behavior by people at work.
   - **(a)** declining morals in society
   - **(b)** lack of religious beliefs
   - **(c)** the absence of whistleblowers
   - **(d)** pressures from bosses and superiors

7. Customers, investors, employees, and regulators are examples of _____ that are important in the analysis of corporate social responsibility (CSR).
   - **(a)** special-interest groups
   - **(b)** stakeholders
   - **(c)** ethics advocates
   - **(d)** whistleblowers

8. A/An _____ is someone who exposes the ethical misdeeds of others.
   - **(a)** whistleblower
   - **(b)** ethics advocate
   - **(c)** ombudsman
   - **(d)** stakeholder

9. A proponent of the classical view of corporate social responsibility would most likely agree with which of these statements?
   - **(a)** Social responsibility improves the public image of business.
   - **(b)** The primary responsibility of business is to maximize business profits.
   - **(c)** By acting responsibly, businesses avoid government regulation.
   - **(d)** Businesses can and should do "good" while doing business.

10. An amoral manager _____.
    - **(a)** always acts in consideration of ethical issues
    - **(b)** chooses to behave unethically
    - **(c)** makes ethics a personal goal
    - **(d)** acts without considering whether or not the behavior is ethical

11. An organization that takes the lead in addressing emerging social issues is being _____, showing the most progressive corporate social responsibility strategy.
    - **(a)** accommodative
    - **(b)** defensive
    - **(c)** proactive
    - **(d)** obstructionist

12. The criterion of _____ identifies the highest level of conviction by an organization to operate in a socially responsible manner.
    - **(a)** economic justice
    - **(b)** legal requirements
    - **(c)** ethical commitment
    - **(d)** discretionary responsibility

13. Which viewpoint emphasizes that business can find ways to profit by doing things that advance the well being of society?
    - **(a)** classical
    - **(b)** shared value
    - **(c)** defensive
    - **(d)** obstructionist

14. Managers show self-governance when they always try to achieve performance objectives in ways that are _____.
    - **(a)** performance effective
    - **(b)** cost efficient
    - **(c)** quality oriented
    - **(d)** ethical and socially responsible

15. The triple bottom line of organizational performance focuses on the "3 P's" of profit, people, and _____.
    - **(a)** principle
    - **(b)** procedure
    - **(c)** planet
    - **(d)** progress

Short-Response Questions

16. Explain the difference between the individualism and justice views of ethical behavior.

17. List four common rationalizations for unethical managerial behavior.

18. What are the major arguments for and against corporate social responsibility?

19. What is the primary difference between immoral and amoral management?

Essay Question

20. A small outdoor clothing company has just received an attractive offer from a business in Bangladesh to manufacture its work gloves. The offer would allow for substantial cost savings over the current supplier. The company manager, however, has read reports that some Bangladeshi businesses break their own laws and operate with child labor. How would differences in the following corporate responsibility strategies affect the manager's decision regarding whether to accept the offer: obstruction, defense, accommodation, and proaction?

ManagementSkills&
Competencies Make yourself **valuable!**

Evaluate Career Situations

What Would You Do?

1. Window to the Future

You've just seen one of your classmates take a picture of an essay question on the exam everyone is taking. The instructor missed it and you're not sure if anyone else saw it. You know that the instructor is giving an exam to another section the next class period. Do you let it pass and pretend it isn't all that important? If you won't let it pass, what will you do?

2. Intern's Assignment

One of your first tasks as a summer intern is to design an ethics training program for the firm's new hires. Your supervisor says that the program should familiarize hires with the corporate code of ethics. But it should also go beyond this to help establish a solid foundation for handling a range of ethical dilemmas in a confident and moral way. What would your training program look like?

3. New Person at the Table

Your employer has a "roundtable" program that brings younger hires together with senior executives on a monthly basis. Each session tackles a topic. This month it's "CSR as a business priority." You've heard that some of the senior execs are skeptical of CSR, believing that business is business and the firm's priority should be on profits. What arguments might you make in support of CSR and the concept of "shared value"?

Reflect on the Self-Assessment

Terminal Values

Instructions

1. Read the following list of things people value. Think about each value in terms of its importance as a guiding principle in your life.

A comfortable life	Inner harmony
An exciting life	Mature love
A sense of accomplishment	National security
A world at peace	Pleasure
A world of beauty	Salvation
Equality	Self-respect
Family security	Social recognition
Freedom	True friendship
Happiness	Wisdom

2. Circle six of these 18 values to indicate that they are most important to you. If you can, rank-order these most important values by writing a number above them—with "1" = the most important value in my life, and so on through "6."

3. Underline the six of these 18 values that are least important to you.

Interpretation

Terminal values reflect a person's preferences concerning the ends to be achieved. They are the goals individuals would like to achieve in their lifetimes. As you look at the items you've selected as most and least important, what major differences are present in the items across the two sets? Think about this and then answer the following questions.

A. What does your selection of most and least important values say about you as a person?

B. What does your selection of most and least important values suggest about the type of work and career that might be best for you?

C. Which values among your most and least important selections might cause problems for you in the future—at work and/or in your personal life? What problems might they cause and why? How might you prepare now to best deal with these problems in the future?

D. How might your choices of most and least important values turn out to be major strengths or assets for you—at work and/or in your personal life, and why?

Contribute to the Class Exercise

Confronting Ethical Dilemmas

Preparation

Read and indicate your response to each of the following situations.

A. Ron Jones, vice president of a large construction firm, receives in the mail a large envelope marked "personal." It contains a competitor's cost data for a project that both firms will be bidding on shortly.

The data are accompanied by a note from one of Ron's subordinates. It says: "This is the real thing!"

Ron knows that the data could be a major advantage to his firm in preparing a bid that can win the contract. What should he do?

B. Kay Smith is one of your top-performing subordinates. She has shared with you her desire to apply for promotion to a new position just announced in a different division of the company. This will be tough on you since recent budget cuts mean you will be unable to replace anyone who leaves, at least for quite some time.

Kay knows all of this and, in all fairness, has asked your permission before she submits an application. It is rumored that the son of a good friend of your boss is going to apply for the job. Although his credentials are less impressive than Kay's, the likelihood is that he will get the job if she doesn't apply. What will you do?

C. Marty was pleased to represent her firm as head of the local community development committee. In fact, her supervisor's boss once held this position and told her in a hallway conversation, "Do your best and give them every support possible."

Going along with this advice, Marty agreed to pick up the bill (several hundred dollars) for a dinner meeting with local civic and business leaders. Shortly thereafter, her supervisor informed everyone that the entertainment budget was being eliminated in a cost-saving effort.

Not wanting to renege on supporting the community development committee, Marty charged the dinner bill to an advertising budget. An internal auditor discovered the charge and reported it to you, the firm's human resource manager.

Marty is scheduled to meet with you in a few minutes. What will you do?

Instructions

1. Working alone, make the requested decisions in each of these incidents. Think carefully about your justification for the decision.
2. Meet in a group assigned by your instructor. Share your decisions and justifications in each case with other group members. Listen to theirs.
3. Try to reach a group consensus on what to do in each situation and why.
4. Be prepared to share the group decisions, and any dissenting views, in general class discussion.

Manage a Critical Incident

Dealing with a Global Supply Chain
Situation

As the co-founder of a small outdoor clothing start-up, you have just received an attractive proposal from a business in Tanzania that wants to manufacture cotton textiles for your warm-up suits. Accepting the offer from the Tanzanian firm would allow for substantial cost savings compared to your current domestic supplier. At this point in your firm's life, every dollar you save really helps. The proposal is now being considered in a meeting that includes you and others in the executive group. Someone mentions that she had recently read reports that some companies in Tanzania use child labor. Her comment immediately broadens the discussion to issues of ethics and business opportunity. Everyone agrees that research on the Tanzanian firm is necessary before any decision can be made on the proposal. You agree and point out that now is a good time to consider not only what course of action is best in this case, but also what policy should be set for dealing with future

situations involving how global suppliers treat their workforces. You stand up and say, "Let's assume the firm can meet all of our delivery times and quality standards," and then write these options on the whiteboard: (1) Accept the proposal. (2) Reject the proposal. (3) Reject the proposal if any laws in Tanzania are being violated. (4) Accept the proposal only if the head of the Tanzanian firm agrees not to employ children.

Questions

Does this list include all possible action alternatives? What others, if any, would you add? What alternative do you support and why? How could you defend your preference in the executive group meeting using concepts and ideas from this chapter?

Collaborate on the Team Activity

Stakeholder Maps
Preparation

Review the discussion of organizational stakeholders in the textbook. (1) Make a list of the stakeholders that would apply to all organizations—for example, local communities, employees, and customers. What others would you add to this starter listing? (2) Choose one organization that you are familiar with from each list that follows. (3) Draw a map of key stakeholders for each organization. (4) For each stakeholder, indicate its major interest in the organization. (5) For each organization, make a list of possible conflicts among stakeholders that the top manager should recognize.

Nonprofit	U.S. Senator
Elementary school	IRS
Community hospital	Child Services
Church	Business
University	Convenience store
United Way	Movie theater
Government	National retailer
Local mayor's office	Local pizza shop
State police	Urgent care medical clinic

Instructions

In teams assigned by your instructor, choose one organization from each list. Create "master" stakeholder maps for each organization. These should include (1) statements of stakeholder interests and (2) lists of potential stakeholder conflicts. Assume the position of top manager for each organization. Prepare a "stakeholder management plan" that represents the high-priority issues the manager should address with respect to stakeholder interest. Make a presentation to the class for each of your organizations and discuss the importance and complexity of stakeholder analysis.

Analyze THE CaseStudy : DELTA Flying High by Managing Effectively

Go to *Management Cases for Critical Thinking* at the end of the book to find this case.

EXTERNAL ENVIRONMENT AND ORGANIZATIONAL CULTURE

KEY TAKEAWAYS

- Identify key elements in the external environment of organizations.

- Discuss how organizations pursue value creation and competitive advantage in a dynamic environment.

- Describe how organizations pursue innovation in a dynamic environment.

- Explain key issues of sustainability as an environmental priority.

SKILLS MAKE YOU **VALUABLE**

- **EVALUATE** *Career Situations for a Complex Environment:* What Would You Do?

- **REFLECT** *On the Self-Assessment:* Tolerance for Ambiguity

- **CONTRIBUTE** *To the Class Exercise:* The Future Workplace

- **MANAGE** *A Critical Incident:* It's Also about Respect

- **COLLABORATE** *On the Team Activity:* Organizational Commitment to Sustainability Scorecard

- **ANALYZE** *The Case Study:* Yahoo!: Cultivating the Right Corporate Culture

We live in a complex and dynamic environment that presents a continual stream of problems and opportunities to us as individuals, to the organizations in which we work, and to society at large. Managers need to understand the environment in order to help lead their organizations to create value for society, accomplish innovation, and contribute to sustainability.

"Today's GM will do the right thing. That begins with my sincere apologies to everyone who has been affected by this recall, especially the families and friends (of those) who lost their lives or were injured. I am deeply sorry." General Motors CEO Mary Barra, testifying before U.S. Congress

"GM engineers knew about the defect, GM investigators knew about the defect, GM lawyers knew about the defect, but GM did not act to protect Americans from that defect. The fact that GM took so long to report this defect says something was very wrong with the company's values." National Highway Traffic Safety Administration (NHTSA) acting administrator David Friedman.

When General Motors belatedly recalled 2.6 million vehicles for ignition switch problems–linked with 13 deaths and known to the company for 10 years, it wasn't just customers and the marketplace that reacted; U.S. regulators and lawmakers did too.[1] GM's new CEO Mary Barra experienced the anger of society when she was called to testify before a Congressional Committee. Although she apologized and pledged a comprehensive review and response, the public wondered why this giant corporation ignored for so many years and with such dire consequences the existence of a defective part that would have cost just about a dollar per car to fix. For starters, GM was fined $35 million by the U.S. government. The final cost of claims and litigation is expected to exceed $2 billion.[2]

This interaction between General Motors, its customers, and U.S. lawmakers is an example of the complex relationship that organizations maintain with their external environments. Whereas some managers embrace the environment, continually scan it for information on trends and issues, and proactively try to deal with challenges, others view it as a source of troublesome problems that are best ignored. GM's Mary Barra claimed that a past culture that valued cost control above other considerations was behind the company's failure to act when the defective ignition switches were first discovered and customers were injured in questionable crashes. As the new CEO, she said: "We have learned a great deal from this recall. . . . We will emerge from this situation a stronger company."[3]

The External Environment

TAKEAWAY 1   What is in the external environment of organizations?

LEARN MORE | Economic conditions • Legal-political conditions • Sociocultural conditions
ABOUT | Technological conditions issues • Natural environment conditions

The **general environment** consists of economic, legal-political, sociocultural, technological, and natural environment conditions in which the organization operates.

The **general environment** of organizations consists of all external conditions that set the context for managerial decision making. You might think of it as a broad envelope of dynamic forces that surround and influence an organization. Figure 4.1 classifies these forces as economic, legal-political, sociocultural, technological, and natural environment conditions. Top managers and C-suite executives bear special responsibility for monitoring these conditions and linking them with the mission, strategies, and internal practices of their organizations. You can say that their job is to make sure that the voice of the environment gets heard within the organization, something that was missing in the General Motors ignition switch debacle but which new CEO Mary Barra has pledged to correct.

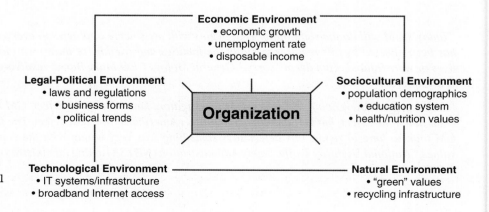

FIGURE 4.1
Sample elements in the general environments of organizations.

Economic Conditions

High unemployment • Long-term joblessness • Rising income inequality
Falling middle-class incomes • Debates on minimum wage

When economic conditions in the external environment begin to reflect extreme imbalances of this kind, what does it mean for organizations and managers?[4] These conditions are part of a larger and ever-changing set of environmental forces. The overall health of the economy in terms of financial markets, inflation, income levels, and job creation are also critical environmental drivers. These macro-economic conditions affect the prospects for companies, consumer spending patterns and lifestyles, and even state and national priorities. They must be assessed, forecasted, and considered when policymakers and executives make decisions.

States now compete on tax incentives to attract new plants from companies like Boeing, and Apple. At stake are hundreds of new jobs and a financial boost for local economies. Global economic trends are always an issue. For years, American companies have pursued **offshoring** by outsourcing work and jobs to lower-cost foreign locations. But new economic signals are now signaling it's time to consider **reshoring**, which moves jobs back home. If you bought a Maytag brand Maxima front-load washer five years ago it would have been made in Germany. Today it is built in Ohio by the parent company Whirlpool.[5] The shift toward reshoring is driven by rising labor costs in foreign countries, higher transoceanic shipping costs, complicated logistics, complaints about poor customer service, public criticism of lost local jobs, and economic incentives for job creation offered by local communities.[6]

> **Offshoring** is the outsourcing of jobs to foreign locations.
>
> **Reshoring** is the movement of jobs from foreign locations back to domestic ones.

Legal-Political Conditions

Immigration reform • Education reform • Tax reform • Health care reform

All the above issues were voted top priorities by 100 chief executives participating in a *Wall Street Journal* conference on business and public policy.[7] They represent just a sample of legal-political conditions with major implications for organizations and managers. These conditions reflect current and proposed laws and regulations, government policies, and the philosophy and objectives of political parties. U.S. lawmakers are debating issues such as regulation of banks and the financial services industry, foreign trade agreements, protection of U.S. jobs and industries, and the minimum wage. Corporate executives follow such debates to monitor trends that can affect the regulation, oversight, and competitive direction of their businesses. What is your position on things like increased regulation in banking and financial services or increases to the minimum wage?

As if the domestic scene wasn't complicated enough, the legal-political conditions in the global business environment also vary significantly from one country to the next. Just as foreign firms have to learn to deal with U.S. laws and politics, U.S. firms must adjust to them when operating in other countries. The European Union fined Microsoft $1.35 billion for antitrust violations involving the practice of bundling media and Windows software and making the source code for interoperability unavailable to competitors.[8] Apple was sued by a Chinese company that had previously trademarked the name "iPad." It ended up paying $60 million to retain rights to use the iPad name in China.[9] Importantly, too, not all countries support international copyright and intellectual property protection. Reports on music, movie, product, and software piracy regularly make the news, affecting companies from SONY Pictures to Louis Vuitton and Microsoft.

National policies also vary on **Internet censorship**—the deliberate blockage and denial of public access to information otherwise available on the Internet, and global firms face many dilemmas in dealing with them. Google, Yahoo!, and Twitter, for example, have all faced problems in China where laws restrict access to Internet sites with content deemed off limits by the government. A Google spokesperson described the global environment as "a delicate balancing act between being a platform for free expression and also obeying local laws around the world."[10]

> **Internet censorship** is the deliberate blockage and denial of public access to information posted on the Internet.

Sociocultural Conditions

Unemployment of African Americans is double that of Whites • White households out-earn African American households by 20 times and Hispanic households by 18 times • Men out-earn women by 23.5 cents per hour

Data like these aren't only of economic significance.[11] They reflect social issues relating to educational opportunity, social network connections, access to technology, mentoring, job options, and the glass ceiling. Think of sociocultural conditions in the general environment as demographics and norms of a society or region, as well as social values pertaining to such things as employment, gender roles, ethics, human rights, and lifestyles.

Generational cohorts consist of people born within a few years of one another and who experience somewhat similar life events during their formative years.

With respect to demographics and norms, for example, the workplace is a mix of **generational cohorts**—people born within a few years of one another and who experience somewhat similar life events during their formative years.[12] And, sometimes these generational subcultures clash. Whereas older generations are "digital immigrants" who have had to learn technology, the younger millennials, Gen Ys, and the iGeneration grew up as "digital natives" in technology-enriched homes, schools, and friendship environments. These differing life experiences affect

Research Brief

Generations Show Differences on Important Values

In an economy with an aging workforce, scholars Jean Twenge, Stacy Campbell, Brian Hoffman, and Charles Lance decided to investigate value differences across generational cohorts—groups of individuals born about the same time and experiencing similar life events during their development years. The authors wanted to understand how values may differ among generations in the same workplace and what the implications might be for managing these differences.

Twenge et al. focused their attention on comparing Baby Boomers (born 1946–1964, grew up during the Vietnam War and civil rights movement) with Generation X (born 1965–1981, saw fall of the Soviet Union and advent of the AIDS epidemic) and with Generation Y or the Millennials (born 1982–1999, grew up digital and saw major corporate ethics scandals). Their data was from a program called Monitoring the Future, which has surveyed high school seniors each year since 1976.

The main findings were in values toward leisure, with GenX increasing over Boomers and Millennials further increasing over GenX. The researchers interpret this as a growing desire for work–life balance. Extrinsic values for money and status, however, increased for GenX and then decreased for Millennials. The researchers say GenX and Millennials may be attracted to work settings that offer work–life balance and support leisure

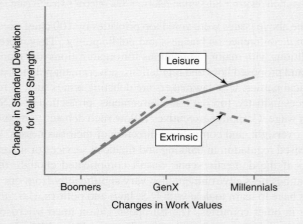

pursuits, things often associated with alternative and more flexible work scheduling.

YOU BE THE RESEARCHER

Do these findings confirm your observations and experiences? Assume you are a summer intern in a large organization and your boss says: "I'd like you to conduct a study to learn what our different generations of employees want from work and what problems they have working with one another." Just how would you design this study so that your findings would have real credibility and value?

everything from how the generations shop, to how they learn, to how they like to work. Characteristics often used to describe digital natives include ease of multitasking, the desire for immediate gratification, continuous contact with others, and less concern with knowing things than with knowing where to find out about things.[13]

With respect to social values, shifting currents and trends affect how organizations focus on employment practices, reputation management, product development, advertising messages, and internal policies. There was a time, for example, when the compensation of university presidents—averaging $480,000 in total compensation—or corporate CEOs like Apple CEO Tim Cook's $40.6 million wasn't a hot-button topic.[14] No more. In a time of persistently high unemployment, limited job opportunities, and income inequality, public values are growing more critical of high executive pay—CEOs at S&P 500 firms average $11.7 million per year while their employees earn $35,239 (a ratio of 331 to 1).[15] There has even been some pressure—unsuccessful to date—for the U.S. Congress to place limits on the pay of top managers in publicly traded firms.

Technological Conditions

63% of smartphone owners say their employers expect more work availability • Average teenagers spend just seven minutes per day reading off line • When e-mail is constantly open, people switch tasks 37 times per hour

No one doubts that continuing technological developments affect everything from the way we work to how we live and how we raise our children. It shouldn't be any surprise that businesses are quickly ramping up their spending on social media for product promotions, reputation

analysis > MAKE DATA YOUR FRIEND

> 75% of women 18–32 believe more must be done to ensure workplace equality.

Social Attitudes Shift on Women at Work, but Concerns for Equality Persist

Social attitudes toward women at work are shifting in a positive direction. But polls and surveys show that a gender wage gap and bias toward women remain. For example:

- More women than men now receive college degrees and comprise almost half the workforce.

- Young women earn 93 cents per dollar earned by young men, while women in general earn 76.5 cents per dollar earned by men, a figure that is actually up slightly from 71.6 cents in 1991.

- Among full-time workers, women earn 79 cents per dollar earned by men.

- The percentage of women who believe they can't have a career and family without sacrifices to each fell from 78% in 1997 to 66% in 2013, while 64% of men now say women can't "have it all."

- 35% of women report experiencing some form of discrimination at work versus 15% of women aged 18–32.

- 84% of women versus 63% of men believe women are paid less than men for the same work.

- 75% of women between 18–32 believe more must be done to ensure workplace equality.

WHAT ARE THE IMPLICATIONS?

What reasons—other than discrimination—can you give for the lingering wage gap between women and men? Do these explanations make the gap more justifiable, or not? What are the implications of this wage gap for the economy, for families, for businesses, and communities? How about the belief that women can't have it all—career and family, without making sacrifices? Is this your belief? What are the implications for society at large as well as for women and their families? If more needs to be done to create workplace equality, what steps should next be taken—by government, by employers, and by educators? Have you seen examples of age, racial- or gender-based imbalance in compensation? What do you think drives any such gaps?

management, internal communication, and more.[16] A continuing wave of social media applications for the workplace ranges from new product development and advertising, to employee networking and data sharing, to virtual meetings and always-available chats. Between new apps for fast-developing smart device technologies and ever-increasing bandwidth, technology continues to penetrate further and further into everyday life.

On the employee side of things, technology easily carries work responsibilities into non-work lives. How often do you hear people complaining that they can "never get away from the job" and that work follows them home, on vacation, and just about everywhere they go with a smart device turned on? How often do you hear warnings about career and reputation risk because of poorly chosen social media decisions? A CareerBuilder.com survey reports that about one-third of executives visiting social-network sites of job candidates said they found information that gave them reasons not to hire the person.[17]

The employer side of ever-present and constantly-changing technology is full of potential problems as well as opportunities. It is a fact that many employees spend lots of time doing personal things online. Some employers call this loss of productivity "social *not*working."[18] This practice isn't limited to the work environment; it's a significant classroom issue as well. In one survey, 65% of business students said they sent at least one text message during each class, but only 49% felt guilty about it.[19] Further down the negative end of the spectrum, recent airplane crashes have raised questions about pilot training and technological dependency. The National Transportation Safety Board (NTSB) is worried that over-reliance on automation causes pilots to lose manual flight skills that are necessary cross-checks and last-resorts in crisis situations.[20]

Natural Environment Conditions

Magnitude 9.0 earthquake and large tsunami hit Japan • 20,000 people killed
Fukushima Daiichi nuclear power station badly damaged • 80,000 residents evacuated
Nuclear radiation may prohibit return to some communities for decades

We tend to think most about natural environment conditions following a disaster—a nuclear plant failure, a major oil spill, or an enormous hurricane.[21] But concerns for the status and preservation of our natural environment are ever-present and global. Calls for being "carbon neutral," "green," and "sustainable" are common on college campuses, in local communities, and in our everyday lives. The intent is to protect natural resources that are essential to society and ensure their availability for future generations.

What are your top environmental concerns and priorities? How about for your community? Is it toxic waste that may be getting dumped in a regional landfill? Could it be global warming prompted by unusually high seasonal temperatures? Or is it fossil fuel consumption and the search for reliable and affordable alternative sources of energy?[22] Just look around and you'll see people and organizations working harder to reduce water consumption, cut back waste and increase recycling, improve energy efficiency, buy and consume more local produce, and eliminate pollution. As consumers, we are asking for and getting more access to "green products and services." As job candidates, we increasingly seek "green job" opportunities. As investors, we can even buy "green mutual funds" and "green bonds."[23]

It is important to recognize that we increasingly expect organizations and their managers to help preserve and respect the environment. When they don't, public criticism can be vocal, harsh, and expensive. Think about public debates over "fracking" in the search for natural gas supplies and the use of coal for electricity generation. Think about the outrage that quickly surfaced over the disastrous BP oil spill in the Gulf of Mexico, the $40-billion-plus cleanup and settlement costs to the company, and the subsequent calls for stronger government oversight and control over corporate practices that put our natural world at risk.[24] And, think about the value placed on a university's sustainability practices by prospective new students.

Learning Check 1

TAKEAWAYQUESTION **1 What is in the external environment of organizations?**

BE SURE YOU CAN • list the key elements in the external environments of organizations • give examples of how present conditions for each element pose immediate challenges to organizations • give examples of how possible future developments for each of these elements might require significant changes in how organizations operate

Environment and Value Creation

TAKEAWAY 2   How do organizations create value and competitive advantage in a dynamic environment?

LEARN MORE ABOUT | Value creation and competitive advantage • Environmental uncertainty

The **specific environment** or **task environment** is composed of the organizations, groups, and persons with whom an organization interacts and conducts business. Its members, referred to as **stakeholders**, are the persons, groups, and institutions affected by the organization's performance.[25] Stakeholders are key constituents that have an interest in how an organization operates. They are influenced by it, and they can influence it in return. The important stakeholders for most organizations include customers, suppliers, competitors, regulators, advocacy groups, investors/ owners, employees, and society at large—including future generations.

> The **specific environment**, or **task environment**, includes the people and groups with whom an organization interacts.
>
> **Stakeholders** are the persons, groups, and institutions directly affected by an organization.

Value Creation and Competitive Advantage

Organizations are expected to contribute to their environments by creating value for—and satisfying the needs of—their multiple stakeholders. For example, businesses create value for customers through product pricing and quality, and for owners in realized profits. Businesses create value for suppliers through the benefits of long-term business relationships. They create value for employees through earned wages and job satisfaction. Businesses create value for local communities through their citizenship. They can even create value for competitors by stimulating market activity and product/process innovations.

Organizations also strive for **competitive advantage** in their environments—something that they do extremely well, is difficult to copy, and gives them an advantage over competitors in the marketplace.[26] Think competitive advantage when you turn to Google for search, shop with "1-Click" at Amazon, and stream movies from Netflix. The ultimate competitive advantage test for an organization's leadership is a good answer to this question: "What does my organization do better than any other?" Many of the answers today are framed in technology utilization and innovation in the following areas:[27]

> **Competitive advantage** is something that an organization does extremely well, is difficult to copy, and that gives it an advantage over competitors in the marketplace.

- *Competitive advantage can be achieved through costs*—finding ways and using technology to operate with lower costs than competitors and thus earn profits with prices that competitors have difficulty matching.

- *Competitive advantage can be achieved through quality*—finding ways and using technology to create products and services that are consistently higher quality than competitors offer.

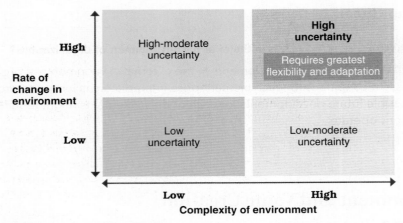

FIGURE 4.2
Dimensions of uncertainty in the external environments of organizations.

- *Competitive advantage can be achieved through delivery*—finding ways and using technology to outperform competitors by delivering products and services to customers faster, more consistently on time, and by developing timely new products.

- *Competitive advantage can be achieved through flexibility*—finding ways and using technology to adjust and tailor products and services to fit customer needs in ways that are difficult or expensive for competitors to match.

Uncertainty, Complexity, and Change

As managers deal with stakeholders, seek to create value, and gain competitive advantage, these pursuits often are complicated by **environmental uncertainty**—a lack of complete information regarding what is present in the environment and what developments may occur. The more uncertain the environment, the harder it is to analyze environmental conditions and predict future states of affairs. The greater the environmental uncertainty, the more risk taking that may be required to act on perceived problems and opportunities.

Two dimensions of environmental uncertainty are shown in Figure 4.2.[28] The first is the *degree of complexity*, or the number of different factors present in the environment. An environment is typically classified as relatively simple or complex. The second is the *rate of change* in and among these factors. An environment is typically classified as being stable or dynamic. The most challenging and uncertain situation is an environment that is both complex and dynamic. High-uncertainty environments require flexibility and adaptability in organizational designs and work practices, as well as decision makers who are comfortable with risk and able to respond quickly as new circumstances arise and new information becomes available.

> **Environmental uncertainty** is a lack of information regarding what exists in the environment and what developments may occur.

Learning Check 2

TAKEAWAYQUESTION 2 **How do organizations create value and gain competitive advantage in a dynamic environment?**

BE SURE YOU CAN • describe how a business can create value for four key stakeholders • explain *competitive advantage* and give examples of how a business might achieve it • analyze the uncertainty of an organization's external environment using degree of complexity and rate of change

Environment and Innovation

TAKEAWAY 3   How do organizations achieve innovation in a dynamic environment?

LEARN MORE ABOUT | Types of innovations • The innovation process • Disruptive innovation and technology

One of the things we can say for sure about organizational environments today is that change, uncertainty, and complexity call for constant **innovation**. It is the process of coming up with new ideas and putting them into practice. And, it's a major driver of competitive advantage.[29] When you think "innovation," what comes to mind? Is it a product like the iPad or Kindle e-reader or Google Glass? Is it something fun like an online game or a Super Soaker water gun? Or is it a customer experience such as using your smart phone to tap an app and pay for a Starbucks coffee, or scan a check to make an electronic bank deposit?

> **Innovation** is the process of taking a new idea and putting it into practice.

Types of Innovations

The innovations we experience every day sort into three broad forms: (1) **Product innovations** result in the creation of new or improved goods and services. (2) **Process innovations** result in better ways of doing things. (3) **Business model innovations** result in new ways of making money for the firm. Consider these examples:

- *Product Innovation*—Groupon put coupons on the Web; Apple introduced the iPod, iPhone, and iPad world; Amazon's Kindle launched a new era of e-readers; Facebook and Instagram made social media part of everyday life, and Twitter introduced communication in 140 characters or less.

- *Process Innovation*—IKEA's "ready to assemble" furniture and fixtures transformed retail shopping; Amazon.com's "1-Click" ordering streamlined the online shopping experience; Nike allows online customers to design their own shoes.

- *Business Model Innovation*—Netflix turned movie rental into a subscription business and Redbox put it into a vending machine; Zynga made "paying for extras" profitable in free online games; eBay created the world's largest online marketplace.

> **Product innovations** result in new or improved goods or services.
>
> **Process innovations** result in better ways of doing things.
>
> **Business model innovations** result in ways for firms to make money.

Although the tendency is to view innovation as being primarily focused in the business and economic context, innovation applies equally well when we talk about the world's social problems—poverty, famine, literacy, disease—and the general conditions for economic and social development. **Social business innovation** uses business models to address important social problems. Think of it as business innovation with a focus on critical social issues.

   Microcredit lending is an example of social business innovation. It was pioneered in Bangladesh, where economist Muhammad Yunus started the Grameen Bank. Recognizing that many of the country's citizens who are poor couldn't obtain regular bank loans because of insufficient collateral, Yunus introduced the "microcredit." He set up the   Bank to lend small amounts of money to these citizens at very low interest rates, with the goal of promoting self-sufficiency through owning small enterprises. At one level, this is a business model innovation—microcredit lending. But at another level, it is a social business innovation—using microcredit lending to help tackle the ever-challenging issue of poverty.[30]

> **Social business innovation** finds ways to use business models to address important social problems.

The Innovation Process

Whatever the goal, whether it be a new product, an improved process, a unique business model, or solving social problems, the innovation process begins with *invention*—the act of discovery—

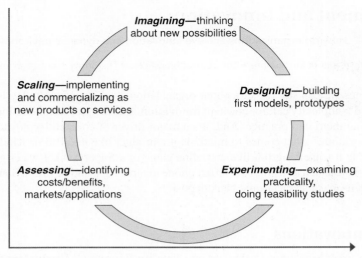

FIGURE 4.3
The five steps in Hamel's "wheel of innovation."

and ends with *application*—the act of use. Consultant Gary Hamel described innovation in the five-step *wheel of innovation* shown in Figure 4.3.[31] Step 1 is *imagining*–thinking about new possibilities. Step 2 is *designing*—building initial models, prototypes, or samples. Step 3 is *experimenting*—examining practicality and financial value through experiments and feasibility studies. Step 4 is *assessing*—identifying strengths and weaknesses, potential costs and benefits, and potential markets or applications. Step 5 is *scaling*—implementing what has been learned and commercializing new products or services. In business, this final step involves commercializing innovation by turning it into actual products, services, or processes that increase profits by improving sales or lowering costs.

Something called **reverse innovation** is now getting lots of attention. It refers to innovation that comes from lower organizational levels and is found in diverse settings or locations.[32] The concept got its start as global firms realized that innovation wasn't just a "home market" activity that creates new products and services for distribution to "foreign markets." Instead, they realized that there were lots of innovations to be found in environments where new products and services had to be created under income and pricing constraints. GE, for example, developed low-priced and portable electrocardiogram and ultrasound machines in India where the prices of its existing lines were prohibitive. The firm brought the new machines through reverse innovation into U.S. markets, where their mobility and low prices made them popular with emergency units.

Reverse innovation is launched from lower organizational levels and diverse locations, including emerging markets.

Disruptive Innovation and Technology

Disruptive innovation creates products or services that become so widely used that they largely replace prior practices and competitors.

The innovation process is sometimes so successful that **disruptive innovation** occurs. Harvard scholar Clay Christensen defines it as the creation of an innovative product or service that starts out small scale and then moves "up market" to where it becomes so widely used that it displaces prior practices and competitors.[33] Historical examples include cellular phones that disrupted traditional landlines, MP3 digital music players that disrupted traditional physical transmission of music from CDs and cassettes, and discount retailers that disrupted traditional full-line department stores. We already see online e-retailers disrupting fixed-place brick and mortar stores, online gaming and movie streaming disrupting "buy and own" models, and tablet devices

wisdom > LEARN FROM ROLE MODELS

Daily Dump's Solution to Waste Management in Bangalore

Sumathy Ramasmy

In 2008, 340 million Indians (30% of the total population) lived in the cities. By 2030, India's urban population is estimated to be 590 million (40% of the total population), and a total of 68 cities in India is expected to have a population of more than 1 million.

India's rapid urbanization has led to challenges with its waste management. Bangalore, known as the Silicon Valley of India, is faced with a waste management problem as approximately 5000 tons of trash is produced every day.

Today, Daily Dump has become an innovative solution to Bangalore's waste management problem. In 2006, Poonam Bir Kasturi founded Daily Dump to introduce home composting as a way to reduce household waste. Armed with the determination to succeed, Kasturi tried various composting methods and used primary data from her household interviews to design her first product, the Kambha composting pot. These three-tier terracotta pots painted with beautiful and unique designs have become useful consumer products in more than 15,000 homes in Bangalore.

However, people's mindset had to be changed if they were to try this home composting product. Daily Dump provided support to first-time users by paying attention to their complaints and listening to customer feedback. In response, Kasturi developed other products such as tools and aprons to help customers to compost their household waste with ease.

Social media has become another medium for Daily Dump to expand its market share across the globe. Cartoons are featured on the website to create interest and encourage consumers around the world to actively participate in the waste management process. By August 2014, Daily Dump's customers have successfully saved 14,470 kg of organic waste from making their way to the landfills.

Furthermore, the use of terracotta pots for composting has breathed new life into India's traditional pottery industry, creating jobs for villagers in Andhra Pradesh. With Daily Dump's steady expansion in India and other countries, the traditional industry will surely see the creation of more jobs and investment opportunities.

To create greater awareness of waste management, Daily Dump has introduced a 'clone' business model. Their products can be cloned by businesses and sold in any country. While the clone model was licenced without a fee at first, an initial fee and a royalty payment for its products were later introduced.

Daily Dump's clones are thriving in Chile, Qatar and Brazil, thus proving that its unique business model has been able to achieve its primary objective–environmentally friendly waste management to ensure a clean environment for all.

FIND INSPIRATION

Identify the stakeholders for Daily Dump. Describe how Daily Dump has created value for each of its stakeholders. Is Daily Dump a sustainable business? Justify your answer.

When Bangalore faced a waste management problem, Kasturi's quick thinking became a solution to many households. Describe three personal traits of Kasturi. Do you see such traits in yourself? How would you develop these traits?

Wisdom: Information from Bryan Boyer and Justin W. Cook, "Designing pathways to successful waste management in India and beyond," 2012, Sitra, The Finnish Innovation Fund; "India's urban awakening: Building inclusive cities, sustaining economic growth,"McKinsey Global Institute, April 2010, http://www.mckinsey.com/insights/urbanization/urban_awakening_in_india, accessed September 1, 2014; http://www.firstpost.com/india/as-garbage-landfills-run-out-of-spacea-pioneering-solution-from-bangalore-1313967.html, accessed September 1, 2014; http://www.dailydump.org, accessed September 3, 2014; Kasturi P.B., Daily Dump, Bangalore, India, interview, September 29, 2014.

disrupting desktop computing. What's on your list for the next great disruptor of today's established products or business practices? Will electric cars like Tesla's Model S disrupt historical internal combustion technology? Will the success of private room rentals through Airbnb drive further developments in the community marketplace model that end up disrupting not just hotels but also businesses in other industries?

Learning Check 3

TAKEAWAYQUESTION 3 **How do organizations achieve innovation in a dynamic environment?**

BE SURE YOU CAN • define *innovation* • discuss differences between process, product, business model, and social business innovations • list the five steps in Hamel's wheel of innovation • explain how innovations get commercialized • define *reverse innovation* and *disruptive innovation* • give an example of a disruptive innovation that you use almost every day

---

Sustainability is a commitment to protect the rights of present and future generations as co-stakeholders of the world's resources.

Sustainable development uses environmental resources to support societal needs today while also preserving and protecting them for future generations.

Environmental capital or **natural capital** is the supply of natural resources—atmosphere, land, water, and minerals—that sustain life and produce goods and services for society.

The **triple bottom line** assesses the economic, social, and environmental performance of organizations.

The **3 P's of organizational performance** are profit, people, and planet.

Environment and Sustainability

TAKEAWAY 4   What is sustainability as an organizational priority?

LEARN MORE ABOUT | Sustainable development • Sustainable business • Human sustainability

Think about climate change, carbon footprints, alternative energy, local foods, and broader links between people, organizations, and nature. They highlight issues of **sustainability**, a commitment to live and work in ways that protect the rights of both present and future generations as co-stakeholders of the world's resources. It applies to everything from the air we breathe and the water we consume, to the spaces we inhabit, to the human labor that gives life to our best-loved foods, beverages, and electronic devices.

Sustainable Development

We live and work at a time when global consumption of fossil fuels is at an all-time high, water shortages are reaching critical proportions in many parts of the world, and air quality in major metropolitan areas around the globe is reaching all-time lows. It only makes sense that **sustainable development** is a major concern for governments, leaders, and the public at large. The term describes the use of environmental resources to support society's needs today, while also preserving and protecting them for use by future generations.[34]

"Renew," "recycle," "conserve," and "preserve" are all well-recognized sustainable development catchwords. They highlight desires to preserve **environmental capital** or **natural capital** as the world's supply of natural resources—atmosphere, land, water, and minerals—that sustain life on Earth.[35] But how do we balance aspirations to consume our environmental capital for everyday prosperity, convenience, comfort, and luxury, with the potential costs of losing it in the future? PepsiCo's CEO Indra Nooyi says: "All corporations operate with a license from society. It's critically important that we take that responsibility very, very seriously; we have to make sure that what corporations do doesn't add costs to society."[36] Nooyi's point directs attention toward a **triple bottom line** that evaluates not only an organization's economic performance but also its social and environmental performance.[37] This is often called the **3 P's of organizational performance**—profit, people, and planet.

Sustainable Business

Pursuit of the triple bottom line and the 3 P's is a hallmark of **sustainable businesses** that both meet the needs of customers and protect or advance the well-being of the natural environment.[38] Sustainable businesses operate in harmony with nature rather than by exploiting it. They set goals for things like "recycling percentage," "carbon reduction," "energy efficiency," "ethical sourcing," and "food security," among others.[39] They employ people with job titles like Corporate Sustainability Officer, Green Building Manager, Staff Ecologist, Sustainability Program Director, and Sustainability Planner. They also pursue **sustainable innovation** or **green innovation** to create new products, practices, and methods that reduce negative impact on the environment and even seek to achieve positive impact.[40]

A sustainable business model seeks win–win outcomes for the organization and the environment. Can you think of some good examples? Actually, a lot of firms approach their markets in this way. For example, Stonyfield Farm saved over $1.7 million in energy costs after putting in a large solar photovoltaic array. Clif Bar cut shrink-wrapping and saved $400,000 a year in plastic costs. Seventh Generation built $40-million-plus of revenues from green personal care and household products.[41] Subaru of Indiana Automotive saved $5.3 million in one year as 98% of plant waste was recycled or reduced, paint solvents were filtered and reused, and compost from food waste was sold to local farmers.[42] Even basic changes in work practices can help with sustainability. Using virtual teams and conferences lowers travel costs; offering work-at-home alternatives helps attract and retain talent; both practices help reduce carbon emissions by cutting back on employee travel.[43]

> A **sustainable business** operates in ways that meet the needs of customers while protecting or advancing the well-being of our natural environment.
>
> **Sustainable innovations** or **green innovations** help reduce an organization's negative impact and enhance its positive impact on the natural environment.

Human Sustainability

The notion of sustainability in management applies to more than the natural environment alone. Scholar Jeffrey Pfeffer offers a strong case for giving greater management attention to social and human sustainability—the "People" part of the 3 P's.[44] He says: "Just as there is concern for protecting natural resources, there could be a similar level of concern for protecting human resources. . . . Being a socially responsible business ought to encompass the effect of management practices on employee physical and psychological well-being."[45]

Pfeffer's concern for human sustainability highlights the importance of including employees as organizational stakeholders. Human sustainability issues like those in the box above remind us that management practices have major consequences for the health and well-being of the individuals who do the everyday work of organizations. A tragic example of the failure to embrace human sustainability is the collapse of an industrial complex in Bangladesh that housed outsourcing suppliers to several well-known global clothing retailers. The incident killed more than 1,100 people and exposed unsafe building and sweatshop conditions in factories throughout the country. The nonprofit Institute for Global Labour and Human Rights is dedicated to improving human sustainability through its mission "to promote and defend human, women's and workers' rights in the global economy."[46]

How to Assess Organizational Commitment to Human Sustainability

To what extent does the organization help support and advance human health and well-being by:

- providing health insurance to employees?
- providing wellness programs for employees?
- avoiding job layoffs?
- structuring work hours to reduce stress?
- structuring work hours to minimize work–family conflict?
- designing jobs to reduce stress?
- designing jobs to give people control over their work?
- being transparent and fair in handling wage and status inequalities?

Learning Check 4

TAKEAWAYQUESTION **4** **What is sustainability as an organizational priority?**

BE SURE YOU CAN • explain the triple bottom line and 3 P's of organizational performance • define the terms *sustainable development* and *environmental capital* • give examples of sustainability issues today • explain and give examples of *sustainable business practices* • discuss human sustainability as a management concern

Management Learning Review
Get Prepared for **Quizzes and Exams**

SUMMARY

TAKEAWAYQUESTION **1**

What is in the external environment of organizations?

- The general environment includes background economic, socio-cultural, legal-political, technological, and natural environment conditions.
- The economic environment influences organizations through the health of the local, domestic, and global economies in terms of such things as financial markets, inflation, income levels, unemployment, and job outlook.
- The legal-political environment influences organizations through existing and proposed laws and regulations, government policies, and the philosophy and objectives of political parties.
- The sociocultural environment influences organizations through the norms, customs, and demographics of a society or region, as well as social values on such matters as ethics, human rights, gender roles, and lifestyles.
- The technological environment influences organizations through continuing advancement of information and computer technologies that affect the way we work, how we live, and how we raise our children.
- The natural environment conditions influence organizations through the abundance of natural resources provided, and the need for organizational practices that both meet the needs of customers and protect future well-being.

FOR DISCUSSION If the interests of a business firm's owners and investors conflict with those of the community, which stakeholder gets preference? What situational factors influence whose interests should take precedence?

TAKEAWAYQUESTION **2**

How do organizations create value and competitive advantage in a dynamic environment?

- The specific environment or task environment consists of suppliers, customers, competitors, regulators, and other stake-holders with which an organization interacts.
- A competitive advantage is achieved when an organization does something very well that allows it to outperform its competitors.

- Environmental uncertainty is created by the rate of change of factors in the external environment and the complexity of this environment in terms of the number of factors that are relevant and important.

FOR DISCUSSION Which of the two or three retail stores that you shop at weekly has the strongest competitive advantage and why?

TAKEAWAYQUESTION **3**

How do organizations achieve innovation in a dynamic environment?

- Product innovations deliver new products and services to customers; process innovations improve operations; and business model innovations find new ways of creating value and making profits.
- Social business innovations use business models to help address social problems such as poverty, famine, disease, and literacy.
- The innovation process involves moving from the stage of invention that involves discovery and idea creation all the way to final application that involves actual use of what has been created.
- Reverse innovation finds innovation opportunities in diverse locations, such as taking products and services developed in emerging markets and finding ways to utilize them elsewhere.
- Disruptive innovation, often involving technological advance-ments, is the creation of a new product or service that starts out small scale and then becomes so widely used that it displaces prior practices and competitors.

FOR DISCUSSION Housing for the homeless is a problem in many communities. In what way might this problem be addressed through some form of social business innovation?

TAKEAWAYQUESTION **4**

What is sustainability as an organizational priority?

- The concept of sustainability describes a commitment to rec-ognize and protect the rights of both present and future gener-ations as co-stakeholders of the world's natural resources.

- The triple bottom line evaluates how well organizations perform on economic, social, and environmental performance criteria; it is also called the 3 P's of organizational performance—profits, people, planet.
- Sustainable development uses environmental resources to support society today while also preserving and protecting those resources for use by future generations.
- Sustainable innovations pursue new ways for minimizing the negative impact and maximizing the positive impact of

organizations on the natural environment by reducing energy and natural resource consumption.

FOR DISCUSSION When the costs of pursuing sustainability goals reduce business profits, which stakeholder interests should take priority, business owners or society at large? Where do you think the balance between profits and sustainability should naturally emerge?

SELF-TEST 4

Multiple-Choice Questions

1. The general environment of an organization would include _____.
   (a) population demographics
   (b) activist groups
   (c) competitors
   (d) customers

2. Internet censorship faced in foreign countries by firms such as Google is an example of how differences in _____ factors in the general environment can cause complications for global business executives.
   (a) economic   (c) natural environment
   (b) legal-political   (d) demographic

3. If the term *offshoring* describes outsourcing of work and jobs to foreign locations, what is it called when firms like Caterpillar move jobs back into the United States from foreign locations?
   (a) protectionism   (c) disrupting
   (b) reshoring   (d) upscaling

4. Work preferences of different generations and public values over things like high pay for corporate executives are examples of developments in the _____ environment of organizations.
   (a) task   (c) socio-cultural
   (b) specific   (d) economic

5. A business that has found ways to use technology to outperform its rivals in the marketplace can be said to have gained _____.
   (a) environmental capital
   (b) competitive advantage
   (c) sustainable development
   (d) environmental certainty

6. Apps for an Apple iPhone or a Google Android phone are examples of _____ innovations, whereas the use of robotics in performing manufacturing tasks previously done by humans is an example of _____ innovation.
   (a) cost-benefit, process
   (b) product, cost-benefit
   (c) value-driven, service-driven
   (d) product, process

7. Micro-credit lending that makes it possible for poor people to get small loans so they can start small businesses is an example of a business model innovation that is also a _____ innovation.
   (a) social business
   (b) technological
   (c) disruptive
   (d) green

8. Two dimensions that determine the level of environmental uncertainty are the number of factors in the external environment and the _____ of these factors.
   (a) location
   (b) rate of change
   (c) importance
   (d) interdependence

9. One of the ways that corporations might better take into account their responsibility for being good environmental citizens is to redefine the notion of profit to: Profit = Revenue − Cost of Goods Sold −_____ .
   (a) operating expenses
   (b) dividends
   (c) costs to society
   (d) loan interest

10. The three P's of organizational performance are Profit, People, and _____.
    (a) Philanthropy
    (b) Principle
    (c) Potential
    (d) Planet

11. What organizational stakeholder must be considered in any serious discussion about how a firm can better fulfill its obligations for sustainable development?
    (a) owners or investors
    (b) customers
    (c) suppliers
    (d) future generations

12. The first step in Hamel's wheel of innovation is _____.
    (a) imagining
    (b) assessing
    (c) experimenting
    (d) scaling

13. When a medical device is developed in India so that it can sell at a low price and still deliver high-quality results, and then that device is transferred for sale in the United States also at a low price, this is an example of _____.
    (a) trickle-down innovation
    (b) disruptive innovation
    (c) reverse innovation
    (d) sustainable innovation

14. What term is used to describe the world's supply of natural resources, such as land, water, and minerals?
    (a) sustainable development
    (b) global warming
    (c) climate justice
    (d) environmental capital

15. Health insurance for employees, flexible work hours to balance work and family responsibilities, and programs to help employees deal with stress in their lives, are ways organizations might try to improve their accomplishments in respect to _____.
    (a) profits
    (b) human sustainability
    (c) innovation
    (d) natural capital

Short-Response Questions

16. Who and/or what should be considered as key stakeholders by a business executive when mapping the task environment for her organization?

17. Exactly how should "sustainability" be best defined when making it part of a goal statement or strategic objective for a business or nonprofit organization?

18. How do product, process, and business model innovations differ from one another?

19. How does the process of reverse innovation work?

Essay Question

20. At a reunion of graduates from a college of business at the local university, two former roommates engaged in a discussion about environment and sustainability. One is a senior executive with a global manufacturer, and the other owns a sandwich shop in the college town.

    Global executive: "We include sustainability in our corporate mission and have a chief sustainability officer on the senior management team. The CSO is really good and makes sure that we don't do anything that could cause a lack of public confidence in our commitment to sustainability."

    Sandwich shop owner: "That's all well and good, but what are you doing on the positive side in terms of environmental care? It sounds like you do just enough to avoid public scrutiny. Shouldn't the CSO be a real advocate for the environment rather than just a protector of the corporate reputation? We, for example, use only natural foods and ingredients, recycle everything that is recyclable, and compost all possible waste."

    Question: If you were establishing a new position called *corporate sustainability officer*, what would you include in the job description as a way of both clarifying the responsibilities of the person hired and establishing clear accountability for what sustainability means to your organization?

Management Skills & Competencies Make yourself **valuable!**

Evaluate Career Situations

What Would You Do?

1. Social Values on the Line

It is uncomfortable just to hear it. One of your friends brought his friend to lunch. When discussing a new female boss, he says: "It really irritates me not only that she gets the job just because she's a woman, but she's also Hispanic. No way that someone like me had a chance against her 'credentials.' Now she has the gall to act as if we're all one big happy team and the rest of us should accept her leadership. As for me, I'll do my best to make it difficult for her to succeed." Your friend looks dismayed but isn't saying anything. What will you say or do? How does this kind of exchange make you feel?

2. Innovation Isn't Everything

A member of your team comes into the office with a complaint. "You're a great boss," she says, "but . . ." Well, it turns out the "but" has to do with an apparent bias on your part for praising in public only those members of the team who come up with new ideas. You seem to overlook or neglect the fact that other team members are working hard and producing good—albeit standard—work every day. Are you ready to accept the point that not all high performers are going to be great innovators? If so, what changes in your behavior might be made to reflect this belief? How can you balance great "conventional" work with efforts to innovate?

3. Humans Count, Too

Your boss is enthusiastic about making sustainability a top organizational priority. In a recent meeting, he kept talking about "nature," "green practices," and "resource protection." You listened and finally said: "What about people—shouldn't they count when it comes to issues of sustainability?" After listening, perhaps after an initial thought to be critical of your response, he said in return: "Give me a proposal that we can discuss at the next staff meeting." What are you going to give him? How can you make sustainability part of the program at your place of work?

Reflect on the Self-Assessment

Tolerance for Ambiguity

Instructions

To determine your level of tolerance for ambiguity, rate each of the following items on this 7-point scale.[47]

1	strongly disagree
3	slightly disagree
5	slightly agree
7	strongly agree

_____ 1. An expert who doesn't come up with a definite answer probably doesn't know too much.

_____ 2. There is really no such thing as a problem that can't be solved.

_____ 3. I would like to live in a foreign country for a while.

_____ 4. People who fit their lives to a schedule probably miss the joy of living.

_____ 5. A good job is one where what is to be done and how it is to be done are always clear.

_____ 6. In the long run, it is possible to get more done by tackling small, simple problems rather than large, complicated ones.

_____ 7. It is more fun to tackle a complicated problem than it is to solve a simple one.

_____ 8. Often the most interesting and stimulating people are those who don't mind being different and original.

_____ 9. What we are used to is always preferable to what is unfamiliar.

_____ 10. A person who leads an even, regular life in which few surprises or unexpected happenings arise really has a lot to be grateful for.

_____ 11. People who insist upon a yes or no answer just don't know how complicated things really are.

_____ 12. Many of our most important decisions are based on insufficient information.

_____ 13. I like parties where I know most of the people more than ones where most of the people are complete strangers.

_____ 14. The sooner we all acquire ideals, the better.

_____ 15. Teachers or supervisors who hand out vague assignments give a chance for one to show initiative and originality.

_____ 16. A good teacher is one who makes you wonder about your way of looking at things.

_____   Total Score

Scoring

To obtain a score, first *reverse* the scale score for the eight "reverse" items, 3, 4, 7, 8, 11, 12, 15, and 16 (i.e., a rating of 1 5 7, 2 5 6, 3 5 5, etc.), then add up the rating scores for all 16 items.

Interpretation

Individuals with a *greater* tolerance for ambiguity are more likely to be able to function effectively in organizations and contexts with high turbulence, a high rate of change, and less certainty about expectations, performance standards, what needs to be done, and so on. They are likely to "roll with the punches" as organizations, environmental conditions, and demands change rapidly.

Individuals with a *lower* tolerance for ambiguity are more likely to be unable to adapt or adjust quickly in turbulence, uncertainty, and change. These individuals are likely to become rigid, angry, stressed, and frustrated when there is a high level of uncertainty and ambiguity in the environment.

Contribute to the Class Exercise

The Future Workplace

Instructions

Form teams as assigned by the instructor.

1. Brainstorm to develop a master list of the major characteristics you expect to find in the workplace in the year 2020. Use this list as background for completing the following tasks:

2. Write a one-paragraph description of what the typical "Workplace 2020" manager's workday will be like.

3. Draw a "picture" representing what the "Workplace 2020" organization will look like.

4. Summarize in list form what you consider to be the personal implications of your future workplace scenario for management students today. That is, explain what this means in terms of using academic and extracurricular activities to best prepare for success in this future scenario.

5. Choose a spokesperson to share your results with the class as a whole and explain their implications for the class members.

Manage a Critical Incident

It's Also about Respect

Situation

For three years you have worked in a small retail store selling gifts and party goods in a college town. This year the owner appointed you as manager and you've run into a perplexing situation. Of the store's eight employees, the only full-timer is a single mother who struggles financially to make ends meet. She lives in public housing, receives food stamps, and overall finds it almost impossible to survive on the minimum wage all employees receive. She just came to you and said that the national debate on raising the minimum wage prompted her to (finally) ask for an increase at least up to the level of the minimum wage ($15 per hour) being advocated by fast-food workers who are threatening strikes. Her point is not just that the wage she receives isn't a "livable" wage, but that "it's also about respect." You have listened to her story and find her case troubling. But you've also got seven part-timers to consider, as well as the owner's needs. At this point you arrange for a meeting with the owner to discuss what you call "wage and motivation issues" at the store. You want to have some concrete ideas ready to drive your discussion with the owner.

Questions

How will you frame your assessment of the situation for the store owner? What alternative courses of action can you suggest? What alternative do you prefer in this situation, and why? How does the preferred alternative handle wage and motivation issues for the full-timer, the part-timers, and yourself?

Collaborate on the Team Activity

Organizational Commitment to Sustainability Scorecard

Instructions

In your assigned teams, do the following:

1. Agree on a definition of "sustainability" that should fit the operations of any organization.

2. Brainstorm and agree on the criteria for an Organizational Commitment to Sustainability Scorecard (OCSS) that can be used to audit an organization's sustainability practices. Be sure that an organization being audited would not only receive scores on individual dimensions or categories of sustainability performance, but also receive a total overall "Sustainability Score" for comparison with other organizations.

3. Present and defend your OCSS to the whole class.

4. Use feedback received from the class presentation to revise your OCSS so that it can be used to conduct an actual organizational sustainability audit.

5. Use your OCSS to complete a sustainability audit for a local organization.

6. Present the results of your audit to the instructor and the whole class. Include in the presentation not only the audit scores, but also: (a) recommendations for how this organization could improve its sustainability practices in the future, and (b) any benchmarks from this organization that might be considered sustainability "best practices" for other organizations to follow.

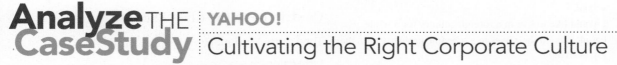

Analyze THE CaseStudy : YAHOO! Cultivating the Right Corporate Culture

Go to *Management Cases for Critical Thinking* at the end of the book to find this case.

INTERNATIONAL MANAGEMENT

5

KEY TAKEAWAYS

- Discuss the implications of globalization for management and organizations.
- Describe global corporations and the issues they face and create.
- Define culture and identify ways to describe diversity in global cultures.
- Identify the benefits of global learning for management and organizations.

SKILLS MAKE YOU **VALUABLE**

- **EVALUATE** *Career Situations:* What Would You Do?
- **REFLECT** *On the Self-Assessment:* Global Intelligence
- **CONTRIBUTE** *To the Class Exercise:* American Football
- **MANAGE** *A Critical Incident:* Silent Team Members
- **COLLABORATE** *On the Team Activity:* Globalization Pros and Cons
- **ANALYZE** *The Case Study:* Hewlett-Packard: Managing on a Global Scale

Our time of global change and turmoil makes the implications of globalization for managers, organizations, and everyday living ever more important to understand. Global corporations offer benefits and create controversies; cultural differences are a source of enrichment and the roots of misunderstandings for travelers, business executives, and government leaders. This chapter introduces the essentials of global management and cultural diversity with a focus on global learning.

Our dynamic, growing global community is rich with information, opportunities, controversies, and complications. We get real-time news from around the world on our smart mobile devices—giving us in the truest sense, the wherewithal to be true global citizens. When such crises as the Japanese tsunami or civil unrest like the Arab Spring occur, social media, including Twitter, Instagram, and Facebook, join major news organizations to get information and news out instantaneously. We play online games like World of WarCraft or Rift with people from around the world in actual time, and colleges and universities in the United States offer a vast array of international study-abroad programs for students.

As for traveling the globe, companies today really are travelers also. IBM has more employees in India than the U.S.[1] Anheuser-Busch, maker of "America's King of Beers," is owned by the Belgian firm InBev. Ben & Jerry's is owned by the British-Dutch firm Unilever. India's Tata

Group owns Jaguar, Land Rover, Tetley, and Eight O'Clock. China's Geely owns Volvo. Japan's Honda, Nissan, and Toyota receive 80% to 90% of their profits from sales in America.[2] Components for Boeing planes come from 5,400 suppliers located in 40 countries![3]

Management and Globalization

TAKEAWAY 1   What are the management challenges of globalization?

LEARN MORE | Global management • Why companies go global • How companies go global
ABOUT | Global business environments

In the **global economy**, resources, markets, and competition are worldwide in scope.

Globalization is the growing interdependence among elements of the global economy.

World 3.0 is a world where nations balance cooperation in the global economy with national identities and interests.

We live and work in the age of the **global economy** in which resources, supplies, product markets, and business competition have a worldwide—rather than a local or national—scope. It is a time heavily influenced by the forces of **globalization**, defined as the growing interdependence among the components in the global economy. Some see globalization as creating a "borderless world" where economic integration becomes so extreme that nation-states hardly matter anymore.[4] But international management scholar Pankaj Ghemawat describes what he calls **World 3.0**, a form of globalization in which national identities remain strong even as countries cooperate in the global economy.[5] National leaders try to balance economic gains from global integration with local needs and priorities.

There's no better way to illustrate the global economy than with the example of the clothes we wear. For example, where did you buy your favorite T-shirt? Where was it made? Where will it end up? In a fascinating book titled *The Travels of a T-Shirt in the Global Economy*, economist Pietra Rivoli tracks the origins and disposition of a T-shirt that she bought while on vacation in Florida.[6]

As can be seen here, Rivoli's T-shirt lived a very complicated global life before she bought it. That life began with cotton grown in Texas. It then moved on to China where the cotton was processed and white T-shirts were manufactured. The T-shirts were then sold to a firm in the United States that silk-screened and sold them to retail shops for resale to American customers. These customers eventually donated the used T-shirts to a charity that sold them to a recycler. The recycler sold them to a vendor in Africa, who then distributed the T-shirts to local markets to be sold yet again to local customers.

It's quite an international story, as this T-shirt travels the global commercial highways and byways of the world. The Limited Brands story, and many other examples like it, leave little doubt as to why Harvard scholar and consultant Rosabeth Moss Kanter once described globalization as "one of the most powerful and pervasive influences on nations, businesses, workplaces, communities, and lives."[7]

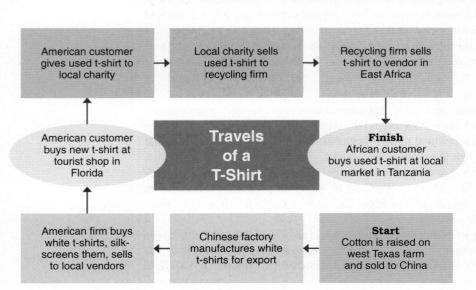

Global Management

Honda in Ohio—Allen Kinzer, now retired, was the first American manager Honda hired for its Marysville, Ohio, plant. Many people were worried whether U.S. workers could adapt to the Japanese firm's production methods, technology, and style.

Says Kinzer: "It wasn't easy blending the cultures; anyone who knew anything about the industry at the time would have to say it was a bold move." Honda now employs 4,200 workers, who produce 440,000 vehicles per year. It is one among literally hundreds of foreign firms offering employment opportunities to U.S. workers.[8]

Haier in South Carolina—The Haier Group is one of China's best-known appliance makers. CEO Zhang Ruimin built a factory in Camden, South Carolina, with the goal of taking a larger share of America's refrigerator market. But the plant was expensive and American workers resented Haier's organizational culture and top-down management style. Work hats that showed different ranks and seniority, for example, didn't go over well in South Carolina. But Zhang stayed with the project, saying, "First the hard, then smooth. That's the way to win."[9]

The prior vignettes introduce the opportunities and complexities of **global management**, which describes management in businesses and organizations with interests in more than one country. For many firms, global management is a way of life today. Procter & Gamble, for example, pursues a global strategy with customers in over 180 countries. The majority of McDonald's sales now come from outside the United States, with the "Golden Arches" prominent on city streets from Moscow and Tokyo to Budapest and Rio de Janeiro. Toyota has 14 plants employing more than 35,000 workers in North America. The success of firms like these depends on attracting and hiring truly **global managers** with a strong global perspective, who are culturally aware, and who are informed about current international issues and events.

Global management involves managing business and organizations with interests in more than one country.

A truly **global manager** is culturally aware and informed on international affairs.

Why Companies Go Global

John Chambers, chairman and CEO of Cisco Systems Inc., once said: "I will put my jobs anywhere in the world where the right infrastructure is, with the right educated workforce, with the right supportive government."[10] Cisco, Honda, Haier, and other firms like these are classic **international businesses** that conduct for-profit transactions of goods and services across national boundaries. Nike is another truly international business—its swoosh is one of the world's most recognized brands.

An **international business** conducts for-profit transactions of goods and services across national boundaries.

Did you know that Nike has no domestic manufacturing infrastructure? All of its products are sourced internationally, including 100-plus factories in China alone. Its competitor, New Balance, takes a different approach. Although extensively leveraging global suppliers and licensing its products internationally, New Balance still produces one out of every four of its shoes at factories in the United States.[11] The two firms follow somewhat different strategies, but each is actively global. Both firms—and others like them—seek these benefits of international business.

Profits—Gain profits through expanded operations.

Customers—Enter new markets to gain new customers.

Suppliers—Get access to materials, products, and services.

Labor—Get access to lower-cost, talented workers.

Capital—Tap into a larger pool of financial resources.

Risk—Spread assets among multiple countries.

◄ Benefits of international business

Today you can add another benefit to this list, *economic development*—where a global firm does business in foreign countries with direct intent to help the local economy. Coffee giants Green Mountain Coffee, Peet's Coffee & Tea, and Starbucks, for example, help Rwandan farmers improve production and marketing methods. They send advisers to teach local coffee growers how to meet high international standards so that their products can be sold worldwide. This commitment to economic development generates a win–win scenario: The global coffee firm gets a quality product at a good price, the local coffee growers gain skills and market opportunities, and the domestic economy improves.[12] A development-focused approach to international business energizes a virtuous circle, where all parties to the relationship keep getting stronger as they work with one another.

How Companies Go Global

The ways of pursuing international business are shown in Figure 5.1. When a business is becoming international, global sourcing, exporting/importing, licensing and franchising are typically the most common ways to begin. These are *market-entry strategies* that involve the sale of goods or services to foreign markets that don't require an expensive investment. Strategic alliances, joint ventures, and wholly owned subsidiaries are *direct investment strategies*. These approaches do require a major capital commitment, but also create rights of ownership and control over operations in the foreign country.

Global Sourcing

In global sourcing, materials or services are purchased around the world for local use.

The first step taken into international business by many firms is **global sourcing**—the process of purchasing materials, manufacturing components, or locating business services around the world. It is an international division of labor in which activities are performed in countries where they can be accomplished effectively at low cost. Global sourcing at Boeing, for example, means that aircraft parts and components flow in from a complex global supply chain for final assembly into 787 Dreamliners at American plants—center fuselage from Italy, landing gear from France, flight deck interiors from Japan, and more. In the service sector, it may mean setting up toll-free customer support call centers in the Philippines, locating research and development centers in Brazil or Russia, or hiring physicians in India to read medical X-rays.[13]

Most manufacturers today—of toys, shoes, electronics, furniture, clothing, aircraft—make extensive use of global sourcing. China is still a major outsourcing destination and in many areas has become the factory for the world. If you use an Apple iPod, iPhone, or iPad, for example, the chances are good that it was assembled by a Taiwanese-owned company called Hon Hai Precision Industry at plants located in China. These plants are huge—employing as many as over 350,000 workers, who produce products not just for Apple, but for other firms like Sony and Hewlett-Packard. You may have heard of Hon Hai through its trade name, Foxconn, and from news coverage of controversies over its treatment of workers.[14] Global firms have to work hard to maintain brand reputations while dealing with complex global supply chains, and aggressive international audits are now common. Even with a rigorous auditing program, however, Apple suffered a blow to its reputation when a financial analyst downgraded the firm's stock for "moral reasons" after discovering some of its global suppliers paid low wages to their workers.[15]

Reshoring shifts foreign manufacturing and jobs back to domestic locations.

Problems with sketchy foreign contractors, rising labor rates, and higher costs for transportation in global supply chains are among the reasons why some firms have started to reduce their outsourcing and do more **reshoring**—moving foreign manufacturing and jobs back home. Further reasons for reshoring include opportunities to access cheaper energy, stable

Increasing involvement in ownership and control of foreign operations

FIGURE 5.1
Common forms of international business—from market entry to direct investment increasing involvement in ownership and control of foreign operations strategies.

wage rates, better quality control, and good public relations by starting or expanding domestic operations. A survey of large U.S.-based manufacturers by the Boston Consulting Group (BCG) found that over half of U.S. firms had either started reshoring or were likely to do so in the future. The report concluded that "Companies are realizing that the economics of manufacturing are swinging in favor of the U.S."[16]

Exporting and Importing

A second form of international business involves **exporting**—selling locally made products in foreign markets. The flipside of exporting is **importing**—buying foreign-made products and selling them in domestic markets.

In **exporting**, local products are sold abroad to foreign customers.

Because the growth of export industries creates local jobs, governments often offer special advice and assistance to businesses seeking to develop or expand export markets. After visiting a U.S. government–sponsored trade fair in China, Bruce Boxerman, president of a then-small Cincinnati firm, Richards Industries, decided to take advantage of the growing market for precision valves. The decision doubled export sales in 10 years and one his employees said: "It wasn't long ago that guys looked at globalization like it is going to cause all of us to lose our jobs. Now it's probably going to save our jobs."[17] And it certainly did. Richards is now the parent company to six product lines and has over 200 sales representatives around the world.

Importing involves the selling in domestic markets of products acquired abroad.

Licensing and Franchising

International business also takes place through the **licensing agreement**, where foreign firms pay a fee for rights to make or sell another company's products in a specified region. The license typically grants access to a unique manufacturing technology, special patent, or trademark. Such licensing, however, involves potential risk.[18] New Balance, for example, licensed a Chinese supplier to produce one of its brands. Even after New Balance revoked the license, the supplier continued to produce and distribute the shoes around Asia. It was only through expensive, drawn-out litigation in China's courts that New Balance was able to deal with the problem.[19]

In a **licensing agreement** a local firm pays a fee to a foreign firm for rights to make or sell its products.

Franchising is a form of licensing in which a foreign firm buys the rights to use another's name and operating methods in its home country. The international version operates in a similar way to domestic franchising agreements. Such firms as McDonald's, Wendy's, and Subway, for example, sell facility designs, equipment, product ingredients, recipes, and management systems to foreign investors, while retaining certain brand, product, and operating controls. One of the challenges associated with international franchising can be the creation of locally popular menu items while retaining coherence with broader branding goals.

In **franchising**, a fee is paid to a foreign business for rights to locally operate using its name, branding, and methods.

Joint Ventures and Strategic Alliances

Foreign direct investment, or FDI, involves setting up and buying all or part of a business in another country. For many countries, the ability to attract foreign business investors has been a key to succeeding in the global economy. The term **insourcing** is often used to describe foreign direct investment, or FDI, that results in local job creation. FDI in the United States totals over $125 billion, for example, and creates just under 6 million local jobs.[20]

Insourcing is job creation through foreign direct investment.

When foreign firms do invest in another country, a common way to start is with a **joint venture**. This is a co-ownership arrangement in which foreign and local partners agree to pool resources, share risks, and jointly operate the new business. Sometimes the joint venture is formed when a foreign partner buys part ownership in an existing local firm. In other cases it is formed as an entirely new operation that the foreign and local partners jointly start up together.

A **joint venture** operates in a foreign country through co-ownership by foreign and local partners.

International joint ventures are types of **global strategic alliances** in which foreign and domestic firms work together for mutual benefit. Partners in alliance hope to generate more market penetration and profits by cooperating than they would have been able to achieve alone. For the local partner, an alliance may bring access to technology and opportunities to learn new skills. For

A **global strategic alliance** is a partnership in which foreign and domestic firms share resources and knowledge for mutual gains.

How to Choose a Joint Venture Partner

- Familiar with firm's major business
- Employs a strong local workforce
- Values its customers
- Has potential for future expansion
- Has strong local market
- Has good profit potential
- Has sound financial standing

the foreign partner, an alliance may bring access to new markets and the expert assistance of locals who understand domestic markets and the local business context.

Joint ventures pose potential business risks and partners must be carefully chosen.[21] Sometimes partners' goals do not match, for example, when the foreign firm seeks profits and cost efficiencies while the local firm seeks maximum employment and acquisition of new technology.[22] Although the loss of business secrets also is a potential risk, the line between acceptable business practice and infringement can be very hard to define in international contexts. Some time ago a new car was marketed in China by a firm partially owned by General Motor's Chinese joint venture partner. The car—called "Chery"—looked very similar to a GM model, and the firm complained that its design had been copied. The competitor denied it and went on to become China's largest independent automaker—Chery International, which sells its cars at home and abroad.[23]

Foreign Subsidiaries

A foreign subsidiary is a local operation completely owned by a foreign firm.

A greenfield venture is a foreign subsidiary built from the ground up by the foreign owner.

One way around some of the risks and problems associated with joint ventures and strategic alliances is full ownership of the foreign operation. A **foreign subsidiary** is a local operation completely owned and controlled by a foreign firm. These subsidiaries may be built from the ground up as a **greenfield venture**. They also can be established by acquisition, wherein the outside firm purchases an entire local operation.

Although a foreign subsidiary represents the highest level of involvement in international operations, it can be very profitable to approach an international venture in this way. When Nissan opened a plant in Canton, Mississippi, an auto analyst said: "It's a smart strategy . . . building more in their regional markets, as well as being able to meet consumers' needs more quickly."[24] The analyst could also have pointed out that this plant allowed Nissan to claim reputational benefits by dealing with American customers as a "local" employer rather than a "foreign" company.

Global Business Environments

When Nissan comes to America or GM goes to China, a lot of what takes place in the foreign business environment is very different from what is common at home. Not only must global managers master the demands of operating with worldwide suppliers, distributors, customers, and competitors, they must also deal successfully with many unique local challenges.

Legal and Political Systems

Some of the most substantial risks in international business come from differences in legal and political systems. Global firms are expected to abide by local laws, many of which may be unfamiliar. The more home-country and host-country laws differ, the harder it is for international businesses to adapt to local rules, regulations, and customs. See, for example, the legal complications faced by Google with the European Union.[25]

Common legal problems faced by international businesses involve incorporation practices and business ownership; negotiation and implementation of contracts with foreign parties; handling of foreign exchange; and intellectual property rights—patents, trademarks, and copyrights. You may be most familiar with the intellectual property issue as it relates to movie and music downloads, sale of fake designer fashion, or software pirating. Companies like Microsoft, Sony, and Louis Vuitton think about this issue in terms of lost profits due to their products or designs being copied and sold as imitations by foreign firms. After a lengthy and complex legal battle, for example, Starbucks won a major intellectual property case it had taken to the Chinese courts. A local firm was using Starbucks'

Chinese name, "Xingbake" (*Xing* means "star" and *bake* is pronounced "bah kuh"), and was also copying its café designs.[26]

Political turmoil, violence, and government changes constitute another area of concern known as **political risk**—the potential loss in value of an investment in or managerial control over a foreign asset because of instability and political changes in the host country. The major threats associated with political risk today come from terrorism,

---

Legal Problems Faced by Google in Europe

- The European Court of Justice rules that individuals have a "right to be forgotten" in some instances and that Google must delete their search results on request.
- Tax authorities in France bill Google for 1 billion Euro in back taxes.
- German economy minister Sigmar Gabriel says that breaking up Google "must be seriously considered" because of its market dominance.
- European Commission under pressure to revise and strengthen an antitrust agreement previously reached with Google over precedence shown to its own businesses in search results.

---

civil wars, armed conflicts, and new government systems and policies. Although these threats can't be prevented, they can be anticipated.

Most global firms use a planning technique called **political-risk analysis** to forecast the probability of disruptive events that can threaten the security of foreign investments. Consider, for example, the criminal drug violence in Mexico. What are some of the implications for business investors? Although involvement in Mexico clearly represents an exercise in political risk, thus far, foreign investment in Mexico is on the increase. The country's proximity to U.S. markets and low-cost skilled labor are still attractive. Gonzalo Cano, quality manager at a large Lego plant in Monterrey, says: "Security is an issue but it does not get in the way. Companies are taking the long view."[27]

Trade Agreements and Trade Barriers

When international businesses believe they are being mistreated in foreign countries, or when local companies believe foreign competitors are disadvantaging them, their respective governments can take these cases to the **World Trade Organization (WTO)**. The WTO is a global organization established to promote free trade and open markets around the world. Its member nations, presently 151 of them, agree to negotiate and resolve disputes about tariffs and trade restrictions.[28]

WTO members are supposed to give one another **most favored nation status**—the most favorable treatment for imports and exports. Yet trade barriers are still common. They include outright **tariffs**, which constitute taxes that governments impose on imports. They also include **nontariff barriers** that discourage imports in nontax ways. These include quotas, import restrictions, and other forms of **protectionism** that give favorable treatment to domestic businesses. Foreign firms complain, for example, that the Chinese government creates barriers that make it hard for them to succeed. A spokesperson for the U.S. Chamber of Commerce says that American multinationals like Caterpillar, Boeing, Motorola, and others have been hurt by "systematic efforts by China to develop policies that build their domestic enterprises at the expense of U.S. firms."[29]

One goal of most tariffs and protectionism is to protect local firms from foreign competition and save local jobs. These issues are reflected in political campaigns and election-year debates. These aren't easy issues to solve. Government leaders face the often conflicting goals of seeking freer international trade, while still protecting domestic industries. Such political dilemmas create controversies for the WTO in its role as a global arbiter of trade issues. For example, in one claim filed with the WTO, the United States complained that China's "legal structure for protecting and enforcing copyright and trademark protections" was "deficient" and not in compliance with WTO rules. China's response was that the suit was out of line with WTO rules and that "we strongly oppose the U.S. attempt to impose on developing members through this case."[30] When both sides of a case like this present defensible positions, it is difficult to establish a clear way to resolving the key issues, particularly when the issues are shaded by cultural differences.

Political risk is the potential loss in value of a foreign investment due to instability and political changes in the host country.

Political-risk analysis tries to forecast political disruptions that can threaten the value of a foreign investment.

World Trade Organization member nations agree to negotiate and resolve disputes about tariffs and trade restrictions.

Most favored nation status gives a trading partner most favorable treatment for imports and exports.

Tariffs are taxes governments levy on imports from abroad.

Nontariff barriers to trade discourage imports in nontax ways such as quotas and government import restrictions.

Protectionism is a call for tariffs and favorable treatments to protect domestic firms from foreign competition.

ethics > KNOW RIGHT FROM WRONG

> Bolivia's president announced that his government was nationalizing "all natural resources, what our ancestors fought for."

Nationalism and Protectionism a Potent Mix

The headline read "Bolivia Seizes Control of Oil and Gas Fields." Although oil industry executives couldn't say that this wasn't anticipated, it still must have been shocking when Bolivia's government announced that it was taking control of the country's oil and gas fields. The announcement said: "We are beginning by nationalizing oil and gas; tomorrow we will add mining, forestry, and all natural resources, what our ancestors fought for."

Immediately following the announcement, Bolivia's armed forces secured all of the country's oil and gas fields. President Evo Morales set forth new terms that gave a state-owned firm 82% of all revenues, leaving 18% for the foreign firms. He said: "Only those firms that respect these new terms will be allowed to operate in the country." The implicit threat was that any firms not willing to sign new contracts would be sent home.

While foreign governments described this nationalization as an "unfriendly move," Morales considered it patriotic. His position was that any existing contracts with the state were in violation of the constitution, and that Bolivia's natural resources belonged to its people.

WHAT DO YOU THINK?

If you were the CEO of one of the global oil firms operating in Bolivia, how would you react to this nationalization? Would you resist and raise the ethics issue of honoring existing contracts with the Bolivian government? Or would you comply and accept the new terms being offered? As an everyday citizen of the world, do you agree or disagree with the argument that Bolivia's natural resources are national treasures that belong to the people, not foreign investors? What ethical issues inform the decision to nationalize Bolivia's oil and gas industry?

Regional Economic Alliances

Regional economic alliances link member countries in agreements to work together for economic gains.

NAFTA is the North American Free Trade Agreement linking Canada, the United States, and Mexico in an economic alliance.

One of the characteristics of globalization is the growth of **regional economic alliances**, where nations agree to work together for economic gains. **NAFTA**, the North American Free Trade Agreement, is an example. Formed in 1994 by the United States, Canada, and Mexico, NAFTA created a trade zone that frees the flow of goods and services, workers, and investment among the three countries.

Many American firms have taken advantage of NAFTA, moving production facilities from the United States to Mexico, largely to benefit from lower wages paid to skilled Mexican workers. This labor shift has both pros and cons, and NAFTA remains a controversial topic in some political debates. Arguments in support credit NAFTA with greater cross-border trade, greater productivity of U.S. manufacturers, and reform of the Mexican business environment. Arguments against blame NAFTA for substantial job losses to Mexico, lower wages for American workers who want to keep their jobs, and a wider trade deficit with Mexico.[31] That said, the NAFTA story is increasingly positive. Intellectual property is well protected under the agreement, and global supply chain issues are making Mexico increasingly attractive as a manufacturing destination. The Boston Consulting Group estimates that by 2015 Mexico will offer manufacturers a 30% labor cost advantage over China.[32]

The **European Union** is a political and economic alliance of European countries.

The **Euro** is now the common European currency.

The **European Union** (EU) is a regional economic and political alliance of global importance. The financial health of the EU is regularly in the news, as upswings and downswings in its economy affect the entire world. The EU comprises 28 member countries that have agreed to support mutual interests by integrating themselves politically—there is now a European Parliament, and economically—member countries have removed barriers that previously limited cross-border trade and business development. Seventeen EU members also are part of a common currency, the **Euro**, which has grown to the point where it is a major alternative and competitor to the U.S. dollar in the global economy.

In Asia and the Pacific Rim, 21 member nations established the **Asia Pacific Economic Cooperation** (APEC) to promote free trade and investment in the Pacific region. Businesses from APEC countries have access to a region of superstar economic status, home to some of the world's fastest growing economies such as China, Republic of Korea, Indonesia, Russia, and Australia. The market potential of member countries, close to 3 billion consumers, far exceeds NAFTA and the EU. Also in Asia, the 10 nations of the Association of Southeast Asian Nations (ASEAN) cooperate with a stated goal of promoting economic growth and progress.

Africa also is increasingly center stage in world business headlines.[33] The region's economies are growing, the middle class is expanding, and there is a promising rise in entrepreneurship.[34] Companies like Harley-Davidson, Walmart, Caterpillar, and Google are making their presence—and continental ambitions—known as they set up offices, invest in dealerships, and buy local companies.[35] The **Southern Africa Development Community** (SADC) links 14 countries in southern Africa in trade and economic development efforts. Its website posts this vision: "a future in a regional community that will ensure economic well-being, improvement of the standards of living and quality of life, freedom and social justice, and peace and security for the peoples of Southern Africa."[36]

> The **Asia Pacific Economic Cooperation** (APEC) links 21 countries to promote free trade and investment in the Pacific region.

> The **Southern Africa Development Community** (SADC) links 14 countries of southern Africa in trade and economic development efforts.

Learning Check 1

TAKEAWAYQUESTION **1 What are the management challenges of globalization?**

BE SURE YOU CAN • define *globalization* and discuss its implications for international management • list five reasons companies pursue international business opportunities • describe and give examples of global sourcing, exporting/importing, franchising/licensing, joint ventures, and foreign subsidiaries • discuss how differences in legal environments can affect businesses operating internationally • explain the goals of the WTO • discuss the significance of regional economic alliances such as NAFTA, the EU, APEC, and SADC

Global Businesses

TAKEAWAY 2   What are global businesses and how do they work?

LEARN MORE | Types of global businesses • Pros and cons of global businesses
ABOUT | Ethics challenges for global businesses

If you travel abroad, many of your favorite brands and products will travel with you. You can have a McDonald's sandwich in over 100 countries, follow it with a Häagen-Dazs ice cream in 50, and then brush up with Procter & Gamble's Crest toothpaste in 180. Economists even use the "Big Mac" index, which compares the U.S. dollar price of the McDonald's sandwich around the world, to track purchasing power parity among the world's currencies.[37]

Types of Global Businesses

Global corporations, also called *multinational enterprises* (MNEs) and *multinational corporations* (MNCs), are business firms with extensive international operations in many foreign countries. The largest global corporations are identified in annual listings such as *Fortune* magazine's Global 500 and the *Financial Times'* FT Global 500. They include familiar names such as Walmart, BP, Toyota, Nestlé, BMW, Hitachi, Caterpillar, Sony, and Samsung, as well as others you may not recognize, such as the big oil and gas producers PetroChina (China), Gazprom (Russia), and Total (France).

There is likely no doubt in your mind that Hewlett-Packard and General Motors are American firms, while Sony and Honda are Japanese. But, this may not be how executives at these companies want their firms to be viewed. These firms and many other global firms act more like **transnational corporations** that do business around the world without being identified with one national home.[38]

> A **global corporation** is a multinational enterprise (MNE) or multinational corporation (MNC) that conducts commercial transactions across national boundaries.

> A **transnational corporation** is a global corporation or MNE that operates worldwide on a borderless basis.

Sample Big Mac Index	
United States	$4.62
Sweden	$6.29
Brazil	$5.25
Euro area	$4.96
Australia	$4.47
Mexico	$2.78
China	$2.64
Russia	$2.62

The Economist magazine has even started publishing a "Domestic Density Index" as a measure of corporate identity using the percentage of sales, employees, and shareholders that are domestic to the home country as well as the nationality of the CEO. Sample domestic identity scores include Coca-Cola (62%), Apple (65%), and GE (63%).[39]

Executives of transnational firms view the entire world as their domain for acquiring resources, locating production facilities, marketing goods and services, and communicating brand images. The goal is described by a global executive as "source everywhere, manufacture everywhere, sell everywhere."[40] The resulting dense, overlapping, and worldwide manufacturing and marketing networks often make it difficult to distinguish one country's firms from the next. When shopping at an Aldi store or browsing Hugo Boss clothes, would you know they're German companies? Which company is really more American—the Indian giant Tata, which gets some 50% of its revenues from North America, or IBM, which gets over 65% of its revenues from outside the United States?[41]

Pros and Cons of Global Businesses

What difference does a company's nationality make? Does it really matter to an American whether local jobs come from a domestic giant like IBM or a foreign firm like Honda? How about size? Does it matter that Exxon/Mobil's revenues are larger than Sweden's gross domestic product (GDP)?[42] What about wealth? Is what some call the **globalization gap**—large multinationals and industrialized nations gaining disproportionately from globalization, a matter for social and personal concern?[43]

The **globalization gap** is where large multinational corporations and industrialized nations gain disproportionately from the benefits of globalization.

Host-Country Issues

Ideally, global corporations and the countries that host them should both reap benefits. But things can go right and wrong in these relationships.[44] Potential host-country benefits shown in Figure 5.2 include a larger tax base, increased employment opportunities, technology transfers, introduction of new industries, and development of local resources. Potential host-country costs include complaints that global corporations extract excessive profits, dominate the local economy, interfere with the local governments, fail to respect local customs and laws, fail to help domestic firms develop, hire the most talented local personnel away from domestic firms, and fail to transfer their most advanced technologies to the host country.

Home-Country Issues

Global corporations also can get into trouble at home in the countries where they were founded and where their headquarters are located. Even as many global firms try to operate as transnationals,

FIGURE 5.2
What should go right and what can go wrong in global corporation and host-country relationships.

What should go right in MNC host-country relationships	What can go wrong in MNC host-country relationships	
Mutual benefits	**Host-country complaints about MNCs**	**MNC complaints about host countries**
Shared opportunities with potential for • Growth • Income • Learning • Development	• Excessive profits • Economic domination • Interference with government • Hire best local talent • Limited technology transfer • Disrespect for local customs	• Profit limitations • Overpriced resources • Exploitative rules • Foreign exchange restrictions • Failure to uphold contracts

home-country governments and citizens still tend to identify them with local and national interests. They also expect global firms to act as good domestic citizens.[45] When a global business cuts back home-country jobs, or closes a domestic operation in order to source work to lower-cost international providers, the loss is controversial. Corporate decision makers are likely to be called on by government and community leaders to reconsider and give priority to domestic social responsibilities. Other home-country criticisms of global firms include sending investment capital abroad and engaging in corruption. American lawmakers are concerned about corporate **tax inversion**, where a U.S.-based MNC buys a firm in a low-tax country in order to shield foreign earnings from U.S. taxes.

Tax inversion is where a U.S.-based MNC buys a firm in a low-tax country in order to shield foreign earnings from U.S. taxes.

Ethics Challenges for Global Businesses

Dateline Bangladesh: The collapse of eight-story Rana Plaza, an industrial building for garment factories, resulted in 1,129 deaths and 2,215 injuries. Although warnings had been issued about cracks in the building, employees faced loss of pay if they refused to work. Rana Plaza factories are connected to a global supply chain producing apparel for brands including Benetton, Cato Fashions, the Children's Place, and Walmart.[46]

We live at a time of increasing global democratization of information and communication technologies, and the ready availability of reports on ethics-tied outcomes from global business activity. Customers, governments and other stakeholders, and the public at large have access to more information about what is happening with MNCs and their complex supply chains than ever before. The consequences of business actions—the good and the bad, and anywhere in the world—have never been more visible and impactful. Although bad decisions will continue to be made, it's harder to hide them from intense public scrutiny and significant public relations and financial backlash.[47]

Corruption

Corruption occurs when people engage illegal practices to further their personal business interests. It's a source of continuing controversy and often makes headline news in the international business context.[48] There is no doubt that corruption poses significant challenges for global managers. The civic society organization Transparency International is devoted to eliminating corrupt practices around the world. Its annual reports and publications track corruption and are a source of insight for both executives and policymakers.[49] But corruption issues aren't always neat and clear-cut. An American executive, for example, says that payoffs are needed to get shipments through customs in Russia even though all legal taxes and tariffs are already paid. Local customs brokers build these payments into their invoices.[50] What do you think? Should the act of paying for what you already deserve to receive be considered a bribe? Should U.S. firms facing such situations be allowed to do whatever is locally acceptable? How do you sort right from wrong when considering how to negotiate local customs and business expectations?

Corruption involves illegal practices to further one's business interests.

The **Foreign Corrupt Practices Act (FCPA)** makes it illegal for U.S. firms and their representatives to engage in corrupt practices overseas.[51] U.S. companies are not supposed to pay or offer bribes or excessive commissions—including nonmonetary gifts—to foreign officials in return for business favors. Critics claim that the FCPA fails to recognize the realities of business practice in many foreign nations. Critics believe the FCPA puts U.S. companies at a competitive disadvantage because they can't offer the same "deals" or "perks" as businesses from other nations, deals locals may regard as standard business practice. But other nations, such as the United Kingdom with its Bribery Act, have begun to pass similar laws and the U.S. Department of Justice isn't backing down. Penalties levied by the U.S. government are now running over $1 billion per year.[52]

The **Foreign Corrupt Practices Act (FCPA)** makes it illegal for U.S. firms and their representatives to engage in corrupt practices overseas.

Child Labor and Sweatshops

The facts are startling: 215 million child laborers worldwide, 115 million of them working in hazardous conditions.[53] **Child labor**—the employment of children to perform work otherwise performed

Child labor is the employment of children for work otherwise done by adults.

by adults, is a major ethics issue that haunts global businesses as they follow the world's low-cost manufacturing from country to country. More than likely, you've heard about child labor used in the manufacture of handmade carpets, but what about your favorite electronic device whose components are largely made by foreign suppliers?[54] Companies find it difficult to always know for certain just who is employed in a foreign factory producing for global brands. After an Apple audit identified 106 underage workers used by 11 of its 400 suppliers, Apple required the firms to return children to their homes, pay for their enrollment in local schools, and pay their families what the children would have earned in annual income.[55]

Sweatshops employ workers at very low wages for long hours in poor working conditions.

Child labor isn't the only ethics-critical labor issue facing global managers. **Sweatshops**—business operations that employ workers at low wages for long hours in poor working conditions—are another key ethical issue. The Bangladesh garment industry, for example, depends on workers, often female and illiterate, who are trying to escape lives of poverty. Their complaints include blocked elevators, filthy tap water, and unclean overflowing toilets in the factories.[56] The Rana Plaza tragedy mentioned earlier exposed unsafe buildings and sweatshop conditions in factories throughout the country. When Walmart audited some 200 factories in its Bangladesh supply chains, 15% failed safety inspections. Walmart now claims it has a "zero tolerance policy" when its standards are violated and will cancel business contracts with any supplier that subcontracts work to others without informing Walmart.[57]

Conflict Minerals

Conflict minerals are ones sourced in the Democratic Republic of Congo and surrounding region and whose sale finances armed groups that perpetuate violence.

It's no secret that the sale of scarce minerals helps support warlords and perpetuates strife in places such as the Democratic Republic of Congo and surrounding region. Called **conflict minerals** because monies gained from their sale help finance armed violence, they also are indispensable to many—if not all—the electrical devices we love and are so dependent upon in everyday living.[58] It just isn't possible to make a phone, tablet, gaming console, or other smart device, without components that use minerals like tin, tungsten, gold, and tantalum, each of which might be mined in conflict areas.[59]

Identifying the source of the minerals used in electronics manufacturing is extremely difficult in the dense and sometimes murky world of global sourcing. Who knows, for example, how many times a supply of tungsten may have been passed from hand to hand and where its original source might be located? Yet, certification of sourced minerals as "conflict free" is exactly what section 1502 of the Dodd-Frank Act of 2010 required of U.S. companies. After the law was appealed, the court ruled that firms would only have to report to the Securities and Exchange Commission that they had investigated their supply chains for conflict minerals.[60] Whether you believe the original Dodd-Frank provision requiring "conflict-free" certification or the later court ruling requiring "investigation" is the right approach, the fact is that companies have a lot to gain in reputation and moral standing by tracing the minerals used in their products and rejecting those sourced in conflict areas. But, this task is exceedingly complex. Apple, for example, says it uses some 200 smelters in 30 countries. HP says as many as 10 middlemen may stand between it and the original sources of some minerals. And Intel, which was one of the first firms to submit an audit report to the SEC, says that its chips are conflict free but that it had visited 85 smelters in 21 countries to establish the audit trail.[61]

Learning Check 2

TAKEAWAYQUESTION **2 What are global businesses and how do they work?**

BE SURE YOU CAN • differentiate a multinational corporation from a transnational corporation • list at least three host-country complaints and three home-country complaints about global business operations • give examples of corruption, sweatshops, and child labor in international businesses

Cultures and Global Diversity

TAKEAWAY 3   What is culture and how does it influence global management?

LEARN MORE ABOUT | Cultural intelligence • Silent languages of culture • Tight and loose cultures
Values and national cultures

Situation: A U.S. executive goes to meet a business contact in Saudi Arabia. He sits in the office with crossed legs and the sole of his shoe exposed. Both are unintentional signs of disrespect in the local culture. He passes documents to the host using his left hand, which Muslims in Saudi Arabia generally consider to be unclean. He declines when coffee is offered, which suggests criticism of the Saudi's hospitality. *Outcome:* A $10 million contract is lost to a Korean executive better versed in the local culture.[62]

"Culture" matters, as we often say, and cultural miscues can be costly in international business and politics. **Culture** is the shared set of beliefs, values, and patterns of behavior common to a group of people.[63] **Culture shock** is the confusion and discomfort a person experiences when in an unfamiliar culture. The box on stages in adjusting to a new culture is a reminder that these feelings must be mastered to travel comfortably and do business around the world. Have you ever had a surprising cross-cultural experience? Have you personally experienced culture shock?

> **Culture** is a shared set of beliefs, values, and patterns of behavior common to a group of people.
>
> **Culture shock** is the confusion and discomfort a person experiences when in an unfamiliar culture.

insight > LEARN ABOUT YOURSELF

Attributes of Leaders in the Asian Century

According to the report, *Asia 2050: Realizing the Asian Century*, seven economies in Asia will lead the region into the Asian Century. These nations—China, India, Indonesia, Japan, South Korea, Malaysia and Thailand—are expected to contribute 45% of global GDP by 2050.

So then, what characteristics should current leaders in Asia develop to lead their organisations and their employees into the Asian Century? A study was conducted to answer this question and the findings were reported in *The Asian Leadership Index 2014.* Senior leaders and emerging leaders were selected from 18 countries across Asia to participate in this research.

Figure 1 below shows the attributes that current leaders must develop or improve to increase employee engagement.

The top five attributes are described as follows:

Communicative: A leader who encourages discussions and debates of ideas

Visionary: A leader who has a vision for the organisation that employees believe in

Emotionally aware: A leader who values the contributions of others

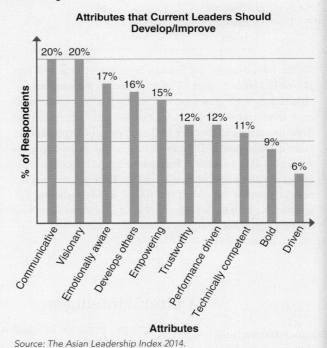

Attributes that Current Leaders Should Develop/Improve

% of Respondents

Communicative	20%
Visionary	20%
Emotionally aware	17%
Develops others	16%
Empowering	15%
Trustworthy	12%
Performance driven	12%
Technically competent	11%
Bold	9%
Driven	6%

Attributes

Source: The Asian Leadership Index 2014.

Continued

Develops others: A leader who coaches and provides feedback

Empowering: A leader who provides employees with the skills and knowledge to carry out the task

Across the region, 20% of the respondents wanted a leader who was communicative and visionary. Respondents in Malaysia, China, Indonesia, Japan and Thailand said they wanted a leader who genuinely encouraged them to discuss and debate ideas and approaches. A communicative leader in India was defined as someone who articulates ideas in ways that employees will understand. In Korea, the employees wanted a leader who listens to them and others.

If the current leaders work on improving these relationship-oriented attributes, employees would be more engaged at their workplace. However, leaders must overcome the high power distance culture common in Asian countries to further develop their attributes.

Based on Geert's dimensions of national culture, the power distance index in the following Asian countries are:

Country	PD Index
Malaysia	100
China	80
Indonesia	78
India	77
Thailand	64
Korea	60
Japan	54

Mr John Mackle, a Canadian high school principal employed in Malaysia, says, "Power distance at the workplace is significantly high compared to Canada." He has vast experience in several leadership roles (as vice-principal, principal, Superintendent and Director of Education) in Canada and his current assignment as Director of Programme in the Canadian International Matriculation Programme would be his first leadership role outside of his home country. Prior to accepting his current position, he visited the school in Malaysia and felt comfortable with the setting as it was structured the same way as other high schools with an Ontario curriculum.

After a year in Malaysia, he feels there are distinct differences in the leadership styles as compared to Canada. In Canada, there is distributed leadership, responsibilities are shared and decision making is team oriented. In Malaysia, the hierarchical nature of leadership results in an unequal distribution of responsibilities. "At first, I was feeling frustrated about this management style, but soon realised that the high power distance is a contributing factor to this type of leadership", says Mr Mackle.

Mr Mackle feels it is important to be respectful of the organisation's management style, for example, the line of command, job titles and loyalty to the organisation. According to him, being successful in adapting to the local culture at the workplace and yet continuing to implement his own leadership style has allowed him to strike a balance between the different workplace cultures.

Mr Mackle has this advice for individuals who want to explore job opportunities abroad, "It would be helpful to find out about the organisation, its vision and mission in general. As leaders, talk the talk and walk the walk, and be prepared to challenge yourself in any country, irrespective of its workplace culture."

PREPARING YOURSELF FOR CULTURAL CHALLENGES

Interview your classmates and teachers from different countries. Prepare a chart on the national culture dimensions for their country. Compare and contrast the index for each dimension and find out their opinion on these dimensions.

Explain how power distance may pose a challenge to the progress of Asian countries as they move into the Asian Century.

Discuss how current leaders can improve the top five attributes identified in the study.

How would you prepare yourself if you are offered a job in a country which has a very different workplace culture as compared to your home country?

Complete the cultural intelligence (CQ) test by answering the four questions on page 112. Discuss your answers with a classmate and reflect on how you can enhance your CQ.

Cultural Intelligence

Ethnocentrism is the tendency to consider one's culture superior to others.

The American's behavior in Saudi Arabia was self-centered. He ignored and showed no concern for the culture of his Arab host. This displayed **ethnocentrism**, a tendency to view one's culture as superior to that of others. Some might excuse him as suffering from culture shock. Perhaps he was exhausted after a long international flight. Maybe he was so uncomfortable upon arrival that all he could think about was making a deal and leaving Saudi Arabia as quickly as possible. Still others might give him the benefit of the doubt as being well-intentioned but not having time to learn enough about Saudi culture before making the trip.

Regardless of possible reasons for the executive's cultural mistakes, they still worked to his disadvantage. They also showed a lack of something critical to success in global management—**cultural intelligence**. Often called "CQ" for "cultural quotient," cultural intelligence is the ability to adapt, adjust, and work well across cultures.[64]

Where do you stand when it comes to cultural intelligence? People with cultural intelligence are flexible in dealing with cultural differences and willing to learn from what is unfamiliar. They use that learning to self-regulate and modify their behaviors to act with sensitivity toward another culture's ways. In other words, someone high in cultural intelligence views cultural differences not as a threat but as an opportunity to learn.[65] You can do a quick test of your CQ by asking and answering these questions:[66]

> **Cultural intelligence** is the ability to adapt, adjust, and work well across cultures.

1. Am I aware of the cultural knowledge I use in cross-cultural situations?

2. Do I know about the cultural values, practices, and religious beliefs of other cultures?

3. Do I enjoy interacting with people from diverse cultures?

4. Do I change my behavior when a cross-cultural situation requires it?

Silent Languages of Culture

The capacities to listen, observe, and learn are key building blocks of cultural intelligence. These skills and competencies can be developed by better understanding what the anthropologist Edward T. Hall calls the "silent" languages of culture.[67] He believes that these silent languages are found in a culture's approach to context, time, and space.

Context

If we look and listen carefully, Hall says we'll recognize how cultures differ in their use of language.[68] Most communication in **low-context cultures** takes place via the written or spoken word. This is common in the United States, Canada, and Germany, for example. Americans in particular tend to say or write what they mean and mean what they say. Things aren't this way in many parts of the world.

> **Low-context cultures** emphasize communication via spoken or written words.

In **high-context cultures**, what is actually said or written may convey only part, and sometimes a very small part, of the real message. The rest must be interpreted from the situation, body language, physical setting, and even past relationships among the people involved. Dinner parties, social gatherings, and golf outings in high-context cultures such as Thailand and Malaysia, for example, are ways for potential business partners to get to know one another. Only after social relationships are established and a context for communication is developed does it become possible to begin making business deals.

> **High-context cultures** rely on nonverbal and situational cues as well as on spoken or written words in communication.

Time

Hall describes differences in how cultures deal with time. People in **monochronic cultures** often do one thing at a time. It is common in the United States, for example, to schedule meetings with specific people and focus on a specific agenda for an allotted period of time.[69] If someone is late to a meeting or brings an uninvited guest, this is viewed unfavorably.

> In **monochronic cultures**, people tend to do one thing at a time.

Members of **polychronic cultures** are more flexible in their views of time. They often try to work on many different things at once, perhaps not in any particular order, and give in to distractions and interruptions. A monochronic American visitor to the office of a polychronic Egyptian

> In **polychronic cultures**, time is used to accomplish many different things at once.

client may be frustrated. He may not get dedicated attention as the client greets and deals with a continuous stream of people flowing in and out of his office.

Space

Proxemics is how people use space to communicate.

The use of space is also one of the silent languages of culture. Hall describes these cultural tendencies in terms of **proxemics**, the study of how people use space to communicate.[70] Americans tend to like and value their own space, perhaps as much space as they can get. We like big offices, big cars, big homes, and big yards. We tend to get uncomfortable in tight spaces and when others stand too close to us in lines. When someone "talks right in our face," we don't like it; the behavior may even be interpreted as an expression of anger.

Members of some cultures are quite comfortable surrounded by smaller spaces and closer physical distances. If you visit Japan, you are likely to notice very quickly that space is precious. Small homes, offices, and shops are the norm; gardens are tiny, but immaculate; public spaces are carefully organized for most efficient use; privacy is highly valued and protected. In many Latin cultures, the *abrazzo*, or strong embrace, is a common greeting. In Vietnam, men often hold hands or link arms as a sign of friendship when talking with one another.

Research Brief

Personality Traits, Behavioral Competencies, and Expatriate Effectiveness

When organizations send employees to work as expatriates in foreign countries, the assignments can be challenging, and the expatriate's performance can turn out lower than anticipated. Nevertheless, many employers fail to make fully informed decisions on expatriate assignments. The results of three empirical studies reported in the *Journal of Applied Psychology* by Margaret Shaffer and her colleagues show that individual differences have an impact on expatriate effectiveness.

The researchers propose a model in which expatriate effectiveness is a function of individual differences in personalities and competencies. Specifically, they examine stable dispositions in terms of the "Big Five" personality traits (conscientiousness, emotional stability, agreeableness, intellectance, and extroversion) and the dynamic competencies of cultural flexibility, task orientation, people orientation, and ethnocentrism.

Data samples were gathered from expatriates working in Hong Kong and Korean expatriates working in other nations. Each of the Big Five traits, except conscientiousness, predicted some aspect of expatriate effectiveness. Emotional stability was

Expatriate Effectiveness Model

Individual Differences
• Stable dispositions
• Dynamic competencies

➡

Expatriate Effectiveness
• Adjustment
• Withdrawal cognitions
• Performance

the strongest predictor of withdrawal cognitions, while intellectance was the only predictor of task and contextual performance. The link between dynamic competencies and performance was less clear, and the researchers believe that study design and/or the presence of unmeasured moderator variables might account for the mixed findings.

YOU BE THE RESEARCHER

There may be international students in your class or on campus who have worked with, or as, expatriates. You may also have family and friends with expatriate experience. Why not interview them to gather their views about how expatriates adapt and perform in foreign cultures? Compare the results of your investigation with the model and findings of this research study.

Tight and Loose Cultures

The nail that sticks up will be hammered down.
Asian Proverb

The squeaking wheel gets the grease.
American Idiom

These two sayings are representative of two very different cultural settings. What are the implications of these two different ways of viewing outliers? Try to picture young children listening to their parents or elders as they offer these words of wisdom. One child grows up being careful to not speak out, stand out, or attract attention. The other grows up trying to speak up and stand out in order to get attention.

The contrast in childhoods just described introduces the concept of *cultural tightness-looseness.* Scholars Michele J. Gelfand, Lisa H. Nishii, and Jana L. Raver describe this as "the strength of social norms and degree of sanctioning within societies."[71] Two things are at issue in this definition: (1) the strength of norms that govern social behavior and (2) the tolerance for any deviations from the norms. Empirical studies have classified 33 societal cultures around the world on their tightness and looseness.[72]

In a **tight culture**, such as ones found in Korea, Japan, or Malaysia, social norms are strong and clear. Members are expected to know the prevailing norms and let them guide their behavior. They tend to self-govern and conform, understanding that deviations are likely to be noticed, discouraged, and even sanctioned. The goal in tight cultures, as suggested in the Asian proverb, is to fit in with society's expectations and not stand out.

> A **tight culture** has rigid social norms expects members to conform with them.

In a **loose culture**, such as ones found in Australia, Brazil, or Hungary, social norms are relaxed and less clear-cut. Members may be more or less concerned with them, and conformity varies a good deal. Deviations from norms tend to be tolerated unless they take the form of criminal behavior or test the extremes of morality. It is acceptable for individuals in loose cultures, as suggested in the American idiom, to show unique identities and express themselves independently of the masses.

> A **loose culture** has relaxed social norms and allows conformity by members to vary a good deal.

It can be challenging to go from a tight to a loose culture, or vice-versa, for travel or work. Being effective requires cultural awareness to understand differences, and self-management to handle these differences well. One of the most common settings where the dynamics of tight and loose cultures emerge is a class group or work team whose members come from different cultures. You've probably been there; what did you see and what might you expect?

A mix of cultural tightness and looseness on a cross-cultural team may result in soft or unstated conflict and missed performance opportunities. Members from tight cultures may be slow to volunteer, criticize, show emotion, or seek praise. They may look toward formal authority for direction while trying to always be on time and prepared. Members from loose cultures may be quick to voice opinions, criticize others, display emotions, and look for recognition. They may not show much respect for authority, and punctuality may be inconsistent. It takes a lot of cultural awareness for a team leader and team members to identify these culturally derived behaviors. It takes a lot of skill to create a

---

Culture Shock: Stages in Adjusting to a New Culture

Confusion: First contacts with the new culture leave you anxious, uncomfortable, and in need of information and advice.

Small victories: Continued interactions bring some "successes," and your confidence grows in handling daily affairs.

The honeymoon: A time of wonderment, cultural immersion, and even infatuation with local ways that are viewed positively.

Irritation and anger: A time when the "negatives" overwhelm the "positives," and the new culture becomes a target of your criticism.

Reality: A time of rebalancing; you are able to enjoy the new culture while accommodating its less desirable elements.

team environment where everyone gets a chance both to contribute to team performance and to take satisfaction from the experience.

Values and National Cultures

The ideas of Geert Hofstede on value differences in national cultures are another useful way for considering how cultural differences can influence management and organizational practices. After studying employees of a global corporation operating in 40 countries, Hofstede identified four cultural dimensions: power distance, uncertainty avoidance, individualism–collectivism, and masculinity–femininity.[73] Later studies added a fifth, now called time orientation.[74]

Figure 5.3 shows how national cultures can vary on these dimensions. Try to imagine what these cultural differences might mean when global business executives try to work and make deals around the world, or when representatives of national governments meet to seek agreements or resolve problems. Remember that Hofstede warns against falling prey to the **ecological fallacy**. This is acting with the mistaken assumption that a generalized cultural value, such as individualism in American culture or masculinity in Japanese culture, applies equally to all members of the culture.[75]

The **ecological fallacy** assumes that a generalized cultural value applies equally well to all members of the culture.

Power distance is the degree to which a society accepts unequal distribution of power.

Individualism– collectivism is the degree to which a society emphasizes individuals and their self-interests.

Uncertainty avoidance is the degree to which a society tolerates risk and uncertainty.

Power Distance

Power distance is the degree that society accepts or rejects the unequal distribution of power among people in organizations and the institutions of society. In high-power-distance cultures, we expect to find great respect for age, status, and titles. People in these cultures tend to be tolerant of power and are prone to follow orders and accept differences in rank. Picture a businesswoman from low-moderate-power-distance America visiting her firm's joint venture partner in high-power-distance Malaysia. Could her tendencies toward informality, for example, using first names to address superiors and dressing casually in the office, create discomfort for local executives less accustomed to such social egalitarianism?

Individualism–Collectivism

Individualism–collectivism is the degree to which a society emphasizes individual accomplishments and self-interests versus the collective accomplishments and interests of groups.[76] The United States had the highest individualism score of any country in Hofstede's data. Do you find the "I" and "me" words used a lot in conversations and meetings, or even when students are making team presentations in class? Such self-referential expressions reflect a cultural tendency toward individualism. This contrasts with the importance placed on group harmony in the Confucian and more collectivist cultures of Asia, as pointed out in the Asian proverb above. What might go wrong when team members from individualistic cultures try to work with those from more collectivist ones?

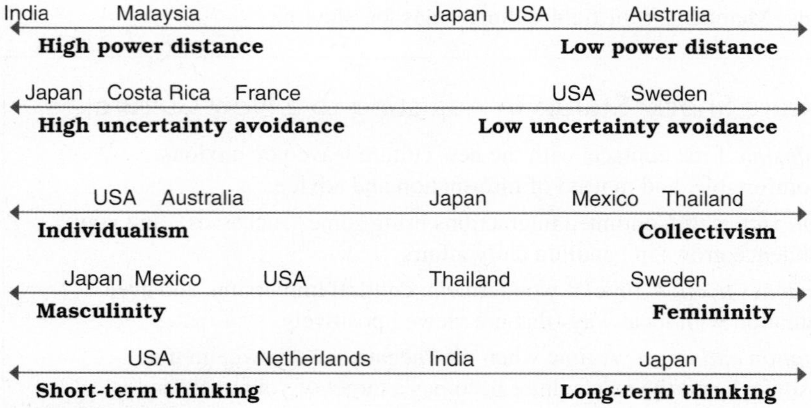

Uncertainty Avoidance

Uncertainty avoidance is the degree to which a society is uncomfortable with risk, change, and situational uncertainty,

India	Malaysia		Japan	USA		Australia
High power distance					**Low power distance**	

Japan	Costa Rica	France			USA	Sweden
High uncertainty avoidance				**Low uncertainty avoidance**		

USA	Australia		Japan		Mexico	Thailand
Individualism					**Collectivism**	

Japan	Mexico		USA	Thailand		Sweden
Masculinity					**Femininity**	

	USA	Netherlands	India		Japan	
Short-term thinking				**Long-term thinking**		

FIGURE 5.3
How countries' short-term thinking and long-term thinking compare on Hofstede's dimensions of national culture.

versus having tolerance for them. Members of low uncertainty-avoidance cultures often display openness to change and innovation. In high uncertainty-avoidance cultures, by contrast, preferences for structure, order, and predictability are likely to be more prevalent. Persons in these cultures may have difficulty dealing with ambiguity, and tend to follow rules, preferring more structure in their lives. Do you think that high uncertainty avoidance is one of the reasons why Europeans seem to favor employment practices that provide job security?

Masculinity–Femininity

Masculinity–femininity is the degree to which a society values assertiveness and materialism versus feelings, relationships, and quality of life.[77] You might think of it as a tendency for members of a culture to show stereotypically masculine versus feminine traits that reflect different attitudes toward gender roles. Visitors to Japan, with the highest masculinity score in Hofstede's research, may be surprised at how restricted career opportunities can still be for women. The *Wall Street Journal* has pointed out that "In Japan, professional women face a set of socially complex issues—from overt sexism to deep-seated attitudes about the division of labor." One female Japanese manager says: "Men tend to have very fixed ideas about what women are like."[78]

Masculinity–femininity is the degree to which a society values assertiveness and materialism.

Time Orientation

Time orientation is the degree to which a society emphasizes short-term versus long-term goals and gratifications.[79] American tendencies toward impatience and desire for quick, even instantaneous, gratification show short-term thinking. Even our companies are expected to achieve short-term results; those failing to meet quarterly financial targets often suffer immediate stock price declines. Many Asian cultures are quite the opposite, displaying Confucian values of persistence, thrift, patience, and a willingness to work for long-term success. This might help explain why Japan's auto executives were more willing than their American counterparts to invest years ago in hybrid engine technologies even though market demand was very low and any return on the investments were likely to take a long time to materialize.

Time orientation is the degree to which a society emphasizes short-term or long-term goals.

Learning Check 3

TAKEAWAYQUESTION 3 **What is culture and how does it influence global management?**

BE SURE YOU CAN • define *culture* and *culture shock* • explain how ethnocentrism can create difficulties for people working across cultures • differentiate between low-context and high-context cultures, and monochronic and polychronic cultures • explain the differences between tight and loose cultures • list and illustrate Hofstede's five dimensions of value differences among national cultures

Global Management Learning

TAKEAWAY 4   How can we benefit from global management learning?

LEARN MORE | Are management theories universal? • Intercultural competencies
ABOUT | Global learning goals

Scholars in the area of **comparative management** study how management perspectives and practices systematically differ among countries and cultures.[80] They use cultural models like those just described for Hall, Gelfand, et al., and Hofstede, in the search for meaningful insights into management around the globe.[81]

Comparative management studies how management practices differ among countries and cultures.

Are Management Theories Universal?

You might think that all the management theories in this book and your course apply universally from one country and culture to the next. The fact is that the world is a complex place and management scholars understand this. If anything, they agree that there is lots left to understand and learn about global management.[82]

Geert Hofstede, whose framework for understanding national cultures was just discussed, urges caution when transferring practices across cultures. He points out that many management theories are really ethnocentric because they come from a single cultural context—often North American.[83] By way of example, he says that the American emphasis on participation in leadership reflects the culture's moderate stance on power distance. It should be understood and respected that the cultures of countries with higher power-distance scores—such as France or Malaysia—will show more tolerance for hierarchy and directive leadership. Hofstede also notes that the American cultural value of individualism is quite prominent in management theories on individual performance, rewards, and job design. These theories may be less applicable in countries where cultural values are more collectivist. Sweden, for example, has a history of designing jobs for groups of workers rather than for individuals.

Intercultural Competencies

Intercultural competencies are skills and personal characteristics that help us be successful in cross-cultural situations.

Even though management theories are not always universal, it may be that **intercultural competencies** are. These are skills and personal characteristics that help us function successfully in cross-cultural situations.

Intercultural competencies are "must haves" for anyone seeking a career as a global manager. They begin with—but add specifics to—the notion of cultural awareness that introduced this chapter. Rather than having just a generalized openness to learning about other cultures and being sensitive to different cultural ways, the focus is on acting competent when working in another culture or in culturally mixed settings. What scholars know in this regard is summarized in three pillars of intercultural competency—perception management, relationship management, and self-management.[84]

In *perception management*, a person must be inquisitive and curious about cultural differences. Being flexible and nonjudgmental are important when interpreting and dealing with situations in which differences are present. In *relationship management*, a person must be genuinely interested in others, be sensitive to one's own emotions and feelings, and be able to make personal adjustments while engaging in cross-cultural interactions. In *self-management*, a person must have a strong sense of personal identity and understand his or her own emotions and values. One must also stay self-confident even in situations that call for personal adaptations because of cultural differences.

Global Learning Goals

In order to compete in the global economy, aspiring and seasoned professionals should continually seek to strengthen personal intercultural competencies, particularly if the goal is to have a successful career as a global manager. A truly global manager will look everywhere and anywhere in the world for new ideas, and will reject the view that the home country and culture have monopolies on the best practices. The intent of comparative management studies is to engage in critical thinking about the ways managers around the world do things and about how they might do them better. As we try to engage in global management learning, however, it is important to hesitate before accepting any idea or practice as a universal prescription for action. Culture and cultural differences always have to be considered. According to Hofstede: "Disregard of other cultures is a luxury only the strong can afford . . . increase in cultural awareness represents an intellectual and spiritual gain."[85]

Learning Check 4

TAKEAWAYQUESTION 4 **How can we benefit from global management learning?**

BE SURE YOU CAN • describe the concept of global organizational learning • define *intercultural competency* and identify three of its major components • answer this question: "Do management theories apply universally around the world?"

Management Learning Review
Get Prepared for **Quizzes and Exams**

SUMMARY

TAKEAWAYQUESTION 1

What are the management challenges of globalization?

- Global managers are informed about world developments and are competent in working with people from different cultures.
- The forces of globalization create international business opportunities to pursue profits, customers, capital, and low-cost suppliers and labor in different countries.
- Market-entry strategies for international business include global sourcing, exporting and importing, and licensing and franchising.
- Direct investment strategies of international business establish joint ventures or wholly owned subsidiaries in foreign countries.
- General environment differences, including legal and political systems, often complicate international business activities.
- Regional economic alliances such as NAFTA, the EU, and SADC link nations of the world with the goals of promoting economic development.
- The World Trade Organization is a global institution that promotes free trade and open markets around the world.

FOR DISCUSSION What aspects of the U.S. legal-political environment could prove difficult for a Chinese firm setting up a factory in America?

TAKEAWAYQUESTION 2

What are global businesses and how do they work?

- A global corporation is a multinational enterprise or multinational corporation with extensive operations in multiple foreign countries.
- A transnational corporation tries to operate globally without a strong national identity and with a worldwide mission and strategies.
- Global corporations can benefit host countries by offering broader tax bases, new technologies, and employment opportunities.
- Global corporations can cause problems for host countries if they interfere in local government, extract excessive profits, and dominate the local economy.

- The U.S. Foreign Corrupt Practices Act prohibits American multinational corporations from engaging in bribery and corrupt practices abroad.

FOR DISCUSSION Is the Foreign Corrupt Practices Act unfair to American firms trying to compete for business around the world?

TAKEAWAYQUESTION 3

What is culture and how does it influence global management?

- Culture is a shared set of beliefs, values, and behavior patterns common to a group of people.
- Culture shock is the discomfort people sometimes experience when interacting with persons from cultures different from their own.
- Cultural intelligence is an individual capacity to understand, respect, and adapt to cultural differences.
- Hall's "silent" languages of culture include the use of context, time, and interpersonal space.
- Hofstede's five dimensions of value differences in national cultures are power distance, uncertainty avoidance, individualism–collectivism, masculinity–femininity, and time orientation.

FOR DISCUSSION Should religion be included in Hall's list of the silent languages of culture?

TAKEAWAYQUESTION 4

How can we benefit from global management learning?

- The field of comparative management studies how management is practiced around the world and how management ideas are transferred from one country or culture to the next.
- The foundations for intercultural competency are perception management, relationship management, and self-management.
- Global management learning must recognize that successful practices in one culture may work less well in others.

FOR DISCUSSION Even though cultural differences are readily apparent, is it the tendency today for the world's cultures to converge and become more alike?

SELF-TEST 5

Multiple-Choice Questions

1. The reasons why businesses go international include gaining new markets, finding investment capital, and reducing _____.
   (a) political risk
   (b) protectionism
   (c) labor costs
   (d) most favored nation status

2. When shoe maker Rocky Brands decided to buy full ownership of a manufacturing company in the Dominican Republic, Rocky was engaging in which form of international business?
   (a) import/export
   (b) licensing
   (c) foreign subsidiary
   (d) joint venture

3. A form of international business that falls into the category of a direct investment strategy is _____.
   (a) exporting
   (b) joint venture
   (c) licensing
   (d) global sourcing

4. The World Trade Organization would most likely become involved in disputes between countries over _____.
   (a) exchange rates
   (b) ethnocentrism
   (c) nationalization
   (d) tariffs

5. Business complaints about copyright protection and intellectual property rights in some countries illustrate how differences in _____ can impact international operations.
   (a) legal environments
   (b) political stability
   (c) sustainable development
   (d) economic systems

6. In _____ cultures, members tend to do one thing at a time; in _____ cultures, members tend to do many things at once.
   (a) monochronic, polychronic
   (b) polycentric, geocentric
   (c) collectivist, individualist
   (d) neutral, affective

7. A culture that places great value on expressing meaning in the written or spoken word is described as _____ by Hall.
   (a) monochromic
   (b) proxemic
   (c) collectivist
   (d) low-context

8. It is common in Malaysian culture for people to value teamwork and to display great respect for authority. Hofstede would describe this culture as high in both _____.
   (a) uncertainty avoidance and feminism
   (b) universalism and particularism
   (c) collectivism and power distance
   (d) long-term orientation and masculinity

9. In Hofstede's study of national cultures, America was found to be the most _____ compared with other countries in his sample.
   (a) individualistic
   (b) collectivist
   (c) feminine
   (d) long-term oriented

10. It is _____ when a foreign visitor takes offense at a local custom such as dining with one's fingers, considering it inferior to practices of his or her own culture.
    (a) universalist
    (b) prescriptive
    (c) monochronic
    (d) enthnocentric

11. When Limited Brands buys cotton in Egypt, has tops sewn from it in Sri Lanka according to designs made in Italy, and then offers the garments for sale in the United States, this form of international business is known as _____.
    (a) licensing
    (b) importing
    (c) joint venturing
    (d) global sourcing

12. The difference between an international business and a transnational corporation is that the transnational _____.
    (a) tries to operate around the world without a strong national identity
    (b) does business in only one or two foreign countries
    (c) is led by ethnocentric managers
    (d) is based outside North America

13. The Foreign Corrupt Practices Act makes it illegal for _____.
    (a) Americans to engage in joint ventures abroad
    (b) foreign businesses to pay bribes to U.S. government officials
    (c) U.S. businesses to make payoffs abroad to gain international business contracts
    (d) foreign businesses to steal intellectual property from U.S. firms operating in their countries

14. When a member of a cross-cultural team is hesitant to speak up and offer ideas, defers to the team leader, and avoids accepting praise for individual work, the person is displaying characteristics consistent with a _____ culture.
    (a) monochronic
    (b) low-context
    (c) tight
    (d) loose

15. Hofstede would describe a culture whose members respect age and authority and whose workers defer to the preferences of their supervisors as _____.
    (a) low masculinity
    (b) high particularism
    (c) high power distance
    (d) monochronic

Short-Response Questions

16. Why do host countries sometimes complain about how global corporations operate within their borders?

17. Why is the "power-distance" dimension of national culture important in management?

18. What is the difference between a culture that is tight and one that is loose?

19. How do regional economic alliances impact the global economy?

20. Kim has just returned from her first business trip to Japan. While there, she was impressed with the intense use of work teams. Now back in Iowa, she would like to totally reorganize the workflows and processes of her canoe manufacturing company and its 75 employees around teams. There has been very little emphasis on teamwork, and she now believes this is "the way to go." Based on the discussion of culture and management in this chapter, what advice would you offer Kim?

ManagementSkills&
Competencies Make yourself **valuable!**

Evaluate Career Situations

What would you do?

1. To Buy or Not to Buy

You've just read in the newspaper that the maker of one of your favorite brands of sports shoes is being investigated for using sweatshop factories in Asia. It really disturbs you, but the shoes are great! One of your friends says it's time to boycott the brand. You're not sure. Do you engage in a personal boycott or not, and why?

2. China Beckons

Your new design for a revolutionary golf putter is a big hit with friends at the local golf course. You decide to have clubs with your design manufactured in China so that you can sell them to pro shops around the country. How can you make sure that your design won't be copied by the Chinese manufacturer and then used to make low-price knock-offs? What should you do in this situation?

3. Cross-Cultural Teamwork

You've just been asked to join a team being sent to Poland for 10 days to discuss a new software development project with your firm's Polish engineers. It is your first business trip out of the country. In fact, you've only been to Europe once, as part of a study-abroad semester in college. How will you prepare for the trip and for work with your Polish colleagues there? What worries you the most under the circumstances? After all, if you do well here, more international assignments are likely to come your way.

Reflect on the Self-Assessment

Global Intelligence

Instructions

Use the following scale to rate yourself on each of these 10 items:[86]

1	Very Poor
2	Poor
3	Acceptable
4	Good
5	Very Good

_____ 1. I understand my own culture in terms of its expectations, values, and influence on communication and relationships.

_____ 2. When someone presents me with a different point of view, I try to understand it rather than attack it.

_____ 3. I am comfortable dealing with situations where the available information is incomplete and the outcomes are unpredictable.

_____ 4. I am open to new situations and am always looking for new information and learning opportunities.

_____ 5. I have a good understanding of the attitudes and perceptions toward my culture as they are held by people from other cultures.

_____ 6. I am always gathering information about other countries and cultures and trying to learn from them.

_____ 7. I am well informed regarding the major differences in the government, political, and economic systems around the world.

_____ 8. I work hard to increase my understanding of people from other cultures.

_____ 9. I am able to adjust my communication style to work effectively with people from different cultures.

_____10. I can recognize when cultural differences are influencing working relationships, and I adjust my attitudes and behavior accordingly.

Interpretation

In order to be successful in the global economy, you must be comfortable with cultural diversity. This requires a global mind-set that is receptive to and respectful of cultural differences, global knowledge that includes the continuing quest to know and learn more about other nations and cultures, and global work skills that allow you to work effectively across cultures.

Scoring

The goal is to score as close to a perfect "5" as possible on each of the three dimensions of global intelligence. Develop your scores as follows:

1. Items $(1 + 2 + 3 + 4)/4 = $ _Global Mind-Set Score_

2. Items $(5 + 6 + 7)/3 = $ _Global Knowledge Score_

3. Items $(8 + 9 + 10)/3 = $ _Global Work Skills Score_

Contribute to the Class Exercise

American Football

Instructions

Form into groups as assigned by the instructor. In the group, do the following:[87]

1. Discuss "American Football"—the rules, the way the game is played, the way players and coaches behave, and the roles of owners and fans.

2. Use "American Football" as a metaphor to explain the way U.S. corporations run and how they tend to behave in terms of strategies and goals.

3. Prepare a class presentation for a group of visiting Japanese business executives. In this presentation, use the metaphor of "American Football" to (1) explain American business strategies and practices to the Japanese and (2) critique the potential strengths and weaknesses of the American business approach in terms of success in the global marketplace.

Manage a Critical Incident

Silent Team Members

The course instructor assigned students to teams for a case study in two parts spaced two weeks apart: Part A requires a preliminary oral presentation and Part B requires a final presentation and written report. Your team has five members, including one each from Japan and Indonesia. The team had three face-to-face meetings while preparing Part A. The Japanese and Indonesian members said very little, although they had extensive notes of information retrieved from research on the Internet. But they were even hesitant to answer when asked direct questions. The other three members created the preliminary presentation and assigned parts for everyone to deliver. The Japanese and Indonesian team members struggled with their parts of the presentation and didn't contribute during the question-and-answer session. The instructor said the team's Part A presentation wasn't focused and well integrated. She said things would have to go much better on Part B if the team expected a high grade. The team is scheduled to meet tonight to recap Part A and start work on Part B.

Questions

What can you say and do at this meeting to set the stage for higher performance on Part B? How might team dynamics and cross-cultural diversity have contributed to the Part A results? What insights from cultural models might explain the behavior of your Japanese and Indonesian teammates? How can they be better engaged so that the team takes best advantage of all of members' talents going forward? What role can you play in future team meetings to help accomplish this goal?

Collaborate on the Team Activity

Globalization Pros and Cons

Question

"Globalization" is frequently in the news. You can easily read or listen to both advocates and opponents. What is the bottom line? Is globalization good or bad, and for whom? What are the important issues to consider as the world becomes even more connected?

Instructions

1. Agree on a good definition for the term "globalization." Review various definitions and find the common ground.

2. Read current events relating to globalization. Summarize the issues and arguments. What is the positive side of globalization? What are the negatives that some might call its "dark" side?

3. Read what scholars say about globalization. Summarize their views on the forces and consequences of globalization for small and large companies, for countries, for people and society at large.

4. Consider globalization from the perspective of your local community and its major employers. Is globalization a threat or an opportunity in this context, and why?

5. Take a position on globalization's pros and cons, and share it with the class. Justify your position.

Analyze THE CaseStudy : HEWLETT-PACKARD
Managing on a Global Scale

Go to **Management Cases for Critical Thinking** at the end of the book to find this case.

Entrepreneurship and Small Business Management

KEY TAKEAWAYS

- Define entrepreneurship and identify entrepreneurs.

- Describe how small businesses get started and common problems they face.

- Explain how entrepreneurs plan, legally structure, and fund new business ventures.

SKILLS MAKE YOU **VALUABLE**

- **EVALUATE** *Career Situations:* What Would You Do?

- **REFLECT** *On the Self-Assessment:* Entrepreneurial Orientation

- **CONTRIBUTE** *To the Class Exercise:* Entrepreneurs among Us

- **MANAGE** *A Critical Incident:* Craft Brewery In—or Out—of the Money?

- **COLLABORATE** *On the Team Activity:* Community Entrepreneurs

- **ANALYZE** *The Case Study:* Lenovo: Tapping the Entrepreneurial Spirit

Entrepreneurship is an attractive opportunity that is enticing more and more college students and experienced workers alike. Many of us have good ideas for business and social entrepreneurship that go unfulfilled. Understanding the nature of entrepreneurs, the challenges of running small businesses, and alternative ways of setting up and funding new ventures can go a long way toward opening the doors to this career pathway.

Just out of the military and starting again? Why not create your own job? John Raftery did. After a four-year tour with the Marines—including two on deployment—he earned an accounting degree with help from the GI Bill. But after being disappointed with slow advancement at an accounting firm, he answered an e-mail about a free Entrepreneurship Bootcamp for Veterans with Disabilities at Syracuse University. Raftery went to the camp and ended up with a business plan to start his own firm, Patriot Contractors, in Waxahachie, Texas.[1]

Struggling with work–life balance as a mother? Why not find flexibility and opportunity in entrepreneurship? Denise Devine did just that. Once a financial executive with Campbell Soup Co., she now has her own line of fiber-rich juice drinks for kids. Called **mompreneurs**, women like Devine find opportunity in market niches for safe, useful, and healthy products they spot as

Mompreneurs pursue business opportunities they spot as mothers.

moms. Says Devine: "As entrepreneurs we're working harder than we did, but we're doing it on our own schedules."[2]

Female, thinking about starting a small business, but don't have the money? Find help from organizations like Count-Me-In. Started by co-founders Nell Merlino and Iris Burnett, it offers "microcredit" loans of $500 to $10,000 to help women start and expand small businesses. A unique credit scoring system doesn't penalize for things such as a divorce, time off to raise a family, or age—all things that might discourage conventional lenders. Merlino says: "Women own 38% of all businesses in this country, but still have far less access to capital than men because of today's process."[3]

These examples are hopefully inspiring. In fact, this is really a chapter of examples. The goal is not only to inform you, but also to get you thinking about starting your own business, becoming your own boss, and making your own special contribution to society as a whole. How does that sound? Could you get excited to join the world of entrepreneurship and small business management?

The Nature of Entrepreneurship

TAKEAWAY 1   What is entrepreneurship and who are the entrepreneurs?

LEARN MORE | Who are the entrepreneurs? • Characteristics of entrepreneurs
ABOUT | Women and minority entrepreneurs • Social entrepreneurship

Entrepreneurship is risk-taking behavior that results in new opportunities.

The term **entrepreneurship** describes strategic thinking and risk-taking behavior that results in the creation of new opportunities. H. Wayne Huizenga started Waste Management with just $5,000 and once owned the Miami Dolphins. He says: "An important part of being an entrepreneur is a gut instinct that allows you to believe in your heart that something will work even though everyone else says it will not."[4] Have you had experiences in your own life where you've continued along a particular path and succeeded, despite the advice of friends or family not to?

Who Are the Entrepreneurs?

A **classic entrepreneur** is someone willing to pursue opportunities in situations others view as problems or threats.

A **classic entrepreneur** is a risk-taking individual who takes action to pursue opportunities others fail to recognize, or even view as problems or threats. Who, for example, would consider starting a bookstore in a place like Nashville, Tennessee, where Borders and Barnes & Noble had already closed shop? Against the advice of family and friends, Ann Patchett did. She reasoned that a place that had previously supported 60,000 square feet of bookstore space still had enough customer potential to support a small center-city store. "Why can't I open 2,500 square feet of bookstore?" she reasoned. That confidence gave birth to Parnassus Books and a sales record that went on to exceed expectations.[5]

A **serial entrepreneur** starts and runs businesses and nonprofits over and over again, moving from one interest and opportunity to the next.

Some people become **serial entrepreneurs** that start and run new ventures over and over again, moving from one interest and opportunity to the next. Serial entrepreneurs can be found both in business and nonprofit settings. H. Wayne Huizenga, mentioned earlier, is a great example. He made his fortune founding and selling businesses like Blockbuster Entertainment, Waste Management, and AutoNation. A member of the Entrepreneurs' Hall of Fame, he describes being an entrepreneur this way: "We're looking for something where we can make something happen: an industry where the competition is asleep, hasn't taken advantage."[6]

A **first-mover advantage** comes from being first to exploit a niche or enter a market.

A common pattern among successful entrepreneurs is **first-mover advantage**. They move quickly to spot, exploit, and deliver a product or service to a new market or an unrecognized niche in an existing one. Consider some other brief examples of entrepreneurs who were willing to take risks and sharp enough to pursue first-mover advantage.[7]

Bloomberg/Getty Images

Caterina Fake. From idea to buyout took only 16 months. That's quite a benchmark for would-be Internet entrepreneurs. Welcome to the world of Flickr, co-founded by Caterina Fake. Flickr took the notion of online photo sharing and turned it into an almost viral Internet phenomenon. Startup capital came from families, friends, and angel investors. The payoff came when Yahoo! bought them out for $30 million. Fake then started Hunch.com, a website designed to help people make decisions (e.g., should I buy that Porsche?). She sold it to eBay for $80 million. She says: "You pick a big, ambitious problem, and look for great people to solve it."[8]

Earl Graves. Earl G. Graves Sr. started *Black Enterprise* magazine with a vision and a $175,000 loan. Its success grew into the diversified business information company Earl G. Graves Ltd.—a multimedia venture spanning television, radio, and digital media including BlackEnterprise.com. Graves's accomplishments led *Fortune* magazine to call him one of the 50 most powerful and influential African Americans in corporate America. The author of the best-selling book *How to Succeed in Business without Being White,* Graves received a Lifetime Achievement Award from the National Association of Black Journalists. He is a member of many business and nonprofit boards, and the business school at his college alma mater—Baltimore's Morgan State University, is named after him. Graves says: "I feel that a large part of my role as publisher of *Black Enterprise* is to be a catalyst for Black economic development in this country."[9]

Louis Johnny/SIPA/NewsCom

Anita Roddick. In 1973, Anita Roddick was a 33-year-old housewife looking for a way to support herself and her two children. She spotted a niche for natural-based skin and health care products, and started mixing and selling them from a small shop in Brighton, England. It became Body Shop, a global retailer selling a product every half-second around the world. Known for her commitment to human rights, the environment, and economic development, Roddick was an early advocate of "profits with principles" and business social responsibility. She once said: "If you think you're too small to have an impact, try going to bed with a mosquito."[10]

NewsCom

Andrew Milligan/PA Photos/Landov

Shawn Corey Carter. You probably know him as Jay Z, and there's an entrepreneurial story behind the name. Carter began rapping on the streets of Brooklyn where he lived with his single mom and three brothers. Hip-hop turned into his ticket to travel. "When I left the block," he told an interviewer, "everyone was saying I was crazy, I was doing well for myself on the streets, and cats around me were like, these rappers . . . just record, tour, and get separated from their families, while some white person takes all their money. I was determined to do it differently."[11] He did. Carter used his music millions to found the media firm Roc Nation, co-found the apparel firm Rocawear, and become part owner of the New Jersey Nets.

Characteristics of Entrepreneurs

Entrepreneurs and entrepreneurship are everywhere. There is no age prerequisite. At the age of 22, Richard Ludlow turned down a full-time job offer and an MBA admission to start New York's Academic Earth. It's an online location for posting and sharing faculty lectures and other educational materials. His goals are both to make a profit and help society by lowering the cost of education. While in high school Jasmine Lawrence created her own natural cosmetics after having problems with a purchased hair relaxer. Products from her firm, Eden Body-Works, can now be found at Walmart and Whole Foods.[12]

> ### Challenging the Myths about Entrepreneurs
>
> • *Entrepreneurs are born, not made.*
>
> Not true! Talent gained and enhanced by experience is a foundation for entrepreneurial success.
>
> • *Entrepreneurs are gamblers.*
>
> Not true! Entrepreneurs are risk takers, but the risks are informed and calculated.
>
> • *Money is the key to entrepreneurial success.*
>
> Not true! Money is no guarantee of success. There's a lot more to it than that; many entrepreneurs start with very little.
>
> • *You have to be young to be an entrepreneur.*
>
> Not true! Age is no barrier to entrepreneurship; with age often comes experience, contacts, and other useful resources.
>
> • *You have to have a degree in business to be an entrepreneur.*
>
> Not true! You may not need a degree at all. Although a business degree is not necessary, it helps to study and understand business fundamentals.

There are lots of entrepreneurs in almost any community. Just look at those individuals who take the risk of buying a local McDonald's or Subway or Papa John's franchise, open a small retail shop selling used video games or bicycles, start a self-employed service business such as financial planning or management consulting, or establish a nonprofit organization to provide housing for the homeless or deliver hot meals to house-bound senior citizens. All of these individuals are entrepreneurs in their own way.[13]

Is there something in your experience that could be a pathway to entrepreneurship? Have you thought about better ways to do things that everyone does? Or a product to do it with? As you think about these questions, don't let the myths shown in the nearby box discourage you.[14]

Attitudes and Personal Interests

Researchers point out that entrepreneurs tend to share certain attitudes and personal characteristics. The general entrepreneurial profile is of an individual who is self-confident, determined, resilient, adaptable, and driven by excellence.[15] They also share personality traits and characteristics like those shown in Figure 6.1 and described here.[16]

Characteristics of ► entrepreneurs

- *Internal locus of control:* Entrepreneurs believe that they are in control of their own destiny; they are self-directing and like autonomy.

- *High energy level:* Entrepreneurs are persistent, hardworking, and willing to exert extraordinary efforts to succeed.

- *Self-confidence:* Entrepreneurs feel competent, believe in themselves, and are willing to make decisions.

- *Tolerance for ambiguity:* Entrepreneurs are risk takers; they tolerate situations with high degrees of uncertainty.

FIGURE 6.1
Personality traits and characteristics of entrepreneurs.

- *Self-reliance and desire for independence:* Entrepreneurs want independence; they are self-reliant; they want to be their own bosses, not work for others.

- *High need for achievement:* Entrepreneurs are motivated to accomplish challenging goals; they thrive on performance feedback.

- *Flexibility:* Entrepreneurs are willing to admit problems and errors, and are willing to change a course of action when plans aren't working.

- *Passion and action orientation:* Entrepreneurs try to act ahead of problems; they want to get things done and not waste valuable time.

Background, Experiences, and Interests

Entrepreneurs tend to have a unique background and personal experiences.[17] Childhood *experiences and family environment* appear to make a difference. Evidence links entrepreneurship with parents who were entrepreneurial and self-employed. Entrepreneurs often are raised in families that encourage responsibility, initiative, and independence. Another issue is *career or work history*. Entrepreneurs who try one venture often go on to others. Prior work experience in the business area or the industry being entered can be helpful.

A report in the *Harvard Business Review* suggests that entrepreneurs may have unique and *deeply embedded life interests*.[18] The article describes entrepreneurs as having strong interests in starting things. They enjoy creative production—things like project initiation, working with the unknown, and finding unconventional solutions. Entrepreneurs also have strong interests in running things. They enjoy enterprise control—being in charge, being accountable, and making decisions while moving others toward a goal. Are these characteristics family and friends might use to describe you?

Entrepreneurs also tend to emerge during certain *windows of career opportunity*. Most start their businesses between the ages of 22 and 45, an age spread that seems to allow for risk taking. However, being older in age shouldn't be viewed as a barrier. When Tony DeSio was 50, he founded the Mail Boxes Etc. chain. He sold it for $300 million when he was 67 and suffering heart problems. Within a year he launched PixArts, another franchise chain based on photography and art. When asked by a reporter what he liked most about entrepreneurship, DeSio replied: "Being able to make decisions without having to go through layers of corporate hierarchy—just being a master of your own destiny."[19]

Female and Minority Entrepreneurs

When economists speak about entrepreneurs, they differentiate between entrepreneurs driven by the search for new opportunities and those driven by absolute need. Entrepreneurs in the latter category pursue **necessity-based entrepreneurship**, meaning that they start new ventures because they have few or no other employment and career options. This was the case for Anita Roddick, the Body Shop founder introduced earlier. She said her entrepreneurship began because she needed "to create a livelihood for myself and my two daughters, while my husband, Gordon, was trekking across the Americas."[20]

Necessity-driven entrepreneurship is one way for women and minorities who have hit the "glass ceiling" in their careers or are otherwise cut off from mainstream employment opportunities to strike out on their own and gain economic independence. One survey of women who left private-sector employment to work on their own reported that 33% of these women were not being taken seriously by their prior employer, and 29% had experienced glass ceiling issues.[21] As to entrepreneurship by women of color, the report *Women Business Owners of Color: Challenges and Accomplishments* points out that glass ceiling issues include not being recognized or valued by their employers, not being taken seriously, and seeing others promoted ahead of them.[22]

The National Foundation for Women Business Owners (NFWBO) reports that women own close to 8 million of U.S. non-farm businesses. These firms are forecasted to create one-third of more than 15 million new jobs predicted by 2018.[23] Although the top four industries for female entrepreneurs are the same as for men—construction, manufacturing, wholesale trade, and retail trade—a Kauffman report notes that only 19.8% of the female business owners earned more than $100,000 per year compared to 32.8% for men. The report states that women "seem to be encountering 'glass walls' that keep their businesses from expanding."[24]

The last U.S. small business census identified almost 2 million small firms owned by African Americans, a growth of 60% over prior numbers, representing 7% of total businesses. Among new startups in 2010, 9% were led by African American entrepreneurs and 23% by Latinos.[25] Even so, obstacles to minority entrepreneurship—as with female entrepreneurship—are real and shouldn't be underestimated. Less than 1% of the available venture capital in the United States goes to minority entrepreneurs. High unemployment and declining wealth among African American households also make it hard to find startup financing. In an effort to address such issues, the U.S. Minority Business Development Agency of the Department of Commerce set up a nationwide network of 40 business development centers with the goal of helping minority-owned businesses grow in "size, scale, and capacity."[26]

Social Entrepreneurship

Entrepreneurship also plays a critical social role in society. For example, it can help to address social issues such as housing and job training for the homeless, bringing technology to poor families, improving literacy among disadvantaged youth, reducing poverty, and improving nutrition. These and other social issues are targets for **social entrepreneurship**, a form of ethical entrepreneurship that seeks novel ways to solve pressing social problems. Social entrepreneurs take risks and create **social enterprises** with the mission to help make lives better for underserved populations.[27]

Necessity-based entrepreneurship takes place because other employment options don't exist.

Social entrepreneurship is a unique form of ethical entrepreneurship that seeks novel ways to solve pressing social problems.

Social enterprises have a social mission to help make lives better for underserved populations.

wisdom > LEARN FROM ROLE MODELS

> *"Founded with a rebellious spirit and a lofty objective: to create boutique-quality, classically crafted eyewear at a revolutionary price point."*

Grad-School Startup Takes on Global Competitors

Kathy Willens/AP

"**D**id you ever wonder why prescription eyeglasses are so expensive?"

When four MBA students at Wharton asked that question they found an oligopoly industry where supply was controlled by just a few firms who had as a result a disproportionate influence on prices. Spotting both a business opportunity and a social calling, they decided to start a company to do what they felt was the right thing to do—make eyeglasses available to people at a reasonable price. Their creation, Warby Parker, is described as being "founded with a rebellious spirit and a lofty objective: to create boutique-quality, classically crafted eyewear at a revolutionary price point."

The founders—David Gilboa, Neil Blumenthal, Andrew Hunt, and Jeffrey Raider—wrote a Web-driven business plan that many questioned at first. Could eyeglasses be sold over the Internet? The Warby Parker answer was: "Of course!" If you're in doubt, and especially if you wear glasses, check out the offerings on warbyparker.com. You can buy stylish glasses for as low as

$95—frames with Rx lenses and free shipping. All this is made possible by the founders' careful analysis of the industry and its supply chains. They source directly from manufacturers and then sell direct to customers, cutting out a lot of costs and profit-taking in the middle of the chain.

Warby Parker is e-commerce and customer friendly—letting you have free home try-ons of up to five "loaner" pairs. On the social side of the business model, if you end up buying from Warby Parker, you're actually also helping someone else who can't afford to buy new glasses for themselves. Warby Parker donates one pair of glasses to someone in need for every pair of glasses that it sells. That adds up quickly when you consider that they sell more than 250,000 pairs a year.

The company's website proudly announces: "Let's do good. We're building a company to do good in the world. . . . We think it's good business to do good." They call their business model "eyewear with a purpose." That purpose is anchored in the fact that over a billion people in the world don't have the eyeglasses they need for school, work, or everyday living. This is a pervasive social problem that Warby Parker aims to help solve through business.

FIND INSPIRATION

Warby Parker's founders discovered that prescription eyeglasses could be sold for less than the current market. By selling for less, they created more value for both customers and for society at large. Instead of buying glasses at a boutique for $695, you can buy a stylish pair online from Warby Parker for $95. Central to the founders' purpose, each purchase sends a free pair of eyeglasses to someone in need. Why aren't there more businesses like Warby Parker? Why aren't there more entrepreneurs who try to match social problems and business opportunities? How about you? Do you have any good ideas matching business opportunity with social need?

Social entrepreneurs and their enterprises, both nonprofit and for-profit, devise new ways to meet needs that are not being served effectively by government or the private sector.[28] *Fast Company* magazine tries to spot and honor social entrepreneurs that run their organizations with "innovative thinking that can transform lives and change the world." Consider these examples of those who strive to live up to these expectations.[29]

- Chip Ransler and Manoj Sinha tackled the lack of power in many of India's poor villages. As University of Virginia business students, they realized that 350 million people lived in India's rice-growing regions without reliable electricity. After discovering that tons of rice husks were being discarded with every harvest, Ransler and Sinha started Husk Power Systems. It creates biogas from the husks and uses the gas to fuel small power plants.

- Rose Donna and Joel Selanikio tackled public health problems in sub-Saharan Africa. After realizing that public health services in developing nations often are bogged down in paperwork, they created software to make the process quicker and more efficient while increasing the reliability of databases. The UN, the World Health Organization, and the Vodafone Foundation are now helping their firm, DataDyne, move the program into 22 other African nations.

- Nissan Bahar and Franky Imbesi tackled lack of computers for African children living in poverty. They created Keepod, which puts an Android operating system on a USB drive that can be used in old PCs. This "operating system on a stick" makes each child an "owner" of a PC even when sharing machines with others. Bahar and Imbesi are testing the model in a Nairobi, Kenya, slum. Local workers buy flash drives for about $7, install the Keepod operating system, resell the drives for $9, and use the profit to pay themselves and fuel further expansion.

Lots of social entrepreneurship takes place without much notice, as most attention often goes to business entrepreneurs making lots of money. However, you can find social entrepreneurs right in your own community. Lewisville, Texas, for example, is the home of the housekeeping service Buckets & Bows, owned by Deborah Sardone. She became alarmed after noticing that many of her clients with cancer struggled hard with everyday household chores. Her response to this problem was to start Cleaning for a Reason. It's a nonprofit that builds networks of linkages with cleaning firms around the country with owners willing to offer free home cleaning to cancer patients.[30]

Learning Check 1

TAKEAWAYQUESTION **1 What is entrepreneurship and who are the entrepreneurs?**

BE SURE YOU CAN • define *entrepreneurship* and differentiate between classic and serial entrepreneurs • list key personal characteristics of entrepreneurs • explain the influence of background and experience on entrepreneurs • discuss motivations for entrepreneurship by women and minorities • define *social entrepreneurship* and *social enterprises*

Entrepreneurship and Small Business

TAKEAWAY 2   How do small businesses get started and what common problems do they face?

LEARN MORE | Why and how small businesses get started • Why small businesses fail
ABOUT | Family-owned small businesses

A small business has fewer than 500 employees, is independently owned and operated, and does not dominate its industry.

The U.S. Small Business Administration (SBA) defines a **small business** as a company that has 500 or fewer employees, is independently owned and operated, and does not dominate its industry. Over 99% of American businesses meet this definition.[31] They provide employment for 46.7% of private-sector workers, create as many as 6 out of every 10 new jobs in the economy, and employ 49.2% of private sector workers.[32] Small businesses employ 43% of high-tech workers such as scientists, engineers, and computer programmers. They produce more patents-per-employee than large firms, receive 35% of federal government contract dollars, and export more than $400 billion of goods and services annually.[33] The most common small business areas are restaurants, skilled professions such as craftspeople and doctors, general services such as hairdressers and repair shops, and independent retailers.[34] The vast majority of small businesses employ fewer than 20 workers, and over half of small businesses are home-based.

How Small Businesses Get Started

There are many reasons why people start their own small businesses—from necessity, as discussed earlier as a stimulus to entrepreneurship, to wanting to be your own boss, control your future, and fulfill a dream.[35] Would you be surprised to learn that the Gallup-Healthways Well-Being Index points to high satisfaction among small business owners? Self-employed business and store owners outrank working adults in 10 other occupations—including professional, manager/executive, and sales—on factors such as job satisfaction and emotional and physical health.[36]

Once a decision is made to go the small business route, the most common ways entrepreneurs get involved are to start a small business, buy an existing one, or buy and run a **franchise**—where a business owner sells the right to operate the same business in another location. A franchise such as Subway, Quiznos, or Domino's Pizza runs under the original owner's business name and guidance. In return, the franchise parent receives a specified share of income or a flat fee from the franchisee.

Any business—large or small, franchise or startup—needs a solid underlying **business model**. Think of a business model as a plan for making a profit by generating revenues that are greater than the costs of doing business. Serial entrepreneur Steven Blank calls business **startups** temporary organizations that are trying "to discover a profitable, scalable business model."[37] A startup is just that—a "start"; it's a new venture the entrepreneur is hoping will take shape and prove successful as the business develops and matures.

Blank's advice for those starting up a new venture is to move fast and create a "minimum viable product" that will attract customers, and that can be further developed and made more sophisticated over time. An example is Facebook, which started with simple message sharing and quickly grew into the complex social media operation we know today. Blank also favors something called a **lean startup**. It takes maximum advantage of resources like open-source software and free Web services to save on costs, while staying small and keeping operations as simple as possible.[38]

Why Small Businesses Fail

Small businesses have a high failure rate—one high enough to be intimidating. The SBA reports that about 50% of new small businesses fail in their first five years of operation, and only one-third survive for 10 years or more.[39] Part of this daunting statistic is a "counting" issue—the government counts as a "failure" any business that closes, whether it is because of the death or retirement of an owner, sale to someone else, or inability to earn a profit.[40] Nevertheless, the fact is that a lot of small business startups don't make it for reasons such as the following (see also Figure 6.2).[41]

- *Insufficient financing*—not having enough money to maintain operations while still building the business and gaining access to customers and markets.

- *Lack of experience*—not having sufficient know-how to run a business in the chosen market or geographic area.

- *Lack of commitment*—not devoting enough time to the requirements of running a competitive business.

- *Lack of strategy and strategic leadership*—not taking the time to craft a vision and mission, or formulate and properly implement a strategy.

- *Ethical failure*—falling prey to the temptations of fraud, deception, and embezzlement.

A **franchise** is when one business owner sells to another the right to operate the same business in another location.

A **business model** is a plan for making a profit by generating revenues that are greater than costs.

A **startup** is a new and temporary venture that is trying to discover a profitable business model for future success.

Lean startups use resources like open-source software, while containing costs, staying small, and keeping operations as simple as possible.

◀ Reasons startups fail

FIGURE 6.2
Eight reasons why many small businesses fail.

- *Lack of expertise*—not having expertise in the essentials of business operations, including finance, purchasing, selling, and production.

- *Growing too fast*—not taking the time to consolidate a position, fine-tune the organization, and systematically meet the challenges of growth.

- *Poor financial control*—not keeping track of the numbers, and failure to control business finances and use money to best advantage.

Family-Owned Small Businesses

In the little town of Utica, Ohio, there is a small child's desk in the corner of the president's office at Velvet Ice Cream Company. Its purpose is to help grow the next generation of leadership for the firm. "That's the way Dad did it," says Luconda Dager, the current head of the firm. "He exposed us all to the business at an early age." She and her two sisters, now both vice presidents, started working at the firm when they were 13 years old. When it came time for Joseph Dager to retire and pass the business on to the next generation, he said: "It is very special for me to pass the baton to my oldest daughter. Luconda has been with us for 15 years. She understands and breathes the ice cream business, and there is no one better suited for this position."[42]

A **family business** is owned and controlled by members of a family.

Velvet Ice Cream is the classic **family business**, owned and financially controlled by family members. The Family Firm Institute reports that family businesses account for 78% of new jobs created in the United States and provide 60% of the nation's employment.[43] Family businesses must solve the same problems of other small or large businesses—meeting the challenges of strategy, competitive advantage, and operational excellence. When everything goes right, as in the Velvet Ice Cream case, the family firm is almost an ideal situation—everyone working together, sharing values and a common goal, and knowing that what they do benefits the family. But it doesn't always work out this way or stay this way. Indeed, family businesses often face unique problems.

A **family business feud** occurs when family members have major disagreements over how the business should be run.

"Okay, Dad, so he's your brother. But does that mean we have to put up with inferior work and an erratic schedule that we would never tolerate from anyone else in the business?"[44] This complaint introduces a problem that can all too often set the stage for failure in a family business—the **family business feud**. Simply put, members of the controlling family get into disagreements about work responsibilities, business strategy, operating approaches, finances, or other matters.

ethics > KNOW RIGHT FROM WRONG

> *For each pair of shoes it sells, this caring capitalism firm donates another pair to needy children.*

Entrepreneurship Meets Caring Capitalism Meets Big Business

Would or do you buy shoes just because the company that sells them also is pledged to philanthropy? Blake Mycoskie, founder of TOMS Shoes, wants you to do just that. He says: "giving back feels good, and that alone is a reason to make it part of your life and part of your business . . . When you incorporate giving into your model, your customers become your marketers."

Mycoskie's journey to entrepreneurship began on the reality TV show, *The Amazing Race,* which whetted his appetite for travel. He had a revelation while visiting Argentina and after coming face to face with lots of young children without shoes. He would return home and start a sustainable business to help address the problem. He named the business TOMS, short for "better tomorrow."

TOMS sells shoes made in a classic Argentinean style, but with a twist. For each pair of shoes sold, TOMS donates a pair to needy children. Mycoskie calls this One for One, a "movement" that involves "people making everyday choices that improve the lives of children." The business model is reflective of what's been called Caring Capitalism or profits with principles. TOMS has expanded to include eyewear. Buy a pair of eyeglasses and the firm will pay for saving someone's eyesight with prescription glasses and medical care. Further product expansion seems likely.

Who knows what the future holds for TOMS if it grows to the point where corporate buyers begin to take an interest in the company. It's happened to profits-with-principles businesses in the past. For example, Ben & Jerry's is now owned by Unilever and Tom's of Maine is owned by Colgate-Palmolive. Many states are now passing laws creating the "benefit corporation" as a new legal entity. It is designed to protect firms whose charters spell out special values; it also requires them to report their social benefit activities and impact.

WHAT DO YOU THINK?

Is TOMS' business model one that other entrepreneurs could—or should—adopt? Is it ethical to link personal philanthropic goals with the products that a for-profit business sells? Which stakeholders' interests take precedence when issues of philanthropic enterprise come into focus? When an entrepreneurial firm is founded on a caring capitalism model, is it ethical for a future buyer of the business to reduce or limit the emphasis on social benefits? What about if/when the company goes public, and shareholders' interests become a relevant issue in the decision-making process? Is the concept of the benefit corporation the way we as a society should be heading?

Although this example is of an intergenerational problem, the feud can be between spouses, among siblings, or between parents and children. It really doesn't matter. Unless family disagreements are resolved to the benefit of the business itself, the firm will have difficulty surviving in a highly competitive environment.

Family businesses also can suffer from the **succession problem**—transferring leadership from one generation to the next. A survey of small and midsized family businesses showed that 66% of these firms planned to keep the business within the family.[45] But the key management questions are: How will the assets be distributed, and who will run the business when the current head leaves? A family business that has been in operation for some time is often a source of both business momentum and financial wealth. Ideally, both are maintained in the succession process. But data on succession are quite sobering. Approximately 30% of family firms survive to the second generation; 12% survive to the third; and only 3% are expected to survive beyond that.[46]

Business advisers recommend having a **succession plan**—a formal statement that describes how the leadership transition and related financial matters will be handled during changeover. A succession plan should include procedures for choosing or designating the firm's new leadership, legal aspects of any ownership transfer, and financial and estate plans relating to the transfer. This plan should be shared and understood by all employees affected by it. The chosen successor

> The **succession problem** is the issue of who will run the business when the current head leaves.

> A **succession plan** describes how the leadership transition and related financial matters will be handled.

should be prepared through experience and training to perform in the new role when the time comes to take over the business.

Small Business Development

Business incubators offer space, shared services, and advice to help get small businesses started.

One way that startup difficulties can be managed is for business owners to join a **business incubator**. Sometimes called *business accelerators*, these are special facilities that offer space, shared administrative services, special equipment, and management advice at reduced costs. The goal is to help new businesses become healthy enough to survive on their own. Some incubators are focused on specific business areas, such as technology, light manufacturing, or professional services; some provide access to expensive equipment like laser cutters and 3-D printing; some are located in rural areas, while others are based in urban centers; some focus only on socially responsible businesses.

Regardless of their focus or location, business incubators seek to increase the survival rates for new startups. Their goal is to help build new businesses that will create new jobs and expand economic opportunities in their local communities. An example is Y Combinator, an incubator located in Mountain View, California. It was founded by Paul Graham with a focus on Web businesses, and supports about 10 startups at any given time. Member entrepreneurs get offices, regular meetings with Graham and other business experts, and access to potential investors. They also receive $15,000 grants in exchange for the incubator taking a 6% ownership stake. Prominent Y Combinator graduates include Airbnb and Dropbox, and more than 500 startups have received its help.[47]

Small Business Development Centers founded with support from the U.S. Small Business Administration provide advice to new and existing small businesses.

Another resource for small business development is the U.S. Small Business Administration. Because small business plays such a significant role in the economy, the SBA works with state and local agencies as well as the private sector to support a network of over 1,100 **Small Business Development Centers** (SBDCs) nationwide.[48] These SBDCs offer guidance to entrepreneurs and small business owners (both actual and prospective) on how to set up and manage business operations. These centers are often associated with colleges and universities, and some give students a chance to work as consultants with small businesses at the same time that they pursue their academic programs.

Learning Check 2

TAKEAWAYQUESTION **2 How do small businesses get started and what common problems do they face?**

BE SURE YOU CAN • give the SBA definition of *small business* • discuss the succession problem in family-owned businesses and possible ways to deal with it • list several reasons why many small businesses fail • explain how business incubators work and how both they and SBDCs can help new small businesses

New Venture Creation

TAKEAWAY 3   How do entrepreneurs start, legally structure, and finance new business ventures?

LEARN MORE | Life cycles of entrepreneurial firms • Writing a business plan
ABOUT | Choosing the form of ownership • Financing the new venture

Whether your interest is low-tech or high-tech, online or bricks and mortar, opportunities for new ventures are always there for true entrepreneurs. Entrepreneurs start with good ideas and the courage to give them a chance. But in order to succeed, entrepreneurs must then master the test

FIGURE 6.3
Stages in the life cycle of an entrepreneurial firm.

of strategy and competitive advantage. Can you identify a market niche or a new market that is being missed by other established firms? Can you generate a first-mover advantage by exploiting a niche or entering a market before other competitors establish themselves? Do you have a viable business model, or a plan, for your business? These are among the questions that entrepreneurs must ask and answer in the process of beginning a new venture.

Life Cycles of Entrepreneurial Firms

Figure 6.3 describes the stages common to the life cycles of entrepreneurial companies. It shows the relatively typical progression from birth to breakthrough to maturity. The firm begins with the *birth stage*—where the entrepreneur struggles to get the new venture established and to survive long enough to test the viability of the underlying business model in the marketplace. The firm then passes into the *breakthrough stage*—where the business model begins to work well, the firm grows, and the complexity of managing the business expands significantly. Finally, the firm enters the *maturity stage*—where the entrepreneur experiences market success and financial stability, while also facing the continuing management challenges associated with remaining competitive in a changing environment.

Entrepreneurs often face control problems and other management dilemmas when their firms start to grow rapidly. The problems often involve the different skills needed for entrepreneurial leadership in the early life cycle stages versus strategic leadership in the later stages of maturity. Entrepreneurial leadership helps to bring ventures into being and steers ventures through the early stages of life. Strategic leadership requires managing and leading the venture into maturity as an ever-evolving and still-growing enterprise. If the founding entrepreneur doesn't have the skills or interests required to meet the firm's strategic leadership needs, its continued success may depend on selling to other owners or passing day-to-day management to professionals with these skills.

Writing a Business Plan

When people start new businesses or launch new units within existing businesses, they can benefit from a good **business plan**. This plan describes the details needed to obtain startup financing and operate a new business.[49] Banks and other sources of finance want to see a business plan before they loan money or invest in a new venture. Senior managers want to see a business plan before they allocate scarce organizational resources to support a new entrepreneurial project. There's good reason for this.

A **business plan** describes the direction for a new business and the financing needed to operate it.

insight > LEARN ABOUT YOURSELF

> *To be strong in self-management, you need lots of self-awareness plus the ability to self-regulate.*

Self-Management Keeps You Growing

Entrepreneurship involves risk, confidence, insight, and more. But for those who have both the desire to attempt new things and **self-management** skills, it's a course with the potential for great personal and financial reward. Self-management skills reflect the ability to be objective in understanding personal strengths and weaknesses, and the capacity to make personal changes to continue improving and growing—both personally and professionally.

Being strong in self-management requires a great deal of self-awareness in addition to the ability to self-regulate. Self-management requires self-knowledge as a person and in relationships with others, the exercise of initiative, acceptance of responsibility for good and bad behavior and accomplishments, and continuing adaptation for self-improvement. Self-management skills are critical for anyone seeking a successful career or wanting to do well in school, at work, and in everyday life. We are operating in challenging times full of uncertainty, change, and increasing complexity. The skills that serve us professionally and personally today may not serve well tomorrow as the relationships and technologies that define our lives continue to evolve.

Look at the self-management tips in the nearby box. These and other foundational tools for career success are available and can be grown and developed. But the motivation and the effort required to succeed through self-management must come from within. Only you can make the commitment to take charge of your personal and professional destiny and become a self-manager.

Self-Management Tips for Career Success

- *Perform to your best.* No matter what the assignment, you must work hard to quickly establish your credibility and work value.
- *Be and stay flexible.* Don't hide from ambiguity. Don't wait for structure. You must always adapt to new work demands, new situations, and new people.
- *Keep the focus.* You can't go forward without talent. Be a talent builder—always adding to and refining your talents to make them valuable to an employer.
- *Do the work.* Practice makes perfect. Like a professional golfer, you have to hit lots and lots of practice balls in order to make perfect shots during the match.
- *Don't give up.* Certainly never give up too soon. You have to stick with it, even during tough times. Remember—resilience counts. If you have talent and know what you love, go for it. Self-management is a way to realize your dreams.

GET TO KNOW YOURSELF BETTER

One of the best ways to check your capacity for self-management is to examine how you approach college, your academic courses, and the rich variety of development opportunities available on and off campus. Ask: What activities am I involved in currently? How well do I balance these activities with academic and personal responsibilities? Do I miss deadlines or turn in assignments pulled together at the last minute? Do I accept poor or mediocre performance? Do I learn from my mistakes?

The detailed thinking required to prepare a business plan can contribute to the success of the new initiative. It forces the entrepreneur to be clear about the business model and think through important issues and challenges—financial, competitive, and managerial—before starting out. Ed Federkeil, who founded a small business called California Custom Sport Trucks, says: "It gives you direction instead of haphazardly sticking your key in the door every day and saying, 'What are we going to do?'"[50] More thoughts on why you need a business plan are presented in the box on the next page.[51]

Although there is no single template, it is generally agreed that a good business plan includes an executive summary, covers certain business fundamentals, is well organized with headings, is easy to read, and runs no more than about 20 pages in length. Here is a sample business plan outline.[52]

• *Executive summary*—overview of the business purpose and the business model for making money.

◄ What goes in a business plan

• *Industry analysis*—nature of the industry, including economic trends, important legal or regulatory issues, and potential risks.

• *Company description*—mission, owners, and legal form.

• *Products and services description*—major goods or services, with competitive uniqueness.

• *Market description*—size of market, competitor strengths and weaknesses, five-year sales goals.

• *Marketing strategy*—product characteristics, distribution, promotion, pricing, and market research.

• *Operations description*—manufacturing or service methods, supplies and suppliers, and control procedures.

Why You Need a Business Plan

• It forces you to be clear about your business model—how your business will make money.

• It makes you identify and confront the potential strengths and weaknesses of your proposed business.

• It makes you examine the market potential for your business's products or services.

• It makes you examine the strengths and weaknesses of the competitors for your proposed business.

• It helps you clarify the mission and key directions for the business, helping you to stay focused.

• It helps you determine how much money will be needed to launch and operate the business.

• It helps you communicate more confidently and credibly with potential lenders and investors.

• *Staffing description*—management and staffing skills needed and available, compensation, and human resource systems.

• *Financial projection*—cash flow projections for one to five years, break-even points, and phased investment capital.

• *Capital needs*—amount of funds needed to run the business, amount available, and amount requested from new sources.

• *Milestones*—a timetable of dates showing when key stages of the new venture will be completed.

Choosing a Form of Ownership

One of the important choices that must be made in starting a new venture is the legal form of ownership. A number of ownership alternatives are most common, and making the choice among these alternatives requires careful consideration of their respective advantages and disadvantages in light of the proposed business.

A **sole proprietorship** is simply an individual or a married couple pursuing business for a profit. This does not involve incorporation. One does business, for example, under a personal name—such as "Tiaña Lopez Designs." A sole proprietorship is simple to start, run, and terminate, and it is the most common form of small business ownership in the United States. However, the business owner is personally liable for business debts and claims.

A **partnership** is formed when two or more people agree to start and operate a business together. It is usually backed by a legal and written partnership agreement. Business partners

A sole proprietorship is an individual pursuing business for a profit.

A partnership is when two or more people agree to contribute resources to start and operate a business together.

agree on the relative contribution of resources and skills to the new venture, and on the sharing of profits and losses. The simplest and most common form is a *general partnership* where the partners share management responsibilities. A *limited partnership* consists of a general partner and one or more "limited" partners who do not participate in day-to-day business management. They share in the profits, but their losses are limited to the amount of their investment. A *limited liability partnership*, common among professionals such as accountants and attorneys, limits the liability of one partner for the negligence of another.

A **corporation**, commonly identified by the "Inc." designation in a company name, is a legal entity that is chartered by the state and exists separately from its owners. The corporation can be for-profit, such as Microsoft, Inc., or nonprofit, such as Count-Me-In, Inc.—a firm featured early in the chapter for helping female entrepreneurs get started with small loans. The corporate form offers two major advantages: (1) It grants the organization certain legal rights (e.g., to engage in contracts), and (2) the corporation becomes responsible for its own liabilities. This separates the owners from personal liability and gives the firm a life of its own that can extend beyond the life of its owners. The disadvantage of incorporation rests largely with the cost of incorporating and the complexity of required documentation.

The **benefit corporation** is a new corporate form for businesses with stated goals to benefit society while making a profit.[53] Businesses that choose this ownership type formally adopt the goals of social entrepreneurship and social enterprises to help solve social and environmental problems. Often called "B Corps" for short, these goals must be stated in the firm's bylaws or rules of incorporation. Each B Corp is required to file an annual "benefit report" as well as an annual financial report so that both social and financial performance can be properly assessed against stated goals. The adoption of this form by a number of larger and well-recognized businesses—Ben & Jerry's, Patagonia, and Etsy, for example—have given the B Corp form growing public visibility.[54]

The **limited liability corporation**, or LLC, has gained popularity because it combines the advantages of the other forms—sole proprietorship, partnership, and corporation. For liability purposes, LLCs function like a corporation and protect owners' assets against claims made against the company. For tax purposes, an LLC functions as a partnership in the case of multiple owners and as a sole proprietorship in the case of a single owner.

Financing a New Venture

Starting a new venture takes money, and that money must often be raised. The cost of setting up a new business or expanding an existing business can easily exceed the amount a would-be entrepreneur has available from personal sources. Initial startup financing might come from personal bank accounts and credit cards. Very soon, however, the chances are that much more money will be needed to sustain and grow the business. There are two major ways an entrepreneur can obtain such outside financing for a new venture.

Debt financing involves going into debt by borrowing money from another person, bank, or financial institution. This loan must be paid back over time, with interest. It also requires collateral that is pledged against business assets or personal assets, such as a home, to secure the loan in case of default. The lack of availability of debt financing became a big issue during the recent financial crisis, and the problem hit entrepreneurs and small business owners especially hard.

Equity financing is an alternative to debt financing. It involves giving ownership shares in the business to outside investors in return for their investment. This money does not need to be paid back. It is an investment, and the investor assumes the risk for potential gains and losses. The equity investor gains some proportionate ownership control in return for taking a risk on the venture.

A corporation is a legal entity that exists separately from its owners.

A benefit corporation, or B Corp, is a corporate form for businesses whose stated goals are to combine making a profit with benefiting society and the environment.

A limited liability corporation (LLC) is a hybrid business form combining the advantages of the sole proprietorship, partnership, and corporation.

Debt financing involves borrowing money that must be repaid over time, with interest.

Equity financing involves exchanging ownership shares for outside investment monies.

Equity financing is usually obtained from **venture capitalists,** companies and individuals that make investments in new ventures in return for an equity stake in the business. Most venture capitalists tend to focus on relatively large investments of $1 million or more, and they usually take a management role, such as a seat on the board of directors, in order to oversee business growth. The hope is that a fast-growing firm will gain a solid market base and be either sold at a profit to another firm or become a candidate for an **initial public offering**, or IPO. An IPO is where shares of stock in the business are first sold to the public and begin trading on a public stock exchange. When an IPO is successful and the share prices are bid up by the market, the original investment made by a venture capitalist and entrepreneur rise in value. The quest for such returns on investment is the business model of the venture capitalist.

When large amounts of venture capital aren't available to the entrepreneur, another financing option is the **angel investor**. An angel investor is a wealthy individual willing to make a personal investment in return for equity in a new venture. Angel investors are especially common and helpful in the very early stages of a startup. Their presence can serve as a positive market signal, raise investor confidence, and help to attract additional venture funding that would otherwise not be available. When Liz Cobb wanted to start her sales compensation firm, Incentive Systems, for example, she contacted 15 to 20 venture capital firms. She was interviewed by 10 and turned down by all of them. After she located $250,000 from two angel investors, the venture capital firms got interested. She was able to obtain her first $2 million in financing and has since built the firm into a 70-plus-employee business.[55]

The rise of social media has given birth to **crowdfunding**, where entrepreneurs go online to obtain startup financing from a "crowd" of willing providers. Kickstarter, for example, focuses on fund-raising for innovative and imaginative projects from software to literature to films and more. Founder Yancy Strickler describes it as "a place of opportunity for anyone to make things happen."[56] Investors don't get ownership rights, but they do get the satisfaction of sponsorship and in some cases early access to the results. Ownership rights are part of the deal at AngelList, a crowdfunding site that offers equity participation and bills itself as the place "Where startups meet investors." AngelList matches entrepreneurs with pools of potential investors—called syndicates—willing to put up as little as $1,000 to back a new venture. All investors are vetted for financial background and legitimacy.[57]

The JOBS Act—Jumpstart Our Business Startups—made it easier for small U.S. companies to sell equity on the Internet. President Obama called crowdfunding a "game changer" when he signed the act in 2012.[58] The U.S. Securities and Exchange Commission, which oversees the practice, has implemented strict guidelines for both investors and the startup entrepreneurs.[59] As you might expect, crowdfunding has both advocates and skeptics. Advocates claim it spurs entrepreneurship by giving small startups a better shot at raising investment capital and helps small investors join in the venture capital area. Skeptics worry that small investors in a crowd may be easy prey for fraudsters because they won't do enough analysis or have the financial expertise to ensure they are making a good investment.[60]

Venture capitalists make large investments in new ventures in return for an equity stake in the business.

An **initial public offering**, or IPO, is an initial selling of shares of stock to the public at large.

An **angel investor** is a wealthy individual willing to invest in a new venture in return for an equity stake.

In **crowdfunding**, entrepreneurs starting new ventures go online to get startup financing from crowds of investors.

Learning Check 3

TAKEAWAYQUESTION 3 **How do entrepreneurs start, legally structure, and finance new business ventures?**

BE SURE YOU CAN • explain the concept of first-mover advantage • illustrate the life cycle of an entrepreneurial firm • identify the major elements in a business plan • differentiate sole proprietorship, partnership, corporation, and limited liability corporation (LLC) • differentiate debt financing and equity financing • explain the roles of venture capitalists and angel investors in new venture financing

Management Learning Review
Get Prepared for **Quizzes and Exams**

SUMMARY

TAKEAWAY QUESTION 1

What is entrepreneurship and who are the entrepreneurs?

- Entrepreneurship is risk-taking behavior that results in the creation of new opportunities.
- A classic entrepreneur is someone who takes risks to pursue opportunities in situations that others may view as problems or threats.
- A serial entrepreneur is someone who starts and runs businesses and other organizations one after another.
- Entrepreneurs tend to be creative, self-confident people who are determined, resilient, adaptable, and driven to excel; they like to be the master of their own destinies.
- Females and minorities are well represented among entrepreneurs, with some being driven by necessity or the lack of alternative, mainstream career options.
- Social entrepreneurs set up social enterprises to pursue novel ways to help solve social problems.

FOR DISCUSSION If "necessity is the mother of invention," will a poor economy result in lots of entrepreneurship and new small business startups?

TAKEAWAY QUESTION 2

How do small businesses get started and what common problems do they face?

- Entrepreneurship results in the founding of many small businesses that offer new jobs and other benefits to local economies.
- The Internet has opened a whole new array of entrepreneurial possibilities for small businesses.
- Family businesses, which are owned and financially controlled by family members, represent the largest percentage of businesses operating worldwide; they sometimes suffer from succession problems.
- Small businesses have a high failure rate, with as many as 60% to 80% failing within five years; many failures result from poor management.

- Entrepreneurs and small business owners can often get help in the startup stages of their venture by working with business incubators and Small Business Development Centers in their local communities.

FOR DISCUSSION Given that so many small businesses fail due to poor management practices, what type of advice and assistance should a Small Business Development Center offer to boost their success rate?

TAKEAWAY QUESTION 3

How do entrepreneurs start, legally structure, and finance new business ventures?

- Entrepreneurial firms tend to follow the life-cycle stages of birth, breakthrough, and maturity, with each stage offering new and different management challenges.
- A new startup should be guided by a good business plan that describes the intended nature of the business, how it will operate, and how financing will be obtained.
- An important choice is the form of business ownership for a new venture, with the proprietorship, corporate, and limited liability forms offering different advantages and disadvantages.
- Two basic ways of financing a new venture are through debt financing—by taking loans, and equity financing—exchanging ownership shares in return for outside investment in the venture.
- Venture capitalists pool capital and make investments in new ventures in return for an equity stake in the business; an angel investor is a wealthy individual who is willing to invest money in return for equity in a new venture.

FOR DISCUSSION If an entrepreneur has a good idea and his or her startup is beginning to take off, is it better to get money for growth by taking an offer of equity financing from an angel investor or taking a business loan from a bank?

SELF-TEST 6

Multiple-Choice Questions

1. _____ is among the personality characteristics commonly found among entrepreneurs.
   (a) External locus of control
   (b) Inflexibility
   (c) Self-confidence
   (d) Low self-reliance

2. When an entrepreneur is comfortable with uncertainty and willing to take risks, these are indicators of someone with a/an _____.
   (a) high tolerance for ambiguity
   (b) internal locus of control
   (c) need for achievement
   (d) action orientation

3. Somewhere around _____ % of American businesses meet the definition of "small business" used by the Small Business Administration.
   (a) 40   (c) 75
   (b) 99   (d) 81

4. When a business owner sells to another person the right to operate that business in another location, this is a business form known as a _____.
   (a) conglomerate
   (b) franchise
   (c) joint venture
   (d) limited partnership

5. A small business owner who is concerned about passing the business on to heirs after retirement or death should prepare a formal _____ plan.
   (a) retirement
   (b) succession
   (c) franchising
   (d) liquidation

6. What is one of the most common reasons why new small business startups often fail?
   (a) The founders lack business expertise.
   (b) The founders are too strict with financial controls.
   (c) The founders don't want fast growth.
   (d) The founders have high ethical standards.

7. When a new business is quick to act and captures a market niche before competitors, this is called _____.
   (a) intrapreneurship
   (b) an initial public offering
   (c) succession planning
   (d) first-mover advantage

8. When a small business is just starting up, the business owner is typically most focused on _____.
   (a) gaining acceptance in the marketplace
   (b) finding partners for expansion
   (c) preparing an initial public offering
   (d) bringing professional skills into the management team

9. At which stage in the life cycle of an entrepreneurial firm does the underlying business model begin to work well and growth starts to occur?
   (a) birth
   (b) early childhood
   (c) maturity
   (d) breakthrough

10. A venture capitalist who receives an ownership share in return for investing in a new business is providing _____ financing.
    (a) debt
    (b) equity
    (c) corporate
    (d) partnership

11. In _____ financing, a business owner borrows money as a loan that must eventually be repaid to the lender along with agreed-upon interest.
    (a) debt
    (b) equity
    (c) partnership
    (d) limited

12. The people who take ownership shares in new ventures in return for providing the entrepreneurs with critical startup funds are called _____.
    (a) business incubators
    (b) angel investors
    (c) SBDCs
    (d) intrapreneurs

13. The _____ form of small business ownership protects owners from any personal losses greater than their original investments; while the _____ form separates them completely from any personal liabilities.
    (a) sole proprietorship, partnership
    (b) general partnership, sole proprietorship
    (c) limited partnership, corporation
    (d) corporation, general partnership

14. The first component of a good business plan is usually a/an _____.
    (a) industry analysis
    (b) marketing strategy
    (c) executive summary of mission and business model
    (d) set of financial milestones

15. If a new venture has reached the point where it is pursuing an IPO, the firm is most likely _____.
    (a) going into bankruptcy
    (b) trying to find an angel investor
    (c) filing legal documents to become a LLC
    (d) successful enough that the public at large will want to buy its shares

Short-Response Questions

16. What is the relationship between diversity and entrepreneurship?

17. What are the major stages in the life cycle of an entrepreneurial firm, and what are the management challenges at each stage?

18. What are the advantages of a limited partnership form of small business ownership?

19. What is the difference, if any, between a venture capitalist and an angel investor?

20. Assume for the moment that you have a great idea for a potential Internet-based startup business. In discussing the idea
with a friend, she advises you to be very careful to tie your
business idea to potential customers and then describe it well
in a business plan. "After all," she says, "you won't succeed
without customers, and you'll never get a chance to succeed
if you can't attract financial backers through a good business
plan." With these words to the wise, you proceed. What questions will you ask and answer to ensure that you are customer-
focused in this business? What are the major areas that you
should address in writing your initial business plan?

ManagementSkills&
Competencies Make yourself **valuable!**

Evaluate Career Situations

What Would You Do?

1. Becoming Your Own Boss
It could be very nice to be your own boss, do your own thing,
and make a decent living in the process. What are your three top
choices for potential business entrepreneurship? How would
you rank them on potential for personal satisfaction and long-
term financial success?

2. Becoming a Social Entrepreneur
Make a list of social problems present in your local community.
Choose one that might be addressed through social entrepreneurship. Explain the basic plan or business model you would
recommend. How will you or another social entrepreneur earn
a living wage from this venture while doing good things for the
community?

3. Making Your Startup Legal
Your small startup textbook-rating website is attracting
followers. One angel investor is willing to put up $150,000 to
help move things to the next level. But, you and your two
co-founders haven't done anything to legally structure the business. You've managed so far on personal resources and a "handshake" agreement among friends. What is the best choice of
ownership to prepare the company for future growth and outside investors?

Reflect on the Self-Assessment

Entrepreneurial Orientation

Instructions

Distribute five points between each pair of statements to indicate the extent to which you agree with "a" and "b."[61]

1. _____ (a) Success as an entrepreneur depends on many
factors. Personal capabilities may have very little to do with
one's success.
_____ (b) A capable entrepreneur can always shape his or her
own destiny.

2. _____ (a) Entrepreneurs are born, not made.
_____ (b) People can learn to be more enterprising even if
they do not start out that way.

3. _____ (a) Whether or not a salesperson will be able to sell his
or her product depends on how effective the competitors are.
_____ (b) No matter how good the competitors are, an effective
salesperson always will be able to sell his or her product.

4. _____ (a) Capable entrepreneurs believe in planning their
activities in advance.
_____ (b) There is no need for advance planning, because no
matter how enterprising one is, there will always be chance
factors that influence success.

5. _____ (a) A person's success as an entrepreneur depends on
social and economic conditions.
_____ (b) Real entrepreneurs can always be successful
irrespective of social and economic conditions.

6. _____ (a) Entrepreneurs fail because of their own lack of
ability and perceptiveness.
_____ (b) Entrepreneurs often fail because of factors beyond
their control.

7. _____ (a) Entrepreneurs are often victims of forces that they
can neither understand nor control.
_____ (b) By taking an active part in economic, social, and
political affairs, entrepreneurs can control events that affect
their businesses.

8. _____ (a) Whether or not you get a business loan depends on
how fair the bank officer you deal with is.
_____ (b) Whether or not you get a business loan depends on
how good your project plan is.

9. _____ (a) When purchasing something, it is wise to collect as
much information as possible and then make a final choice.
_____ (b) There is no point in collecting a lot of information;
in the long run, the more you pay, the better the product is.

10. _____ (a) Whether or not you make a profit in business
depends on how lucky you are.
_____ (b) Whether or not you make a profit in business
depends on how capable you are as an entrepreneur.

11. _____ (a) Some types of people can never be successful entrepreneurs.
_____ (b) Entrepreneurial ability can be developed in different types of people.

12. _____ (a) Whether or not you will be a successful entrepreneur depends on the social environment into which you were born.
_____ (b) People can become successful entrepreneurs with effort and capability irrespective of the social strata from which they originated.

13. _____ (a) These days, business and personal success depend on the actions of government, banks, and other outside institutions.
_____ (b) It is possible to succeed without depending too much on outside institutions. What is required is insight and a knack for dealing with people.

14. _____ (a) Even perceptive entrepreneurs falter quite often because the market situation is very unpredictable.
_____ (b) When an entrepreneur's prediction of the market situation is wrong, he or she is to blame for failing to read things correctly.

15. _____ (a) With effort, people can determine their own destinies.
_____ (b) There is no point in spending time planning. What is going to happen will happen.

16. _____ (a) There are many events beyond the control of entrepreneurs.
_____ (b) Entrepreneurs are the creators of their own experiences.

17. _____ (a) No matter how hard a person works, he or she will achieve only what is destined.
_____ (b) The rewards one achieves depend solely on the effort one makes.

18. _____ (a) Organizational success can be achieved by employing competent and effective people.
_____ (b) No matter how competent the employees are, the organization will have problems if socioeconomic conditions are not good.

19. _____ (a) Leaving things to chance and letting time take care of them helps a person to relax and enjoy life.
_____ (b) Working for things always turns out better than leaving things to chance.

20. _____ (a) The work of competent people will always be rewarded.
_____ (b) No matter how competent one is, it is hard to succeed without contacts.

Scoring

_____ *External Orientation Score.* Total your points for the following items: 1a, 2a, 3a, 4b, 5a, 6b, 7a, 8a, 9b, 10a, 11a, 12a, 13a, 14a, 15b, 16a, 17a, 18b, 19a, 20b.
_____ *Internal Orientation Score.* Total your points for the following items: 1b, 2b, 3b, 4a, 5b, 6a, 7b, 8b, 9a, 10b, 11b, 12b, 13b, 14b, 15a, 16b, 17b, 18a, 19b, 20a.

Interpretation

This Inventory measures the extent to which a person is internally or externally oriented in entrepreneurial activities. Scores greater than 50 indicate more of that orientation. Those who score high on entrepreneurial internality tend to believe that entrepreneurs can shape their own destinies through their own capabilities and efforts. Those who score high on entrepreneurial externality believe that the success of entrepreneurs depends on factors such as chance, political climate, community conditions, and economic environment—factors beyond their own capabilities and control.

Contribute to the Class Exercise

Entrepreneurs among Us

Question

Who are the entrepreneurs or potential entrepreneurs in your class? What kinds of businesses are they involved in?

Instructions

Interview one another to find out who is already an entrepreneur and who would like to be one. Discuss your classmates' entrepreneurial examples and aspirations. Make an inventory of entrepreneurship insights and lessons available within the class. Critique them in terms of successes and failures, both real and potential. Choose one or two to share with the class as a whole. What challenges have these entrepreneurs faced? What funding directions have they pursued? What kinds of relationships have they developed in the process?

Manage a Critical Incident

Craft Brewery In—or Out—of the Money?

As the loan officer of a small community bank, you've just been approached for a commercial business loan. A group of three entrepreneurs are asking for $250,000 to start a craft brewery producing beers with a local flavor. There is already one microbrewery in your town of 20,000 full-timers and another 20,000 university students. It has been linked with a popular tavern and music venue for several years, and recently expanded its brewing capacity to allow distribution into regional markets. The entrepreneurs proposing the new craft brewery include a brewer who learned his trade in Portland, Oregon, and won a national award for a strong, vanilla-mint specialty brew. The plan is to take his expertise and create spin-off brews that will be both national award-winners and local favorites. They want the bank financing to purchase and equip a brewing facility on the outskirts of town.

Questions

What will you look for as positive and negative signals in the business plan? When you meet with the would-be entrepreneurs, what will be the first five questions you will ask and what answers will you want to receive before deciding whether to lend them the funds? Overall, what are the major risks associated with this proposal and what is the probability of it being successful enough to justify a startup loan?

Collaborate on the Team Activity

Community Entrepreneurs

Entrepreneurs are everywhere. Some might live next door to you, many own and operate the small businesses in and around your community, and you might even be one of them—or aspiring to be.

Question

Who are the entrepreneurs in your community and what are they accomplishing?

Instructions

1. Read the local news, talk to your friends and other locals, and think about where you shop. Make a list of the businesses and other organizations that have an entrepreneurial character. Be as complete as possible—look at both commercial businesses and nonprofits.

2. For each of the organizations, do further research to identify the people who are the entrepreneurs responsible for them.

3. Contact as many of the entrepreneurs as possible and interview them. Try to learn how they got started, why, what obstacles or problems they encountered, and what they learned about entrepreneurship that could be passed along to others. Ask for their "founding stories" and ask for advice they might give to aspiring entrepreneurs.

4. Analyze your results for class presentation and discussion. Look for patterns and differences in terms of the entrepreneurs as people, their entrepreneurial experiences, and potential insights into business versus social entrepreneurship.

5. Consider writing short cases of the entrepreneurs you find especially interesting. What kinds of stories would you tell? How would these stories probably end?

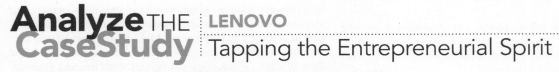

Analyze THE | LENOVO
CaseStudy : Tapping the Entrepreneurial Spirit

Go to *Management Cases for Critical Thinking* at the end of the book to find this case.

THE DECISION-MAKING PROCESS

7

KEY TAKEAWAYS

- Discuss the role of information in the management process.

- Identify how managers approach problems and decisions.

- Describe the six steps in the decision-making process.

- Describe the potential pitfalls and sources of creativity in managerial decision making.

SKILLS MAKE YOU **VALUABLE**

- **EVALUATE** *Career Situations:*
  What Would You Do?

- **REFLECT** *On the Self-Assessment:*
  Cognitive Style

- **CONTRIBUTE** *To the Class Exercise:*
  Lost at Sea

- **MANAGE** *A Critical Incident:*
  Asking for a Raise

- **COLLABORATE** *On the Team Project:*
  Crisis Management Realities

- **ANALYZE** *The Case Study:*
  Amazon.com: One E-Store to Rule
  Them All

Decisions . . . decisions . . . decisions. We all make them and we all have to live with their consequences, both for ourselves and for others affected by them. Managers must gather and use information effectively in order to solve problems and explore opportunities. They must be familiar with the steps in the decision-making process and understand current issues that potentially influence the quality of their decisions and outcomes.

When the San José copper and gold mine collapsed in Chile, 32 miners and their shift leader, Luis Urzúa, were trapped inside.[1] "The most difficult moment was when the air cleared and we saw the rock," said Urzúa. "I had thought maybe it was going to be a day or two days, but not when I saw the rock. . . ." In fact, the miners were trapped 2,300 feet below the surface for 69 days. Getting them out alive was a problem that captured the attention of the entire world.

After the rescue shaft was completed, Urzúa was the last man out. "The job was hard," he said. "They were days of great pain and sorrow." But the decisions Urzúa made as shift leader—organizing the miners into work shifts, keeping them busy, studying mine diagrams, making escape plans, raising morale—all contributed to the successful rescue of the miners. After embracing Urzúa when he arrived at the surface, Chile's President Sebastian Pinera said: "He was a shift boss who made us proud."

Most managers will never have to face such an extreme crisis, but decision making and problem solving are a critical aspect of every manager's job. Not all decisions are going to be easy; some will have to be made under tough conditions; and, not all decisions will turn out right. But as with the case of Luis Urzúa trapped in the Chilean mine with 32 other miners, the goal is to do the best you can under the circumstances.

Information, Technology, and Management

TAKEAWAY 1   What is the role of information in the management process?

LEARN MORE | Information and information systems • Data mining and analytics
ABOUT | Business intelligence and executive dashboards

Tests of our abilities to make good decisions occur every day in situations that may not be crisis driven, but which nevertheless have real consequences for ourselves and others. The challenges begin with the fact that our society is now highly information-driven, digital, socially networked, transparent, and continuously evolving. Career and personal success increasingly require three "must-have" competencies: **technological competency**—the ability to understand new technologies and to use them to their best advantage; **information competency**—the ability to locate, gather, organize, and display information; and **analytical competency**—the ability to evaluate and analyze information to make actual decisions and solve real problems.[2] How about it—are you ready?

Information and Information Systems

This sign should be on every manager's desk—*Warning: Data ≠ Information!* **Data** are raw facts and observations. In contrast, **information** is data made useful and meaningful for decision making. We all have lots of access to data, but we don't always gather and use this data to create useful information that meets the test of these five criteria:

1. *Timely*—The information is available when needed; it meets deadlines for decision making and action.

2. *High quality*—The information is accurate, and it is reliable; it can be used with confidence.

3. *Complete*—The information is complete and sufficient for the task at hand; it is as current and up to date as possible.

4. *Relevant*—The information is appropriate for the task at hand; it is free from extraneous or irrelevant material.

5. *Understandable*—The information is clear and easily understood by the user; it is free from unnecessary detail.

People and organizations perform best when they have available to them the right information at the right time and in the right place. This is the function served by **management information systems** that use the latest technologies to collect, organize, and distribute data. Information departments or centers are now mainstream features on organization charts, and the CIO (chief information officer), CKO (chief knowledge officer), CTO (chief technology officer), or CDO (chief digital officer) are prominent members of the C-suite within top management teams. The number and variety of information-driven career fields are growing fast.

Information systems serve the variety of needs described in Figure 7.1. Within organizations, people need vast amounts of *internal information* to make decisions and solve problems in their daily work. They need information from their immediate work setting and from other parts of the

---

Technological competency is the ability to understand new technologies and to use them to their best advantage.

Information competency is the ability to locate, gather, and organize information for use in decision making.

Analytical competency is the ability to evaluate and analyze information to make actual decisions and solve real problems.

Data are raw facts and observations.

Information is data made useful for decision making.

Management information systems collect, organize, and distribute data for use in decision making.

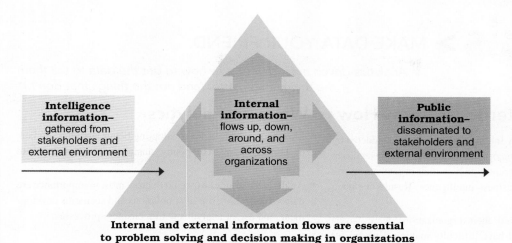

| Intelligence information—gathered from stakeholders and external environment | Internal information—flows up, down, around, and across organizations | Public information—disseminated to stakeholders and external environment |

**Internal and external information flows are essential
to problem solving and decision making in organizations**

FIGURE 7.1
Internal and external information needs in organizations.

organization. Internal information flows downward in the form of goals, instructions, and feedback. It flows horizontally in ways that assist in cross-functional coordination and problem solving. And, it flows upward as performance reports, suggestions for improvement, and even policy and personnel disputes. At the organization's boundaries, information in the external environment is accessed. Managers use this *intelligence information* to deal with customers, competitors, and other stakeholders such as government agencies, creditors, suppliers, shareholders, and community members. Organizations also send vast amounts of *public information* to stakeholders and the external environment. This often takes the form of advertising, public relations campaigns, social media posts, and financial reports that serve a variety of purposes, ranging from image-building to product promotion to financial documentation to damage control.

Data Mining and Analytics

Data mining is the process of analyzing data to produce useful information for decision makers. There is now so much computing power available that we increasingly talk about **big data**, which is collected in huge quantities and is difficult to mine without using sophisticated mathematical and analytical techniques. UPS, for example, spends over $1 billion per year on technology. In one big data program, some 250 million data points are run through an algorithm with over 1,000 pages of code to calculate optimum daily routes for drivers. The company expects to save some $50 million per year from eliminating excess driving miles.[3]

Even when data is available, we don't always use it well. The challenge in data mining, especially when mining big data, comes down to strength in **analytics**. This is sometimes called *business analytics* or *management analytics*, which is the systematic evaluation and analysis of data to make informed decisions. Think, for example, of the vast amounts of data being collected by social media sites. These sites—Facebook, Twitter, LinkedIn, and others—mine the data for their own business uses, and they also sell the data to others. Would you be surprised that the United Nations buys social data from Twitter? It does, and it mines this data for insights into social unrest around the world.[4] Organizations of all types are investing heavily in big data initiatives, hiring people with strong analytics skills, and setting up analytics units and teams to make available data valuable. The top management role of Chief Data Officer is appearing in more C-suites and the job of data scientist is appearing more and more often in help wanted ads.

Data mining is the process of analyzing data to produce useful information for decision makers.

Big data exists in huge quantities and is difficult to process without sophisticated mathematical and computing techniques.

Management with **analytics** involves systematic gathering and processing of data to make informed decisions.

analysis > MAKE DATA YOUR FRIEND

> *Analytics-driven managers "know how to get the data to tell them the things that matter (and not the things that don't.)"*

Intelligent Enterprises Know How to Win with Analytics

A survey on "The New Intelligent Enterprise" conducted by the *Sloan Management Review* asked 3,000 executives from around the world to report on how their organizations use and deal with data for business intelligence. Results included the following:

- 60% of executives said their organizations were "overwhelmed" by data and have difficulty making it useful for performance results.

- Organizations outperforming competitors were three times better at managing and acting on data.

- Top performers were two times more likely than low performers to say they needed to get even better with analytics.

- Top performers use analytics most often in finance, strategy, operations, and sales and marketing.

- Most frequent obstacles to adopting better analytics are lack of understanding, competing management priorities, and lack of skills.

- Analytic techniques expected to grow most in importance are data visualization, use of simulations and scenarios development, and use of analytics within business processes.

YOUR THOUGHTS?

What are the implications for your career planning and development? The consulting firm McKinsey & Co. projects that by 2018, the United States will be short of 1.5 million managers who have the skills to "use data to shape business decisions." Are you prepared to compete for jobs and promotions in career situations where analytics count? How could your local schools, small businesses, and even government agencies gain by better harnessing the power of information and analytics?

Business Intelligence and Executive Dashboards

Business intelligence taps information systems to extract and report data in organized ways that are helpful to decision makers.

Business intelligence is the process of tapping or mining information systems to extract data that is most potentially useful for decision makers. It sorts and reports data in organized ways that help decision makers detect, digest, and deal with patterns posing important implications. Some of that data provides *competitive information*. At Amazon, for example, a "competitive intelligence" team buys products from other retailers to check on their quality, speed, and customer service. Data on the purchases is presented to top management and analyzed to keep Amazon ahead of the competition.[5] Some of that data provides *big picture information*. For example, companies can now easily share the latest financial results across different levels in the organization so that employees know current profits and how they compare to past results and desired targets. Other data provides *function-specific information*. An example is ensuring that manufacturing workers are always aware of costs, marketing people are aware of sales expenses relative to sales revenues, and customer service employees know cost per service contact.[6]

Executive dashboards visually display graphs, charts, and scorecards of key performance indicators and information on a real-time basis.

One of the trends in business intelligence is the use of **executive dashboards** that visually display and update key performance metrics in the form of graphs, charts, and scorecards in real time. The Chief Financial Officer of the manufacturing firm Ceradyne says: "If numbers are the language of business, then dashboards are the way we drive the business forward." He adds that they "take the daily temperature of a business."[7] Picture a sales manager whose office wall has a large flat-panel computer display much like the one you might use for TV and games at home. But this display calls up one or more dashboards filled with a wide range of real-time information including, for example, sales by product, salesperson, and sales area, as well as tracking comparisons with past performance and current sales targets. How can a manager with this kind of information fail to make well-informed decisions?

Learning Check 1

TAKEAWAYQUESTION **1 What is the role of information in the management process?**

BE SURE YOU CAN • define and give examples of *technological competency, information competency, and analytical competency* • differentiate data and information • list the criteria of useful information • describe the role of information systems in organizations • explain the importance of analytics and business intelligence • discuss how IT is reducing barriers within organizations and between organizations and their environments

Problem Solving and Managerial Decisions

TAKEAWAY 2   How do managers address problems and make decisions?

LEARN MORE | Managers as problem solvers • Problem-solving approaches and styles
ABOUT | Types of problem-solving decisions • Types of decision environments

Information is the anchor point for effective decision making. It helps us sense the need for a decision, frame an approach to the decision, and discuss the decision with others.[8] An essential part of a manager's job, as depicted in Figure 7.2, is to serve as a nerve center for the flow of information.[9] Managers are information processors who continually use relationships and technology to gather, share, and receive information. Managers who fulfill this aspect of their role well are always turned on and always connected.

Managers as Problem Solvers

Sometimes the problems are big things—how a small local retailer can compete with the big chains. Other times they're smaller but still consequential things—how to handle the Fourth of

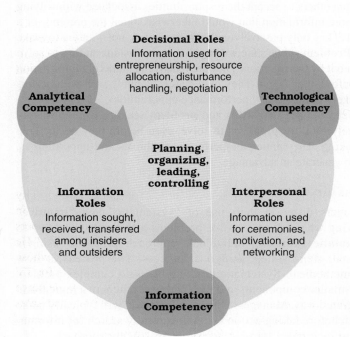

FIGURE 7.2
The manager as an information processor and nerve center for planning, organizing, leading, and controlling.

Problem solving involves identifying and taking action to resolve problems.

A decision is a choice among possible alternative courses of action.

A performance threat is a situation in which something is obviously wrong or has the potential to go wrong.

A performance opportunity is a situation that offers the chance for a better future if the right steps are taken.

July holiday staffing when everyone on the team wants the day off. Sometimes it's being able to recognize and correct an outright mistake—such as when the wrong item has been shipped to an important customer. What we are talking about in all such situations is a manager's skill with **problem solving**, the process of identifying a discrepancy between an actual and a desired state of affairs, and then taking corrective action to resolve the problem.

Success in problem solving comes depends on information to make good **decisions**—choices among alternative possible courses of action. Managers, in this sense, make decisions while facing a continuous stream of daily problems. The most obvious situation is a **performance threat** in which something is already wrong or has the potential to go wrong. This happens when actual performance is less than desired or is moving in an unfavorable direction. Examples are when turnover or absenteeism suddenly increases in the work unit, when a team member falls behind in work, or when a customer complains about service delays. Another important situation emerges as a **performance opportunity** that offers the chance for better future performance if the right steps are taken. This happens when an actual situation either turns out better than anticipated or offers the potential to exceed expectations.

Problem-Solving Approaches and Styles

Problem: Airline aisles are clogged during boarding with frustrated passengers. Airline executives know that minutes saved in boarding can mean money saved.

Analysis: A study by astrophysicist Jason Steffen shows that boarding alternating rows back to front and boarding window–middle–aisle for each row beats other methods.

Result: Airline executives may be as stuck in their thinking as their passengers are in the aisles. Most have no plans to change current boarding systems.[10]

Openness to Problem Solving

Problem avoiders ignore information indicating a performance opportunity or threat.

Problem solvers try to solve problems when they occur.

Problem seekers constantly process information looking for problems to solve, even before they occur.

Even when presented with good information, managers often differ in their openness to problem solving. Some are more willing than others to accept the responsibilities associated with solving a problem. **Problem avoiders** ignore information that would otherwise signal the presence of a performance opportunity or threat. They only passively gather information, not wanting to make decisions or deal with problems. **Problem solvers** are willing to make decisions and try to solve problems, but only when forced into it by the situation. They are reactive in gathering information to solve problems after, but not before, they occur. They may deal reasonably well with performance threats, but they also are likely to miss many performance opportunities.

There is quite a contrast between the last two styles and **problem seekers** who constantly process information and proactively look for problems to solve, even before they occur. True problem seekers are forward thinking. They anticipate performance threats and opportunities, and they take preemptive action to generate an advantage.

Systematic and Intuitive Thinking

Systematic thinking approaches problems in a rational and analytical fashion.

Systematic and Intuitive Thinking

Systematic thinker approaches problems in a step-by-step and linear fashion

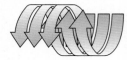

Intuitive thinker approaches problems in flexible and spontaneous fashion

Managers differ in their use of "systematic" and "intuitive" thinking when trying to solve problems and make decisions. In **systematic thinking**, individuals approach problems using a rational, step-by-step, analytical process. The process is slow and methodical. Systematic thinking breaks a complex problem into smaller components and then addresses them in a logical and integrated way. Managers who are systematic will typically make a plan before taking action and will carefully search for information to facilitate a step-by-step problem-solving approach.

Someone using **intuitive thinking** is more flexible and spontaneous in problem solving.[11] This process involves a quick and broad evaluation of the situation as well as possible alternative courses of action. Managers who are intuitive will generally deal with many aspects of a problem at once, jumping from one issue to another, and consider "hunches" based on experience or spontaneous ideas. This approach is often imaginative and tends to work best in situations where facts are limited and there are few decision precedents.[12]

Amazon.com's Jeff Bezos recognizes that it's not always possible for the firm's top managers to make systematic fact-based decisions. There are times, he says, when "you have to rely on experienced executives who've honed their instincts" and are able to make good judgments.[13] There's clearly a place for both systematic and intuitive decision making in management. Intuition balanced by support from good solid analysis, experience, and effort can be a great combination.[14]

Multidimensional Thinking

Managers often deal with portfolios of problems that encompass multiple and interrelated issues. This requires **multidimensional thinking**—an ability to view many problems simultaneously, in relationship to one another and across both long and short time horizons.[15] The best managers are able to "map" multiple problems into a network that can be actively managed over time as priorities, events, and demands continuously change. They are able to make decisions and take actions in the short run that benefit longer-run objectives. And, they also avoid being sidetracked while sorting through a shifting mix of daily problems. Harvard scholar Daniel Isenberg calls this skill **strategic opportunism**—the ability to remain focused on long-term objectives while being flexible enough to resolve short-term problems and opportunities in a timely way.[16]

Cognitive Styles

When US Airways Flight 1549 was in trouble and pilot Chesley ("Sully") Sullenberger decided to land in the Hudson River, he had both a clear head and a clear sense of what he had been trained to do. The landing was successful and all of the 155 passengers and crew aboard the Airbus A320-214 survived. Called a "hero" for his efforts, Sullenberger described his thinking this way:[17]

> I needed to touch down with the wings exactly level . . . with the nose slightly up. I needed to touch down at . . . a descent rate that was survivable. And I needed to touch down just above our minimum flying speed but not below it. . . . I needed to make all these things happen simultaneously.

This example highlights **cognitive styles**, or the way individuals deal with information while making decisions. If you take the end-of-chapter self-assessment, it will allow you to examine your cognitive style in problem solving as a contrast of tendencies toward information gathering—*sensation versus intuition*—and information evaluation—*feeling versus thinking*. Most likely, Sully Sullenberger would score high in both sensation and thinking, and that is probably an ideal type for a pilot.

People with different cognitive styles are likely to approach problems and make decisions in very different ways. It is helpful to understand the four styles shown here along with their characteristics, both for yourself and as you see them in others.[18]

- *Sensation Thinkers*—STs tend to emphasize the impersonal rather than the personal and take a realistic approach to problem solving. They like hard "facts," clear goals, certainty, and situations characterized by high levels of control.

Intuitive thinking approaches problems in a flexible and spontaneous fashion.

Multidimensional thinking is an ability to address many problems at once.

Strategic opportunism focuses on long-term objectives while being flexible in dealing with short-term problems.

Cognitive styles are shown by the ways individuals deal with information while making decisions.

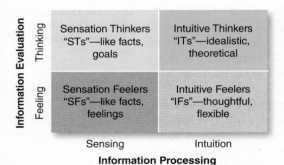

Information Evaluation

Thinking — Sensation Thinkers "STs"—like facts, goals | Intuitive Thinkers "ITs"—idealistic, theoretical

Feeling — Sensation Feelers "SFs"—like facts, feelings | Intuitive Feelers "IFs"—thoughtful, flexible

Sensing   Intuition

Information Processing

- *Intuitive Thinkers*—ITs are comfortable with abstraction and unstructured situations. They tend to be idealistic, prone to intellectual and theoretical positions; they are logical and impersonal but also tend to avoid details.

- *Intuitive Feelers*—IFs prefer broad and global issues. They are insightful and also tend to avoid details, being comfortable with intangibles; they value flexibility and human relationships.

- *Sensation Feelers*—SFs tend to emphasize both analysis and human relations. They primarily have a realistic approach and prefer facts to speculation; they are open communicators and sensitive to feelings and values.

Structured and Unstructured Problems

Structured problems are straightforward and clear with respect to information needs.

A programmed decision applies a solution from past experience to a routine problem.

Unstructured problems have ambiguities and information deficiencies.

A nonprogrammed decision applies a specific solution crafted for a unique problem.

Managers sometimes face **structured problems** that are familiar, straightforward, and clear with respect to information needs. Because these problems are routine and occur over and over again, they can be dealt with through **programmed decisions** that use solutions or decision rules already available from past experience. Although not always predictable, routine problems can be anticipated. This allows for decisions to be programmed in advance and then executed as needed. In human resource management, for example, problems are common whenever decisions are made about pay raises and promotions, vacation requests, committee assignments, etc. Forward-looking managers use this understanding to decide in advance how to handle complaints and conflicts when and if they arise, essentially standardizing their approach to these decisions.

Managers also deal with **unstructured problems** that are new or unusual situations characterized by ambiguities and information deficiencies. These problems require **nonprogrammed decisions** where novel solutions are specifically crafted to meet the demands of the unique situation at hand. Many, if not most, problems faced by higher-level managers are unstructured, often involving the choice among different strategies and objectives in uncertain situations.

Crisis Problems

A crisis decision occurs when an unexpected problem arises that can lead to disaster if not resolved quickly and appropriately.

Think back to the opening example of shift leader Luis Urzúa and the Chilean mine disaster. This case represents one of the most challenging of all decision situations—a **crisis decision**. This appears as an unexpected problem that can lead to disaster if not resolved quickly and appropriately. The ability to handle a crisis could well be the ultimate test of any manager's decision-making capabilities.[19] Urzúa certainly passed this test with flying colors. Not everyone does as well in crisis situations. In fact, we sometimes react to a crisis by doing exactly the wrong things.

Researchers tell us that managers often err in crisis situations by isolating themselves and trying to solve the problem alone or as part of a small closed group.[20] But, this tendency to close ranks limits access to crucial information at the very time that it is most needed. And it not only sets things up for poor decisions—it may create even more problems as the situation escalates. When Toyota recalled over 5 million vehicles for quality defects—a real disaster for the brand—one observer said: "Crisis management does not get any more woeful than this."[21] The poor crisis management was blamed on a corporate culture that discouraged transparency and public disclosure of quality problems. Toyota's CEO Akio Toyoda's and the firm were criticized for "initially denying, minimizing and mitigating the problems."[22]

Good information systems and active problem seeking can help managers get on top of crisis situations. Good preparation helps as well; there's no need to wait for crises to hit before figuring out how to best deal with them. Managers can be assigned to crisis management teams ahead of time, and crisis management plans can be developed to deal with various contingencies. Just as police departments and community groups plan ahead and train to handle civil and natural disasters, managers and work teams also can plan ahead and train to deal with organizational crises. Many organizations offer crisis management workshops that address issues like the rules shown in the box on the right. The intent of these programs is to prepare managers for unexpected high-impact events that threaten an organization's health and well-being.

Six Rules for Crisis Management

1. *Figure out what is going on*—Take the time to understand what's happening and the conditions under which the crisis must be resolved.
2. *Remember that speed matters*—Attack the crisis as quickly as possible, trying to catch it when it is as small as possible.
3. *Remember that slow counts, too*—Know when to back off and wait for a better opportunity to make progress with the crisis.
4. *Respect the danger of the unfamiliar*—Understand the danger of all-new territory where you and others have never been before.
5. *Value the skeptic*—Don't look for and get too comfortable with agreement; appreciate skeptics and let them help you see things differently.
6. *Be ready to "fight fire with fire"*—When things are going wrong and no one seems to care, you may have to start a crisis to get their attention.

Problem-Solving Environments

Figure 7.3 shows that problems must be solved in three different decision conditions or environments—certainty, risk, and uncertainty. Although managers have to make decisions in each of these environments, the conditions of risk and uncertainty are common at higher levels of management where problems are more complex and unstructured.

Certain Environment

The most favorable decision situation for a manager or team leader is to face a problem in a **certain environment**. This is an ideal decision-making situation because full and complete factual information is available about possible alternative courses of action and their outcomes. The decision maker's task is simple: Study the alternatives and choose the best solution. Certain environments are nice, neat, and comfortable for decision makers. However, very few managerial problems are like this.

A **certain environment** offers complete information on possible action alternatives and their consequences.

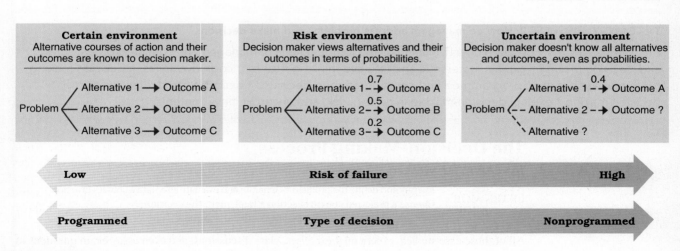

FIGURE 7.3

Three environments for problem solving and decision making.

Risk Environment

A risk environment lacks complete information but offers "probabilities" of the likely outcomes for possible action alternatives.

A basic fact of managerial decision making is that many, if not most, management problems emerge in **risk environments** where facts and information on action alternatives and their consequences are incomplete. Decision making in risk environments requires the use of *probabilities* to estimate the likelihood that a particular outcome will occur (e.g., 4 chances out of 10). Because probabilities are only possibilities, people vary in how they act under risk conditions. Some of us are risk takers and some are risk avoiders; some of us gain from taking risks and others lose.

Domino's Pizza CEO J. Patrick Doyle is a risk taker. When deciding to change the firm's pizza recipe, he ran a television ad admitting that customers really disliked the old one because it was "totally devoid of flavor" and had a crust "like cardboard." Whereas some executives might want to hide or downplay such customer reviews, Doyle used them to help launch the new recipe. He says it was a "calculated risk" and that "we're proving to our customers that we are listening to them by brutally accepting the criticism that's out there."[23]

General Motors' former Vice Chairman of Global Product Development, Bob Lutz, wasn't a risk taker. He once said: "GM had the technology to do hybrids back when Toyota was launching the first Prius, but we opted not to ask the board to approve a product program that'd be destined to lose hundreds of millions of dollars."[24] He and other GM executives either miscalculated the probabilities of positive payoffs from hybrid vehicles or didn't believe the probabilities were high enough to justify the financial risk. Their Japanese competitors, facing the same risk environment, decided differently and gained the early mover advantage.

Uncertain Environment

An **uncertain environment** lacks so much information that it is difficult to assign probabilities to the likely outcomes of alternatives.

When facts are few and information is so poor that managers are unable to even assign probabilities to the likely outcomes of alternatives, an **uncertain environment** exists. This is the most difficult decision-making condition. The high level of uncertainty forces managers to rely heavily on intuition, judgment, informed guessing, and hunches—all of which leave considerable room for error. Perhaps there is no better example of the challenges of uncertainty than the situation faced by government and business leaders as they struggle to deal with global economic turmoil. Even as they struggle to find the right paths forward, great political, social, and economic uncertainties make their tasks difficult and the outcomes of their decisions hard to predict.

Learning Check 2

TAKEAWAYQUESTION 2 **How do managers address problems and make decisions?**

BE SURE YOU CAN • describe how IT influences the four functions of management • define *problem solving* and *decision making* • explain systematic and intuitive thinking • list four cognitive styles in decision making • differentiate between programmed and nonprogrammed decisions • describe the challenges of crisis decision making • explain decision making in certain, risk, and uncertain environments

The Decision-Making Process

TAKEAWAY 3   What are the steps in the decision-making process?

LEARN MORE ABOUT | Identify and define the problem • Generate and evaluate alternative courses of action
Choose a preferred course of action • Implement the decision
Evaluate results • At all steps—check ethical reasoning

All of those case studies, experiential exercises, class discussions, and even essay exam questions in your courses are intended to get students to experience some of the complexities involved in managerial decision making, the potential problems and pitfalls, and even the pressures of crisis situations.

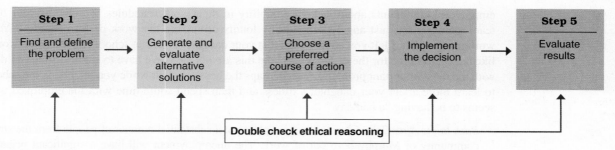

FIGURE 7.4
Steps in the decision-making process.

From the classroom forward, however, it's all up to you. Only you can determine whether you step up and make the best out of very difficult problems, or collapse under pressure.

Figure 7.4 describes five steps in the **decision-making process**: (1) Identify and define the problem, (2) generate and evaluate alternative solutions, (3) choose a preferred course of action, (4) implement the decision, and (5) evaluate results.[25] Importantly, ethical reasoning should be double-checked at all five steps. The decision-making process can be understood within the context of the following short case.

> *The Ajax Case*. On December 31, the Ajax Company decided to close down its Murphysboro plant. Market conditions were forcing layoffs, and the company could not find a buyer for the plant. Some of the 172 employees had been with the company as long as 18 years; others as little as 6 months. All were to be terminated. Under company policy, they would be given severance pay equal to one week's pay per year of service.

This case reflects how competition, changing times, and the forces of globalization can take their toll on organizations, the people who work for them, and the communities in which they operate. Think about how you would feel as one of the affected employees. Think about how you would feel as the mayor of this small town in Illinois. Think about how you would feel as a corporate executive forced to make the difficult business decision to close the plant down.

The decision-making process begins with identification of a problem and ends with evaluation of results.

Step 1—Identify and Define the Problem

The first step in decision making is to find and define the problem. Information gathering and deliberation are critical in this stage. The way a problem is defined can have a major impact on how it is resolved, and it is critical here to clarify exactly what a decision should accomplish. The more specific the goals, the easier it is to evaluate results after the decision is actually implemented. But, three common mistakes can occur in this critical first step in decision making.[26]

Mistake number one is defining the problem too broadly or too narrowly. To take a classic example, the problem stated as "build a better mousetrap" might be better defined as "get rid of the mice." Managers should define problems in ways that give them the best possible range of problem-solving options.

Mistake number two is focusing on symptoms instead of causes. Symptoms are indicators that problems may exist, but they shouldn't be mistaken for the problems themselves. Although managers should be alert to spot problem symptoms (e.g., a drop in performance), they must also dig deeper to address root causes (such as discovering that workers need training in the use of a new IT system).

Mistake number three is choosing the wrong problem to deal with at a particular point in time. For example, which of these three problems would you address first on a busy workday? 1—An e-mail message from your boss requesting a proposal "as soon as possible" on how to handle employees' complaints about lack of flexibility in their work schedules. 2—One of your best team members has just angered another by loudly criticizing her work performance. 3—Your working spouse has left you a voice mail that your daughter is sick at school and the nurse would like her to go home for the day. Choices like this are not easy. We have to set priorities and deal with the most important problems first. Perhaps the boss can wait while you telephone the school to learn more about your daughter's illness and then spend some time with the employee who seems to be having "a bad day."

Back to the Ajax Case. Closing the Ajax plant put a substantial number of people from the small community of Murphysboro out of work. The unemployment will have a significant negative impact on individuals, their families, and the town as a whole. The loss of the Ajax tax base will further hurt the community. The local financial implications of the plant closure will be great, and potentially devastating. The problem for Ajax management is how to minimize the adverse impact of the plant closing on the employees, their families, and the community.

Step 2—Generate and Evaluate Alternative Courses of Action

Once a problem is defined, it is time to assemble the facts and information that can be used to solve it. This is where we clarify exactly what is known and what needs to be known. Extensive information gathering should identify alternative courses of action as well as their potential consequences. Key stakeholders in the problem should be identified, and the effects of possible courses of action on each of these should be considered. Importantly, a course of action can only be as good as the quality of the alternatives considered. The better the pool of alternatives and the more that is known about them, the more likely it is that a good decision will be made.

It is important at this stage to avoid a very common decision-making error—*abandoning the search for alternatives and evaluation of their consequences too quickly*. This often happens due to impatience, time pressure, and plain old lack of commitment. But just because an alternative is convenient doesn't make it the best. It may well have less potential than others that might be discovered with the right approach and adequate time commitment.

Unintended consequences are unanticipated positive or negative side effects that result from a decision.

Decisions often have **unintended consequences** in the form of unanticipated positive or negative side effects. If alternatives are given proper attention, some of these could be identified ahead of time and their implications used to modify and strengthen a decision. A growing number of states and localities, for example, are passing minimum wage laws higher than federal standards. Although the intent is to help low-wage workers fight poverty and cope with living costs, unintended consequences have appeared as affected employers struggle to maintain profits in face of higher labor costs. On the positive side, the higher wages have sometimes driven innovation—for example, a Carl's Jr. owner in California now filters shortening more frequently to extend its life and save costs. On the negative side, the higher wages have sometimes caused layoffs and reduced work hours—for example, a White Castle owner in Illinois eliminated two jobs to protect profit margins without raising prices.[27]

One way to strengthen the search for alternatives is to actively seek consultation and the involvement of others. Adding more people to the process helps brings new perspectives and information to bear on a problem, generates more alternatives for consideration, reveals more about the possible consequences of the alternatives, and can result in a chosen course of action that is better for everyone involved in—and potentially affected by—the decision. Another way to strengthen the search for alternatives is to put each through a systematic and rigorous **cost-benefit analysis**. This compares what an alternative will cost in relation to what it will return in respect to expected benefits. At a minimum, the benefits of an alternative should be greater than its costs to stay in consideration. And, it should also be ethically sound.

Cost-benefit analysis involves comparing the costs and benefits of each potential course of action.

insight > LEARN ABOUT YOURSELF

> *Lacking in confidence, procrastination becomes easy. Too many of us have difficulty deciding, and we have difficulty acting.*

Self-Confidence Builds Better Decisions

Does confidence put a spring into your step and a smile on your face? It's a powerful force, something to be nurtured and protected. Managers need the **self-confidence** not only to make decisions but to take the actions required to implement them. Once decisions are made, managers are expected to rally people to utilize resources and take effective action. This is how problems actually get solved and opportunities get explored. But lacking in confidence, procrastination becomes easy. Too many of us have difficulty deciding, and we have difficulty acting.

How would you proceed with the situation in the box—option A, or B, or C?

Jeff McCracken was the team leader who actually had to deal with this situation. He acted deliberately, with confidence, and in a collaborative fashion. After extensive consultations with the team, he decided to salvage the old track. The team worked 24 hours a day and finished in less than a week. McCracken called it a "colossal job" and said the satisfaction came from "working with people from all parts of the company and getting the job done without anyone getting hurt."

Self-confidence doesn't have to mean acting alone, but it does mean being willing to act. Management consultant Ram Charan calls self-confidence a willingness to "listen to your own voice" and "speak your mind and act decisively." It is, he says, an "emotional fortitude" that counteracts "emotional insecurities."

Decision Time

Situation: A massive hurricane has damaged a railroad bridge over a large lake. The bridge is critical for relief efforts to aid a devastated city. You are leading a repair team of 100. Two alternatives are on the table: Rebuild using new tracks, or rebuild with old track salvaged from the lake.

Question: How do you proceed?

A. Decide to rebuild with new tracks; move quickly to implement.

B. Decide to rebuild with old tracks; move quickly to implement.

C. Consult with team; make decision; move quickly to implement.

GET TO KNOW YOURSELF BETTER

Opportunities to improve your self-confidence are everywhere, but you have to act in order to take advantage of them. What about your involvement in student organizations, recreational groups, intramural sports teams, and community activities? Do a self-check: Make a list of things you are already doing that offer ways to build your self-confidence. What are you gaining from these experiences? Make another list that describes what you could do to gain more experience and add more self-confidence to your skills portfolio between now and graduation. Becoming an officer in a club where you are a member? Starting a new student organization? Organizing a community service project for you and your friends? Becoming a tutor for a class where you did well? Volunteering at a local food bank or homeless shelter?

Back to the Ajax Case. The Ajax plant is going to be closed. Given that, the possible alternative approaches that can be considered are (1) close the plant on schedule and be done with it; (2) delay the plant closing until all efforts have been made to sell it to another firm; (3) offer to sell the plant to the employees and/or local interests; (4) close the plant and offer transfers to other Ajax plant locations; or (5) close the plant, offer transfers, and help the employees find new jobs in and around the town of Murphysboro.

Step 3—Choose a Preferred Course of Action

This is the point where an actual decision is made to select a preferred course of action. Just how this choice occurs and who makes it must be successfully resolved in each problem situation. Management theory recognizes rather substantial differences between the classical and behavioral models of decision making as shown in Figure 7.5.

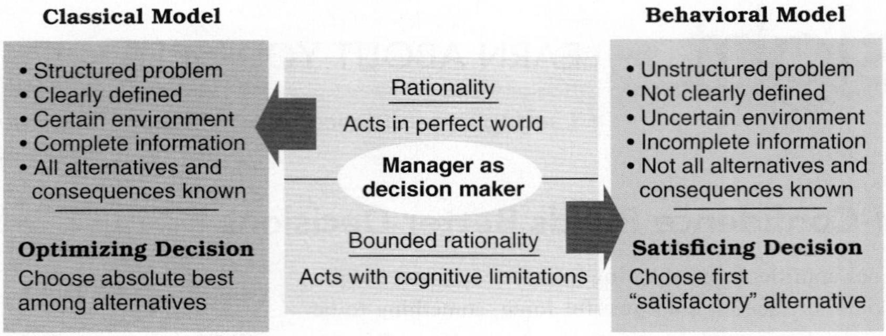

Classical Model

- Structured problem
- Clearly defined
- Certain environment
- Complete information
- All alternatives and consequences known

Optimizing Decision
Choose absolute best among alternatives

Rationality
Acts in perfect world

Manager as decision maker

Bounded rationality
Acts with cognitive limitations

Behavioral Model

- Unstructured problem
- Not clearly defined
- Uncertain environment
- Incomplete information
- Not all alternatives and consequences known

Satisficing Decision
Choose first "satisfactory" alternative

FIGURE 7.5
Differences in the classical and behavioral decision-making models.

Classical Decision Model

The **classical decision model** views the manager as acting rationally in a certain world. The assumption is that a rational choice of the preferred course of action will be made by a decision maker who is fully informed about all possible alternatives. Here, managers face a clearly defined problem and know all possible action alternatives, as well as their consequences. As a result, managers make an **optimizing decision** that gives the absolute best solution to the problem.

Behavioral Decision Model

Behavioral scientists question the assumptions of perfect information underlying the classical model of decision making. Perhaps best represented by the work of scholar Herbert Simon, behavioral decision making instead recognizes that there are *cognitive limitations* on our human information-processing capabilities.[28] These limits make it hard for managers to become fully informed and make optimizing decisions. They create a **bounded rationality**, such that managerial decisions are rational only within the boundaries set by the available information and known alternatives, both of which are incomplete.

Because of cognitive limitations and bounded rationalities, the **behavioral decision model** assumes that people act with only partial knowledge about the available action alternatives and their consequences. As a consequence, the first alternative that appears to offer a satisfactory resolution to the problem is likely to be chosen. Simon, who won a Nobel Prize for his work, calls this the tendency to make **satisficing decisions**—choosing the first satisfactory alternative that comes to your attention. The behavioral model is useful in describing how many decisions get made in the ambiguous and fast-paced problem situations faced by managers today.

> *Back to the Ajax Case.* Ajax executives decided to close the plant, offer transfers to company plants in another state, and offered to help displaced employees find new jobs in and around Murphysboro.

Step 4—Implement the Decision

Once a decision is made, actions must be taken to fully implement it. Nothing new can or will happen unless action is taken to actually solve the problem. Managers not only need the determination and creativity to arrive at a decision, they also need the ability and willingness to implement it.

Difficulties encountered when decisions get implemented may trace to **lack-of-participation error**. This is a failure to adequately involve in the process individuals whose support is necessary

---

The **classical decision model** describes decision making with complete information.

An **optimizing decision** chooses the alternative giving the absolute best solution to a problem.

Bounded rationality describes making decisions within the constraints of limited information and alternatives.

The **behavioral decision model** describes decision making with limited information and bounded rationality.

A **satisficing decision** is the choice of the first satisfactory alternative that comes to one's attention.

Lack-of-participation error is failure to involve in a decision the persons whose support is needed to implement it.

to put the decision into action. Managers who use participation wisely get the right people involved in problem solving from the beginning. When they do, implementation typically follows quickly, smoothly, and to the satisfaction of all stakeholders.

> *Back to the Ajax Case*. Ajax ran ads in the local and regional newspapers. The ad called attention to an "Ajax skill bank" composed of "qualified, dedicated, and well-motivated employees with a variety of skills and experiences." Interested employers were urged to contact Ajax for further information.

Step 5—Evaluate Results

The decision-making process is not complete until results are evaluated. If the desired outcomes are not achieved or if undesired side effects result, corrective action should be taken. Evaluation is a form of managerial control. It involves gathering data to measure performance results and compare these results against established goals. If results are less than what was desired, it is time to reassess and return to earlier steps. In this way, problem solving becomes a dynamic and ongoing activity within the management process. Evaluation is always easier when clear goals, measurable targets, and timetables are established at the outset of the process.

> *Back to the Ajax Case*. How effective were Ajax's decisions? We don't know for sure. But after the advertisement ran for two weeks, the plant's industrial relations manager said: "I've been very pleased with the results." That's all we know, and more information would certainly be needed for a good evaluation of how well management handled this situation. Wouldn't you like to know how many of the displaced employees got new jobs locally and how the local economy held up? You can look back on the case as it was described and judge for yourself. Perhaps you would have approached the situation and the five decision-making steps somewhat differently.

At All Steps—Check Ethical Reasoning

Each step in the decision-making process can and should be linked with ethical reasoning.[29] The choices made often have moral dimensions that might easily be overlooked. For example, job eliminations in the prior Ajax case might not be sufficiently considered for their implications on all stakeholders, including the affected persons, their families, and the local community. We sometimes have to take special care to stay tuned into *virtues*—things like fairness, kindness, compassion, and generosity—and guard against *vices*—things like greed, anger, ignorance, and lust.[30]

One way to check ethical reasoning in decision making is to ask and answer pointed questions that bring critical thinking into the process. Gerald Cavanagh and his associates, for example, suggest that a decision should test positive on these four ethics criteria.[31]

1. *Utility*—Does the decision satisfy all constituents or stakeholders?
2. *Rights*—Does the decision respect the rights and duties of everyone?
3. *Justice*—Is the decision consistent with the canons of justice?
4. *Caring*—Is the decision consistent with my responsibilities to care?

Another way to test ethical reasoning is to consider a decision in the context of full transparency and the prospect of shame.[32] Three **spotlight questions** can be powerful in this regard. *Ask:* "How would I feel if my family found out about this decision?" *Ask:* "How would I feel if this decision were published in the local newspaper or posted on the Internet?" *Ask:* "What would the person you know or know of who has the strongest character and best ethical judgment do in this situation?"

> The **spotlight questions** test the ethics of a decision by exposing it to scrutiny through the eyes of family, community members, and ethical role models.

It is also helpful to check decisions against the hazards of undue rationalizations. Caution is called for when you hear yourself or others saying: "It's just part of the job" . . . "We're fighting fire with fire" . . . "Everyone is doing it" . . . "I've got it coming" . . . "It's legal and permissible" . . . "I'm doing it just for you." Such comments or thoughts are warning signs. If these signs are heeded, it can prompt a review of the decision and perhaps lead to a more ethical outcome.

Learning Check 3

TAKEAWAYQUESTION **3 What are the steps in the decision-making process?**

BE SURE YOU CAN • list the steps in the decision-making process • apply these steps to a sample decision-making situation • explain cost-benefit analysis in decision making • discuss differences between the classical and behavioral decision models • define *optimizing* and *satisficing* • explain how lack-of-participation error can hurt decision making • list useful questions for double-checking the ethical reasoning of a decision

Decision-Making Pitfalls and Creativity

TAKEAWAY 4   What are current issues in managerial decision making?

LEARN MORE ABOUT | Decision errors and traps • Creativity in decision making

Once we accept the fact that we are likely to make imperfect decisions at least some of the time, it makes sense to try to understand why. Two common mistakes are falling prey to decision errors and traps, and not taking full advantage of creativity. Both can be easily avoided.

Decision Errors and Traps

Test: Would you undergo heart surgery if the physician tells you the survival rate is 90%? Chances are you would. But if the physician tells you the mortality rate is 10%, the chances of you opting for surgery are likely to be substantially lower!

What is happening here? Well-intentioned people often rely on simplifying strategies when making decisions with limited information, time pressures, and even insufficient energy. Psychologist Daniel Kahneman describes this as a triumph of *System 1 thinking*—automatic, effortless, quick, and associative—over *System 2 thinking*—conscious, slow, deliberate, and evaluative.[33] In the above test, the simplification of System 1 thinking is called "framing" because the decision to have surgery or not varies according to whether the information is presented as a survival rate—encouraging, or a mortality rate—threatening.[34] This and other simplifying strategies or rules of thumb are known as **heuristics**.[35] Although heuristics can be helpful in dealing with complex and ambiguous situations, they also lead to common decision-making errors.[36]

Heuristics are strategies for simplifying decision making.

Framing Error

Framing error is trying to solve a problem in the context in which it is perceived.

Managers sometimes suffer from **framing error** that occurs when a problem is evaluated and resolved in the context in which it is perceived—either positively or negatively. Suppose, for example, data show that a particular product has a 40% market share. A negative frame views the product as deficient because it is missing 60% of the market. The likely discussion would focus on: "What are we doing wrong?" Alternatively, the frame could be a positive one, looking at the 40% share as a strong market foothold. In this case, the discussion is more likely to proceed with "How can we do things better?" Sometimes people use framing as a tactic for presenting information in a way that gets other people to think within the desired frame. In politics, this is often referred to as "spinning" the data.

Availability Bias

The **availability bias** occurs when people assess a current event or situation by using information that is "readily available" from memory. An example is deciding not to invest in a new product based on your recollection of a recent product failure. The potential bias is that the readily available information is fallible and irrelevant. For example, the product that recently failed may have been a good idea that was released to market at the wrong time of year, or it may have belonged to an entirely different product category.

> The **availability bias** bases a decision on recent information or events.

Representativeness Bias

The **representativeness bias** occurs when people assess the likelihood of something happening based on its similarity to a stereotyped set of occurrences. An example is deciding to hire someone for a job vacancy simply because he or she graduated from the same school attended by your last and most successful new hire. The potential bias is that the representative stereotype masks factors important and relevant to the decision. For instance, the abilities and career expectations of the job candidate may not fit the job requirements; the school attended may be beside the point.

> The **representativeness bias** bases a decision on similarity to other situations.

Anchoring and Adjustment Bias

Anchoring and adjustment bias occurs when decisions are influenced by inappropriate deference to a previous value or starting point. An example is a manager who sets a new salary level for an employee by simply raising her prior year's salary by a small percentage. Although the

> The **anchoring and adjustment bias** bases a decision on incremental adjustments from a prior decision point.

Research Brief

Escalation Increases Risk of Unethical Decisions

When Marc and Vera L. Street reviewed research on escalating commitments to previously chosen courses of action, they realized that little has been done to investigate if escalation tendencies lead to unethical behaviors. To address this void, the researchers conducted an experiment with 155 undergraduate students working on a computerized investment task. They found that exposure to escalation situations increases tendencies toward unethical acts and that the tendencies further increase with the magnitude of the escalation.

Street and Street believe this link between escalation and poor ethics is driven by desires to get out of and avoid the increasing stress of painful situations. Additional findings from the study showed that students with an external locus of control were more likely to choose an unethical decision alternative than their counterparts with an internal locus of control.

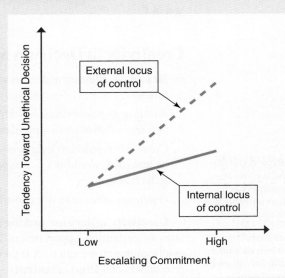

YOU BE THE RESEARCHER

This study was done in the college classroom and under simulated decision conditions. How would you design a study that tests the same hypotheses in the real world? Also, is it possible to design a training program that would use the "Spotlight Questions" to help people better deal with unethical decision options in escalation situations?

increase may appear reasonable to the manager, the decision actually undervalues the employee relative to the job market. The small incremental salary adjustment, reflecting anchoring and adjustment bias, may end up prompting her to look for another, higher-paying job.

Confirmation Error

One of our tendencies after making a decision is to try and find ways to justify it. In the case of unethical acts, for example, we try to "rationalize" them after the fact. This is called **confirmation error**. It means that we notice, accept, and even seek out only information that confirms or is consistent with a decision we have just made. Contrary information that suggests what we are doing is incorrect or unethical is downplayed or denied.

A **confirmation error** occurs when focusing only on information that confirms a decision already made.

Escalating commitment is the continuation of a course of action even though it is not working.

How to Avoid the Escalation Trap in Decision Making

- Set advance limits on your involvement and commitment to a particular course of action; stick with these limits.
- Make your own decisions; don't follow the leads of others, since they are also prone to escalation.
- Carefully assess why you are continuing a course of action; if there are no good reasons to continue, don't.
- Remind yourself of what a course of action is costing; consider saving these costs as a reason to discontinue.
- Watch for escalation tendencies in your behaviors and those of others.

Escalating Commitment

Another decision-making trap is **escalating commitment**. This occurs as a decision to increase effort and perhaps apply more resources to pursue a course of action that is not working.[37] Managers prone to escalation let the momentum of a situation and personal ego overwhelm them. They are unwilling to admit they were wrong and unable to "call it quits," even when the facts indicate that this is the best alternative. This is a common decision error, perhaps one that you are personally familiar with. It is sometimes called the *sunk-cost fallacy*. The nearby box offers advice on how to avoid tendencies toward escalating commitments to previously chosen courses of action.[38]

Creativity in Decision Making

Situation—Elevator riders in a new high-rise building are complaining about long waiting times.

Building engineers' advice—Upgrade the entire system at substantial cost. Why? He assumed that any solutions to a slow elevator problem had to be mechanical ones.

Creativity consultant's advice—Place floor-to-ceiling mirrors by the elevators. Why? People, he assumed, would not notice waiting times because they were distracted by their and others' reflections.

Outcome—the creativity consultant was right.[39]

Creativity in decision making shows up as a novel idea or unique approach to solving problems or exploiting opportunities.[40] The potential for creativity is one of our greatest personal assets, although we often let it go unrecognized. One reason is that we focus too much on what researchers call **Big-C creativity**—when extraordinary things are done by exceptional people.[41] Think Big-C creativity when you use or see someone using an iPhone or iPad—Steve Jobs' creativity, or browse Facebook—Mark Zuckerberg's creativity.

Don't get sidetracked by Big-C creativity alone. There is a lot of **Little-C creativity** around also. It occurs when average people come up with unique ways to deal with daily events and situations. Think Little-C creativity, for example, the next time you solve relationship problems at home, build something for the kids, or even find ways to pack too many items into too small a suitcase.

Creativity is the generation of a novel idea or unique approach that solves a problem or crafts an opportunity.

Big-C creativity occurs when extraordinary things are done by exceptional people.

Little-C creativity occurs when average people come up with unique ways to deal with daily events and situations.

Just imagine what can be accomplished with all the creative potential—Big-C and Little-C—present in an organization. How do you turn that potential into creative decisions? David Kelley, founder of the design firm IDEO, believes that a lot, perhaps most, of us start to lose our creativity skills in primary school.[42] It's something about being taught to look for answers to assigned problems and fearing failure when taking standardized tests. But, he also believes our creativity can be reenergized when we stop fearing failure and commit to **design thinking**. First comes *experiencing*—defining problems by research and observation; not simply accepting the parameters of a problem or issue as delivered. Second comes *ideation*—visualizing and brainstorming potential solutions in collaboration with others. Third comes *prototyping*—testing and modifying the potential solution over and over to achieve the best outcome.

Design thinking unlocks creativity in decision making through a process of experiencing, ideation, and prototyping.

Personal Creativity Drivers

The figure on the right identifies task expertise, task motivation, and creativity skills as personal creativity drivers.[43] This three-component model points us in useful directions for personal creativity development as well as toward management actions that can boost creativity in teams or work units.

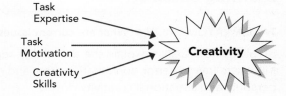

Creative decisions are more likely to occur when an individual has a lot of *task expertise*. Creativity grows from something one is good at or knows about, while extending it in new directions. And, creative decisions are more likely when someone is highly *task-motivated*. Creativity tends to occur in part because people work exceptionally hard to resolve a problem or exploit an opportunity.

Creative decisions also emerge when people have strong personal *creativity skills*. Creative people tend to work with high energy, hold their ground in the face of criticism, and respond in a resourceful way in difficult situations. They have strong associative skills, meaning they are good at making connections among seemingly unrelated facts or events. Creative people also have strong behavioral skills of questioning, observing, networking, and experimenting.[44] They are good at synthesizing information to find correct answers (convergent thinking), looking at diverse ways to solve problems (lateral thinking), and thinking "outside of the box" (divergent thinking).[45]

Situational Creativity Drivers

If you mix creative people and traditional organization and management practices, what will you get? You may not get much. It takes more than individual creativity alone to make innovation a way of life in organizations. Situational creativity drivers are important too.

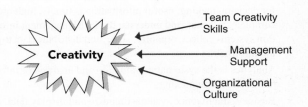

Managers should, of course, staff their organizations and teams with creative members. But they should also realize these *team creativity skills* are most likely to blossom when buoyed by *management support* and the right *organizational culture*. This means things like having a team leader with the patience to allow for creative processes to work themselves through a decision situation. It means having top management that is willing to accept and even celebrate failure, and to provide the resources—time, technology, and space—that are helpful to the creative processes. It also means making creativity a top organizational priority and a core value of the organizational culture.

Think creativity gained the next time you see a young child playing with a really neat toy. It may be from Fisher-Price Toys—part of Mattel, Inc. In the firm's headquarters, you'll find a special place called the "Cave," and it's not your typical office space. Picture bean-bag chairs, soft lighting, and casual couches. It's a place for brainstorming, where designers, marketers, engineers, and others can meet work together without any strings attached to come up with the next great toy for preschoolers. Consultants recommend that such innovation spaces be separated from the normal workplace and be large enough for no more than 15 to 20 people.[46]

Think creativity wasted the next time you watch TV on a beautiful, large, flat-panel screen. In 1964, George H. Heilmeier showed his employers at RCA Labs his new discovery—a liquid-crystal display, or LCD. They played with it until 1968 when RCA executives decided the firm was so heavily invested in color TV tubes that they weren't really interested. Today the market is dominated by Japanese, Korean, and Taiwanese producers, with not a single U.S. maker in the market. Ironically, Heilmeier received the Kyoto Prize, considered the Nobel Prize of Japan, for his pioneering innovation.[47]

Learning Check 4

TAKEAWAYQUESTION 4 **What are current issues in managerial decision making?**

BE SURE YOU CAN • explain the availability, representativeness, and anchoring and adjustment heuristics • illustrate framing error, confirmation error, and escalating commitment in decision making • identify key personal and situational creativity drivers

Management Learning Review
Get Prepared for **Quizzes and Exams**

SUMMARY

TAKEAWAYQUESTION 1

What is the role of information in the management process?

- Technological, information, and analytical competencies are all needed to take advantage of information technology in decision making.

- Data are raw facts and figures; information is data made useful for decision making; useful information is timely, high quality, complete, relevant, and understandable. Management information systems collect, organize, store, and distribute data to meet the information needs of managers.

- Analytics is the systematic evaluation and analysis of information for decision making.

- Business intelligence systems organize and display data, often in the form of dashboards, so that patterns and trends are evident to decision makers.

FOR DISCUSSION What are the potential downsides to the ways IT is changing organizations?

TAKEAWAYQUESTION 2

How do managers address problems and make decisions?

- Managers serve as information nerve centers in the process of planning, organizing, leading, and controlling activities in organizations.

- Managers can display problem avoidance, problem solving, and problem seeking in facing problems.

- Managers vary in the use of systematic and intuitive thinking, and in tendencies toward multidimensional thinking.

- Managers must understand the different cognitive styles people use in decision making.

- Programmed decisions are routine solutions to recurring and structured problems; nonprogrammed decisions are unique solutions to novel and unstructured problems.

- Crisis problems occur unexpectedly and can lead to disaster if not handled quickly and properly.

- Managers face problems and make decisions under conditions of certainty, risk, and uncertainty.

FOR DISCUSSION When would a manager be justified in acting as a problem avoider?

TAKEAWAYQUESTION 3

What are the steps in the decision-making process?

- The steps in the decision-making process are (1) find and define the problem, (2) generate and evaluate alternatives, (3) decide on the preferred course of action, (4) implement the decision, and (5) evaluate the results.

- An optimizing decision, following the classical model, chooses the absolute best solution from a known set of alternatives.
- A satisficing decision, following the behavioral model, chooses the first satisfactory alternative to come to attention.
- To check the ethical reasoning of a decision at any step in the decision-making process, it is helpful to ask the ethics criteria questions of utility, rights, justice, and caring.
- To check the ethical reasoning of a decision at any step in the decision-making process, it is helpful to ask the spotlight questions that expose the decision to transparency in the eyes of family, community members, and ethical role models.

FOR DISCUSSION Do the steps in the decision-making process have to be followed in order?

TAKEAWAYQUESTION 4

What are current issues in managerial decision making?

- Common decision errors and traps include the availability, representativeness, and anchoring and adjustment biases, as well as framing error, confirmation error, and escalating commitment.
- Creativity in decision making can be enhanced by the personal creativity drivers of individual creativity skills, task expertise, and motivation.
- Creativity in decision making can be enhanced by the situational creativity drivers of group creativity skills, management support, and organizational culture.

FOR DISCUSSION Which decision trap seems most evident as an influence on bad choices made by business CEOs today?

S E L F - T E S T   7

Multiple-Choice Questions

1. Among the ways information technology is changing organizations today, _____ is one of its most noteworthy characteristics.
   - **(a)** eliminating the the need for top managers
   - **(b)** reducing information available for decision making
   - **(c)** breaking down barriers internally and externally
   - **(d)** decreasing need for environmental awareness

2. Whereas management information systems use the latest technologies to collect, organize, and distribute data, _____ involves tapping the available data to extract and report it in organized ways that are most useful to decision makers.
   - **(a)** analytics
   - **(b)** business intelligence
   - **(c)** anchoring and adjustment
   - **(d)** optimizing

3. A manager who is reactive and works hard to address problems after they occur is known as a _____.
   - **(a)** problem seeker
   - **(b)** problem avoider
   - **(c)** problem solver
   - **(d)** problem manager

4. A/An _____ thinker approaches problems in a rational and an analytic fashion.
   - **(a)** systematic
   - **(b)** intuitive
   - **(c)** internal
   - **(d)** external

5. A person likes to deal with hard facts and clear goals in a decision situation; she also likes to be in control and keep things impersonal. This person's cognitive style tends toward _____.
   - **(a)** sensation thinking
   - **(b)** intuitive thinking
   - **(c)** sensation feeling
   - **(d)** intuitive feeling

6. The assigning of probabilities for action alternatives and their consequences indicates the presence of _____ in the decision environment.
   - **(a)** certainty
   - **(b)** optimizing
   - **(c)** risk
   - **(d)** satisficing

7. The first step in the decision-making process is to _____.
   - **(a)** identify alternatives
   - **(b)** evaluate results
   - **(c)** find and define the problem
   - **(d)** choose a solution

8. Being asked to develop a plan to increase international sales of a product is an example of the types of _____ problems that managers must be prepared to deal with.
   - **(a)** routine
   - **(b)** unstructured
   - **(c)** crisis
   - **(d)** structured

9. Costs, timeliness, and _____ are among the recommended criteria for evaluating alternative courses of action.
   - **(a)** ethical soundness
   - **(b)** competitiveness
   - **(c)** availability
   - **(d)** simplicity

10. A common mistake made by managers in crisis situations is that they _____.
    - **(a)** try to get too much information before responding
    - **(b)** rely too much on group decision making
    - **(c)** isolate themselves to make the decision alone
    - **(d)** forget to use their crisis management plan

11. The _____ decision model views managers as making optimizing decisions, whereas the _____ decision model views them as making satisficing decisions.
    - **(a)** behavioral, human relations
    - **(b)** classical, behavioral
    - **(c)** heuristic, humanistic
    - **(d)** quantitative, behavioral

12. When a manager makes a decision about someone's annual pay raise only after looking at his or her current salary, the risk is that the decision will be biased because of _____.
    (a) a framing error   (c) anchoring and adjustment
    (b) escalating commitment   (d) strategic opportunism

13. When a problem is addressed according to the positive or negative context in which it is presented, this is an example of _____.
    (a) framing error   (c) availability and adjustment
    (b) escalating commitment   (d) strategic opportunism

14. When a manager decides to continue pursuing a course of action that facts otherwise indicate is failing to deliver desired results, this is called _____.
    (a) strategic opportunism   (c) confirmation error
    (b) escalating commitment   (d) the risky shift

15. Personal creativity drivers include creativity skills, task expertise, and _____.
    (a) emotional intelligence   (c) organizational culture
    (b) management support   (d) task motivation

Short-Response Questions

16. What is the difference between an optimizing decision and a satisficing decision?

17. How can a manager double-check the ethics of a decision?

18. How would a manager use systematic thinking and intuitive thinking in problem solving?

19. How can the members of an organization be trained in crisis management?

Essay Question

20. As a participant in a new mentoring program between your university and a local high school, you have volunteered to give a presentation to a class of sophomores on the challenges in the new "electronic office." The goal is to sensitize these high school students to developments in information technology and motivate them to take the best advantage of their high school academics so as to prepare themselves for the workplace of the future. What will you say to them?

Management Skills & Competencies Make yourself valuable!

Evaluate Career Situations

What Would You Do?

1. **Tired of Excuses**

   Little problems are popping up at the most inconvenient times. They make your work as team leader sometimes difficult and even aggravating. Today it's happened again. Trevor just called in "sick," saying his doctor advised him yesterday that it was better to stay home than to come to work and infect others with the flu. It makes sense, but it's also a hardship for you and the team. What can you do to best manage this type of situation since it's sure to happen again?

2. **Social Loafing Problem**

   You are under a lot of pressure because your team is having performance problems. They trace, in part at least, to persistent social loafing by one team member in particular. You have come up with a reason to remove her from the team. But, the decision you are about to make fails all three of the ethics spotlight questions. As team leader, what will you do now?

3. **Task Force Selection**

   You have finally caught the attention of senior management. Top executives asked you to chair a task force to develop a creative new product that can breathe fresh life into an existing product line. To begin, you need to select the members of the task force. What criteria will you use to choose members who are most likely to bring high levels of creativity to this team?

Reflect on the Self-Assessment

Cognitive Style

Instructions

This assessment is designed to get an impression of your cognitive style based on the work of psychologist Carl Jung. For each of the following 12 pairs, place a "1" next to the statement that best describes you. Do this for each pair, even though the description you choose may not be perfect.[48]

1. (a) I prefer to learn from experience.
   (b) I prefer to find meanings in facts and how they fit together.

2. (a) I prefer to use my eyes, ears, and other senses to find out what is going on.
   (b) I prefer to use imagination to come up with new ways to do things.

3. (a) I prefer to use standard ways to deal with routine problems.

(b) I prefer to use novel ways to deal with new problems.

4. (a) I prefer ideas and imagination.

(b) I prefer methods and techniques.

5. (a) I am patient with details, but get impatient when they get complicated.

(b) I am impatient and jump to conclusions, but I am also creative, imaginative, and inventive.

6. (a) I enjoy using skills already mastered more than learning new ones.

(b) I like learning new skills more than practicing old ones.

7. (a) I prefer to decide things logically.

(b) I prefer to decide things based on feelings and values.

8. (a) I like to be treated with justice and fairness.

(b) I like to be praised and to please other people.

9. (a) I sometimes neglect or hurt other people's feelings without realizing it.

(b) I am aware of other people's feelings.

10. (a) I give more attention to ideas and things than to human relationships.

(b) I can predict how others will feel.

11. (a) I do not need harmony; arguments and conflicts don't bother me.

(b) I value harmony and get upset by arguments and conflicts.

12. (a) I am often described as analytical, impersonal, unemotional, objective, critical, hardnosed, rational.

(b) I am often described as sympathetic, people-oriented, unorganized, uncritical, understanding, ethical.

Self-Assessment Scoring

Sum your scores as follows, and record them in the parentheses. (Note that the *Sensing* and *Feeling* scores will be recorded as negatives.)

(–   ) *Sensing (S Type)* 5 1a 1 2a 1 3a 1 4a 1 5a 1 6a

(   ) *Intuitive (N Type)* 5 1b 1 2b 1 3b 1 4b 1 5b 1 6b

(   ) *Thinking (T Type)* 5 7a 1 8a 1 9a 1 10a 1 11a 1 12a

(–   ) *Feeling (F Type)* 5 7b 1 8b 1 9b 1 10b 1 11b 1 12b

Interpretation

This assessment contrasts personal tendencies toward information gathering (sensation vs. intuition) and information evaluation (feeling vs. thinking) in one's approach to problem solving. The result is a classification of four cognitive styles and their characteristics. Read the descriptions provided in the chapter text and consider the implications of your suggested style, including how well you might work with people whose styles are very different.

Contribute to the Team Exercise

Lost at Sea

Situation

You are sailing on a private yacht in the South Pacific when a fire of unknown origin destroys the yacht and most of its contents. You and a small group of survivors are now in a large raft with oars. Your location is unclear, but you estimate that you are about 1,000 miles south-southwest of the nearest land. One person has just found in her pockets five $1 bills and a packet of matches. Everyone else's pockets are empty. The items below are available to you on the raft.[49]

	Individual ranking	Team ranking	Expert ranking
Sextant			
Shaving mirror			
5 gallons water			
Mosquito netting			
1 survival meal			
Maps of Pacific Ocean			
Floatable seat cushion			
2 gallons oil-gas mix			
Small transistor radio			
Shark repellent			
20 square feet black plastic			
1 quart 20-proof rum			
15 feet nylon rope			
24 chocolate bars			
Fishing kit			

Instructions

1. *Working alone,* rank the 15 items in order of their importance to your survival ("1" is most important and "15" is least important).

2. *Working in an assigned group,* arrive at a "team" ranking of the 15 items. Appoint one person as team spokesperson to report your team ranking to the class.

3. *Do not write in Column C* until your instructor provides the "expert" ranking.

Manage a Critical Incident

Asking for a Raise

Situation: You want a raise.[50]

Problem: The question is: How do you get your boss to decide that you deserve one?

Insight: Researchers tell us that when negotiating a raise, it's better to not use a round number as a target—such as "about $65,000," and better to use a precise number—such as "$63,750." The round number suggests a person has only a general idea of the market for their skills, whereas the precise number gives the impression that they've done the research and know their facts.

Task: Describe what you will say and do to get your boss to agree that you deserve a raise. Prepare a narrative that presents the exact words, justifications, and dollar target you would use to ask for a raise in your current job. Alternatively, assume you have been working in your chosen career field for five years, have developed lots of expertise and earned high performance reports, and now want a raise.

Collaborate on the Team Project

Crisis Management Realities

Questions: What types of crises do business leaders face, and how do they deal with them?

Instructions

- Identify three crisis events from the recent local, national, and international business news.
- Read at least three different news reports on each crisis, trying to learn as much as possible about its specifics, how it was dealt with, what the results were, and the aftermath of the crisis.
- For each crisis, use a balance sheet approach to list sources or causes of the conflict and management responses to it. Analyze the lists to see if there are any differences based on the nature of the crisis faced in each situation. Also look for any patterns in the responses to them by the business executives.
- Score each crisis (from 1 5 low to 5 5 high) in terms of how successfully it was handled. Be sure to identify the criteria that you use to describe "success" in handling a crisis situation. Make a list of "Done Rights" and "Done Wrongs" in crisis management.
- Summarize the results of your study into a report on "Realities of Crisis Management."

Analyze THE CaseStudy : AMAZON.COM One E-Store to Rule Them All

Go to *Management Cases for Critical Thinking* at the end of the book to find this case.

FUNDAMENTALS OF PLANNING

8

KEY TAKEAWAYS

- Identify the importance of planning and steps in the planning process.

- List and give examples of the types of plans used by managers.

- Discuss useful planning tools and techniques.

- Explain how goals and participation influence planning success.

SKILLS MAKE YOU **VALUABLE**

- **EVALUATE** *Career Situations:* What Would You Do?

- **REFLECT** *On the Self-Assessment:* Time Management Profile

- **CONTRIBUTE** *To the Team Exercise:* Personal Career Planning

- **MANAGE** *A Critical Incident:* Policy on Paternity Leave for New Dads

- **COLLABORATE** *On a Team Activity:* The Future Workplace

- **ANALYZE** *The Case Study:* Avago Technologies: Planning for the Speed of Business

Most of our days are chock full of time pressure and multiple activities—expected and unexpected. A good plan can help us to stay on course and get a reasonable number of things accomplished. Managers need plans, too, but the planning environment within organizations can be complicated. Now is a good time to study the essential planning processes and techniques.

No one can know for sure what the future holds, but no one doubts its likely complications. A meeting of the World Economic Forum in Davos, Switzerland, for example, identified five key risks for the world at large—extreme weather events, climate change, cyber-attacks, rising unemployment and underemployment, and growing income disparities.[1] What are the implications for companies like Amazon or Nike, or for our schools and local governments? What might they mean to you?

Like all of us, managers need the ability to look ahead, make good plans, and help themselves and others meet future challenges. But it can be easy to get so engrossed in the details of the present moment that we forget about what happens next. Other times an accelerated rush to the future can go off track because of a wide range of uncertainties and few or no familiar reference points. The likelihood is that even the best of plans—organizational and personal—will have to be adjusted or modified to fit unforeseen new circumstances. This requires the insight and courage to be flexible, and the discipline to stay focused on goals even as events change and problems arise.

Why and How Managers Plan

TAKEAWAY 1   Why and how do managers plan?

LEARN MORE | Importance of planning • The planning process • Benefits of planning
ABOUT | Planning and time management

The management process involves planning, organizing, leading, and controlling the use of resources to achieve performance objectives. The first of these functions, **planning**, sets the stage for the others by providing a sense of direction. It is a process of setting objectives and determining how best to accomplish them. At its core, planning involves deciding exactly what needs to be accomplished and how best to go about it.

Planning is the process of setting objectives and determining how to accomplish them.

Importance of Planning

When planning is done well, it creates a solid platform for the other management functions. It helps with *organizing*—allocating and arranging resources to accomplish tasks, *leading*—guiding and inspiring others to achieve high levels of task accomplishment, and *controlling*—monitoring task accomplishments and taking corrective action when needed.

The centrality of planning in management is shown in Figure 8.1. Good planning helps us become better at what we are doing and to stay action-oriented. An Eaton Corporation annual report, for example, once stated: "Planning at Eaton means making the hard decisions before events force them upon you, and anticipating the future needs of the market before the demand asserts itself."[2]

The Planning Process

The five basic steps in the planning process are:

1. *Define your objectives*—Identify desired outcomes or results in very specific ways. Know where you want to go; be specific enough that you will know you have arrived when you get there, or know how far off the mark you are at various points along the way.

2. *Determine where you stand vis-à-vis objectives*—Evaluate current accomplishments relative to the desired results. Know where you stand in reaching the objectives; know what strengths work in your favor and what weaknesses may hold you back.

Objectives and **goals** are specific results that one wishes to achieve.

3. *Develop premises regarding future conditions*—Anticipate future events. Generate alternative "scenarios" for what may happen; identify for each scenario things that may help or hinder progress toward your objectives.

4. *Analyze alternatives and make a plan*—List and evaluate possible actions. Choose the alternative most likely to accomplish your objectives; describe what must be done to follow the best course of action.

5. *Implement the plan and evaluate results*—Take action and carefully measure your progress toward objectives. Follow through by doing what the plan requires; evaluate results, take corrective action, and revise plans as needed.

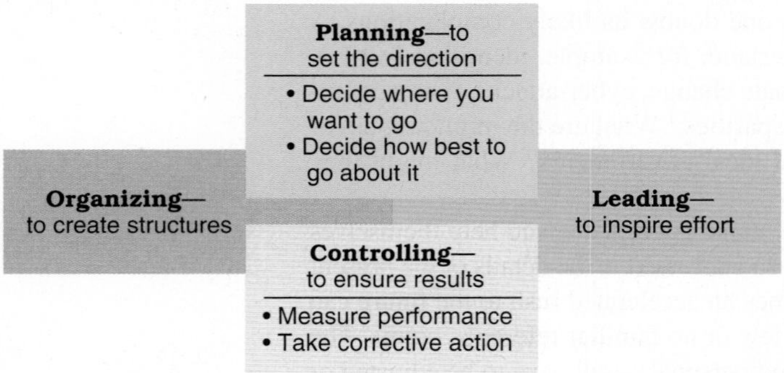

Planning should focus attention on **objectives** and **goals** that are specific results or desired outcomes. But the objectives and goals have to be good ones; they should push you to achieve substantial and not trivial accomplishments. Jack Welch, former CEO of

Planning—to set the direction
• Decide where you want to go
• Decide how best to go about it

Organizing—to create structures

Leading—to inspire effort

Controlling—to ensure results
• Measure performance
• Take corrective action

FIGURE 8.1
The roles of planning and controlling in the management process.

...mance targets that we have to work extra hard and really stretch to reach." Do you agree that Welch's concept of stretch goals adds real strength to the planning process for both organizations and individuals?

It's important not to forget the action side of planning. The process should always create a realistic and concrete **plan**, a statement of action steps to be taken in order to accomplish objectives and goals. These steps must be clear and compelling, so that the all-important follow-through takes place. Plans alone don't deliver results; implemented plans do. Like other decision making in organizations, the best planning includes the active participation of those whose work efforts will eventually determine whether or not the plans get put successfully into action.

It's also important to remember that planning is not something managers do only on occasion or while working alone in quiet rooms, free from distractions, and at scheduled times. It is an ongoing process, enacted continuously while dealing with a busy work setting filled with distractions, interpersonal dynamics, and ever-constant performance pressures.

Stretch goals are performance targets that one must work extra hard and stretch to reach.

A **plan** is a statement of intended means for accomplishing objectives.

Benefits of Planning

The pressures organizations face come from many sources. Externally, these include changing social norms and ethical expectations, government regulations, uncertainties of a global economy, new technologies, and the sheer cost of investments in labor, capital, and other supporting resources. Internally, they include the quest for operating efficiencies, new structures and technologies, alternative work arrangements, greater workplace diversity, and concerns for work–life balance. As you would expect, planning under such conditions has a number of benefits for both organizations and individuals.

Planning Improves Focus and Flexibility

Good planning improves focus and flexibility, both of which are important for performance success. An organization with focus recognizes what it does best, understands the needs of its customers, and knows how to serve customers well. An individual with focus knows where he or she wants to go in a situation, career, and life in general. An organization with flexibility is willing and able to change and adapt to shifting circumstances without losing focus, and operates with an orientation toward the future rather than the past. An individual with flexibility adjusts career plans to fit new opportunities and constraints as they arise.

Planning Improves Action Orientation

Planning focuses attention on priorities and helps avoid the **complacency trap**—simply being carried along by the flow of events. It is a way for people and organizations to stay ahead of the competition and become better at what they are doing. Planning keeps the future visible as a performance target and reminds us that the best decisions are often those made before events force problems upon us.

The **complacency trap** is being carried along by the flow of events.

Management consultant Stephen R. Covey points out that the most successful executives "zero in on what they do that 'adds value' to an organization."[4] Instead of working on too many things, they work on the things that really count. Covey says that good planning makes managers more (1) results oriented—creating a performance-oriented sense of direction; (2) priority oriented—making sure the most important things get first attention; (3) advantage oriented—ensuring that all resources are used to best advantage; and (4) change oriented—anticipating problems and opportunities so they can be dealt with most effectively.

Planning Improves Coordination and Control

Planning improves coordination.[5] Individuals, groups, and subsystems in organizations are all engaged in multiple tasks and activities simultaneously. But their efforts must also be combined into meaningful contributions to the organization as a whole. Good plans promote coordination of the activities of employees and organizational subsystems so that their accomplishments advance critical performance initiatives.

Planning that is done well facilitates control. The link between planning and controlling begins when objectives and standards are set. They make it easier to measure results and take action to improve things as necessary. After launching a costly information technology upgrade, for example, executives at McDonald's realized that the system couldn't deliver on its promises. They stopped the project, took a loss of $170 million, and refocused the firm's plans and resources on projects with more direct impact on customers.[6]

This is how planning and controlling work closely together in the management process. Without planning, control lacks objectives and standards for measuring how things are going and identifying what could be done to make them go better. Without control, planning lacks the follow-through necessary to ensure that things work out as planned. With both good planning and good control, it's a lot easier to spot when things aren't going well and make the necessary adjustments.

Planning and Time Management

When Daniel Vasella was CEO of Novartis AG and responsible for operations spread across 140 countries, he admitted to being calendar-bound and said: "I'm locked in by meetings, travel and other constraints. . . . I have to put down in priority things I like to do." Kathleen Murphy is president of Fidelity Personal Investing. She's also calendar-bound, with conferences and travel booked well ahead. Meetings can be scheduled at half-hour intervals and workdays can last 12 hours. She spends lots of time traveling, but tries to make good use of her time on planes. "No one can reach me by phone," she says, "and I can get reading and thinking done."[7]

These are common executive stories—tight schedules, little time alone, lots of meetings and phone calls, and not much room for spontaneity. The keys to success in such classic management scenarios rest, in part at least, with another benefit of good planning—time management.

Check out the box with useful tips on developing time management skills. A lot of this skill comes down to discipline and priorities. Lewis Platt, former chairman of Hewlett-Packard, once said: "Basically, the whole day is a series of choices." These choices have to be made in ways that allocate your time to the most important priorities. Platt says that he was "ruthless about priorities" and that you "have to continually work to optimize your time."[8]

Most of us have experienced the difficulties of balancing available time with our many commitments and opportunities. As suggested in the chapter opener, it is easy to lose track of time and fall prey to what consultants identify as "time wasters." All too often we allow our time to be dominated by other people or to be misspent on nonessential activities.[9] To-do lists can help, but they have to contain the right things. In daily living and in management situations, it is important to distinguish between things that you must do (top priority), should do (high priority), would be nice to do (low priority), and really don't need to do (no priority).

Personal Time Management Tips

1. *Do* say "No" to requests that divert you from what you really should be doing.
2. *Don't* get bogged down in details that you can address later or leave for others.
3. *Do* have a system for screening telephone calls, e-mails, and requests for meetings.
4. *Don't* let drop-in visitors or instant messages use too much of your time.
5. *Do* prioritize what you will work on in terms of importance and urgency.
6. *Don't* become calendar-bound by letting others control your schedule.
7. *Do* follow priorities and work on the most important and urgent tasks first.

Learning Check 1

Types of Plans Used by Managers

TAKEAWAY 2   What types of plans do managers use?

LEARN MORE | Long-range and short range plans • Strategic and tactical plans
ABOUT | Operational plans

"I am the master of my fate: I am the captain of my soul." How often have you heard this phrase? The lines are from "Invictus," written by British poet William Earnest Henley in 1875. He was sending a message, one of confidence and control, as he moved forward into the future. That notion, however, worries a scholar by the name of Richard Levin. His response to Henley is: "Not without a plan you're not."[10]

Managers use a variety of plans as they face different kinds of challenges in organizations. In some cases, the planning environment is stable and predictable; in others, it is more dynamic and uncertain. Different situations call for different types of plans.

Long-Range and Short-Range Plans

In the not-too-distant past, **long-term plans** looked three or more years into the future, while **short-term plans** covered one year or less. But, the increasing environmental complexity and dynamism of recent years has severely tested the concept of "long-term" planning. Most executives would likely agree that these complexities and uncertainties challenge how we actually go about planning and how far ahead we can really plan. At the very least, we can conclude that there is a lot less permanency to long-term plans today and that they are sub-ject to frequent revisions.

Even though the time frames of planning may be shrinking, top management is still responsible for setting longer-term plans and directions for the organization as a whole. They set the context for lower-level management to work on useful short-terms plans. Unless everyone understands an organization's long-term plans and objectives, there is always risk that the pressures of daily challenges will divert attention from "important tasks." Without a sense of long-term direction, employees can end up working hard and still not achieve significant—or mission-critical—results.

Management researcher Elliot Jaques believes that people vary in their capa-bility to think with different time horizons.[11] In fact, he suggests that most people work comfortably with only 3-month time spans; a smaller group works well with a 1-year span; and only the very rare person can handle a 20-year time frame. These are provocative and personally challenging ideas. Although a team leader's planning may fall primarily in the weekly or monthly range, a chief executive is expected to have a vision extending years into the future. Career progress to higher levels of management requires the conceptual skills to work well with longer-range time frames.

Long-term plans typically look three or more years into the future.

Short-term plans typically cover one year or less.

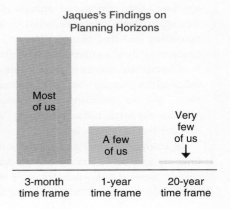

Jaques's Findings on Planning Horizons

Most of us — 3-month time frame

A few of us — 1-year time frame

Very few of us ↓ — 20-year time frame

Strategic and Tactical Plans

A strategic plan identifies long-term directions for the organization.

A vision clarifies the purpose of the organization and expresses what it hopes to be in the future.

When a sports team enters a game, it typically does so with a "strategy" in hand. Most often this strategy is set by the head coach in conjunction with assistant and position coaches. The goal is clear: Win the game. As the game unfolds, however, situations arise that require actions to solve problems or exploit opportunities. They call for "tactics" that deal with a current situation in ways that advance the overall strategy for winning. The same logic holds true for organizations. Plans at the top of the traditional organizational pyramid tend to have a strategic focus. Those at the middle and lower levels of the organization are more tactical.

Strategic plans are focused on the organization as a whole or a major component. They are longer-term plans that set broad action directions and create a frame of reference for allocating resources for maximum performance impact. Strategic plans ideally set forth the goals and objectives needed to accomplish the organization's **vision** in terms of mission or purpose and what it hopes to be in the future.

Research Brief

You've Got to Move Beyond Planning by the Calendar

Organizations today need executives who can make faster and better decisions, and that means strategic planning must be done continuously. Michael C. Mankins and Richard Steele, writing in the *Harvard Business Review*, express their concerns that planning is too often viewed as an annual activity focused more on documenting plans for the record than on action. Little wonder, they suggest, that only 11% of executives in a survey of 156 firms with sales of $11 billion were highly satisfied that strategic planning is worthwhile.

The research, conducted in collaboration with Marakon Associates and the Economist Intelligence Unit, inquired as to how long-range strategic planning was conducted and how effective these planning activities were. Results showed that executives perceived a substantial disconnect between the way many firms approached strategic planning and the way they approached strategic decisions. Some 66% of the time, executives said that strategic planning at their firms was conducted only at set times, and very often was accomplished by a formal and structured process. Survey respondents also indicated that planning was often considered as only a "periodic event" and not something to be engaged in continuously. Mankins and Steele call such planning "calendar driven," and they question its effectiveness.

In calendar-driven planning, the researchers found that firms averaged only 2.5 major strategic decisions per year, with "major" meaning a decision that could move profits by more

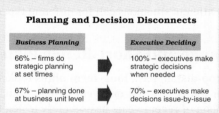

Planning and Decision Disconnects

Business Planning	Executive Deciding
66% – firms do strategic planning at set times	100% – executives make strategic decisions when needed
67% – planning done at business unit level	70% – executives make decisions issue-by-issue

than 10%. They also point out that when planning is disconnected from the calendar, companies make higher-quality and more strategic decisions. The researchers call this alternative planning approach "continuous review" and argue it is more consistent with the way executives actually make decisions and business realities.

YOU BE THE RESEARCHER

Why can tying planning to certain calendar dates end up being dysfunctional for a business? On the other hand, how can we plan almost continuously? Choose two or three organizations in your community for field research. Arrange interviews with their senior executives. Find out if they plan on a set schedule and if so, what that schedule might be. Probe further to find out how effective they consider planning in their organization to be, and what changes they might like to see made.

Tactical plans are developed and used to implement strategic plans. They specify how the organization's resources can be used to put strategies into action. In the sports context, you might think of tactical plans as having "special teams" or as "special plays" ready to meet a particular threat or opportunity. Tactical plans in business often take the form of **functional plans** that indicate how different components of the enterprise will contribute to the overall strategy. Such functional plans might include:

- *Production plans*—dealing with work methods and technologies.
- *Financial plans*—dealing with money and capital investments.
- *Facilities plans*—dealing with physical space and work layouts.
- *Logistics plans*—dealing with suppliers and acquiring resource inputs.
- *Marketing plans*—dealing with selling and distributing goods or services.
- *Human resource plans*—dealing with and building a talented workforce.

> A **tactical plan** helps to implement all or parts of a strategic plan.
>
> **Functional plans** indicate how different operations within the organization will help advance the overall strategy.

Operational Plans

Operational plans guide behavior and describe what needs to be done in the short term to support strategic and tactical plans. They include both *standing plans* like policies and procedures that are used over and over again, and *single-use plans* like budgets that apply to one specific task or time period.

> An **operational plan** identifies short-term activities to implement strategic plans.

Policies and Procedures

A **policy** communicates broad guidelines for making decisions and taking action in specific circumstances. Organizations operate with lots of policies that set expectations for many aspects of employee behavior. Typical human resource policies cover things like employee hiring, termination, performance appraisals, pay increases, promotions, and discipline. For example, Judith Nitsch made sexual harassment a top priority when starting her engineering-consulting business.[12] Nitsch defined a sexual harassment policy, took a hard line on its enforcement, and appointed both a male and a female employee for others to talk with about sexual harassment concerns.

> A **policy** is a standing plan that communicates broad guidelines for decisions and action.

Procedures describe specific rules for what actions are to be taken in various situations. They are stated in employee handbooks and often called SOPs—standard operating procedures. Whereas a policy sets a broad guideline, procedures define precise actions to be taken. In the prior example, Judith Nitsch was right to establish a sexual harassment policy for her firm. But, she should also put into place procedures that ensure everyone receives fair, equal, and nondiscriminatory treatment under the policy. Everyone in her firm should know both how to file a sexual harassment complaint and just how that complaint will be handled.

> A **procedure** is a rule describing actions that are to be taken in specific situations.

Budgets

Budgets are single-use plans that commit resources for specific time periods to activities, projects, or programs. Managers typically spend a fair amount of time bargaining with higher levels to get adequate budgets to support the needs of their work units or teams. They are also expected to achieve work objectives while keeping within allocated budgets. Being "over budget" is generally bad, while coming in "under budget" is generally good.

> A **budget** is a plan that commits resources to projects or activities.

Managers deal with and use a variety of budgets. *Financial budgets* project cash flows and expenditures; *operating budgets* plot anticipated sales or revenues against expenses; *nonmonetary budgets* allocate resources like labor, equipment, and space. A *fixed budget* allocates an established amount of resources for a specific purpose, such as $50,000 for equipment purchases in a given year. A *flexible budget* allows resources to vary in proportion with emergent levels of activity, such as having extra money available to hire temporary workers when workloads exceed certain levels.

Because budgets link planned activities with the resources needed to accomplish them, they are useful for activating and tracking performance. But budgets can get out of control, creeping higher and higher without getting sufficient critical reviews. In fact, one of the most common budgeting problems is that resource allocations get "rolled over" from one time period to the next without rigorous scrutiny; the new budget is simply an incremental adjustment over the previous one. In a major division of Campbell Soups, for example, managers once discovered that 10% of the marketing budget was going to sales promotions no longer relevant to current product lines.

A zero-based budget allocates resources as if each budget were brand new.

A **zero-based budget** deals with this rollover budget problem by approaching each new budget period as it if were brand new. In zero-based budgeting, there is no guarantee that any past funding will be renewed; all proposals, old and new, must compete for available funds at the start of each new budget cycle. What do you think? Does zero-based budgeting make sense in government and other organizations that struggle to balance goals and available resources?

Learning Check 2

TAKEAWAY QUESTION **2 What types of plans do managers use?**

BE SURE YOU CAN • differentiate between short-range and long-range plans • differentiate between strategic and operational plans and explain how they relate to one another • define *policy* and *procedure* and give examples of each in a university setting • define *budget* and explain how zero-based budgeting works

Planning Tools and Techniques

TAKEAWAY 3   What are some useful planning tools and techniques?

LEARN MORE | Forecasting • Contingency planning • Scenario planning
ABOUT | Benchmarking • Staff planning

Planning delivers the most benefits when its foundations are strong. Useful planning tools and techniques include forecasting, contingency planning, scenario planning, benchmarking, and staff planning.

Forecasting

Forecasting attempts to predict the future.

What are top executives around the world thinking about as they make plans for the future? Are they on top of the right trends? Planning in business and our personal lives often involves **forecasting**, the process of predicting what will happen in the future.[13] Periodicals such as *Business Week*, *Fortune*, and *The Economist* regularly report forecasts of industry conditions, interest rates, unemployment trends, and national economies, among other issues. Some are based on *qualitative forecasting*, which uses expert opinions to predict the future. Others involve *quantitative forecasting*, which uses mathematical models and statistical analyses of historical data and surveys to predict future events.

Although useful, all forecasts should be treated cautiously. They are planning aids, not substitutes. Forecasts rely on human judgment—and they can be wrong. It is said that a music agent once told Elvis Presley: "You ought to go back to driving a truck, because you ain't going nowhere." And when it came time to make the second pick in the 1984 NBA draft, the Portland Trail Blazers chose Sam Bowie. The next-in-line Chicago Bulls used their third pick to choose Michael Jordan.

Contingency Planning

Picture the scene: A professional golfer is striding down the golf course with an iron in each hand. The one in her right hand is "the plan"; the one in her left is the "backup plan." Which club she uses will depend on how the ball lies on the fairway. One of her greatest strengths is being able to adjust to the situation by putting the right club to work in the circumstances she encounters.

Planning is often like that. By definition, it involves thinking ahead. The more uncertain the planning environment, the more likely it is that an original forecast or intention will turn out to be inadequate or wrong. The golfer deals with this uncertainty by having backup clubs available. This amounts to **contingency planning**—identifying alternative courses of action that can be implemented if circumstances change. A really good contingency plan will even contain "trigger points" to indicate when to activate preselected alternatives. In the face of uncertainties, this can be an indispensable tool for managerial and personal planning.

Poor contingency planning was center stage when debates raged over how BP managed the disastrous Deepwater Horizon oil spill in the Gulf of Mexico. Everyone from the public at large to U.S. lawmakers to oil industry experts criticized BP not only for failing to contain the spill quickly, but also for failing to anticipate and have contingency plans in place to handle such an ecological crisis.[14]

> *A BP spokesperson initially said*—"You have here an unprecedented event . . . the unthinkable has become thinkable and the whole industry will be asking questions of itself."

> *An oil industry expert responded*—"There should be a technology that is preexisting and ready to deploy at the drop of a hat. . . . It shouldn't have to be designed and fabricated now, from scratch."

> *Former BP CEO Tony Hayward finally admitted*—"There are some capabilities that we could have available to deploy instantly, rather than creating as we go."

The lesson here is hard-earned but very clear. Contingency planning can't prevent crises from occurring. But when things do go wrong, there's nothing better to have in place than good contingency plans.

Contingency planning identifies alternative courses of action to take when things go wrong.

Scenario Planning

Scenario planning is a long-term version of contingency planning. It involves identifying several possible future scenarios or states of affairs and then making plans to deal with each scenario should it actually occur.[15] In this sense, scenario planning forces us to think really far ahead and to be open to a wide range of possibilities.

The scenario planning approach was developed years ago at Royal Dutch/Shell when top managers asked themselves a perplexing question: "What would Shell do after its oil supplies ran out?" Although recognizing that scenario planning can never be inclusive of all future possibilities, a Shell executive once said that it helps "condition the organization to think" and better prepare for "future shocks."

Shell uses scenario planning to tackle such issues as climate change, sustainable development, fossil-fuel alternatives, human rights, and biodiversity. Most typically it involves descriptions of "worst cases" and "best cases." With regard to diminishing oil supplies, for example, a worst-case scenario might be that global conflict and devastating effects on the natural environment occur as nations jockey with one another to secure increasingly scarce supplies of oil and other natural resources. A best-case scenario might be that governments work together to find pathways that take care of our resource needs while supporting the search for sustainability of global resources. It's anyone's guess which scenario will materialize or if something else altogether will happen. But these words of former Shell CEO Jeroen van der Veer highlight the value of the scenario planning process: "This will require hard work and time is short."[16]

Scenario planning identifies alternative future scenarios and makes plans to deal with each.

ethics > KNOW RIGHT FROM WRONG

> *"We aren't really interested in the more-aid-less-aid debate. We're interested in seeing what works and what doesn't."*

What Really Works When Fighting World Poverty?

Developing countries send more than $100 billion in aid to poor countries; private foundations and charities spend $70-billion-plus billion more fighting poverty and its effects around the world. Their plans and goals are praiseworthy, but is all of that money being well spent, and to the greatest effect?

Not all of it is being well spent, that's for sure. That's one of the problems being tackled by the Poverty Action Lab at the Massachusetts Institute of Technology. The director, Abhijit Banerjee, a development economist, says: "We aren't really interested in the more-aid-less-aid debate. We're interested in seeing what works and what doesn't." The lab criticizes "feel-good" approaches and pushes for rigorous evaluations of poverty-fighting programs using scientific methods. Here's an example.

The Indian antipoverty group Seva Mandir was concerned about teacher absenteeism and low performance by rural school children. Its original plan was to pay extra tutors to assist teachers in 120 rural schools. The Poverty Lab Plan suggested paying extra tutors in 60 schools, making no changes in the other 60, and then comparing outcomes to see if the plan worked. An evaluation of results showed no difference in children's performance, even with the higher costs of extra tutors.

A new plan was made to buy cameras for 60 teachers, have them take time/date-stamped photos with children at the start and end of each school day, and have the photos analyzed each month. Teachers would receive bonuses or fines based on their absenteeism and student performance. Again, no changes were made in the other 60 schools. Evaluation revealed that teacher absenteeism was 20% lower and student performance was significantly higher in the camera schools. With the Poverty Lab's help, Seva Mandir concluded that investing in closely monitored pay incentives could improve teacher attendance in rural schools.

WHAT DO YOU THINK?

Look around your organization and at cases reported in the news. How often do we draw conclusions that "plans are working" based on feel-good evaluations or anecdotal reports rather than solid scientific evaluations? What are the consequences at work and in society when plans are implemented at great cost, but without systematic, defensible systems for evaluation? Even if the objectives of a project are honorable, what ethical issues arise in situations where it isn't clear that the project is having the intended benefit?

Benchmarking

Benchmarking uses external and internal comparisons to plan for future improvements.

Best practices are things people and organizations do that lead to superior performance.

Planners sometimes become too comfortable with the ways things are going and become overconfident that the past is a good indicator of the future. It is often better to keep challenging the status quo and not simply to accept things as they are. One way to do this is through **benchmarking**—which is the use of external and internal comparisons to better evaluate current performance and identify possible ways to improve for the future.[17]

The purpose of benchmarking is to determine what other people and organizations are doing very well, and then plan how to incorporate these ideas into one's own operations. It is basically a way of learning from the successes of others. One benchmarking technique is to search for **best practices**—things people and organizations do that help them to achieve superior performance.

Well-run organizations emphasize *internal benchmarking* that encourages members and work units to learn and improve by sharing one another's best practices. They also use *external benchmarking* to learn from competitors and non-competitors alike. Xerox, for example, has benchmarked L.L. Bean's warehousing and distribution methods, Ford's plant layouts, and American Express's billing and collections. Ford benchmarked BMW's 3 series.[18] And in the apparel industry, the Spanish retailer Zara has become a benchmark for excellence in "fast fashion."[19]

Staff Planning

As organizations grow, so do their planning challenges and so does the use of staff planners. These specialists are experts in all steps of the planning process, as well as in the use of planning tools and techniques. They can help bring focus and expertise to a wide variety of planning tasks. But one risk is a tendency for a communication gap to develop between the staff planners and line managers. Unless everyone works closely together, the resulting plans may be based on poor information. Also, an organization's employees may end up with little commitment to implement the plans made by the staff, no matter how good they are.

Learning Check 3

TAKEAWAYQUESTION 3 **What are some useful planning tools and techniques?**

BE SURE YOU CAN • define *forecasting, contingency planning, scenario planning,* and *benchmarking* • explain the benefits of contingency planning and scenario planning • describe the pros and cons of using staff planners

Implementing Plans to Achieve Results

TAKEAWAY 4   How can plans be well implemented?

LEARN MORE ABOUT | Goal setting • Goal alignment • Goal management • Participation and involvement

In a book entitled *Doing What Matters*, Jim Kilts, the former CEO of Gillette, quotes an old management adage: "In business, words are words, promises are promises, but only performance is reality."[20] The same applies to plans. They are, we might say, words with promises attached. These promises are only fulfilled when plans are implemented so that their purposes are achieved. And, the foundations for successful implementation are set with the planning processes of goal setting, goal alignment, and participation and involvement.

Goal Setting

Although most of us are aware of the importance of goal setting in management, we may mistakenly think that goal setting is an easy thing to accomplish. The reality is that how goals are set can have a big impact on how well they function as performance targets and motivators. There's a significant difference between having "no goals" or even just everyday run-of-the-mill "average goals," and having really "great goals" that inspire effort and result in plans being successfully implemented.

Great goals—think SMART goals—tend to have the five characteristics shown in the figure on the right. They are *specific*— clearly targeted key results and outcomes to be accomplished. They are *measurable*—described so results can be measured without ambiguity. They are *attainable*—include a challenging stretch factor while still being realistic and possible to achieve. They are *relevant*—focused on important results, not just on activities or effort expended. And they are *timely*—linked to specific timetables and "due dates."

One of the more difficult aspects of goal setting is making performance objectives as measurable as possible. It's best to achieve

wisdom > LEARN FROM ROLE MODELS

> *"I wanted to give this opportunity to girls who had a light so bright that not even poverty could dim that light."*

Oprah Thinks Now and Embraces the Future

HO/REUTERS/Newscom

Having grown up poor, Oprah Winfrey says she is grateful for getting a good education, calling it "the most vital aspect of my life." She's now sharing that lesson through the Oprah Winfrey Leadership Academy for young women in South Africa.

When the academy opened, Winfrey said: "I wanted to give this opportunity to girls who had a light so bright that not even poverty could dim that light." Her goal was for the new academy to "be the best school in the world."

Nelson Mandela, first president of non-apartheid South Africa, spoke at the opening ceremony and praised her vision. "The key to any country's future is in educating its youth," said Mandela. "Oprah is therefore not only investing in a few young individuals, but in the future of our country." One of the first students said: "I would have had a completely different life if this hadn't happened to me."

Even the best intentions couldn't guarantee that everything would go according to Winfrey's plan. Not long after the academy launched, it was hit by scandal over alleged abuse of students by a dorm matron. Oprah quickly apologized to the students and their families, and rededicated herself to the school.

"I think that crisis is there to teach you about life," she said. "The school is going to be even better because that happened."

FIND THE INSPIRATION

In what ways do Oprah's objectives for the leadership academy reflect her life and past experiences? Can you make plans that will include social contributions in the future? Are you adaptable in your plans as Oprah appears to be, or more fixed? What are the implications of your approach for your professional and personal goals, and what you accomplish?

---

agreement on a *measurable end product*—for example, "to reduce travel expenses by 5% by the end of the fiscal year." But performance in some jobs, particularly managerial positions, can be hard to quantify. Rather than abandon the quest for a good objective in such cases, it is often possible to agree on *verifiable work activities*. Their accomplishment serves as an indicator of performance progress. An example is "to improve communications with my team in the next three months by holding weekly team meetings." Whereas it can be difficult to measure "improved communications," it is much easier to document whether the "weekly team meetings" have been held.

Goal Management

Scandal—The Ohio state auditor charged that teachers and principals in the Columbus school district were pressured to change student test scores and attendance rosters in order to improve the district's performance scorecard on goals that affected state funding. Failing grades were changed to passing for at least 7,000 students.[21]

Scandal—An internal audit of the U.S. Department of Veterans Affairs system charged that managers covered up long appointment waiting times and used bogus lists in order meet tight scheduling goals and receive personal bonuses. More than 120,000 veterans failed to get care, and at least 23 died awaiting treatment.[22]

It isn't enough to set smart goals with and for others, and for yourself—the goals and the quest for their accomplishment must also be well managed. The fact is that goals can have a "dark" as well as positive side.[23] Look again at the scandals just reported. The ethics and performance failures in both cases were linked in part to unrealistic goals tied to performance rewards. In the Ohio school district, the teachers and principals—not the students—became the cheaters. In the VA scandal, the audit report described the negative effects of unrealistic goals set for patient waiting times this way: "Imposing this expectation on the field before ascertaining the resources required and its ensuing broad promulgation represent an organizational leadership failure . . . pressures were placed on schedulers to utilize unofficial lists or engage in inappropriate practices in order to make waiting times appear more favorable."[24]

Researchers point out that goals can have negative consequences when they are set unrealistically high, when individuals are expected to meet high goals over and over again, and when people striving to meet high goals aren't given the support they need to build abilities and learn what is needed to accomplish them.[25] The downsides of poorly managed stretch goals include high stress for the goal seeker, poor performance results, and possible unethical or illegal behavior. Good management of goal setting helps to avoid such problems. Scholars Gary Latham and Gerard Seijts point out that it is important to distinguish between **learning goals** that create the knowledge and skills required for performance and **outcome goals** that set targets for actual performance results. If outcome goals are emphasized at the expense of learning goals that are prerequisite to them, undesirable effects are likely. Latham and Seijts say: "It is foolish and even immoral for organizations to assign employees stretch goals without equipping them with the resources to succeed—and still punish them when they fail to reach those goals. This lack of guidance often leads to stress, burnout, and in some instances, unethical behavior."[26]

Learning goals set targets to create the knowledge and skills required for performance.

Outcome goals set targets for actual performance results.

Goal Alignment

It is one thing to set great goals, make them part of a plan, and then manage and support them well. It is an entirely different thing to make sure goals and plans are well integrated across many people, work units, and levels of an organization as a whole. Goals set everywhere in the organization should ideally help advance its overall mission or purpose. Yet, we sometimes work very hard to accomplish things that simply don't make much of a difference in organizational performance. This is why goal alignment is an important part of managerial planning.

Figure 8.2 shows how a **hierarchy of goals** or **hierarchy of objectives** helps with goal alignment. When such a hierarchy is well defined, the accomplishment of lower-level goals and objectives provides the foundation for the accomplishment of higher-level goals and objectives. The example in the figure is built around quality goals in a manufacturing setting. Strategic goals set by top management cascade down the organization step by step to become quality management objectives for lower levels. Everything ideally works together in a consistent "means–end" fashion so that the organization consistently performs as "the world's number one supplier of recyclable food containers."

In a **hierarchy of goals** or **hierarchy of objectives**, lower-level goals and objectives support accomplishment of higher-level goals and objectives.

Conversations between team leaders and team members or between supervisors and subordinates at each step in the hierarchy are essential to achieving goal alignment. The conversations should result in agreement on: (1) performance objectives for a given time period, (2) plans through which objectives will be accomplished, (3) standards for measuring whether objectives have been accomplished, and (4) procedures for reviewing performance results. This process is sometimes called *management by objectives* (MBO), but in reality, it is just old-fashioned good management.[27]

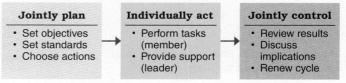

Goal Alignment Between Team Leader and Team Member

Jointly plan	**Individually act**	**Jointly control**
• Set objectives • Set standards • Choose actions	• Perform tasks (member) • Provide support (leader)	• Review results • Discuss implications • Renew cycle

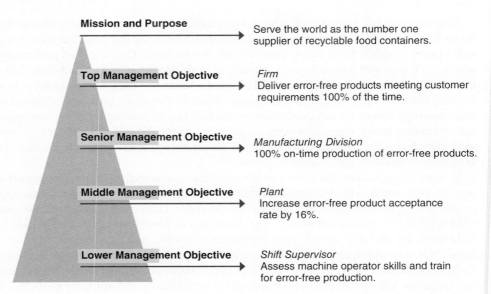

FIGURE 8.2
Goal alignment in a sample hierarchy of objectives.

Participation and Involvement

Planning is a process and not an event. And "participation" and "involvement" are two of its core components. **Participatory planning** includes in all planning steps the people who will be affected by the plans and asked to help implement them. One of the things that research is most clear about is that when people participate in setting goals, they gain motivation to work hard to accomplish them.[28] This power of participation is unlocked in planning when people who are involved in the process gain commitment to work hard and support the implementation of plans.

Figure 8.3 shows the role of participation and involvement in the planning process. Notice that participation can and should be engaged in all planning steps. Think of it using the metaphor of

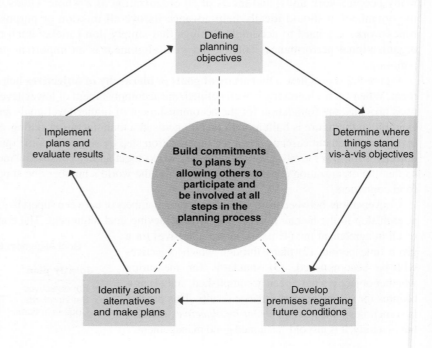

FIGURE 8.3
How participation and involvement help build commitment to plans.

a big kitchen table. Everyone from family members to guests sits around the table and enjoys the meal while joining in the conversation. The same can happen with planning, if the manager invites others to the table. When he or she does, the conversation focuses on defining objectives, assessing the present and potential future state of affairs, identifying action alternatives, and discussing implementation successes and failures.

There are many benefits when and if this participatory planning approach is followed in practice. Participation can increase the creativity and information available for planning. It can also increase the understanding and acceptance of plans, as well as commitment to their success. Even though participatory planning takes more time, it can improve performance results by improving both the quality of the plans that are made and the effectiveness of their implementation.

Learning Check 4

TAKEAWAYQUESTION **4 How can plans be well implemented?**

BE SURE YOU CAN • list the criteria of great goals • describe the value of a hierarchy of objectives • give examples of improvement and personal development objectives • explain how goal alignment can take place between a team leader and team members

Management Learning Review
Get Prepared for **Quizzes and Exams**

SUMMARY

TAKEAWAYQUESTION **1**

Why and how do managers plan?

- Planning is the process of setting performance objectives and determining what should be done to accomplish them.
- A plan is a set of intended actions for accomplishing important goals and objectives.
- Five steps in the planning process are: (1) Define your objectives, (2) determine where you stand vis-à-vis your objectives, (3) develop your premises regarding future conditions, (4) identify and choose among alternative ways of accomplishing objectives, and (5) implement action plans and evaluate results.
- The benefits of planning include better focus and flexibility, action orientation, coordination, control, and time management.

FOR DISCUSSION Which step in the planning process is likely to cause the most difficulties for managers?

TAKEAWAYQUESTION **2**

What types of plans do managers use?

- Short-range plans tend to cover a year or less; long-range plans extend up to three years or more.
- Strategic plans set critical long-range directions; operational plans are designed to implement strategic plans.
- Policies, such as a sexual harassment policy, are plans that set guidelines for the behavior of organizational members.

- Procedures and rules are plans that describe actions to be taken in specific situations, such as the steps to be taken when persons believe they have been subjected to sexual harassment.
- Budgets are plans that allocate resources to activities or projects.

FOR DISCUSSION Is there any real value to long-term planning in today's rapidly changing environment?

TAKEWAYQUESTION **3**

What are some useful planning tools and techniques?

- Forecasting, which attempts to predict what might happen in the future, is a planning aid but not a planning substitute.
- Contingency planning identifies alternative courses of action that can be implemented if and when circumstances change.
- Scenario planning analyzes the implications of alternative versions of the future.
- Planning through benchmarking utilizes external and internal comparisons to identify best practices for possible adoption.
- Staff planners with special expertise are often used to assist in the planning process, but the risk is a lack of involvement by managers and others who must implement the plans.

FOR DISCUSSION Shouldn't all plans be supported by contingency plans?

TAKEWAYQUESTION **4**
How can plans be well implemented?

- Great or SMART goals are specific, measurable, attainable, relevant, and timely.
- Goals can have negative consequences, including unethical or illegal behavior, when they are poorly managed and set unrealistically high.
- A hierarchy of objectives helps to align goals from top to bottom in organizations.

- Goal alignment is facilitated by a participative process that clarifies performance objectives for individuals and teams and identifies support that can and should be provided by managers.
- Participation and involvement open the planning process to valuable inputs from people whose efforts are essential to the effective implementation of plans.

FOR DISCUSSION Given its potential advantages, why isn't goal alignment a characteristic of all organizations?

S E L F - T E S T 8

Multiple-Choice Questions

1. Planning is the process of _____ and _____.
   (a) developing premises about the future, evaluating them
   (b) measuring results, taking corrective action
   (c) measuring past performance, targeting future performance
   (d) setting objectives, deciding how to accomplish them

2. The benefits of planning include _____.
   (a) improved focus   (c) more accurate forecasts
   (b) lower labor costs   (d) higher profits

3. In order to help implement its corporate strategy, a business firm would likely develop a _____ plan for the marketing department.
   (a) functional   (c) production
   (b) single-use   (d) zero-based

4. _____ planning identifies alternative courses of action that can be taken if and when certain situations arise.
   (a) Zero-based   (c) Strategic
   (b) Participative   (d) Contingency

5. The first step in the control process is to _____.
   (a) measure actual performance
   (b) establish objectives and standards
   (c) compare results with objectives
   (d) take corrective action

6. A sexual harassment policy is an example of _____ plans used by organizations.
   (a) long-range
   (b) single-use
   (c) standing-use
   (d) operational

7. When a manager is asked to justify a new budget proposal on the basis of projected activities rather than past practices, this is an example of _____ budgeting.
   (a) zero-based   (c) fixed
   (b) variable   (d) contingency

8. One of the benefits of participatory planning is _____.
   (a) reduced time for planning
   (b) less need for forecasting
   (c) greater attention to contingencies
   (d) more commitment to implementation

9. The ideal situation in a hierarchy of objectives is that lower-level plans become the _____ for accomplishing higher-level plans.
   (a) means   (c) scenarios
   (b) ends   (d) benchmarks

10. When managers use the benchmarking approach to planning, they _____.
    (a) use flexible budgets
    (b) identify best practices used by others
    (c) are seeking the most accurate forecasts that are available
    (d) focus more on the short term than the long term

11. One of the problems in relying too much on staff planners is _____.
    (a) a communication gap between planners and implementers
    (b) lack of expertise in the planning process
    (c) short-term rather than long-term focus
    (d) neglect of budgets as links between resources and activities

12. The planning process isn't complete until _____.
    (a) future conditions have been identified
    (b) stretch goals have been set
    (c) plans are implemented and results evaluated
    (d) budgets commit resources to plans

13. When a team leader is trying to follow an approach known as management by objectives, who should set a team member's performance objectives?
    (a) the team member
    (b) the team leader
    (c) the team leader and team member
    (d) the team member, the team leader, and a lawyer

14. A good performance objective is written in such a way that it _____.
    (a) has no precise timetable
    (b) is general and not too specific
    (c) is almost impossible to accomplish
    (d) can be easily measured

15. Which type of plan is used to guide resource allocations for long-term advancement of the organization's mission or purpose?
    (a) tactical   (c) strategic
    (b) operational   (d) functional

Short-Response Questions

16. List five steps in the planning process and give examples of each.
17. How might planning through benchmarking be used by the owner of a local bookstore?
18. How does planning help to improve focus?
19. Why does participatory planning facilitate implementation?

Essay Question

20. Put yourself in the position of a management trainer. You have been asked to make a short presentation to the local Small Business Enterprise Association at its biweekly luncheon. The topic you are to speak on is "How Each of You Can Use Objectives to Achieve Better Planning and Control." What will you tell them and why?

Management Skills & Competencies Make yourself **valuable!**

Evaluate Career Situations

What Would You Do?

1. The Planning Retreat

It's been a bit over two years since your promotion to division manager. You're now accountable for delivering about 10% of your firm's total revenues, and oversee more than 100 people working in five different departments. This year you'd like to make the annual planning retreat really valuable to everyone. All managers from team leaders to functional heads will be present. You will have them off site for a full day. What goals will you state for the retreat in the e-mail you send out with the retreat agenda? Knowing the steps in the planning process, what will the retreat agenda look like, and why?

2. Sexual Harassment

One of the persons under your supervision has a "possible" sexual harassment complaint about the behavior of a co-worker. She says that she understands the organization's sexual harassment policy, but the procedures are not clear. You're not clear, either, and take the matter to your boss. She tells you to draft a set of procedures that can be taken to top management for approval. What procedures will you recommend so that sexual harassment complaints like this one can be dealt with in a fair way?

3. Getting "Buy In"

A consulting firm has been hired to help write a strategic plan for your organization. The plan would be helpful, but you are worried about getting buy-in from all members, not just those at the top. What conditions can you set for the consultants so that they not only provide a solid strategic plan, but also create strong commitments to implementing it from members of your organization?

Reflect on the Self-Assessment

Time Management Profile

Instructions

Complete the following questionnaire by indicating "Y" (yes) or "N" (no) for each item. Be frank and allow your responses to create an accurate picture of how you tend to respond to these kinds of situations.

1. When confronted with several items of urgency and importance, I tend to do the easiest first.
2. I do the most important things during that part of the day when I know I perform best.
3. Most of the time I don't do things someone else can do; I delegate this type of work to others.
4. Even though meetings without a clear and useful purpose upset me, I put up with them.
5. I skim documents before reading and don't finish any that offer little value for my time.
6. I don't worry much if I don't accomplish at least one significant task each day.
7. I save the most trivial tasks for that time of day when my creative energy is lowest.
8. My workspace is neat and organized.
9. My office door is always "open"; I never work in complete privacy.
10. I schedule my time completely from start to finish every workday.
11. I don't like to-do lists, preferring to respond to daily events as they occur.
12. I block out a certain amount of time each day or week that is dedicated to high-priority activities.

Scoring

Count the number of "Y" responses to items 2, 3, 5, 7, 8, 12. Enter that score here [ ]. Count the number of "N" responses to items 1, 4, 6, 9, 10, 11. Enter that score here [ ]. Add the two scores together here [ ].

Self-Assessment Interpretation

The higher the total score, the more closely your behavior matches recommended time management guidelines. Reread those items where your response did not match the desired response. Why don't they match? Do you have reasons why your behavior in this instance should be different from the recommended time management guideline? Think about what you can do to adjust your behavior to be more consistent with these guidelines.

Contribute to the Team Exercise

Personal Career Planning

Instructions

Part 1—Complete the following activities as an individual assignment. Part 2—Share your results with your team. Part 3—Prepare a team summary of each member's career plans and present it for discussion with the class and instructor.

Activity 1 Strengths and Weaknesses Inventory Different occupations require special talents, abilities, and skills. Each of us, you included, has a repertoire of existing strengths and weaknesses that are "raw materials" we presently offer a potential employer. Actions can (and should!) be taken over time to further develop current strengths and to turn weaknesses into strengths. Make a list identifying your most important strengths and weaknesses in relation to the career direction you are likely to pursue after graduation. Place a * next to each item you consider most important to focus on for continued personal development.

Activity 2 Five-Year Career Objectives Make a list of three career objectives that you hope to accomplish within five years of graduation. Be sure they are appropriate given your list of personal strengths and weaknesses.

Activity 3 Five-Year Career Action Plans Write a specific action plan for accomplishing each objective. State exactly what you will do, and by when, in order to meet these objectives. If you will need special support or assistance, identify it and state how you will obtain it. An outside observer should be able to read your action plan for each objective and end up feeling confident that he or she knows exactly what you are going to do and why.

Manage a Critical Incident

Policy on Paternity Leave for New Dads

As the Human Resource Director for a medium-sized business with 800 employees, you've been asked by the CEO to draft a paternity leave policy. At present new moms get up to 8 weeks off with pay and an option for another 4 without pay. New dads are informally allowed to take up to a week off. After doing some research, you find that about 85% of new dads take one or two weeks off with the birth of a new child. But few new dads take more than that, even when it's available, because of a variety of worries about their careers and job security.[29]

Questions

What is your plan for drafting this new paternity leave policy? How will you go about getting good information and making sure the new policy is a good fit with your organization and its employees? What is your plan for making sure that new dads take full advantage of the new policy and aren't afraid to use it because of job and career concerns? In short, you need to not only develop the new policy but make sure it is accepted by all of the stakeholders affected by the policy.

Collaborate on a Team Activity

The Future Workplace

Instructions

Form groups as assigned by the instructor. Brainstorm to develop a master list of the major characteristics you expect to find in the workplace in the year 2020. Use this list as background for completing the following tasks:

1. Write a one-paragraph description of what the typical "Workplace 2020" manager's workday will be like.

2. Draw a "picture" representing what the "Workplace 2020" organization will look like.

3. Summarize in list form what you consider to be the major planning implications of your future workplace scenario for management students today. That is, explain what this means in terms of using academic and extracurricular activities to best prepare for success in this future scenario.

4. Choose a spokesperson to share your results with the class as a whole and explain their implications for the decisions most likely to lead to professional success for the members of the class.

Analyze THE CaseStudy : AVAGO TECHNOLOGIES
Planning for the Speed of Business

Go to *Management Cases for Critical Thinking* at the end of the book to find this case.

FUNDAMENTALS OF CONTROL

9

KEY TAKEAWAYS

- Identify the types of controls used by managers and the reasons for them.

- List and describe the steps in the control process.

- Explain the use of common control tools and techniques.

SKILLS MAKE YOU **VALUABLE**

- **EVALUATE** *Career Situations:*
  What Would You Do?

- **REFLECT** *On the Self-Assessment:*
  Internal/External Control

- **CONTRIBUTE** *To the Class Exercise:*
  After Meeting/Project Remorse

- **MANAGE** *A Critical Incident:*
  High Performer but Late for Work

- **COLLABORATE** *On the Team Project:*
  Building a Balanced Scorecard

- **ANALYZE** *The Case Study:*
  British Petroleum: Getting Drilled About Their Operations

Facts are informative and measurement helps keep us on target. Why, then, are we so often late to the party when it comes to exercising good control in our jobs and personal lives? We miss deadlines, we default on commitments, and we disappoint ourselves and others. There is a lot to learn about making control a personal asset, something that helps improve our performance as well as the performance of our teams and organizations.

Keeping in touch . . . staying informed . . . being in control: These are important responsibilities for every manager. But "control" is a word like "power." If you aren't careful when and how it's used, just the thought of it carries a negative connotation. Yet, control plays a positive and necessary role in everyday living and in the management process. Having things "under control" helps to get things done; when things are "out of control," it is generally more difficult.

Nike and Target are high-profile companies with different control stories. At Nike, the story is positive. The firm's stylish shoes are made by innovative micro-level precision engineering that is great for controlling costs of materials, time, and labor.[1] At Target, the story is negative. The firm experienced a massive data security breach that resulted in the loss of some 110 million credit card registries with personal data to cyber hackers, and cost the CEO his job.[2] What lies behind these different control stories? Are management practices just better and more sophisticated at Nike? Did Target executives lack sufficient technology expertise to put the right control systems into place?

Why and How Managers Control

TAKEAWAY 1   Why and how do managers exercise control?

LEARN MORE
ABOUT | The importance of controlling • Types of controls • Internal and external control

Control is important for the success of any organization, and we practice a lot of control quite naturally. Think of the things you do for fun—playing golf or tennis or Frisbee, reading, dancing, driving a car, or riding a bike. Through activities such as these, you've already become quite expert in the control process. How? Most probably by having an objective in mind, always checking to see how well you are doing, and making continuous adjustments to get it right.

Importance of Controlling

Controlling is the process of measuring performance and taking action to ensure desired results.

The management function of planning involves setting goals and making plans. It is closely linked with **controlling**, the process of measuring performance and making sure that plans turn out as intended. And, information is the foundation of control. Henry Schacht, former CEO of Cummins Engine Company and also of Lucent Technologies, linked control to what he called "friendly facts." He stated: "Facts that reinforce what you are doing are nice, because they help in terms of psychic reward. Facts that raise alarms are equally friendly, because they give you clues about how to respond, how to change, where to spend the resources."[3]

Figure 9.1 shows how controlling fits in with the other management functions. *Planning* sets the direction and the parameters for resource allocation. *Organizing* brings people and material resources together in working combinations. *Leading* inspires people to best utilize these resources. *Controlling* makes sure that the right things happen, in the right way, and at the right time. It's a way of ensuring that performance is consistent with plans and that accomplishments throughout a team or organization are coordinated in a means–ends fashion.

An **after-action review** is a systematic assessment of lessons learned and results accomplished in a completed project.

One of the great benefits of effective control is organizational learning. Consider, for example, the program of **after-action review** pioneered by the U.S. Army and now used in many corporate settings. It is a process for a structured review of lessons learned and results accomplished in a completed project, task force assignment, or special operation. Participants answer questions such as: "What was the intent?" "What actually happened?" "What did we learn?"[4] The after-action review helps make continuous improvement a shared norm. It encourages those involved to take responsibility for how they acted, what they achieved, and how they can be more effective in the future. The end-of-chapter team exercise is modeled on this approach.

Feedforward control ensures that directions and resources are right before the work begins.

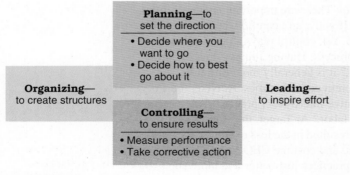

Planning—to
set the direction

• Decide where you
  want to go
• Decide how to best
  go about it

Organizing—
to create structures

Leading—
to inspire effort

Controlling—
to ensure results

• Measure performance
• Take corrective action

FIGURE 9.1
The role of controlling in the management process.

Types of Controls

The open-systems perspective shown in Figure 9.2 is one of the best ways to understand control. It shows how feedforward, concurrent, and feedback controls are linked with different phases of the input–throughput–output cycle.[5] The use of each of these control types increases the likelihood of high performance.

Feedforward Controls

Feedforward controls, also called *preliminary controls*, take place before a work activity begins. They ensure that objectives are clear, that proper directions

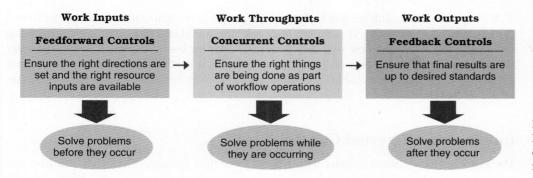

FIGURE 9.2
Feedforward,
concurrent, and
feedback controls.

are established, and that the right resources are available to accomplish the objectives. The goal is to solve problems before they occur by asking an important but often neglected question: "What needs to be done before we begin?"

Feedforward controls are preventive in nature. Managers using them take a forward-thinking and proactive approach to control. At McDonald's, for example, preliminary control of food ingredients plays an important role in the firm's quality program. The company requires that suppliers of its hamburger buns produce them to exact specifications, covering everything from texture to uniformity of color. Even in overseas markets, the firm works hard to develop local suppliers that can offer dependable quality.[6]

Concurrent Controls

Concurrent controls focus on what happens during the work process. Sometimes called *steering controls,* they make sure objective-focused actions are executed according to plan. You can also think of this as control through direct supervision. In today's increasingly complex virtual world, that supervision is as likely to be computer driven as face-to-face. Picture this scene at the Hyundai Motors headquarters in Seoul, South Korea, in what the firm calls its Global Command and Control Center.[7]

Concurrent control focuses on what happens during the work process.

> With dozens of computer screens relaying video and data, it [the Global Command and Control Center] keeps watch on Hyundai operations around the world. Parts shipments are traced from the time they leave the supplier until they reach a plant. Cameras peer into assembly lines from Beijing to Montgomery and keep a close watch on Hyundai's giant Ulsan, Korea, plant, the world's largest integrated auto factory.

The goal of concurrent controls is to solve problems as they emerge. The key question is, "What can we do to improve things right now?" In the Hyundai example, operations are monitored and business intelligence is gathered in real time using sophisticated information systems that help managers to quickly spot and correct any problems in the manufacturing cycle. The same kind of process intervention also happens at McDonald's, but there, concurrent control takes place face to face. Ever-present shift leaders constantly observe what is taking place in the unit as a whole, while helping out with the work necessary to keep the unit running. They are trained to intervene immediately when something is done improperly and to correct things on the spot.

Feedback Controls

Feedback controls, also called *post-action controls,* take place after work is completed. They focus on the quality of end results rather than on inputs and activities. Feedback controls are largely reactive; the goals are to solve problems after they occur and to prevent future problems from occurring. They ask the question: "Now that we are finished, how well did we do?"

Feedback control takes place after an action is completed.

We are all familiar with feedback controls and probably recognize their weak points from a customer service perspective. Restaurants often ask how you liked a meal after it is eaten; course evaluations tell instructors how well they performed after the course is over; a budget summary identifies cost overruns after a project is completed. Such feedback about mistakes that have already been made may not enable their immediate correction, but it can help to improve performance in the future.

Internal and External Control

Managers have two broad options with respect to control systems. First, they can trust and expect people to control their own behavior. This puts priority on internal or self-control. Second, they can exercise external control by structuring situations to increase the likelihood that things will happen as planned.[8] The alternatives here include bureaucratic or administrative control, clan or normative control, and market or regulatory control. The most effective control typically involves a mix of these internal and external options.

Self-Control

Self-control is internal control that occurs through self-management and self-discipline in fulfilling work and personal responsibilities.

We all exercise internal control in our daily lives. We do so with regard to managing our money, our relationships, our eating and drinking, our health behaviors, our study habits, and more. Managers can take advantage of this human capacity for **self-control** by unlocking, allowing, and supporting it. This means helping people to be good at self-management, giving them freedom, and encouraging them to exercise self-discipline in performing their jobs. Any workplace that emphasizes participation, empowerment, and involvement will rely heavily on self-control.

Managers can gain a lot by assuming that people are ready and willing to exercise self-control in their work.[9] But, an internal control strategy requires a great deal of trust. When people are willing to work on their own and exercise self-control, managers have to have the confidence to give them the freedom to do so. Self-control is most likely when the process used to set objectives and standards is participative. The potential for self-control also increases when capable people have a clear sense of the organization's mission and have the resources necessary to do their jobs well. The potential for self-control is also greater in inclusive organizational cultures in which everyone treats everyone else with respect and consideration.

It's important to think about self-control as a personal capacity, even a life skill. How good are you at taking control of your time and maintaining a healthy work–life balance? Do you ever wonder who's in control, you or your phone? It used to be that we sometimes took work home in a briefcase, did a bit, closed the case up, and took it back to work the next day. Now work is always there, on the computer, in our e-mails, and streamed as text messages. All this is habit forming, and some of us handle this intrusion into our non-work lives better than others.[10]

Bureaucratic Control

Bureaucratic control influences behavior through authority, policies, procedures, job descriptions, budgets, and day-to-day supervision.

One form of external control uses authority, policies, procedures, job descriptions, budgets, and day-to-day supervision to make sure that people act in harmony with organizational interests. It's called **bureaucratic control**, and you can think of it as control that flows through the organization's hierarchy of authority. Organizations typically have policies and procedures regarding sexual harassment, for example. Their goal is to make sure members behave toward one another respectfully and with no suggestion of sexual pressure or impropriety.

> *"Resilient people are like trees bending in the wind. . . . They bounce back."*

Resiliency Offers Strength from Within

Managerial control is all about how to increase the probability that things go right for organizations even as they deal with an increasing number of operational complexities. It's the same for us—every day, in our work and personal lives. We need to spot and understand where things are going according to plan or going off course. We need to have the courage and confidence to change approaches that aren't working well. Our success, simply put, depends a lot on **resiliency**—the ability to call on inner strength and keep moving forward even when things are tough.

Think of resiliency in personal terms—caring for an aging parent with a terrible disease or single parenthood with small children. Think of it in career terms—juggling personal and work responsibilities, continuously attending to e-mails, voice mails, instant messages, and rushing to many scheduled and unscheduled meetings. We need to be managed, we need to exercise control, and we need staying power to perform over the long term. Resiliency helps us hold on and keep things moving forward even in the face of personal and professional adversity.

Resilient people face up to challenges; they don't hide or back away from them. They develop strategies, make plans, and find opportunity even in challenging situations. Dr. Steven M. Southwick, professor of psychiatry at Yale University, says: "Resilient people are like trees bending in the wind. . . . They bounce back." Does this description fit you . . . or not? Why?

Resiliency Quick Test

Score yourself from 1 = don't at all agree, to 5 = totally agree, on the following items:

- I am an upbeat person for the most part.
- Uncertainty and ambiguity don't much bother me.
- I tend to adapt quickly as things change.
- I can see positives even when things go wrong.
- I am good at learning from experience.
- I am good at problem solving.
- I am strong and hold up well when times are tough.
- I have been able to turn bad situations into positive gains.

GET TO KNOW YOURSELF BETTER

Take the Resiliency Quick Test. A score of 35 or better suggests you are highly resilient; with any lower score, you should question how well you hold up under pressure. Double-check the test results by looking at your behavior. Write notes on how you handle situations like a poor grade at school, a put-down from a friend, a denial letter from a job application, or criticism from a supervisor or co-worker on your job. Summarize what you've learned in a memo to yourself about how you might benefit from showing more resiliency in difficult situations.

Organizations also use budgets for personnel, equipment, travel expenses, and the like to keep behavior targeted within set limits.

Another level of bureaucratic control comes from laws and regulations in the organization's external environment. An example is the Sarbanes-Oxley Act of 2002 (SOX), which establishes procedures to regulate financial reporting and governance in publicly traded corporations.[11] SOX was passed in response to major corporate scandals over the accuracy of financial reports provided by some firms. Under SOX, chief executives and chief financial officers must personally sign off on financial reports and certify their accuracy. Those who misstate their firm's financial records can go to jail and pay substantial personal fines. The complexity and pressures of increased government regulations have led many firms to appoint chief compliance officers, CCOs, and set up compliance departments. They are most effective when the CCO reports directly to the chief executive or to the board of directors.[12] Actions are also being taken to strengthen governance by boards. Stricter management oversight is evident in moves for directors to become more actively involved in leadership and to separate the CEO and board chairman roles.[13]

analysis > MAKE DATA YOUR FRIEND

> *Office workers get distracted as often as once every 3 minutes; it can take 23 minutes to refocus after a major interruption.*

Those Small Distractions Can Be Goal Killers

Most of us work with good intentions. But when distractions hit, focus gets lost, plans fall by the wayside, and progress suffers. Whether it's chatting with co-workers, following social media, or tackling electronic in-boxes, interruptions are more plentiful than we might admit.

- Office workers get distracted as often as once every 3 minutes and it takes an average of 23 minutes to refocus after a major interruption.
- Handling up to 100 electronic messages can kill up to one-half of a workday.
- Facilitators of disruptions include open-plan office spaces, use of multiple electronic devices, and constant checking of social media and messaging windows.

Lacy Roberson, eBay's director of learning and organization development, calls the situation "an epidemic" and says it's hard for people to get their work done with all the interruptions and the strain that they cause. The fight against disruptions causes some employees to start their day very early or to stay late to get their jobs done. Employers are starting to fight back and to try to protect "real work" time.

"No devices" is a rule at some eBay meetings. Intel is experimenting with allowing workers blocks of "think time" where they don't answer messages or attend meetings. Abbot Laboratories is retraining workers to use the telephone rather than e-mail for many internal office communications.

YOUR THOUGHTS?

How prone are you to letting distractions consume your time? Does this problem apply to your personal affairs and relationships, not just work? It's interesting that some employers are trying to step in and set policies that might minimize the negative impact of distractions, particularly electronic ones. Where's the self-control? Aren't there things we can all do to protect our time and keep our work and goals on track?

Clan Control

Clan control
influences behavior through norms and expectations set by the organizational culture.

Whereas bureaucratic control emphasizes hierarchy and authority, **clan control** influences behavior through norms and expectations set by the organizational culture. Sometimes called *normative control,* it harnesses the power of group cohesiveness and collective identity to influence behavior in teams and organizations.

Clan control happens as people who share values and identify strongly with one another behave in consistent ways. Just look around the typical college classroom and campus. You'll see clan control reflected in how students dress, use language, and act in class and during leisure time. They often behave according to the expectations of peers and the groups with whom they identify. The same holds true in organizations, where clan control influences the members of teams and work groups to display common behavior patterns.

Market Control

Market control is essentially the influence of market competition on the behavior of organizations and their members.

Market control is essentially the influence of customers and competition on the behavior of organizations and their members. Business firms show the influence of market control in the way that they adjust products, pricing, promotions, and other practices in response to consumer feedback and what competitors are doing. A good example is the growing emphasis on green products and sustainability practices. When a firm like Walmart starts to get positive publicity from its expressed goals of powering all of its stores with renewable energy, for example, the effect is felt by its competitors.[14] They have to adjust their practices in order to avoid losing the public relations advantage to Walmart. "For American companies, there's a lot of peer pressure," said the director of the Governance & Accountability Institute when reporting that voluntary filings by S&P 500 firms of sustainability reports had risen from 53% to 72% in just one year.[15] In this sense, the time-worn phrase "keeping up with the competition" is really another way of expressing the dynamics of market controls in action.

Learning Check 1

TAKEAWAYQUESTION **1 Why and how do managers exercise control?**

BE SURE YOU CAN • define *controlling* as a management function • explain benefits of after-action reviews • illustrate how a fast-food restaurant uses feedforward, concurrent, and feedback controls • discuss internal control and external control systems • give examples of bureaucratic, clan, and market controls

The Control Process

TAKEAWAY 2   What are the steps in the control process?

LEARN MORE | Establishing objectives and standards • Measuring actual results
ABOUT | Comparing results with objectives and standards • Taking corrective action

The control process involves the four steps shown in Figure 9.3: (1) establish performance objectives and standards; (2) measure actual performance; (3) compare actual performance with objectives and standards; and (4) take corrective action as needed. Although essential to management, these steps apply equally well to personal and career decisions as well. Consider this—without career objectives, how do you know where you really want to go? How can you allocate your time and other resources to take best advantage of available opportunities? Without measurement, how can you assess whether any progress has been made? How can you adjust your current behavior to improve the prospects for positive future results?

The **Pareto Principle** states that 80% of consequences come from 20% of causes.

Step 1—Establish Objectives and Standards

The control process begins with planning, when performance objectives and standards for measuring them are set. The objectives and standards define what one wants to accomplish in terms of key results. However, the word *key* in the prior sentence deserves special emphasis. The focus when setting objectives and standards should be on "critical" or "essential" results that will make a real performance difference. Unfortunately we often expend too much time and effort on things that just aren't all that important, and we let the big or really consequential things get away from us in the process. To stay on focus, productivity experts suggest remembering the **Pareto Principle** that 80% of consequences (think—real impact) come from 20% of causes (think—work accomplished).[16]

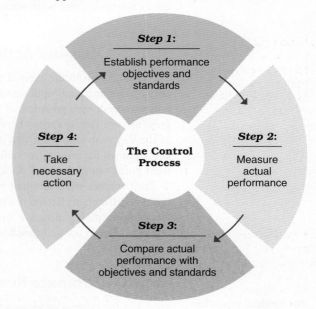

FIGURE 9.3
Four steps in the control process.

Output Standards

An **output standard** measures performance results in terms of quantity, quality, cost, or time.

The control process uses **output standards** that measure actual outcomes or work results. Businesses use many output standards, such as earnings per share, return on investment, sales growth, and market share. Others include quantity and quality of production, costs incurred, service or delivery time, and error rates. Based on your experience at work and as a consumer, you can probably come up with even more examples of relevant output standards.

When Allstate Corporation launched a new diversity initiative, it created a "diversity index" to quantify performance across a range of diversity issues. The standards included how well employees met the goals of bias-free customer service and how well managers met the firm's diversity expectations.[17] When General Electric became concerned about managing ethics in its 320,000-member global workforce, it created measurement standards to track compliance. Each business unit was required to report quarterly on how many of its members attended ethics training sessions and signed the firm's "Spirit and Letter" ethics guide.[18]

How about output standards for other types of organizations, such as a symphony orchestra? When the Cleveland Orchestra wrestled with performance standards, the members weren't willing to rely on vague generalities like "we played well" or "the audience seemed happy" or "not too many mistakes were made." Rather, they decided to track standing ovations, invitations to perform in other countries, and how often other orchestras copied their performance style.[19]

Input Standards

An **input standard** measures work efforts that go into a performance task.

The control process also uses **input standards** that measure work efforts. These are common in situations where outputs are difficult or expensive to measure. Examples of input standards for a college professor might be an orderly course syllabus, meeting all class sessions, and returning exams and assignments in a timely fashion. Of course, as this example might suggest, measuring inputs doesn't mean that outputs such as high-quality teaching and learning are necessarily achieved. Other examples of input standards at work include conformance with rules, efficient use of resources, and work attendance.

Step 2—Measure Actual Performance

The second step in the control process is to measure actual performance. It is the point where output standards and input standards are used to carefully document results. Linda Sanford, currently a senior vice president at IBM, has had a high-performance career with the company. She grew up on a family farm where measuring results was a way of life. Sanford says: "At the end of the day, you saw what you did, knew how many rows of strawberries you picked." At IBM she is known for walking around the factory, just to see "at the end of the day how many machines were going out of the back dock."[20]

Performance measurement in the control process must be accurate enough to identify significant differences between what is really taking place and what was originally planned. Without measurement, effective control is impossible. With measurement tied to key results, however, an old adage often holds true: "What gets measured happens."

Step 3—Compare Results with Objectives and Standards

The **control equation** states: Need for Action = Desired Performance − Actual Performance.

Step 3 in the control process is to compare objectives with results. You can remember its implications by this **control equation**:

$$\text{Need for Action} = \text{Desired Performance} - \text{Actual Performance}$$

ethics > KNOW RIGHT FROM WRONG

> *Twitter removes tweets in response to government requests in specific countries.*

Global Censorship of Search and Social Media

London—Reporters Without Borders criticized Twitter's censorship policy after the company said it will remove tweets in response to government requests in specific countries. These tweets will remain available elsewhere in the world, and deleted tweets will be replaced with the message "Deleted at government request." CEO Dick Costolo says: "You can't reside in countries and not operate within the law." Lucie Morillon of Reporters Without Borders counters that "if Twitter is ready to abide by repressive countries then there are real consequences for journalists, bloggers . . . the chain of information is broken."

Beijing—Skype is told by the Chinese government that its software must filter words that the Chinese leadership considers offensive from text messages. If the company doesn't, it can't do business in the country. After refusing at first, company executives finally agreed. Phrases such as "Falun Gong" and "Dalai Lama" are deleted from text messages delivered through Skype's Chinese joint venture partner, Tom Online. Skype co-founder Niklas Zennstrom, says: "I may like or not like the laws and regulations to operate businesses in the UK or Germany or the U.S., but if I do business there I choose to comply."

New Delhi—An Indian citizen sues Google in local court claiming that some of its content is offensive to certain religious communities. The New Delhi district court issued an order for Google to remove the content. Google complies on its India site but keeps the content available outside of the country. A Google spokesperson says: "This step is in accordance with Google's longstanding policy of responding to court orders." But, free speech advocates in India claim it is censorship.

WHAT DO YOU THINK?

Is it ethical for companies who want to do business in China or elsewhere to go along with policies that would clearly be considered to be a violation of human rights in other places? What determines whether companies should comply with local censorship requests? Should they follow local rules, challenge the status quo, or simply decline to operate in those markets? When should business executives stand up and challenge laws and regulations that are used to deny customers the rights or privacy that they expect?

The question of what constitutes "desired" performance plays an important role in the control equation. Some organizations use *engineering comparisons.* United Parcel Service (UPS), for example, carefully measures the routes and routines of its drivers to establish the times expected for each delivery. When a delivery manifest is scanned as completed, the driver's time is registered in a performance log that is closely monitored by supervisors. Organizations also use *historical comparisons*, where past experience becomes the baseline for evaluating current performance. They also use *relative comparisons* that benchmark performance against that being achieved by other people, work units, or organizations.

Step 4—Take Corrective Action

The final step in the control process is to take actions needed to correct problems or make improvements. **Management by exception** is the practice of giving attention to situations that show the greatest need for action. It saves time, energy, and other resources by helping managers focus their attention on high-priority areas.

Managers should be alert to two types of exceptions. The first is where actual performance is less than desired. This *problem situation* must be understood so that corrective action can restore performance to the desired level. The second is where actual performance turns out higher than what was desired. This *opportunity situation* must be understood with the goal of continuing or increasing the high level of accomplishment in the future.

Management by exception focuses attention on substantial differences between actual and desired performance.

Learning Check 2

TAKEAWAYQUESTION **2 What are the steps in the control process?**

BE SURE YOU CAN • list the steps in the control process • explain why planning is important to controlling • differentiate between output and input standards • state the control equation • define *management by exception*

Projects are one-time activities with many component tasks that must be completed in proper order and according to budget.

Project management is the responsibility for overall planning, supervision, and control of projects.

A **Gantt chart** graphically displays the scheduling of tasks required to complete a project.

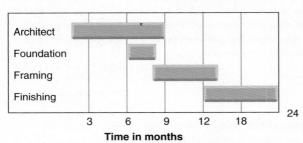

Time in months

CPM/PERT is a combination of the critical path method and the program evaluation and review technique.

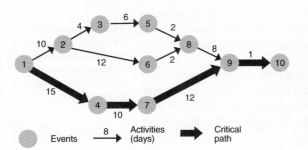

Control Tools and Techniques

TAKEAWAY 3 What are the common control tools and techniques?

LEARN MORE | Project management and control • Inventory control • Breakeven analysis
ABOUT | Financial controls • Balanced scorecards

Managers in most organizations use a variety of different control systems and techniques. Some of the most common ones include special techniques of project management, inventory control, breakeven analysis, and financial controls, as well as the use of balanced scorecards.

Project Management and Control

It might be something personal, like an anniversary party for your parents or grandparents; a fundraiser for a local homeless shelter; or the launch of a new product or service at your place of work. It might be the completion of a new student activities building on campus, or the implementation of a new advertising campaign for a sports team. What these examples and others like them share in common is that they encompass relatively complicated sets of interrelated tasks with multiple components that have to happen in a certain sequence, and that must be completed by a specified date. We call them **projects**, complex one-time events with unique components and an objective that must be met within a set time frame.

Project management takes responsibility for overall planning, supervision, and control of projects. A project manager's job is to ensure that a project is well planned and then completed according to plan—on time, within budget, and consistent with objectives. Two useful techniques for project management and control are Gantt charts and CPM/PERT.

A **Gantt chart** graphically displays the scheduling of tasks that go into completing a project. As developed in the early 20th century by Henry Gantt, an industrial engineer, this tool has become a core element of project management. The visual overview of what needs to be done on a project allows for easy progress checks to be made at different time intervals. It also helps with event or activity sequencing to make sure key aspects of a project get accomplished in time for later work to build on them. One of the biggest problems with projects, for example, is when delays in early activities create problems for later activities.

A more advanced use of the Gantt chart is a technique known as **CPM/PERT**—a combination of the critical path method and the program evaluation and review technique. Project planning based on CPM/PERT uses a network chart like the one shown here. Such charts break a project into a series of smaller sub-activities that have clear beginning and end points. These points become "nodes" in the chart, and the arrows between nodes show in what order the sub-activities must be completed. The full diagram shows all the interrelationships that must be coordinated for the entire project to be successfully completed.

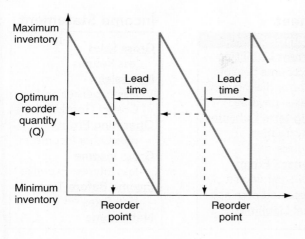

Use of CPM/PERT techniques helps project managers track activities to make sure they happen in the right sequence and on time. If you look at the network in the figure on the previous page, you should notice that the time required for each activity can be easily computed and tracked. The longest pathway from start to conclusion in a CPM/PERT network is called the **critical path**. It represents the quickest time in which the entire project can be finished, assuming everything goes according to schedule and established project plans. In the example, the critical path is 38 days.

> The **critical path** is the longest pathway in a CPM/PERT network.

> **Inventory control** ensures that inventory is only big enough to meet immediate needs.

> The **economic order quantity** method places new orders when inventory levels fall to predetermined points.

> **Just-in-time scheduling (JIT)** routes materials to workstations just in time for use.

> The **breakeven point** occurs where revenues just equal costs.

> **Breakeven analysis** performs what-if calculations under different revenue and cost conditions.

Inventory Control

Cost control is always an important performance concern. And a very good place to start is with inventory. The goal of **inventory control** is to make sure that any inventory is only big enough to meet immediate needs, so that carrying costs are minimized.

The **economic order quantity** form of inventory control, shown in the above figure, automatically orders a fixed number of items every time an inventory level falls to a predetermined point. The order sizes are mathematically calculated to minimize inventory costs. A good example is your local supermarket. It routinely makes hundreds of daily orders on an economic order quantity basis.

Another popular approach to inventory control is **just-in-time scheduling (JIT)**. These systems reduce costs and improve workflow by scheduling materials to arrive at a workstation or facility just in time for use. Because JIT nearly eliminates the carrying costs of inventories, it is an important business productivity tool.

Breakeven Analysis

A frequent control question asked by business executives is: "What is the **breakeven point**?" In Figure 9.4 you'll see that breakeven occurs at the point where revenues are just equal to costs. You can also think of the breakeven point as where losses end and profit begins. A breakeven point is computed using this formula:

Breakeven Point = Fixed Costs ÷ (Price − Variable Costs)

Managers using **breakeven analysis** perform what-if calculations under different projected cost and revenue conditions. *Question*—Suppose the proposed target price for a new product is $8 per unit, fixed costs are $10,000, and variable costs are $4 per unit. What sales volume is required to break even? (*Answer*: breakeven at 2,500 units.) *Question*— What happens if you can keep variable costs to $3 per unit? (*Answer*: breakeven at 2,000 units.) *Question*—If you can produce only 1,000 units in the beginning and at the original costs, at what price must you sell them to break even? (Answer: $14.) Business executives perform these types of cost control analyses every day.

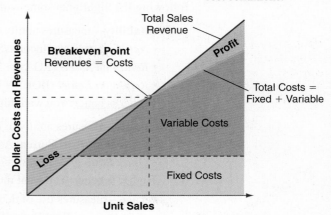

FIGURE 9.4
Use of breakeven analysis to make informed "what-if" decisions.

Balance Sheet

Assets	Liabilities
Current Assets	**Current Liabilities**
• Cash	• Accounts payable
• Receivables	• Accrued expenses
• Inventories	• Taxes payable
Fixed Assets	**Long-term Liabilities**
• Land	• Mortgages
• Buildings	• Bonds
Less Depreciation	**Owner's Equity**
	• Outstanding stock
	• Retained earnings
Total Assets =	**Total Liabilities**

Income Statement

Gross Sales
 less Returns
Net Sales
 less Expenses and
 Cost of Goods Sold
Operating Profits
 plus Other Income
Gross Income
 less Interest Expense
Income Before Taxes
 less Taxes
Net Income

FIGURE 9.5
Basic foundations of a balance sheet and income statement.

Financial Controls

The pressure is ever present for all organizations to use their financial resources well. And, the global economic recession has left no doubt that an important part of managerial control involves the analysis of financial performance. Control depends on measurement, and there are a number of ways that financial performance can be measured and tracked for control purposes.

The foundation for analysis using financial controls rests with the firm's balance sheet and income statement. Each looks at finances in slightly different ways, and together they provide a good picture of the financial health of an organization. The **balance sheet** shows assets and liabilities at a point in time. It will be displayed in an Assets = Liabilities format. The **income statement** shows profits or losses at a point in time. It will be displayed in a Sales − Expenses = Net Income format. You are likely to remember both from an accounting course or as summarized in Figure 9.5.

Special measures of financial performance help managers use information from balance sheets and income statements for control purposes. They include financial ratios that indicate *liquidity*—the ability to generate cash to pay bills; *leverage*—the ability to earn more in returns than the cost of debt; *asset management*—the ability to use resources efficiently and operate at minimum cost; and *profitability*—the ability to earn revenues greater than costs. The following list highlights some widely used financial ratios.

A balance sheet shows assets and liabilities at one point in time.

An income statement shows profits or losses at one point in time.

 Profitability—measures ability to earn revenues greater than costs
 • *Net Margin* = Net Income/Sales
 • *Return on Assets* (ROA) = Net Income/Total Assets
 • *Return on Equity* (ROE) = Net Income/Owner's Equity
 <u>Higher is better</u>: You want higher net income relative to sales, assets, and equity.

 Liquidity—measures ability to meet short-term obligations
 • *Current Ratio* = Current Assets/Current Liabilities
 • *Quick Ratio or Acid Test* = Current Assets − Inventories/Current Liabilities
 <u>Higher is better</u>: You want more assets and fewer liabilities.

Leverage—measures use of debt
 • *Debt Ratio* = Total Debts/Total Assets
 <u>Lower is better</u>: You want fewer debts and more assets.

Asset Management—measures asset and inventory efficiency
- *Asset Turnover* = Sales/Total Assets
- *Inventory Turnover* = Sales/Average Inventory
<u>Higher is better:</u> You want more sales relative to assets and inventory.

Financial ratios are very common in executive dashboards that organize business intelligence information for decision making. The ratios lend themselves in a straightforward way to visual displays that provide neat historical comparisons within the firm and for industry benchmarking. They can also be used to set financial targets or goals to share with employees and tracked to indicate performance success or failure. Civco Medical Instruments, for example, distributes a monthly financial report to all employees. These reports always have the facts about how well the firm is doing. This helps employees focus on what they can do better to improve the firm's bottom line.[21]

Balanced Scorecards

If an instructor takes class attendance and assigns grades based on it, students tend to come to class. If an employer tracks the number of customers employees serve per day, employees tend to serve more customers. So if "what gets measured happens," shouldn't managers take advantage of "scorecards" to record and track performance results?

Strategic management consultants Robert S. Kaplan and David P. Norton advocate using the **balanced scorecard** for management control.[22] They say it gives top managers "a fast, but comprehensive view of the business." The basic principle is that to do well and to win, you have to keep score. Like sports teams, organizations tend to perform better when their members always know the score.

Developing a balanced scorecard for any organization begins with a clarification of the organization's mission and vision—what it wants to be and how it wants to be perceived by its key stakeholders. Next, the following questions are used to develop specific scorecard goals and measures:

- *Financial Performance*—"How well do our actions directly contribute to improved financial performance? To improve financially, how should we appear to our shareholders?" Sample goals: survive, succeed, and prosper. *Sample measures:* cash flow, sales growth and operating income, increased market share, and return on equity.

- *Customer Satisfaction*—"How well do we serve our customers and clients? To achieve our vision, how should we appear to our customers?" Sample goals: new products, responsive supply. *Sample measures:* percentage sales from new products, percentage on-time deliveries.

- *Internal Process Improvement*—"How well do our activities and processes directly increase the value we provide our customers and clients? To satisfy our customers and shareholders, at what internal business processes should we excel?" Sample goals: manufacturing excellence, design productivity, new product introduction. *Sample measures:* cycle times, engineering efficiency, new product time.

- *Innovation and Learning*—"How well are we learning, changing, and improving things over time? To achieve our vision, how will we sustain our ability to change and improve?" Sample goals: technology leadership, time to market. *Sample measures:* time to develop new technologies, new product introduction time versus competition.

When balanced scorecard measures are taken and routinely recorded for critical managerial review, Kaplan and Norton expect managers to make better decisions and organizations to perform better in these four performance areas. Like the financial ratios discussed earlier, the balanced scorecard is a good fit for executive dashboards and visual displays of business intelligence. Again, what gets measured happens.

A **balanced scorecard** tallies organizational performance in financial, customer service, internal process, and innovation and learning areas.

Think about the possibilities of using balanced scorecards in all types of organizations. How can this approach be used, for example, by an elementary school, a hospital, a community library, a mayor's office, or a fast-food restaurant? How might the performance dimensions and indicators vary among these different organizations? And if balanced scorecards make sense, why is it that more organizations don't use them?

Learning Check 3

TAKEAWAYQUESTION 3 **What are the common control tools and techniques?**

BE SURE YOU CAN • define project management • explain how Gantt charts and CPM/PERT analysis can assist in project management • explain how inventory controls and breakeven analysis can assist in cost control • list and explain common ratios used in financial control • identify the four main balanced scorecard components and give examples of how they might be used in organizations of various types

Management Learning Review
Get Prepared for **Quizzes and Exams**

SUMMARY

TAKEAWAYQUESTION 1

Why and how do managers exercise control?

* Controlling is the process of measuring performance and taking corrective action as needed.
* Feedforward controls are accomplished before a work activity begins; they ensure that directions are clear and that the right resources are available to accomplish them.
* Concurrent controls make sure that things are being done correctly; they allow corrective actions to be taken while the work is being done.
* Feedback controls take place after an action is completed; they address the question "Now that we are finished, how well did we do, and what did we learn for the future?"
* Internal control is self-control and occurs as people take personal responsibility for their work.
* External control is based on the use of bureaucratic, clan, and market control systems.

FOR DISCUSSION Can strong input and output controls make up for poor concurrent controls?

TAKEAWAYQUESTION 2

What are the steps in the control process?

* The first step in the control process is to establish performance objectives and standards that create targets against which later performance can be evaluated.
* The second step in the control process is to measure actual performance and specifically identify what results are being achieved.

* The third step in the control process is to compare performance results with objectives to determine if things are going according to plans.
* The fourth step in the control process is to take action to resolve problems or explore opportunities that are identified when results are compared with objectives.

FOR DISCUSSION What are the potential downsides to management by exception?

TAKEAWAYQUESTION 3

What are the common control tools and techniques?

* A project is a unique event that must be completed by a specified date; project management is the process of ensuring that projects are completed on time, on budget, and according to objectives.
* Gantt charts assist in project management and control by displaying how various tasks must be scheduled in order to complete a project on time.
* CPM/PERT analysis assists in project management and control by describing the complex networks of activities that must be completed in sequence for a project to be completed successfully.
* Economic order quantities and just-in-time deliveries are common approaches to inventory cost control.
* The breakeven equation is: Breakeven Point = Fixed Costs ÷ (Price − Variable Costs).
* Breakeven analysis identifies the points where revenues will equal costs under different pricing and cost conditions.
* Financial control of business performance is facilitated by a variety of financial ratios, such as those dealing with liquidity, leverage, assets, and profitability.

- The balanced scorecard measures overall organizational performance in four areas: financial, customers, internal processes, and innovation.

FOR DISCUSSION Should all employees of a business be regularly informed of the firm's overall financial performance?

SELF-TEST 9

Multiple-Choice Questions

1. After objectives and standards are set, what step comes next in the control process?
   (a) Measure results.
   (b) Take corrective action.
   (c) Compare results with objectives.
   (d) Modify standards to fit circumstances.

2. When a soccer coach tells her players at the end of a game, "I'm pleased you stayed with the game plan," she is using a/an _____ to a measure performance, even though in terms of outcomes, her team lost.
   (a) input standard
   (b) output standard
   (c) historical comparison
   (d) relative comparison

3. When an automobile manufacturer is careful to purchase only the highest-quality components for use in production, this is an example of an attempt to ensure high performance through _____ control.
   (a) concurrent
   (b) statistical
   (c) inventory
   (d) feedforward

4. Management by exception means _____.
   (a) managing only when necessary
   (b) focusing attention where the need for action is greatest
   (c) the same thing as concurrent control
   (d) the same thing as just-in-time delivery

5. When a supervisor working alongside an employee corrects him or her when a mistake is made, this is an example of _____ control.
   (a) feedforward
   (b) concurrent
   (c) internal
   (d) clan

6. If an organization's top management visits a firm in another industry to learn more about its excellent record in hiring and promoting minority and female candidates, this is an example of using _____ for control purposes.
   (a) a balanced scorecard
   (b) relative comparison
   (c) management by exception
   (d) progressive discipline

7. The control equation states: _____ = Desired Performance − Actual Performance.
   (a) Problem Magnitude
   (b) Management Opportunity
   (c) Planning Objective
   (d) Need for Action

8. When a UPS manager compares the amount of time a driver takes to make certain deliveries against standards set through a quantitative analysis of her delivery route, this is known as _____.
   (a) a historical comparison
   (b) an engineering comparison
   (c) relative benchmarking
   (d) concurrent control

9. Projects are unique one-time events that _____.
   (a) have unclear objectives
   (b) must be completed by a specific time
   (c) have unlimited budgets
   (d) are largely self-managing

10. The _____ chart graphically displays the scheduling of tasks required to complete a project.
    (a) exception
    (b) Taylor
    (c) Gantt
    (d) after-action

11. When one team member advises another team member that "your behavior is crossing the line in terms of our expectations for workplace civility," she is exercising a form of _____ control over the other's inappropriate behaviors.
    (a) clan
    (b) market
    (c) internal
    (d) preliminary

12. In a CPM/PERT analysis, the focus is on _____ and the event that link them together with the finished project.
    (a) costs, budgets
    (b) activities, sequences
    (c) timetables, budgets
    (d) goals, costs

13. If fixed costs are $10,000, variable costs are $4 per unit, and the target selling price per unit is $8, what is the breakeven point?
    (a) 2
    (b) 500
    (c) 2,500
    (d) 4,800

14. Among the financial ratios used for control, Current Assets/Current Liabilities is known as the _____.
    (a) debt ratio
    (c) current ratio
    (b) net margin
    (d) inventory turnover ratio

15. With respect to return on assets (ROA) and the debt ratio, the preferred directions when analyzing them from a control standpoint are _____.
    (a) decrease ROA, increase debt
    (b) increase ROA, increase debt
    (c) increase ROA, decrease debt
    (d) decrease ROA, decrease debt

Short-Response Questions

16. List the four steps in the controlling process and give examples of each.

17. How might feedforward control be used by the owner/manager of a local bookstore?

18. How does Douglas McGregor's Theory Y relate to the concept of internal control?

19. What four questions could be used to organize the presentation of a real-time balanced scorecard in the executive dashboard for a small business?

Essay Question

20. Assume that you are given the job of project manager for building a new student center on your campus. List just five of the major activities that would need to be accomplished to complete the new building in two years. Draw a CPM/PERT network diagram that links the activities together in required event scheduling and sequencing. Make an estimate for the time required for each sequence to be completed and identify the critical path.

Management Skills & Competencies Make yourself valuable!

Evaluate Career Situations

What Would You Do?

1. Adrift in Career

A work colleague comes to you and confides that she feels "adrift in her career" and "just can't get enthused about what she's doing anymore." You think this might be a problem of self-management and personal control. How can you respond most helpfully? How might she use the steps in the management control process to better understand and improve her situation?

2. Too Much Socializing

You have a highly talented work team whose past performance has been outstanding. You've recently noticed team members starting to act like the workday is mainly a social occasion. Getting the work done too often seems less important than having a good time. Recent data show that performance is on the decline. How can you use controls in a positive way to restore performance to high levels in this team?

3. Yes or No to Graduate School

You've had three years of solid work experience after earning your undergraduate degree. A lot of your friends are talking about going to graduate school, and the likely target for you would be an MBA degree. Given all the potential costs and benefits of getting an MBA, how can breakeven analysis help you make the decision: (a) to go or not go, (b) to go full time or part time, and (c) even where to go?

Reflect on the Self-Assessment

Internal/External Control

Instructions

Circle either "a" or "b" to indicate the item you most agree with in each pair of the following statements.[23]

1. (a) Promotions are earned through hard work and persistence.
   (b) Making a lot of money is largely a matter of breaks.

2. (a) Many times the reactions of teachers seem haphazard to me.
   (b) In my experience, I have noticed that there is usually a direct connection between how hard I study and the grades I get.

3. (a) The number of divorces indicates that more and more people are not trying to make their marriages work.
   (b) Marriage is largely a gamble.

4. (a) It is silly to think that one can really change another person's basic attitudes.
   (b) When I am right, I can convince others.

5. **(a)** Getting promoted is really a matter of being a little luckier than the next guy.

   (b) In our society, an individual's future earning power is dependent on his or her ability.

6. **(a)** If one knows how to deal with people, they are really quite easily led.

   (b) I have little influence over the way other people behave.

7. **(a)** In my case, the grades I make are the results of my own efforts; luck has little or nothing to do with it.

   (b) Sometimes I feel that I have little to do with the grades I get.

8. **(a)** People such as I can change the course of world affairs if we make ourselves heard.

   (b) It is only wishful thinking to believe that one can really influence what happens in society at large.

9. **(a)** Much of what happens to me is probably a matter of chance.

   (b) I am the master of my fate.

10. **(a)** Getting along with people is a skill that must be practiced.

    (b) It is almost impossible to figure out how to please some people.

Scoring

Give yourself 1 point for 1a, 2b, 3a, 4b, 5b, 6a, 7a, 8a, 9b, 10a. Total scores of: 8–10 = high *internal* locus of control, 6–7 = moderate *internal* locus of control, 5 = *mixed* locus of control, 3–4 = moderate *external* locus of control, 0–2 = high *external* locus of control.

Interpretation

This instrument offers an impression of your tendency toward an *internal locus of control or external locus of control*. Persons with a high internal locus of control tend to believe they have control over their own destinies. They may be most responsive to opportunities for greater self-control in the workplace. Persons with a high external locus of control tend to believe that what happens to them is largely in the hands of external forces or other people. They may be less comfortable with self-control and more responsive to external controls in the workplace.

Contribute to the Class Exercise

After-Meeting/Project Remorse

Instructions

A. Everyone on the team should complete the following assessment after participating in a meeting or a group project.[24]

1. How satisfied are you with the outcome of the meeting project?

   Not at all satisfied　　1 2 3 4 5 6 7　　Totally satisfied

2. How would the other members of the meeting/project group rate your influence on what took place?

   No influence　　1 2 3 4 5 6 7　　Very high influence

3. In your opinion, how ethical was any decision that was reached?

   Highly unethical　　1 2 3 4 5 6 7　　Highly ethical

4. To what extent did you feel *pushed into* going along with the decision?

   Not pushed into　　1 2 3 4 5 6 7　　Very pushed
   it at all　　　　　　　　　　　　　　　　into it

5. How committed are you to the agreements reached?

   Not at all　　1 2 3 4 5 6 7　　Highly
   committed　　　　　　　　　　　　committed

6. Did you understand what was expected of you as a member of the meeting or project group?

   Not at all clear　　1 2 3 4 5 6 7　　Perfectly clear

7. Were participants in the meeting/project group discussions listening to each other?

   Never　　1 2 3 4 5 6 7　　Always

8. Were participants in the meeting/project group discussions honest and open in communicating with one another?

   Never　　1 2 3 4 5 6 7　　Always'

9. Was the meeting/project completed efficiently?

   Not at all　　1 2 3 4 5 6 7　　Very much

10. Was the outcome of the meeting/project something that you felt proud to be a part of?

    Not at all　　1 2 3 4 5 6 7　　Very much

B. Share results with all team members and discuss their meaning.

C. Summarize and share with the instructor and class the implications of this exercise for: (a) the future success of this team if it was to work on another project, and (b) each individual team member as he or she goes forward to work in other teams and on other group projects in the future.

Manage a Critical Incident

High Performer but Late for Work

You are an elementary school principal. One of your best teachers—perhaps the best—is causing a bit of an uproar. She is in her second year on staff after graduating from college and is doing a wonderful job with the second graders. They're happy, the parents are happy, and you're happy. The other teachers aren't happy, at least some of them aren't. Two of the more outspoken and senior teachers came to you today with a request. "Do something about her," they said. "She is consistently late in the mornings. You know our policy is for the teacher to be in the classroom at least 30 minutes before school starts." You are aware of her tardiness, but you also know that she consistently stays late and is most often the last teacher out of the building at the end of the day. She isn't aware that her co-workers have complained about her. You can't put this off because the grumbling is starting to spread.

Questions

What do you do, and why? How can you turn this into an opportunity to develop an approach that accommodates a range of personal work styles and different classroom approaches, all while holding up high performance standards?

Collaborate on the Team Activity

Building a Balanced Scorecard
Instructions

In your assigned teams, do the following:

1. Choose a local organization of interest to team members and about which you collectively have some information and insights.

2. Build a Balanced Scorecard that can be used for control purposes by this organization's top management. Make sure your scorecard covers these four areas—financial performance, customer satisfaction, internal process improvement, and innovation and learning.

3. For each of the four scorecard performance areas, be very specific in identifying what you recommend as possible performance goals and areas of performance measurement.

4. Design a scorecard format that makes analysis easy and informative. If possible, demonstrate how your proposed scorecard might fit into an Executive Dashboard.

5. Present your proposed Balanced Scorecard to the entire class, along with justification for all suggested goals and measures. Explain in your presentation why you believe this scorecard could help the organization perform better in the future.

Analyze THE CaseStudy : BRITISH PETROLEUM
Getting Drilled About Their Operations

Go to *Management Cases for Critical Thinking* at the end of the book to find this case.

THE STRATEGIC MANAGEMENT PROCESS

10

KEY TAKEAWAYS

- Discuss the process and importance of strategic management.
- Identify the essential elements in strategic analysis.
- Explain alternative corporate strategies.
- Explain alternative business-level strategies.
- Describe the foundations for strategy implementation.

SKILLS MAKE YOU **VALUABLE**

- **EVALUATE** *Career Situations:* What Would You Do?
- **REFLECT** *On the Self-Assessment:* Intuitive Ability
- **CONTRIBUTE** *To the Class Exercise:* Strategic Scenarios
- **MANAGE** *A Critical Incident:* Kickstarting a Friend's Business Idea
- **COLLABORATE** *On the Team Activity:* Contrasting Strategies
- **ANALYZE** *The Case Study:* Sony Corporation: An Evolution of Technology

Strategic management is one of the most significant planning challenges faced by managers. All organizations face a complex array of forces. Uncertainties of many types—market, economic, political, social, and more—must be understood and analyzed in order to craft strategies for competitive success. As with organizations, each of us faces personal life and career challenges that test our abilities with strategic management. We, too, need to make and implement strategies to achieve our goals.

Salman Khan's innovative online Khan Academy has the goal of "changing education for the better by providing a free world-class education for anyone anywhere." The success of Khan helped spur the development of MOOCs—massive open online courses—as "disrupters" of the traditional university model of face-to-face delivery of pay-per-credit courses. Some MOOCs are free. They're being launched in increasing numbers from top universities, and start-ups like Coursera and Udacity are marketing them on a global scale. What's the future of these online alternatives? Will MOOCs make higher education more accessible and affordable? Will they change the traditional college experience for better or worse? Or, will they soon fade away and be remembered as just another passing trend?[1]

Our institutions of higher education are taking center stage among industries facing strategic challenges—MOOCs are on the move, politicians are attacking college costs, graduates worry about paying off student loans. University, government, and business leadership are being tested by changing times, tastes, and technologies. And *Fast Company* magazine says: "If you want to make a difference as a leader, you've got to make time for strategy."[2]

Leaders struggling with strategy need to remember lessons from the past. There was a time when Henry Ford could say: "The customer can have any color he wants as long as it's black." Those days are long gone for businesses large and small, they're gone for hospitals and local governments, and they're gone for universities as well. A senior IBM executive described this shift in strategic landscape as the "difference between a bus which follows a set route, and a taxi which goes where customers tell it to go."[3]

There are a lot of strategy and strategic management ideas and insights in this chapter. As you read and think about them, remember that everything applies equally well to your own career. What's your personal strategy for career and life success? Are you acting like a bus following a set route, a taxi following opportunities, or some combination of both?

Strategic Management

TAKEAWAY 1   What is strategic management?

LEARN MORE | Competitive advantage • Strategy and strategic intent • Levels of strategy
ABOUT | Strategic management process

Forces and challenges like those just described confront managers in all organizations and industries. Today's environment places a great premium on "competitive advantage" and how it is achieved—or not—through "strategy" and "strategic management."[4]

Competitive Advantage

Competitive advantage is the ability to do something so well that one outperforms competitors.

The term **competitive advantage** describes an organization's ability to use resources so well that it performs better than the competition. Typical sources of competitive advantage are:[5]

- *Technology*—using technology to gain operating efficiencies, market exposure, and customer loyalty.

- *Cost and quality*—operating with greater efficiency and product or service quality.

- *Knowledge and speed*—doing better at innovation and speed of delivery to market for new ideas.

- *Barriers to entry*—creating a market stronghold that is protected from entry by others.

- *Financial resources*—having better investments or loss absorption potential than competitors.

Sustainable competitive advantage is the ability to outperform rivals in ways that are difficult or costly to imitate.

Achieving and retaining competitive advantage is an increasingly difficult challenge to master. Whenever organizations do things very well, rivals try to duplicate and copy their approach. The ultimate goal is creating **sustainable competitive advantage**—competitive advantage that is durable and difficult or costly for others to copy or imitate. When you think sustainable competitive advantage, think about Apple's iPad. One analyst observes: "Apple moved the goal posts before most of their competitors even took the field."[6] The iPad was first to market as an innovative product linking design, technology, and customer appeal. It was also backed by Apple's super-efficient supply chain, which made it a high-margin product. The iPad is still a top seller, but tablet consumers can now choose competing products offering many similar features. Lawsuits between Apple and Samsung over copyrights, such as the "slide to unlock" feature, illustrate what is at stake in the battles for competitive advantage.[7]

Strategy and Strategic Intent

If sustainable competitive advantage is the goal, "strategy" is the means to achieve it.[8] A **strategy** is a comprehensive action plan that identifies the long-term direction for an organization and that guides resource utilization to achieve sustainable competitive advantage. It is a "best guess" about what must be done for future success in the face of competition and changing market conditions. And, it usually involves risk taking. At Facebook, for example, the firm's mission is "to give people the power to share and make the world more open and connected."[9] Given this mission, CEO Mark Zuckerberg struggled to match a web-based and computer-focused legacy strategy with new trends in mobile. He made an important decision to commit the company to a "mobile first" strategy that shifted the direction for innovation and app development away from computers and toward smartphones. The new strategy quickly paid off with increased mobile ad revenues and a higher share price.[10]

> A **strategy** is a comprehensive plan guiding resource allocation to achieve long-term organization goals.

Just as with our personal assets, organizational resources like time, money, and people get wasted when they are spent on things that don't result in real accomplishments. The presence of a strategy helps ensure that resources are used with consistent **strategic intent**—that is, with all energies directed toward accomplishing a long-term target or goal.[11] In the Facebook case just described, CEO Mark Zuckerberg backed his mobile first strategy by halting any company meeting he was attending where someone began by talking about computers instead of smartphones.[12] Patagonia backs its commitment to sustainability in the apparel industry by programs like Common Thread, which reduces use of new materials by allowing customers to return purchased items for repair, reuse, and recycling.[13]

> **Strategic intent** focuses and applies organizational energies on a unifying and compelling goal.

Levels of Strategy

> *Google buys Nest Labs for $3.2 billion . . . Rovio Lets Angry Birds Roam Free . . . Chip maker thrives on virtual manufacturing.*

These headlines display the three levels of strategy in organizations shown in Figure 10.1. At the corporate level of strategy, Google adds to its business lines by purchasing the smart-home company Nest Labs. At the business level of strategy, Rovio Entertainment shifts from selling Angry Birds to offering it free but selling add-on features. At the functional level of strategy, a semiconductor chip maker operates with a virtual factory.[14] In order to really understand the stories behind these headlines, you need to understand the strategy and how it fits with both the business purpose and the current competitive conditions.

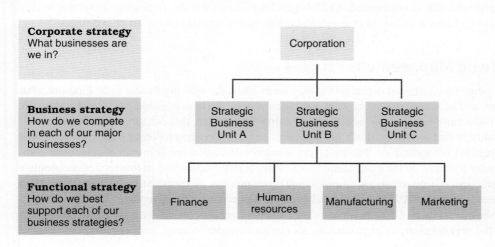

Corporate strategy
What businesses are we in?

Business strategy
How do we compete in each of our major businesses?

Functional strategy
How do we best support each of our business strategies?

Corporation

Strategic Business Unit A | Strategic Business Unit B | Strategic Business Unit C

Finance | Human resources | Manufacturing | Marketing

FIGURE 10.1
Corporate-level strategy, business-level strategy, and functional strategy.

Corporate-Level Strategy

A corporate strategy sets long-term direction for the total enterprise.

At the highest level, **corporate strategy** directs the organization as a whole toward sustainable competitive advantage. It describes the scope of operations by answering this *corporate-level strategic question*: "In what industries and markets should we compete?" The purpose of corporate strategy is to set direction and guide resource allocations for the entire enterprise. It identifies how large and complex organizations can compete across multiple industries and markets. General Electric, for example, owns more than 100 businesses in a wide variety of areas, including aircraft engines, appliances, capital services, medical systems, and power systems. Typical corporate-level strategic decisions for GE relate to initiatives such as new business acquisitions and existing business expansions and cutbacks.

Business-Level Strategy

A business strategy identifies how a division or strategic business unit will compete in its product or service domain.

Business strategy sets the direction for a single business unit or product line. It involves asking and answering this *business-level strategic question*: "How are we going to compete for customers in this industry and market?" Typical business strategy decisions include choices about product and service mix, facilities locations, and new technologies. Business strategy is the corporate strategy in single-product enterprises. The term *strategic business unit* (SBU) is often used to describe a business that operates as part of a larger enterprise, such as online retailer Zappos within the Amazon umbrella and smart home firm Nest Labs within Google's suite of businesses.

Whereas the enterprise on a whole will have a corporate strategy, each SBU will have its own focused business strategy. Porsche Automobile Holding SE, for example, is owned by Volkswagen Group. Historically a two-door sports car company, Porsche adjusted its business strategy and successfully marketed a sport utility vehicle, the Cayenne, that became the brand's volume sales leader. It was followed by another success—a four-door sedan, the Panamera.[15] These shifts in business-level strategy, which are core to Porsche operations, don't bear directly on the corporate-level strategy of Volkswagen as a whole.

Functional Strategy

A functional strategy guides activities within one specific area of operations.

Functional strategy guides the use of organizational resources to implement business strategy. The *functional-level strategic question* is: "How can we best utilize resources within a function to implement our business strategy?" Answers to this question might focus on ways to improve products, gain efficiencies, and enhance customer service. The attention in functional strategy focuses on activities within a specific functional area such as marketing, manufacturing, finance, or human resources. Picochip, for example, produces specialized microchips using a "virtual" model where all chip production is outsourced. CEO Nigel Toon says what the firm saves from not having expensive factories it invests in research and development on state-of-the-art chip designs.[16]

Strategic Management Process

Strategic management is the process of formulating and implementing strategies.

Strategic analysis is the process of analyzing the organization, the environment, and the organization's competitive position and current strategies.

Developing strategy for an organization may seem like a deceptively simple task: Find out what products and services customers want, provide these at the best possible price, and make sure competitors can't easily copy what you are doing. In practice, this can get very complicated.[17] The reality is that strategies don't just happen; they must be developed and then implemented effectively. At the same time that managers in one organization are doing all of this, their competitors are trying to do the exact same thing—only better. Succeeding in this mix of competitive pressures depends on **strategic management**, the process of formulating and implementing strategies to accomplish long-term goals and sustain competitive advantage.

As shown in Figure 10.2, the strategic management process begins with **strategic analysis** to assess the organization, its environment, its competitive positioning, and its current strategies.

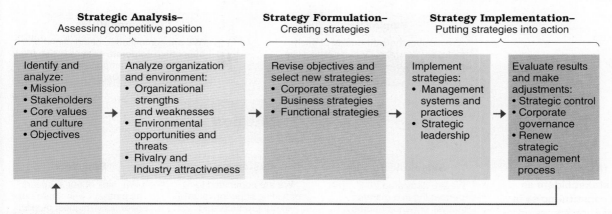

FIGURE 10.2
Major elements in the strategic management process.

Next in the process is **strategy formulation**, developing a new or revised strategy. The final phase is **strategy implementation**, using resources to put strategies into action, and then evaluating results so that the implementation can be improved or the strategy changed. As the late management consultant and guru Peter Drucker once said: "The future will not just happen if one wishes hard enough. It requires decision—now. It imposes risk—now. It requires action—now. It demands allocation of resources, and above all, it requires work—now."[18]

> **Strategy formulation** is the process of crafting strategies to guide the allocation of resources.
>
> **Strategy implementation** is the process of putting strategies into action.

Learning Check 1

TAKEAWAYQUESTION **1 What is strategic management?**

BE SURE YOU CAN • define *competitive advantage*, *strategy*, and *strategic intent* • explain the concept of sustainable competitive advantage • differentiate corporate, business, and functional strategies • differentiate strategy formulation from strategy implementation • list the major phases in the strategic management process

Essentials of Strategic Analysis

TAKEAWAY 2   What are the essentials of strategic analysis?

LEARN MORE ABOUT | Analysis of mission, values, objectives
SWOT analysis of organization and environment
Five forces analysis of industry attractiveness

When it comes to the essentials of strategic analysis, there is a core set of strategic questions that any top manager should be prepared to answer. (1) What is our business mission? (2) Who are our customers? (3) What do our customers value? (4) What have been our results? (5) What is our plan?[19]

Analysis of Mission, Values, and Objectives

The strategic management process begins with an analysis of mission, values, and objectives. This sets the stage for assessing the organization's resources and capabilities, as well as opportunities and threats in its external environment.

FIGURE 10.3
External stakeholders as strategic constituencies in an organization's mission statement.

Mission and Stakeholders

*A **mission** statement expresses the organization's reason for existence in society.*

The **mission** or purpose of an organization describes its reason for existence in society.[20] Strategy consultant Michael Hammer believes that a mission should represent what the strategy or underlying business model is trying to accomplish. In order to clarify the mission, he suggests asking: "What are we moving to?" "What is our dream?" "What kind of a difference do we want to make in the world?" "What do we want to be known for?"[21]

Patagonia's mission is to "Build the best product, cause no unnecessary harm, use business to inspire and implement solutions to the environmental crisis."[22] This mission statement identifies not only a business direction but also a distinctive value commitment that gives Patagonia a unique identity as it competes with much larger rivals in its industry.

*ered **Stakeholders** are individuals and groups directly affected by the organization and its strategic accomplishments.*

A clear sense of mission helps inspire the support and respect of an organization's **stakeholders**. These are individuals and groups—including customers, shareholders, employees, suppliers, creditors, community groups, future generations, and others—who are directly affected by the organization and its accomplishments. Figure 10.3 gives an example of how stakeholder interests can be linked with an organization's mission.

Core Values and Culture

*Core **values** are broad beliefs about what is or is not appropriate behavior.*

Organizational values and culture should be analyzed in the strategic management process to determine how well they align with the mission.[23] **Core values** are broad beliefs about what is or is not appropriate behavior. Patagonia founder and chairman Yvon Chouinard says: "Most people want to do good things, but don't. At Patagonia it's an essential part of your life."[24] He leads Patagonia with a personal commitment to sustainability and expects the firm to live up to it as a core value. Among other things, Patagonia donates employee time and more than 1% of sales to support environmental groups, uses recycled polyester and organic cotton, and emphasizes "simplicity and utility" in product designs.[25]

*Organizational **culture** is the predominant value system for the organization as a whole.*

The presence of core values helps build a clear organizational identity. It gives the organization a sense of character as seen through the eyes of employees and external stakeholders. This character is part of what is called **organizational culture** or the predominant value system of the organization as a whole.[26] A clear and strong organizational culture helps guide the behavior of members in ways that are consistent with the organization's mission and core values. When browsing Patagonia's website for job openings, for example, the message about the corporate culture is clear: "We're especially interested in people who share our love of the outdoors, our passion for quality, and our desire to make a difference."[27]

Objectives

Whereas a mission statement lays out an organization's purpose and core values set standards for accomplishing it, **operating objectives** direct activities toward key performance areas. Typical operating objectives for a business include the following:[28]

Operating objectives are specific results that organizations try to accomplish.

- *Profitability*—operating with a net profit.

- *Sustainability*—helping to preserve, not exploit, the environment.

- *Social responsibility*—acting as a good community citizen.

- *Financial health*—acquiring capital; earning positive returns.

- *Cost efficiency*—using resources well to operate at low cost.

- *Customer service*—meeting customer needs and maintaining loyalty.

- *Product quality*—producing high-quality goods or services.

- *Market share*—gaining a specific share of possible customers.

- *Human talent*—recruiting and maintaining a high-quality workforce.

- *Innovation*—developing new products and processes.

Well-chosen operating objectives can turn a broad sense of mission into specific performance targets. In the case of Patagonia, mission, values, and operating objectives fit together as a coherent whole. Chouinard says that he wants to run Patagonia "so that it's here 100 years from now and always makes the best-quality stuff." Although one of the firm's objectives is revenue growth, this doesn't mean growth at any cost. Chouinard's objective is modest growth, not extreme or uncontrolled growth.[29]

SWOT Analysis of Organization and Environment

A technique known as **SWOT analysis** is a useful first step in analyzing the organization and its environment. As Figure 10.4 describes, it is an internal analysis of *organizational strengths and*

A **SWOT analysis** examines organizational strengths and weaknesses and environmental opportunities and threats.

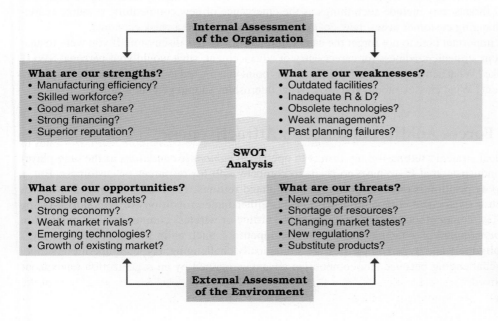

Internal Assessment of the Organization

What are our strengths?
- Manufacturing efficiency?
- Skilled workforce?
- Good market share?
- Strong financing?
- Superior reputation?

What are our weaknesses?
- Outdated facilities?
- Inadequate R & D?
- Obsolete technologies?
- Weak management?
- Past planning failures?

SWOT Analysis

What are our opportunities?
- Possible new markets?
- Strong economy?
- Weak market rivals?
- Emerging technologies?
- Growth of existing market?

What are our threats?
- New competitors?
- Shortage of resources?
- Changing market tastes?
- New regulations?
- Substitute products?

External Assessment of the Environment

FIGURE 10.4
SWOT analysis of strengths, weaknesses, opportunities, and threats.

weaknesses as well as an external analysis of *environmental opportunities and threats*. Although the following examples and discussion apply SWOT to organizations, you can also apply it in your own career and life planning.

A SWOT analysis begins with a systematic evaluation of the organization's resources and capabilities—its basic strengths and weaknesses. You can think of this as an analysis of organizational capacity to achieve its objectives. A major goal is to identify **core competencies**—things that the organization does exceptionally well in comparison with competitors. They are capabilities that—by virtue of being rare, costly to imitate, and not substitutable—become potential sources of competitive advantage.[30] An organization's core competencies may be found in special knowledge or expertise, superior technologies, efficient supply chains, or unique distribution systems, among many other possibilities. As an individual, core competencies may include your unique combination of intelligence, knowledge, experience, personality, and enthusiasm.

> A **core competency** is a special strength that gives an organization a competitive advantage.

Organizational weaknesses represent the other end of the competency spectrum. The goal here is to identify things that inhibit performance and hold the organization back from fully accomplishing its objectives. Examples might be outdated products, lack of financial capital, shortage of talented workers, and poor or poorly used technology. At the individual level, weaknesses may include limited work experience, underdeveloped computing skills, knowing only one language, or no industry-specific certifications.

Take Advantage of Insights from SWOT Analysis

- Build on and use strengths to create core competencies.
- Avoid relying on weaknesses that can't be turned into strengths.
- Move toward opportunities to capture advantage.
- Avoid threats or act in ways that minimize their impact.

Once weaknesses are identified, plans can be set to eliminate or reduce them, or possibly to turn them into strengths. Even if some weaknesses cannot be corrected, it is critical that they be understood. Strategies should ideally build on strengths and minimize the negative impact of weaknesses.

No SWOT analysis is complete until opportunities and threats in the external environment also are assessed. As shown in Figure 10.4, opportunities may be present as possible new markets, a strong economy, weaknesses in competitors, and emerging technologies. Environmental threats may include such things as the emergence of new competitors, resource scarcities, changing customer tastes, new government regulations, and a weak economy.

It's important here to not forget the career implications of this discussion. If you were to analyze your strategic readiness for career entry or advancement, what would your personal SWOT look like? What actions does this SWOT analysis point you toward to better prepare for the future you want? What classes should you take? What internships should you apply for?

Five Forces Analysis of Industry Attractiveness

The ideal strategic setting for any firm is to operate in *monopoly conditions* as the only player in an industry—that is, to have no rivals to compete with for resources or customers. But, a monopoly position is rare except in highly regulated settings. The reality for most businesses is intense rivalry and competition that unfolds either under conditions of *oligopoly*—facing just a few competitors, such as in consolidated airline or wireless communications industries, or *hypercompetition*—facing several direct competitors, such as in the fast-food industry.[31] Both oligopoly and hypercompetition are strategically challenging. Hypercompetition is especially challenging because any competitive advantage gained by an organization tends to be short-lived.

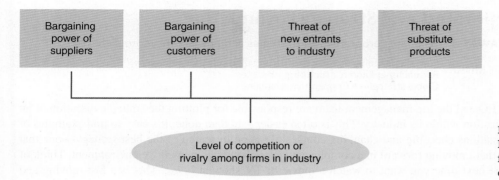

FIGURE 10.5
Porter's model of five strategic forces affecting industry competition.

Harvard scholar and consultant Michael Porter describes the five forces shown in Figure 10.5 as a tool for strategic analysis in competitive industries.[32] He calls these five forces the "industry structure":

1. *Industry competition*—the intensity of rivalry among firms in the industry and the ways they behave competitively toward one another.

2. *New entrants*—the threat of new competitors entering the market, based on the presence or absence of barriers to entry.

3. *Substitute products or services*—the threat of substitute products or services, or ability of customers to get what they want from other sellers.

4. *Bargaining power of suppliers*—the ability of resource suppliers to influence the price that a firm has to pay for their products or services.

5. *Bargaining power of customers*—the ability of customers to influence the price that they will pay for the firm's products or services.

The status of these five forces determines an industry's attractiveness or potential to generate long-term business returns. The less attractive the industry structure, the harder it is to make good strategic choices and realize sustained competitive advantage. According to a five forces analysis, an *unattractive industry* has intense rivalry among competitors, substantial threats in the form of possible new entrants and substitute products, and suppliers and buyers with bargaining power over price and quality. An *attractive industry*, by contrast, has less competition, fewer threats from new entrants or substitutes, and lower supplier and buyer bargaining power.

Five Forces Analysis	
Attractive Industry	**Unattractive Industry**
• Few competitors	• Many competitors
• High barriers to entry	• Low barriers to entry
• Few substitute products	• Many substitute products
• Low power of suppliers	• High power of suppliers
• Low power of customers	• High power of customers

Learning Check 2

TAKEAWAYQUESTION **2   What are the essentials of strategic analysis?**

BE SURE YOU CAN • explain how a good mission statement helps organizations relate to stakeholders • define *core values* and *organizational culture* • List several operating objectives for organizations • define *core competency* • explain SWOT analysis • use Porter's five forces model to assess the attractiveness of an industry

Corporate-Level Strategy Formulation

TAKEAWAY 3   What are corporate-level strategies and how are they formulated?

LEARN MORE
ABOUT

Portfolio planning model • Growth and diversification strategies
Retrenchment and restructuring strategies
Global strategies • Cooperative strategies

The CEO and the top management team are responsible for plotting the strategic direction of an organization within its industry. This is often easier said than done. It's easy to find examples of organizations choosing and changing courses of action in search of the best strategy—one that keeps them moving forward in a complex and ever-changing competitive environment. Think of this the next time you want to watch a movie or TV show at home. This is a fast-moving and highly competitive landscape where Netflix, Apple, Amazon, and the cable and telephone companies are constantly trying to figure out how to capture and retain your attention. They have to constantly worry about and deal with one another, and any number of startups seeking to offer alternatives to their products.

Portfolio Planning Model

Google's CEO Larry Page faces a difficult strategic question all the time: How should he allocate Google's resources across a diverse mix of opportunities? Growth by acquisition has added great diversity to what started out as a search engine and software company. Page now has to manage everything from search, YouTube, robotics and smart homes to wind farms, self-driving cars, and more.[33] If you think about it, Page's strategic management questions are similar to those we all face in managing personal assets. How, for example, do you create a good mix of cash, stocks, bonds, and real estate investments? What do you buy more of, what do you sell, and what do you hold? These are the same questions that executives ask all the time. They are *portfolio-planning* questions, and they have major strategic implications. Shouldn't they be made systematically rather than randomly?[34]

The Boston Consulting Group offers a portfolio planning approach known as the **BCG Matrix**. Although more complicated models of strategic portfolio planning are available, the BCG Matrix is a widely accepted and well-understood foundation for understanding the portfolio planning approach to strategic resource allocation decisions.

The BCG Matrix shown in Figure 10.6 asks managers to analyze business and product strategies based on two major factors: (1) market growth rate for the industry, and (2) market share held by the firm.[35] The analysis shown in the figure sorts businesses or products into four strategic types: Dogs, Stars, Question Marks, and Cash Cows. Each type comes with a recommended core or master strategy—*growth*, *stability*, or *retrenchment*.[36] These strategies become the guidelines for making resource allocation decisions.

- *Grow the Stars*. Businesses or products with high market shares in high-growth markets are "Stars" in the BCG Matrix. They produce large profits through substantial penetration of expanding markets. The preferred strategy for Stars is growth, and the BCG Matrix recommends making further resource investments in them. Not only are Stars high performers in the present—they offer similar potential for the future. If we look at Apple today, the iPad would be a Star.

- *Milk the Cash Cows*. Businesses or products with high-market shares in low-growth markets are "Cash Cows" in the BCG Matrix. They produce good profits and a strong cash flow, but with little upside potential. Because the markets offer limited growth opportunity, the preferred strategy for Cash Cows is stability or modest growth. Like real dairy cows, the BCG Matrix advises firms to "milk" these businesses. They should invest just enough to keep them stable or growing just a bit. This keeps them generating cash that can be reinvested in other more

BCG Matrix analyzes business opportunities according to market growth rate and market share.

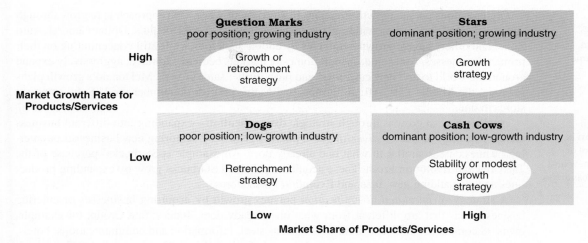

FIGURE 10.6
The BCG matrix approach for portfolio planning in corporate-level strategy formulation.

promising areas. For Apple, we might wonder: Is yesterday's Star—the iPhone—becoming (or already) a Cash Cow?

- *Grow or Retrench the Question Marks.* Businesses or products with low-market shares in high-growth markets are "Question Marks" in the BCG Matrix. Although they may not generate much profit at the moment, the upside potential is there because of the growing markets. But nothing is guaranteed. Question Marks make for difficult strategic decision making. The BCG Matrix recommends targeting only the most promising Question Marks for growth, while retrenching those that are less promising. What's the most promising Question Mark at Apple today? That's a good question, and perhaps the answer is Apple TV. Will it be the Star of the future, or a Dog?

- *Retrench the Dogs.* Businesses or products with low-market shares in low-growth markets are "Dogs" in the BCG Matrix. They produce little, if any, profit, and they have low potential for future improvement. The preferred strategy for Dogs in the BCG Matrix is retrenchment. Not too long ago, Apple's iPhone was a Star; then it became a Cash Cow. Is it now well on the road to being tomorrow's Dog?

Growth and Diversification Strategies

Among the core or master strategies just illustrated in the BCG matrix, **growth strategies** seek to expand the size and scope of operations. The goal is to increase total revenue, product or service lines, and operating locations. When you hear terms like "acquisition," "merger," and "global expansion," for example, they indicate a growth strategy.

A **growth strategy** involves expansion of the organization's current operations.

Growth is a common and popular business strategy. And although there is a tendency to equate growth with effectiveness, it is possible to get caught in an "expansion trap" where growth outruns an organization's capacity to manage it. Mark Zuckerberg faced this problem at Facebook. The firm grew incredibly fast and spending outran revenues. The *Wall Street Journal* claimed it had "growing pains," and Zuckerberg even asked: "Is being a CEO always this hard?" His response was to hire an experienced Google vice president, Sheryl Sandberg, to become chief operating officer and lead Facebook's continued expansion.[37] This decision took some humility on Zuckerberg's part, and it's also one that history has shown to be a great move for Facebook.

Growth through concentration is within the same business area.

Organizations pursue growth strategies in a variety of ways. One approach is to grow through **concentration**—expanding within in the same business area. McDonald's, Dollar General, Auto Zone, and others pursue growth strategies by adding locations while still concentrating on their primary businesses. And some, as their domestic markets become saturated, aggressively expand around the world to find new customers and push further sales growth. McDonald's growth plans for Asia, the Middle East, Africa, Europe, and Latin America outnumber the U.S. by some six stores to one.[38]

Growth through diversification is by acquisition of or investment in new and different business areas.

Another way to grow is through strategic **diversification**—expanding into different business areas. A strategy of *related diversification* pursues growth by acquiring new businesses or entering business areas similar to what one already does. An example is Starbucks' purchase of the Tazo Tea and Evolution Fresh. These acquisitions helped Starbucks grow by expanding product lines and also adding new Tazo and Evolution Fresh stores.

A strategy of *unrelated diversification* pursues growth by acquiring businesses or entering business areas that are different from what one already does. India's Tata Group, for example, owns 98 companies in diverse industries such as steel, information and communications, hotels, energy, and consumer products. Its brands include Eight O'Clock Coffee and Tetley Tea as well as Jaguar and Land Rover. About Tata's growth by unrelated diversification, Chairman Ratan N. Tata says: "We have been thinking bigger . . . we have been bolder . . . we have been more aggressive in the marketplace."[39]

Growth through vertical integration occurs by acquiring upstream suppliers or downstream distributors.

Growth by diversification is sometimes done by **vertical integration** where a business moves upstream (farther from customers) to acquire its suppliers—*backward vertical integration,* or moves downstream (closer to customers) to acquire its distributors—*forward vertical integration.* Examples of backward vertical integration include Apple Computer—buying chip manufacturers to give it more privacy and sophistication in developing microprocessors for its products; Rolex—buying a foundry for the precious metals it uses in its luxury watches; and Delta Airlines—buying an oil refinery to supply part of its aviation fuel needs. The beverage industry provides a good example of forward vertical integration. Both Coca-Cola and PepsiCo own some major bottlers that make drinks from their concentrates and distribute their products regionally.[40] Even a trip to the local farmer's market shows forward vertical integration in practice. All those stands of vegetables and fruits are run by farmers moving downstream from production to distribution of their produce directly to customers.

Retrenchment and Restructuring Strategies

Retrenchment, restructuring, and turnaround strategies pursue radical changes to solve problems.

When organizations are in trouble, perhaps experiencing problems brought about by a bad economy or too much growth and diversification, the focus shifts toward **retrenchment, restructuring, and turnaround strategies** that pursue radical changes to solve problems. At one end of the extreme, a firm may be insolvent and unable to pay its bills. In some cases, retrenchment may take the form of **Chapter 11 bankruptcy**, which under U.S. law gives firms protection while they reorganize to restore solvency. Both Chrysler and General Motors used this strategy during the recent economic crisis. In other cases an insolvent firm goes into outright **liquidation**, where business ceases and assets are sold off to pay creditors.

Chapter 11 bankruptcy under U.S. law protects a firm from creditors while management reorganizes to restore solvency.

Liquidation is where a business closes and sells its assets to pay creditors.

Short of bankruptcy and liquidation, distressed organizations can try other retrenchment strategies to get back on a path toward competitiveness. Restructuring by **downsizing** decreases the size of operations, often by drastically reducing the workforce.[41] Facing revenue declines, for example, HP's CEO Meg Whitman decided to lay off 14% of the firm's workforce—some 50,000 workers. By making the cuts and saving over $1.6 billion in costs, she hoped to restore growth by making new investments in technology and workforce skills.[42] When you learn of organizations downsizing, however, you should be skeptical of those making "across-the-board" cuts. Research shows that downsizing is most successful when cutbacks are done selectively and

A downsizing strategy decreases the size of operations.

with specific performance objectives. The term *rightsizing* is sometimes used to describe down-sizing with a clear strategic focus.[43]

Restructuring by **divestiture** involves selling off parts of the organization to refocus what remains on core competencies, cutting costs, and improving operating efficiency. You'll see this strategy followed by organizations that become overdiversified and whose executives have problems managing so much complexity. For example, eBay bought Skype with high expectations and later sold it to private investors at a loss. At the time of sale, eBay's CEO said: "Skype is a strong standalone business, but it does not have synergies with our e-commerce and online payments business."[44] In other words, the original purchase was a costly and bad idea. Skype is now owned by Microsoft, where the strategic question is: Will the expected synergies pay off, or will there be yet another divestiture in Skype's future?

Restructuring by **turnaround** is an attempt to fix an organization's specific performance problems. It often occurs along with a change in top management. Check the latest on Yahoo!, a company that has struggled for traction even though its brand is well established. Founder Jerry Yang stepped down as CEO after investors complained he made a mistake by refusing a buyout offer from Microsoft. Carol Bartz was then hired in a turnaround attempt. She was fired after 30 months on the job and replaced by Scott Thompson. His first major move was to sue Facebook, a strategic partner, over patent infringements. He lasted less than a year. The next to step in as CEO was Marissa Mayer, a Google star. She has made many changes in the firm's structure, culture, operations, and strategies, and earned respect from the financial markets. Yet, Yahoo's future remains a question mark to many investors and analysts.[45]

> **Divestiture** sells off parts of the organization to refocus attention on core business areas.

> A **turnaround strategy** tries to fix specific performance problems.

Global Strategies

A key issue in corporate strategy today is how to embrace the global economy and its mix of business risks and opportunities.[46] An easy way to spot differences in global strategies is to notice how products are developed and advertised around the world. A firm pursuing a **globalization strategy** tends to view the world as one large integrated market. It makes most decisions from the corporate headquarters and tries as much as possible to standardize products and advertising for use everywhere. The latest Gillette razors from Procter & Gamble, for example, are likely to be sold and advertised similarly around the world.

Firms using a **multidomestic strategy** try to customize products and advertising as much as possible in order to fit local preferences in different countries or regions. McDonald's is a good example. Although you can get your standard fries and Big Mac in most locations, you can have a McVeggie in India, a McArabia Kofta in Saudi Arabia, and a Croque McDo in France.

A third approach is the **transnational strategy** where a firm tries to operate without a strong national identity and blend seamlessly with the global economy. Resources and management talents are acquired worldwide, while manufacturing and other business functions are located wherever in the world they can be accomplished at the lowest cost. Ford is an example. Its global strategy uses design, manufacturing, and distribution expertise all over the world to build core car platforms that build vehicles using common parts and components. These platforms produce cars like the Focus and Fiesta that are then sold around the world with slight modifications to meet regional tastes.

> A **globalization strategy** adopts standardized products and advertising for use worldwide.

> A **multidomestic strategy** customizes products and advertising to best fit local needs.

> A **transnational strategy** seeks efficiencies of global operations with attention to local markets.

Cooperative Strategies

It's quite common today to hear about **strategic alliances** where two or more organizations join in a targeted partnership to pursue an area of mutual interest. This is basically a strategy of cooperating for common gains. In an *outsourcing alliance*, one organization contracts to purchase important services, perhaps IT or human resources, from another. In a *supplier alliance,*

> In a **strategic alliance**, organizations join in partnership to pursue an area of mutual interest.

preferred supplier relationships guarantee a smooth and timely flow of quality supplies among partners. In a *distribution alliance*, firms join together as partners to sell and distribute products or services.

Co-opetition is the strategy of working with rivals on projects of mutual benefit.

One interesting strategic direction is called **co-opetition**, or strategic alliances among competitors.[47] The idea behind co-opetition is that organizations can still cooperate even as they compete with one another. The airline industry is a great example. United Airlines and Lufthansa are major international competitors, but they also cooperate as "Star Alliance" partners. The alliance provides their customers code-sharing on flights and shared frequent-flyer programs. There's also co-opetition in the auto industry where the cost of developing new technologies provides the stimulus to cooperate. Daimler cooperates with BMW to co-develop new motors and components for hybrid cars; it cooperates with Nissan to co-develop electric car batteries.[48]

Learning Check 3

TAKEAWAYQUESTION **3 What are corporate-level strategies and how are they formulated?**

BE SURE YOU CAN • describe the BCG matrix as a strategic portfolio planning tool • list and explain the major types of growth and diversification strategies • list and explain the major types of retrenchment and restructuring strategies • list and give examples of global strategies • define *strategic alliance* and explain cooperation as a business strategy

Business-Level Strategy Formulation

TAKEAWAY 4 What are business-level strategies and how are they formulated?

LEARN MORE ABOUT | Competitive strategies model • Differentiation strategy
Cost leadership strategy • Focus strategy

Harvard's Michael Porter says that "the company without a strategy is willing to try anything."[49] But with a good strategy in place, he believes a business can achieve superior profitability or above-average returns within its industry. The key question in formulating business-level strategy is: "How can we best compete for customers in our market and with our products or services?"

Competitive Strategies Model

Figure 10.7 shows Porter's model for choosing competitive strategies based on the market scope of products or services, and the source of competitive advantage for the product or service. With respect to *market scope*, the strategic planner asks: "How broad or narrow is the market or target market?" With respect to *source of competitive advantage*, the question is: "Do we seek competitive advantage primarily through low price or product uniqueness?" Answers to these questions create a matrix like the one shown in the figure. Three business-level strategies are possible—cost leadership, differentiation, and focus. There are two combinations of the focus strategy—focused cost leadership and focused differentiation.

A differentiation strategy offers products that are unique and different from the competition.

Differentiation Strategy

A **differentiation strategy** seeks competitive advantage through uniqueness. This means developing goods and services that are clearly different from the competition. The strategic objective is to attract customers who stay loyal to the firm's products and lose interest in those of its competitors.

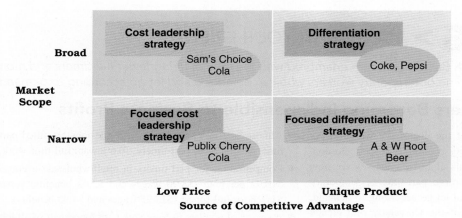

FIGURE 10.7
Porter's competitive strategies framework with soft-drink industry examples.

Success with a differentiation strategy requires organizational strengths in marketing, research and development, and creativity. An example in the apparel industry is Polo Ralph Lauren, retailer of upscale classic fashions and accessories. In Ralph Lauren's words: "Polo redefined how American style and quality is perceived. Polo has always been about selling quality products by creating worlds and inviting our customers to be part of our dream."[50]

The differentiation strategy examples in Figure 10.7 are Coke and Pepsi from the soft drinks industry. These firms continually battle for customer attention and loyalty. Although part of their differentiation may be actual taste, another part is pure perception. Coke and Pepsi spend enormous amounts on advertising to create beliefs that their products are somehow distinctly different from one another.

Cost Leadership Strategy

A **cost leadership strategy** seeks competitive advantage by operating with lower costs than competitors. This allows organizations to make profits selling products or services at low prices their competitors can't profitably match. The objective is to continuously improve operating efficiencies in purchasing, production, distribution, and other organizational systems.

Success with the cost leadership strategy requires tight cost and managerial controls, as well as products or services that are easy to create and distribute. This is what might be called the "Walmart" strategy—a firm takes every possible step to keep costs so low that they can offer customers the lowest prices and still make a reasonable profit. The example in Figure 10.7 is Sam's Choice Colas, where because of economies of scale and branding, these beverages can be offered at a fraction of the cost of "name brand" alternatives. An example from the financial services industry is the Vanguard Group. It keeps operating costs low to attract customers who want to buy mutual funds with low expense ratios and minimum fees.

You might be wondering if it's possible to combine cost leadership

A **cost leadership strategy** seeks to operate with low cost so that products can be sold at low prices.

Porter's Competitive Strategies

- *Differentiation*—Make products that are unique and different.
- *Cost leadership*—Produce at lower cost and sell at lower price.
- *Focused differentiation*—Use differentiation and target needs of a special market.
- *Focused cost leadership*—Use cost leadership and target needs of a special market.

analysis > MAKE DATA YOUR FRIEND

> *Businesses seem enamored with the idea of hiring fewer full-timers and more part-time or temporary workers who can be added and let go according to demand.*

Disposable Workers Becoming Indispensible to Business Profits

We're now in the era of the disposable worker, says Northwestern University economist Robert Gordon. The facts certainly support his claim. Businesses are now hiring fewer full-timers and more part-time or temporary workers who can be added and let go according to demand. Professor Susan J. Lambert of the University of Chicago blames some of the switch to disposable workers on the decline of labor union influence in the U.S. Others simply point out the cost advantages to employers who only have to pay for workers as needed.

- A McKinsey survey of 2,000 employers found 58% planning to hire more workers on a part-time, temporary, and contract basis.

- The U.S. Bureau of Labor Statistics reports that 1 million full-time jobs have been cut and 500,000 part-time positions added by retail and wholesale employers in the past six years.

- Almost 3 of every 10 retail/wholesale jobs are filled part-time. Among those part-timers, 30.6% want full-time work.

- Compensation for part-timers in retail/wholesale averaged $10.92 per hour ($8.90 wages and $2.02 benefits) versus $17.18 for full-timers ($12.25 wages and $4.93 benefits).

- A survey of retailers in New York City found half of all jobs filled by part-timers. Only 1 in 10 of them had set work schedules.

YOUR THOUGHTS?

Is this switch to employing more disposable workers a good long-term strategy for businesses? How about public sector organizations like governments, schools, and local services? What are the possible downsides to the employer and the remaining full-time employees? How might this trend affect you? Is this something that you have already factored into your career plan?

---

with differentiation. Porter says: "No." He refers to this combination as a *stuck-in-the-middle strategy* and believes it is rarely successful because differentiation increases costs. "You can compete on price or you can compete on product, but you can't compete on both," marketers tend to say. Porter agrees.

Focus Strategy

A focus strategy concentrates on serving a unique market segment better than anyone else.

A focused differentiation strategy offers a unique product to a special market segment.

A focused cost leadership strategy seeks the lowest costs of operations within a special market segment.

A **focus strategy** concentrates attention on a special market segment in the form of a niche customer group, geographical region, or product/service line. The objective is to serve the needs of the segment better than anyone else. Competitive advantage is achieved by combining focus with either differentiation or cost leadership.[51]

NetJets offers private, secure, and luxury air travel for those who can pay a high fee, such as wealthy media stars and executives. This is a **focused differentiation strategy** because the firm sells a unique product to a special niche market. Also in airlines, carriers such as Ryan Air and Easy Jet in Europe offer heavily discounted fares and "no-frills" flying. This is a **focused cost leadership** strategy because it offers low prices to attract budget travelers. The airlines still make profits by keeping costs low. They fly to regional airports and cut out free services such as bag checks and in-flight snacks.[52]

Figure 10.7 shows both types of focus strategies in the soft drink industry. Specialty drinks such as A&W Root Beer, Dr. Pepper, and Mountain Dew represent the focused differentiation strategy. Each focuses on a special market segment and tries to compete on the basis of product uniqueness. Drinks like Sam's Diet Cola, Publix Cherry Cola, and Big K Cola with Lime represent the focused cost leadership strategy. They also focus on special market segments, but try to compete by keeping operating costs low so that their soda brands can be profitably sold to consumers at low prices.

Learning Check 4

TAKEAWAYQUESTION **4 What are business-level strategies and how are they formulated?**

BE SURE YOU CAN • list and explain the four competitive strategies in Porter's model • explain the differences between focused differentiation and focused cost leadership strategies • clarify the roles of both price and cost in a cost leadership strategy • illustrate how Porter's competitive strategies apply to products in a market familiar to you

Strategy Implementation

TAKEAWAY 5   What are the foundations for strategy implementation?

LEARN MORE ABOUT | Management practices and systems • Strategic control and corporate governance | Strategic leadership

A discussion of the corporate history on Patagonia, Inc.'s website includes this statement: "During the past thirty years, we've made many mistakes but we've never lost our way for very long."[53] Not only is the firm being honest in the information it shares with the public, it also is communicating an important point about strategic management—mistakes will be made. Sometimes those mistakes will be in poor strategy selection. Other times they will be failures of implementation.

Management Practices and Systems

In order to successfully put strategy into action, the entire organization and all of its resources must be mobilized in support. This involves the complete management process—from planning and controlling through organizing and leading. No matter how well or elegantly conceived, a strategy requires supporting structures and workflows staffed by talented people. The strategy needs leaders who can motivate employees so that individuals and teams do their best work. The strategy also needs to be properly monitored and controlled to ensure that the desired results are achieved.

    Failures of substance in strategic management show up in poor analysis and bad strategy selection. *Failures of process* reflect poor handling of the ways in which strategic management is accomplished. A common process failure is the **lack of participation error**. It shows up as a lack of commitment to action and follow-through by individuals excluded from the strategic planning process.[54] Another process failure is *goal displacement*. This is the tendency to get so bogged down in details that the planning process becomes an end in itself, rather than a means to an end.

Lack of participation error is a failure to include key persons in strategic planning.

Strategic Control and Corporate Governance

Top managers exercise **strategic control** by making sure strategies are well implemented and that poor strategies are scrapped or modified quickly to meet performance demands of changing conditions. We expect them to always be "in control"—measuring results, evaluating the success of existing strategies, and taking action to improve things in the future. Yet the financial crisis and recent economic recession showed that strategic control was inadequate at many firms, including the automakers and big banks.

Strategic control makes sure strategies are well implemented and that poor strategies are scrapped or modified.

ethics > KNOW RIGHT FROM WRONG

> *The work is meaningless, no conversation is allowed on the production lines, and bathroom breaks are limited.*

Life and Death at an Outsourcing Factory

Foxconn is a major outsourcing firm owned by Hon Hai Precision Industry of Taiwan and has extensive operations in China. It makes products for Apple, Dell, and Hewlett-Packard, among others. Foxconn has over a million workers in China, with some 250,000 working in one huge complex stretching over 1 square mile in Shenzen. The site includes dormitories, restaurants, recreational facilities, and a hospital in addition to the factory spaces. Because of a number of employee suicides, netting has been draped from the dormitories to prevent employees from jumping to their death from roofs of the buildings.

One worker complains that the work is meaningless, no conversation is allowed on the production lines, and bathroom breaks are limited. Another says: "I do the same thing every day. I have no future." A supervisor points out that the firm provides counseling services since most workers are young and this is the first time they have been away from their homes. "Without their families," says the supervisor, "they're left without direction. We try to provide them with direction and help."

Recent moves by Hon Hai involve shifting more production to sites in rural China that are closer to many workers' homes and expanding automation through the use of more assembly-line robots. Wages have been increased and employees get counseling. This goes along with a broader commitment to the "highest possible safety practices," says a company spokesperson.

WHAT DO YOU THINK?

What ethical responsibilities do firms have when they contract for outsourcing in foreign plants? Whose responsibility is it to make sure workers are well treated—the global firm or the local supplier? What are our responsibilities as consumers? Should we support bad practices by buying products from firms with outsourcing partners are known to treat workers poorly? What role can and should the market play in improving conditions for workers worldwide?

Corporate governance is the system of control and performance monitoring of top management.

When strategic control fails at the level of top management, it is supposed to kick in at the level of **corporate governance**. This is the system of control and monitoring of top management performance exercised by boards of directors in business firms and boards of trustees in nonprofits. Corporate governance is intended to ensure that the strategic management of the organization is successful.[55] But, boards are sometimes too compliant and uncritical in endorsing or confirming what top management is doing. Instead of questioning, criticizing, and requiring change, they condone the status quo. Weak corporate governance doesn't subject top management to rigorous oversight and accountability. The result is organizations that end up doing the wrong things, doing bad things, or just performing poorly.

When governance fails, blame sometimes can be traced back to the composition of the board and expectations for how it operates. Most boards consist of *inside directors* chosen from the ranks of senior management and *outside directors* chosen from other organizations and positions external to the organization. In some boards, insiders are too powerful, and the CEO may even be the board chairperson. In others, the board lacks outside members whose skills match with the organization's strategic challenges. In still others, board members may be insufficiently observant or critical because they are friends of top management or at least sympathetic to them. Current directions to strengthen board oversight and control of management include separating the roles of CEO and board chair, appointing outside directors with relevant expertise, and having board members take on more active leadership roles.[56]

Strategic Leadership

Ford's former CEO Alan Mulally led the company out of recession and back onto a path toward growth. Paul Ingrassia, an auto analyst, called his success "one of the great turnarounds in corporate

Research Brief

Female Directors on Corporate Boards Linked with Positive Management Practices

Richard Vernardi, Susan Bosco, and Katie Vassill examined gender diversity of board membership and corporate performance. The research question guiding their article in *Business and Society* was: "Do firms listed in *Fortune's* '100 Best Companies to Work For' have a higher percentage of female directors than do Fortune 500 companies?" The researchers chose the "100 Best" listing because it includes firms whose employees consider them to have positive organizational cultures and supportive work practices. The evaluations were measured on a 225-item Great Place to Work Trust Index, sent to a random sample of employees in each company. Documentation of female board representatives was obtained by examining company annual reports.

Results confirmed expectations: the percentage of female directors was higher for firms on the "100 Best" list than for those in the Fortune 500 overall. The researchers suggest that gender diversity on boards of directors may bring about positive organizational changes that make firms better places to work. They also cite the growing presence of women on corporate boards as evidence that firms are changing board memberships to be "more representative of its employee and customer pools."

YOU BE THE RESEARCHER

Why would the presence of more female directors on a board result in a better workplace? Does board diversity, including

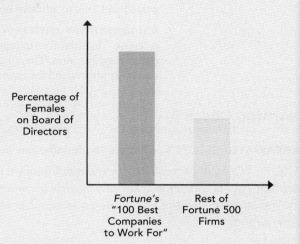

minorities and women, lead to different agendas, deliberations, concerns, and strategies? Does it lead to better strategy implementation through greater employee involvement and loyalty? Look at organizations with which you are familiar. Can you see where greater membership diversity in general, not just at the top, makes a difference in the way an organization performs?

---

history" and praised Mulally's efforts "to simplify, relentlessly and systematically, a business that had grown way too complicated and costly to be managed effectively."[57] What Mulally showed at Ford is **strategic leadership**—the capability to inspire people to successfully engage in a process of continuous change, performance enhancement, and implementation of organization strategies.[58]

One of the big lessons learned in studying how businesses perform during economic crisis is that a *strategic leader has to maintain strategic control*. This means that the CEO and other members of top management should always be in touch with the strategy. They must know how well it is being implemented, whether the strategy is generating performance success or failure, and if the strategy needs to be modified or changed. The following list identifies other key responsibilities of strategic leadership.[59]

- *A strategic leader has to be the guardian of trade-offs*. It is the leader's job to ensure that the organization's resources are allocated in ways that are consistent with the strategy. This requires the discipline to sort through many competing ideas and alternatives, to stay on course, and not to get sidetracked.

Strategic leadership inspires people to continuously change, refine, and improve strategies and their implementation.

- *A strategic leader needs to create a sense of urgency.* The leader can't allow the organization and its members to grow slow and complacent. Even when doing well, the leader retains focus on getting better and being alert to conditions that require adjustments to the strategy.

- *A strategic leader needs to make sure that everyone understands the strategy.* Unless strategies are understood, the daily tasks and contributions of individuals and teams lose context and purpose. Everyone might work very hard, but without alignment to strategy the impact is dispersed and fails to advance common goals.

- *A strategic leader needs to be a teacher.* It is the leader's job to teach the strategy and make it a "cause." In order for strategy to work, it must become an ever-present commitment throughout the organization. This means that a strategic leader must be a great communicator. Everyone must understand the strategy and how it makes their organization different from others.

Learning Check 5

TAKEAWAYQUESTION 5 **What are the foundations for strategy implementation?**

BE SURE YOU CAN • explain how the management process supports strategy implementation • define *corporate governance* • explain why boards of directors sometimes fail in their governance responsibilities • define *strategic control* and *strategic leadership* • list the responsibilities of a strategic leader in today's organizations

Management Learning Review
Get Prepared for **Quizzes and Exams**

SUMMARY

TAKEAWAYQUESTION 1

What is strategic management?

- Competitive advantage is achieved by operating in ways that allow an organization to outperform its rivals; a competitive advantage is sustainable when it is difficult for competitors to imitate.

- A strategy is a comprehensive plan that sets long-term direction and guides resource allocation for sustainable competitive advantage.

- Corporate strategy sets direction for an entire organization; business strategy sets direction for a business division or product/service line; functional strategy sets direction for the operational support of business and corporate strategies.

- Strategic management is the process of formulating and implementing strategies that achieve goals in a competitive environment.

FOR DISCUSSION Can an organization have a good strategy and still fail to achieve competitive advantage?

TAKEAWAYQUESTION 2

What are the essentials of strategic analysis?

- The strategic management process begins with analysis of mission, clarification of core values, and identification of objectives.

- A SWOT analysis systematically assesses organizational strengths and weaknesses, and environmental opportunities and threats.

- Porter's five forces model analyzes industry attractiveness in terms of competitive rivalry, new entrants, substitute products, and the bargaining powers of suppliers and buyers.

FOR DISCUSSION Would a monopoly get a perfect score for industry attractiveness in Porter's five forces model?

TAKEAWAYQUESTION 3

What are corporate-level strategies and how are they formulated?

- Growth strategies pursue greater sales and broader markets by concentration that expands in related product or business areas, and diversification that expands in new and different product and business areas.

- Restructuring strategies pursue ways to correct performance problems by such means as liquidation, bankruptcy, downsizing, divestiture, and turnaround.

- Global firms take advantage of international business opportunities through globalization, multidomestic, and transnational strategies.

- Cooperative strategies create strategic alliances with other organizations to achieve mutual gains, including such things as outsourcing alliances, supplier alliances, and even co-opetition among competitors.
- The BCG matrix is a portfolio planning approach that classifies businesses or product lines as "Stars," "Cash Cows," "Question Marks," or "Dogs" for purposes of strategy formulation.

FOR DISCUSSION Is it good news or bad news for investors when a firm announces that it is restructuring? Why?

TAKEAWAYQUESTION 4

What are business-level strategies and how are they formulated?

- Potential sources of competitive advantage in business-level strategy formulation are found in things like lower costs, better quality, more knowledge, greater speed, and strong financial resources.
- Porter's model of competitive strategy bases the choice of business-level strategies on two major considerations—market scope of product or service, and source of competitive advantage for the product or service.
- A differentiation strategy seeks competitive advantage by offering unique products and services that are clearly different from those of competitors.
- A cost leadership strategy seeks competitive advantage by operating at low costs that allow products and services to be sold to customers at low prices.

- A focus strategy seeks competitive advantage by serving the needs of a special market segment or niche better than anyone else; it can be done as focused differentiation or focused cost leadership.

FOR DISCUSSION Can a business ever be successful with a combined cost leadership and differentiation strategy?

TAKEAWAYQUESTION 5

What are the foundations for strategy implementation?

- Management practices and systems—including the functions of planning, organizing, leading, and controlling—must be mobilized to support strategy implementation.
- Pitfalls that inhibit strategy implementation include failures of substance—such as poor analysis of the environment; and failures of process—such as lack of participation by key players in the planning process.
- Boards of directors play important roles in control through corporate governance, including monitoring how well top management fulfills strategic management responsibilities.
- Top managers exercise strategic control by making sure strategies are well implemented and are changed if not working.
- Strategic leadership inspires the process of continuous evaluation and improvement of strategies and their implementation.

FOR DISCUSSION Can strategic leadership by top managers make up for poor corporate governance by board members? Why or why not?

SELF-TEST 10

Multiple-Choice Questions

1. The most appropriate first question to ask in strategic planning is _____.
   (a) "Where do we want to be in the future?"
   (b) "How well are we currently doing?"
   (c) "How can we get where we want to be?"
   (d) "Why aren't we doing better?"

2. The ability of a firm to consistently outperform its rivals is called _____.
   (a) vertical integration
   (b) competitive advantage
   (c) incrementalism
   (d) strategic intent

3. In a complex conglomerate such as General Electric that owns a large number of different businesses, a/an _____ level strategy sets strategic direction for a strategic business unit.
   (a) institutional
   (b) corporate
   (c) business
   (d) functional

4. The _____ is a predominant value system for an organization as a whole.
   (a) strategy
   (b) core competency
   (c) mission
   (d) corporate culture

5. Cost efficiency and product quality are two examples of _____ objectives of organizations.
   (a) official   (c) informal
   (b) operating   (d) institutional

6. An organization that is downsizing by laying off workers to reduce costs is implementing a _____strategy.
   (a) growth
   (b) cost differentiation
   (c) restructuring
   (d) vertical integration

7. When PepsiCo acquired Tropicana, a maker of orange juice, the firm's strategy was growth by _____.
   (a) related diversification
   (b) concentration
   (c) vertical integration
   (d) cooperation

8. In Porter's five forces framework, having _____ increases industry attractiveness.
   (a) many rivals
   (b) many substitute products
   (c) low bargaining power of suppliers
   (d) few barriers to entry

9. A _____ in the BCG matrix would have a high market share in a low-growth market, and the correct grand or master strategy is _____.
   (a) Dog, growth
   (b) Cash Cow, stability
   (c) Question Mark, stability
   (d) Star, retrenchment

10. Strategic alliances that link together airlines in code sharing and joint marketing agreements are examples of how businesses can use _____ strategies.
    (a) divestiture   (c) cooperation
    (b) growth   (d) backward integration

11. The two questions asked by Porter to identify competitive strategies for a business or product line are: 1—What is the market scope? 2—What is the _____?
    (a) market share
    (b) source of competitive advantage
    (c) core competency
    (d) industry attractiveness

12. According to Porter's model of competitive strategies, a firm that wants to compete with its rivals in a broad market by selling a very low-priced product would need to successfully implement a _____ strategy.
    (a) retrenchment   (c) cost leadership
    (b) differentiation   (d) diversification

13. When Coke and Pepsi spend millions on ads trying to convince customers that their products are unique, they are pursuing a _____ strategy.
    (a) transnational   (c) diversification
    (b) concentration   (d) differentiation

14. The role of the board of directors as an oversight body that holds top executives accountable for the success of business strategies is called _____.
    (a) strategic leadership
    (b) corporate governance
    (c) logical incrementalism
    (d) strategic opportunism

15. An example of a process failure in strategic planning is _____.
    (a) lack of participation
    (b) weak mission statement
    (c) bad core values
    (d) insufficient financial resources

Short-Response Questions

16. What is the difference between corporate strategy and functional strategy?

17. What would a manager look at in a SWOT analysis?

18. What is the difference between focus and differentiation as competitive strategies?

19. What is strategic leadership?

Essay Question

20. Kim Harris owns and operates a small retail store selling the outdoor clothing of an American manufacturer to a predominately college-student market. Lately, a large department store outside of town has started selling similar but lower-priced clothing manufactured in China, Thailand, and Bangladesh. Kim believes she is starting to lose business to this store. Assume you are part of a student team assigned to do a management class project for Kim. Her question for the team is: "How can I best deal with my strategic management challenges in this situation?" How will you reply?

Management Skills & Competencies Make yourself **valuable!**

Evaluate Career Situations

What Would You Do?

1. The Mission Statement

You've just been given a great assignment to serve as personal assistant to the company president of a mid-sized firm operating just outside a major city in the U.S. It will last for six months and then, if you've done a good job, the expectation is you'll be moved into a fast-track management position. The president comes to you and says: "It's time to revisit the mission statement and our corporate values. Set things up for us." There are about a dozen people on the top management team and the company as a whole employs 700-plus, all in one location. How will you proceed to get the mission and values of this company updated?

2. Cooperate or Compete, or Both?

A neighborhood business association has this set of members: coffee shop, bookstore, drugstore, dress shop, hardware store, and bicycle shop. The owners of these businesses are interested in how they might cooperate for better success. As a business consultant to the association, what strategic alliances would you propose as ways to join sets of these businesses together for mutual gain?

3. Saving a Bookstore

For some years you've owned a small specialty bookshop in a college town. You sell some textbooks but mainly cater to a broader customer base. The store always has the latest fiction, nonfiction, and children's books in stock. You've recently experienced a steep decline in overall sales, even for those books that would normally be considered bestsellers. You suspect this is because of the growing popularity of e-books and e-readers such as the Amazon Kindle and Barnes & Noble Nook. Some of your friends say it's time to close the store and call it quits because your market is dying. Is it hopeless? Or, can a new business strategy save you?

Reflect on the Self-Assessment

Intuitive Ability

Instructions

Complete this survey as quickly as you can. Be honest with yourself. For each question, select the response that most appeals to you.[60]

1. When working on a project, do you prefer to
   (a) be told what the problem is but be left free to decide how to solve it?
   (b) get very clear instructions for how to go about solving the problem before you start?

2. When working on a project, do you prefer to work with colleagues who are
   (a) realistic?
   (b) imaginative?

3. Do you most admire people who are
   (a) creative?
   (b) careful?

4. Do the friends you choose tend to be
   (a) serious and hard working?
   (b) exciting and often emotional?

5. When you ask a colleague for advice on a problem you have, do you
   (a) seldom or never get upset if he or she questions your basic assumptions?
   (b) often get upset if he or she questions your basic assumptions?

6. When you start your day, do you
   (a) seldom make or follow a specific plan?
   (b) usually first make a plan to follow?

7. When working with numbers, do you find that you
   (a) seldom or never make factual errors?
   (b) often make factual errors?

8. Do you find that you
   (a) seldom daydream during the day and really don't enjoy doing so when you do it?
   (b) frequently daydream during the day and enjoy doing so?

9. When working on a problem, do you
   (a) prefer to follow the instructions or rules that are given to you?
   (b) often enjoy circumventing the instructions or rules that are given to you?

10. When you are trying to put something together, do you prefer to have
    (a) step-by-step written instructions on how to assemble the item?
    (b) a picture of how the item is supposed to look once assembled?

11. Do you find that the person who irritates you *the most* is the one who appears to be
    (a) disorganized?
    (b) organized?

12. When an unexpected crisis comes up that you have to deal with, do you
    (a) feel anxious about the situation?
    (b) feel excited by the challenge of the situation?

Scoring

Total the number of "a" responses selected for questions 1, 3, 5, 6, 11; enter the score here [a = ____]. Total the number of "b" responses for questions 2, 4, 7, 8, 9, 10, 12; enter the score here [b = ____]. Add your "a" and "b" scores and enter the sum here [a + b = ____]. This is your intuitive score. The highest possible intuitive score is 12; the lowest is 0.

Interpretation

In his book *Intuition in Organizations* (Newbury Park, CA: Sage, 1989), pp. 10–11, Weston H. Agor states: "Traditional analytical techniques . . . are not as useful as they once were for guiding major decisions. . . . If you hope to be better prepared for tomorrow, then it only seems logical to pay some attention to the use and development of intuitive skills for decision making." Agor developed the preceding survey to help people assess their tendencies to use intuition in decision making. Your score offers a general indication of your strength in this area. It may also suggest a need to further develop your skill and comfort with more intuitive decision-making approaches.

Contribute to the Class Exercise

Strategic Scenarios

Preparation

In today's turbulent economic environment, it is no longer safe to assume that an organization that was highly successful in the past will continue to be so in the near future—or that it will even be in existence. Changing times exact the best from strategic planners. Think about the situations currently facing the following well-known organizations. Think, too, about the futures they may face in competitive markets.

Chipotle	Domino's Pizza	Sony
Apple Computer	Nordstrom	Zynga
Netflix	National Public Radio	AT&T
Ann Taylor	*New York Times*	Federal Express

Instructions

Form into groups. Choose one or more organizations from the list (or as assigned by your instructor) and answer for this organization the following questions:

1. What in the future might seriously threaten the success, perhaps the very existence, of this organization? As a group, develop at least three such *future scenarios*.
2. Estimate the probability (0% to 100%) of each future scenario occurring.
3. Develop a strategy for each scenario that will enable the organization to deal with it successfully.

Thoroughly discuss these questions within the group and arrive at your best possible consensus answers. Be prepared to share and defend your answers in general class discussion.

Manage a Critical Incident

Kickstarting a Friend's Business Idea

You've worked hard, made a fair amount of money, and have a nice stock portfolio. You're also known among your friends as "the guy with the money." As with lottery winners, you've become a bit of a target—some want handouts, some loans, and others just do their share of freeloading. But now one of your friends has come with a business proposal. She's just back from a trip to Southeast Asia and is raving about all the neat fabrics available in local markets in places like Cambodia, Thailand, and Vietnam. She's also a great fan of the TV show *Project Runway*. So, she wants to import fabrics, buy some sewing machines and materials, rent a small storefront, and set up a shop called The Design Place. The basic idea is that a customer can come in, find fabrics, use the workspace, and then design and sew their own clothing. She thinks the idea will be a winner, but has come to your for advice and—she hopes—some startup financing.

Questions

What questions will you ask and what will you say to help your friend do a good strategic analysis of her business idea? Without knowing any more than you do now, what do you believe is the real strategic potential of The Design Place? Are there examples of do-it-yourself stores within other product spaces that could serve as guides for your evaluation and help in developing her business proposal?

Collaborate on the Team Activity

Contrasting Strategies

Question

How do organizations in the same industry fare when they pursue similar or very different strategies?[61]

Instructions

1. Research recent news reports and analyst summaries for each of the following organizations:
   - Coach and Kate Spade
   - Southwest Airlines and Delta Airlines
   - *The New York Times* and *USA Today*
   - Under Armour and Lululemon
   - National Public Radio and Sirius Satellite Radio
   - Tesla and General Motors
   - Amazon and Alibaba
2. Use this information to write a short description of the strategies that each seems to be following in the quest for success.
3. Compare the strategies for each organizational pair. Identify whether or not, and why, one organization has a strategic advantage in the industry.
4. Choose other pairs of organizations and do similar strategic comparisons for them.
5. Prepare a summary report highlighting (a) the strategy comparisons and (b) suggestions on how organizations in the same industry can choose strategies to best compete with one another.

Analyze THE CaseStudy
SONY CORPORATION
An Evolution of Technology

Go to *Management Cases for Critical Thinking* at the end of the book to find this case.

FUNDAMENTALS OF ORGANIZING

11

KEY TAKEAWAYS

- Describe organizing as a management function and the difference between formal and informal organization structures.

- Identify the traditional organizational structures, and the strengths and weaknesses of each.

- Identify newer horizontal organizational structures, and the strengths and weaknesses of each.

- Explain how organizational designs are changing in the modern workplace.

SKILLS MAKE YOU **VALUABLE**

- **EVALUATE** *Career Situations:* What Would You Do?

- **REFLECT** *On the Self-Assessment:* Empowering Others

- **CONTRIBUTE** *To the Class Exercise:* Organizational Metaphors

- **MANAGE** *A Critical Incident:* Crowdsourcing Evaluations to Cut Management Levels

- **COLLABORATE** *On the Team Activity:* Designing a Network University

- **ANALYZE** *The Case Study:* Toyota: Designing as Effective Structure

Organizing puts people together with resources in ways designed to help them achieve performance goals. Although organizations still make use of traditional structures, new approaches are being crafted around horizontal relationships, teams, and collaboration. Key trends in organizational design are reshaping structures for better alignment with the people, tasks, and demands of the new workplace.

It is much easier to talk about high-performing organizations than to create them. And in true contingency fashion there is no one best way to do things; no one organizational form can meet the needs of all circumstances. What works well at one moment in time can quickly become outdated or even dysfunctional in the next. This is why you often read and hear about organizations making changes to their structures and personnel and reorganizing operations to improve their performance.

Management scholar and consultant Henry Mintzberg says that people need to understand how their organizations work if they are to work well within them.[1] Whenever job assignments and reporting relationships change, whenever an organization grows or shrinks, whenever old ways of doing things are reconfigured, people naturally struggle to understand the new ways of working. They ask questions such as: "Who's in charge?" "How do the parts connect to one another?" "How should processes and people come together?" "Whose ideas have to flow where?" They also worry about the implications of the new arrangements for their jobs and careers.

Organizing as a Management Function

TAKEAWAY 1   What is organizing as a management function?

LEARN MORE
ABOUT | What is organization structure? • Formal structures • Informal structures

Organizing
arranges, connects,
and integrates people
and resources to
accomplish a common
purpose.

Organizing is the process of arranging, connecting, and integrating people and other resources to accomplish a goal. Its purpose as one of the basic functions of management is to create a division of labor and then coordinate processes and results to achieve a common purpose.

Figure 11.1 shows the central role that organizing plays in the management process. Once plans are created, the manager's task is to ensure that they are carried out. Once strategy is set and plans are made, organizing launches the processes of implementation and accomplishment by clarifying jobs and working relationships. It identifies who does what, who is in charge of whom, and how different people and parts of the organization relate to and work with one another. All of this, of course, can be done in many different ways. The challenge for managers is to choose the best organizational form to fit the firm's strategy and other situational/market demands.

What Is Organization Structure?

Organization structure is a system of tasks, reporting relationships, and communication linkages.

The way in which the various parts of an organization are arranged is usually referred to as the **organization structure**. It is the system of tasks, workflows, reporting relationships, and communication channels that connect the work and activities of diverse individuals and groups within a firm. An organization's structure should both effectively allocate tasks through a division of labor and coordinate performance results. A structure that accomplishes both well helps to implement an organization's strategy.[2] But as stated earlier, the problem for managers is that it is much easier to describe what a good structure does than it is to create one.

Formal Structures

An **organization chart** describes the arrangement of work positions within an organization.

Formal structure is the official structure of the organization.

You may know the concept of structure best in the form of an **organization chart**. It diagrams reporting relationships and the arrangement of work positions within an organization.[3] A typical organization chart identifies positions and job titles as well as the lines of authority and communication between them. It shows the **formal structure**, or how the organization is intended to function.

Reading an organization chart should help you learn the basics of an organization's formal structure. But caution is in order, charts can be useful . . . or confusing and out of date. At their best, they provide a snapshot of how an organization is supposed to work in respect to:

- *Division of work*—Positions and titles show work responsibilities.
- *Supervisory relationships*—Lines show who reports to whom.
- *Communication channels*—Lines show formal communication flows.
- *Major subunits*—Positions reporting to a common manager are shown.
- *Levels of management*—Vertical layers of management are shown.

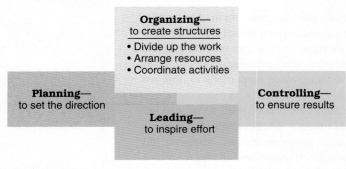

FIGURE 11.1
Organizing viewed in relationship with the other management functions.

Informal Structures and Social Networks

Underneath an organization's formal structure lies an **informal structure**. This is a "shadow" organization made up of social networks comprising the unofficial, but often critical, working relationships that connect organizational members.

No organization can be fully understood without gaining insight into its spiderweb of informal networks as well as the formal organizational structure.[4] If the informal structure could be drawn, it would show who talks and interacts with whom, regardless of their formal titles and relationships. The lines of the informal structure would cut across levels and move from side to side. They would show people interacting through social media, meeting for coffee, joining in exercise groups, and participating in leisure activities—all driven by friendship and enjoyment rather than formal requirements.

A tool known as **social network analysis**, or **sociometrics**, is one way of identifying patterns in informal structures and their embedded social relationships.[5] Such an analysis can be done by surveys that ask people to identify others to whom they turn for help most often, with whom they communicate regularly, and who give them energy and motivation.[6] It can also be done by analysis of data mined from an organization's internal social media sites, and even by data gathered from special electronic badges worn by employees and that record their interactions during daily work.[7] Lines are then drawn to create a social network map or informal structure that shows how a lot of work really gets done and who the "influencers" really are, in contrast to the formal descriptions in the organization chart. This information can be used to update the organization chart to better reflect the way things actually work. It also recognizes the legitimacy of the informal networks people use in their daily work and identifies talented people whose value as connectors and networkers may otherwise go unnoticed by management.[8]

Informal structures and social networks are in many ways essential to organizational success. They allow people to make contacts with others who can help them get things done. They stimulate informal learning as people work and interact together throughout the workday. And, they are also sources of emotional support and friendship that satisfy members' social needs.

Of course, informal structures also have potential disadvantages. They can be susceptible to rumor, carry inaccurate information, breed resistance to change, and even divert work efforts from important objectives. The Society for Human Resource Management (SHRM), for example, reported that when the bad economy caused massive job losses, firms experienced an increase in workplace eavesdropping and in "gossip and rumors about downsizings and layoffs."[9] Another problem sometimes found in informal structures is the presence of "in" and "out" groups. Those who perceive themselves as "outsiders" may become less engaged in their work and more dissatisfied. Some American managers of Japanese firms, for example, have complained about being excluded from what they call the "shadow cabinet" composed of Japanese executives who hold the real power and sometimes interact with one another while excluding others.[10]

Informal structure is the set of social networks found in unofficial relationships among the members of an organization.

Social network analysis or **sociometrics** identifies the informal structures and their embedded social relationships that are active in an organization.

Informal Structures and the Shadow Organization

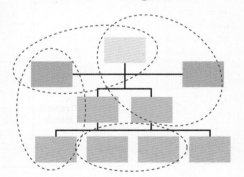

Learning Check 1

TAKEAWAYQUESTION **1 What is organizing as a management function?**

BE SURE YOU CAN • define *organizing* as a management function • explain the difference between formal and informal structures • discuss the potential advantages and disadvantages of informal structures in organizations

Traditional Organization Structures

TAKEAWAY 2   What are the traditional organization structures?

LEARN MORE ABOUT | Functional structures • Divisional structures • Matrix structures

A guiding principle of organizing is that performance should improve when tasks are divided up and people are allowed to become experts in specific jobs. But there are different ways to accomplish this division of labor, and each has potential advantages and disadvantages. The traditional alternatives are the functional, divisional, and matrix structures.[11]

Functional Structures

> A **functional structure** groups together people with similar skills who perform similar tasks.

In **functional structures**, people with similar skills and who perform similar tasks are grouped together into formal work units. Members of functional departments share technical expertise, interests, and responsibilities. The first example in Figure 11.2 shows a functional structure you might find in medium-sized business, with top management arranged by the functions of marketing, finance, information systems, and human resources. Under this structure, sales tasks are the responsibility of the Chief Sales Officer, information systems tasks are the responsibility of the Chief Information Officer, and so on. Figure 11.2 also shows how functional structures are used in other types of organizations such as banks and hospitals.

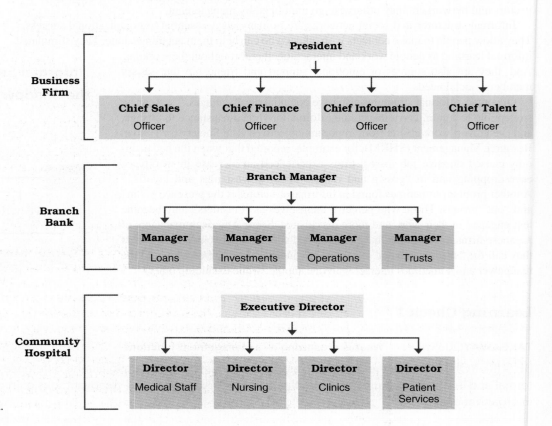

FIGURE 11.2 Functional structures in a business, branch bank, and community hospital.

Advantages of Functional Structures

The key point of the functional structure is to put together people with the same expertise and help them work well together. If each function does its work properly, the expectation is that the organization as a whole will be successful. These structures work well for organizations with only a few products or services. They also tend to work best in relatively stable environments where problems are predictable and the demands for change and innovation are limited. The major advantages of functional structures include the following:

- Economies of scale with efficient use of resources.
- Task assignments consistent with expertise and training.
- High-quality technical problem solving.
- In-depth training and skill development within functions.
- Clear career paths within functions.

Disadvantages of Functional Structures

One of the major problems with functional structures is the tendency for each department or function to focus primarily on its own concerns, avoid communications with other functions, and neglect "big picture" issues. There is too little cross-functional collaboration as a sense of common purpose gets lost and self-centered and narrow viewpoints become emphasized.[12] This is often called the **functional chimneys** or **functional silos problem**— a lack of communication, coordination, and problem solving across functions. It happens because the functions become formalized not only on the organization chart, but also in people's mind-sets; they end up viewing the function as the center of the organizational world rather than one among many key components. The functional chimney or silos problem tends to get more common as organizations grow larger and more rigid. When GM CEO Mary Barra was asked what she would do to prevent future failures like the ignition switch debacle that scandalized the company and caused several deaths, for example, she said one of her priorities was to reorganize so that safety information didn't get lost in "silos" within the firm.[13]

The **functional chimneys** or **functional silos problem** is a lack of communication, coordination, and problem solving across functions.

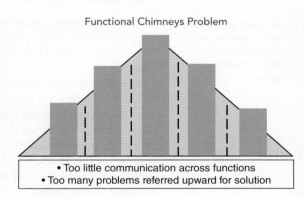

Functional Chimneys Problem

- Too little communication across functions
- Too many problems referred upward for solution

Divisional Structures

A second organizing alternative is the **divisional structure**. As illustrated in Figure 11.3, this structure puts together people who work on the same product or process, serve similar customers, or are located in the same area or geographical region.

Divisional structures are common in complex organizations with diverse operations that extend across many products, territories, customer segments, and work processes.[14] The idea is to overcome some of the disadvantages of a functional structure, such as the functional chimneys problem. For example, Toyota changed to a divisional structure in its North American operations. The new design brought together the engineering, manufacturing, and sales functions under common leadership rather than having each function reporting to its own top executive. As one industry analyst said: "The problem is every silo reported back to someone different, but now they need someone in charge of the whole choir."[15]

A **divisional structure** groups together people working on the same product, in the same area, with similar customers, or on the same processes.

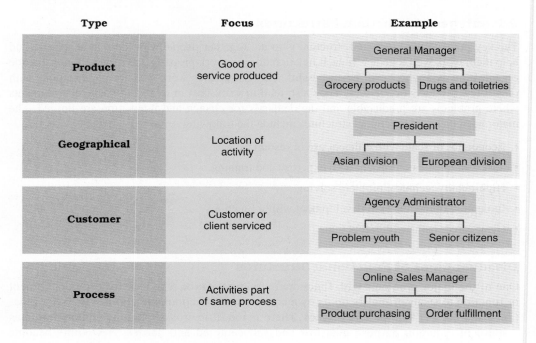

FIGURE 11.3
Divisional structures based on product, geography, customer and process.

Product Structures

A product structure groups together people and jobs focused on a single product or service.

Product structures group together jobs and activities focused on a single product or service. They clearly link costs, profits, problems, and successes in a market area with a central point of accountability. This prompts managers to be responsive to changing market demands and customer tastes.

Product structures in large organizations can even extend into global operations. When Fiat took over Chrysler, for example, CEO Sergio Marchionne said he wanted a "leaner, flatter structure" to improve decision making and communication flow. His choice was to use product divisions. Each of the firm's three brands—Chrysler, Jeep, and Dodge—was given its own chief executive and assigned responsibility for its own profits and losses.[16] This same approach has been applied at Procter & Gamble, which is now organized around four product divisions—Global baby, feminine and family care; Global health and grooming; Global fabric and home care; and Global beauty.[17]

Geographical Structures

A geographical structure groups together people and jobs performed in the same location.

Geographical structures, sometimes called *area structures*, group jobs and activities being performed in the same location. They are typically used to differentiate products or services in various locations, such as in different parts of a country. They also help global companies focus attention on the unique cultures and requirements of particular regions. As United Parcel Service (UPS) operations expanded worldwide, for example, the company announced a shift from a product structure to a geographical structure. Two geographical divisions were created—the Americas and Europe/Asia. Each area was given responsibility for its own logistics, sales, and other business functions.

Customer Structures

A customer structure groups together people and jobs that serve the same customers or clients.

Customer structures group together jobs and activities serving the same customers or clients. The goal is to best serve the diverse needs of different customer groups. This is a common structure in the consumer products industry. 3M Corporation structures itself to focus attention on such diverse markets as consumer and office, specialty materials, industrial, health care, electronics and communications, and safety. Customer structures also are useful in services. Banks, for example, use them to give separate attention to consumer and commercial loan customers. If you look again at Figure 11.3, you'll see that it also shows a government agency using the customer structure to serve different client populations.

Process Structures

A **work process** is a group of related tasks that collectively creates something of value for customers.[18] An example is order fulfillment by an online retailer, a process that takes an order from point of customer initiation all the way through product delivery. A **process structure** groups together jobs and activities that are part of the same processes. Figure 11.3 shows how a product structure might emerge in product-purchasing teams and order-fulfillment teams for a mail-order catalog business.

A **work process** is a group of related tasks that collectively creates a valuable work product.

A **process structure** groups jobs and activities that are part of the same processes.

Advantages and Disadvantages of Divisional Structures

Organizations use divisional structures for a variety of reasons, including the desire to avoid the functional chimneys problem and other limitations of functional structures. The potential advantages of divisional structures include:

- More flexibility in responding to environmental changes.
- Improved coordination across functional departments.
- Clear points of responsibility for product or service delivery.
- Expertise focused on specific customers, products, and regions.
- Greater ease in changing size by adding or deleting divisions.

As with other structural alternatives, however, divisional structures have potential disadvantages as well. They can reduce economies of scale and increase costs through the duplication of resources and efforts across divisions. They can also create unhealthy rivalries as divisions compete for resources and top management attention, emphasizing division needs over broader organizational goals.

Matrix Structures

The **matrix structure**, often called the *matrix organization*, combines functional and divisional structures. It is an attempt to gain the advantages and avoid the disadvantages of each. This is accomplished by creating permanent teams in a matrix that cuts across functions to support specific products, projects, or programs.[19] As shown in Figure 11.4, workers in a matrix structure simultaneously belong to at least two formal groups—a functional group and a product, program, or project team. They also report to two supervisors—one within the function and the other within the team.

The matrix organization has gained a strong foothold in the workplace, with applications in such diverse settings as manufacturing (e.g., aerospace, electronics, pharmaceuticals), service industries (e.g., banking, brokerage, retailing), professional fields (e.g., accounting, advertising, law), and the nonprofit sector (e.g., city, state, and federal agencies, hospitals, universities). Matrix structures also are found in multinational corporations, where they offer the flexibility to deal with regional differences while still supporting multiple product, program, or project needs.

A **matrix structure** combines the functional and divisional approaches to create permanent cross-functional project teams.

Advantages and Disadvantages of Matrix Structures

The primary benefits of matrix structures derive from team members working closely together across functional lines and sharing expertise and information in a timely way. This structure goes

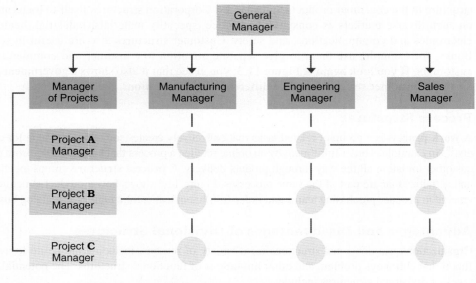

FIGURE 11.4
Matrix structure in a small, multiproject business firm.

⬤ Persons assigned to both projects and functional departments

a long way toward eliminating functional chimneys problems and poor cross-functional communication. The potential advantages of matrix structures include:

- Better communication and cooperation across functions.
- Improved decision making; problem solving takes place at the team level where the best information is available.
- Increased flexibility in adding, removing, or changing operations to meet changing demands.
- Better customer service; there is always a program, product, or project manager informed and available to answer questions.
- Better performance accountability through the program, product, or project managers.
- Improved strategic management; top managers are freed from lower-level problem solving to focus time on more strategic issues.

As you might expect, matrix structures also have potential disadvantages. The additional team leaders needed to staff a matrix structure result in higher costs. The two-supervisor system is susceptible to power struggles. Problems and frustrations occur when functional supervisors and team leaders don't coordinate well and end up sending conflicting messages and priorities, or even competing with one another for authority. Matrix teams may develop something called "groupitis," where strong team loyalties cause a loss of focus on larger organizational goals. And, team meetings in the matrix can take lots of time.

Learning Check 2

TAKEAWAYQUESTION 2 **What are the traditional organization structures?**

BE SURE YOU CAN • explain the differences between functional, divisional, and matrix structures • list advantages and disadvantages of a functional structure, divisional structure, and matrix structure • draw charts to show how each type of traditional structure could be used in organizations familiar to you

Horizontal Organization Structures

TAKEAWAY 2   What are the types of horizontal organization structures?

LEARN MORE ABOUT | Team structures • Network structures • Boundaryless structures

The matrix structure is a step toward better cross-functional integration within organizations. But it is just one part of a broader movement to increase collaboration in organizations by building horizontal structures that harness the power of teams, technology, and connections. The goal is to increase communication, teamwork, and flexibility, but reduce hierarchy and functional silos, and empower human talent.[20] Consultant and scholar Gary Hamel says that one of the driving forces toward horizontal structures comes from "younger workers" who are "impatient with old hierarchies and value systems."[21]

Team Structures

Organizations with **team structures** make extensive use of both permanent and temporary teams to solve problems, complete special projects, and accomplish day-to-day tasks.[22] As illustrated in Figure 11.5, these are often **cross-functional teams** composed of members drawn from different areas of work responsibility.[23] Like the matrix structure, the intention of team structures is to break down functional silos, foster horizontal connections, and create faster decision making at the levels where work gets done.

Team structures use many **project teams** that are convened to complete a specific task or "project." An example is a team tasked with guiding the changeover to a new IT system. Such project teams are temporary and disband once the task is completed. The intention is to convene a team of people who have the needed talents, focus their efforts intensely to solve a problem or take advantage of a special opportunity, and then release them once the project is finished.

Advantages and Disadvantages of Team Structures

The advantage of a team structure is that it helps to break down interpersonal barriers and mobilize diverse talents. Because teams focus shared knowledge and expertise on specific problems, they can improve performance by increasing the speed and quality of decisions. They can also boost morale. People working in teams often experience a greater sense of task involvement and identification, as well as increased enthusiasm for the job.

The complexities of teams and teamwork contribute to the potential disadvantages of team structures. These include conflicting loyalties for members with both team and functional assignments. They also include issues of time management and group process. By their very

A team structure uses permanent and temporary cross-functional teams to improve lateral relations.

A cross-functional team brings together members from different functional departments.

Project teams are convened for a particular task or project and disband once it is completed.

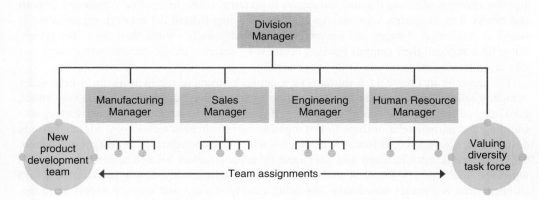

FIGURE 11.5 How a team structure uses cross-functional teams for improved lateral relations.

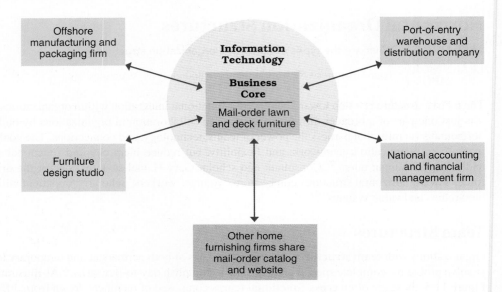

FIGURE 11.6
A network structure for a
Web-based retail business.

nature, teams spend a lot of time in meetings. Whether meetings are face-to-face or virtual, not all meeting time is productive. The quality of outcomes depends on how well tasks, relationships, and team dynamics are managed. But, all of these challenges can be mastered with the right team talents, good technology, and leadership.

Network Structures

A network structure
uses information
technologies to link
with networks of
outside suppliers and
service contractors.

Organizations using a **network structure**, like the one in Figure 11.6, have a central core of full-time employees surrounded by "networks" of outside contractors and partners supplying essential services.[24] Because the central core is relatively small and surrounding networks can be expanded or contracted as needed, the network structure helps lower costs and improve flexibility in dealing with changing environments.[25]

A strategic alliance
is a cooperation
agreement with
another organization to
jointly pursue activities
of mutual interest.

Instead of doing everything for itself with full-time employees, the network organization employs a minimum staff and contracts out as much work as possible. This is done through **strategic alliances**, which are cooperative agreements with partner firms to pursue mutual business interests. Some are *outsourcing strategic alliances* in which firms contract to purchase services such as accounting or document processing from another organization. Others may be *supplier strategic alliances* that link businesses in preferred relationships that guarantee a smooth and timely flow of quality supplies. An example of a step toward the network organization is found in residential colleges and universities that traditionally owned their own dormitories. Some have reduced their campus housing business by entering public–private partnerships that turn dormitories over to private firms to operate.[26]

The example in Figure 11.6 shows how a network structure might work for a mail-order company selling lawn and deck furniture online and through a catalog. The firm is very small, consisting of few full-time "core" employees. Beyond that, it is structured as a network of outsourcing and partner relationships linked together by information technology. Merchandise is designed on contract with a furniture designer—which responds quickly as designs are shared. The furniture is manufactured and packaged by subcontractors located around the world—wherever materials are found at the lowest cost and best quality. Stock is maintained and shipped from a contract warehouse—ensuring quality storage and on-time expert shipping.

 **> LEARN ABOUT YOURSELF**

> *Do you have a problem "letting go," or letting others do their share?*

Empowerment Gets More Things Done

It takes a lot of trust to be comfortable with **empowerment**—letting others make decisions and exercise discretion in their work. But if you aren't willing and able to empower others, you may try to do too much on your own and end up accomplishing too little.

The fundamental, underlying reason for organizations is synergy—bringing together the contributions of many people to achieve something that is much greater than any individual could accomplish alone. Empowerment enables synergy to flourish. It means collaborating with others to accomplish firm objectives—allowing others to do things that you might be good at doing yourself. Many managers fail to empower others, and the result is their organizations often underperform.

How often do you get stressed out by group projects in your classes, feeling like you're doing all the work? Do you have a problem "letting go," or letting others do their share of group assignments? The reason may be the fear of losing control. People with control anxiety often end up trying to do too much. This unfortunately raises the risks of missed deadlines and poor performance.

If the prior description fits you, your assumptions probably align with those in the upper left box in the Empowerment Quick Test. Alternatively, you could be in the lower right box and perhaps find that you work smarter and better while also making others happier.

GET TO KNOW YOURSELF BETTER

Are you someone who easily and comfortably empowers others? Or, do you suffer from control anxiety, with little or no

EMPOWERMENT QUICK TEST

In a team situation, which square best describes your beliefs and behaviors?

- It's faster to do things myself than explain how to do them to others
- Some things are just too important not to do yourself

?

- People make mistakes, but they also learn from them
- Many people are ready to take on more work, but are too shy to volunteer

willingness to delegate? The next time you are in a study or work group, be a self-observer. The question is: How well do you handle empowerment? Write a short narrative that accurately describes your behavior to someone who wasn't present. Focus on both your tendencies to empower others and how you respond when others empower you. Compare that narrative with the results from the Self-Assessment—Empowering Others. Is there a match?

Accounting and financial matters are contracted with an outside firm that provides better technical expertise than the merchandiser could afford to employ on a full-time basis. The website is managed by an independent contractor and hosted on rented server space. The quarterly catalog is produced in cooperation with two other firms that sell different home furnishings with a related price appeal.

Advantages and Disadvantages of Network Structures

Network structures are lean and streamlined. They help organizations stay cost-competitive by reducing overhead and increasing operating efficiency. Network concepts allow organizations to employ outsourcing strategies and contract out specialized business functions. Within the operating core of a network structure, interesting jobs are created for employees who coordinate the entire system of relationships.

Network structures have potential disadvantages as well. The more complex the organization's mission, the more complicated it is to control and coordinate the network of contracts and alliances. If one part of the network breaks down, the entire system can fail. The organization may lose control over contracted activities. Firms also may experience a lack of loyalty among contractors who are used infrequently rather than on a long-term basis. Outsourcing also can become so aggressive as to be dangerous to the firm, especially when critical activities such as finance, logistics, and human resources management are outsourced.[27]

Boundaryless Structures

A boundaryless organization eliminates internal boundaries among subsystems and external boundaries with the external environment.

It is popular today to talk about creating a **boundaryless organization** that eliminates many internal subsystem boundaries as well as boundaries with the external environment.[28] The boundaryless structure, as shown in Figure 11.7, can be viewed as a combination of the team and network structures, with the added feature of "temporariness." A photograph that documents this organization's configuration today will look different from one taken tomorrow, as the form naturally adjusts to new environmental pressures and circumstances.

Spontaneous teamwork and communication replace formal lines of authority within the boundaryless organization. Meetings and information sharing are continuous. People work together in teams that form and disband as needed. There is little hierarchy but lots of empowerment and use of technology. Impermanence is accepted. Knowledge sharing is both a goal and an essential component of the structure. At consulting giant PricewaterhouseCoopers, for example, knowledge sharing brings together 160,000 employees spread across 150 countries in a virtual-learning and problem-solving network. Individuals collaborate electronically through online databases where information is stored, problems are posted, and questions are asked and answered in real time by those with experience and expertise relevant to current problems.[29]

A virtual organization uses mobile IT to engage a shifting network of strategic alliances.

The **virtual organization** takes the boundaryless concept to the extreme.[30] It operates as a shifting network of alliances that are engaged as needed using mobile IT solutions. The virtual organization calls an alliance into action to meet specific operating needs and objectives.

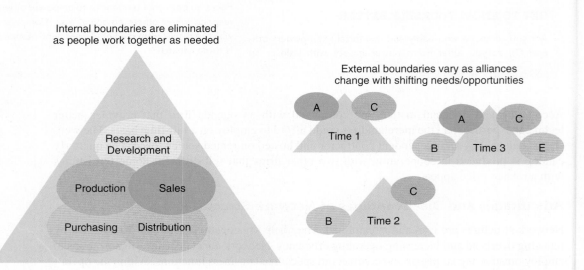

FIGURE 11.7
The boundaryless organization eliminates internal and external barriers.

When the work is complete, the alliance rests until it is next called into action. This mix of mobilized alliances shifts continuously. Do you see similarities with the Twitter or LinkedIn communities? The virtual organization concept is similar to how we manage relationships online—logging in, logging off, accomplishing tasks with different individuals and groups as needed, and all taking place instantaneously, temporarily, and without the need for face-to-face contact.

Learning Check 3

TAKEAWAYQUESTION **3 What are the types of horizontal organization structures?**

BE SURE YOU CAN • describe how organizations can be structured to use cross-functional teams and project teams • define *network structure* • illustrate how a new retail venture might use a network structure to organize its various operations • discuss the potential advantages and disadvantages of a network structure • explain the concept of the boundaryless organization

Organizational Designs

TAKEAWAY 4 How are organizational designs changing the workplace?

LEARN MORE | Contingency in organizational design
ABOUT | Mechanistic and organic organization designs • Trends in organizational designs

Organizational design is the process of choosing and implementing structures to accomplish an organization's mission and objectives.[31] Because every organization faces its own set of unique challenges and opportunities, no one design can be applied in all circumstances. The best design at any given moment achieves a good match between structure and situational contingencies—including task, technology, environment, and people.[32] The choices among design alternatives are broadly framed in the distinction between mechanistic or bureaucratic designs at one extreme, and organic or adaptive designs at the other end.

Organizational design is the process of creating structures that accomplish mission and objectives.

Contingency in Organizational Design

A classic **bureaucracy** is a form of organization based on logic, order, and the legitimate use of formal authority.[33] It is a vertical structure, and its distinguishing features include a clear-cut division of labor, strict hierarchy of authority, formal rules and procedures, and promotion based on competency.

According to sociologist Max Weber, bureaucracies should be orderly, fair, and highly efficient.[34] But the bureaucracies we know often are associated with "red tape." Instead of being orderly and fair, they often are seen as cumbersome and impersonal, to customers' and clients' needs.[35] Rather than view all bureaucratic structures as inevitably flawed, however, management theory asks two contingency questions. When is bureaucracy a good choice for an organization? When it isn't, what alternatives are available?

Pioneering research conducted in England during the early 1960s by Tom Burns and George Stalker helps answer these questions.[36] After investigating 20 manufacturing firms, they concluded that two quite different organizational forms could be successful, depending on the firm's external environment. A more bureaucratic form, which Burns and Stalker called "mechanistic," thrives in stable environments. But, bureaucratic organizations have difficulty in environments that are rapidly changing and uncertain. In these dynamic environments, a much

A **bureaucracy** emphasizes formal authority, order, fairness, and efficiency.

analysis > MAKE DATA YOUR FRIEND

> *"It doesn't matter what industry you're in. People have blind spots about where they are weak."*

Managers May Overestimate Their Managing Skills

A survey by Development Dimensions International, Inc., finds that managers may be overestimating their management skills. "It doesn't matter what industry you're in. People have blind spots about where they are weak," says DDI vice president Scott Erker. These results are from a sample of 1,100 first-year managers:

- 72% never question their ability to lead others.
- 58% claim planning and organizing skills as strengths.
- 53% say they are strong in decision making.
- 50% say they are strong in communication.

- 32% claim proficiency in delegating.
- Skills rated as needing most development were delegating, gaining commitment, and coaching.

YOUR THOUGHTS?

Would you, like the managers in this survey, overestimate your strengths in management skills? What might explain managers' tendencies toward overconfidence? What would you identify as being among the skills on which you most need improvement? What might account for the fact that 72% of managers never question their ability to lead others?

---

*A **mechanistic design** is centralized, with many rules and procedures, a clear-cut division of labor, narrow spans of control, and formal coordination.*

less bureaucratic form, called "organic," performs best. Figure 11.8 portrays these two approaches as opposite extremes on a continuum of organizational design alternatives.

Mechanistic and Organic Designs

Organizations with more **mechanistic designs** are highly bureaucratic. As shown in the figure, they are vertical structures that typically operate with centralized authority, many rules and

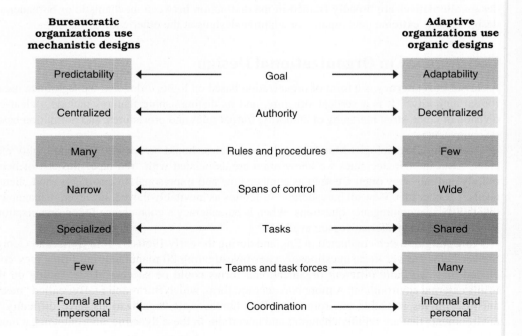

FIGURE 11.8
Organizational design alternatives: from bureaucratic to adaptive organizations.

procedures, a precise division of labor, narrow spans of control, and formal coordination. They can be described as "tight" structures of the traditional pyramid form.[37]

Mechanistic designs work best for organizations doing routine tasks in stable environments. A local fast-food restaurant is a good example. Each store is a relatively small operation that operates much like others in the franchise chain and according to rules established by the corporate management. Service personnel work in orderly and disciplined ways, guided by training, rules, and procedures, and by close supervision of crew leaders who work alongside them. Even personal appearance is carefully regulated, with everyone working in uniform. This mechanistic design performs well as it repetitively delivers items that are part of a standard menu. You quickly discover the design limits, however, if you try to order something not on the menu. The chains also are slow to adjust when consumer tastes change.

When organizations are in dynamic and uncertain environments, their effectiveness depends on being able to adapt quickly to changing customer tastes and preferences. This requires the more **organic designs** described in Figure 11.8.[38] These are horizontal structures that operate with decentralized authority, fewer rules and procedures, less precise division of labor, wider spans of control, and more personal means of coordination.

Organic designs create **adaptive organizations** that can perform well in environments that demand flexibility in dealing with changing conditions. They are relatively "loose" systems where a lot of work gets done through informal structures and networking.[39] They are built on a foundation of trust that gives employees the freedom to use their own ideas and expertise to do things on their own initiative, and without waiting for orders from a "boss." This means giving workers freedom to get the job done.

Trends in Organizational Designs

The complexity, uncertainty, and change inherent in today's environment are prompting more organizations to shift toward horizontal and organic structures. A number of trends in organization design are evident as structures and practices are adjusted to gain performance efficiency and effectiveness in challenging conditions. The growth of new technologies, particularly in information systems and social media, is helping to drive these trends by improving information availability and ease of communication within organizations.

Fewer Levels of Management

A typical organization chart shows the **chain of command**, or the line of authority that vertically links each position with successively higher levels of management. When organizations get bigger, they also tend to get taller as levels of management are added to the chain of command. But Nucor, a North Carolina-based steel producer, shows that this needn't be the case. Nucor's management hierarchy is flat and compact. Its structure is described as "simple" and "streamlined" in order to "allow employees to innovate and make quick decisions."[40]

One of the influences on management levels is **span of control**—the number of persons directly reporting to a manager. Narrow spans of control are characteristic of **tall structures** with many levels of management. Because tall organizations have more managers, they are more costly. They also tend to be less efficient, less flexible, and less customer-sensitive. Wider spans of control run with **flat structures** that have fewer levels of management. This not only reduces overhead costs and improves agility; it can also be good for workers who gain empowerment and independence because of reduced supervision.[41]

An **organic design** is decentralized, with fewer rules and procedures, open divisions of labor, wide spans of control, and more personal coordination.

An **adaptive organization** operates with a minimum of bureaucratic features and encourages worker empowerment and teamwork.

Tall Structure (narrow span of control)

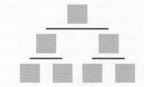

Flat Structure (wide span of control)

The **chain of command** links all employees with successively higher levels of authority.

Span of control is the number of subordinates directly reporting to a manager.

Tall structures have narrow spans of control and many hierarchical levels.

Flat structures have wide spans of control and few hierarchical levels.

ethics > KNOW RIGHT FROM WRONG

> *"I even feel guilty now taking time to watch my daughter play soccer on Saturday mornings."*

Help! I've Been Flattened into Exhaustion

Dear Stress Doctor:

My boss came up with the great idea of laying off some managers, assigning more workers to those of us who haven't been laid off, and calling us "coaches" instead of supervisors. She says this is all part of a new management approach to operate with a flatter structure and more empowerment.

For me, this means a lot more work coordinating the activities of 17 operators instead of the 6 that I previously supervised. I can't get everything cleaned up on my desk most days, and I end up taking a lot of work home.

As my organization "restructures" and cuts back staff, it puts a greater burden on the rest of us. We get exhausted, and our families get short-changed and angry. I even feel guilty now taking time to watch my daughter play soccer on Saturday mornings. Sure, there's some decent pay involved, but that doesn't make up for the heavy price in terms of lost family time.

But you know what? My boss doesn't get it. I never hear her ask: "Camille, are you working too much? Don't you think it's time to get back on a reasonable schedule?" No! What I often hear instead is "Look at Andy; he handles our new management model really well, and he's a real go-getter. I don't think he's been out of here one night this week before 8 PM."

What am I going to do, just keep it up until everything falls apart one day? Is a flatter structure with fewer managers always best? Am I missing something here with the whole "new management"?

Sincerely,
Overworked in Cincinnati

WHAT DO YOU THINK?

Is it ethical to restructure, cut management levels, and expect remaining managers to do more work? Or is it simply the case that managers used to the "old" ways of doing things need extra training and care while learning "new" management approaches? What about this person's boss—is she on track with her management skills? Aren't managers supposed to help people understand their jobs, set priorities, and fulfill them, while still maintaining a reasonable work–life balance?

Trend: Organizations are cutting unnecessary levels of management and shifting to wider spans of control. Managers are taking responsibility for larger teams whose members operate with less supervision.

More Delegation and Empowerment

Delegation is the process of distributing and entrusting work to others.

Self-enhancement bias is the tendency to view oneself as more capable, intelligent, and ethical than others.

The authority-and-responsibility principle is that authority should equal responsibility when work is delegated.

All managers must decide what work they should do themselves and what should be left for others. At issue here is **delegation**—the process of entrusting work to others by giving them the right to make decisions and take action. Unfortunately, many managers and team leaders don't do enough delegation, and one of the reasons is **self-enhancement bias**. This is the tendency to view oneself as more capable, intelligent, and ethical than others. Self-enhancement bias makes it hard to "let go" and give others a chance to work independently without close supervision.[42]

When it comes to delegating, a classical principle of organization warns managers to make sure the person being delegated to has sufficient authority to perform. The **authority-and-responsibility principle** states that authority should equal responsibility when work is delegated by a supervisor to a subordinate. When done well, the process of delegation involves these three action steps:

- *Step 1*—The manager assigns responsibility by carefully explaining the work or duties someone else is expected to do. This responsibility is an expectation for the other person to perform assigned tasks.

- *Step 2*—The manager grants authority to act. Along with the assigned task, the right to take necessary actions (for example, to spend money, direct the work of others, or use resources) is given to the other person.

- *Step 3*—The manager creates accountability. By accepting an assignment, the person takes on a direct obligation to the manager to complete the job as agreed.

On those days when you complain that "I just can't get everything done," the real problem may be that you are trying to do everything yourself. Unwillingness to delegate is a common management failure. Whether this comes from a lack of trust in others or from personal inflexibility, it can be dangerous. Too little delegation overloads managers with work that could be done by others and leaves them with too little time to do their own work.

Delegation that is done well leads to **empowerment**. This concept was defined in the chapter opener as letting others make decisions and exercise discretion in their work. Empowerment occurs when delegation provides decision-making authority to individuals most capable of doing the work. It builds performance potential by allowing individuals freedom to use their talents, contribute ideas, and do their jobs in the best possible ways. And because empowerment creates a sense of ownership, it also increases commitment to follow through on decisions and work hard to accomplish goals.

Empowerment allows others to make decisions and exercise discretion in their work.

Trend: Managers are delegating more. They are finding ways to empower people at all organizational levels to make more decisions that affect themselves and their work.

Decentralization with Centralization

Should most decisions be made at the top levels of an organization, or should they be dispersed by extensive delegation across all levels? The former approach is referred to as **centralization**; the latter is called **decentralization**. And the decision to operate one way or another is a strategic choice. At Rovio, the Finnish company making Angry Birds, for example, one person used to be in charge of game development—centralization. But as the firm grew, CEO Mikael Hed realized this centralization wasn't working anymore. His response was to divide the unit up into smaller "tribes" and give each "their own profit and loss sheet, their own management, their own targets"—decentralization.[43]

Centralization is the concentration of authority for most decisions at the top level of an organization.

A closer look at the Rovio story would likely show that centralization/decentralization isn't necessarily an either/or choice. A game maker is already a high-tech setting, and CEO Hed should be able to operate with greater decentralization without giving up centralized control.[44] High-speed, advanced IT systems allow top managers to easily stay informed about a wide range of day-to-day performance matters throughout an organization. Because they have information so readily available, they can allow more decentralized decision making. If something goes wrong, say in one of Rovio's tribes, the information systems sound an alarm, enabling almost immediate corrective actions to be taken.

Decentralization is the dispersion of authority to make decisions throughout all organization levels.

Trend: Delegation, empowerment, and horizontal structures are contributing to more decentralization in organizations; at the same time, advances in information technology help top managers maintain centralized control.

Reduced Use of Staff

When it comes to coordination and control in organizations, the issue of line–staff relationships is critical. People in **staff positions** provide expert advice and guidance to line personnel. In a large retail chain, for example, line managers in each store typically make daily operating decisions regarding direct merchandise sales. But, staff specialists at the corporate

Staff positions provide technical expertise for other parts of the organization.

or regional levels often provide direction and support so that all the stores operate with the same credit, purchasing, employment, marketing, and advertising procedures.

Problems in line–staff distinctions can and do arise, and organizations sometimes find that staff size grows to the point where its costs outweigh its benefits. This is why cutbacks in staff positions are common during downsizing and other turnaround efforts. There is no one best solution to the problem of how to divide work between line and staff responsibilities. What is best for any organization is a cost-effective staff component that satisfies, but doesn't overreact to, needs for specialized technical assistance to line operations. But overall, the trend toward reduced use of staff across all industries is increasing.

Trend: Organizations are lowering costs and increasing efficiency by employing fewer staff personnel and using smaller staff units.

Learning Check 4

TAKEAWAYQUESTION 4 **How are organizational designs changing the workplace?**

BE SURE YOU CAN • define *organizational design* • describe the characteristics of mechanistic and organic designs • explain when the mechanistic design and the organic design work best • describe trends in levels of management, delegation and empowerment, decentralization and centralization, and use of staff

Management Learning Review
Get Prepared for **Quizzes and Exams**

SUMMARY

TAKEAWAYQUESTION 1

What is organizing as a management function?

- Organizing is the process of arranging people and resources to work toward a common goal.
- Organizing decisions divide up the work that needs to be done, allocate people and resources to do it, and coordinate results to achieve productivity.
- Structure is the system of tasks, reporting relationships, and communication that links people and positions within an organization.
- The formal structure, such as that in an organization chart, describes how an organization is supposed to work.
- The informal structure of an organization consists of the informal relationships that develop among members.

FOR DISCUSSION **If organization charts are imperfect, why bother with them?**

TAKEAWAYQUESTION 2

What are the traditional organization structures?

- In functional structures, people with similar skills who perform similar activities are grouped together under a common manager.

- In divisional structures, people who work on a similar product, work in the same geographical region, serve the same customers, or participate in the same work process, are grouped together under common managers.
- A matrix structure combines the functional and divisional approaches to create permanent cross-functional project teams.

FOR DISCUSSION **Why use functional structures if they are prone to functional chimneys problems?**

TAKEAWAYQUESTION 3

What are the types of horizontal organization structures?

- Team structures use cross-functional teams and task forces to improve lateral relations and problem solving at all levels.
- Network structures use contracted services and strategic alliances to support a core organizational center.
- Boundaryless structures or boundaryless organizations combine team and network structures with the advantages of technology to accomplish tasks and projects.

- Virtual organizations use information technology to mobilize a shifting mix of strategic alliances to accomplish tasks and projects.

FOR DISCUSSION **What problems could reduce the effectiveness of team-oriented organization structures?**

TAKEAWAYQUESTION **4**

How are organizational designs changing the workplace?

- Contingency in organizational design basically involves finding designs that best fit situational features.

- Mechanistic designs are bureaucratic and vertical, performing best for routine and predictable tasks.
- Organic designs are adaptive and horizontal, performing best in conditions requiring change and flexibility.
- Key organizing trends include fewer levels of management, more delegation and empowerment, decentralization with centralization, and fewer staff positions.

FOR DISCUSSION **Which of the organizing trends is most likely to change in the future, and why?**

SELF-TEST 11

Multiple-Choice Questions

1. The main purpose of organizing as a management function is to _____.
   (a) make sure that results match plans
   (b) arrange people and resources to accomplish work
   (c) create enthusiasm for the work to be done
   (d) match strategies with operational plans

2. _____ is the system of tasks, reporting relationships, and communication that links together the various parts of an organization.
   (a) Structure
   (b) Staff
   (c) Decentralization
   (d) Differentiation

3. Rumors and resistance to change are potential disadvantages often associated with _____.
   (a) virtual organizations
   (b) informal structures
   (c) delegation
   (d) specialized staff

4. An organization chart showing vice presidents of marketing, finance, manufacturing, and purchasing all reporting to the president is depicting a _____ structure.
   (a) functional
   (b) matrix
   (c) network
   (d) product

5. The functional chimneys problem occurs when people in different functions _____.
   (a) fail to communicate with one another
   (b) try to help each other work with customers
   (c) spend too much time coordinating decisions
   (d) focus on products rather than functions

6. A manufacturing business with a functional structure has recently developed three new product lines. The president of the company might consider shifting to a/an _____ structure to gain a stronger focus on each product.
   (a) virtual
   (b) informal
   (c) divisional
   (d) network

7. _____ structure tries to combine the best elements of the functional and divisional forms.
   (a) Virtual
   (b) Boundaryless
   (c) Team
   (d) Matrix

8. The "two-boss" system of reporting relationships is found in the _____ structure.
   (a) functional
   (b) matrix
   (c) network
   (d) product

9. Better lower-level teamwork and more top-level strategic management are among the expected advantages of a _____ structure.
   (a) divisional
   (b) matrix
   (c) geographical
   (d) product

10. "Tall" organizations tend to have long chains of command and _____ spans of control.
    (a) wide
    (b) narrow
    (c) informal
    (d) centralized

11. A student volunteers to gather information on a company for a group case analysis project. The other members of the group agree and tell her to go ahead and choose the information sources. In terms of delegation, this group is giving the student _____ to fulfill the agreed-upon task.
    (a) responsibility
    (b) accountability
    (c) authority
    (d) decentralization

12. The current trend in the use of staff in organizations is to _____.
    (a) give staff personnel more authority over operations
    (b) reduce the number of staff personnel
    (c) remove all staff from the organization
    (d) combine all staff functions in one department

13. The bureaucratic organization described by Max Weber is similar to the _____ organization described by Burns and Stalker.
    (a) adaptive
    (b) mechanistic
    (c) organic
    (d) adhocracy

14. Which type of organization design best fits an uncertain and changing environment?
    (a) mechanistic
    (b) bureaucratic
    (c) organic
    (d) traditional

15. An organization that employs just a few "core" or essential full-time employees and outsources a lot of the remaining work shows signs of using a _____ structure.
    (a) functional
    (b) network
    (c) matrix
    (d) mechanistic

Short-Response Questions

16. What symptoms might indicate that a functional structure is causing problems for the organization?

17. Explain by example the concept of a network organization structure.

18. Explain the practical significance of this statement: "Organizational design should be done in contingency fashion."

19. Describe two trends in organizational design and explain their importance to managers.

Essay Question

20. Faisal Sham supervises a group of seven project engineers. His unit is experiencing a heavy workload, as the demand for different versions of one of his firm's computer components is growing. Faisal finds that he doesn't have time to follow up on all design details for each version of the product. Until now he has tried to do this all by himself. Two of the engineers have shown an interest in helping him coordinate work on the various designs. As a consultant, how would you advise Faisal in terms of delegating work to them?

ManagementSkills& Competencies Make yourself **valuable!**

Evaluate Career Situations

What Would You Do?

1. The New Branch Manager
As the newly promoted manager of a branch bank, you will be leading a team of 22 people. Most members have worked together for a number of years. How can you discover the informal structure or "shadow organization" of the branch and your team? Once you understand them, how will you try to use informal structures to advantage while establishing yourself as an effective manager in this situation?

2. Advisor to the Business School
The typical university business school is organized on a functional basis, with department heads in accounting, finance, information systems, management, and marketing all reporting to a dean. You are on your alma mater's advisory board, and the dean is asking for advice. What suggestions might you give for redesigning this structure to increase communication and collaboration across departments, as well as improve curriculum integration for students in all areas of study?

3. **Entrepreneur's Dilemma**

As the owner of a small computer repair and services business, you would like to allow employees more flexibility in their work schedules. But you also need consistent coverage to handle drop-in customers as well as at-home service calls. There are also times when customers need what they consider to be "emergency" help outside of normal 8 a.m. to 5 p.m. office times. You've got a meeting with employees scheduled for next week. Your goal is to come out of the meeting with a good plan to deal with this staffing dilemma. How can you achieve this goal?

Reflect on the Self-Assessment

Empowering Others

Instructions

Think of times when you have been in charge of a group in a work or student situation. Complete the following questionnaire by recording how you feel about each statement according to this scale:[45]

1	2	3	4	5
Strongly disagree	Disagree	Neutral	Agree	Strongly agree

When in charge of a team, I find that:

1. Most of the time, other people are too inexperienced to do things, so I prefer to do them myself.

2. It often takes more time to explain things to others than to just do them myself.

3. Mistakes made by others are costly, so I don't assign much work to them.

4. Some things simply should not be delegated to others.

5. I often get quicker action by doing a job myself.

6. Many people are good only at very specific tasks, so they can't be assigned additional responsibilities.

7. Many people are too busy to take on additional work.

8. Most people just aren't ready to handle additional responsibilities.

9. In my position, I should be entitled to make my own decisions.

Scoring

Total your responses to get an overall score. Possible scores range from 9 to 45.

Interpretation

The lower your score, the more willing you appear to be to delegate to others. Willingness to delegate is an important managerial characteristic. It is how you, as a manager, can empower others and give them opportunities to assume responsibility and exercise self-control in their work. With the growing importance of horizontal organizations and empowerment, your willingness to delegate is worth thinking about seriously.

Contribute to the Class Exercise

Organizational Metaphors

Instructions

Form into groups as assigned by the instructor and do the following:

1. Think about organizations and how they work.

2. Select one of the following sets of organizational metaphors.
   (a) human brain—spiderweb
   (b) rock band—chamber music ensemble
   (c) cup of coffee—beehive
   (d) cement mixer—star galaxy
   (e) about the fifth date in an increasingly serious relationship—a couple celebrating their 25th wedding anniversary

3. Brainstorm how each metaphor in your set can be used to explain how organizations work.

4. Brainstorm how each metaphor is similar to and different from the other in this explanation.

5. Draw pictures or create a short skit to illustrate the contrasts between your two metaphors of an organization.

6. Present your metaphorical views of organizations to the class.

7. Be prepared to explain what can be learned from your metaphors and engage in class discussion.

Manage a Critical Incident

Crowdsourcing Evaluations to Cut Management Levels

Performance reviews in your firm have always been completed by managers and then discussed with workers. But you've been reading about 360° reviews that include feedback from peers and others working with or for the person being evaluated. You're also aware that new technology makes it easy to conduct evaluations online and even to make them happen in almost real time, on a project-by-project basis, without a manager leading the process. As soon as a task is completed by an individual or team, a 360° review can be done online and the feedback immediately used for future performance improvement. You'd like to start crowdsourcing evaluations at your firm in order to save costs by cutting management levels, and also to improve the flow and timeliness of performance feedback. Before going further, you sit down to make a list of the pros and cons of the idea.

Questions

What's on your list of pros and cons, and why? You next decide to make another list of resources and support from key persons that would be needed to implement the practice. What's on this second list and why?

Collaborate on the Team Activity

Designing a Network University

Instructions

In your assigned team, do the following.

1. Discuss the concept of the network organization structure as described in the textbook.

2. Create a network organization structure for your college or university. Identify the "core staffing" and what will be outsourced. Identify how outsourcing will be managed.

3. Draw a diagram depicting the various elements in your "Network U."

4. Identify why "Network U" will be able to meet two major goals: (a) create high levels of student learning and (b) operate with cost efficiency.

5. Present and justify your design for "Network U" to the class.

Analyze THE CaseStudy : TOYOTA Designing as Effective Structure

Go to *Management Cases for Critical Thinking* at the end of the book to find this case.

ORGANIZATIONAL CHANGE AND DEVELOPMENT

KEY TAKEAWAYS

- Explain the concept of organizational culture and discuss how it affects organizational behavior and performance.

- Describe how a multicultural organization handles subcultures and diversity issues.

- Identify alternative approaches to organizational change and the types of change strategies and resistance to change found in organizations.

SKILLS MAKE YOU **VALUABLE**

- **EVALUATE** *Career Situations:* What Would You Do?

- **REFLECT** *On the Self-Assessment:* Change Leadership IQ

- **CONTRIBUTE** *To the Class Exercise:* Force-Field Analysis

- **MANAGE** *A Critical Incident:* Proposal for Open Office Design and Hotdesking

- **COLLABORATE** *On the Team Activity:* Organizational Culture Walk

- **ANALYZE** *The Case Study:* Apple Inc.: People and Design

Any organization has a "culture" that acts a personality and sets a tone for everyday operations. Some organizational cultures have a more positive influence than others on members' attitudes, behaviors, commitments and performance accomplishments, as well as customer loyalty. One of the most important career decisions we make is to choose an employer that offers a good "fit" between personal preferences and its work culture. Part of that fit relates to how the culture handles change and the ways managers act, or not, as change leaders.

"Culture" is a word we hear a lot these days as we become more aware of diversity in everyday living. And when it comes to the world at large, cultural differences between people and nations are often in the news. However, there's another type of culture that can be just as important: the cultures of organizations. Just as nations, ethnic and religious groups, nations, and families have cultures, organizations do, too. These cultures help distinguish organizations from one another and give members a sense of collective identity. The "fit" between the individual and an organization's culture is very important. The right fit is good for both employers and job seekers, and finding the right fit in your work and membership organizations is a real career issue.

"Change" is another hot-button word we also face in our lives and at work. Just as people are being asked to adapt and be ever more flexible, organizations are, too. Managers are expected to support change initiatives launched from the C-suite; they also are expected to be change leaders in their own teams and work units. Some organizational cultures push change, while others resist it. This is a good time to check your readiness to master career challenges and change processes in today's organizations.

Organizational Cultures

TAKEAWAY 1   What is organizational culture?

LEARN MORE | Understanding organizational cultures • Observable culture
ABOUT | Values and the core culture

Think of the stores where you shop; the restaurants that you patronize; the place where you work. What is the "vibe" like? Do you notice, for example, that atmospheres in the stores of major retailers like Anthropologie, Gap, Hollister, and Banana Republic seem to fit their brands and customer identities?[1] Are you envious when someone says about their workplace: "It's just like a family" or "We have fun while we're working" or "The whole place just pulls together to get the job done"? Such aspects of the internal environments of organizations are important in management, and the term used to describe them is **organizational culture**. Sometimes called the *corporate culture*, this is the system of shared beliefs and values that shapes and guides the behavior of an organization's members.[2] Organizational culture can be thought of as the personality of the organization or the atmosphere within which people work.

The organizational culture is what you see and hear when walking around an organization as a visitor, a customer, or an employee. Look carefully, check the atmosphere, and listen to the conversations. Whenever someone speaks of "the way we do things here," for example, that person is providing insight into the organization's culture. Just as nations, ethnic groups, and families have cultures, organizations also have cultures that create unique identities and help to distinguish them from one another. These cultures have a strong impact on an organization's performance and the quality of work experiences of its members.[3]

> **Organizational culture** is the system of shared beliefs and values that guides behavior in organizations.

Understanding Organizational Cultures

At Zappos.com, a popular shoe e-tailer, CEO Tony Hsieh has built a fun, creative, and customer-centered culture. He says: "The original idea was to add a little fun." And then everyone joined in the idea that "We can do it better." Now the notion of an unhappy Zappos customer is almost unthinkable. "They may only call once in their life," says Hsieh, "but that is our chance to wow them."[4] Hsieh's advice is that if you "get the culture right, most of the other stuff, like brand and the customer service, will just happen."[5] Amazon.com CEO Jeff Bezos liked Zappos so much he bought the company. The Girl Scouts are among a number of organizations that send executives to study Zappos' culture and bring back ideas for improving their own.

It takes a keen eye to be able to identify and understand an organization's culture. But such understanding can be a real asset to employees and job seekers alike. No one wants to end up in a situation with a bad person–culture fit. Management scholars offer ideas for reading an organization's culture by asking and answering questions like the following:[6]

How tight or loose is the structure? • Do most decisions reflect change or the status quo? • What outcomes or results are most highly valued? • How widespread are empowerment and worker involvement? • What is the competitive style, internal and external? • What value is placed on people, as customers and employees? • Is teamwork a way of life in this organization?

Types of Organization Cultures

One of the popular descriptions of organizational cultures is shown in the figure on the right. Based on a model called the competing values framework, it identifies four different culture types.[7] *Hierarchical cultures* emphasize tradition and clear roles; *dependable cultures* emphasize process and slow change; *enterprising cultures* emphasize creativity and competition; and, *social cultures* emphasize collaboration and trust. According to LeadershipIQ, employees give enterprising cultures the highest marks for engagement and motivation, and as good places to work.[8] How do these

Alternative Organizational Cultures

Team Culture	**Hierarchical Culture**
• Authority shared, distributed • Teams and teamwork rule • Collaboration, trust valued • Emphasis on mutual support	• Authority runs the system • Traditions, roles clear • Rules, hierarchy valued • Emphasis on predictability
Entrepreneurial Culture	**Rational Culture**
• Authority goes with ideas • Flexibility and creativity rule • Change and growth valued • Emphasis on entrepreneurship	• Authority serves the goals • Efficiency, productivity rule • Planning, process valued • Emphasis on modest change

organization culture options sound to you? Are you prepared to identify the cultures in organizations you interview with and, perhaps, even rule out those with a potentially poor person–culture fit?

Strong Organizational Cultures

Zappos's Tony Hsieh was quoted earlier as saying: "If we get the culture right, most of the other stuff, like brand and the customer service, will just happen."[9] And he's mostly right. Although culture isn't the only determinant of what happens in organizations, it does help to set values, shape attitudes, reinforce beliefs, direct behavior, and establish performance expectations.[10] It is in these ways that an organization's culture influences its moral character and performance tone.

In **strong organizational cultures**, the culture is clear, well defined, and widely shared by members. When the strong culture is positive, it acts as a performance asset by helping fit together the nature of the business and the talents of the employees. It discourages dysfunctional behaviors and encourages helpful ones, while keeping the vision clear and goals compelling for all to rally around.[11] But when the strong culture is negative, its power is equally strong in the other direction. In responding to a devastating product recall scandal, for example, General Motors' CEO Mary Barra pledged to change a strong and negative organizational culture for the better. She claimed GM's historical culture of cost containment and avoidance of responsibility encouraged covering up rather than addressing problems. She criticized the "GM Nod" where meeting participants would nod in agreement but take no action, and the "GM Salute" symbolized by crossed arms indicating "responsibility belongs to someone else, not me."[12]

Strong organizational cultures are clear, well defined, and widely shared among members.

Strong and positive organizational cultures don't happen by chance. They are created by leaders who set and model the right tone, and they are reinforced through **socialization**. This is the process of onboarding new members so that they learn the culture and the values of the organization.[13] Socialization often begins in an anticipatory way with education, such as when business students learn the importance of professional appearance, integrity, and interpersonal skills. It continues with an employer's onboarding orientation and training programs. Disney's highly regarded strong culture, for example, is supported by major investments in socializing and training new hires. Founder Walt Disney is quoted as saying: "You can dream, create, design and build the most wonderful place in the world, but it requires people to make the dream a reality."[14]

Socialization is the onboarding process through which new members learn the culture of an organization.

Observable Culture of Organizations

Organizational culture is usually described from the perspective of the two levels shown in Figure 12.1. The outer level is the "observable" culture, and the inner level is the "core" culture.[15] As suggested by the figure, it is useful to think of organizational culture as an iceberg with an observable component—the part that stands out above the surface and is visible to the discerning eye, and a core component—the foundation that lies below the surface and is hard to see.

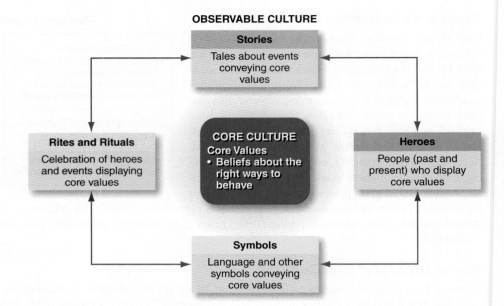

FIGURE 12.1
Levels of organizational culture—observable culture and core culture in the organizational "iceberg."

The **observable culture** is visible in the way members behave, and in the stories, heroes, rituals, and symbols that are part of daily organizational life.

The **observable culture** is visible and is readily apparent at the surface of every organization. It is expressed in the way that people dress at work, how they arrange their offices, how they speak to and behave toward one another, the nature of their conversations, and how they talk about and treat customers and clients. Test this out the next time you go to a store, restaurant, or service establishment. How do people look, act, and behave? How do they treat one another? How do they treat customers? What's in their conversations? Are they enjoying themselves? When you answer these questions, you are starting to identify the organization's observable culture.

The observable culture also is found in the stories, heroes, rituals, and symbols that are part of daily organizational life. It can be something simple like joining in spontaneous celebrations of work accomplishments or personal milestones such as a co-worker's birthday. In workplaces like Apple, Zappos, and Amazon, it's in the stories told about the founders and the firm's startup history.

At colleges and universities, it includes the pageantry of graduation and honors ceremonies, and in sports teams, it's evident in the pregame rally, sideline pep talk, and all the "thumping and bumping" that takes place after a good play. When you are trying to understand the observable culture of an organization, look for the following:[16]

The observable ▶ culture of organizations

- *Heroes*—the people singled out for special attention and whose accomplishments are recognized with praise and admiration; they include founders and role models.

- *Ceremonies, rites, and rituals*—the ceremonies and meetings, planned and spontaneous, that celebrate important events and accomplishments.

- *Legends and stories*—oral histories and tales, told and retold among members, about dramatic incidents in the life of the organization.

- *Metaphors and symbols*—the special use of language and other nonverbal expressions that communicate important themes and values of the organization.

The **core culture** consists of the core values, or underlying assumptions and beliefs that shape and guide people's behaviors in an organization.

Values and the Core Culture of Organizations

A second and deeper level of organizational culture, the **core culture**, consists of the **core values** or underlying assumptions and beliefs that shape and guide people's behaviors. You know core

Core values are beliefs and values shared by organization members.

values, so to speak, when you experience them. This may be when you are trying to claim lost luggage at an airline counter and are treated really well, or are returning a product to a retail store and are greeted with a smile and "no questions asked." Values set in the core culture are a strong influence on how such transactions play out. And when customer experiences aren't positive, the culprit may well be weak or just plain bad core values.

Values in some of the best companies have been found to emphasize performance excellence, innovation, social responsibility, integrity, worker involvement, customer service, and teamwork.[17] Examples of values at strong-culture firms include "service above all else" at Nordstrom; "Creating ongoing win–win partnerships with our suppliers" at Whole Foods; "Innovation, Inspiration, Reliability and Integrity" at Under Armour; "the best electric car and electric power trains in the world" at Tesla; and, "We strive to live up to our name in the way we conduct our business" at Honest Tea.[18]

Value-Based Management

How would you react if you found out senior executives in your organization talked up values such as honesty and ethical behavior, but then acted very differently—altering financial reports or spending company funds on expensive private parties, personal travel, or luxury products? Most likely you'd be upset, and justifiably so. It's important not to be fooled by values statements alone when trying to understand an organization's core culture. It's easy to write a set of values, post them on the Web, and talk about them. It's a lot harder to live up to them every day.

If core values are to have any positive effect, everyone in the organization—from top to bottom—must reflect these values in their day-to-day actions. It's in this context that managers and team leaders have a special responsibility to "walk the talk" in order to make the expressed values real. The term **value-based management** describes managers who actively help to develop, communicate, and enact core values every day. Although you might tend to associate value-based management with top executives, the responsibility extends to all managers and team leaders. Like the organization as a whole, every work team or group has its own a culture. The nature of this culture and its influence on team outcomes has a lot to do with how the team leader behaves as a values champion and role model.

Value-based management actively develops, communicates, and enacts shared values.

An incident at Tom's of Maine provides an example of value-based management in action.[19] After making a substantial investment in a new deodorant, founder Tom Chappell learned that customers were very dissatisfied with the product. He made the decision to reimburse customers and pull the product from the market, even though it would cost the company more than $400,000. Tom had founded the company on values of fairness and honesty in all matters. Rather than trying to save costs by avoiding or denying the customer dissatisfaction, he did what he believed was the right thing. He listened, accepted responsibility for a poor product, and made the customers right. By so doing, he lived up to the company's stated values and set a positive example for others to follow in the future. When faced with similar dilemmas, their responses could be checked by asking: What would Tom do? This incident also shows Tom Chappell's strengths as a **symbolic leader**, someone whose words and actions consistently communicate core values.[20]

A **symbolic leader** is someone whose words and actions consistently communicate core values.

Workplace Spirituality

The notion of **workplace spirituality** is sometimes discussed along with value-based management. Although the first tendency might be to associate "spirituality" with religion, the term is used more broadly in management. It describes an organizational culture that helps people find meaning and a sense of shared community in their work. The core value underlying workplace spirituality is respect for human beings. The guiding principle is that people are inwardly enriched when they are engaged in meaningful work and feel personally connected with others inside and outside of the organization.[21]

Workplace spirituality creates meaning and shared community among organizational members.

A culture of workplace spirituality will have a strong ethical foundation, value human dignity, respect diversity, and focus on linking jobs with real contributions to society. Anyone who works in a culture of workplace spirituality should derive pleasure from knowing that what is being accomplished is personally meaningful, created through community, and valued by others. Anyone who leads a culture of workplace spirituality values people by emphasizing meaningful purpose, trust and respect, honesty and openness, personal growth and developments, worker-friendly practices, and ethics and social responsibility.[22]

Learning Check 1

TAKEAWAYQUESTION **1 What is organizational culture?**

BE SURE YOU CAN • define *organizational culture* and explain the importance of strong cultures to organizations • define and explain the onboarding process of *socialization* • distinguish between the observable and core cultures • explain how value-based management helps build strong culture organizations • describe how workplace spirituality is reflected in an organization's culture

Multicultural Organizations and Diversity

TAKEAWAY 2   What is a multicultural organization?

LEARN MORE ABOUT | Multicultural organizations • Organizational subcultures
Power, diversity, and organizational subcultures

U.S. laws make it illegal to discriminate in hiring and employment decisions based on race, religion, national origin, ethnicity, able-bodiedness, or sex. Those who believe they have been a victim of discrimination can appeal to the U.S. Equal Employment Opportunity Commission. But, did you know that workers who are gay, lesbian, transgender, or bisexual aren't covered by current laws? The proposed Employment Non-Discrimination Act (ENDA) is intended to add gender identity and sexual orientation to the list of anti-discrimination protections. As of this writing, ENDA has passed the Senate but still needs House of Representatives approval. Its supporters at recent count included 59 of the Fortune 500 companies.[23] Don't you wonder why it doesn't include all 500 of these major firms?

Multicultural Organizations

Multiculturalism in organizations involves inclusiveness, pluralism, and respect for diversity.

A **multicultural organization** has core values that respect diversity and support multiculturalism.

Characteristics of ▶ multicultural organizations

In the book *Beyond Race and Gender*, consultant R. Roosevelt Thomas, Jr., points out that the way people are treated at work—with respect and inclusion, or with disrespect and exclusion— is a direct reflection of the organization's culture and leadership.[24] We use the term **multiculturalism** to describe inclusiveness, pluralism, and respect for diversity in the workplace. The core values of a truly **multicultural organization** communicate support for multiculturalism and empower the full diversity of all members. Common characteristics of multicultural organizations include:[25]

- *Pluralism*—Members of both minority cultures and majority cultures are influential in setting key values and policies.

- *Structural integration*—Minority-culture members are well represented in jobs at all levels and in all functional responsibilities.

- *Informal network integration*—Various forms of mentoring and support groups assist in the career development of minority-culture members.

- *Absence of prejudice and discrimination*—A variety of training and task-force activities address the need to eliminate culture-group biases.

- *Minimum intergroup conflict*—Diversity does not lead to destructive conflicts between members of majority and minority cultures.

A key argument in support of multiculturalism is that organizations with inclusive cultures will gain performance advantages because their workforces offer a wide mix of talents and perspectives.[26] In other words, multiculturalism in organizations is a performance asset. The *Gallup Management Journal*, for example, reports that a racially and ethnically inclusive workplace is good for morale. In a study of 2,014 American workers, those who felt included were more likely to stay with their employers and recommend them to others.[27] And, a Catalyst study of gender diversity found that firms with at least three female board members achieved a higher return on equity than did firms with no female board representation.[28] But Thomas Kochan and colleagues at MIT advise caution. They warn that the *presence* of diversity alone does not guarantee these types of positive outcomes. The performance advantages of multiculturalism emerge only when *respect* for diversity is firmly embedded in the organizational culture.[29]

Organizational Subcultures

Organizations—like societies at large—contain a mixture of **organizational subcultures** or **co-cultures**. They exist within the larger organizational culture and consist of members who share similar values and beliefs based on their work responsibilities, personal characteristics, and social identities. Subcultures formed around in-group similarities and out-group differences often make it hard to tap the full potential of a diverse workforce and create a truly multicultural organization. As it does in everyday life, **ethnocentrism**—the belief that one's subculture or co-culture is superior to all others, can creep into organizations and negatively affect the way people relate to one another.

Age differences create **generational subcultures** in organizations.[30] It's common today for the mix of generations in an organization's workforce to span from post–World War II baby boomers to the latest Internet generation.[31] Harris and Conference Board polls report that younger workers tend to be more dissatisfied than older workers.[32] Studies also describe younger workers as having a much shorter time orientation, giving greater priority to work–life balance, and expecting to hold several jobs during the course of their career.[33] Just imagine the possible conflicts when recent college graduates end up working for older managers who grew up with quite different life experiences and values. And how about the reverse, when older workers end up on teams with much younger leaders?

Gender subcultures form in organizations among persons with shared gender identities and displaying common patterns of behavior. When men work together, for example, an "alpha male" subgroup culture may emphasize a competitive behavior set of sports metaphors, games, and stories that focus on winning and losing.[34] When women work together, the interactions and patterns of the subgroup culture may emphasize a supportive behavior set of personal relationships and collaboration.[35] And, female leaders can suffer a **double-bind dilemma** due to subculture expectations. This occurs when they get criticized as being "too soft" when they act consistent with female subculture stereotypes, but also get criticized as being "too hard" when acting consistent with male subculture stereotypes. In other words, female leaders may be "damned if they do, and damned if they don't," and find it hard to get credit for effective leadership.[36]

The many possible subcultures in organizations also include **occupational and functional subcultures** that form around shared professions and skills.[37] People from different occupations and functions can have difficulty understanding and working well with one another. Employees in a business firm, for example, may consider themselves "systems people" or "marketing people" or "finance people." When such identities are overemphasized, members of functional groups spend most of their time with each other, develop a shared "jargon" or common technical language, and view their roles in the organization as more important than

Organizational subcultures or **co-cultures** consist of members who share similar beliefs and values based on their work, personal characteristics, or social identities.

Ethnocentrism is the belief that one's membership group and subculture or co-culture is superior to all others.

Generational subcultures form among persons who work together and share similar ages, such as millennials and baby boomers.

Gender subcultures form among persons who share gender identities and display common patterns of behavior.

The **double-bind dilemma** is where female leaders get criticized when they act consistent with female subculture stereotypes and when they act consistent with male subculture stereotypes.

Occupational and functional subcultures form among persons who share the same skills and work responsibilities.

analysis > MAKE DATA YOUR FRIEND

Quotas to Increase Women in Senior Management

In 2013, women made up 35% of the global workforce while 24% of the senior management positions were held by women. This was an increase from 2012 (21%) and 2011 (20%).

According to the *Grant Thornton International Business Report (IBR) 2013*:

- Senior leadership positions held by women on a regional basis comprised: (Asia Pacific—29%, EU—25%, Latin America—23%, and North America—21%).

- China has the highest number of women in senior management positions in the world. In 2013, approximately 51% of the senior positions were held by women as compared to 25% the previous year.

- Women form 15% of India's workforce. In 2013, women held 19% of senior management roles but these figures are set to increase as more companies intend to employ women, especially in senior positions.

- On average, ASEAN countries recorded 32% of women in senior management. The chart below shows a comparison of five ASEAN countries with the global and regional average.

In 2013, Malaysia had the highest number of women in their workforce (40%) in ASEAN, but only 26% of the senior management positions were held by women.

Can the introduction of quotas increase the number of women in senior managerial positions?

According to the *Grant Thornton IBR 2014*, the introduction of quotas to increase the number of women on the executive boards is favoured by 45% of listed companies worldwide.

The chart below shows regional support for quotas as compared to the global average. The Asia Pacific region shows strong support at 71%.

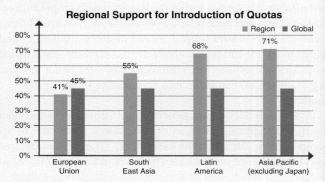

Regional Support for Introduction of Quotas

DISCUSSION QUESTIONS:

1. Discuss the challenges faced by women who are vying for senior management positions.
2. Suggest how employers can help women to overcome these challenges.
3. Evaluate the pros and cons of introducing quotas to increase the number of women in senior positions.
4. In your opinion, is implementing a quota an effective measure to increase women's role in senior management?

Women in Senior Management - 2013

those of the other functions. It's easy under such conditions for teamwork across the occupational or functional boundaries to suffer.

Ethnic subcultures and **national subcultures** form in the workplace among people sharing the same background in terms of ethnicity or nationality. Although our world of work is one of diverse cultural communities, it's often more complicated than appears at first glance. We're growing more interested in foreign languages, but what happens when co-workers hear a group of software engineers that share a language—say Mandarin or Hindi, speaking it together? We love fashion and are used to all different manners of dress, but how do we react when three

Ethnic subcultures or national subcultures form among people who work together and have roots in the same ethnic community or nationality.

women in head scarves and ankle-length skirts walk into the office coffee room while chatting back and forth? We are happy when foreign employers create domestic jobs, but how do local managers for a multinational like Honda or Toyota feel when their Japanese colleagues play rounds of golf together? We emphasize the importance of understanding and respecting cross-cultural differences when traveling internationally. Can't the same attention help us better deal with diversity among ethnic and national subcultures in the workplace?

Power, Diversity, and Organizational Subcultures

The term "diversity" basically means the presence of interpersonal differences. Those differences may or may not be distributed equally among organizational subcultures and power structures. What happens when one subculture is in the "majority" while others are "minorities"?

Glass Ceilings and the Leaking Pipeline

Even though demographics and hiring practices are changing, there is still likely to be more workforce diversity at lower and middle levels than at the top. Look at Figure 12.2. It depicts the **glass ceiling** as an invisible barrier that limits the professional advancement of women and minorities in some organizations. What are the implications for women and minority members seeking to advance and prosper in an organization where the majority culture consists almost exclusively of white males? How easy is it for women and people of color to move up when promotions are controlled by decision makers who are part of an alternative and dominant culture?

If women now hold over 50% of management jobs, why do they hold only about 5% of CEO positions and 17% of board seats at Fortune 500 firms?[38] One reason why more women haven't gotten to the top is that they often hit plateaus or "fall off the cliff" at earlier career stages. The **leaking pipeline problem** describes situations where qualified and high-performing females with top management potential drop out of upward-tracking career paths. Their decisions aren't always due to personal goals on the one hand or outright gender prejudice or discrimination on the other. Subtle forces in male-dominant organizational cultures may make it hard for women to

The **glass ceiling** is an invisible barrier to advancement by women and minorities in organizations.

The **leaking pipeline problem** is where glass ceilings and other obstacles cause qualified and high-performing women to drop out of upward career paths.

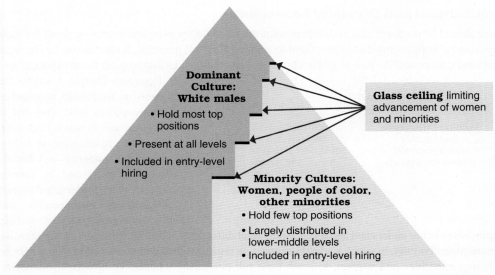

FIGURE 12.2
Glass ceilings as barriers to women and minority cultures in traditional organizations.

advance.[39] They may lack female role models and have difficulty finding top managers to advocate and sponsor their career progress. Executive mind-sets may have a hard time tolerating women who want both a family and a career. Even in organizations with family-friendly human resource policies, women may still feel forced to choose between job advancement and family—a choice that often puts family first and sacrifices career opportunities like promotions and assignments in new locations.[40]

Harassment and Discrimination

Subculture challenges faced by minority and female employees can range from misunderstanding and a lack of sensitivity on the one hand to overt sexual harassment and discrimination on the other. Data from the U.S. Equal Employment Opportunity Commission (EEOC) show that sex discrimination is a factor in approximately 30% of bias suits filed by workers.[41] The EEOC also reports an increase in pregnancy-related discrimination complaints.[42] And, researchers identify risks of discrimination in hiring. In a study that distributed to recruiters fake résumés showing equal credentials but different family details, men with children were the most hirable—viewed as responsible, and women with children were the least hirable—viewed as likely to sacrifice work for family responsibilities.[43]

Pay discrimination is another issue. A senior executive in the computer industry reported her surprise at finding out that the top performer in her work group, an African American male, was paid 25% less than anyone else. This wasn't because his pay had been cut to that level, she said. It was because his pay increases had always trailed those given to his white co-workers. The differences added up significantly over time, but no one noticed or stepped forward to make the appropriate adjustment.[44]

Biculturalism is when minority members display characteristics of majority cultures in order to succeed.

Members of minority cultures may resort to **biculturalism** in attempts to adapt to uncomfortable situations and avoid harassment or discrimination by majorities. This means they try to display majority culture characteristics that seem necessary to succeed in the work environment. For example, gay and lesbian employees may hide their sexual orientation from co-workers out of fear of prejudice or discrimination. Similarly, an African American employee may train herself to not use words or phrases that might be considered to be subculture "slang" when communicating with white co-workers.

Multicultural and Diversity Leadership

There should be no doubt that all workers want the same things everyone wants—respect for their talents and a work setting that allows them to achieve their full potential. It takes an inclusive organizational culture and the best in multicultural and diversity leadership to meet these expectations.

Affirmative Action
Create upward mobility for minorities and women

Valuing Differences
Build quality relationships with respect for diversity

Managing Diversity
Achieve full utilization of diverse human resources

R. Roosevelt Thomas describes the continuum of leadership approaches to diversity shown here. The first is *affirmative action*, in which leadership commits the organization to hiring and advancing minority and female employees. The second is *valuing diversity*, in which leadership commits the organization to education and training programs designed to help

Managing diversity is a leadership approach that creates an organizational culture that respects diversity and supports multiculturalism.

employees to better understand and respect individual differences. The third and most comprehensive is **managing diversity**, in which leadership creates an organizational culture that allows all members, including minorities and women, to reach their full potential.[45] Leaders committed to managing diversity build organization cultures that are what Thomas calls "diversity mature."[46] They have a strong diversity mission that is integrated into the organizational mission as a strategic imperative.

Learning Check 2

TAKEAWAYQUESTION **2**   **What is a multicultural organization?**

BE SURE YOU CAN • define *multiculturalism* and explain the concept of a multicultural organization • identify common organizational subcultures • discuss glass ceilings and employment problems faced by minorities and women • describe the leaking pipeline problem • explain Thomas's concept of managing diversity

Organizational Change

TAKEAWAY 3   **What is the nature of organizational change?**

LEARN MORE | Models of change leadership • Transformational and incremental change
ABOUT | Phases of planned change • Change strategies • Resistance to change

What if an organization's culture is flawed, doesn't drive high performance, and needs to be changed? What if organizational subcultures clash and adjustments must be made? What can leaders do if diversity isn't valued on a team or in an organization? We use the word *change* so much that culture changes like these may seem easy, almost routine. But that's not always the case.[47] Former British Airways CEO Sir Rod Eddington once said that "Altering an airline's culture is like trying to perform an engine change in flight."[48] Executive coach Ben Dattner says: "Organizations can go on autopilot just as individuals do."[49]

Models of Change Leadership

A **change leader** is someone who takes initiative to change existing patterns of behavior by a person or within a social system. These are managers who act as *change agents* and make things happen, even when inertia has made systems and people reluctant to embrace new ways of doing things. Managers who are strong change leaders are alert to cultures, situations, and people needing change, open to good ideas and opportunities, and ready and able to support the implementation of new ideas in actual practice.

    Every manager and team leader should ideally act as a change leader. But the reality is that most of us have tendencies to stay with the status quo, accepting things as they are and not wanting to change. Figure 12.3 contrasts a true "change leader" with a "status quo manager." Whereas the status quo manager is backward-looking, reactive, and comfortable with habit, the change leader is forward-looking, proactive, supportive of new ideas, and comfortable with criticism.

> A **change leader** takes initiative in trying to change the behavior of another person or within a social system.

Change leaders		**Status quo managers**
• Confident of ability • Willing to take risks • Seize opportunity • Expect surprises • Make things happen	promote and actively support → **Change, creativity, and innovation** ← avoid and even discourage	• Threatened by change • Bothered by uncertainty • Prefer predictability • Support the status quo • Wait for things to happen

FIGURE 12.3
Change leaders versus status quo managers.

Top-Down Change

In top-down change, the change initiatives come from senior management.

Top-down change is where senior managers initiate changes with the goal of improving organizational performance. Although it sounds straightforward that "what the boss wants the boss will get," research indicates that as many as 70% of large-scale change efforts in American firms actually fail; only 20% of European firms report "substantial success" with large-scale change, while 63% report "occasional" success.[50]

The most common reason for the failure of top-down change is poor implementation. And without doubt, people are more likely to be committed to implement plans that they have played a part in creating. Change programs have little chance of success without the support of those who must implement them. When change is driven from the top without lower-level inputs and participation, it can easily fail.

Bottom-Up Change

In bottom-up change, change initiatives come from all levels in the organization.

Bottom-up change taps into ideas initiated from lower organizational levels and lets them percolate upward. A major risk as organizations grow in size is that good ideas get lost in the labyrinth. One way managers can unlock the potential for bottom-up change is by holding "diagonal slice meetings" that bring together employees from across functions and levels. They are asked for ideas about what might be wrong and what changes might be made to improve things. Another way is to build an organizational culture that values empowerment and encourages everyone regardless of rank or position to use their job knowledge and common sense to improve things.

Bottom-up change was harnessed at General Electric under former CEO Jack Welch, when he started a widely benchmarked program called Work-Out. In Work-Out sessions, employees confront their managers in a "town meeting" format with the manager in front listening to suggestions. The managers are expected to respond immediately and support positive change initiatives raised during the session. Welch felt that approaches like this facilitate change because they "bring an innovation debate to the people closest to the products, services, and processes."[51]

Organizational Change Pyramid

Few strategic, large-scale changes to reposition organization

Major changes to improve performance through new structures, systems, technologies, products, and people

Frequent, smaller-scale changes to fine tune performance, enable short-term gains, and provide continuous improvements in operations

Transformational and Incremental Change

Planned changes at the top levels of an organization are likely to be large-scale and strategic repositioning changes focused on big issues that affect the organization as a whole. Lower-level changes often deal with adjustments in structures, systems, technologies, products, and people to support strategic positioning. Both types of changes—high-level transformational and on-the-ground incremental—are important in the organizational change pyramid shown here.[52]

Transformational change results in a major and comprehensive redirection of the organization.

Transformational change is radical or frame-breaking change that results in a major and comprehensive redirection of the organization.[53] It is led from the top and creates fundamental shifts in strategy, culture, structures, and even the organization's underlying sense of purpose or mission. As you might expect, transformational change is intense, highly stressful, complex, and difficult to achieve. Popular advice to would-be leaders of transformational changes includes these guidelines:[54]

How to lead ▶ transformational change

- Establish a sense of urgency for change.

- Form a powerful coalition to lead the change.

- Create and communicate a change vision.

- Empower others to move change forward.
- Celebrate short-term wins, and recognize those who help.
- Build on success; align people and systems with new ways.
- Stay with it; keep the message consistent; champion the vision.

Incremental change is modest, frame-bending change. It basically bends or nudges current systems and practices to better align them with emerging problems and opportunities. The intent isn't to break and remake the system, but rather to move it forward through continuous improvements. Common incremental changes in organizations involve the evolution of products, processes, technologies, and work systems.

One shouldn't get the idea, by the way, that incremental change is inferior to transformational change. Both are critical in the organizational change pyramid just shown. Incremental changes keep organizational processes and structures tuned up—like the engine in an automobile—in between transformations—when the old vehicle is replaced with a new one.

Incremental change bends and adjusts existing ways to improve performance.

Phases of Planned Change

Managers seeking to lead organizational change can benefit from a simple but helpful model developed many years ago by the psychologist Kurt Lewin. He recommends that any planned change be viewed as a process with the three phases. Phase 1 is *unfreezing*—preparing a system for change; phase 2 is *changing*—making actual changes in the system; and phase 3 is *refreezing*—stabilizing the system after change.[55] In today's fast-paced organizational environments, we can also talk about another phase called *improvising*—making adjustments as needed while change is taking place.[56]

Unfreezing

Planned change has a better chance for success when people are ready for it and open to doing things differently. **Unfreezing** is the phase in which the change agent prepares a situation for change by developing felt needs for change among those affected by a change initiative. The goal is to get people to view change as a way to solve a real problem or pursue a meaningful opportunity. Common errors at the unfreezing stage are not creating a sense of urgency for change and neglecting to build a coalition of influential persons who support it.

Some call unfreezing the "burning bridge" phase of change, arguing that in order to get people to jump off a bridge, you might just have to set it on fire! Managers can simulate the burning bridge by engaging people with facts and information that communicate the need for change—environmental pressures, declining performance, and examples of benchmarks or alternative approaches. As you have probably experienced, conflict can help people to break old habits and recognize new ways of thinking about or doing things.

Unfreezing is the phase during which a situation is prepared for change.

Changing

Figure 12.4 shows that unfreezing is followed by the **changing** phase, where actual changes are made in such organizational targets as tasks, people, culture, technology, and structures. Lewin believes that many change agents commit the error of entering the changing phase prematurely. They are too quick to change things and end up creating harmful resistance. In this sense, the change process is like building a house; you need to put a good foundation in place before you begin framing the rooms. With a poor foundation, the house will likely fall at some point. Similarly, if you try to implement change before people are prepared and feel a need for it, your attempt is more likely to fail.

Changing is the phase where a planned change actually takes place.

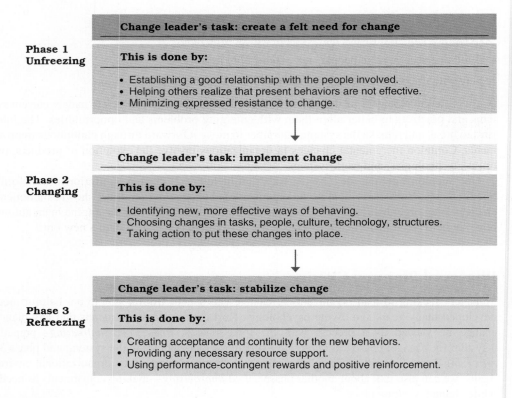

FIGURE 12.4
Lewin's three phases of planned organizational change.

Refreezing

Refreezing is the phase at which change is stabilized.

The final phase in Lewin's planned change process is **refreezing**. Here, managers are concerned with stabilizing the change. Refreezing is accomplished by linking change with appropriate rewards, positive reinforcement, and resource support. It is important in this phase to evaluate results, provide feedback to those involved, and make any required modifications to the original change that either undershot or overshot evolving contingencies.

When refreezing is done poorly, changes are too easily forgotten or abandoned with the passage of time. The most common error at the refreezing stage is declaring victory too soon and withdrawing support before the change has really become a fixed aspect of normal routines. In today's dynamic environment, there may also not be a lot of time for refreezing before change becomes necessary again. We end up preparing for more change even before the present one is fully implemented.

Improvising

Although Lewin's model depicts change as a linear, step-by-step process, the reality is that change is dynamic and complex. Managers must not only understand each phase of a planned change, they must be prepared to deal with them simultaneously. They should also be willing and able to engage in the process of **improvisational change** where adjustments are continually made as aspects of the change initiative are implemented.[57]

Improvisational change makes continual adjustments as changes are being implemented.

Consider the case of bringing new technology into an organization or work unit. A technology that is attractive in theory may appear complicated in practice to new potential users. The full extent of its benefits or inadequacies may not become known until it is actually tried out. A change leader can succeed in such situations by continually gathering feedback on how the change is progressing, and then improvising the process to revise and customize the new technology to best meet users' needs and address their concerns about the complexity of the new system.

Change Strategy	Power Bases	Managerial Behavior	Likely Results
Force–Coercion Using formal authority to create change by decree and position power	Legitimacy Rewards Punishments	*Direct forcing* and unilateral action *Political maneuvering* and indirect action	Faster, but low commitment and only temporary compliance
Rational Persuasion Creating change through rational persuasion and empirical argument	Expertise	*Informational efforts* using credible knowledge, demonstrated facts, and logical argument	
Shared power Developing support for change through personal values and commitments	Reference	*Participative efforts* to share power and involve others in planning and implementing change	Slower, but high commitment and longer-term internalization

FIGURE 12.5
Alternative change strategies and their leadership implications.

Change Strategies

Strategy is a major issue when managers actually try to move people and systems toward a planned change. Figure 12.5 summarizes three common strategies used to make things happen during the planned change process—force-coercion, rational persuasion, and shared power.[58] Managers, as change agents and leaders, should understand each strategy and its likely results.

Force-Coercion Strategies

A **force-coercion strategy** uses formal authority as well as rewards and punishments as the primary inducements to get behind change. A change agent that seeks to create change through force-coercion believes that people are motivated by self-interest and by what the situation offers in terms of potential personal gains or losses.[59] In *direct forcing*, change agents take unilateral action to "command" that change take place. In *political maneuvering*, change agents work indirectly to gain special advantage over other persons and thereby make them change. This involves bargaining, obtaining control of important resources, forming alliances, or granting small favors.

The force-coercion strategy of change usually produces only limited, unsatisfactory results. Although it can be quickly tried, most people respond to this strategy out of fear of punishment or hope for reward. The likely outcome of this approach is temporary compliance; the new behavior continues only as long as the rewards and punishments persist. For this reason, force-coercion may be most useful as an unfreezing strategy that helps people break old patterns and encourages willingness to try new approaches.

> A **force-coercion strategy** pursues change through formal authority and/or the use of rewards or punishments.

Rational Persuasion Strategies

Change agents using a **rational persuasion strategy** attempt to bring about change through persuasion supported by special knowledge, empirical data, and rational arguments. Change agents following this strategy believe that people are inherently rational and guided by reason. Once the value of a specific course of action is demonstrated by information and relevant facts, it is assumed that reason and rationality will cause the person to adopt it. A good rational persuasion strategy helps both unfreeze and refreeze a change situation. Although slower than force-coercion, it is likely to result in longer-lasting and more internalized change.

To succeed with the rational persuasion strategy, a manager must convince others that making a change will leave them better off than they were before the change. This persuasive power can come directly from the change agent if she has personal credibility as an "expert."

> A **rational persuasion strategy** pursues change through empirical data and rational argument.

insight > LEARN ABOUT YOURSELF

> *Some people struggle with the unfamiliar. They prefer structure, security, and clear directions.*

Get Comfortable with Tolerance for Ambiguity

The next time you are driving somewhere and following a familiar route only to encounter a "detour" sign, test your **tolerance for ambiguity**. Is the detour just a minor inconvenience? Do you go forward without any further thought? Or is it a big deal, perhaps causing you anxiety and anger? Do you show a tendency to resist change in your normal routines? Change creates anxiety and breaks us from past habits and conditions. Uncertainty puts many things out of our immediate control. Depending on your tolerance for ambiguity, you may be more or less comfortable dealing with these realities.

Which alternatives in the Tolerance for Ambiguity Double Check best describe you? What are the insights for your tolerance for ambiguity? It takes personal flexibility and a lot of confidence to cope well with unpredictability, whether it's in a college course or in a work situation. Some people struggle with the unfamiliar. They prefer structure, security, and clear directions. They get comfortable with fixed patterns in life and can be afraid of anything "new."

Have we been talking about you? Or are you willing and able to work with less structure? Do you enjoy flexibility, setting your own goals, and making decisions? Are you excited by the prospect of change and new—as yet undefined—opportunities? It's important to find a good fit between your personal preferences for ambiguity and the pace and nature of change in the career field and organizations where you ultimately choose to work. To achieve this fit, you have to understand your own tolerance for ambiguity and how you are likely to react in change situations.

Tolerance for Ambiguity Double Check

An instructor who gives precise assignments and accepts no deviations *or* one who gives open-ended assignments and lets students suggest alternatives?

 In a typical course, do you prefer...

An instructor who keeps modifying the course syllabus using student feedback *or* one who gives out a detailed syllabus and sticks to it?

GET TO KNOW YOURSELF BETTER

Write a short narrative describing your "ideal" employer in terms of organization culture, management styles, and frequency of major changes. Add a comment that explains how this ideal organization fits your personality, including insights from self-assessments completed in other chapters. What does this say about how you may have to change and adapt in order to fulfill your career aspirations?

It can also be borrowed in the form of advice from consultants and other outside experts, or gained from credible demonstration projects and identified benchmarks. Many firms, for example, benchmark Disney to demonstrate to their own employees the benefits of a customer-oriented culture. A Ford vice president says: "Disney's track record is one of the best in the country as far as dealing with customers."[60] In this sense, the power of rational persuasion is straightforward: if the culture works for Disney, it can also work for us.

Shared Power Strategies

> **A shared power strategy** pursues change by participation in assessing change needs, values, and goals.

A **shared power** strategy uses collaboration to identify values, assumptions, and goals from which support for change naturally emerges. Sometimes called a *normative–reeducative strategy*, this approach is empowerment based and also is highly participative. It involves others in examining personal needs and values, group norms, and operating goals as they relate to the issue in focus. Power is shared as the change agent and others work together to develop consensus to support needed change. Because it entails a high level of involvement, this strategy is often slow and time consuming. But power sharing is likely to result in longer-lasting, internalized change.

A change agent shares power by recognizing that people have varied needs and complex motivations. The agent understands that organizational change requires a shift in attitudes, values, skills, and significant relationships, not just changes in knowledge, information, or practices. Thus, change agents need to be sensitive to the way group pressures can support or inhibit change. Every attempt is made to gather opinions, identify feelings and expectations, and incorporate them fully into the change process.

The great "power" of sharing power in the change process lies with unlocking the creativity, experience, and energies of people within the system. Some managers hesitate to engage this strategy for fear of losing control or having to compromise on important organizational goals. But Harvard scholar Teresa M. Amabile points out that they should have the confidence to share power regarding means and processes, if not overall goals. "People will be more creative," she says, "if you give them freedom to decide how to climb particular mountains. You needn't let them choose which mountains to climb."[61]

Research Brief

Top Management Must Get—and Stay—Committed for Shared Power to Work in Tandem with Top-Down Change

Harry Sminia and Antonie Van Nistelrooij's case study of a public-sector organization in the Netherlands sheds light on what happens when top-down change and organization development based on shared power are used simultaneously.

Writing in the *Journal of Change Management*, they describe how top management initiated a strategic change involving

Intended and Realized Change

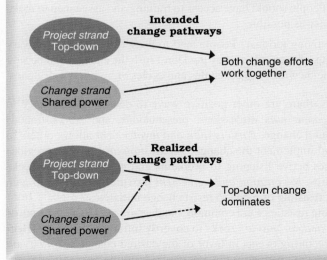

organization design, procedures, work standards, and systems. Called the "project strand," this change was well structured with deadlines and a management hierarchy. Simultaneously, a "change strand" was initiated with organization development interventions to develop information and create foundations helpful to the success of the project strand. The change strand involved conferences, workshops, and meetings. The goal was for both strands to operate in parallel and eventually converge in joint implementation.

What the researchers found was that top management favored the project strand and resisted challenges to its decision-making prerogatives that came from the change strand. Eventually, the shared power aspects of the change pretty much disappeared and activities centered around completing the project on schedule. Sminia and Van Nistelrooij conclude that the change was hampered by "management refusal to share power with the employees."

YOU BE THE RESEARCHER

Is it realistic to expect that top-down and bottom-up changes can operate simultaneously? Can any shared power change strategy be successful without full and continuing support from top management? How would you design research projects to test these questions?

Why People May Resist Change

- *Fear of the unknown*—not understanding what is happening or what comes next.
- *Disrupted habits*—feeling upset to see the end of the old ways of doing things.
- *Loss of confidence*—feeling incapable of performing well under the new ways of doing things.
- *Loss of control*—feeling that things are being done "to" you rather than "by" or "with" you.
- *Poor timing*—feeling overwhelmed by the situation or that things are moving too fast.
- *Work overload*—not having the physical or emotional energy to commit to the change.
- *Loss of face*—feeling inadequate or humiliated because the "old" ways weren't "good" ways.
- *Lack of purpose*—not seeing a reason for the change and/or not understanding its benefits.

Resistance to Change

When people resist change, they are most often defending something important to them that now appears to be threatened by the impending change. A change leader can achieve a lot by listening to the reasons employees voice for their resistance, and then using this information as a resource for improving the change and change process.[62] Check the common sources of resistance as shown in the box. You've most likely seen (or even experienced!) some if not all of these.

Instead of viewing resistance to change as something that has to be "overcome," it is often more appropriately viewed as feedback. The presence of resistance usually means that something can be done to achieve a better "fit" among the planned change, the situation, and the people involved. Feedback in the form of resistance—if listened to—can provide lots of clues on what's causing problems with a planned change effort and what might be done to improve things. In fact, one of the easiest ways to add discipline to your change leadership is to track progress by always monitoring these resistance to change checkpoints.[63]

Four resistance to ▶ change checkpoints

1. *Check benefits*—Do the people involved see a clear advantage in making the change? Everyone should know "what is in it for me" or "what is in it for our group or the organization as a whole."

2. *Check compatibility*—Is the change perceived as breaking comfort levels? It's best to keep the change as close as possible to the existing values and ways of doing things. Minimizing the scope of change helps to keep it more acceptable and less threatening.

3. *Check simplicity*—How complex is the change? It's best to keep the change as easy as possible to understand and to use. People should have access to training and assistance to make the transition to new ways as easy as possible.

4. *Check triability*—Are things moving too fast? People tend to do better when they can try the change little by little, making adjustments as they go. Don't rush the change, and be sure to adjust the timing to best coincide with work schedules and cycles of high/low workloads.

In addition to these checkpoints, there are other positive ways to deal with resistance to change.[64] *Education and communication* uses discussions, presentations, and demonstrations to educate everyone beforehand about a change. *Participation and involvement* allows others to contribute ideas and help design and implement the change. *Facilitation and support* provides encouragement and training, engages active listening to problems and complaints, and seeks ways to reduce performance pressures. *Negotiation and agreement* provides incentives to gain support from those who are actively resisting or ready to resist change initiatives.

Two other approaches for managing resistance are common, but they are also risky in terms of negative side effects. *Manipulation and co-optation* seeks to covertly influence others by selectively providing information and structuring events in favor of the desired change. *Explicit and implicit coercion* forces people to accept change by threatening undesirable consequences for noncompliance with what is being asked in the change process.

Learning Check 3

TAKEAWAYQUESTION **3 What is the nature of organizational change?**

BE SURE YOU CAN • define *change leader* and *change agent* • discuss the pros and cons of top-down change and bottom-up change • differentiate between incremental and transformational change • describe Lewin's three phases of planned change • discuss improvising as an approach to planned change • discuss the pros and cons of the force-coercion, rational persuasion, and shared power change strategies • list several reasons why people resist change • describe strategies for dealing with resistance to change

Management Learning Review
Get Prepared for **Quizzes and Exams**

SUMMARY

TAKEAWAYQUESTION 1

What is organizational culture?

- Organizational culture is an internal environment that establishes a personality for the organization and influences the behavior of members.
- The observable culture is found in the rites, rituals, stories, heroes, and symbols of the organization; the core culture consists of the core values and fundamental beliefs on which the organization is based.
- In organizations with strong cultures, members behave with shared understandings and act with commitment to core values.
- Key dimensions of organizational culture include hierarchical culture, dependable culture, enterprising culture, and social culture.
- Among trends in managing organizational cultures, value-based management and workplace spirituality are popular directions and considerations.

FOR DISCUSSION Which of the various dimensions of organizational culture are most important to you as an employee?

TAKEAWAYQUESTION 2

What is a multicultural organization?

- Multicultural organizations operate with internal cultures that value pluralism, respect diversity, and build strength from an environment of inclusion.
- Organizations have many subcultures, including those based on occupational, functional, ethnic, age, and gender differences.
- Challenges faced by members of minority subcultures in organizations include sexual harassment, pay discrimination, job discrimination, and the glass ceiling effect.

- Managing diversity is the process of developing an inclusive work environment that allows everyone to reach their full potential.

FOR DISCUSSION What can the leader of a small team do to reduce diversity prejudice being expressed by one team member?

TAKEAWAYQUESTION 3

What is the nature of organizational change?

- Change leaders are change agents who take initiative to change the behavior of people and organizational systems.
- Organizational change can proceed with a top-down emphasis, with a bottom-up emphasis, or a combination of both.
- Incremental change makes continuing adjustments to existing ways and practices; transformational change makes radical changes in organizational directions.
- Lewin's three phases of planned change are unfreezing—preparing a system for change; changing—making a change; and refreezing—stabilizing the system. To this can be added a fourth—improvising as needed.
- Change agents should understand the force-coercion, rational persuasion, and shared power change strategies.
- People resist change for a variety of reasons, including fear of the unknown and force of habit.
- Good change agents deal with resistance in a variety of ways, including education, participation, support, and facilitation.

FOR DISCUSSION Can a change leader ever be satisfied that the refreezing stage of planned change has been accomplished in today's dynamic environments?

SELF-TEST 12

Multiple-Choice Questions

1. Pluralism and the absence of discrimination and prejudice in policies and practices are two important hallmarks of _____.
   (a) the glass ceiling effect
   (b) a multicultural organization
   (c) quality circles
   (d) affirmative action

2. When members of minority cultures feel that they have to behave in ways similar to the majority culture, this is called _____.
   (a) biculturalism   (c) the glass ceiling effect
   (b) symbolic leadership   (d) inclusivity

3. Engineers, scientists, and information systems specialists are likely to become part of separate _____ subcultures in an organization.
   (a) ethnic   (c) functional
   (b) generational   (d) occupational

4. Stories told about an organization's past accomplishments and heroes such as company founders are all part of what is called the _____ culture.
   (a) observable   (c) functional
   (b) underground   (d) core

5. Honesty, social responsibility, and customer service are examples of _____ that can become foundations for an organization's core culture.
   (a) rites and rituals   (c) subsystems
   (b) values   (d) ideas

6. Which leadership approach is most consistent with an organizational culture that values the full utilization of all diverse talents of all the organization's human resources?
   (a) Managing diversity
   (b) Affirmative action
   (c) Status quo
   (d) Rational persuasion

7. When members of a dominant subculture, such as white males, make it hard for members of minority subcultures, such as women, to advance to higher level positions in the organization, this is called the _____ effect.
   (a) dominator
   (b) glass ceiling
   (c) brick wall
   (d) end-of-line

8. An executive pursuing transformational change would give highest priority to which one of these change targets?
   (a) an out-of-date policy
   (b) the organizational culture
   (c) a new information system
   (d) job designs in a customer service department

9. _____ change results in a major change of direction for an organization, while _____ change makes small adjustments to current ways of doing things.
   (a) Frame-breaking; radical
   (b) Frame-bending; incremental
   (c) Transformational; frame-breaking
   (d) Transformational; incremental

10. The presence or absence of a felt need for change is a key issue in the _____ phase of the planned change process.
    (a) improvising   (c) unfreezing
    (b) evaluating   (d) refreezing

11. When a manager listens to users, makes adaptations, and continuously tweaks and changes a new MIS as it is being implemented, the approach to technological change can be described as_____.
    (a) top-down   (c) organization development
    (b) improvisational   (d) frame breaking

12. A manager using a force-coercion strategy will rely on _____ to bring about change.
    (a) expertise   (c) formal authority
    (b) benchmarking   (d) information

13. The most participative of the planned change strategies is _____.
    (a) force-coercion   (c) shared power
    (b) rational persuasion   (d) command and control

14. True internalization and commitment to a planned change is most likely to occur when a manager uses a/an _____ change strategy.
    (a) education and communication
    (b) rational persuasion
    (c) manipulation and co-optation
    (d) shared power

15. Trying to covertly influence others, offering only selective information, and structuring events in favor of the desired change is a way of dealing with resistance by _____.
    (a) participation
    (b) manipulation and co-optation
    (c) force-coercion
    (d) facilitation

Short-Response Questions

16. What core values might be found in high-performance organizational cultures?

17. Why is it important for managers to understand subcultures in organizations?

18. What are the three phases of change described by Lewin, and what are their implications for change leadership?

19. What are the major differences in potential outcomes of using the force-coercion, rational persuasion, and shared power strategies of planned change?

EssayQuestion

20. Two businesswomen, former college roommates, are discussing their jobs and careers over lunch. You overhear one saying to the other: "I work for a large corporation, while you own a small retail business. In my company, there is a strong corporate culture and everyone feels its influence. In fact, we are always expected to act in ways that support the culture and serve as role models for others to do so as well. This includes a commitment to diversity and multiculturalism. Because of the small size of your firm, things like corporate culture, diversity, and multiculturalism are less important to worry about." Do you agree or disagree with this statement? Why?

ManagementSkills& Competencies Make yourself **valuable!**

Evaluate Career Situations

What Would You Do?

1. Two Job Offers

You will soon have to choose between two really nice job offers. They are in the same industry, but you wonder which employer would be the "best fit." You have a sense that their "cultures" are quite different. Fortunately, you've been invited back to spend a full day at each before making your decision. One of your friends suggests that doing a balance-sheet assessment of cultural pluses and minuses for each employer could be helpful. What aspects of organizational culture would you identify as important to your job choice? Given the items on your list, what can you look for or do in the coming visits to discover the real organizational cultures' pluses and minuses for each item?

2. Team Culture Nightmare

The promotion to team manager puts you right where you want to be in terms of career advancement. Even though you've had to move to a new location, it's a great opportunity . . . if you can do well as team leader. That's the problem. Now that you're in the job, you realize that the culture of the team is really bad. Some of the ways you've heard members describe it to one another are "toxic," "dog-eat-dog," "watch your back," and "keep your head down." Realizing that culture change takes time but that's it's also necessary in this situation, what can you do right away as the new team leader to set the team on course for a positive change to its culture?

3. Tough Situation

Times are tough at your organization, and, as the director of human resources, you have a problem. The company's senior executives have decided that 10% of the payroll has to be cut immediately. Instead of laying off about 30 people, you would like to have everyone cut back their work hours by 10%. This way the payroll would be cut but everyone would get to keep their jobs. But you've heard that this idea isn't popular with all of the workers. Some are already grumbling that it's a "bad idea" and the company is just looking for excuses "to cut wages." How can you best handle this situation as a change leader?

Reflect on the Self-Assessment

Change Leadership IQ

Instructions

Indicate whether each of the following statements is true (T) or false (F).[65]

T F 1. People invariably resist change.

T F 2. One of the most important responsibilities of any change effort is that the leader clearly describes the expected future state.

T F 3. Communicating what will remain the same after change is as important as communicating what will be different.

T F 4. Planning for change should be done by a small, knowledgeable group, and then that group should communicate its plan to others.

T F 5. Managing resistance to change is more difficult than managing apathy about change.

T F 6. Complaints about a change effort are often a sign of change progress.

T F 7. Leaders find it more difficult to change organizational goals than to change the ways of reaching those goals.

T F 8. Successful change efforts typically involve changing reward systems to support change.

T F 9. Involving more members of an organization in planning a change increases commitment to making the change successful.

T F 10. Successful organizational change requires certain significant and dramatic steps or "leaps," rather than moderate or "incremental" ones.

Scoring

Questions 2, 3, 6, 8, 9, 10 are true; the rest are false. Tally the number of correct items to indicate the extent to which your change management assumptions are consistent with findings from the discipline.

Contribute to the Class Exercise

Force-Field Analysis

Instructions

1. Form into your class discussion groups and review this model of **force-field analysis**—the consideration of forces driving in support of a planned change and forces resisting the change.

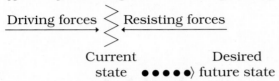

Driving forces ⤳ Resisting forces

Current state ●●●●⟩ Desired future state

2. Use force-field analysis and make lists of driving and resisting forces for one of the following situations:

   (a) *"Home Schooling" at College Level.* Things are changing in colleges and universities as budget declines create pressures for a rethinking of educational programming. Home schooling has grown popular at primary and secondary levels. Why can't it work for college as well, at least for the first two years? At least one vice president at the local university is in favor of making a proposal to move her campus to a 3rd/4th-year-only status and have years 1 and 2 go fully online. She wonders what she should prepare for when sharing her ideas with the rest of the executive team.

   (b) *Scheduling Dilemma.* A new owner has just taken over a small walk-in-and-buy-by-the-slice pizza shop in a college town. There are presently eight employees, three of whom are full-time and five of whom are part-time. The shop is open seven days a week from 10:30 a.m. to midnight. The new owner believes there is a market niche available for late-night pizza and would like to stay open each night until 4 a.m. She wants to make the change as soon as possible.

   (c) *Instructor's Choice.* A situation assigned by the instructor.

3. Choose the three driving forces that are most significant for the proposed change. For each force, develop ideas on how it could be further increased or mobilized in support of the change.

4. Choose the three resisting forces that are most significant for the proposed change. For each force, develop ideas on how it could be reduced or turned into a driving force.

5. Be prepared to participate in a class discussion led by your instructor.

Manage a Critical Incident

Proposal for Open Office Design and Hotdesking

You are just starting to work with an architect on designs for a new office space for your fast-growing tech startup. She proposes a design that does away with private offices, includes two or three personal cubicles with flexible dividers, and provides lots of flexible open spaces for casual and arranged meetings. She also proposes a shift to "hotdesking" for the sales representatives because they spend a lot of time away from the office. This means that they will not have permanent space and will instead "sign up" to use temporary cubicle desks when they come into the office. You really like the total design concept because it supports collaboration and teamwork while also saving space and facilities costs as the firm grows. But, you're worried about possible resistance from employees who are used to having private offices and their own desks. You sit down to write a list of "pros" and "cons" for the architect's proposal. You also make some notes on how to engage the staff with these ideas in order to head off any problems.

Questions

What's on your list and what's in your notes? What kind of change leadership approach do you think will be most likely to work with this group and situation?

Collaborate on the Team Activity

Organizational Culture Walk

Question

What organizational cultures do we encounter and deal with every day, and what are their implications for employees, customers, and organizational performance?

Instructions

1. In your team, make two lists. List A should identify the things that represent the core cultures of organizations. List B should identify the things that represent the observable cultures of organizations. For each item on the two lists, identify one or more indicators that you might use to describe this aspect of the culture for an actual organization.

2. Take an *organizational culture walk* through a major shopping area of your local community. Choose at least three business establishments. Visit each as customers. As you approach, put your "organizational culture senses" to work. Start gathering data on your lists A and B. Keep gathering it while you are at the business and right through your departure. Take good notes, and gather your thoughts together after leaving. Do this for each of the three organizations you choose.

3. Analyze and compare your data to identify the major cultural attributes of the three organizations and how they influence customers and organizational performance.

4. Use your results to make some general observations and report on the relationship between organizational cultures and performance as well as among organizational cultures, employee motivation, and customer satisfaction.

Analyze THE CaseStudy : APPLE INC. People and Design

Go to *Management Cases for Critical Thinking* at the end of the book to find this case.

HUMAN RESOURCE MANAGEMENT

13

As a manager or team leader, in many ways it's all about talent—the talent that you hire, nurture, develop, and support to help organizations and teams succeed. We're also talking about your talent, which you possess and develop—or not—to stay marketable and successful in your career field. Human resource management locates, cultivates, and sustains talent in organizations, and it's one of a manager's most important responsibilities.

> The key to managing people in ways that lead to profit, productivity, innovation, and real organizational learning ultimately lies in how you think about your organization and its people. . . . When you look at your people, do you see costs to be reduced? . . . Or, when you look at your people, do you see intelligent, motivated, trustworthy individuals—the most critical and valuable strategic assets your organization can have?

With these words from his book *The Human Equation: Building Profits by Putting People First*, scholar Jeffrey Pfeffer challenges managers to invest in people and their talents.[1] His research shows that organizations investing more in people outperform those that don't. These high-performing organizations thrive on strong foundations of **human capital**—the economic value of people with job-relevant knowledge, skills, abilities, experience, ideas, energies, and commitments. The best employers put people first and benefit from doing so.

Human capital is the economic value of people with job-relevant knowledge, skills, abilities, ideas, energies, and commitments.

Human Resource Management

TAKEAWAY 1   What is human resource management?

LEARN MORE | Human resource management process • Strategic human resource management
ABOUT | Legal environment of human resource management

A marketing manager at IDEO, a Palo Alto-based consulting design firm, once said: "If you hire the right people . . . if you've got the right fit . . . then everything will take care of itself."[2] This is what **human resource management**, or HRM, is all about—attracting, developing, and maintaining a talented and energetic workforce. Organizations that can't do this well, and don't have talented and committed employees to do the required work, have very little chance of being competitive in the long-term.

There are many career opportunities in a wide variety of areas in human resource management. HRM specialists within organizations deal with hiring, compensation and benefits, training, employee relations, and more. Common HR job titles include human resource planner, corporate recruiter, training and development specialist, compensation analyst, salary and benefits manager, and director of diversity. A growing number of consulting and outsourcing firms employ HR professionals to offer their clients specialized services in the same areas. And in the C-suite of senior executives, the title of Chief Talent Officer is becoming more popular and it gives direct testimony to what a commitment to HR is all about. Attention to the many facets of human resource management is essential for organizations in environments complicated by legal issues, economic turmoil, new corporate strategies, shifting labor markets, and changing social values.

Human Resource Management Process

The goal of human resource management is to support organizational performance by aligning people and their talents with organizational strategies and objectives. All managers, not just human resource specialists, share the responsibility to ensure that highly capable and enthusiastic people are in the right positions and working with the support they need to be successful. The three major tasks in human resource management are typically described as:

**Tasks of human ▶
resource management**

1. *Attracting a quality workforce*—talent acquisition through human resource planning, employee recruitment, and employee selection.

2. *Developing a quality workforce*—talent development through employee onboarding and orientation, training and development, and performance management.

3. *Maintaining a quality workforce*—talent retention through career development, work–life balance, compensation and benefits, retention and turnover, and labor–management relations.

A key concept in HRM is "fit"—individual-job fit and individual-organization culture fit. In fact, an organization's HRM approach should always focus on establishing both a good fit between the employee and the specific job to be accomplished, and between the employee and the overall culture of the organization. **Person–job fit** is the extent to which an individual's knowledge, skills, experiences, and personal characteristics are consistent with the requirements of their work.[3] **Person–organization fit** is the extent to which an individual's values, interests, and behavior are consistent with the culture of the organization.[4]

Strategic Human Resource Management

When Sheryl Sandberg left her senior management position with Google to become Facebook's chief operating officer, one of her first steps was to strengthen the firm's human resource management systems. She updated the approach for performance reviews, started new recruiting

---

Human resource management is a process of attracting, developing, and maintaining a talented workforce.

Person–job fit is the extent to which an individual's knowledge, skills, experiences and personal characteristics are consistent with the requirements of their work.

Person–organization fit is the extent to which an individual's values, interests, and behavior are consistent with the culture of the organization.

wisdom > LEARN FROM ROLE MODELS

> *Zappos' "work-hard play-hard" setting includes free food and fully paid medical and dental insurance.*

Tony Hsieh Taps HRM to Keep Zappos One Step Ahead

Brad Swonetz/Redux Pictures

As the CEO of Zappos.com, a popular online retailer that sells shoes, clothing, handbags, and more, Tony Hsieh (pronounced *shay*) has led the company through an amazing period of growth. He's also forged a creative and unique approach to human resources management, designed to hire and retain only those individuals who are truly committed to the company's values.

Before becoming "Zapponians," prospective hires go through two interviews. In the first, Zappos interviewers assess applicants' technical proficiency. In the second, they evaluate applicants'

ability to fit into the Zappos culture, which is characterized by 10 core values. Hsieh actually created the "cultural fit interview" himself. He included questions such as: "On a scale of 1 to 10, how weird are you?" "If they say 'one,' we won't hire them . . . . We like 7s or 8s," says Hsieh. He also notes that "qualified egotists need not apply" because one of our core values is to "be humble."

Once hired, all employees, including executives, are required to go through a four-week customer loyalty training, where they not only spend time on the phone with customers but also work at the company's giant warehouse in Kentucky. At the end of this "KY Boot Camp," boot camp trainees are offered a $2,000 bonus to quit and walk away. When asked why he offers to pay new employees to leave the company, Hsieh says that he wants only people who are committed to his long-term vision. Interestingly, 97% of the trainees turn down the buyout.

Hsieh also believes in creating a "work hard, play hard" atmosphere. To keep Zapponians inspired, he throws a weekly costume party at the main office. Hsieh also has implemented several employee-friendly practices such as providing free food in the company's cafeterias and vending machines as well as paying 100% of employees' medical and dental expenses.

FIND THE INSPIRATION

Is Hsieh's approach to human resource management just an interesting oddity? Or, is it representative of the direction more organizations should follow to attract today's new generation of talented workers? What aspects of the Zappos approach could be used by just about any employer? What parts might not fit at all? If Hsieh moves on to other opportunities, can his HRM practices survive at Zappos without his continued leadership?

methods, and launched new management training programs.[5] Sandberg's initiatives are consistent with the concept of **strategic human resource management**—mobilizing human capital through the HRM process to best implement organizational strategies.[6]

One indicator that HRM is truly strategic to organizations is when it is headed by a senior executive reporting directly to the chief executive officer. At Google, that position is Vice President of People Operations . . . Netflix has a Chief Talent Officer . . . Under Armour has a Senior

Strategic human resource management mobilizes human capital to implement organizational strategies.

Vice President of Human Resources. By locating the senior HRM position in the C-suite, these organizations allow it to play a strategic role in building a high-performing workforce while supporting core values and the corporate culture.

Employee value propositions are packages of opportunities and rewards that make diverse and talented people want to belong to and work hard for the organization.

The foundations for strategic human resource management are set with **employee value propositions** that align people with organizational strategies and objectives. Called EVPs, these are packages of opportunities and rewards, such as pay, benefits, meaningful work, and advancement possibilities, that make diverse and talented people want to belong to and work hard for the organization. Organizations with compelling EVPs have the edge over others in hiring and retaining talented people in scarce labor markets. Starbucks, for example, teamed up with Arizona State University to offer online degree programs for employees who work at least 20 hours per week. In return for paying part of the tuition bills, Starbucks expects to attract and retain talented workers while lowering its hiring and training costs.[7]

Legal Environment of Human Resource Management

Hire a relative? Promote a friend? Fire an enemy? Hold on! Managers and employers can't simply do whatever they want when it comes to human resource management practices. Everything has to be done within the framework of government laws and regulations about employment practices.

Laws Protecting Against Discrimination

Job discrimination occurs when someone is denied a job or work assignment for reasons that are not job relevant.

If valuing people is at the heart of human resource management, **job discrimination** is its nemesis. It occurs when organizations deny someone employment or a promotion for reasons unrelated to their performance potential. Think of this the next time you or someone else wonders: "Why didn't I get invited for a job interview? Is it because my first name is Shaniqua?" "Why didn't I get that promotion? Is it because I'm obviously pregnant?"

The cornerstone of U.S. laws designed to protect workers from job discrimination is Title VII of the Civil Rights Act of 1964, amended by the Equal Employment Opportunity Act of 1972 and the Equal Employment Opportunity Act (EEOA) of 1991. These acts provide for **equal employment opportunity** (EEO), giving everyone the right to employment without regard to sex, race, color, ethnicity, national origin, able-bodiedness, or religion. It is illegal under Title VII to consider any of these factors in decisions related to hiring, promoting, compensating, terminating, or in any way changing someone's terms of employment.

Equal employment opportunity is the requirement that employment decisions be made without regard to sex, race, color, ethnicity, national origin, able-bodiedness, or religion.

The intent of equal employment opportunity is to ensure the rights of all citizens to gain and keep employment based only on their ability to do the job and their performance once on the job. This right is federally enforced by the Equal Employment Opportunity Commission (EEOC). This agency has the power to file civil lawsuits against organizations that do not provide timely resolution of charges of discrimination lodged against them. The laws generally apply to all public and private organizations with 15 or more employees.

Affirmative action is an effort to give preference in employment to women and minority group members who have traditionally been underrepresented.

Under Title VII, organizations are expected to show **affirmative action** by setting goals and having plans that ensure equal employment opportunity for members of protected groups, those historically underrepresented in the workforce. The purpose of affirmative action is to ensure that women and minorities are represented in the workforce in proportion to their labor market availability.[8] The pros and cons of affirmative action are debated at both the federal and state levels. Criticism tends to focus on the use of group membership, such as female or minority status, as a criterion in employment decisions.[9] Issues include claims of *reverse discrimination* by members of majority populations. White males, for example, may believe that preferential treatment given to women and minorities interferes with their own employment rights.

Bona fide occupational qualifications are employment criteria justified by the capacity to perform a job.

As a general rule, legal protections for equal employment opportunity do not restrict an employer's right to establish **bona fide occupational qualifications** (BFOQs). These are criteria for employment that can be clearly justified as being a reasonable necessity for the normal operation of a business and are clearly related to a person's capacity to perform a job. The use of bona fide occupational qualifications based on race and color is not allowed under any circumstances. Those based on sex, religion, age, able-bodiedness, and national origin are possible, but organizations must take great care to support these requirements.[10] Examples of a BFOQ include age-based mandatory retirement for pilots and bus drivers based on issues of public safety. Religion may be a BFOQ in religious education contexts where the faculty must adhere to the beliefs of the denomination running the school. Able-bodiedness may be a BFOQ where space constraints, such as in aircraft where flight attendants must operate within narrow aisles, physically preclude the introduction of wheelchairs.

Employment Issues and Controversies

The legal environment is complex and dynamic, and it's important to stay informed about new laws and changes to existing laws. As Figure 13.1 shows, major U.S. laws prohibiting employment discrimination provide extensive protections. Matters relating to race, sex, religion, disabilities, age, and pregnancy are generally well covered, but open issues and controversies still exist.[11]

In the case of *bias due to sexual orientation and gender identity*, federal legal protection is still pending. The Employment Non-Discrimination Act of 2013 (ENDA) allows cases of discrimination against lesbians, gays, bisexual, and transgender workers to be filed with the EEOC.[12] As of this writing, ENDA has passed the Senate but still needs House of Representatives approval or an executive order for its contents to go into effect. Currently, legal protections for lesbian, gay, bisexual, transgender (LGBT) workers vary by state. Discrimination on the basis of sexual orientation is legal in 29 states, and discrimination on the basis of gender identity is legal in 33 states.[13]

Equal Pay Act of 1963	Requires equal pay for men and women performing equal work in an organization.
Title VII of the Civil Rights Act of 1964 (as amended)	Prohibits discrimination in employment based on race, color, religion, sex, or national origin.
Age Discrimination in Employment Act of 1967	Prohibits discrimination against persons over 40; restricts mandatory retirement.
Occupational Health and Safety Act of 1970	Establishes mandatory health and safety standards in workplaces.
Pregnancy Discrimination Act of 1978	Prohibits employment discrimination against pregnant workers.
Americans with Disabilities Act of 1990	Prohibits discrimination against a qualified individual on the basis of disability.
Civil Rights Act of 1991	Reaffirms Title VII of the 1964 Civil Rights Act; reinstates burden of proof by employer, and allows for punitive and compensatory damages.
Family and Medical Leave Act of 1993	Allows employees up to 12 weeks of unpaid leave with job guarantees for childbirth, adoption, or family illness.

FIGURE 13.1

Sample of U.S. laws against employment discrimination.

Sexual harassment is behavior of a sexual nature that affects a person's employment situation.

Sexual harassment remains an important workplace concern. It occurs when a person experiences conduct or language of a sexual nature that affects his or her employment situation. The EEOC defines sexual harassment as behavior of a sexual nature that creates a hostile work environment, interferes with a person's ability to do a job, or impedes a person's promotion potential. *Quid pro quo sexual harassment* is where job decisions are made based on whether the employee submits to or rejects sexual advances. *Hostile work environment sexual harassment* occurs when any unwelcome form of sexual conduct (inappropriate touching, teasing, dirty jokes, vulgar conversations, or the display of sexually explicit images) creates an intimidating, hostile, or offensive work setting. Organizations should have clear sexual harassment policies in place, along with fair and equitable procedures for implementing them.

Comparable worth holds that persons performing jobs of similar importance should be paid at comparable levels.

The Equal Pay Act of 1963 requires that men and women in the same organization be paid equally for doing work that is equivalent in terms of skills, responsibilities, and working conditions. But a lingering issue over gender disparities in pay involves **comparable worth**, the notion that persons performing jobs of similar importance should be paid at comparable levels. Why should a long-distance truck driver, for example, be paid more than a teacher in an elementary school? Does it make any difference that truck driving is a traditionally male occupation and teaching is a traditionally female occupation? Advocates of comparable worth argue that historical disparities in pay across occupations can result from gender bias. They would like to have the issue legally resolved.

Independent contractors are hired as needed and are not part of the organization's permanent workforce.

Our new economy has given rise to a growing number of people who work in temporary or part-time jobs, hire themselves out with temporary staffing agencies, or freelance as **independent contractors** for a changing mix of employers. Organizations are hiring more temporary and part-time workers and using more independent contractors in the attempt to reduce costs and increase staffing flexibility. Critics say this employment trend has created a category of "disposable workers" who are caught in "a race to the bottom" and labor in a system where "when they're used up it's on to the next one."[14] These individuals often work without benefits—or with reduced benefits—such as health insurance, retirement plans, sick pay, and holiday leave. Many, called **permatemps**, are employed in a temporary status for an extended period of time. The legal status of part-timers and independent contractors is regularly in the news and varies from state to state in the U.S.[15]

Permatemps are workers that are employed in a temporary status for an extended period of time.

Workplace privacy is the right to privacy while at work.

Privacy is another hot-button employment and societal issue in our high-tech work world. The Pew Research Center finds that 86% of Americans already try to hide their online footprints as consumers and web browsers, and 68% believe current laws protecting their electronic privacy aren't strong enough.[16] **Workplace privacy** is the right of individuals to privacy on the job.[17] Although it is legal for employers to monitor the work performance and behavior of their employees, employer practices can become invasive and cross legal and ethical lines in everything from recruitment to day-to-day task performance. Software can easily monitor e-mails, record Internet searches, follow keystrokes, document performance moment to moment, check social media activity and online profiles for key words, and track employee movements during the workday. All of this information can also be stored in vast databases without an employee's permission. Until the legal status of electronic surveillance is cleared up, one consultant says the best approach is to "assume you have no privacy at work."[18]

Learning Check 1

TAKEAWAYQUESTION 1 **What is human resource management?**

BE SURE YOU CAN • explain the human resource management process • define *discrimination, equal employment opportunity, affirmative action,* and *bona fide occupational qualification* • identify major laws that protect against discrimination in employment • discuss legal issues of sexual harassment, comparable worth, independent contractors, and workplace privacy

ethics > KNOW RIGHT FROM WRONG

> Since when is someone's Facebook profile meant to be an online résumé?

Personality Test? Drug Test? Social Media Test?

It used to be that preparing for a job interview meant being ready to answer questions about your education, work experience, interests, and activities. Now there's another question to prepare for: What's your Instagram user name and password?

Believe it or not, it's true. Many interviewers are now asking for access to an applicants' social media pages. They don't want just a quick glance at the public profile; they want access to the private profile, too. It's time to get worried when the recruiter says: "Please friend me."

"It's akin to requiring someone's house keys," says a law professor. One job candidate turned over a password because "I needed the job to feed my family. I had to." Another refused the interviewer's request and withdrew her application. She didn't want to work for an employer that would even ask to view her private Web pages.

A survey by Microsoft Research found 70% of recruiters saying that they had rejected applicants based on information they found online. Although a social media profile can be a treasure chest of information for recruiters and employers, it is less clear whether it is ethical to tap this resource to measure candidates' characters and make employment decisions. Since when is a Facebook profile meant to be an online résumé?

Sometimes recruiters make negative hiring decisions after finding relatively mild forms of questionable behavior such as using poor grammar, posting negative comments about prior employers, or uploading drinking pictures. This may be information or pictures that the individual has little control over. What happens if a "friend" posts a picture of someone from a party from years ago, or if inaccurate or untrue information is posted as a joke among friends?

WHAT DO YOU THINK?

What are the ethical issues involved with regard to recruiters asking for access to personal Facebook—or other online social network—pages? Should it be held against applicants if they refuse? Is it okay for managers to search online sites to check up on what employees are doing outside of work? Should what someone does outside of work cost them their job? On the other hand, shouldn't individuals who knowingly post online information understand that it may end up in the hands of their employers? Where do the lines of responsibility fall?

Attracting a Quality Workforce

TAKEAWAY 2   How do organizations attract a quality workforce?

LEARN MORE ABOUT | Human resource planning • Recruitment process • Selection techniques

The first responsibility of human resource management is talent acquisition. Its goal is to attract a high-quality workforce that has the talents needed for the organization to meet its performance goals. An advertisement once run by the Motorola Corporation put it this way: "Productivity is learning how to hire the person who is right for the job." To attract the right people, an organization must know exactly what it is looking for in terms of the jobs to be done and the talents required to do them well. It must create an employee value proposition that makes the organization stand out as a preferred employer. And, it must have the human resource management systems in place so that it can excel at employee recruitment and selection.

Human Resource Planning

Human resource planning is the process of analyzing an organization's staffing needs and determining how to best fill them. As shown in Figure 13.2, human resource planning begins with assessing staffing needs and the current workforce, and deciding what additions, replacements,

Human resource planning analyzes staffing needs and identifies actions to fill those needs.

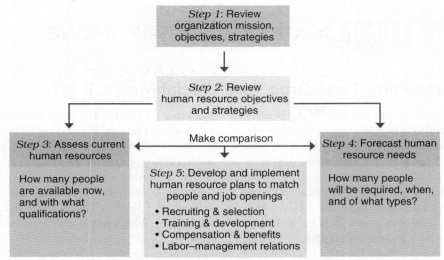

FIGURE 13.2
Steps in strategic human resource planning.

A **job analysis** studies exactly what is done in a job, and why.

A **job description** details the duties and responsibilities of a job holder.

Job specifications list the qualifications required of a job holder.

Recruitment is a set of activities designed to attract a talented pool of job applicants.

and upgrades are required for the future. The process involves **job analysis**—the systematic evaluation of job facets to determine what is done when, where, how, why, and by whom.[19] This information is then used to write or update **job descriptions** that describe specific job duties and responsibilities. The information in a job analysis is used to create **job specifications** that identify the qualifications—such as education, prior experience, and skills—needed by someone hired for a given job.

Recruitment Process

Recruitment is a set of activities designed to attract a talented pool of job applicants to an organization. Three steps in the traditional recruitment process are: (1) advertisement of a job vacancy, (2) preliminary contact with potential job candidates, and (3) initial screening to create a pool of applicants potentially meeting the organization's staffing needs. Today, recruitment increasingly involves social media where employers advertise jobs, individuals post interests and talents, and connections between would-be new hires and employers take place. At the extreme, you may be asked on a pre-recruitment basis to join a private social media site run by the employer. If you want to get hired at Zappos, for example, the front door is Zappos Insiders.[20] It's a social network set up by Zappos to allow potential employees to link with existing ones, show their personalities and talents, and learn what's going on at the firm. When a job vacancy opens, those with good reputations on Zappos Insiders get the first calls.

External recruitment seeks job applicants from outside the organization.

Social recruiting is where employers browse social media sites looking for prospective job candidates.

External and Internal Recruitment

The recruiting that takes place on college campuses is an example of **external recruitment** in which job candidates are sought from outside the hiring organization. External recruits are found through company websites and social media, virtual job fairs, specialized recruiting sites such as Monster and CareerBuilder, employment agencies and headhunters, university placement centers, personal contacts, and employee referrals. Through **social recruiting**, employers browse social media sites like LinkedIn, Facebook, Reddit, and Twitter, looking for people whose online

analysis > MAKE DATA YOUR FRIEND

Role of Social Media in Today's Recruitment

Social media has become an integral part of our lives today. According to the graph below, the number of social network users is expected to grow by 28% from 2014 to 2017.

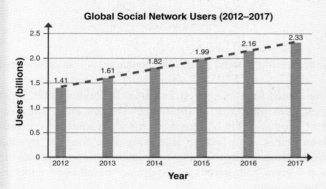

Global Social Network Users (2012–2017)

Year	Users (billions)
2012	1.41
2013	1.61
2014	1.82
2015	1.99
2016	2.16
2017	2.33

Increasingly, social networks have become a useful tool for human resource managers for recruitment purposes. In 2011, LinkedIn (95%), Facebook (58%) and Twitter (42%) were the most favoured social networks to search for candidates.

In March 2012, recruitment and branding managers across the Asia Pacific region participated in a survey conducted by Alexander Mann Solutions and Chapman Consulting Group. The study revealed the following interesting facts on the use of social media for recruitment:

- In Australia, social media was mainly used to post vacancies to create a wider reach. Branding the organisation and checking resumes were other reasons for using social media.
- In Singapore, brand-building and cost-saving were the main reasons for the use of social media. Almost 40% of respondents were using social media to vet resumes and 16% decided to reject applicants after going through their profiles on social media.
- In Hong Kong, social media was primarily used for posting jobs. Others reasons included cost-saving, brand-building and vetting of potential employees.
- In China, HR managers were more reserved about the usage of social media for recruitment when compared to the other countries in the Asia Pacific region. Social media is less valued as a channel for job posting or branding of the organisation.

In June 2014, the top five social networks, ranked by active users worldwide, were:

- Facebook
- Qzone
- Google+
- LinkedIn
- Twitter

Another survey of job seekers from 31 countries, conducted by the Kelly Global Workforce Index 2013, had these results:

- 53% used social media to share information about job opportunities with their friends
- 44% were contacted about a job opportunity through social media
- 39% used social media to help them make decisions about employment
- 16% were hired in the past 12 months for a job which originated from social media

Respondents from Gen Y (42%), Gen X (47%) and baby boomers (42%) also said they had been contacted by potential employers via social media in the past 12 months. Thus, social media has become a widely used job search tool for all generations.

This survey also indicated that job seekers across Asia preferred to use social media to look for opportunities. In Thailand, Indonesia, Malaysia and India, social media was selected over traditional methods such as newspaper advertisements and recruitment agencies when looking for employment.

The graph below shows job seekers' preferences when choosing social media to look for employment opportunities.

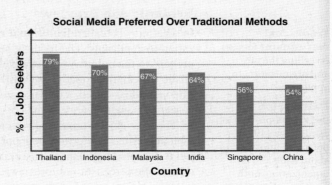

Social Media Preferred Over Traditional Methods

Country	% of Job Seekers
Thailand	79%
Indonesia	70%
Malaysia	67%
India	64%
Singapore	56%
China	54%

(Continued)

Today, social media has transformed the way job seekers search for employment. With this in mind, recruiters too are using social media as an important tool to source for candidates.

DISCUSSION QUESTIONS:

1. Is social media a good tool for recruiters to attract quality workforce to an organisation? Justify your answer.

2. Have you used social media to seek for a job? Describe some of the information that helped you to make a decision.

3. If social media is widely used for recruitment, would you be cautious about information posted on your Facebook or Twitter? Why or why not?

profiles show potential—things like leadership, special skills, and connections—as prospective job candidates.

Internal recruitment
seeks job applicants
from inside the
organization.

Internal recruitment involves the search for applicants from within the organization. Most organizations have a procedure for announcing vacancies through newsletters, electronic postings, and in-house social media sites. They also rely on managers and team leaders to recommend internal candidates for advancement. The college internship is a form of internal recruitment that is an increasingly important pathway to employment. It brings a student into the organization on a temporary basis and gives both parties an experience-based opportunity to consider one another for long-term employment.

There are advantages and disadvantages to both external and internal recruitment. External recruitment brings in outside applicants with fresh perspectives, expertise, and work experience. But extra effort is needed to get reliable information about these candidates. A major downside of recruiting externally is that a hiring decision might turn out bad because either not enough information was gathered about the applicant, or what was discovered turned out to be inaccurate.

Internal recruitment is usually quicker and focuses on employees with well-known performance records. A history of internal recruitment builds workforce loyalty and motivation by showing that there are opportunities to advance within the organization. It also helps to reduce turnover rates and facilitates retention of high-quality employees. But internal recruiting also has downsides as well. Limiting job searches to internal talent pools increases the risk that the best candidate may not be chosen for a position. A valuable opportunity to bring in outside expertise and viewpoints also may be lost at the very moment when new insights, skills, and creativity are most needed by the organization.

Realistic Job Previews

**Traditional
recruitment** focuses
on selling the job
and organization to
applicants.

**Realistic job
previews** provide job
candidates with all
pertinent information
about a job and an
organization, both
positive and negative.

In what may be called **traditional recruitment**, the emphasis is on selling the job and organization to applicants. The focus is on communicating the most positive features of the position, perhaps to the point where negatives are downplayed or even concealed. This may create unrealistic expectations that cause costly turnover when new hires become disillusioned and quit. The individual suffers a career disruption; the employer suffers lost productivity and the added costs of having to recruit again.

The alternative to traditional recruitment is a **realistic job preview** that provides candidates with all pertinent information about the job and organization without distortion, and before the job is accepted.[21] Rather than seeking to "sell" applicants on the positive features of the job or organization, realistic job previews are intended to be open and balanced. Both favorable and unfavorable aspects of work are covered.

The interviewer in a realistic job preview might use phrases such as "Of course, there are some downsides . . ."; "Something that you will want to be prepared for is . . ."; and "We have found that some new hires have difficulty with. . . ." Not surprisingly, such conversations may lead some applicants to decide that the job is not for them. But, this helps to avoid mismatches that could prove troublesome later on. For those who do take the job, knowing both the positive and negative features ahead of time builds realistic expectations that better prepare them for the inevitable ups and downs of a new position. The expected benefits of realistic recruiting practices include higher levels of early job satisfaction, greater trust in the organization, and less inclination to quit prematurely.

Selection Techniques

Once a a pool of job candidates exists, the next step is to determine whom to hire. This process of **selection**, as shown in Figure 13.3, involves gathering and assessing information about job candidates and making a hiring decision.

Selection is choosing individuals to hire from a pool of qualified job applicants.

Reliability and Validity

The selection process is always a prediction exercise in which the reliability and validity of techniques used are very important. **Reliability** means that the selection technique is consistent with regard to how it measures something. That is, it returns the same results time after time. For example, a personality test is reliable if the same individual receives a similar score when taking the test on two separate occasions. **Validity** means that there is a clear relationship between what the selection device is measuring and eventual job performance. That is, there is clear evidence that once on the job, individuals with high scores on an employment test, for example, outperform individuals with low scores.

Reliability means that a selection device repeatedly gives consistent results.

Validity means that scores on a selection device have a demonstrated correlation with future job performance.

Interviews Ins and Outs

Very few individuals are hired for managerial and professional positions without passing through one or more screening interviews. They are used to evaluate applicants on technical skill sets and experience, communication skills and personal impression, and potential person–organization culture fit. The traditional *face-to-face interview* is still the most used, but the *telephone interview*

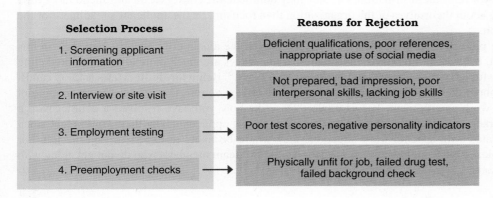

Selection Process	Reasons for Rejection
1. Screening applicant information	Deficient qualifications, poor references, inappropriate use of social media
2. Interview or site visit	Not prepared, bad impression, poor interpersonal skills, lacking job skills
3. Employment testing	Poor test scores, negative personality indicators
4. Preemployment checks	Physically unfit for job, failed drug test, failed background check

FIGURE 13.3
Steps in the selection process: The case of a rejected job applicant.

How to Succeed in a Telephone or Video Interview

- *Prepare ahead of time*—Study the organization; carefully list your strengths and capabilities; be ready to take notes.
- *Take the call or video link in private*—Make sure you are in a quiet room, with privacy and without the possibility of interruptions.
- *Dress professionally*—Dress right to increase your confidence and set a tone for your side of the conversation; don't dress in casual clothes.
- *Practice your "interview voice" and "screen presence"*—Impression counts; speak slowly and clearly, look at the camera; look pleasant, interested, and happy to be there.
- *Have reference materials handy*—Keep your résumé and other supporting documents within easy reach.
- *Have a list of questions*—Don't be caught unprepared; intersperse your best questions during the interview.
- *Ask what happens next*—Find out how to follow up; ask what other information you can provide; ask about the time frame for a decision.
- *Follow up*—Don't forget to send a thank-you note and reiterate your interest in the job.

and the *virtual or online video interview* are increasingly common. The likelihood for most college graduates today is that success in a telephone or online virtual interview will determine whether they ever get to the face-to-face on-site interview stage.

Even well-qualified job applicants may perform poorly in a job interview. They may be unprepared for questions related to the specific organization with which they are interviewing. They may be nervous or may be poor communicators. Or, they may simply fail at answering unusual and demanding questions.

Google is famous for asking questions like: "A man pushed his car to a hotel and lost his fortune. What happened?" Other employers are now pushing the interview envelope as well. Whole Foods might ask: "What's your perfect last meal?" Expedia might ask: "If you could go camping anywhere, where would you put your tent?" Xerox wants to know why tennis balls are fuzzy.[22] These types of interview questions are designed less for testing "right" answers and more for finding, through a candidate's responses, how well they might fit with the organization overall and its culture specifically. But you have to be prepared for standard questions as well—"What are your strengths and weaknesses?" "Where do you see yourself in five years?" "What can you offer us that someone else cannot?"[23]

It may surprise you to find out that interviews often have relatively low validity as selection devices. This is especially true of **unstructured interviews** where the interviewer doesn't work from a formal and pre-established list of questions that is asked of all interviewees. Some interviewers rush to judgment based on first impressions of candidates and fail to dig deeper for relevant information. Or, they may dominate the conversation and spend more time talking about themselves or the organization than focusing on the applicant's readiness for the position.

The predictive validity of interviews increases as the amount of structure increases. In this respect, behavioral interviews and situational interviews are much more effective at predicting successful job performance than traditional interviews.[24] **Behavioral interviews** ask job candidates about their past behavior, focusing specifically on actions that are likely to be important in the work environment. For example: "Describe how you have resolved a conflict with a co-worker or team mate." **Situational interviews** ask applicants how they would react when confronted with specific work situations they would be likely to experience on the job. For example: "How would you as team leader handle two team members who do not get along with one another?"[25]

In **unstructured interviews**, the interviewer does not work from a formal and pre-established list of questions that is asked of all interviewees.

Behavioral interviews ask job applicants about past behaviors.

Situational interviews ask job applicants how they would react in specific situations.

Employment Tests

Employment tests are often used to identify a candidate's intelligence, aptitudes, personality, interests, and even ethics. But organizations need to be careful about the way that they use tests and make sure that they are documented as valid predictors of job performance. **Biodata methods** usually take the form of multiple-choice, self-report questionnaires. They collect "hard" biographical information and also include "soft" items that inquire about more abstract characteristics such as value judgments, aspirations, motivations, attitudes, and expectations. When used in conjunction with ability tests, biodata methods can increase the reliability and validity of the selection process.[26] Google, for example, analyzes data collected by its biodata surveys and compares them with those of current top performers.[27]

Other types of employment tests involve actual demonstrations of job-relevant skills and personal characteristics. An **assessment center** evaluates candidates' potential by observing their performance in experiential activities designed to simulate daily work. When using **work sampling**, companies ask applicants to do actual job tasks while being graded by observers on their performance. Generally speaking, organizations should use a combination of methods in order to increase the predictive validity of the selection process.

> **Biodata methods** collect certain biographical information that has been proven to correlate with good job performance.
>
> An **assessment center** examines how job candidates handle simulated work situations.
>
> In **work sampling**, applicants are evaluated while performing actual work tasks.

Learning Check 2

TAKEAWAYQUESTION **2 How do organizations attract a quality workforce?**

BE SURE YOU CAN • explain the difference between external recruitment and internal recruitment • discuss the value of realistic job previews to employers and to job candidates • differentiate reliability and validity as two criteria of selection tools • discuss the pros and cons of job interviews and employment tests

Developing a Quality Workforce

TAKEAWAY 3   How do organizations develop a quality workforce?

LEARN MORE ABOUT | Onboarding and socialization • Training and development
Performance management

The second responsibility of human resource management is talent development. This begins when new hires are brought on board with care so their first experiences are positive ones. When people join an organization, they have to "learn the ropes" and become familiar with "the way things are done." Newcomers need to learn about the organization's culture so they can best fit into the work setting. The best employers don't leave all of this to chance. They step in and try to guide this learning process in the right direction. Talent development also means that all employees must be continually trained and developed through well-chosen job experiences and placements to keep their abilities and skills at the highest possible levels.

Onboarding and Socialization

The first formal experience newcomers have often begins with some form of **onboarding** or **orientation** activities designed to familiarize new employees with their jobs, co-workers, and key aspects of the organization as a whole. A good onboarding program brings new hires into the organization with a clear understanding of the organization's mission and goals, culture, and key policies and procedures. It also introduces them to their jobs, co-workers, and performance expectations in a positive and, ideally, motivating way. For example, all new hires at the Disney World Resort in Buena Vista, Florida, learn during onboarding that everyone, regardless of their specific job title—be it entertainer, ticket seller, or groundskeeper—is a "cast member" who is there "to make the customer happy."

> **Onboarding** or **orientation** familiarizes new hires with the organization's mission and culture, their jobs and co-workers, and performance expectations.

Socialization is a process of learning and adapting to the organizational culture.

Socialization is a process through which new members learn and adapt to the ways of the organization.[28] The socialization that begins with onboarding and which continues during the first six months or so of employment often determines how well a new employee is going to fit in and perform. A technique used by Neil Blumenthal, co-founder of the online eyewear retailer Warby Parker, is to "provide realistic short-term goals to establish quick wins, which will get the employee into a rhythm where he or she is motivated."[29] When done well, socialization sets the right foundations for high performance, job satisfaction, and work enthusiasm. When weak or neglected, however, it largely leaves integration to chance as newcomers learn about the organization and their jobs through interactions with co-workers.[30] Even though learning from experienced workers can be helpful to a new hire, it also is possible for newcomers to learn the wrong kinds of things and pick up bad attitudes.

Training and Development

Training provides learning opportunities to acquire and improve job-related skills.

Training is a set of activities that helps people acquire and improve their job-related skills. This applies both to an employee's initial training and to upgrading skills to meet changing job requirements. Organizations that value their human resources invest in extensive training and development programs to ensure that everyone always has the capabilities needed to perform well and manage their personal lives.[31]

In **job rotation**, people switch tasks to learn multiple jobs.

Coaching occurs as an experienced employee offers performance advice to a less experienced co-worker.

Mentoring assigns new hires and early-career employees as protégés to more senior employees.

In **reverse mentoring**, younger employees mentor seniors to improve their technology skills.

On-the-job training takes place on the job in the work setting. A common approach is **job rotation**, which allows people to spend time working in different jobs or departments or even geographical locations, and thus expand the range of their job capabilities.[32] Another approach is **coaching**, in which an experienced person provides performance advice to a newcomer or less experienced co-worker. **Mentoring** is a form of coaching in which early-career employees are formally assigned as protégés to senior, veteran job holders. The mentoring relationship gives new employees regular access to advice on developing skills and getting better informed about the organization. More organizations, including Mastercard and Cisco, are now also using **reverse mentoring** where younger employees mentor seniors to improve their technology skills. At Capgemini Consulting, global practice leader Didier Bonnet says "the main aim is to raise the digital IQ of business leaders in the firms."[33]

Management development is training to improve knowledge and skills in the management process.

Off-the-job training is accomplished outside the work setting. It provides an opportunity to enhance job-critical skills or even to develop skills that might be needed before a promotion or transfer. An example is **management development**—formal training designed to improve a person's knowledge and skill in the fundamentals of management. New managers just starting out often benefit from training that emphasizes team leadership and communication. Middle managers may benefit from training to better understand multifunctional viewpoints or techniques for motivating employees. Top managers may benefit from advanced management training to sharpen their decision-making and negotiation skills, as well as to expand their awareness of corporate strategy and direction.

Performance Management

A **performance management system** sets standards, assesses results, and plans for performance improvements.

An important part of human resource management is the design and implementation of a successful **performance management system**. This system ensures that performance standards and objectives are set, that performance is regularly assessed, and that steps are taken to improve employees' future performance following the provision of performance feedback by managers.

Performance assessment or **performance review** is the process of formally evaluating performance and providing feedback to a job holder.

Performance assessment or **performance review**, also called *performance appraisal* and *performance evaluation*, is the process of formally assessing employees' work accomplishments and providing feedback. Such a performance review serves both evaluation and development purposes.[34] The *evaluation purpose* focuses on past performance and measures results against standards. Performance is documented for the record and for the purpose of allocating rewards such as financial incentives and bonuses. The manager provides an evaluation of the job holder's accomplishments and areas of weakness. The *development purpose* focuses on future performance. Performance goals and obstacles are identified, along with areas where training or supervisory support may be needed. The manager acts in a counseling role and gives attention to job holders' developmental needs.

Surveys report that 42% of workers and 58% of HR managers dislike their performance assessment systems.[35] One of the reasons is that the reviews aren't frequent enough, often an "annual" ritual. Another is the tendency to focus on the evaluation of performance and neglect the discussion of pathways for performance development.[36] Use of ongoing **performance coaching** helps minimize these problems. It provides employees with frequent and developmental feedback as more of an ongoing dialogue than a formal, scheduled event. The coaching helps clarify performance expectations and prevent small problems from getting out of control. At the same time, it increases trust and improves the quality of supervisor–subordinate relationships.

Another important reason for dissatisfaction with performance assessments is the nature of the process itself. All parties involved in the giving and receiving of performance feedback can find the event uncomfortable, emotional, and even anger inducing. Along with this, the assessment content–message and measures being delivered—are often open to disagreement and debate. This is why good choices must be made among alternative performance assessment methods, and why they should be as reliable and valid given the circumstances.[37] A reliable assessment method yields the same result over time or for different raters. A valid method is unbiased and measures only factors directly relevant to job performance.

> **Performance coaching** provides frequent and developmental feedback for how a worker can improve job performance.

Trait-Based Performance Assessment

Trait-based approaches are designed to measure the extent to which employees possess characteristics or traits that are considered important in the job. For example, trait-based measures often assess characteristics such as dependability, initiative, conscientiousness, and leadership. One of the oldest and most widely used performance appraisal methods is a **graphic rating scale**. It is basically a checklist for rating individuals on traits or performance characteristics such as quality of work, job attitude, and punctuality. Although this approach is quick and easy, it tends to be very subjective and, as a result, also tends to have poor reliability and validity.

> A **graphic rating scale** uses a checklist of traits or characteristics to evaluate performance.

Behavior-Based Performance Assessment

Behavior-based approaches evaluate employees on specific actions that are viewed as important parts of the job. The **behaviorally anchored rating scale**, or BARS, describes actual behaviors for various levels of performance achievement in a job. In the case of the customer-service representative illustrated in Figure 13.4, "extremely poor" performance is clearly defined as rude or disrespectful treatment of customers.

The BARS is more reliable and valid than the graphic rating scale because it anchors performance assessments to specific descriptions of work behavior. Behavior-based appraisals also are more consistent with the developmental purpose of performance appraisal because they provide specific feedback to employees as to areas in need of improvement. But one problem is that a BARS evaluation may be influenced by **recency bias**. This is the tendency for evaluations to focus on recent behaviors rather than on behavior occurring throughout the evaluation period.

The **critical-incident technique** is a behavior-based approach that can diminish recency bias. With this technique, a running log or inventory is kept of employees' effective and ineffective job behaviors. Using the case of the customer-service representative, a critical-incidents log might contain the following entries: Positive example—"Took extraordinary care of a customer who had purchased a defective product from a company store in another city"; negative example—"Acted rudely in dismissing the complaint of a customer who felt that a sale item was erroneously

> A **behaviorally anchored rating scale** uses specific descriptions of actual behaviors to rate various levels of performance.

> **Recency bias** overemphasizes the most recent behaviors when evaluating individuals' performance.

> The **critical-incident technique** keeps a log of employees' effective and ineffective job behaviors.

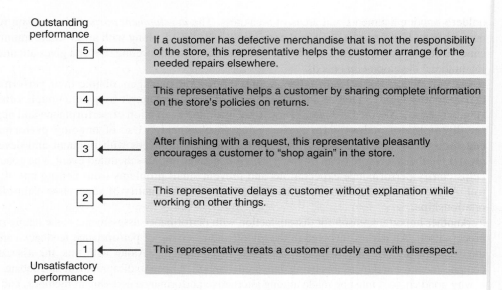

Outstanding performance

5 ← If a customer has defective merchandise that is not the responsibility of the store, this representative helps the customer arrange for the needed repairs elsewhere.

4 ← This representative helps a customer by sharing complete information on the store's policies on returns.

3 ← After finishing with a request, this representative pleasantly encourages a customer to "shop again" in the store.

2 ← This representative delays a customer without explanation while working on other things.

1 ← This representative treats a customer rudely and with disrespect.

Unsatisfactory performance

FIGURE 13.4
Sample of a behaviorally anchored rating scale for performance appraisal.

advertised." Such a written record can be discussed in specific terms with the employee and used for both evaluative and developmental purposes.

Results-Based Performance Assessment

Results-based approaches target just what their name implies. Rather than employees' traits or their specific behaviors, results-based assessments focus on accomplishments. This type of assessment is typically quantitative and objective, making it ideal in some circumstances. But results-based measures can sometimes create more problems than they solve. In some jobs, the outcomes that are the easiest to measure quantitatively aren't necessarily the most important. For instance, although the number of hours a technician spends on a customer's custom speaker installation is easy to measure, it is less important than how effective the installation is, which is more complicated to evaluate. In addition, results-based measures may ignore the impact of circumstances beyond the employee's control, such as inadequate technology or poor performance by another member of their team. When people are evaluated only on goal attainment, they also may adopt unethical approaches to accomplish goals.[38]

Leniency is the tendency to give employees a higher performance rating than they deserve.

One of the common performance appraisal errors is **leniency**—the tendency for supervisors to rate employees more favorably than they deserve in order to avoid the unpleasant task of giving negative feedback.[39] Although leniency tends to be less pronounced in results-based performance appraisals, it may be further reduced by the use of **multiperson comparisons** that formally compare one manager's evaluations with ratings provided by another manager. In *rank ordering*, all employees being rated are arranged in order of performance achievement. The best performers go at the top of the list, while the worst performers go at the bottom; no ties are allowed. In a *forced distribution*, each employee is placed into a frequency distribution, which requires that a certain percentage of employees fall into specific performance classifications, such as the top 10%, the next 40%, the next 40%, and the bottom 10%. These systems are usually put in place to guard against supervisors giving their employees too lenient or overly positive evaluations.[40]

A **multiperson comparison** compares one person's performance with that of others.

360-Degree Feedback

360-degree appraisals include superiors, subordinates, peers, and even customers in the appraisal process.

It also is increasingly popular to include more than immediate supervisors in the performance appraisal process.[41] In **360-degree appraisals**, feedback is gathered from multiple sources in order to provide a more comprehensive evaluation of employees' performance. These typically include input not only from an employee's supervisor but from peers, subordinates, and even customers—stakeholders inside and outside the organization who depend on the job holder's performance. Most 360-degree appraisals also include a self-evaluation by job holders. Assessments from all of these sources are used to identify employees' strengths, weaknesses, and development needs.[42]

Learning Check 3

TAKEAWAYQUESTION **3 How do organizations develop a quality workforce?**

BE SURE YOU CAN • define *orientation* and *socialization* and describe their importance to organizations • give examples of on-the-job and off-the-job training • discuss strengths and weaknesses of trait-based, behavior-based, and results-based performance appraisals • explain how 360-degree appraisals work

Maintaining a Quality Workforce

TAKEAWAY 4   How do organizations maintain a quality workforce?

LEARN MORE | Flexibility and work–life balance • Compensation and benefits
ABOUT | Retention and turnover • Labor–management relations

The third responsibility in human resource management is talent retention. "Hiring good people is tough . . . keeping them can be even tougher," states an article in the *Harvard Business Review*.[43] The point is that it isn't enough to hire and train workers to meet an organization's immediate needs; employees must also be successfully nurtured, supported, and retained. A Society for Human Resource Management survey of employers shows that popular tools for maintaining a quality workforce include flexible work schedules and personal time off, competitive salaries, and good benefits—especially health insurance.[44]

Flexibility and Work–Life Balance

Today's increasingly fast-paced, complex, and multifaceted lifestyles have contributed to increased concerns about **work–life balance**—how people balance the demands of their careers with their personal and family needs.[45] Not surprisingly, the "family friendliness" of an employer is now frequently used as a screening criterion by job candidates. It is also used in "best employer" rankings found in publications such as *Working Mother*, *Fortune*, and *Forbes,* and online sources such as Linked In and Vault.Com.

Work–life balance involves balancing career demands with personal and family needs.

Work–life balance is enhanced when workers have flexibility in scheduling work hours, work location, and even such things as vacations and personal time off. Flexibility allows people to more easily balance their personal lives and work responsibilities. Research shows that workers who have flexibility, at least with regard to when they begin and end their workday, are less likely to leave their jobs.[46] The health-care company Pfizer encourages employees to customize their work schedules around families' needs. In one year, 86% of all employees adjusted their hours at some point, while 50% occasionally worked from their homes or other off-site locations.[47]

Flexibility programs are becoming essential for many employers to attract and retain the talented workers they need. Some firms are helping workers handle family matters through initiatives such as on-site day care and elder care, and concierge services for miscellaneous needs such as dry cleaning and getting a haircut. Others have moved into innovative programs like work sabbaticals—FedEx, Genentech, Patagonia, and General Mills are now offering sabbaticals as a way to motivate (and retain) their best performers.[48] A few even offer limitless vacation time. At investment research firm

Morningstar, employees can take as much vacation time as they want whenever they want. The same goes for online investment information website Motley Fool and software company HubSpot.[49]

Compensation and Benefits

Base compensation is a salary or hourly wage paid to an individual.

It may be that no other work issue receives as much attention as pay. **Base compensation** in the form of a market-competitive salary or hourly wage helps in hiring the right people. The way pay increases are subsequently handled can have a significant impact on employees' job attitudes, motivation, and performance, and it can also influence their tendencies to look for a better job elsewhere.

Benefits also rank right near the top of the list in importance with pay as a way of helping to attract and retain workers. How many times does a graduating college student hear, "Be sure to get a job with benefits!"?[50] But with rising costs, these benefits—retirement plans and health insurance in particular—are becoming harder to negotiate. Most employers that still offer them require employees to pay at least part of the costs.[51]

Merit Pay Systems

Merit pay awards pay increases in proportion to performance contributions.

The trend in compensation today is largely toward "pay-for-performance."[52] If you are part of a **merit pay** system, your pay increases will be based at least in part on some assessment of how well you perform. The idea is that a good merit raise is a positive signal to high performers; no merit raise or a low merit raise sends a negative signal to low performers. Because their pay is contingent on performance, both groups are expected to work harder in the future.

Although they make sense in theory, merit systems are also not free of problems. A survey reported by the *Wall Street Journal* found that only 23% of employees understood their companies' reward systems.[53] Typical questions include: Who assesses performance? What happens if the employee doesn't agree with the assessment? Is the system fair and equitable to everyone involved? Is there enough money available to make the merit increases meaningful?

Bonuses and Profit-Sharing Plans

Bonus pay plans provide one-time payments based on performance accomplishments.

Profit-sharing plans distribute to employees a proportion of net profits earned by the organization.

Gain-sharing plans allow employees to share in cost savings or productivity gains realized by their efforts.

Employee stock ownership plans (ESOPs) help employees purchase stock in their employing companies.

How would you like to someday receive a letter like this one, once sent to two top executives by Amazon.com's chairman Jeff Bezos? "In recognition and appreciation of your contributions," his letter read, "Amazon.com will pay you a special bonus in the amount of $1,000,000."[54] **Bonus pay** plans provide one-time or lump-sum payments to employees who meet specific performance targets or make some other extraordinary contribution, such as an idea for a work improvement. These pay plans have been most common at the executive level, but many companies now use them more extensively across all levels. At Applebee's, for example, "Applebucks" are small cash bonuses given to reward employee performance and increase loyalty to the firm.

In contrast to straight bonuses, **profit-sharing** plans give employees a proportion of the net profits earned by the organization during a performance period. **Gain-sharing** plans extend the profit-sharing concept by allowing groups of employees to share in any savings or "gains" realized when their efforts or ideas result in measurable cost reductions or productivity increases. As incentive systems, profit-sharing plans, gain-sharing plans, and bonus plans have the advantage of helping to ensure that individual employees work hard by linking their pay to the performance of the organization as a whole.

Stock Ownership and Stock Options

Some employers provide employees with ways to accumulate stock in their companies and thus develop a sense of ownership. The idea is that stock ownership will motivate employees to work hard so that the company becomes and stays successful. **Employee stock ownership plans**, or ESOPs, help employees purchase stock in their employing companies, sometimes at special discounted rates. For example, almost 95% of employees are stock owners at Anson Industries, a Chicago construction firm.[55] An administrative assistant says it has made a difference in her job performance: "You have a different attitude . . . everyone here has the same attitude because it's our money." Of course, there are downside risks of ESOPs. When a company's market value falls, so too does the value of any employee-owned stock.

Another approach is to grant employees **stock options** linked to their performance or as part of their hiring packages. Stock options give owners rights to buy shares of stock at a future date at a fixed price. Employees gain financially if the stock price rises above the option price, but the stock options lose value if the stock price drops. The logic is that option holders will work hard so that the company performs well and they can reap some of the financial benefits. The Hay Group, a global human resource management consulting firm, reports that the most admired U.S. companies are also those that offer stock options to a greater proportion of their workforces.[56]

> **Stock options** give the right to purchase shares at a fixed price in the future.

Benefits

Employee benefits packages include nonmonetary forms of compensation that are intended to improve the work and personal lives of employees. Some benefits are required by law, such as contributions to Social Security, unemployment insurance, and workers' compensation insurance. Many organizations offer additional benefits in order to attract and retain highly qualified employees. They include health care insurance, retirement plans, pay for time not worked—such as personal days and vacations, sick leave, and maternity and paternity leave. But, the majority of U.S. workers still don't have access to such discretionary benefits. Although the Family and Medical Leave Act requires employers to offer unpaid leaves for medical and family problems, for example, President Obama told a Summit on Working Families: "There is only one country in the world that does not offer paid maternity leave, and that is us."[57] And when it comes to the "working sick" problem, some 40 million Americans lack paid sick leave benefits.[58]

> **Employee benefits** are nonmonetary forms of compensation such as health insurance and retirement plans.

The ever-rising costs of benefits, particularly medical insurance and retirement, are a major concern for employers. Many are attempting to gain control over health care expenses by shifting more of the insurance costs to employees and by restricting choices among health care providers. Some also are encouraging healthy lifestyles as a way to decrease health insurance claims.

Flexible benefits programs are increasingly common. These plans allow employees to choose a set of benefits within a certain dollar amount. The trend also is toward more **family-friendly benefits** that help employees balance work and non-work responsibilities. These include child care, elder care, flexible schedules, parental leave, and part-time employment options, among others. Increasingly common as well are **employee assistance programs** that help employees deal with troublesome personal problems. Such programs may offer assistance in dealing with stress, counseling on alcohol and substance abuse, referrals for domestic violence and sexual abuse, and sources for family and marital counseling.

> **Flexible benefits** programs allow employees to choose from a range of benefit options.
>
> **Family-friendly benefits** help employees achieve better work–life balance.
>
> **Employee assistance programs** help employees cope with personal stresses and problems.

Retention and Turnover

Retirement is one of those experiences that can increase employees' fears and apprehensions as it approaches. Many organizations offer special counseling and other forms of support for retiring employees, including advice on company benefits, financial management, estate planning, and use of leisure time. Increasingly on the radar at many firms are **early retirement incentive programs**. These programs give workers financial incentives to retire early. The potential benefits for employers include the opportunity to lower payroll costs by reducing positions, replacing higher-wage workers with less expensive newer hires, and creating openings that can be used to hire workers with different, more current skills and talents.

> **Early retirement incentive programs** offer workers financial incentives to retire early.

The most extreme replacement decisions involve **termination**, or the involuntary and permanent dismissal of an employee. In some cases, termination is based on performance problems or

> **Termination** is the involuntary dismissal of an employee.

violations of organizational policy. In other cases, the employees involved may be performing well, but may be terminated as part of strategic restructuring through workforce reduction. In all cases, terminations should be handled fairly, according to organizational policies and in full legal compliance with all relevant federal and state statues.

Many employment relationships are governed by the **employment-at-will** doctrine. This principle assumes that employers can terminate employees at any time for any reason. Likewise, employees may quit their job at any time for any reason. In other cases, the principle of **wrongful discharge** gives workers legal protections against discriminatory firings, and employers must have a bona-fide job-related cause to terminate the employee. In situations where workers belong to unions, terminations also are potentially subject to labor contract rules and specifications.

Labor–Management Relations

Labor unions are organizations to which workers belong and that deal with employers on the workers' behalf.[59] They are found in many industrial and business occupations, as well as among public-sector employees including teachers, police officers, firefighters, and government workers. Unions have historically played an important role in American society. Although they often are associated with wage and benefit issues, workers also join unions because of things like poor relationships with supervisors, favoritism or lack of respect by supervisors, little or no influence with employers, and failure of employers to provide a mechanism for grievance and dispute resolution.[60]

The National Labor Relations Act of 1935 (known as the Wagner Act) protects employees by recognizing their right to join unions and engage in union activities. It is enforced by the National Labor Relations Board (NLRB). The Taft-Hartley Act of 1947 protects employers from unfair labor practices by unions and allows workers to decertify unions. And, the Civil Service Reform Act of 1978 clarifies the right of government employees to join and to be represented by labor unions.

Although union membership has been on the decline in the United States, dropping from 20.1% in 1983 to just under 12% in 2013, unions have historically had a significant impact on the lives of the majority of American citizens. Notable accomplishments attributed to unions include (1) the "weekend," which emerged from the Fair Labor Standards Act of 1938, a federal standard for a shorter workweek and leisure time; (2) an end to child labor, which had been normative in the United States until 1938 with the first passage of federal legislation regulating child labor; (3) employer-based health care, which emerged in the 1950s; and (4) the Family Medical Leave Act, which provides for job-protected leave for employees to care for infants or a family member with an illness.[61] Notwithstanding the downward membership trend, unions remain an important force in the workplace.[62] They serve as a collective "voice" for their members and act as bargaining agents to negotiate **labor contracts** with employers. These contracts specify the rights and obligations of employees and management with respect to wages, work hours, work rules, seniority, hiring, grievances, and other conditions of employment. They are developed through **collective bargaining**, the process through which labor and management representatives negotiate, administer, and interpret labor contracts. It typically involves face-to-face meetings between labor and management representatives. During this time, a variety of demands, proposals, and counterproposals are exchanged. Several rounds of bargaining may be required before a contract is reached or a dispute over a contract issue is resolved.

As you might expect, the collective bargaining process is time-consuming and expensive, and it can lead to problems. When negotiations break down and labor–management relations take on an adversarial character, the conflict can be prolonged and extremely costly for both sides. This happens primarily when labor and management view each other as "win–lose" adversaries. In these

Employment-at-will means that employees can be terminated at any time for any reason.

Wrongful discharge is a doctrine giving workers legal protections against discriminatory firings.

A labor union is an organization that deals with employers on the workers' collective behalf.

A labor contract is a formal agreement between a union and an employer about the terms of work for union members.

Collective bargaining is the process of negotiating, administering, and interpreting a labor contract.

situations the collective bargaining becomes more of a battle than a constructive dialogue. The ideal process, by contrast, is characterized by a mutual "win–win" approach with a focus on achieving benefits to labor in terms of fair treatment and to management in terms of workforce quality.

Learning Check 4

TAKEAWAYQUESTION 4 **How do organizations maintain a quality workforce?**

BE SURE YOU CAN • define *work–life balance* • explain why compensation and benefits are important elements in human resource management • explain potential benefits and problems for merit pay plans • differentiate among bonuses, profit sharing, and stock options • define *flexible benefits plans* and discuss their advantages • define *labor union* and *collective bargaining*

Management Learning Review
Get Prepared for **Quizzes and Exams**

SUMMARY

TAKEAWAYQUESTION 1

What is human resource management?

- The human resource management process involves attracting, developing, and maintaining a quality workforce.
- Human resource management becomes strategic when it is integrated into the organization's strategic management process.
- Employees have legal protections against employment discrimination; equal employment opportunity requires that employment and advancement decisions be made without discrimination.
- Current legal issues in human resource management include sexual harassment, comparable worth, rights of independent contractors, and employee privacy.

FOR DISCUSSION What gaps in legal protection against employment discrimination still exist?

TAKEAWAYQUESTION 2

How do organizations attract a quality workforce?

- Human resource planning analyzes staffing needs and identifies actions to fill these needs over time.
- Recruitment is the process of attracting qualified job candidates to fill positions.
- Realistic job previews provide candidates with both positive and negative information about the job and organization.
- Selection involves gathering and assessing information about job candidates and making decisions about whom to hire.
- The selection process often involves screening applicants for qualifications, interviewing applicants, administering employment tests, and doing preemployment checks.

FOR DISCUSSION Is it realistic to expect that when interviewing with a potential employer, you will get a "realistic" job preview?

TAKEAWAYQUESTION 3

How do organizations develop a quality workforce?

- Orientation is the process of formally introducing new employees to their jobs, performance expectations, and the organization.
- On-the-job training includes job rotation, coaching, modeling, and mentoring; off-the-job training includes approaches like management development programs.
- Performance appraisal serves both evaluation and development purposes.
- Common performance appraisal methods focus on evaluating employees' traits, behaviors, or performance achievements.

FOR DISCUSSION What are the potential downsides to using 360-degree feedback in the performance review process?

TAKEAWAYQUESTION 4

How do organizations maintain a quality workforce?

- Complex demands of job and family responsibilities have made work–life balance programs increasingly important in human resource management.
- Compensation and benefits packages must be attractive so that an organization stays competitive in labor markets.
- Merit pay plans link compensation and performance; bonuses, profit sharing, and stock options are also forms of incentive compensation.
- Retention decisions in human resource management involve promotions, retirements, and/or terminations.
- The collective bargaining process and labor–management relations are carefully governed by law.

FOR DISCUSSION What creative options can employers offer to attract and retain motivated lower-wage employees?

SELF-TEST 13

Multiple-Choice Questions

1. Human resource management is the process of _____, developing, and maintaining a high-quality workforce.
   (a) attracting   (c) appraising
   (b) compensating   (d) training

2. _____ programs are designed to ensure equal employment opportunities for persons historically underrepresented in the workforce.
   (a) Realistic recruiting
   (b) External recruiting
   (c) Affirmative action
   (d) Employee assistance

3. The Age Discrimination in Employment Act prohibits discrimination against persons _____.
   (a) 40 years and older
   (b) 50 years and older
   (c) 65 years and older
   (d) of any age

4. _____ is the idea that jobs that are similar in terms of their importance to the organization should be compensated at the same level.
   (a) Affirmative action
   (b) Realistic pay
   (c) Merit pay
   (d) Comparable worth

5. A _____ is a criterion that can be legally justified for use in screening candidates for employment.
   (a) job description
   (b) bona fide occupational qualification
   (c) job specification
   (d) BARS

6. The first step in strategic human resource management is to _____.
   (a) forecast human resource needs
   (b) forecast labor supplies
   (c) assess the existing workforce
   (d) review organizational mission, objectives, and strategies

7. In human resource planning, a/an _____ is used to determine exactly what is done in an existing job.
   (a) critical-incident technique
   (b) assessment center
   (c) job analysis
   (d) multiperson comparison

8. If an employment test yields different results over time when taken by the same person, it lacks _____; if it bears no relation to actual job performance, it lacks _____.
   (a) equity, reliability
   (b) specificity, equity
   (c) realism, idealism
   (d) reliability, validity

9. Which phrase is most consistent with a recruiter offering a job candidate a realistic job preview?
   (a) "There are just no downsides to this job."
   (b) "No organization is as good as this one."
   (c) "There just aren't any negatives."
   (d) "Let me tell you what you might not like once you start work."

10. Socialization of newcomers occurs during the _____ step of the staffing process.
    (a) recruiting   (c) selecting
    (b) orientation   (d) training

11. The _____ purpose of performance appraisal is being addressed when a manager describes training options that might help an employee improve future performance.
    (a) development   (c) judgment
    (b) evaluation   (d) legal

12. When a team leader is required to rate 10% of team members as "superior," 80% as "good," and 10% as "unacceptable" for their performance on a project, this is an example of the _____ approach to performance appraisal.
    (a) graphic
    (b) forced distribution
    (c) behaviorally anchored rating scale
    (d) realistic

13. An employee with domestic problems due to substance abuse would be pleased to learn that his employer had a/an _____ plan to help on such matters.
    (a) employee assistance
    (b) cafeteria benefits
    (c) comparable worth
    (d) collective bargaining

14. Whereas bonus plans pay employees for special accomplishments, gain-sharing plans reward them for _____.
    (a) helping to increase social responsibility
    (b) regular attendance
    (c) positive work attitudes
    (d) contributing to cost reductions

15. In labor–management relations, the process of negotiating, administering, and interpreting a labor contract is known as _____.
    (a) arbitration   (c) reconciliation
    (b) mediation   (d) collective bargaining

Short-Response Questions

16. What are the different advantages of internal and external recruitment?

17. Why is orientation an important part of the human resource management process?

18. Why is a BARS potentially superior to a graphic rating scale for use in performance appraisals?

19. How does mentoring work as a form of on-the-job training?

EssayQuestion

20. Sy Smith is not doing well in his job. The problems began to appear shortly after Sy's job was changed from a manual to computer-based operation. He has tried hard but is just not doing well in learning to use the computer; as a result, he is having difficulty meeting performance expectations. As a 55-year-old employee with over 30 years with the company, Sy is both popular and influential among his work peers. Along with his performance problems, you have also noticed that Sy seems to be developing a more negative attitude toward his job. As Sy's manager, what options would you consider in terms of dealing with the issue of his retention in the job and in the company? What would you do, and why?

ManagementSkills&
Competencies Make yourself **valuable!**

Evaluate Career Situations

What Would You Do?

1. **Tattoos in the Office**
A co-worker has come to you with a problem. He has tattoo "sleeves" on both arms that extend to the wrists. Even in a long-sleeved shirt they are difficult to cover. He's upset because he learned that someone else got the promotion he had been hoping for. Everyone respects his high performance, diligence, and loyalty to the company. But it's also common knowledge that the boss "doesn't like tattoos." What advice can you give to your colleague about handling the current situation regarding the lost promotion? What advice, if any, can you offer about having both a career and tattoos?

2. **Bad Appraisal System**
As the new head of retail merchandising at a local department store, you are disappointed to find that the sales associates are evaluated on a graphic rating scale that uses a simple list of traits to gauge their performance. You believe that better alternatives are available, ones that will not only meet the employer's needs but also be helpful to the sales associates themselves. After raising this issue with your boss, she says "Fine, I hear you. Give me a good proposal and I'll take it to the store manager for approval." What will you propose, and how will you justify it as being good for both the sales associates and the boss?

3. **The Union Wants In**
There's a drive to organize the faculty of your institution and have them represented by a union. The student leaders on campus are holding a forum to gather opinions on the pros and cons of a unionized faculty. Because you represent a popular student organization in your college, you are asked to participate in the forum. You are expected to speak for about 3 minutes in front of the other student leaders. So, are you for or against faculty unionization? What will you say at the forum, and why?

Reflect on the Self-Assessment

Performance Assessment Assumptions

Instructions

In each of the following pairs, check the statement that best reflects your assumptions about performance assessment and appraisal.[63]

Performance assessment is:

1. **(a)** a formal process that should be done annually.
   (b) an informal process that should be done continuously.
2. **(a)** a process best planned for the person being assessed.
   (b) a process best planned with the person being assessed.
3. **(a)** done as an organizational requirement.
   (b) done regardless of organizational requirements.
4. **(a)** a time for team leaders to evaluate performance of team members.
   (b) a time for team members to evaluate their team leaders.
5. **(a)** a time to clarify performance standards for a worker.
   (b) a time to clarify a worker's career needs.
6. **(a)** a time to confront poor performance.
   (b) a time to express appreciation.
7. **(a)** an opportunity to improve direction and control.
   (b) an opportunity to increase enthusiasm and commitment.
8. **(a)** only as good as the organization's procedures for it.
   (b) only as good as the manager's coaching skills.

Scoring

There is no formal scoring for this assessment, but if you look carefully and think through your answers, there may be a pattern worth thinking more about.

Interpretation

The "a" responses represent a more traditional approach to performance appraisal that emphasizes its evaluation function.

This role largely puts the supervisor in the role of documenting a subordinate's performance for control and administrative purposes. The "b" responses represent more emphasis on the counseling or development role. Here, the supervisor is concerned with helping the subordinate perform better and learn how he or she might be of help.

Contribute to the Class Exercise

Upward Appraisal

Instructions

Form into work groups as assigned by the instructor. After the instructor leaves the room, complete the following tasks.[64]

1. Create a master list of comments, problems, issues, and concerns about the course experience to date that members would like to communicate to the instructor.

2. Select one person from the group to act as the spokesperson who will give your feedback to the instructor when he or she returns to the classroom.

3. The spokespersons should meet to rearrange the room (placement of tables, chairs, etc.) for the feedback session. This arrangement should allow the spokespersons and instructor to communicate in view of the other class members.

4. While spokespersons are meeting, group members should discuss what they expect to observe during the feedback session.

5. The instructor should be invited in; spokespersons should deliver feedback while observers make notes.

6. After the feedback session is complete, the instructor will call on observers for comments, ask the spokespersons for their reactions, and engage the class in general discussion about the exercise and its implications.

Manage a Critical Incident

Athletic Director's Dilemma

You are the athletic director at a large private university with a highly comprehensive, highly competitive intercollegiate athletics program. Every year the football team is ranked in the top 25 and is always in the hunt for an NCAA Division I national championship. The football team captain at your university has just been in your office. He presented you with a petition signed by 70% of the players that requests permission to start the process leading to unionization. The players aren't asking to be paid, but they believe it is in their best interests to have union protection when it comes to their physical well-being, academic progress, and financial affairs. Since you are at a private university, the players are within their rights and can speak with unions such as the National College Players Association about representing them. The next step in the process will be for the players to distribute formal "union cards" for signatures. If at least 30% sign the cards, they could ask the National Labor Relations Board to endorse their request to unionize. This is a complete surprise to you.

Questions

You have to contact the university president, but you want to be well prepared. What notes will you make about on goals, critical issues, possible outcomes, and stakeholders in this situation? What will be on your list of possible recommendations? What will be your preferred course of action, and why?

Collaborate on the Team Activity

Future of Labor Unions

Question: What is the future for labor unions in America?

Instructions

1. Perform library research to identify trends in labor union membership in the United States.

2. Analyze the trends to identify industries and settings where unions are gaining and losing strength. Develop possible explanations for your findings.

3. Talk with members of labor unions—friends, family, community members—to gather their viewpoints on the benefits of unions and issues affecting the future of unions in the United States.

4. Talk with managers in different types of organizations to get their views on unions, how they work, and the advantages and disadvantages they present to management.

5. Consider examining data on labor union trends in other countries.

6. Prepare a report that uses the results of your research to answer the project question.

Analyze THE CaseStudy
COCA-COLA
Staying Focused on Talent

Go to *Management Cases for Critical Thinking* at the end of the book to find this case.

Essentials of Leadership

14

"Leadership" is one of those words that we hear and use all the time but may rarely stop to think much about. In fact, leadership is a very complicated process that demands a great deal from leaders and followers alike, and requires lots of background understanding and personal insight. This review of the research foundations of leadership and its implications for leadership development can help you build skills and reach your full leadership potential.

A glance at the shelves in your local bookstore will quickly confirm that "leadership" is one of the most popular topics in the field of management. The consensus is that leaders become great by bringing out the best in the people who follow them. As the late Grace Hopper, management expert and the first female admiral in the United States Navy, once said: "You manage things; you lead people."[1] Leadership scholar and consultant Barry Posner believes: "The present moment is the domain of managers. The future is the domain of leaders."[2] Consultant and author Tom Peters claims the leader is "rarely—possibly never?—the best performer."[3] All seem to agree that leaders thrive through and from the successes of others.

Although the leadership message seems clear, the task of leading isn't easy. Managers and team leaders often face daunting responsibilities. Resources can be scarce and performance expectations high. Time frames for getting things accomplished can be short, while problems to be resolved are complex, ambiguous, and multidimensional.[4] It takes high self-awareness and hard work to be a great leader. There are many challenges to be mastered on the pathways toward leadership success at work, in our communities, and at home with families and loved ones. This chapter offers an opportunity to find out more about the leader who resides in you.

The Nature of Leadership

TAKEAWAY 1   What is the nature of leadership?

LEARN MORE | Leadership and power • Leadership and vision • Leadership and service
ABOUT | Leadership and followership

Leadership is the process of inspiring others to work hard to accomplish important tasks.

It helps to think of **leadership** as the process of inspiring others to work hard to accomplish important tasks.[5] As shown in Figure 14.1, it also is one of the four functions that constitute the management process. *Planning* sets the direction and objectives; *organizing* brings together resources to turn plans into action; *leading* builds the commitments and enthusiasm for people to apply their talents to help accomplish plans; and *controlling* makes sure plans turn out right.

Leadership and Power

Leadership success begins with the ways we use power to influence the behavior of other people. Harvard professor Rosabeth Moss Kanter once called *power* "America's last great dirty word."[6] She was concerned that too many people, including managers, are uncomfortable with the concept of power. They don't realize how critical it is for leadership.

Power is the ability to get others to do something you want done or to make things happen the way you want.

Power is the ability to get others to do something you want done, or to make things happen the way you want. The "positive" face of power is that it is the foundation of effective leadership. This means using power not with the desire to influence others for the sake of personal satisfaction, but for the good of the group or organization as a whole.[7]

Theoretically, anyone in a managerial position—team leader, department head, supervisor—has power, but how well it is used varies from person to person. Leaders gain power both from the position they hold and from their personal qualities.[8] You can remember this as an equation: Managerial Power = Position Power + Personal Power. The three bases of position power are reward power, coercive power, and legitimate power; three important bases of personal power are expertise, information and networking, and referent power.

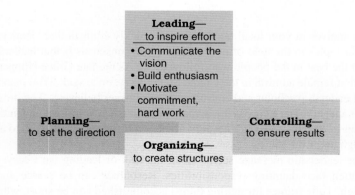

FIGURE 14.1
Leading viewed in relationship to the other management functions.

Position Power

When it comes to the position of being a manager, **reward power** is the ability to influence through rewards. It is the capacity to offer something of value—a positive outcome—as a way to influence others' behavior. This involves use of incentives such as pay raises, bonuses, promotions, special assignments, and verbal or written compliments. In mobilizing reward power, a manager says, in effect: "If you do what I ask, I'll reward you." As you might expect, this approach works as long as people want the reward and the manager/leader makes it continuously available. But take the value of the reward or the reward itself away, and the power is quickly lost.

Coercive power is the ability to achieve influence through punishment. It is the capacity to punish or withhold positive outcomes to influence others' behavior. A manager may attempt to coerce by threatening with verbal reprimands, pay penalties, and even termination. In mobilizing coercive power, a manager says, in effect: "If you don't do what I want, I'll punish you." How would you feel if threatened in these ways? If you're like most people, you'll resent both the threat and the person making it. You might do what you're told or at least go through the motions. But, you're unlikely to continue once the threat is gone.

Legitimate power is the ability to influence through authority. It is the right to exercise control by virtue of organizational position or status. In mobilizing legitimate power, a manager says, in effect: "I am the boss; therefore, you need to do what I ask." When your instructor assigns homework, exams, and team projects, most often you do what the instructor requested. Why? You do it because the requests seem legitimate in the context of the course. But if the instructor moves outside of the boundaries of the course, such as telling you to attend a campus sports event, the legitimacy is lost and you are much less likely to comply.

Power of the POSITION: *Based on things managers can offer to others.*
Rewards: "If you do what I ask, I'll give you a reward."
Coercion: "If you don't do what I ask, I'll punish you."
Legitimacy: "Because I am the boss; you *must* do as I ask."

Reward power is the capacity to offer something of value as a means of influencing other people.

Coercive power is the capacity to punish or withhold positive outcomes as a means of influencing other people.

Legitimate power is the capacity to influence others by virtue of formal authority, or the rights of office.

Personal Power

After all is said and done, position power alone isn't sufficient for any manager. It's very often the amount of personal power you can mobilize through expertise and reference that makes the difference between success and failure in a leadership situation, and even in your career.

Expert power is the ability to achieve influence through special skills, knowledge, and reputation. It is the capacity to influence others' behavior because of expertise and a high-performance reputation. When a manager uses expert power, the implied message is one of credibility: "You should do what I want because of what I know and what I have accomplished." This expertise is part of our **human capital**, which is the ability to get things done based on what we know and can do. It can be earned from credentials, experience, and visible performance achievements. But, it has to be maintained by protecting credibility, not overstepping boundaries or pretending to expertise that isn't really there. Although some people, such as medical doctors and attorneys, are granted at least temporary expertise due to credentials, they can quickly lose it through mistakes and bad behavior. Most of us acquire expertise one step at a time. Gaining it, in fact, may be among of your biggest early career challenges.

Information and networking power is the ability to achieve influence through access to information and contacts with other people.[9] It is the capacity to influence others due to centrality in information flows and social networks, and as a result of being trusted as a credible information source and reliable networking partner. When a manager uses information and networking power, the implied message is: "I have access to information and people, I can get things done." This power is linked to the informal structures and social networks—both interpersonal and media driven—that give life to day-to-day organizational dynamics. It is part of what is called **social capital**, the ability to get things done based on who you know.

Expert power is the capacity to influence others' because of specialized knowledge.

Human capital is the ability to get things done based on what we know and can do.

Information and networking power is the ability to influence others through access to information and contacts with other people.

Social capital is the ability to get things done because of who you know.

Power of the PERSON:
Based on how managers are viewed by others.

Expertise—as a source of special knowledge and information.

Reference—as a person with whom others like to identify.

Referent power is the capacity to influence other people because of their desire to identify personally with you.

Vision is a clear sense of the future.

Visionary leadership brings to the situation a clear sense of the future and an understanding of how to get there.

Servant leadership is follower-centered and committed to helping others in their work.

Empowerment enables others to gain and use decision-making power.

Referent power is the ability to achieve influence through identification. It is the capacity to influence others' behavior because of their admiration and their desire for positive identification with you. Referent power derives from charisma or interpersonal attractiveness. When a manager uses referent power, the implied message is: "You should do what I want in order to maintain a positive, self-defined relationship with me." It's helpful to view referent power as something that can be developed and maintained through good interpersonal relationships that encourage others' admiration and respect. It is a lot easier to get others to do what you want when they like you than when they don't.

Leadership and Vision

"Great leaders," it is said, "get extraordinary things done in organizations by inspiring and motivating others toward a common purpose."[10] Their power is enhanced by their ability to communicate a compelling **vision**—a hoped-for future that if achieved will improve on the present state of affairs. But simply talking up a vision isn't enough. Truly exceptional leaders excel at transforming their vision into accomplishments.

The term **visionary leadership** describes the behaviors of leaders who offer a clear and compelling sense of the future, as well as an understanding of the actions needed to get there successfully.[11] This means having a clear vision, communicating the vision, and getting people motivated and inspired to pursue the vision in their daily work. Think of it this way. Visionary leadership gives meaning to people's work; it makes what they do seem worthwhile and valuable. Noted educational leader Lorraine Monroe says: "The job of a good leader is to articulate a vision that others are inspired to follow."[12] Her views match those of the late John Wooden, member of the college basketball hall of fame and coach of 10 NCAA Division I men's national championship teams at UCLA. Wooden once said: "Effective leadership means having a lot of people working toward a common goal." If you can achieve that with no one caring who gets the credit, you're going to accomplish a lot.[13]

Leadership and Service

Institutions function better when the idea, the dream, is to the fore, and the person, the leader, is seen as servant to the dream.
　　　　　—Robert Greenleaf of the Greenleaf Center for Servant Leadership[14]

The real leader is a servant of the people she leads. A really great boss is not afraid to hire smart people. You want people who are smart about things you are not smart about.
　　　　　—Lorraine Monroe of the Monroe Leadership Institute[15]

When thinking about leadership, power, and vision, it is critical to remember personal integrity as described in the chapter opener. According to Peter Drucker, the concept of "service" is central to integrity, and leaders who have integrity act as "servants of the organization."[16] More and more today you'll hear conversations about **servant leadership** that is based on serving others and helping them fully use their talents so that organizations benefit society.[17] Ask this question: Who is most, the leader or the followers? For those who believe in servant leadership the correct answer clear—the followers. A servant leader is "other-centered" and not "self-centered."

When servant leaders shift the focus away from themselves and toward others, what happens? The answer is **empowerment**. This is the process of allowing others to exercise power and achieve organizational influence. Servant leaders realize that power is not a "zero-sum" quantity. They reject the idea that in order for someone to gain power, another has to give it up.[18] They empower others by

wisdom > LEARN FROM ROLE MODELS

> *"The job of the leader is to uplift her people . . . as individuals of infinite worth. . . ."*

Educator Turns Leadership Vision into Inspiration

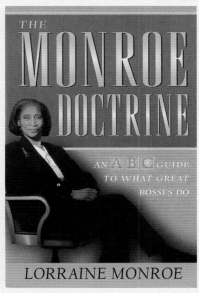

Dr. Lorraine Monroe's career in the New York City public schools began as a teacher. She went on to serve as assistant principal, principal, and vice-chancellor for curriculum and instruction. She then founded the Frederick Douglass Academy, a public school in Harlem, where she grew up. Like its namesake, an escaped slave who later became a prominent abolitionist and civil rights leader, the school became highly respected for educational excellence.

Through her experiences, Monroe formed a set of beliefs centered on a leader being vision-driven and follower-centered. They are summarized in what is called the "Monroe Doctrine." It begins with this advice: The job of the leader is to uplift her people—not just as members of and contributors to the organization, but as individuals of infinite worth in their own right. "We can reform society," she says, "only if every place we live—every school, workplace, church, and family—becomes a site of reform."

Monroe believes leaders must always start at the "heart of the matter" and that "the job of a good leader is to articulate a vision that others are inspired to follow." She also believes in ensuring that all workers know they are valued, that their advice is welcome, and that workers and managers should always try to help and support one another. "I have never undertaken any project," she says, "without first imagining on paper what it would ultimately look like. . . . All the doers who would be responsible for carrying out my imaginings have to be informed and let in on the dream."

FIND THE INSPIRATION

Is visionary leadership something that works only at the very top of organizations? Should the leader of a work team also have a vision? What about this notion that leaders should be follower-centered? Does that mean that followers get to determine what gets done and when? What are the lessons of the Monroe Doctrine for everyday leaders at all levels in organizations of all types and sizes? How could this doctrine serve you?

---

providing them with the information, responsibility, authority, and trust to make decisions and act independently. They also expect that people who are empowered will work hard so that the organization is better equipped to pursue its cause or mission.

Leadership and Followership

The discussion of servant leadership and empowerment is a nice transition into the subject of "followership." What roles do followers play in leadership? How do followers influence leadership success and failure? Do follower perceptions and expectations of effective leadership vary in discoverable ways? These are but a few of the questions that leaders and followers alike should be asking in teams and organizations.

Followership is the act of joining with a leader to accomplish tasks and goals.

If leadership is the act of inspiration, **followership** is the act of joining with a leader to accomplish tasks and goals.[19] The work of scholar Mary Uhl-Bien and others strongly suggests that the emphasis in this definition should be on the word "joining." They view leadership as something that is "co-produced" by leaders and followers, rather than being a singular result of a leader's actions alone. They criticize tendencies toward the *romance of leadership* and the *subordination of followership*, which together create situations where leaders get credit for accomplishments and the contributions of followers get overlooked.[20]

In research on followership, the perceptions of both leaders and followers are of interest. Some followers, for example, tend to see themselves as passive players whose job it is to obey and take little responsibility for shared leadership. They are comfortable being told what to do and may get stressed and uncomfortable with a leader who emphasizes empowerment and independence. Other followers may see themselves as proactive partners with responsibility to make real leadership contributions. They are likely to be unhappy in a top-down leadership climate, but act energized and motivated in a shared leadership climate. From an empowering leader's perspective, followers tend to get high ratings for showing initiative, enthusiasm, and loyalty, and get low ratings for showing incompetence and conformity.[21]

Learning Check 1

TAKEAWAYQUESTION **1 What is the nature of leadership?**

BE SURE YOU CAN • define *power* • illustrate three types of position power and discuss how managers use each • illustrate three types of personal power and discuss how managers use each • define *vision* • explain the concept of visionary leadership • explain the notion and benefits of servant leadership • define *empowerment* and *followership* • explain the *romance of leadership* and *subordination of followership*

Leadership Traits and Behaviors

TAKEAWAY 2   What are the important leadership traits and behaviors?

LEARN MORE ABOUT | Leadership traits • Leadership behaviors • Classic leadership styles

Societies have recognized for centuries that while some people do really well as leaders, others do not. The question still debated is: "Why?" Historically, the answer has been sought by studying leader traits, behaviors, and situational contingencies. Although they differ in how leadership effectiveness is explained, each approach still offers useful insights into leadership development.

Leadership Traits

Question—*What personal traits and characteristics are associated with leadership success?*

An early direction in leadership research involved the search for universal traits or distinguishing personal characteristics that separate effective from ineffective leaders.[22] Sometimes called the "great person theory," the results from many years of research in this direction can be summarized as follows:

Physical characteristics such as a person's height, weight, and physique make no difference in determining leadership success. On the other hand, certain personal traits are common among the best leaders. A study of more than 3,400 managers, for example, revealed that followers tend to consistently admire leaders who are honest, competent, forward looking, inspiring, and credible.[23]

A comprehensive review by Shelley Kirkpatrick and Edwin Locke identifies these personal traits of many successful leaders:[24]

- *Drive*—Successful leaders have high energy, display initiative, and are tenacious.

- *Self-confidence*—Successful leaders trust themselves and have confidence in their abilities.

- *Creativity*—Successful leaders are creative and original in their thinking.

- *Cognitive ability*—Successful leaders have the intelligence to integrate and interpret information.

- *Job-relevant knowledge*—Successful leaders know their industry and its technical foundations.

- *Motivation*—Successful leaders enjoy influencing others to achieve shared goals.

- *Flexibility*—Successful leaders adapt to fit the needs of followers and the demands of situations.

- *Honesty and integrity*—Successful leaders are trustworthy, honest, predictable, and dependable.

◀ Personal leadership traits

Leadership Behaviors

Question—*How is leadership success affected by the ways leaders behave when engaging with followers?*

After the early trait studies, researchers turned their attention to the issue of how leaders behave when dealing with followers.[25] If the most effective behaviors could be identified, they reasoned, then it would be possible to train leaders to become skilled at using these behaviors.

A stream of research that began in the 1940s, spearheaded by studies at Ohio State University and the University of Michigan, focused attention on two dimensions of leadership behavior: (1) concern for the task to be accomplished, and (2) concern for the people doing the work. The Ohio State studies used the terms *initiating structure* and *consideration* for the respective dimensions; the University of Michigan studies called them *production-centered* and *employee-centered*.[26] Regardless of the terminology used, the characteristics of each dimension of leadership behavior were quite clear.

- *A leader high in concern for task*—plans and defines the work to be done, assigns task responsibilities, sets clear work standards, urges task completion, and monitors performance results.

- *A leader high in concern for people*—acts with warmth and supportiveness toward followers, maintains good social relations with them, respects their feelings, is sensitive to their needs, and shows trust in them.

The results of leader behavior research at first suggested that followers of people-oriented leaders would be the most productive and satisfied.[27] However, researchers eventually moved toward the high-high position that effective leaders were high in concerns for both people and task.[28] This type of leader focuses on task accomplishments while also sharing decisions with team members, empowering them, encouraging participation, and supporting teamwork.

Classic Leadership Styles

Question—*How do different leadership styles combine concerns for task and concerns for people?*

Work in the leader behavior tradition made it easy to talk about different **leadership styles**—the recurring patterns of behaviors exhibited by leaders. When people talk about the leaders with whom they work, even today, their vocabulary often describes classic styles of leadership shown in Figure 14.2.[29] These styles represent different combinations of concerns for task and concerns for people in the leadership experience.

Leadership style is a recurring pattern of behaviors exhibited by a leader.

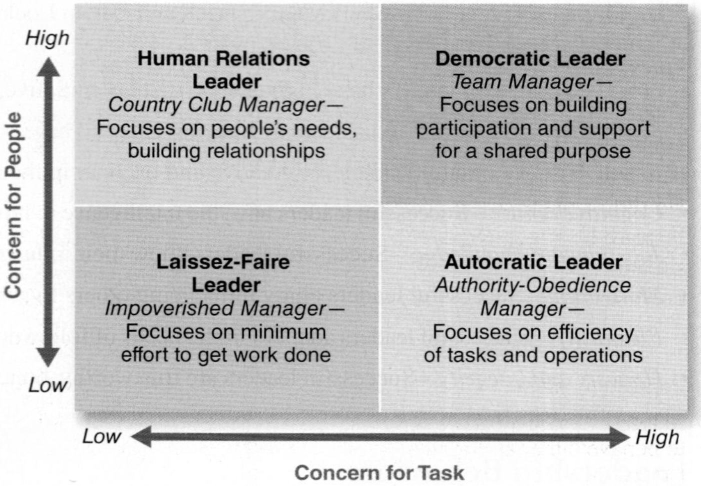

FIGURE 14.2
Classic leadership styles combining concerns for task and concerns for people.

An **autocratic** leader acts in a command-and-control fashion.

A **human relations** leader emphasizes people over task.

A **laissez-faire** leader has a "do the best you can and don't bother me" attitude.

A **democratic** leader emphasizes both tasks and people.

A leader identified with an **autocratic style** emphasizes task over people, retains authority and information, and acts in a unilateral, command-and-control fashion. A leader with a **human relations style** does just the opposite and emphasizes people over task. A leader with a **laissez-faire style** shows little concern for the task, lets the group make decisions, and acts with a "do the best you can and don't bother me" attitude. A leader with a **democratic style**, the "high-high" team manager, is committed to both task and people. This leader tries to get things done while sharing information, encouraging participation in decision making, and otherwise helping others develop their skills and capabilities.

Learning Check 2

TAKEAWAYQUESTION **2 What are the important leadership traits and behaviors?**

BE SURE YOU CAN • contrast the trait and leader-behavior approaches to leadership research • identify five personal traits of successful leaders • illustrate leader behaviors consistent with a high concern for task • illustrate leader behaviors consistent with a high concern for people • describe behaviors associated with four classic leadership styles

Contingency Approaches to Leadership

TAKEAWAY 3 What are the contingency approaches to leadership?

LEARN MORE ABOUT | Fiedler's contingency model • Hersey-Blanchard situational leadership model
House's path–goal leadership theory • Leader-member exchange theory
Leader-participation model

Over time, scholars became increasingly uncomfortable with both the trait and leader behavior approaches. They concluded that no one set of traits or behaviors or styles works best all of the time. In response, they developed a number of contingency approaches to explain the conditions for leadership success in different situations.

Fiedler's Contingency Model

Question—*Which leadership styles work best in the different types of situations that leaders face?*

One of the first contingency leadership models was developed by Fred Fiedler. He proposed that good leadership depends on a match or fit between a person's leadership style and situational demands.[30] Fiedler viewed leadership style as part of personality and therefore as difficult to change. He didn't place much hope in trying to change styles and train leaders to behave in new ways. Instead, he suggested that the key to success was to put existing leadership styles to work in the situations where they fit best. In order to achieve these style–situation matches, leaders have to understand both their personal styles and the situational strengths and weaknesses of those styles.[31]

Understanding Leadership Styles and Situations

Leadership style in Fiedler's model is measured using the **least-preferred co-worker scale**, known as the LPC scale, which can be found as the end-of-chapter self-assessment. It describes tendencies to behave either as a *task-motivated leader* (low LPC score) or *relationship-motivated leader* (high LPC score).

The **least-preferred co-worker scale**, LPC, is used in Fiedler's contingency model to measure leadership style.

Leadership situations in Fiedler's model are assessed according to the amount of control they offer the leader. Three contingency variables measure situational control. The *quality of leader–member relations* (good or poor) measures the degree to which the group supports the leader. The degree of *task structure* (high or low) measures the extent to which task goals, procedures, and guidelines are clearly spelled out. The amount of *position power* (strong or weak) measures the degree to which the position gives the leader power to reward and punish subordinates.

Figure 14.3 shows eight leadership situations that result from different combinations of these contingency variables. They range from the most favorable situation of high control (good leader–member relations, high task structure, strong in position power) to the least favorable situation of low control (poor leader–member relations, low task structure, weak in position power).

Matching Leadership Style and Situation

Fiedler's research showed that neither the task-oriented nor the relationship-oriented leadership style was effective all the time. Instead, as summarized here and shown in Figure 14.3, each style seemed to work best when used in the right situation.

- *Task-motivated style*—This leader will be most successful in either very favorable high-control situations or very unfavorable low-control situations.

- *Relationship-motivated style*—This leader will be most successful in situations of moderate control.

FIGURE 14.3
Predictions on style–situation fit from Fiedler's contingency leadership model.

Consider some examples. Assume you are the leader of a team of market researchers. The researchers seem highly supportive of you, and their job is clearly defined regarding what needs to be done. You have the authority to evaluate their performance and to make pay and promotion recommendations. This is a high-control situation consisting of good leader–member relations, high task structure, and high position power. Figure 14.3 shows that a task-motivated leader would be most effective in this situation.

Suppose now that you are the faculty chairperson of a committee asked to improve student–faculty relationships in a university. Although the goal is clear, no one can say for sure how to accomplish it, and task structure is low. Because the committee is voluntary and members are free to quit any time, the chairperson has little position power. Because student members thought that the chair should be a student rather than a faculty member, leader–member relations are mixed. According to the figure, this low-control situation also calls for a task-motivated leader.

Finally, assume that you are the new head of a fashion section in a large department store. Because you were selected over one of the popular sales associates you now supervise, leader–member relations are poor. Task structure is high because the associate's job is well defined. Your position power is low because associates work under a seniority system and fixed wage schedule. From Figure 14.3, you can see that Fiedler identifies a relationship-motivated leader as the best fit for this moderate-control situation.

Hersey-Blanchard Situational Leadership Model

Question—*How should leaders adjust their leadership styles according to the task readiness of followers?*

In contrast to Fiedler's notion that leadership style is hard to change, the Hersey-Blanchard situational leadership model suggests that successful leaders do adjust their styles. But they do so wisely and based on the task readiness, or task maturity, of followers.[32] "Readiness," in this sense, refers to how able and willing or confident followers are performing required tasks. The four leadership styles to choose from are shown in Figure 14.4 as:

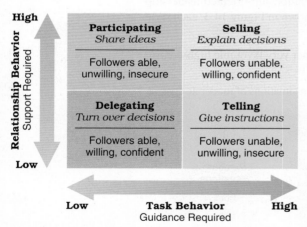

FIGURE 14.4
Leadership implications of the Hersey-Blanchard situational leadership model.

- *Delegating*—allowing the group to take responsibility for task decisions; a low-task, low-relationship style.

- *Participating*—emphasizing shared ideas and participative decisions on task directions; a low-task, high-relationship style.

- *Selling*—explaining task directions in a supportive and persuasive way; a high-task, high-relationship style.

- *Telling*—giving specific task directions and closely supervising work; a high-task, low-relationship style.

The delegating style works best in high-readiness situations with able, willing, and confident followers. The telling style works best at the other extreme of low readiness, where followers are unable and unwilling, or insecure. The participating style is recommended for low-to-moderate-readiness followers—able but unwilling, or insecure. Finally, the selling style is most effective for moderate-to-high-readiness followers—unable, but willing or confident.

Hersey and Blanchard also believed that leadership styles should be adjusted as followers change over time. If the correct styles are used in lower-readiness situations, followers will "mature" and grow in ability, willingness, and confidence. This allows leaders to become less directive and more participative as followers mature. Although the Hersey-Blanchard model is intuitively appealing, limited research has been accomplished on it to date.[33]

House's Path–Goal Leadership Theory

Question—*How can leaders use alternative leadership styles to add value in different types of situations?*

The path–goal theory advanced by Robert House seeks the right fit between leadership style and situation.[34] Unlike Fiedler, House believed that a leader can use all of the following leadership styles and actually shift back and forth among them:

- *Directive leadership*—letting followers know what is expected; giving directions on what to do and how; scheduling work to be done; maintaining definite performance standards; clarifying the leader's role in the group.

- *Supportive leadership*—doing things to make work more pleasant; treating team members as equals; being friendly and approachable; showing concern for the well-being of subordinates.

- *Achievement-oriented leadership*—setting challenging goals; expecting the highest levels of performance; emphasizing continuous performance improvement; displaying confidence in meeting high standards.

- *Participative leadership*—involving team members in decision making; consulting with them and asking for suggestions; using these suggestions when making decisions.

◄ Path-goal leadership styles

Path–Goal Contingencies

House's path–goal theory suggests that the key task of any leader is to "add value" to a situation. They do this by shifting among the four leadership styles in ways that contribute something that is missing or needs strengthening. They avoid redundancy by not trying to do things that are already taken care of. When team members are already expert and competent at their tasks, for example, it is unnecessary and even dysfunctional for the leader to tell them how to do things.

> ### Four Leadership Styles in House's Path–goal Theory
>
> 1. *Directive leader*—lets others know what is expected; gives directions, maintains standards
> 2. *Supportive leader*—makes work more pleasant; treats others as equals, acts friendly, shows concern
> 3. *Achievement-oriented leader*—sets challenging goals; expects high performance, shows confidence
> 4. *Participative leader*—involves others in decision making; asks for and uses suggestions

There is a variety of research-based guidance on how to contingently match path–goal leadership styles with situational characteristics. When job assignments are unclear, *directive leadership* helps to clarify task objectives and expected rewards. When worker self-confidence is low, *supportive leadership* can increase confidence by emphasizing individual abilities and offering needed assistance. When task challenge is insufficient in a job, *achievement-oriented leadership* helps to set goals and raise performance aspirations. When performance incentives are poor, *participative leadership* might clarify individual needs and identify appropriate rewards.[35]

Substitutes for Leadership

Path–goal theory contributed to the recognition of what we call **substitutes for leadership**.[36] These are aspects of the work setting and the people involved that reduce the need for active

Substitutes for leadership are factors in the work setting that direct work efforts without the involvement of a leader.

leader involvement. In effect, substitutes provide leadership from within the situation and thus make leadership from the outside unnecessary.

Possible substitutes for leadership include follower characteristics such as ability, experience, and independence; task characteristics such as the presence or absence of routine and the availability of feedback; and organizational characteristics such as clarity of plans and formalization of rules and procedures. When these substitutes for leadership are present, managers are advised in true path–goal fashion to avoid duplicating them. Instead, they should concentrate on making other and more important leadership contributions.

Leader–Member Exchange Theory

Question—*How do in-group and out-group dynamics influence leader–follower relationships?*

One of the things you may have noticed is the tendency of leaders to develop "special" relationships with some team members, even to the point where not everyone is always treated in the same way. This notion is central to leader–member exchange theory, or LMX theory as it is often called.[37]

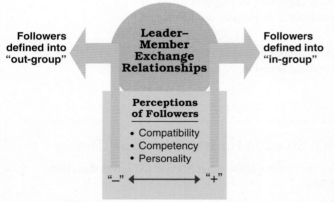

FIGURE 14.5
Elements of leader–member exchange (LMX) theory.

Described in Figure 14.5, LMX theory recognizes that not everyone is treated the same by leaders. People fall into "in-groups" and "out-groups," and the group you are in can make a big difference in your experience with the leader.[38] In-group members enjoy special and trusted high-exchange relationships with leaders and often get special rewards, assignments, privileges, and access to information. For a follower in the leader's in-group, it's motivating and satisfying to receive such favorable treatment. Out-group members have a low-quality exchange relationship and may be marginalized, ignored, and receive fewer benefits than in-group members with higher-quality exchange relationships. For out-group members, it can be frustrating to receive fewer rewards, less information, and little or no special attention.

Just look around. You're likely to see examples of this in classroom situations between instructors and certain students, and in work teams between leaders and certain team members. The notion of leader in-groups and out-groups seems to make sense and corresponds to working realities experienced by many people. Interestingly, research shows that members of leaders' in-groups get more positive performance evaluations and report higher levels of job satisfaction. They also are more loyal followers and are less prone to turnover than are out-group members.[39]

Leader-Participation Model

Question—*How should leaders make decisions in different types of problem situations?*

The Vroom-Jago leader-participation model links leadership success with the use of decision-making methods that best fit problem situations.[40] An **authority decision** is made by the leader and then communicated to the team. A **consultative decision** is made by the leader after gathering information from team members either individually or as a group. A **group or team decision** is made by the team either on its own or with the leader's participation as a contributing member.[41]

Figure 14.6 shows that a leader's choice among alternative decision-making methods is governed by three factors: (1) *Decision quality*—based on who has the information needed for problem

An **authority decision** is made by the leader and then communicated to the group.

A **consultative decision** is made by a leader after receiving information, advice, or opinions from group members.

A **group or team decision** is made by team members.

solving; (2) *Decision acceptance*—based on the importance of follower acceptance to the decision's eventual implementation; and (3) *Decision time*—based on the time available to make and implement the decision. Each decision method has advantages and disadvantages with respect to these factors. As a consequence, effective leaders continually shift among the methods as they deal with daily problems and opportunities.

Authority decisions work best when leaders have the expertise needed to solve problems and are confident acting alone. They also work best when followers are likely to accept and implement leader's decisions, and when there is little or no time available for group discussion. Consultative and group decisions work best when the leader lacks the expertise or information needed to solve a problem. They also work best when the problem is unclear, follower acceptance is uncertain but necessary for implementation, and adequate time is available.

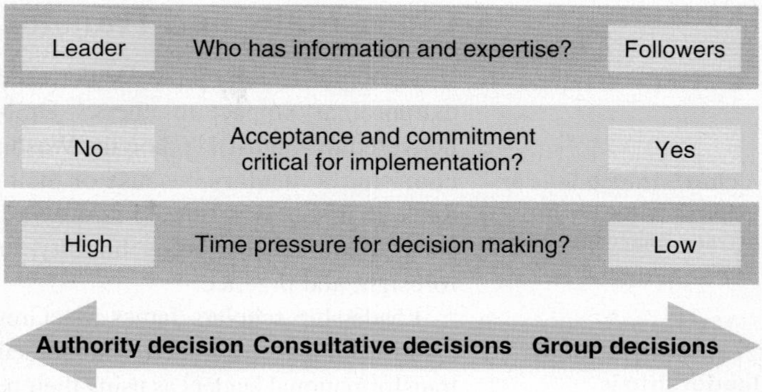

Vroom and Jago believed that consultative and group decisions offer special benefits.[42] Participation helps improve decision quality by bringing more information to bear on the problem. It helps improve decision acceptance as participants gain understanding and commitment. It also contributes to leadership development by allowing others to gain experience in the problem-solving process. Of course, the lost efficiency of consultative and group decisions is a potential negative. Participative decision making is time consuming and leaders don't always have time available to involve group members in the process. When problems must be resolved immediately, an authority decision may be the only option.[43]

Leader	Who has information and expertise?	Followers
No	Acceptance and commitment critical for implementation?	Yes
High	Time pressure for decision making?	Low

←————— **Authority decision Consultative decisions Group decisions** —————→

FIGURE 14.6
Leadership implications of Vroom-Jago leader-participation model.

Learning Check 3

TAKEAWAYQUESTION 3 What are the contingency approaches to leadership?

BE SURE YOU CAN • contrast the leader-behavior and contingency leadership approaches • explain Fiedler's contingency model • identify the four leadership styles in the Hersey-Blanchard situational model • explain House's path–goal theory • define *substitutes for leadership* • explain LMX theory • contrast the authority, consultative, and group decisions in the Vroom-Jago model

Personal Leadership Development

TAKEAWAY 4   What are the challenges of personal leadership development?

LEARN MORE ABOUT | Charismatic and transformational leadership
Emotional intelligence and leadership • Gender and leadership
Moral leadership • Drucker's "good old-fashioned" leadership

There is no one answer to the question of what makes a particular person—say you—an effective leader. And, there is always room to grow. Personal leadership development is best viewed as a goal that you are more likely to reach if you know key leadership concepts and scholarly models. But, success in personal leadership development also requires lots of self-awareness and a commitment to continuous learning as you move from one practical experience to the next.

Charismatic and Transformational Leadership

It is popular to talk about "superleaders," people whose vision and strong personality have an extraordinary impact on others.[44] Dr. Martin Luther King, Jr.'s famous "I Have a Dream" speech delivered in August 1963 on the Washington Mall is a good example. Some call people like King **charismatic leaders** because of their ability to inspire others in exceptional ways. We used to think charisma was limited to only a few lucky people. It's now considered one of several personal qualities—including honesty, credibility, and competence—that can be developed with foresight and practice.

Leadership scholars James MacGregor Burns and Bernard Bass link charismatic qualities like enthusiasm and inspiration with something called **transformational leadership**.[45] They describe transformational leaders as using their personalities, character, and insight to inspire followers. These leaders get others so excited about their jobs and organizational goals that these followers strive for extraordinary performance accomplishments. Indeed, the easiest way to spot a truly transformational leader is through his or her followers. They are likely to be enthusiastic about the leader, loyal, devoted to his or her ideas, and willing to work exceptionally hard to achieve the leader's vision.

The pathway to transformational leadership starts with the willingness to bring real emotion to the leader–follower relationship. It involves acting with integrity and living up to the trust of others. It requires both having a compelling vision of the future and the ability to communicate

> A **charismatic leader** inspires followers in extraordinary ways.

> **Transformational leadership** is inspirational and arouses extraordinary effort and performance.

insight > LEARN ABOUT YOURSELF

> *Our personal character gets revealed by how we treat those with no power.*

There's No Substitute for Integrity

Whether you call it ethical leadership or moral leadership, the lesson is the same: Respect flows toward leaders who behave with **integrity**. If you have integrity, you'll be honest, credible, and consistent in all that you do. This seems obvious. "This is what we have been taught since we were kids," you might say.

So, why are there so many well-publicized examples of leaders who act without integrity? Where, so to speak, does integrity go when some people find themselves in positions of leadership? CEO coach Kenny Moore says that our personal character gets "revealed by how we treat those with no power." Look closely at how people in leadership positions treat everyday workers—servers, technicians, custodians, and clerks, for example. Moore says that the ways we deal with people who are powerless "brings out our real dispositions."

The "integrity line" in the figure marks the difference between where we should and should not be. Below the line are leaders who lie, blame others for personal mistakes, want others to fail, and take credit for others' ideas. They're conceited, and they're also selfish. Above the integrity line are honest, consistent, humble, and selfless leaders. Some call such leaders "servants" of the organization and its members.

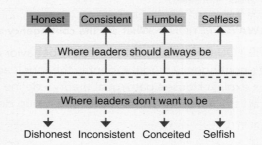

Leadership and the Integrity Line

| Honest | Consistent | Humble | Selfless |

Where leaders should always be

Where leaders don't want to be

Dishonest   Inconsistent   Conceited   Selfish

GET TO KNOW YOURSELF BETTER

Why is it that in the news and in everyday experience we so often end up wondering where leadership integrity has gone? Ask: How often have I worked for someone who behaved below the "integrity line"? How did I feel about it, and what did I do? Write a set of notes on your behavior in situations where your own leadership integrity could be questioned. What are some of the lessons available from this experience? Who are your leadership exemplars, the ones you most admire and would like to emulate? At this point in your life, who is the real leader in you?

that vision in ways that influence others to work hard together to achieve it. Transformational leaders excel in part because of their strong sense of high aspiration, confidence, and contagious enthusiasm.

Emotional Intelligence and Leadership

The role of personality in transformational leadership relates to another area of inquiry in leadership development—**emotional intelligence**. Popularized by the work of Daniel Goleman, emotional intelligence, or EI for short, is the ability to understand emotions in yourself and others and use this understanding to handle social relationships effectively.[46] "Great leaders move us," say Goleman and his colleagues. "Great leadership works through emotions."[47]

Emotional intelligence is the ability to manage our emotions in social relationships.

Emotional intelligence shows up in research as an important influence on leadership success, particularly in more senior management positions. In Goleman's words: "the higher the rank of the person considered to be a star performer, the more emotional intelligence capabilities showed up as the reason for his or her effectiveness."[48] This is a pretty strong endorsement for Goleman's position that not only is EI a key leadership asset; it is one that we can each develop.

Consider the five emotional intelligence competencies shown in the figure.[49] A leader strong in emotional intelligence possesses *self-awareness*. This is the ability to understand one's own moods and emotions, and to understand their impact on one's own work and on others' work. Emotionally intelligent leaders are good at *self-management*, or self-regulation. This is the ability to think before acting and to control otherwise disruptive impulses. Emotional intelligence in leadership involves *motivation and persistence* in being willing to work hard for reasons other than money and status. Leaders who are high in emotional intelligence display *social awareness*, or empathy. They have the ability to understand the emotions of others and to use this understanding to relate to them more effectively. A leader high in emotional intelligence is good at *relationship management*. This is the ability to establish rapport with others and to build social capital through relationships and informal social networks.

Gender and Leadership

When Sara Levinson was president of NFL Properties, Inc., she asked the all-male members of her NFL management team this question: "Is my leadership style different from a man's?" "Yes," they replied, and even suggested that the very fact that she was asking the question was evidence of the difference. They said her leadership style emphasized communication as well as gathering ideas and opinions from others. When Levinson probed further by asking: "Is this a distinctly 'female' trait?", the men said they thought it was.[50]

Are there gender differences in leadership? In pondering this question, three background points deserve highlighting. First, social science research largely supports the **gender similarities hypothesis**. That is, males and females are very similar to one another in terms of psychological properties.[51] Second, research leaves no doubt that both women and men can be equally effective as leaders.[52] Third, research does show that men and women are sometimes perceived as using different styles, and perhaps arriving at leadership success from different angles.[53]

The **gender similarities hypothesis** holds that males and females have similar psychological properties.

When men and women are perceived differently as leaders, the perceptions tend to fit traditional stereotypes.[54] Men may be expected to act as "take-charge" leaders who are task-oriented, directive, and assertive while trying to get things done in traditional command-and-control ways. Women may be expected to act as "take-care" leaders who behave in supportive

Research Brief

Charismatic Leaders Display Positive Emotions That Followers Find Contagious

When leaders show positive emotions, the effect on followers is positive, creating positive moods and also creating tendencies toward positive leader ratings and feelings of attraction to the leader. These are the major conclusions from four research studies conducted by Joyce E. Bono and Remus Ilies, and reported in *Leadership Quarterly*.

Bono and Ilies set out to examine how charismatic leaders "use emotion to influence followers." They advanced hypotheses as indicated in the figure. They expected to find that charismatic leaders display positive emotions, that positive leader emotions create positive follower moods, and that positive follower moods generate both positive ratings of the leader and attraction toward the leader. These hypotheses were examined in a series of four empirical studies.

The researchers concluded that positive emotions are an important aspect of charismatic leadership. They found that leaders who rated high in charisma chose words with more positive emotional content for vision statements and speeches. They also found that the positive emotions of leaders were transferred into positive moods among followers; that is, the positive leader moods were contagious. They also found that followers with positive moods had more positive perceptions of leader effectiveness.

These studies, by Bono and Ilies, focused only on positive leader emotions. This leaves open the questions of how leaders

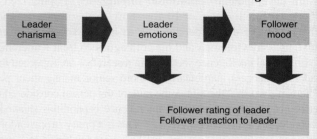

Leader Charisma and Emotional Contagion

Leader charisma → Leader emotions → Follower mood

Follower rating of leader
Follower attraction to leader

use negative emotions and how these emotions affect followers. Also, the researchers suggest we need to know more about the impact of leader moods on follower performance and creativity.

YOU BE THE RESEARCHER

Is this logic of emotional contagion insightful? What are the implications? Should we conclude that a leader can never allow herself or himself to have a "bad" day, and can never communicate, verbally or nonverbally, anything other than positive emotional messages? Is it realistic for managers to live up to these expectations to always be positive? Could you design a research study to examine these questions?

In the leadership double bind, women get criticized for displaying stereotypical male leadership characteristics and also for displaying stereotypical female leadership characteristics.

Interactive leaders are strong communicators and act in democratic and participative ways with followers.

and nurturing ways. These stereotyped expectations can create what has been called a **leadership double bind** for women. In this situation, a female leader gets criticized when displaying stereotypical male leadership characteristics and also gets criticized for showing female ones. In other words, the female leader can't win when either breaking or conforming to stereotyped expectations.[55]

Studies also report favorable perceptions of female leaders. Harvard scholar Rosabeth Moss Kanter says: "Women get high ratings on exactly those skills required to succeed in the global information age, where teamwork and partnering are so important."[56] For example, female leaders have been rated by peers, subordinates, and supervisors as more participative than male leaders and as strong on motivating others, emotional intelligence, persuading, fostering communication, listening to others, mentoring, and supporting high-quality work.[57] In research using 360-degree assessments, female managers were rated more highly than male managers in all but one area of leadership—visioning. The possible explanation was that because women are less directive as leaders, they aren't perceived as visionaries.[58]

The pattern of positive leader behaviors sometimes attributed to women is called **interactive leadership**.[59] Interactive leaders are democratic, participative, connecting, and inclusive. They approach problems and decisions through collaboration and teamwork, show respect for others, and use connections to share power and information. They build good interpersonal relations through communication and involvement and have the confidence to seek consensus.[60] They also tend to get things done more through personal power and good interpersonal relationships than through command-and-control use of position power.[61]

One of the risks in any discussion of gender and leadership is falling prey to stereotypes that place individual men and women into leadership boxes in which they don't necessarily belong.[62] Perhaps it would be most appropriate to set gender issues aside, accept the gender similarities hypothesis, and focus instead on the notion of interactive leadership. The likelihood is that an interactive leader is likely to be a very good fit with the needs of today's organizations and their members. There also is no reason why men and women can't adopt this style equally well.[63]

Moral Leadership

As highlighted in the chapter opener on integrity, society expects organizations to be run with **moral leadership**. This is leadership with ethical standards that clearly meet the test of being "good" and "correct."[64] Strength in moral leadership begins with personal integrity, a concept fundamental to the notion of transformational leadership. People who lead with **integrity** act in an honest, credible, and consistent way to put their values into action. A leader with integrity earns the trust of followers. When followers believe leaders are trustworthy, they try to behave in ways that live up to their leader's expectations.

If moral leadership is the goal, why don't we see more of it? Are you surprised by a *Business Week* survey that found just 14% of top executives at large U.S. firms rated "having strong ethical values" as a top leadership characteristic?[65] How about a Harris poll that found only 37% of U.S. adults in a survey described their top managers as acting with "integrity and morality"?[66] One of the risks we face in living up to the expectations of moral leadership is **moral overconfidence**, falling prey to an overly positive view of one's strength of character.[67] Leaders with moral overconfidence may act unethically without realizing it or while using inappropriate rationalizations to justify their behavior. "I'm a good person, so I can't be wrong," might just be a signal of a leader's moral overconfidence.[68]

The concept of servant leadership fits with the concept of a moral leader. So, too, does the notion of **authentic leadership**. Fred Luthans and Bruce Avolio describe an authentic leader as one with a high level of self-awareness and a clear understanding of his or her personal values.[69] An authentic leader acts in ways that are consistent with those values, being honest and avoiding self-deception. Because of this approach, an authentic leader is perceived by followers as genuine, gains their respect, and develops a capacity to positively influence their behaviors.[70] The values and actions of authentic leaders create a positive ethical climate in their organizations.[71]

> **Moral leadership** is always "good" and "right" by ethical standards.

> Leaders show **integrity** by acting with honesty, credibility, and consistency in putting values into action.

> **Moral overconfidence** is an overly positive view of one's strength of character.

> **Authentic leadership** activates positive psychological states to achieve self-awareness and positive self-regulation.

Drucker's "Good Old-Fashioned" Leadership

The late and widely respected consultant Peter Drucker took a time-tested and very pragmatic view of leadership. His many books and articles remind us that leadership effectiveness must have strong foundations, something he refers to as the "good old-fashioned" hard work of a successful leader.[72]

Drucker believed that the basic building block for success as a leader is defining and establishing a sense

Peter Drucker's Straight Talk on Leadership

- Define and communicate a clear vision.
- Accept leadership as a responsibility, not a rank.
- Surround yourself with talented people.
- Don't blame others when things go wrong.
- Keep your integrity; earn the trust of others.
- Don't be clever, be consistent.

of mission. A good leader sets the goals, priorities, and standards. And, a good leader keeps them always clear and visible. As Drucker put it: "The leader's first task is to be the trumpet that sounds a clear sound."[73] Drucker also believed that leadership should be accepted as a responsibility rather than a rank. He pointed out that good leaders surround themselves with talented people, aren't afraid to develop strong and capable followers, don't blame others when things go wrong, and accept the adage that has become a hallmark of leadership—"The buck stops here."

Finally, Drucker also stressed the importance of earning and keeping others' trust. The key is the leader's personal integrity, the point on which the chapter began. Followers of good leaders trust in their leadership. They believe the leader means what he or she says, and know that his or her actions will be consistent with what is said. "Effective leadership is not based on being clever," says Drucker, "it is based primarily on being consistent."[74]

Learning Check 4

TAKEAWAYQUESTION 4 **What are the challenges of personal leadership development?**

BE SURE YOU CAN • define *transformational leadership* • explain how emotional intelligence contributes to leadership success • discuss research insights on the relationship between gender and leadership • define *interactive leadership* • discuss integrity as a foundation for moral leadership • list Drucker's essentials of good old-fashioned leadership

Management Learning Review
Get Prepared for **Quizzes and Exams**

SUMMARY

TAKEAWAYQUESTION 1

What is the nature of leadership?

- Leadership is the process of inspiring others to work hard to accomplish important tasks.
- The ability to communicate a vision—a clear sense of the future—is essential for effective leadership.
- Power is the ability to get others to do what you want them to do through leadership.
- Sources of position power include rewards, coercion, and legitimacy or formal authority; sources of personal power include expertise, referent, and information and networking power.
- Servant leadership is follower-centered and focused on empowering others and helping them to fully utilize their talents.
- Followership is the act of joining with a leader to accomplish tasks and goals.
- There is a tendency to give credit to leaders—the romance of leadership, and overlook the contributions of followers—the subordination of followership.

FOR DISCUSSION When is a leader justified in using coercive power?

TAKEAWAYQUESTION 2

What are the important leadership traits and behaviors?

- Traits that seem to have a positive impact on leadership include drive, integrity, and self-confidence.
- Research on leader behaviors has focused on alternative leadership styles based on concerns for tasks and concerns for people.
- One suggestion of leader-behavior researchers is that effective leaders are team-based and participative, showing both high task and people concerns.

FOR DISCUSSION Are any personal traits indispensable "must haves" for success in leadership?

TAKEAWAYQUESTION 3

What are the contingency approaches to leadership?

- Contingency leadership approaches point out that no one leadership style always works best; the best style is one that properly matches the demands of each unique situation.

- Fiedler's contingency model matches leadership styles with situational differences in task structure, position power, and leader–member relations.
- The Hersey-Blanchard situational model recommends using task-oriented and people-oriented behaviors, depending on the "maturity" levels of followers.
- House's path–goal theory points out that leaders add value to situations by using supportive, directive, achievement-oriented, or participative styles.
- The Vroom-Jago leader-participation model advises leaders to choose decision-making methods—individual, consultative, group—that best fit the problems to be solved.

FOR DISCUSSION What are the career development implications of Fiedler's contingency model of leadership?

TAKEAWAYQUESTION **4**

What are the challenges of personal leadership development?

- Transformational leaders use charisma and emotion to inspire others toward extraordinary efforts and performance excellence.
- Emotional intelligence—the ability to manage our relationships and ourselves effectively—is an important leadership capability.
- The interactive leadership style emphasizes communication, involvement, and interpersonal respect.
- Managers are expected to be moral leaders who communicate high ethical standards and show personal integrity in all dealings with other people.

FOR DISCUSSION Is transformational leadership always moral leadership?

SELF-TEST 14

Multiple-ChoiceQuestions

1. Someone with a clear sense of the future and the actions needed to get there is considered a _____ leader.
   (a) task-oriented
   (c) transactional
   (b) people-oriented
   (d) visionary

2. Leader power = _____ power + _____ power.
   (a) reward, punishment
   (b) reward, expert
   (c) legitimate, position
   (d) position, personal

3. A manager who says "Because I am the boss, you must do what I ask" is relying on _____ power.
   (a) reward   (b) legitimate
   (c) expert   (d) referent

4. When a leader assumes that others will do as she asks because they want to positively identify with her, she is relying on _____ power to influence their behavior.
   (a) expert
   (b) referent
   (c) legitimate
   (d) reward

5. The personal traits now considered important for managerial success include _____.
   (a) self-confidence
   (b) gender
   (c) age
   (d) height

6. In the leader-behavior approaches to leadership, someone who does a very good job of planning work, setting standards, and monitoring results would be considered a/an _____ leader.
   (a) task-oriented
   (b) control-oriented
   (c) achievement-oriented
   (d) employee-centered

7. When leader behavior researchers concluded that "high-high" was the pathway to leadership success, what were they referring to?
   (a) High initiating structure and high integrity.
   (b) High concern for task and high concern for people.
   (c) High emotional intelligence and high charisma.
   (d) High job stress and high task goals.

8. A leader whose actions indicate an attitude of "do as you want, and don't bother me" would be described as having a(n) _____ leadership style.
   (a) autocratic
   (b) country club
   (c) democratic
   (d) laissez-faire

9. In Fiedler's contingency model, both highly favorable and highly unfavorable leadership situations are best dealt with by a _____ leader.
   (a) task-motivated
   (b) laissez-faire
   (c) participative
   (d) relationship-motivated

10. _____ leadership model suggests that leadership style is strongly anchored in personality and therefore hard to change.
    (a) Trait
    (b) Fiedler's
    (c) Transformational
    (d) Path-goal

11. House's _____ theory of leadership says that successful leaders find ways to add value to leadership situations.
    (a) trait
    (b) path–goal
    (c) transformational
    (d) life-cycle

12. A leader who _____ would be described as achievement-oriented in the path–goal theory.
    (a) sets challenging goals for others
    (b) works hard to achieve high performance
    (c) gives directions and monitors results
    (d) builds commitment through participation

13. The critical contingency variable in the Hersey-Blanchard situational model of leadership is _____.
    (a) followers' maturity   (c) task structure
    (b) LPC   (d) LMX

14. Vision, charisma, integrity, and symbolism are all on the list of attributes typically associated with _____ leaders.
    (a) contingency
    (b) informal
    (c) transformational
    (d) transactional

15. The interactive leadership style, sometimes associated with women, is characterized by _____.
    (a) inclusion and information sharing
    (b) use of rewards and punishments
    (c) command and control
    (d) emphasis on position power

Short-Response Questions

16. Why does a person need both position power and personal power to achieve long-term managerial effectiveness?

17. What is the major insight of the Vroom-Jago leader-participation model?

18. What are the three variables that Fiedler's contingency model uses to diagnose the favorability of leadership situations, and what does each mean?

19. How does Peter Drucker's view of "good old-fashioned leadership" differ from the popular concept of transformational leadership?

Essay Question

20. When Marcel Henry took over as leader of a new product development team, he was both excited and apprehensive. "I wonder," he said to himself on the first day in his new assignment, "if I can meet the challenges of leadership." Later that day, Marcel shared this concern with you during a coffee break. Based on the insights offered in this chapter, how would you describe the implications of current thinking on transformational leadership and moral leadership for his personal leadership development?

Management Skills & Competencies Make yourself **valuable!**

Evaluate Career Situations

What Would You Do?

1. Autocratic Boss

Some might say it was bad luck. Others will tell you it's life and you'd better get used to it. You've just gotten a new team leader, and within the first week, it was clear to everyone that she is as "autocratic" as can be. The previous leader was very "democratic," and so is the higher-level manager, with whom you've always had a good working relationship. Is there anything you and your co-workers can do to remedy this situation without causing anyone, including the new boss, to lose their jobs?

2. New to the Team

You've just been hired as a visual effects artist by a top movie studio. The team you are joining has already been together for about two months. There's obviously an in-group when it comes to team leader and team member relationships. This job is important to you; the movie is going to be great résumé material. But you're worried about the leadership dynamics and your role as a newcomer to the team. What can you do to get on board as soon as possible, work well with the team leader, and be valued by other team members?

3. Out of Comfort Zone

Okay, it's important to be "interactive" in leadership. By personality, though, you tend to be a bit withdrawn. If you could do things by yourself, that's the way you would approach your work. That's your comfort zone. Yet you are talented and ambitious. Career growth in your field requires taking on management responsibilities. So, here you are agreeing to take over as a team leader in your first upward career move. Can you succeed by leading within your comfort zone? If not, what can you do to "stretch" your capabilities into new leadership territories?

Reflect on the Self-Assessment

Least-Preferred Co-Worker Scale

Instructions

Think of all the different people with whom you have ever worked—in jobs, in social clubs, in student projects, or other areas of your life. Next think of the one person with whom you could work least well—that is, the person with whom you had the most difficulty getting a job done. This is the one person—a peer, boss, or subordinate—with whom you would least want to work. Describe this person by circling numbers at the appropriate points on each of the following pairs of bipolar adjectives. Work fast. There are no right or wrong answers.[75]

Pleasant	8	7	6	5	4	3	2	1	Unpleasant
Friendly	8	7	6	5	4	3	2	1	Unfriendly
Rejecting	1	2	3	4	5	6	7	8	Accepting
Tense	1	2	3	4	5	6	7	8	Relaxed
Distant	1	2	3	4	5	6	7	8	Close
Cold	1	2	3	4	5	6	7	8	Warm
Supportive	8	7	6	5	4	3	2	1	Hostile
Boring	1	2	3	4	5	6	7	8	Interesting
Quarrelsome	1	2	3	4	5	6	7	8	Harmonious
Gloomy	1	2	3	4	5	6	7	8	Cheerful
Open	8	7	6	5	4	3	2	1	Guarded
Backbiting	1	2	3	4	5	6	7	8	Loyal
Untrustworthy	1	2	3	4	5	6	7	8	Trustworthy
Considerate	8	7	6	5	4	3	2	1	Inconsiderate
Nasty	1	2	3	4	5	6	7	8	Nice
Agreeable	8	7	6	5	4	3	2	1	Disagreeable
Insincere	1	2	3	4	5	6	7	8	Sincere
Kind	8	7	6	5	4	3	2	1	Unkind

Self-Assessment Scoring

Compute your "least-preferred co-worker" (LPC) score by totaling all the numbers you circled; enter that score here [LPC _____].

Interpretation

The LPC scale is used by Fred Fiedler to identify a person's dominant leadership style. He believes that this style is a relatively fixed part of our personality and is therefore difficult to change. Thus, he suggests the key to leadership success is finding (or creating) good "matches" between style and situation. If your score is 73 or above, Fiedler considers you a "relationship-motivated" leader. If your score is 64 or below, he considers you a "task-motivated" leader. If your score is between 65 and 72, Fiedler leaves it up to you to determine which leadership style is most like yours.

Contribute to the Class Exercise

Most Needed Leadership Skills
Instructions

1. Work individually to make a list of the leadership skills you believe you need to develop further in order to be ready for success in your next full-time job.
2. Share your list with teammates, discuss the rationale for your choices, and listen to what they have to say about the list of skills.
3. Prepare a master list of the five leadership skills that your team believes are most important for further development.
4. For each skill on the team list, prepare a justification that describes what the skill involves, why it is important to leadership success, and why it is still a candidate for further skills development among your teammates.
5. Present your leadership skills development list along with justifications to the whole class for discussion.

Manage a Critical Incident

Playing Favorites as a Team Leader

One of your colleagues just returned from a leadership training session at which the instructor presented the LMX, or leader-member exchange, theory. Listening to her talk about the training prompted thoughts about your own leader behaviors, and you came to a somewhat startling conclusion: You may be playing "favorites." In fact, the last person you recommended for promotion was a good friend and a member of your bi-weekly poker night club. Of course he was competent and is doing a good job in the new position. But as you think more about it, there were also two others on the team who may well have been equally good choices. Did you give them a fair chance when preparing your promotion recommendation, or did you short-change them in favor of your friend?

Questions

Well, it's a new day for the team, and basically the start of the rest of your leadership career. What can you do as a team leader to make sure that tendencies toward favoritism don't disadvantage some members? What warning signs can you watch for to spot when and if you are playing favorites?

Collaborate on the Team Activity

Leadership Believe-It-or-Not

You would think leaders would spend lots of time talking with the people who make products and deliver services, trying to understand problems and asking for advice. But *Business Week* reports a survey showing that quite the opposite is true. Persons with a high school education or less are asked for advice by only 24% of their bosses; for those with a college degree, the number jumps to 54%.

Question

What stories do your friends, acquaintances, family members, and you tell about their bosses that are truly hard to believe?

Instructions

1. Listen to others and ask others to talk about the leaders they have had in the past or currently do have. What strange-but-true stories are they telling?

2. Create a journal that can be shared with class members that summarizes, role-plays, or otherwise communicates the real-life experiences of people whose bosses sometimes behave in ways that are hard to believe.

3. For each of the situations in your report, try to explain the boss's behaviors.

4. For each of the situations, assume that you observed or heard about it as the boss's supervisor. Describe how you would "coach" or "counsel" the boss to turn the situation into a "learning moment" for positive leadership development.

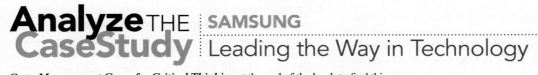

Analyze THE CaseStudy : SAMSUNG Leading the Way in Technology

Go to *Management Cases for Critical Thinking* at the end of the book to find this case.

FOUNDATIONS OF INDIVIDUAL BEHAVIOR

KEY TAKEAWAYS

■ Identify perceptual tendencies and distortions that influence behavior.

■ Explain common personality differences along with their implications for work and careers.

■ Discuss the components of attitudes and the importance of job satisfaction.

■ Illustrate how emotions, moods, and stress influence behavior in work and social situations.

SKILLS MAKE YOU **VALUABLE**

■ **EVALUATE** *Career Situations:*
What Would You Do?

■ **REFLECT** *On the Self-Assessment:*
Self-Monitoring

■ **CONTRIBUTE** *To the Class Exercise:*
Job Satisfaction Preferences

■ **MANAGE** *A Critical Incident:*
Facing Up to Attributions

■ **COLLABORATE** *On the Team Activity:*
Difficult Personalities

■ **ANALYZE** *The Case Study:*
Intel: Processing Individuals to Succeed

When people work, play, and live together, they experience lots of ups and downs. There are relationship and communication miscues, and bonds of friendship that fill life with pleasure. Within this natural ebb and flow are individual differences in perceptions, personalities, attitudes, moods, and emotions. Those who understand and respect differences are likely to succeed where those who are self-centered and insensitive more likely will not.

In his books *Leadership Is an Art* and *Leadership Jazz*, Max DePree, former chairperson of the publicly-traded furniture manufacturer Herman Miller, Inc., talks about a millwright who worked for his father. When the man died, DePree's father, wishing to express his sympathy to the family, went to their home. There he listened as the widow read some beautiful poems which, to his father's surprise, the millwright had written. DePree says that he and his father often wondered, "Was the man a poet who did millwright's work, or a millwright who wrote poetry?" He summarized the lesson this way: "It is fundamental that leaders endorse a concept of persons," basically meaning you have to care enough to find and respect the whole person residing behind the face.[1]

Contrast DePree's story with that of Karen Nussbaum, founder of the national membership organization 9to5 which is "dedicated to putting working women's issues on the public agenda."[2] 9to5 grew from an incident Nussbaum experienced in her job as a secretary at Harvard University.

Individual Behavior Sets

- *Performance behaviors*—task performance, customer service, productivity
- *Withdrawal behaviors*—absenteeism, turnover, job disengagement
- *Citizenship behaviors*—helping, volunteering, job engagement
- *Dysfunctional behaviors*—antisocial behavior, intentional wrongdoing

---

"One day I was sitting at my desk at lunchtime, when most of the professors were out," she says. "A student walked into the office and looked me dead in the eye and said, 'Isn't anyone here?'"[3] Nussbaum pledged to "remake the system so that it does not produce these individuals." Among the action priorities of 9to5 are family-supporting jobs, paid sick leave, equal pay for female employees, and elimination of discriminatory hiring practices based on gender or sexual orientation.[4]

Perceptions, personalities, attitudes, emotions, and moods can have a positive or a negative influence on individual behavior as shown in the above box. When employees are treated without respect at work, as reflected in Nussbaum's story, they may respond with low performance, poor customer service, absenteeism, and even antisocial behavior. In contrast, when individuals work in supportive settings, positive work behavior is much more likely to emerge—including higher levels of work performance, less withdrawal and dysfunction, and helpful citizenship behavior.

Perception

TAKEAWAY 1   How do perceptions influence individual behavior?

LEARN MORE | Perception and psychological contracts • Perception and attribution
ABOUT | Perception tendencies and distortions • Perception and impression management

Perception is the process through which people receive, organize, and interpret information from the environment.

Perception is the process through which people receive and interpret external information from the environment. It affects the impressions we form of ourselves, other people, and our daily experiences. You can think of perception as a screen or filter through which information passes into our consciousness and affects how we think about the world. Because perceptions are influenced by factors such as cultural background, values, and other personal and situational circumstances, people can and do perceive the exact same people, events, situations or circumstances in very different ways. Importantly, we most often behave in accordance with our perceptions.[5]

Perception and Psychological Contracts

A **psychological contract** is the set of individual expectations about the employment relationship.

One of the ways in which perceptions influence work behavior is through the **psychological contract,** or what the individual employee expects both to give and to receive from the employment relationship.[6] Figure 15.1 shows that a healthy psychological contract offers a balance between the contributions individuals make on behalf of their organization and inducements they receive. These contributions include time, energy, effort, creativity, commitment, and loyalty. Inducements are what the organization gives to employees in exchange for these contributions. These inducements include pay, fringe benefits, training and opportunities for personal growth and advancement, a sense of professional identity, and job security.

The **employee value proposition** describes the organization's intentions for creating value for both the employee and employer sides of the psychological contract.

Human resource managers use the term **employee value proposition,** or EVP to describe the organization's intentions for creating value on the employee and employer sides of the psychological contract. The ideal EVP is one where the exchanges made on each side of the psychological contract are perceived as fair by both parties. Problems are likely to occur when the psychological contract is perceived as out of balance or broken. For example, employees who perceive they are receiving too little in exchange for what they contribute might compensate by reducing their performance and withdrawing through absenteeism or tardiness.

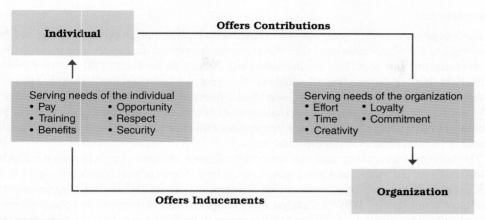

FIGURE 15.1
Components in the psychological contract.

Perception and Attribution

What happens when you perceive that someone else in a job or student team isn't performing up to the expectations of the team or their supervisor/instructor? How do you personally explain this less-than-ideal level of performance? Given your explanation, how do you react? These questions involve **attribution**, which is the process of developing explanations for events.

Attribution theory describes how people try to explain perceptions of their own behavior and the behavior of other people, often making errors in the process.[7] The **fundamental attribution error** occurs when someone's performance problems are blamed more on internal failures of the individual than on external factors relating to the environment. In the case of poor-quality work, for example, a team leader might blame a team member's lack of job skills or laziness—an unwillingness to work hard enough to get the job done. In response, the leader may try to resolve the problem through rewards, punishment, or even replacement. Because the fundamental attribution error neglects possible alternative, external explanations for poor-quality work, such as unrealistic time pressures, bad technology, or poor training, opportunities to improve these factors can be easily missed.

> **Attribution** is the process of explaining events.
>
> **Fundamental attribution error** overestimates internal factors and underestimates external factors driving individual behavior.

Fundamental Attribution Error *"It's their fault."* ← **They are performing poorly**   **I am performing poorly** → **Self-Serving Bias** *"It's not my fault."*

Attribution theory also recognizes tendencies toward **self-serving bias**. This happens when individuals blame their own personal failures or problems on external causes, while attributing successes to internal causes. You can recognize it as the "It's not my fault!" error when something is wrong but as the "It was me, I did it!" error when things go right. Think of the self-serving bias the next time your favorite team loses a close game—"It was bad officiating!" or when your team wins a close one—"It was great coaching and playmaking!" Self-serving bias creates a false sense of confidence. We don't place responsibility for outcomes in a consistent way, which also causes us to overlook opportunities for personal change and development. Because the outcome influences where we ultimately place responsibility, we can't learn effectively from either our victories or our defeats.

> **Self-serving bias** explains personal success by internal causes and personal failures by external causes.

Perception Tendencies and Distortions

A variety of perceptual tendencies and distortions also influence the way we communicate with and behave toward one another. Inappropriate use of stereotypes, halo effects, selective perception, and projections can cause us to lose sight of important individual differences.

Stereotypes

A **stereotype** occurs when attributes commonly associated with a group are assigned to an individual.

A **stereotype** occurs when someone is identified with a particular group or category, and then oversimplified attributes associated with that group or category are used to describe the individual, to make assumptions about how the individual will behave, or the kinds of things the individual is likely to think or assume. We all make use of stereotypes and they aren't always negative or ill-intended. But stereotypes based on individual differences such as gender, age, race, religion, able-bodiedness, national origin, or sexual orientation can, and unfortunately do, bias our perceptions of other people.[8] And because perceptions influence behavior, we may behave toward people in incorrect and even disrespectful ways.

The problem with making decisions under the influence of stereotypes is that each individual is just that—an individual, and not a generic archetype. For example, female managers in the U.S. get a smaller proportion of international assignments—about 25% fewer assignments—than their male counterparts.[9] Why? A Catalyst study blames gender stereotypes that place women at a disadvantage for global jobs. The perception seems to be that women lack the abilities or willingness to work abroad effectively.[10] The many women serving successfully in these roles as well as the high-powered women heading major global companies—like Indra Nooyi of Pepsico, Ursula Burns of Xerox, Mary Barra of General Motors, Marillyn Hewson of Lockheed Martin, and Virginia Rometty of IBM—would surely disagree.

Halo Effects

A **halo effect** occurs when one attribute is used to develop an overall impression of a person or situation.

A **halo effect** occurs when one personal attribute is used to develop an overall impression of a person or of a situation. When meeting someone new, for example, the halo effect may cause one trait, such as a pleasant smile or a firm handshake, to trigger an overall positive perception of that individual. A unique hairstyle or style of clothes, by contrast, may trigger a generalized negative impression. Halo effect errors often show up during performance evaluations. One factor, such as a person's punctuality or pleasant personality, may become the "halo" for a positive overall performance assessment, even though an accurate evaluation of the full set of available performance facts would not have led to the same positive appraisal.

Selective Perception

Selective perception is the tendency to define problems from one's own point of view.

Selective perception is the tendency to single out those aspects of an individual or situation that reinforce one's existing beliefs, values, or needs.[11] Information that makes us feel uncomfortable tends to get screened out, while information that makes us feel comfortable is allowed in. What this often means in organizations is that people from different departments or functions—such as marketing and information systems—see organizational events from their own point of view but fail to recognize the validity of others' point of view. One way to reduce or avoid selective perception is to be sure to gather inputs and opinions from people with divergent points of view.

Projection

Projection is the assignment of personal attributes to other individuals.

Projection involves the assignment of personal attributes to other individuals. A classic projection error is to assume that other people share our own needs, desires, and values. For example, suppose that you enjoy a lot of responsibility and challenge in your work. Suppose, also, that you are the newly appointed head of a team whose jobs you see as dull and routine. You might move quickly to redesign jobs within the team so that members take on more responsibilities and perform more challenging tasks. But this may not be a good decision. Instead of designing jobs to best fit the team members' needs, you might just have spent a lot of time and effort designing their jobs to fit with your own needs. The members may, in fact, have been satisfied doing jobs that seem routine to you. Projection errors can be controlled through self-awareness and a willingness to try to see things from others' points of view.

Perception and Impression Management

Richard Branson, CEO of the Virgin Group, is one of the richest and most famous executives in the world.[12] He's also known for informality and being a casual dresser. One of his early successes was launching Virgin Airlines as a competitor to British Airways (BA). The former head of BA, Lord King, said: "If Richard Branson had worn a shirt and tie instead of a goatee and jumper, I would not have underestimated him."[13] This anecdote reveals how much impressions can influence our experiences with others—both positive and negative.

Scholars discuss **impression management** as the systematic attempt to influence how others perceive us.[14] Impression management is really a matter of routine in everyday life. The way we dress, talk, act, and surround ourselves with objects (e.g., headphones, jewelry, car) conveys what we perceive to be a desirable image to others. We try to create an image of ourselves. When well done, impression management can help to develop personal relationships with attractive people, advance in jobs and careers, form professional relationships with people we admire, and even create inroads to group memberships, internships, and prestigious universities. Some of the basic impression management tactics are worth remembering. Dress in ways that convey positive appeal—for example, know when to "dress up" and when to "dress down." Use words to flatter other people in ways that generate positive feelings toward you. Make eye contact and smile when engaged in conversations to create a personal bond. Display a high level of energy that suggests lots of work commitment and initiative.[15]

> **Impression management** is the systematic attempt to influence how others perceive us.

Learning Check 1

TAKEAWAYQUESTION **1   How do perceptions influence individual behavior?**

BE SURE YOU CAN • define *perception* • explain the benefits of a healthy psychological contract • explain fundamental attribution error and self-serving bias • define *stereotype, halo effect, selective perception*, and *projection* and illustrate how each can adversely affect work behavior • explain impression management

Personality

TAKEAWAY 2   What should we know about personalities in the workplace?

LEARN MORE ABOUT | Big Five personality dimensions • Myers-Briggs Type Indicator
Technology personality • Personal conception and emotional adjustment traits

How often do you complain about someone's "bad personality," tell a friend how much you like someone because of their "nice personality," or worry that co-workers mistake your "quiet shyness" for a lack of competency? These same kinds of personality-driven impressions of other people emerge at work as frequently as they do in our everyday lives. Perhaps you have been part of conversations like these: "I can't give him that job; with a personality like that, there's no way he can work with customers." "Put Erika on the project—her personality is perfect for the intensity that we expect from the team." "Cynthia should present our team's proposal—she's got a really outgoing personality."

We use the term **personality** in management to describe the profile of enduring characteristics that makes each of us unique as an individual. No one can doubt that an individual's personality can influence how she or he behaves and how that behavior is regarded by others. The implications of personality extend from how we face problems and pursue tasks, to how we handle relationships with everyone from family to friends to co-workers.

> **Personality** is the profile of characteristics making a person unique from others.

Big Five Personality Dimensions

Although there are many different personality traits, some of the most widely recognized are a short list of five that are especially significant in the workplace. Known as the *Big Five*,[16] these personality dimensions are:

Extraversion is being outgoing, sociable, and assertive.

Agreeableness is being good-natured, cooperative, and trusting.

Conscientiousness is being responsible, dependable, and careful.

Emotional stability is being relaxed, secure, and unworried.

Openness to experience is being curious, receptive to new ideas, and imaginative.

1. **Extraversion**—the degree to which someone is outgoing, sociable, and assertive. An extravert is comfortable and confident in interpersonal relationships; an introvert is more withdrawn and reserved.

2. **Agreeableness**—the degree to which someone is good-natured, cooperative, and trusting. An agreeable person gets along well with others; a disagreeable person is a source of conflict and discomfort for others.

3. **Conscientiousness**—the degree to which someone is responsible, dependable, and careful. A conscientious person focuses on what can be accomplished and meets commitments; a person who lacks conscientiousness is careless, often trying to do too much and failing, or doing little.

4. **Emotional stability**—the degree to which someone is relaxed, secure, and generally unworried. A person who is emotionally stable is calm and confident; a person lacking in emotional stability is anxious, nervous, and tense.

5. **Openness to experience**—the degree to which someone is curious, open to new ideas, and imaginative. An open person is broad-minded, receptive to new things, and comfortable with change; a person who lacks openness is narrow-minded, has few interests, and is resistant to change.

A considerable body of evidence from published academic research links these personality dimensions with a range of individual behaviors at work and in life overall. For example, conscientiousness is a good predictor of job performance for most occupations. Extraversion often is associated with success in management and sales.[17] Indications are that extraverts tend to be happier than introverts in their lives overall, that conscientious people tend to be less risky, and that those more open to experience are actually more creative.[18]

You can easily spot the Big Five personality traits in people with whom you work, study, and socialize in your everyday life. But don't forget that these traits also apply to you! Others form impressions of your personality, and respond to it, just as you do with theirs. Managers often use personality judgments when making job assignments, building teams, and otherwise engaging in the daily social give-and-take of work within an organization.

Sample Myers-Briggs Types

- ESTJ (extraverted, sensing, thinking, judging)—decisive, logical, and quick to dig in; common among managers.
- ENTJ (extraverted, intuitive, thinking, judging)—analytical, strategic, quick to take charge; common for leaders.
- ISJF (introverted, sensing, judging, feeling)—conscientious, considerate, and helpful; common among team players.
- INTJ (introverted, intuitive, thinking, judging)—insightful, free thinking, determined; common for visionaries.

Myers-Briggs Type Indicator

The Myers-Briggs Type Indicator is another popular approach to personality assessment. It "types" personalities based on a questionnaire that probes into how people act or feel in various situations. Called the *MBTI* for short, it was developed by Katherine Briggs and her daughter Isabel Briggs-Myers from foundations set forth in the work of psychologist Carl Jung.[19]

Jung's model of personality differences included three main distinctions. The first is how people differ in the ways they in which they relate to others—by extraversion (outgoing and sociable) or introversion (shy and quiet). The second is how they differ in the ways in which they gather information—by sensation (emphasizing details, facts, and routine) or by intuition (looking for the "big picture" and being willing to deal with various possibilities). The third is how they differ in the ways in which they evaluate information—by thinking (using reason and analysis) or by feeling (responding to the feelings and desires of others). Briggs and Briggs-Myers used all three of Jung's personality dimensions in developing the MBTI. But, they added a fourth dimension that describes how people differ in the ways in which they relate to the outside world—judging or perceiving. The four MBTI dimensions are:

- *Extraverted vs. introverted (E or I)*—social interaction: whether a person tends toward being outgoing and sociable or shy and quiet.

- *Sensing vs. intuitive (S or I)*—gathering data: whether a person tends to focus on details or on the big picture in dealing with problems.

- *Thinking vs. feeling (T or F)*—decision making: whether a person tends to rely on logic or emotions in dealing with problems.

- *Judging vs. perceiving (J or P)*—work style: whether a person prefers order and control or acts with flexibility and spontaneity.

◄ MBTI personality dimensions

Sixteen possible MBTI personality types result from the various combinations of the four dimensions just described.[20] A sample of Myers-Briggs types often found in work settings is shown in the box. These kinds of systematic, easily understandable personality classifications have made the Myers-Briggs Type Indicator an extremely popular management tool.[21] Employers and trainers like it because people can be taught to understand their own personality types, for example as an ESTJ or ISJF, and to learn how to work better with people with different personalities.

Technology Personality

Recent thinking also suggests that personality differences extend to the ways in which people interact with technology. Someone's **technology personality** is reflected in the frequency of technology and social media use as well as the ways in which it is used.[22] The following seven technology personality types have been identified in the adult U.S. population. Why not pause and use this list to check your technology personality and consider its implications for your work and social relationships?

Technology personality reflects levels of social media use and how media are used to connect to others.

◄ Technology personality types

1. *Always On*—8%—early adopters who use technology to create content, actively engage others, and make connections with people they'd like to know, not merely the people they know already.

2. *Live Wires*—35%—very connected, use technology to stay in touch with family and friends, own smartphones and tablets.

3. *Social Skimmers*—6%—highly connected, use social media sites, have substantial on-line networks and connect with family and friends using mobile technology; primarily use technology to gather information rather than to engage others.

4. *Broadcasters*—8%—less connected, selectively use technology to tell others what they're doing, are less likely to be active on social media, and tend not to text.

5. *Toe Dippers*—27%—low connectivity, use technology to converse, own desktops and laptops, with less than 25% owning a smart phone; most likely to prefer person-to-person contact with others.

6. *Bystanders*—15%—relatively unconnected, mostly own only desktops; use technology primarily to keep up with the news and less frequently to connect with family and friends.

7. *Never-Minders*—2%—relative outliers, who do not use cell phones, texting or social media, are apprehensive about technology use, and see technology as isolating.

Personal Conception and Emotional Adjustment Traits

In addition to the Big Five dimensions, the Myers-Briggs Type Indicator, and the more recent possibility of a technology personality, psychologists have long studied a wide range of other personality traits. As shown in Figure 15.2, some traits with special relevance to people at work include the personal conception traits of locus of control, authoritarianism, Machiavellianism, and self-monitoring, as well as the emotional adjustment trait of Type A orientation.[23] In general, you can think of a *personal conception trait* as describing how people's personality influences how they tend relate to the environment, while an *emotional adjustment trait* describes how they are inclined to handle stress and uncomfortable situations.

Locus of Control

Locus of control is the extent to which one believes that what happens is within one's control.

Scholars have long had a strong interest in **locus of control**, recognizing that some people believe they are in control of their destiny, while others believe that what happens to them is beyond their control.[24] "Internals" are self-confident and accept responsibility for their own actions and the outcomes they lead to. "Externals" are more likely to blame others and outside forces for what happens to them. Research suggests that internals tend to be more satisfied and less alienated from their work than externals.

Authoritarianism

Authoritarianism is the degree to which a person tends to defer to authority.

Authoritarianism is the degree to which a person yields to authority and accepts interpersonal status differences.[25] Someone with an authoritarian personality tends to behave in a rigid, control-oriented way when serving as a leader. This same person is likely to behave in a subservient way and to comply with rules when serving as a follower. The tendency of people with an authoritarian personality to obey rules and follow procedures can cause problems if they follow orders to the point of acting unethically or even illegally.

Machiavellianism describes the extent to which someone is emotionally detached and manipulative.

Machiavellianism

In his 16th-century book *The Prince*, Niccolo Machiavelli gained lasting fame for giving his prince advice on how to use power to achieve personal goals.[26] The personality trait of **Machiavellianism** describes the extent to which someone is emotionally detached and manipulative in his or her use of power.[27] A person with a "high-Mach" personality is viewed as exploitative and unconcerned about others, often acting with the assumption that the end (i.e., goal) justifies the means (i.e., how the goal is accomplished). A person with a "low-Mach" personality, by contrast, is deferential in allowing others to exert power over him or her, and does not seek to manipulate others.

Self-monitoring is the degree to which someone is able to adjust behavior in response to external factors.

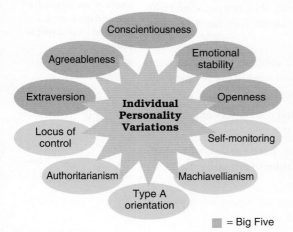

FIGURE 15.2
Common personality dimensions that influence human behavior at work.

Self-Monitoring

Self-monitoring reflects the degree to which individuals are able to adjust and modify their behavior in response to the immediate

insight > LEARN ABOUT YOURSELF

> *Individuals blinded by ambition can end up sacrificing substance for superficiality, and even sacrificing right for wrong.*

Keep Ambition on Your Side

When it comes to understanding people's behavior, their attitudes, and their professional interactions with others, one of the most important distinctions can be their level of **ambition**, which is the desire to succeed, accomplish things, and achieve high goals. Ambition shows up in personality as a sense of competitiveness and the urge to get better or to be the best at something.

We tend to think of ambition as a positive individual quality to be admired and developed. Scholar and consultant Ram Charan calls it a "personal differentiator" that separates "people who perform from those who don't." But, there's also a potential downside. Charan points out that individuals blinded by ambition can end up sacrificing substance for superficiality, and even sacrificing right for wrong.

Overly ambitious people may exaggerate their accomplishments to themselves and others. They also may try to do too much and end up accomplishing less than they would otherwise have accomplished. Ambitious people who lack integrity can also get trapped by corruption and misbehavior driven by ambition.

Personal Traits Associated with High Performers

- Ambition—to achieve
- Drive—to solve
- Tenacity—to persevere
- Confidence—to act
- Openness—to experience
- Realism—to accept
- Learning—to grow
- Integrity—to fulfill

GET TO KNOW YOURSELF BETTER

Review the "personal differentiators" in the small box above. How do you score? Can you say that your career ambition is backed with a sufficient set of personal traits and skills to make success a real possibility? Ask others to comment on the ambition you display as you go about your daily activities. Write a short synopsis of two situations—one in which you showed ambition and one in which you did not.

---

situation and to external factors.[28] A person high in self-monitoring tends to be a learner, comfortable with feedback, and is both willing and able to change. Because high self-monitors are flexible in changing behavior from one situation to the next, it may be hard to get a clear read on exactly where they stand on any particular issue. A person low in self-monitoring, by contrast, is predictable and tends to act in a consistent way regardless of circumstances or who happens to be present within a particular situation.

Type A Personality

A **Type A personality** is high in achievement orientation, impatience, and perfectionism. One of the key aspects of the Type A personality is the tendency for Type A individuals to bring stress on themselves, even in situations others are likely to find relatively stress free. The following patterns of behavior reveal Type A personality tendencies in yourself and others:[29]

- Always moving, walking, and eating rapidly.
- Acting impatient, hurrying others, put off by waiting.
- Doing, or trying to do, several things at once.
- Feeling guilty when relaxing.
- Hurrying or interrupting the speech of others.

A Type A personality is a person oriented toward extreme achievement, impatience, and perfectionism.

Learning Check 2

TAKEAWAYQUESTION **2 What should we know about personalities in the workplace?**

BE SURE YOU CAN • list the Big Five personality traits and give work-related examples of each • list and explain the four dimensions used to assess personality in the MBTI • explain and illustrate different technology personality types • list five personal conception and emotional adjustment personality traits and give work-related examples for each

Attitudes

TAKEAWAY 3 How do attitudes influence individual behavior?

LEARN MORE | What is an attitude? • What is job satisfaction? • Job satisfaction trends
ABOUT | Job satisfaction outcomes

When Challis M. Lowe was executive vice president at Ryder System, she was one of only two African American women among the five highest-paid executives in over 400 U.S. companies.[30] She rose to the executive VP level after a 25-year career that included several changes of employers and lots of stressors—working-mother guilt, a failed marriage, gender bias on the job, race-based barriers, and an MBA degree earned part-time. Through it all, she said: "I've never let being scared stop me from doing something. Just because you haven't done it before doesn't mean you shouldn't try." That, simply put, is what can be characterized as a "can-do" attitude!

What Is an Attitude?

An attitude is a predisposition to act in a certain way.

Attitudes are predispositions to act in a certain way toward people and events in our environment.[31] In order to fully understand attitudes, it helps to recognize the three components shown in the small box. First, the *cognitive component* reflects beliefs or opinions. You might believe, for example, that your management course is very interesting. Second, the *affective or emotional component* of an attitude reflects a specific feeling. For example, you might feel very good about being a management major. Third, the *behavioral component* of an attitude reflects an intention to behave in a way that is consistent with the belief and feeling. Using the same example again, you might say to yourself: "I am going to work hard and try to get an A in all of my management courses."

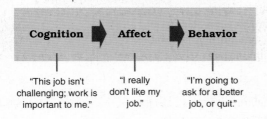

Components of Individual Attitudes

Cognition ▶ Affect ▶ Behavior

"This job isn't challenging; work is important to me." "I really don't like my job." "I'm going to ask for a better job, or quit."

The intentions reflected in an attitude may or may not be confirmed through actual behavior. Despite having a positive attitude and good intentions in your management courses, for example, demands on your time from family, friends, or leisure activities have the potential to keep you from studying and preparing for your class. You end up not working hard enough to get an A, and fail to live up to your original intentions to get a good grade in the course.

Cognitive dissonance is discomfort felt when attitude and behavior are inconsistent.

The psychological concept of **cognitive dissonance** describes the discomfort felt when one's attitude and behavior are inconsistent with one another.[32] For most people, dissonance is very uncomfortable and results in changing the attitude to fit the behavior— "Oh, I really don't like management that much anyway," changing future behavior to fit the attitude—dropping out of intramural sports to get extra study time in order to get a good grade in the course, or rationalizing to force the two to be compatible—"Management is an okay major, but being a manager also requires the experience I'm gaining in my extracurricular activities."

wisdom > LEARN FROM ROLE MODELS

> *"You can decide you're going to be happy today . . . the little things in life are the big things."*

Little Things Are Big Things at Life Is Good

Erick Jacobs/The New York Times/Redux Pictures

*I*magine! Yes, you can! Go for it! Life is good. We'll make that: *Life is really good!* These are the kinds of thoughts that can help turn your dreams into reality. They're also part and parcel of a multimillion-dollar company that really *is* named Life is Good.

It all began with two brothers—Bert and John Jacobs—making T-shirts for street sales. Picture a card table set up at a Boston street fair and two young brothers setting out 48 T-shirts printed with a smiling face—Jake—and the words "Life is good." Then picture the cart empty, with all of the shirts sold for $10 apiece, and the two brothers happily realizing they *might*—just might—have come up with a viable business idea.

From that modest beginning, Bert—Chief Executive Optimist—and John—Chief Creative Optimist—built a company devoted to humor and humility. John says: "It's important that we're saying 'Life is good,' not 'Life is great' or 'Life is perfect'; there's a big difference. . . . Don't determine that you're going to be happy when you get the new car or the big promotion or meet that special person. You can decide that you're going to be happy today." According to Bert: "The little things in life are the big things." That's the message of the Life Is Good brand.

How did the two brothers turn their belief in happiness and that life is good into a successful firm? They didn't start with business degrees or any real experience. They developed their business with good instincts, creativity, and a very positive view on life. They stuck to their values while learning about business as their firm grew. They still live the brand while enjoying leisure pursuits like kayaking and ultimate Frisbee. They also support philanthropic enterprises like Camp Sunshine for children with serious illnesses and Playmakers for traumatized children.

FIND THE INSPIRATION

Bert and John Jacobs built a successful company with a positive message and approach to life that has an almost universal appeal. Just how far can positive thinking carry these entrepreneurs? Does there come a point where continuing to build and expand a business requires systematic, professional management approaches and tactics? How about us, personally? Is there more to be gained by looking for positives than negatives in our everyday experiences and relationships with others? What about when it comes to our own lives—your life—who's in charge of the "good" factor?

What Is Job Satisfaction?

People hold attitudes about many aspects of their experiences at work—supervisors, co-workers, tasks, policies, goals, pay, and promotion opportunities, among many others. One of the most often discussed work attitudes is **job satisfaction**, which is the degree that employees feel positively or negatively about various aspects of work.[33] The following facets of job satisfaction are commonly discussed and measured:

Job satisfaction is the degree to which an individual feels positive or negative about a job.

- *Work itself*—Does the job offer responsibility, interest, challenge?
- *Quality of supervision*—Are task help and social support available?
- *Co-workers*—How much harmony, respect, and friendliness is there?
- *Opportunities*-—Are there avenues for promotion, learning, and growth?

- *Pay*—Is compensation, actual and perceived, fair and substantial?
- *Work conditions*—Do conditions offer comfort, safety, support?
- *Security*—Is the job and employment secure?

Job Satisfaction Trends

If you watch the news on television or get news from the Internet, you'll regularly find reports on employees' job satisfaction. You'll also find reports on lots of job satisfaction studies from the academic literature. The results from these various sources and studies don't always agree. But they do show that job satisfaction tends to be higher in small firms and lower in large firms, that it tends to be correlated with overall life satisfaction, that it is higher for workers above 50 years old, and that bosses tend to be more satisfied than workers.[34]

The general trend in job satisfaction has been down for several years, with the percentages recently falling below 45%.[35] Conference Board surveys find fewer and fewer people saying that they are satisfied with their jobs. In 1987, about 61% of workers said they were satisfied. By 2008, that number had dropped to 49%, and by 2010, after the effects of the recession were in full force, it dropped further to 45%. Younger workers under 25 were the least happy with their jobs, with 64% reporting dissatisfaction. Among other findings, only 51% of all workers surveyed said their jobs were interesting, 56% liked their co-workers, and 51% were satisfied with their supervisors. These data suggest "something troubling about work in America," according to a Conference Board analyst.[36]

Research Brief

Business Students More Satisfied with Their Lives Perform Better

Wondering if "a happy student is a high-performing student," Joseph C. Rode, Marne L. Arthaud-Day, Christine H. Mooney, Janet P. Near, Timothy T. Baldwin, William H. Bommer, and Robert S. Rubin hypothesized that students' satisfaction with their lives and student domains would, along with cognitive abilities, have a positive influence on academic performance.

A sample of 673 business students completed satisfaction and IQ questionnaires, and their academic performance was measured by self-reported GPAs and performance on a 3-hour simulation exercise. The findings confirmed the expected relationships between students' leisure and family satisfaction and overall life satisfaction. Also confirmed were links between both life satisfaction and IQ scores, and self-reported GPA and simulation performance. Expected relationships between students' university and housing satisfaction and overall life satisfaction proved not to be significant.

Rode et al. point out that "it is time to more fully acknowledge that college students also live 'integrated lives' and are heavily influenced by the milieu that surrounds them."

Life satisfaction influences on academic performance

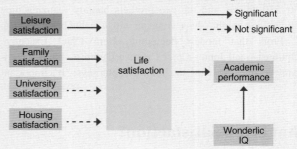

YOU BE THE RESEARCHER

Does your everyday experience as a student support these results or contradict them? Build a model that describes how you would predict student academic performance, not limiting yourself to directions used in this study. If it is true that students' academic performance is influenced by overall life satisfaction, what does this mean to an instructor or to a college administrator?

Job Satisfaction Outcomes

Effective managers and team leaders help their employees and teammates to achieve not just higher levels of work performance, but also higher job satisfaction as well. People deserve to have satisfying work experiences, and job satisfaction is an important goal, if for no other reason than on quality-of-work-life grounds alone. But, is job satisfaction important in other than a "feel-good" sense? In other words, does job satisfaction matter when it comes to measurable organization-critical outcomes? Here is what we know about the consequences of job satisfaction.

Job Satisfaction and Withdrawal Behaviors

There is a strong relationship between job satisfaction and the **withdrawal behaviors** of temporary absenteeism and actual job turnover. With regard to *absenteeism*, workers who are more satisfied with their jobs are absent less often than workers who are dissatisfied with their jobs. With regard to *turnover*, satisfied workers also are more likely to stay in their positions while dissatisfied workers are more likely to quit their jobs.[37]

Both findings are important. Absenteeism and turnover are costly in terms of the recruitment and training needed to replace workers, as well as in the productivity lost while new workers are learning how to perform the job tasks of the vacated positions up to expectations.[38] In fact, the results from one recent study revealed that changing retention rates up or down results in magnified changes to corporate earnings. It also warns about the negative impact of declining employee loyalty and high turnover on corporate performance.[39] Job satisfaction can hit the bottom line in many ways.

> **Withdrawal behaviors** occur as temporary absenteeism and actual job turnover.

Job Satisfaction and Employee Engagement

A survey of 55,000 American workers by the Gallup organization suggests that business profits rise with higher levels of **employee engagement**—a strong sense of belonging or connection with one's job and employer.[40] Engagement shows up as a willingness to help others, always trying to do something extra to improve work performance, and feeling and speaking positively about the organization. The Gallup research shows that the things that counted most toward employee engagement were workers believing that they had the opportunity to do their best every day, that their opinions count, that fellow workers are committed to quality, and that there is a direct connection between their work and the company's mission.[41] Of course the flip side of engagement is disengagement. It shows up as low commitment, lack of loyalty, absenteeism and turnover, and even disruptive and harmful work behaviors. Gallup reports that roughly 18% of workers in its surveys report being "actively disengaged" from their work.[42]

> **Employee engagement** is a strong positive feeling about one's job and the organization.

Employee engagement is strongly connected with two other attitudes that influence work behavior. **Job involvement** is the extent to which an employee feels dedicated to a job. Someone with high job involvement psychologically identifies with her or his job, and, for example, would be expected to work beyond expectations to complete a special project, or stay late to help a co-worker finish an assignment. **Organizational commitment** reflects the degree of loyalty an employee feels toward the organization. Individuals with a high level of organizational commitment identify strongly with the organization and take pride when viewing themselves as an organization member. Researchers find that strong *emotional commitment* to the organization—based on values and interests of others—has as much as four times more positive influence on performance than *rational commitment*—which is based primarily on pay and self-interest.[43]

> **Job involvement** is the extent to which an individual feels dedicated to a job.
>
> **Organizational commitment** is the loyalty an individual feels toward the organization.

Job Satisfaction and Organizational Citizenship

Have you ever wondered about those people who are always willing to "go beyond the call of duty" or "go the extra mile" in their work?[44] Such actions represent **organizational citizenship**

> **Organizational citizenship behavior** is a willingness to "go beyond the call of duty" or "go the extra mile" in one's work.

behavior, OCB, and also are linked with job satisfaction.[45] A good organizational citizen does things that, although not formally required, help advance the performance of co-workers, the work unit, and the organization as a whole. Examples of OCBs include a service worker who goes to extraordinary lengths to take care of a customer, a team member who is always willing to take on extra tasks, or an employee who always volunteers to stay late with no extra pay just to make sure a key assignment gets done right.

Of course, the flip side of positive organizational citizenship is antisocial and counterproductive behavior that disrupts work processes, relationships, teamwork, satisfaction, and performance.[46] Two of its common forms are incivility and bullying.[47] **Incivility** is antisocial behavior that shows up as individual or group displays of disrespectful acts, social exclusion, and use of language that is hurtful to others. **Bullying** is antisocial behavior, again individual or group, that is intentionally aggressive, intimidating, demeaning, and/or abusive toward the recipients. Both incivility and bullying behaviors occur on a continuing basis, making them clearly different from what might be considered just one-time "bad" behaviors.

Incivility is antisocial behavior in the forms of disrespectful acts, social exclusion, and use of hurtful language.

Bullying is antisocial behavior that is intentionally aggressive, intimidating, demeaning, and/or abusive.

Job Satisfaction and Job Performance

Airline passengers are easily frustrated, but a report on passenger satisfaction by J. D. Power & Associates states a conclusion that probably seems obvious: Customers tend to be more satisfied when airline employees smile when dealing with them. The report went on to state "One of the things we see is that when you see companies that have high internal employee satisfaction, they have high customer satisfaction as well."[48] Although it makes sense that an employee's job satisfaction in service industries will be linked with customer satisfaction, scholars report that the satisfaction and performance relationship is generally more complicated.[49] Three plausible arguments are depicted in the box.

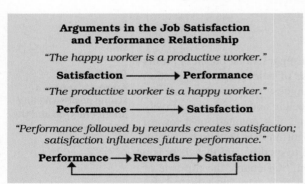

Arguments in the Job Satisfaction and Performance Relationship

"The happy worker is a productive worker."

Satisfaction ⟶ Performance

"The productive worker is a happy worker."

Performance ⟶ Satisfaction

"Performance followed by rewards creates satisfaction; satisfaction influences future performance."

Performance ⟶ Rewards ⟶ Satisfaction

There is probably a modest link between job satisfaction and objective or quantifiable performance.[50] But, it is important to stress the word *modest* when describing this relationship. We shouldn't rush to conclude that making employees happy or increasing their job satisfaction is a foolproof way to improve their job performance. The reality is that some employees will tend to like their jobs, be very satisfied, and still will not perform very well. That is just part of the complexity regarding the potential impact of individual differences on job performance. Consider the implications of this sign that once hung in a tavern near a Ford plant in Michigan: "I spend 40 hours a week here, am I supposed to work too?"

There also is a link between high levels of work performance and job satisfaction. High-performing employees are likely to feel satisfied with their work. Here again, caution is called for; not everyone is likely to fit the model. Some employees may get their jobs done effectively and efficiently, meet high performance expectations, but still not feel satisfied with their job. Given that job satisfaction is a good predictor of absenteeism and turnover, managers are well advised to take steps to avoid losing highly productive but unhappy workers. Unless changes are made to increase their job satisfaction, productive employees may choose to leave, hurting firm performance.

Finally, job satisfaction and job performance most likely have a reciprocal influence on one another—each playing a role in the level of the other. But the relationship between job satisfaction and performance also is most likely to hold only under certain conditions, particularly those related to rewards. We know that job performance followed by rewards that employees value and perceive as fair tends to create job satisfaction. This experienced satisfaction is likely to increase motivation to work hard and achieve high performance in the future in order to gain additional rewards.

Learning Check 3

TAKEAWAYQUESTION **3 How do attitudes influence individual behavior?**

BE SURE YOU CAN • define *attitude* and list the three components of an attitude • define *job satisfaction* and list its components • explain the potential consequences of high and low job satisfaction • define *employee engagement, job involvement, organizational commitment,* and *organizational citizenship behavior* • explain three arguments in the job satisfaction and performance relationship

Emotions, Moods, and Stress

TAKEAWAY 4   How do emotions, moods, and stress influence individual behavior?

LEARN MORE ABOUT | Emotions • Moods • Stress and strain

Situation: The Boeing 787 Dreamliner is falling further behind on its promised delivery schedule. Boeing's former head of Asia-Pacific sales, John Wojick, is in a meeting with the chief sales officer. After a "heated" discussion over delivery dates and customer promises, Wojick "storms" out. He says: "Quite frankly we were failing at meeting our commitment to customers. Some of us may have been able to handle our emotions a little better than others." Now Boeing's senior vice president of global sales, Wojick is described as having "an understated manner" and an underlying "fiery temper."[51]

Looking at this incident we might say that Wojick was emotional about the fact that his customers weren't being well served. His temper flared and his anger got the better of him during the meeting. Whether that was good or bad for his clients . . . for him . . . and for his boss, is an open question. But, for a time at least, he and his boss both probably ended up in bad moods because of their stressful confrontation.

Emotions

Emotional intelligence is an important human skill for managers and an essential leadership capability. Daniel Goleman defines "EI" as the ability to understand emotions in ourselves and in others, and to use this understanding to manage relationships effectively.[52] His point is that we perform at our best when we are good at recognizing and dealing with emotions. Emotional intelligence helps us to avoid letting our emotions "get the better of us." Emotional intelligence also allows individuals to show restraint when the emotions of others would otherwise get the better of them.[53]

An **emotion** is a strong feeling directed toward someone or something. For example, you might feel positive emotion or elation when an instructor congratulates you on a fine class presentation; you might feel negative emotion or anger when an instructor criticizes you in front of the class. In both cases the object of your emotion is the instructor, but the impact of the instructor's behavior on your feelings is quite different. How you respond to the aroused emotions is likely to differ as well—perhaps breaking into a wide smile with the compliment, or making a nasty side comment after the criticism.

Emotional intelligence is an ability to understand emotions and manage relationships effectively.

Emotions are strong feelings directed toward someone or something.

Understanding Emotions

"I was really mad when Prof. Nitpicker criticized my presentation."

- Linked with a specific cause
- Tends to be brief or episodic
- Specific effect on attitude, behavior
- Might turn into a mood

Moods

Moods are generalized positive and negative feelings or states of mind.

Whereas emotions tend to be short term and clearly targeted, **moods** are more generalized positive and negative feelings or states of mind that may persist for a longer period of time.[54] Everyone seems to have occasional moods, and we each know the full range of possibilities they represent. How often do you wake up in the morning and feel excited, refreshed, and happy? In contrast, how often do you wake up feeling low, depressed, and generally unhappy? What are the consequences of these different moods for your behavior with friends and family, and your performance at work or at school?

Mood contagion is the spillover of one's positive or negative moods to others.

Positive and negative emotions can spill over and become "contagious," causing others to display similarly positive and negative moods. This **mood contagion** can easily influence one's co-workers and teammates, as well as family and friends.[55] When a leader's mood contagion is positive, for example, researchers find that followers display more positive moods, report being more attracted to their leaders, and rate their leaders more favorably.[56] And in social media, emotion and mood contagion has been identified in networks of online connections. In a study of Facebook posts, James Fowler and colleagues found that positive updates tend to generate positive posts by others while negative updates tend to generate negative ones. The contagion effect is higher for positive posts. Fowler's interpretation of these data is that "people are not just choosing other people like themselves to associate with but actually causing their friends' emotional expressions to change . . . emotional expressions spread online . . . positive expressions spread more than negative."[57]

With regard to CEO moods, a *BusinessWeek* article claims it pays to be likable.[58] If a CEO goes to a meeting in a good mood and gets described as "cheerful," "charming," "humorous," "friendly," and "candid," she or he may be viewed as being on a professional upswing. But if the CEO is in a bad mood and comes away perceived as "prickly," "impatient," "remote," "tough," "acrimonious," or even "ruthless," she or he may be more likely to be perceived as being on a professional downhill slide. Many CEOs, C-suite executives, and ambitious managers are hiring executive coaches to help them learn how to better manage emotions and moods to come across as personable and friendly at public relations events and in professional relationships.[59]

Understanding Moods

"I just feel lousy today and don't have any energy. I've been down all week."

- Hard to identify the cause
- Tends to linger, and be long-lasting
- General effect on attitude, behavior
- Can be "negative" or "positive"

Stress and Strain

Stress is a state of tension caused by extraordinary demands, constraints, or opportunities.

Closely aligned with emotions and moods is **stress**, a state of tension caused by extraordinary demands, constraints, or opportunities.[60] It is certainly a powerful life force to be reckoned with. In one survey of college graduates, for example, 31% reported working over 50 hours per week, 60% rushed meals, 34% ate lunches "on the run," and 47% of those under 35 and 28% of those over 35 had feelings of job burnout.[61] A study by the Society for Human Resources Management (SHRM) found that 70% of those surveyed worked over and above scheduled hours, including putting in extra time on the weekends; over 50% said that the pressure to do the extra work was "self-imposed."[62]

Stressors

A stressor is anything that causes tension.

Stressors are the experiences and events that cause tensions in our lives. Whether they come from work or non-work situations, from personality, or from trauma, stressors influence our attitudes, emotions and moods, behavior, job performance, and even health.[63] Having the Type A personality discussed earlier is an example of a personal stressor. Stressful life situations include such things as family events (e.g., the birth of a new child, marriage, divorce, moving), economics (e.g., a sudden loss of extra income), and personal affairs (e.g., a preoccupation with a bad relationship). Importantly, stressors from one space—work or non-work—can spill over to affect other areas of one's life.

Work can be full of stressors. In fact, 34% of workers in one survey reported that their jobs were so stressful that they thought of quitting.[64] We can experience work stressors like long hours of work, excessive e-mails, unrealistic deadlines, difficult supervisors or co-workers, unwelcome or unfamiliar work, and unrelenting change. Potential stressors also include excessively high or low task demands, role conflicts or ambiguities, poor interpersonal relations, and career progress that is too slow or too fast. Two troublesome stress syndromes caused by managerial miscues are *set up to fail*—holding performance expectations are impossible to reach or for which the available support is inadequate to the task, and *mistaken identity*—put people in jobs that don't match their talents, or that they simply don't like.[65]

Constructive Stress and Destructive Strain

Outcomes associated with the process of experiencing and dealing with stress vary from person to person and also from situation to situation. At times we experience **constructive stress**, sometimes called **eustress**, that is energizing and performance enhancing.[66] This is a positive stress outcome that encourages increased effort, stimulates creativity, and enhances diligence, while still not overwhelming the individual or causing negative health or behavioral outcomes. Individuals with a Type A personality, for example, are likely to work long hours and are less likely to be satisfied with poor performance. Challenging task demands move them toward ever-higher levels of task accomplishment. Even non-work stressors such as new family responsibilities may cause them to work harder in anticipation of greater financial rewards.

All too often it seems, we experience **destructive stress** or **strain** that shows up as a dysfunctional or negative impact on physical well-being, mental health, and behavior.[67] Medical researchers, for example, are concerned that too much strain harms health by reducing resistance to disease and increasing the likelihood of physical and/or mental illness. Other possible adverse health problems include hypertension, ulcers, substance abuse, overeating, depression, and muscle aches, among a wide range of other negative health outcomes.[68]

Figure 15.3 shows that people experiencing destructive stress at work may react through turnover, absenteeism, errors, accidents, dissatisfaction, and reduced work performance. A common outcome is **job burnout**, feelings of physical and mental exhaustion that can be personally incapacitating. A less common but very troubling outcome is **workplace rage**, aggressive behavior

Constructive stress or **eustress** is a positive stress outcome that can increase effort, stimulate creativity, and encourage diligence in one's work.

Destructive stress or **strain** is a negative stress outcome that impairs the performance and well-being of an individual.

Job burnout is a feeling of physical and mental exhaustion from work stress.

Workplace rage is showing aggressive behavior toward co-workers or the work setting.

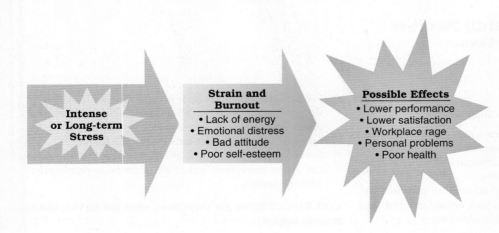

Intense or Long-term Stress

Strain and Burnout
• Lack of energy
• Emotional distress
• Bad attitude
• Poor self-esteem

Possible Effects
• Lower performance
• Lower satisfaction
• Workplace rage
• Personal problems
• Poor health

FIGURE 15.3
Potential negative consequences of a destructive job stress–burnout cycle.

toward co-workers and the work setting in general. Most often this rage is temporary and moderate, such as lost tempers. But, it can also explode into disturbing acts of violence and personal tragedy.[69]

Stress and Strain Management

Personal wellness is the pursuit of one's full potential through a personal health-promotion program.

The best strategy to manage work stress and strain is to prevent it from becoming excessive in the first place. A top priority for individuals and employers is **personal wellness**. Individually personal wellness means taking personal responsibility for your physical and mental health through a disciplined approach to such things as smoking, alcohol use, diet, exercise, and physical fitness. As an employer this could mean setting up wellness programs and assistance plans to help employees follow through with wellness commitments to healthy living, and insurance plans that include preventative services.

Strain also can be managed by taking actions to cope with and, hopefully, minimize the impact of personal and non-work stressors. Family difficulties may be relieved by a change in work schedule, or the anxiety these stressors cause may be reduced by a supportive supervisor.[70] Work stressors can sometimes be dealt with by role clarification through frank and open communication between supervisors and co-workers. Jobs can sometimes be redesigned to eliminate a poor fit between individuals' abilities and job demands.

Some employers are trying to reduce the tendency to "work too much" as a way of helping people "do better work." Surveys by Glassdoor, for example, show that only 25% of American workers used all their vacation days, and that 15% didn't take any at all.[71] The consulting firm KPMG uses a wellness scorecard to track and counsel workers who skip vacations and work excessive hours of overtime. Harvard scholar Leslie Perlow says the goal is to avoid "a feeling of having no time truly free from work, no control over work and no opportunity to ask questions to clarify foggy priorities."[72] The work–life balance issue—and getting a break from work—is critical for relieving the negative consequences of work stressors, including significant employee health outcomes.[73]

Learning Check 4

TAKEAWAYQUESTION 4 **How do emotions, moods, and stress influence individual behavior?**

BE SURE YOU CAN • define *emotion, mood,* and *stress* • explain how emotions and moods influence behavior • identify the common stressors found in work and in personal life • differentiate between constructive stress and destructive strain • define *job burnout* and *workplace rage* • discuss personal wellness as a stress management strategy

Management Learning Review
Get Prepared for **Quizzes and Exams**

SUMMARY

TAKEAWAYQUESTION 1

How do perceptions influence individual behavior?

- Perception acts as a filter through which people receive and process information from the environment.
- Because people perceive things differently, they may interpret and respond to situations differently.
- A healthy psychological contract occurs with perceived balance between work contributions, such as time and effort, and inducements received, such as pay and respect.

- Fundamental attribution error occurs when we blame others for performance problems while excluding possible external causes; self-serving bias occurs when we take personal credit for successes and blame failures on external factors.
- Stereotypes, projection, halo effects, and selective perception can distort perceptions and result in errors as people relate with one another.

FOR DISCUSSION Are there times when self-serving bias is actually helpful?

TAKEAWAY QUESTION 2

What should we know about personalities in the workplace?

- Personality is a set of traits and characteristics that cause people to behave in unique ways.
- The personality factors included in the Big Five model are extraversion, agreeableness, conscientiousness, emotional stability, and openness to experience.
- The Myers-Briggs Type Indicator profiles personalities in respect to tendencies toward extraversion–introversion, sensing–intuitive, thinking–feeling, and judging–perceiving.
- Additional personality dimensions of work significance include the personal conception traits of locus of control, authoritarianism, Machiavellianism, and behavioral self-monitoring, as well as the emotional adjustment trait of Type A orientation, and technology personality.

FOR DISCUSSION What dimension would you add to make the "Big Five" the "Big Six" personality model?

TAKEAWAY QUESTION 3

How do attitudes influence individual behavior?

- An attitude is a predisposition to respond in a certain way to people and things.
- Cognitive dissonance occurs when a person's attitude and behavior are inconsistent.
- Job satisfaction is an important work attitude that reflects a person's evaluation of the job, co-workers, and other aspects of the work setting.

SELF-TEST 15

Multiple-Choice Questions

1. In the psychological contract, job security is a/an _____, whereas loyalty is a/an _____.
   (a) satisfier factor, hygiene factor
   (b) intrinsic reward, extrinsic reward
   (c) inducement, contribution
   (d) attitude, personality trait

2. Self-serving bias is a form of attribution error that involves _____.
   (a) blaming yourself for problems caused by others
   (b) blaming the environment for problems you caused
   (c) poor emotional intelligence
   (d) authoritarianism

3. If a new team leader changes job designs for persons on her work team mainly "because I would prefer to work the new way rather than the old," the chances are that she is committing a perceptual error known as _____.
   (a) halo effect   (c) selective perception
   (b) stereotype   (d) projection

4. If a manager allows one characteristic of a person, say a pleasant personality, to bias performance ratings of that individual

- Job satisfaction influences work attendance and turnover and is related to other attitudes, such as job involvement and organizational commitment.
- Three possible explanations for the job satisfaction-to-performance relationship: satisfaction causes performance, performance causes satisfaction, and rewards cause both performance and satisfaction.

FOR DISCUSSION What should a manager do with an employee who has high job satisfaction but relatively low performance?

TAKEAWAY QUESTION 4

How do emotions, moods, and stress influence individual behavior?

- Emotions are strong feelings that are directed at someone or something; they influence behavior, often with intensity and for short periods of time.
- Moods are generalized positive or negative states of mind that can persistently influence one's behavior.
- Stress is a state of tension experienced by individuals facing extraordinary demands, constraints, or opportunities.
- Stress can be constructive in the form of eustress or destructive as strain; a moderate level of strain typically has a positive impact on performance.
- Strain can be managed through both prevention and coping strategies, including a commitment to personal wellness.

FOR DISCUSSION Is a Type A personality required for managerial success?

overall, the manager is committing a perceptual distortion known as _____.
(a) halo effect   (c) selective perception
(b) stereotype   (d) projection

5. Use of special dress, manners, gestures, and vocabulary words when meeting a prospective employer in a job interview are all examples of how people use _____ in daily life.
   (a) projection
   (b) selective perception
   (c) impression management
   (d) self-serving bias

6. A person with a/an _____ personality would most likely act unemotionally and manipulatively when trying to influence others to achieve personal goals.
   (a) extraverted   (c) self-monitoring
   (b) sensation-thinking   (d) Machiavellian

7. When a person believes that he or she has little influence over things that happen in life, this indicates a/an _____ personality.
   (a) low emotional stability   (c) high self-monitoring
   (b) external locus of control (d) intuitive-thinker

8. Among the Big Five personality traits, _____ indicates someone who is responsible, dependable, and careful with respect to tasks.
   (a) authoritarianism
   (b) agreeableness
   (c) conscientiousness
   (d) emotional stability

9. The _____ component of an attitude is what indicates a person's belief about something, whereas the _____ component indicates a specific positive or negative feeling about it.
   (a) cognitive, affective
   (b) emotional, affective
   (c) cognitive, attributional
   (d) behavioral, attributional

10. The term used to describe the discomfort someone feels when his or her behavior is inconsistent with an expressed attitude is _____.
    (a) alienation
    (b) cognitive dissonance
    (c) job dissatisfaction
    (d) person–job imbalance

11. Job satisfaction is known from research to be a good predictor of _____.
    (a) job performance
    (b) job burnout
    (c) conscientiousness
    (d) absenteeism

12. A person who is always willing to volunteer for extra work or to help someone else with his or her work is acting consistent with strong _____.
    (a) job performance
    (b) self-serving bias
    (c) emotional intelligence
    (d) organizational citizenship

13. Which statement about the job satisfaction–job performance relationship is most likely based on research?
    (a) A happy worker will be a productive worker.
    (b) A productive worker will be a happy worker.
    (c) A productive worker well rewarded for performance will be a happy worker.
    (d) There is no link between being happy and being productive in a job.

14. A/an _____ represents a rather intense but short-lived feeling about a person or a situation, whereas a/an _____ describes a more generalized positive or negative state of mind.
    (a) stressor, role ambiguity
    (b) external locus of control, internal locus of control
    (c) self-serving bias, halo effect
    (d) emotion, mood

15. Through _____, the stress people experience in their personal lives can create problems for them at work while the stress experienced at work can create problems for their personal lives.
    (a) eustress
    (b) self-monitoring
    (c) spillover effects
    (d) selective perception

Short-Response Questions

16. What is a healthy psychological contract?

17. What is the difference between self-serving bias and fundamental attribution error?

18. Which three of the Big Five personality traits do you believe most affect how well people work together in organizations, and why?

19. Why is it important for a manager to understand the Type A personality?

Essay Question

20. When Scott Tweedy picked up a magazine article on how to manage health care workers, he was pleased to find some advice. Scott was concerned about poor or mediocre performance on the part of several respiratory therapists in his clinic. The author of the article said that the "best way to improve performance is to make your workers happy." Scott was glad to have read this article and made a pledge to himself to start doing a much better job of making his employees happy. But should Scott follow this advice? What do we know about the relationship between job satisfaction and performance, and to apply this knowledge to the performance problems Scott has observed at his clinic?

Management Skills & Competencies Make yourself **valuable!**

Evaluate Career Situations

What Would You Do?

1. Putting Down Seniors

While standing on line at the office coffee machine, you overhear the person in front of you saying this to his friend: "I'm really tired of having to deal with the old-timers in here. It's time for them to call it quits. There's no way they can keep up the pace and handle all the new technology we're getting these days." You can listen and forget, or you can listen and act. What would you do or say here, and why? What does this comment suggest regarding age-based attributions of technology personality?

2. Compulsive Co-worker

You've noticed that one of your co-workers is always rushing, always uptight, and constantly criticizing herself while on the job. She never takes breaks when the rest of you do, and even at lunch it's hard to get her to stay and just talk for a while. Your guess is that she's fighting stressors from some sources other than work and the job itself. How can you help her out? What might you say?

3. Bad Mood in the Office

Your department head has just told you that some of your teammates have complained to him that you have been in a really bad mood lately. They like you and point out that this isn't characteristic of you at all. But, they also think your persistent bad mood is rubbing off on others in this situation. What can you do? Is there anything your supervisors or co-workers might do to help you get out of your funk?

Reflect on the Self-Assessment

Self-Monitoring

Instructions

Indicate your agreement with the following statements by circling the value that aligns with your belief. For example, if you believe that a statement is always false, circle the 0 next to that statement.[74]

5 = Certainly, always true
4 = Generally true
3 = Somewhat true, but with exceptions
2 = Somewhat false, but with exceptions
1 = Generally false
0 = Certainly, always false

1. In social situations, I have the ability to alter   5 4 3 2 1 0
   my behavior if I feel that something else is
   called for.

2. I am often able to read people's true emotions   5 4 3 2 1 0
   correctly through their eyes.

3. I have the ability to control the way I come   5 4 3 2 1 0
   across to people, depending on the impression
   I wish to give them.

4. In conversations, I am sensitive to even the   5 4 3 2 1 0
   slightest change in the facial expression of
   the person I'm conversing with.

5. My powers of intuition are quite good when it   5 4 3 2 1 0
   comes to understanding others' emotions and
   motives.

6. I can usually tell when others consider a joke   5 4 3 2 1 0
   in bad taste, even though they may laugh
   convincingly.

7. When I feel that the image I am portraying   5 4 3 2 1 0
   isn't working, I can readily change it to
   something that does.

8. I can usually tell when I've said something   5 4 3 2 1 0
   inappropriate by reading the listener's eyes.

9. I have trouble changing my behavior to suit   5 4 3 2 1 0
   different people and different situations.

10. I have found that I can adjust my behavior to   5 4 3 2 1 0
    meet the requirements of any situation I find
    myself in.

11. If someone is lying to me, I usually know it at   5 4 3 2 1 0
    once from that person's manner of expression.

12. Even when it might be to my advantage, I   5 4 3 2 1 0
    have difficulty putting up a good front.

13. Once I know what the situation calls for, it is   5 4 3 2 1 0
    easy for me to regulate my actions accordingly.

Scoring

Add the circled numbers except for 9 and 12. These are reverse-scored and you should add them into your total using these conversions: 5 = 0, 4 = 1, 3 = 2, 2 = 3, 1 = 4, 0 = 5. High self-monitoring is indicated by scores above 53.

Interpretation

This instrument offers an indication of your awareness of how you are being perceived by others and their reactions to your behavior in social situations. Persons with a high self-monitoring score tend to be quite aware of their public persona—the impression that they are leaving others with. They can use their ability to self-monitor to create a favorable social impression. Their behavior tends to change to match the demands of the situation. Persons with a low self-monitoring score, by contrast, are less aware of the impact that their words, actions, and expressions are having on others. They tend to maintain a fairly consistent self-presentation style and manner, regardless of their audience or the circumstances.

Contribute to the Class Exercise

Job Satisfaction Preferences

Preparation

Rank the following items for how important (1 = least important to 9 = most important) they are to your future job satisfaction.[75]
My job will be satisfying when it—

(a) is respected by other people.

(b) encourages continued development of knowledge and skills.

(c) provides job security.

(d) provides a feeling of accomplishment.

(e) provides the opportunity to earn a high income.

(f) is intellectually stimulating.

(g) rewards good performance with recognition.

(h) provides comfortable working conditions.

(i) permits advancement to high administrative responsibility.

Instructions

Form into groups as designated by your instructor. The group should be split by gender into two subgroups—one composed of men and one composed of women. Each group should first rank the items on their own. Then, the men should develop a consensus ranking of the items as they think women ranked them, and the women should do a consensus ranking of the items as they think men ranked them. The two subgroups should then get back together to share and discuss their respective rankings, paying special attention to reasons for the rankings attributed to the opposite gender group. A spokesperson for the men and for the women in each group should share their subgroup's rankings and highlights of the total group discussion with the class.

Optional Instructions

Form into groups consisting entirely of men or women. Each group should meet and decide which of the work values members of the opposite sex will rank first. Do this again for the work value ranked last. The reasons should be discussed, along with the reasons why each of the other values probably was not ranked first or last. A spokesperson for each group should share group results with the rest of the class.

Manage a Critical Incident

Facing Up to Attributions

You are the senior section manager for a medium-sized manufacturing firm producing high-tech digital devices. You've worked with this company for 8 years and supervise teams of materials engineers. As senior manager, you manage these teams, keep them working together effectively, and find ways to cut costs and increase profits. Because of recent government regulations, your manufacturing processes have undergone substantial changes. The firm has had to hire outside consultants to help with the manufacturing transition. The consultants have been tasked with training the engineers on the new protocol and evaluating their performance, which has declined substantially since the transition. Although historically the engineers have been very productive and received high performance evaluations, this last quarter the majority received poor evaluations and has been formally reprimanded by upper management. You have also been reprimanded for the reduced performance. The consultants have

attributed the performance declines to poor leadership and poor motivation. You know that neither the leadership these teams are given nor their motivation has changed.

Questions

What role might fundamental attribution errors and self-serving bias be playing here? What are the potential consequences of these poor performance evaluations and formal reprimands, and what can you do to offset any negatives? How might you explain the declining performance of the engineers, and what might you do to stop these declines?

Collaborate on the Team Activity

Difficult Personalities

Question

What personalities cause the most problems when people work together in teams, and what can be done to best deal with them?

Instructions

1. Do a survey of friends, family, co-workers, and even the public at large to get answers to these questions:

    (a) When you work in a team, what personalities do you have the most difficulty dealing with?

    (b) How do these personalities affect you, and how do they affect the team as a whole?

    (c) In your experience and for each of the "difficult personalities" that you have described, what have you found to be the best way of dealing with them?

    (d) How would you describe your personality, and are there any circumstances or situations in which you believe others could consider your personality "difficult" to deal with?

    (e) Do you engage in any self-management when it comes to your personality and how it fits when you are part of a team?

2. Gather the results of your survey, organize them for analysis, and then analyze them to see what patterns and insights your study has uncovered.

3. Prepare a report to share your study with the rest of your class.

Analyze THE INTEL
CaseStudy : Processing Individuals to Succeed

Go to *Management Cases for Critical Thinking* at the end of the book to find this case.

MOTIVATION THEORY AND PRACTICE

16

KEY TAKEAWAYS

- Explain theories of how individual needs motivate behavior.

- Identify the influences of expectancy, equity, goal-setting, and self-efficacy processes on motivation.

- Discuss the roles reinforcement principles and strategies play in motivation.

- Explain how job designs and alternative work schedules influence motivation.

SKILLS MAKE YOU **VALUABLE**

- **EVALUATE** *Career Situations:*
  What Would You Do?

- **REFLECT** *On the Self-Assessment:*
  Student Engagement Survey

- **CONTRIBUTE** *To the Class Exercise:*
  Why We Work

- **MANAGE** *A Critical Incident:*
  Great Worker Won't Take Vacation

- **COLLABORATE** *On the Team Activity:*
  CEO Pay . . . Too High, or Just Right?

- **ANALYZE** *The Case Study:*
  United Parcel Service: Delivering on Their Success

There are times when all of us lack the motivation to do something and other times when we are so "psyched" it's hard to stop what we're doing. These contrasting situations have intrigued and perplexed generations of social scientists. Even though there's more work for researchers to do, we've learned a lot about the conditions under which people—ourselves and others—can be highly motivated to work hard on the job, at school, and in leisure pursuits.

Did you know that J. K. Rowling's first Harry Potter book was rejected by 12 publishers; that the Beatles' "sound" cost them a deal with Decca Records; and, that Walt Disney lost a newspaper job because he supposedly "lacked imagination"?[1] Thank goodness they each didn't give up. Their "motivation" to stay engaged, hard working, and confident in their work paid off abundantly—for them and for the millions who have enjoyed the fruits of their labors.

Did you also know that only about 13% of global workers surveyed by Gallup report that they are actively "engaged" while 24% say they are actively "disengaged" on any given workday . . . that 25% of American employers believe their workers have low morale . . . that up to 40% of workers say that they have trouble staying motivated?[2] Such data raise questions like: Why do some people work enthusiastically, persevere in the face of difficulty, and often exceed the requirements of their job? Why do others hold back, quit at the first negative feedback, and do the minimum needed to avoid reprimand or termination? What can be done to ensure that every person, at every task, in every job, on every workday achieves the best possible performance?[3]

Individual Needs and Motivation

TAKEAWAY 1   How do individual needs influence motivation?

LEARN MORE | Hierarchy of needs theory • ERG theory • Two-factor theory
ABOUT | Acquired needs theory

Motivation accounts for the level, direction, and persistence of effort expended at work.

A **need** is an unfulfilled physiological or psychological desire.

The term **motivation** describes forces within individuals that account for the level, direction, and persistence of effort they expend at work. Simply put, a highly motivated person works hard at a job while an unmotivated person does not. One of a manager's most important responsibilities is to create conditions under which people feel consistently inspired to work hard.

Most discussions of motivation begin with the concept of individual **needs**—individuals' unfulfilled physiological or psychological desires. Although each of the following theories discusses a slightly different set of needs, all agree that needs create tensions that lead individuals to act in ways to help meet their needs. They suggest that managers should attempt to help people satisfy important needs through their work, and try to eliminate obstacles that block the satisfaction of needs.

Hierarchy of Needs Theory

Lower-order needs are physiological, safety, and social needs in Maslow's hierarchy.

Higher-order needs are esteem and self-actualization needs in Maslow's hierarchy.

The **deficit principle** states that a satisfied need does not motivate behavior.

The **progression principle** states that a need isn't activated until the next lower-level need is satisfied.

Abraham Maslow's theory of human needs is an important foundation in the history of management thought. The **lower-order needs** in his hierarchy include physiological, safety, and social concerns, while **higher-order needs** include esteem and self-actualization concerns.[4] Lower-order needs focus on desires for physical and social well-being; higher-order needs focus on desires for psychological development and growth.

Maslow used two principles to describe how these needs affect human behavior. The **deficit principle** provides that a satisfied need no longer motivates behavior. People are expected to act in ways that satisfy deprived needs—that is, needs for which there is a "deficit." The **progression principle** states that the need at one level does not become activated until the next-lower-level need in the hierarchy is already satisfied. People are expected to advance step by step up the hierarchy in their quest for need satisfaction. This progression principle ends at the level of self-actualization. According to the theory, the need to self-actualize can never be met fully. In fact, the more the need for self-actualization is satisfied, the stronger it is theorized to grow.

Figure 16.1 illustrates how managers can use Maslow's ideas to better meet the needs of the people with whom they work. Notice that higher-order self-actualization needs are served by opportunities like creative and challenging work and job autonomy; esteem needs are served by respect, responsibility, praise, and recognition. The satisfaction of lower-order social, safety, and physiological needs depends on aspects of the work environment, such as positive interactions with others, compensation and benefits, and reasonable working conditions.

ERG Theory

Existence needs are desires for physical well-being.

Relatedness needs are desires for good interpersonal relationships.

Growth needs are desires for personal growth and development.

One of the most promising efforts to build on Maslow's work is the ERG theory proposed by Clayton Alderfer.[5] This theory collapses Maslow's five needs categories into three. **Existence needs** are desires for physiological and material well-being. **Relatedness needs** are desires for satisfying interpersonal relationships. **Growth needs** are desires for continued psychological growth and development.

Existence and relatedness needs are similar to the lower-order needs in Maslow's hierarchy, while growth needs are essentially the higher-order needs in Maslow's hierarchy. Beyond that, the dynamics of ERG theory differ somewhat from Maslow's hierarchy of needs.

ERG theory doesn't include the progression principle that certain needs must be satisfied before other needs become activated. Instead, it maintains the various needs can influence individuals' behavior at any given time. Alderfer also rejects the deficit principle that only unsatisfied

What satisfies higher-order needs?

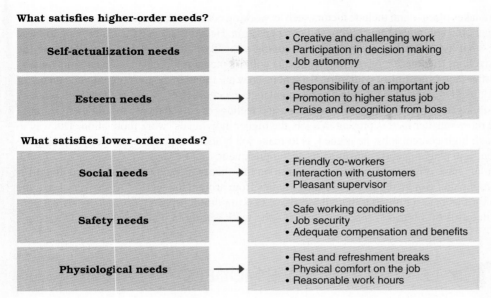

What satisfies lower-order needs?

needs have motivational impact. According to his **frustration-regression principle**, an already satisfied need can become reactivated and influence behavior when a higher-level need cannot be satisfied. Workers who are stuck in simple and repetitive jobs that offer little room for growth and limited opportunities for promotion, for example, will be frustrated in attempts to satisfy their growth needs. Their response could be to refocus attention on getting better work schedules, working conditions, and even pay and benefits to further fulfill their existence needs.

The **frustration-regression principle** states that an already satisfied need can become reactivated when a higher-level need is blocked.

Two-Factor Theory

Frederick Herzberg developed the two-factor theory of motivation from a pattern discovered in almost 4,000 interviews.[6] When asked what they disliked about their jobs, respondents talked mostly about issues related directly to the nature of the work itself. Herzberg called these **satisfier factors**, or motivator factors. When asked what they liked, respondents talked more about issues related to the actual work environment. Herzberg called these **hygiene factors**. As shown in Figure 16.2, Herzberg argued that these two factors affect people in different ways.

Two-factor theory links hygiene factors with job dissatisfaction. Job dissatisfaction goes up as hygiene quality goes down. Hygiene factors are found in the job context—the environment in which

A **satisfier factor** is found in job content, such as challenging and exciting work, recognition, responsibility, advancement opportunities, or personal growth.

A **hygiene factor** is found in the job context, such as working conditions, interpersonal relations, organizational policies, and compensation.

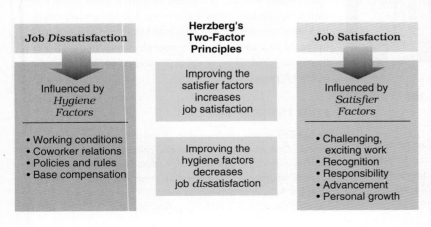

the work takes place—and include factors such as working conditions, interpersonal relations, organizational policies and administration, and compensation. Herzberg argued that improving in these factors, such as remodeling work spaces or adding a quality cafeteria, can help to decrease job dissatisfaction. But, these hygiene improvements will not increase job satisfaction and motivation.

Satisfier factors are linked with job satisfaction. They are found in the job content—the nature of the work itself—and include things like job challenge, recognition for work well done, a sense of responsibility, the opportunity for advancement, and feelings of personal growth. Herzberg believed that the more satisfier factors present in a job, the higher individuals' work motivation. The way to build such high-content jobs, he argued, is to make job holders responsible for not just doing the work, but also planning and controlling its accomplishment.

Scholars have criticized Herzberg's research on this theory as being method-bound and difficult to replicate.[7] But he reports confirming studies from around the world.[8] At the very least, the two-factor theory is a reminder that all jobs have two important aspects: *job content*—what people do in terms of job tasks—and *job context*—the work setting in which they do it. Herzberg's

wisdom > LEARN FROM ROLE MODELS

> *The nonprofit's mission is combining "rigorous research with innovative solutions to improve the health and quality of life of young people with chronic illness."*

Video Game Motivates High-Risk Kids to Take Medicines

HopeLab/AP/Wide World Photos

Although many of us play video games just for fun, teens with cancer can now play games that can help them to beat the disease. Picture a teenager who has a tough time keeping up with cancer medication schedules. Now imagine him playing the video game called Re-Mission and maneuvering a nanobot called Roxxi through the body of a cancer patient to destroy cancer cells. Then think about an article in the medical journal *Pediatrics* that reports teen patients who play the game at least one hour a week do a better job of sticking to their medication schedules.

What's taking place is the brainchild of HopeLab, founded by Pam Omidyar. An immunology researcher and gaming enthusiast, Omidyar saw the possible link between games and fighting disease. The nonprofit's mission is combining "rigorous research with innovative solutions to improve the health and quality of life of young people with chronic illness."

One of HopeLab's products is Zamzee, described as a "game-based website." It includes an activity meter where kids earn points for movement and activity. A recent research study looking at possible benefits concluded that "kids using Zamzee increased their moderate-to-vigorous physical activity (MVPA) by an average of 59%—or approximately 45 additional minutes of MVPA per week."

FIND THE INSPIRATION

Re-Mission is one positive step in the war against childhood cancer. One of HopeLab's current priorities is to use video gaming in the fight against childhood obesity. Think about how creative approaches to motivation might be used to improve peoples' lives in other ways as well.

advice to managers also makes good sense: (1) Correct poor job context to eliminate potential job dissatisfaction; (2) build satisfier factors into job content to maximize job satisfaction.

Acquired Needs Theory

David McClelland and his colleagues developed yet another approach to the study of human needs. They began by asking people to view pictures and write stories about what they saw.[9] These stories were then content-analyzed for themes that display the strengths of three needs—achievement, power, and affiliation. According to McClelland, people acquire or develop these needs over time as a result of individual life experiences.

> ### Work Preferences of High-Need Achievers
> • Challenging but achievable goals
> • Feedback on performance
> • Individual responsibility

Because each need can be linked with a distinct set of work preferences, he encourages managers to understand these needs in themselves and in others, and to try and create work environments responsive to them.

Need for achievement is the desire to do something better or more efficiently, to solve problems, or to master complex tasks. People with a high need for achievement like to put their competencies to work; they take moderate risks in competitive situations, and are willing to work alone. As a result, high-need achievers' work preferences include individual responsibility for results, achievable but challenging goals, and performance feedback.

Need for power is the desire to control other people, to influence their behavior, or to be responsible for them. People with a high need for power are motivated to behave in ways that have a clear impact on other people and events. They enjoy being in control of situations and being recognized for this responsibility. Importantly, though, McClelland distinguishes between two forms of the power need. The *need for personal power* is exploitative and involves manipulation for the pure sake of personal gratification. This type of power need does not lead to management success. The *need for social power* involves the use of power in socially responsible ways directed toward group or organizational objectives rather than personal gains. This need for social power is essential to effective managerial leadership.

Need for affiliation is the desire to establish and maintain friendly and warm relations with other people. People with a high need for affiliation seek companionship, social approval, and satisfying interpersonal relationships. They tend to like jobs that involve working with people and offer opportunities for social approval. This is consistent with managerial work. But, McClelland believes that managers must be careful that high needs for affiliation don't interfere with decision making. There are times when managers and leaders must act in ways that others disagree with. If the need for affiliation limits the ability to make these tough decisions, managerial effectiveness gets lost. In McClelland's view, successful executives are likely to have a high need for social power that is greater than an otherwise strong need for affiliation.

Need for achievement is the desire to do something better, to solve problems, or to master complex tasks.

Need for power is the desire to control, influence, or be responsible for other people.

Need for affiliation is the desire to establish and maintain good relations with people.

Learning Check 1

TAKEAWAYQUESTION **1 How do individual needs influence motivation?**

BE SURE YOU CAN • define *motivation* and *needs* • describe work practices that satisfy higher-order and lower-order needs in Maslow's hierarchy • contrast Maslow's hierarchy with ERG theory • describe work practices that influence hygiene factors and satisfier factors in Herzberg's two-factor theory • explain McClelland's needs for achievement, power, and affiliation • describe work conditions that satisfy people with a high need for achievement

Process Theories of Motivation

TAKEAWAY 2   What are the process theories of motivation?

LEARN MORE | Equity theory • Expectancy theory • Goal-setting theory • Self-efficacy theory
ABOUT |

Although the details vary, each of the needs theories offers insights on individual differences and how managers can deal effectively with them. Another set of motivation theories, the process theories, add further to this understanding. These include the equity, expectancy, goal-setting, and self-efficacy theories.

Equity Theory

Fact: In 1965, the average CEO pay in S&P companies was 24 times that of the typical worker; in 1980, it was 42 times; in 2001, it was 202 times; by 2012, it was 354 times.

How do these data strike you?[10] Do they motivate you as an aspiring CEO? Or, do they concern you as someone who empathizes with hourly and lower-wage workers? For many people, facts like these bring the words "equity" and "fairness" to mind. In fact, one of the best known motivation theories is the equity theory of motivation, brought to us through the work of J. Stacy Adams.[11] It is based on the idea that we all want to be treated fairly in comparison to others. The theory suggests that being unfairly treated (whether we receive too little or too much when compared to someone else) makes people uncomfortable. When this happens, we're motivated to eliminate the discomfort and restore a sense of perceived equity to the situation.

Equity and Social Comparison

Figure 16.3 shows how the equity dynamic works. According to equity theory, people compare their outcomes-to-inputs ratio to the outcomes-to-inputs ratios of others (called a *referent*). Outcomes are what an individual receives from work—including things like pay, benefits, job security, advancement opportunities, autonomy, interesting work experiences, and anything else that the employee values. Inputs are the qualifications an individual possesses and the contributions made to the organization—including things like education, experience, special skills and training, the quality and quantity of work completed, and a positive attitude and loyalty.

Perceived inequities occur whenever people feel that the outcomes they receive for their work contributions are unfair in comparison to the outcomes received by others. Equity comparisons are especially common whenever managers allocate rewards such as pay raises, preferred job assignments, work privileges, and even office space or new technology. Equity comparisons can be made with co-workers—individual equity comparisons, others at different levels within the same organization—internal equity comparisons, or even people employed by other organizations—external equity comparisons.

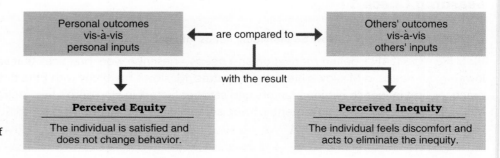

FIGURE 16.3
Equity theory and the role of social comparison.

Equity Dynamics

A key point in the equity theory is that people behave according to their perceptions. For example, in the case of a pay raise, it isn't the reward's absolute value or the manager's intentions that influence individuals' behavior; the recipient's perceptions determine the motivational impact of the raise.

An individual who perceives that she or he is being treated unfairly in comparison to others will be motivated to act in ways that reduce the perceived inequity. There are two basic types of inequity: over-reward or positive inequity and under-reward or negative inequity. **Over-reward inequity** occurs when individuals perceive that they are receiving more than what is fair. That is, the outcomes-to-inputs ratio is greater than that of a referent other. While such perceptions do occur, it is much more common for individuals to experience **under-reward inequity**. The perception here is of receiving less than what is deserved in comparison to someone else. Adams predicted that people try to deal with such perceived negative inequity in the following ways:

- Changing their work inputs by putting less effort into their jobs—"If that's all I'm going to get, I'm going to do a lot less."

- Changing the rewards received by asking for better treatment—"Next stop, the boss's office; I should get what I deserve."

- Changing the inputs or outcomes of their referent—"Bob either needs to work as hard as the rest of us or else he shouldn't get the same bonus that we get."

- Changing the person to whom you compare yourself to make things seem better— "Well, if I look at Marissa's situation, I'm still doing pretty well."

- Changing the situation by leaving the job—"No way I'm going to stick around here if this is the way you get treated."

In **over-reward inequity** (positive inequity) an individual perceives that rewards are more than what is fair.

In **under-reward inequity** (negative inequity) an individual perceives that rewards are less than what is fair.

◀ How people deal with under-reward inequity

ethics > KNOW RIGHT FROM WRONG

> *"Why don't I pass this information along anonymously so that everyone knows what's going on?"*

Information Goldmine Creates Equity Dilemma

A worker opens the top of the office photocopier and finds a document someone has left behind. It's a list of performance evaluations, pay, and bonuses for 80 co-workers. She reads the document, and finds something very surprising. Someone she considers a "nonstarter" is getting paid more than others regarded as "super workers." New hires are also being brought in at much higher pay and bonuses than those of current staff. To make matters worse, she's in the middle of the list and not near the top, where she would have expected to be. The fact is she makes a lot less money than many others.

Looking at the data, she begins to question why she is spending extra hours working evenings and weekends at home, trying to do a really great job for the firm. She wonders to herself: "Should I pass this information around anonymously so that everyone knows what's going on? Or should I quit and find another employer who fully values me for my talents and hard work?"

In the end she decided to quit, saying: "I just couldn't stand the inequity." She also decided not to distribute the information to others in the office because "it would make them depressed, like it made me depressed."

WHAT DO YOU THINK?

What would you do in this situation? You're going to be concerned and perhaps upset. Would you hit "print," make about 80 copies, and put them in everyone's mailboxes—or even just leave them stacked in a couple of convenient locations? That would get the information out into the gossip chains pretty quickly. But is this ethical? If you don't send out the information, on the other hand, is it ethical to let other workers go about their days with inaccurate assumptions about the firm's pay practices? By quitting and not sharing the information, did this worker commit an ethics mistake?

Equity Research and Insights

The research on equity theory is most conclusive with respect to perceived negative inequity. Those who feel under-rewarded appear to be more likely to make active attempts to restore equity than those who feel over-rewarded.[12] But, there is some evidence that equity dynamics can occur among people who feel perceived positive inequity from being over-rewarded. In such cases, attempts to restore perceived equity may involve increasing the quantity or quality of work, taking on more difficult assignments, or advocating for others to be compensated more fairly.

Managers should anticipate that perceptions of negative inequity arise when especially visible rewards such as pay or promotions are given. They should make sure that processes for allocating rewards are objectively fair, and also that they are perceived to be fair. One way to do this is to be as transparent as possible. At a minimum, managers should communicate the intended value of the rewards being given, clarify the performance appraisals on which they are based, and suggest appropriate comparison points. This advice is particularly relevant in organizations using merit-based pay-for-performance systems. A common problem in these systems is that what constitutes "meritorious" performance can be a source of debate. Any disagreement over performance ratings increases the likelihood of negative equity dynamics problems.

Equity Sensitivity

Equity sensitivity reflects that people have different preferences for equity and react differently to perceptions of inequity.

While equity theory is based on the premise that all employees desire fairness, research suggests that equity considerations are not equally important to all individuals. The idea of **equity sensitivity** proposes that people have different preferences for equity and thus react differently to perceptions of inequity. Differences in equity sensitivity are usually described as follows.[13] *Benevolents* are less concerned about being under-rewarded. They more readily accept situations of negative inequity while situations of positive inequity make them very uncomfortable. *Sensitives* have a strong preference for equitable distribution of rewards. They react as the basic theory proposes. *Entitleds* have a desire to be over-rewarded. They try to create situations of positive inequity for themselves and react very negatively in situations of perceived negative inequity.

Expectancy Theory

Expectancy is a person's belief that working hard will result in high task performance.

Victor Vroom's expectancy theory of motivation asks the question: What determines people's willingness to work hard at organizational-critical tasks?[14] The answer is that motivation depends on the relationships between three expectancy factors depicted in Figure 16.4 and described here:

- **Expectancy**—a person's belief that working hard will result in achieving a desired level of task performance (this is sometimes called effort-performance expectancy).

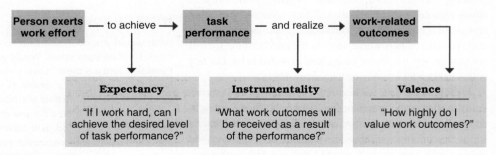

FIGURE 16.4
Elements in the expectancy theory of motivation.

- **Instrumentality**—a person's belief that successful performance will be followed by rewards and other work-related outcomes (this is sometimes called performance-outcome expectancy).

- **Valence**—the value a person assigns to the possible rewards and other work-related outcomes.

Instrumentality is a person's belief that various outcomes will occur as a result of task performance.

Valence is the value a person assigns to work-related outcomes.

Motivation = Expectancy × Instrumentality × Valence

In expectancy theory, motivation (M), expectancy (E), instrumentality (I), and valence (V) are related to one another in a multiplicative fashion: $M = E \times I \times V$. In other words, motivation is determined by expectancy times instrumentality times valence. Mathematically, a zero at any location on the right side of the equation (that is, for E, I, or V) will result in zero motivation. What this means in practice is that all three factors must be high and positive for motivation to also be high.[15]

Suppose, for example, that a manager is wondering whether or not the prospect of earning a promotion will be motivational to a job holder. Expectancy theory predicts that a person's motivation to work hard for a promotion will be low if any one or more of the following three conditions apply. First, if expectancy is low, motivation will suffer. This is a negative answer to the "If I

> ## Managing by Expectancy Theory
>
> *Create high expectancies*—Select capable workers, train them well, support them with adequate resources.
>
> *Create high instrumentalities*—Clarify rewards earned by performance, give rewards on performance-contingent basis.
>
> *Create positive valences*—Identify individual needs, offer rewards that satisfy these needs.

try hard, will I succeed?" question. The person may lack confidence that he or she can achieve the performance level necessary to get promoted. So, why try? Second, if instrumentality is low, motivation will suffer. This is a negative answer to the "If I succeed, will I be rewarded?" question. The person may lack confidence that a high level of task performance will result in being promoted. Perhaps the manager is notorious for promoting close friends or hiring from the outside, so why try? Third, if valence is low, motivation will suffer. This is a negative answer to the "What does the possible reward for this hard work and performance achievement mean to me?" question. The person may place little value on receiving a promotion because it would require longer hours away from home or because it would require relocation to another city. It simply isn't a desired reward. So, why try for it?

Expectancy Theory Applications

Expectancy theory reminds managers and team leaders that people answer the question "Why should I work hard today?" in different ways. Every person has unique needs, preferences, and concerns at work. Knowing this, a manager should try to build work environments that respect individual differences so that expectancies, instrumentalities, and valences all support motivation.

To maximize expectancy, people must believe in their abilities. They must believe that if they try, they can perform. This is an issue of perceived competency. Managers can build positive expectancies by selecting workers with the right abilities for the jobs to be done, providing them with the best training and development, and supporting them with resources so that the jobs can be accomplished. *To maximize instrumentality, people must see the link between high performance and work outcomes.* This is an issue of rewards for accomplishments. Managers can create positive instrumentalities by clarifying the possible rewards for high performance and then allocating these rewards fairly and on a performance-contingent basis. *To maximize positive valence, people must value the outcomes associated with high performance*. This is an issue of individual differences. Managers can use the content theories to help understand what needs are important to different individuals. Steps can then be taken to link these needs with outcomes having positive valences and that can be earned through high performance.

Goal-Setting Theory

Steven A. Davis rose through a series of management jobs to become CEO of Bob Evans Farms in Columbus, Ohio.[16] His parents gave him lots of encouragement as a child. "They never said that because you are an African-American, you can only go this far or do only this or that," he says, "they just said 'go for it'." Davis set goals when he graduated from college—to be a corporate vice president in 10 years and a president in 20. Expectancy theory would suggest that his parents increased his motivation by creating high positive expectancy during his school years. Goal-setting theory would suggest that Davis found lots of motivation through the goals he set as a college graduate.

Goal-Setting Essentials

The basic premise of Edwin Locke's goal-setting theory is that task goals can be highly motivating if they are properly set and well managed.[17] Goals give people direction in their work. They clarify the performance expectations in supervisory relationships, between co-workers, and across organizational subunits. They establish a frame of reference for task feedback. Goals also set a foundation for behavioral self-management.

The motivational benefits of goal setting occur when managers and team leaders work with others to set the right goals in the right ways. The box below points out that goal specificity, goal difficulty, goal acceptance, and goal commitment are all important. Managers can use goal setting in these and related ways to enhance employees' work performance and job satisfaction.

Goal Setting and Participation

Participation goes a long way toward unlocking the motivational power of task goals. When managers and team members join in a participative process of goal setting and performance review, members are likely to experience greater motivation. Participation increases understanding of task goals, increases acceptance and commitment to them, and creates more readiness to receive feedback bearing on goal accomplishment.

It isn't always possible to allow participation when selecting which goals need to be pursued. But it can be possible to allow participation in deciding how best to pursue them. It's also true that the constraints of time and other factors in some situations may not allow for participation. But Locke's research suggests that workers respond positively to externally imposed goals if supervisors assigning them are trusted, and if workers believe they will be adequately supported in their attempts to achieve them.

Goal-Setting Downsides

It is important to remember that poorly set and managed goals can have a downside

---

How to Make Goal Setting Work for You

- *Set specific goals:* They lead to higher performance than do more generally stated ones, such as "do your best."

- *Set challenging goals:* When viewed as realistic and attainable, more difficult goals lead to higher performance than do easy goals.

- *Build goal acceptance and commitment:* People work harder for goals they accept and believe in; they resist goals forced on them.

- *Clarify goal priorities:* Make sure that expectations are clear as to which goals should be accomplished first, and why.

- *Provide feedback on goal accomplishment:* Make sure that people know how well they are doing with respect to goal accomplishment.

- *Reward goal accomplishment:* Don't let positive accomplishments pass unnoticed; reward people for doing what they set out to do.

that actually turns the motivation to accomplish them into performance negatives rather than positives.[18] A good example is the scandal over patient waiting times in U.S. Veterans Affairs hospitals and clinics, where more than 120,000 veterans failed to get care and at least 23 died while awaiting treatment.[19] A VA audit report described the negative effects of working with unrealistic goals— a maximum of 14 days for patient waiting times—this way: "simply not attainable" . . . "an organizational leadership failure." The audit also said that the pressures to meet unattainable goals to achieve pay bonuses motivated some schedulers "to utilize unofficial lists or engage in inappropriate practices in order to make waiting times appear more favorable."[20] Lawmakers at a congressional hearing claimed the VA had an "outlandish bonus culture" and that the fabricated records were motivated by a "quest for monetary gain."[21]

These patterns of behavior in the Veterans Affairs case are consistent with research that identifies goal-setting downsides when managers and leaders set or allow unrealistically high goals, when individuals are expected to meet high goals over and over again, and when people striving to meet high goals aren't given the support they need to accomplish them.[22] Scholars Gary Latham and Gerard Seijts sum up the research implications this way: "It is foolish and even immoral for organizations to assign employees stretch goals without equipping them with the resources to succeed— and still punish them when they fail to reach those goals. This lack of guidance often leads to stress, burnout, and in some instances, unethical behavior."[23]

Self-Efficacy Theory

Closely related to both the expectancy and goal-setting approaches to motivation is self-efficacy theory, also referred to as social learning theory. Based on the work of psychologist Albert Bandura, **self-efficacy** refers to a person's belief that she or he is capable of performing a specific task.[24] You can think of self-efficacy using such terms as confidence, competence, and ability. From a manager's perspective, the major point is that anything done to boost employees' feelings of self-efficacy is likely to pay off with increased motivation.

Self-efficacy is a person's belief that she or he is capable of performing a task.

Mahatma Gandhi once said: "If I have the belief that I can do it, I shall surely acquire the capacity to do it, even if I may not have it at the beginning."[25] This is the essence of self-efficacy theory. When people believe themselves to be capable, they will set higher goals for themselves, be more motivated to work hard at these goals, and persist longer in the face of any obstacles that impede their progress. The *Wall Street Journal* has called this "the unshakable belief some people have that they have what it takes to succeed."[26]

There are clear links between Bandura's self-efficacy theory, elements of Vroom's expectancy theory, and Locke's goal-setting theory. With respect to Vroom, a person with higher self-efficacy will have greater expectancy that he or she can achieve a high level of task performance. With respect to Locke, a person with higher self-efficacy should be more willing to set challenging performance goals. In terms of expectancy and goal setting, managers who help create feelings of self-efficacy in others should boost their motivation to work.

Bandura identifies four major ways that we can enhance self-efficacy.[27] First is *enactive mastery*—when a person gains confidence through positive experience. The greater your initial success and the more experience you have with a task, the more confident you become at doing it. Second is *vicarious modeling*—learning by observing others. When someone else is good at a task and we observe how they do it, we gain confidence in being able to do it ourselves. Third is *verbal persuasion*—when someone tells us that we can or encourages us to perform a task. Hearing others praise our efforts and link those efforts with performance successes can be very motivational. Fourth is *emotional arousal*—when we are highly stimulated or energized to perform well in a situation. A good analogy for arousal is how athletes get "psyched up" and highly motivated to compete.

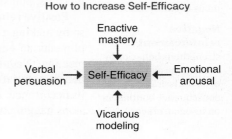
How to Increase Self-Efficacy

Learning Check 2

BE SURE YOU CAN • explain the role of social comparison in Adams's equity theory • describe how people with felt negative inequity behave • define *equity sensitivity* • define *expectancy, instrumentality,* and *valence* • explain Vroom's expectancy theory equation: M = E × I × V • explain Locke's goal-setting theory • define *self-efficacy* and explain four ways to increase it

Reinforcement Theory

TAKEAWAY 3   What role does reinforcement play in motivation?

LEARN MORE | The law of effect • Reinforcement strategies
ABOUT | Positive reinforcement • Punishment

The motivation theories discussed so far have tried to explain why people do things in terms of satisfying needs, resolving felt inequities, evaluating expectancies, and pursuing task goals. Reinforcement theory, by contrast, views human behavior as determined by its environmental consequences. Instead of looking within the individual to explain what drives motivation, this perspective focuses on the external environment and its consequences.

The Law of Effect

The law of effect states that behavior followed by pleasant consequences is likely to be repeated; behavior followed by unpleasant consequences is not.

Operant conditioning is the control of behavior by manipulating its consequences.

Positive reinforcement strengthens behavior by making a desirable consequence contingent on its occurrence.

Negative reinforcement strengthens behavior by making the avoidance of an undesirable consequence contingent on its occurrence.

The basic premise of reinforcement theory is based on what E. L. Thorndike called the **law of effect**. It states: Behavior that results in a pleasant outcome is likely to be repeated; behavior that results in an unpleasant outcome is not likely to be repeated.[28] This law underlies the concept of **operant conditioning**, which was popularized by psychologist B. F. Skinner as the process of applying the law of effect to control behavior by manipulating its consequences.[29] You may think of operant conditioning as learning by reinforcement. When applied in management, its goal is to use reinforcement principles to systematically reinforce desirable work behavior and discourage undesirable work behavior.[30]

Reinforcement Strategies

Figure 16.5 shows four strategies of reinforcement that can be used in operant conditioning—positive reinforcement, negative reinforcement, punishment, and extinction. The figure uses a quality example to illustrate how these strategies can be used to influence work behavior. Note that both positive and negative reinforcement strategies strengthen desired work behavior when it occurs; punishment and extinction strategies weaken or eliminate undesirable behaviors.

    Positive reinforcement strengthens or increases the frequency of desirable behavior. It does so by making a pleasant consequence contingent on its occurrence. *Example:* A manager compliments an employee on his or her creativity in making a helpful comment during a staff meeting. **Negative reinforcement** also strengthens or increases the frequency of desirable behavior, but it does so by making the avoidance of an unpleasant consequence contingent on its occurrence. *Example:* A manager who has been nagging a worker every day about tardiness stops nagging when the individual shows up on time for work.

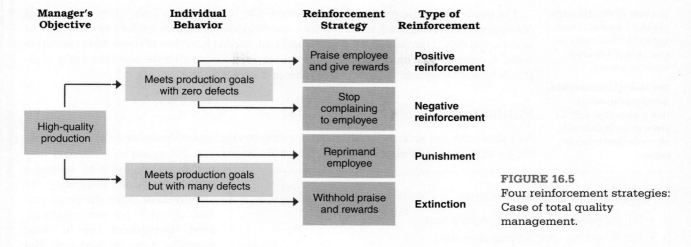

Manager's Objective	Individual Behavior	Reinforcement Strategy	Type of Reinforcement

FIGURE 16.5
Four reinforcement strategies: Case of total quality management.

Punishment decreases the frequency of an undesirable behavior—or eliminates it entirely. It does so by making an unpleasant consequence contingent on its occurrence. *Example:* A manager issues a written reprimand to an employee whose careless work is creating quality problems. **Extinction** also decreases the frequency of or eliminates an undesirable behavior, but does so by making the removal of a pleasant consequence contingent on its occurrence. *Example:* A manager observes that a disruptive employee is receiving social approval from co-workers who laugh at his jokes during staff meetings; the manager counsels co-workers to ignore the jokes and stop providing approval of this behavior.

Punishment discourages behavior by making an unpleasant consequence contingent on its occurrence.

Extinction discourages behavior by making the removal of a desirable consequence contingent on its occurrence.

Positive Reinforcement

Positive reinforcement deserves special attention among the reinforcement strategies. It should be part of any manager's motivational toolkit. Sir Richard Branson, founder of Virgin Group, is a believer. "For the people who work for you or with you, you must lavish praise on them at all times," he says. "If a flower is watered, it flourishes. If not, it shrivels

Guidelines for Positive Reinforcement

- Clearly identify desired work behaviors.
- Maintain a diverse inventory of rewards.
- Inform everyone what must be done to get rewards.
- Recognize individual differences when allocating rewards.
- Follow the laws of immediate and contingent reinforcement.

up and dies." Besides, he adds, "It is much more fun looking for the best in people."[31] David Novak, CEO of Yum! Brands, Inc., is also a believer. He claims that one of his most important tasks as CEO is "to get people fired up" and that "you can never underestimate the power of telling someone he's doing a good job." Novak advocates celebrating "first downs and not just touchdowns," which means publicly recognizing and rewarding small wins that keep everyone motivated for the long haul.[32]

The box presents useful guidelines for positive reinforcement. One way to put them into action is through a process known as **shaping**.[33] This is the creation of a new behavior by the positive reinforcement of successive approximations to it. **Continuous reinforcement** administers a reward each time a desired—or approximated—behavior occurs. **Intermittent reinforcement** rewards behavior only periodically. Continuous reinforcement tends to work best to encourage desired behaviors through shaping, while intermittent reinforcement works best to maintain it.

Shaping is positive reinforcement of successive approximations to the desired behavior.

Continuous reinforcement rewards each time a desired behavior occurs.

Intermittent reinforcement rewards behavior only periodically.

The law of contingent reinforcement is that a reward should only be given when a desired behavior occurs.

The law of immediate reinforcement is that a reward should be given as soon as possible after a desired behavior occurs.

The power of positive reinforcement is governed by two important laws.[34] First is the **law of contingent reinforcement**. It states that for a reward to have maximum reinforcing value, it must be delivered only if the desired behavior is exhibited. Second is the **law of immediate reinforcement**. It states that the more immediate the delivery of a reward after the occurrence of a desirable behavior, the greater the reinforcing value of the reward.

Punishment

As a reinforcement strategy, punishment attempts to eliminate undesirable behavior by making an unpleasant consequence contingent on its occurrence. For example, a manager may punish an employee by issuing a verbal reprimand, suspending the employee, or fining the employee. Just as with positive reinforcement, punishment can be done poorly or it can be done well. But because punishment can have a harmful effect on relationships, it should be used sparingly. The box (left) offers advice on how best to handle punishment as a reinforcement strategy.

Guidelines for Punishment

- Tell the person what is being done wrong.
- Tell the person what is being done right.
- Focus on the undesirable behavior, not on personal characteristics.
- Make sure the punishment matches the behavior so that it is neither too harsh nor too lenient.
- Administer the punishment in private.
- Follow the laws of immediate and contingent reinforcement.

Learning Check 3

TAKEAWAYQUESTION 3 **What role does reinforcement play in motivation?**

BE SURE YOU CAN • explain the law of effect and operant conditioning • illustrate how positive reinforcement, negative reinforcement, punishment, and extinction influence work behavior • explain the reinforcement technique of shaping • describe how managers can use the laws of immediate and contingent reinforcement • list guidelines for positive reinforcement and punishment

Motivation and Job Design

TAKEAWAY 4   What is the link between job design and motivation?

LEARN MORE ABOUT | Job simplification • Job enlargement • Job enrichment
Alternative work schedules

Job design is arranging work tasks for individuals and groups.

One place where motivation theories can have a significant impact is **job design**, the process of arranging work tasks for individuals and groups. Building jobs so that satisfaction and performance go hand in hand is in many ways an exercise in generating "fit" between task requirements and people's needs, capabilities, and interests.[35] The alternatives range from job simplification at one extreme to job enrichment at the other.

Job Simplification

Job simplification employs people in clearly defined and specialized tasks with narrow job scope.

Job simplification standardizes work procedures and employs people in well-defined and highly specialized tasks.[36] Simplified jobs, such as those in classic automobile assembly lines, limited menu restaurants such as McDonalds, and call center phone solicitation, are narrow in *job scope*—the number and variety of different tasks a person performs.

The logic of job simplification is straightforward. Because these jobs don't require complex skills, workers should be more easily and quickly trained, less difficult to supervise, and easily replaced if they leave. Because tasks are well defined, workers should become more efficient by performing them over and over again. But, things don't always work out as planned.[37] Routine, structured, and repetitive tasks can cause problems if workers become bored and alienated. Productivity can decline when unhappy workers do poor work. Costs can increase when low job satisfaction leads to more absenteeism and turnover.

One way to eliminate the problems with job simplification is **automation**, the total mechanization of a job. One example is in manufacturing where robots are being used to perform tasks previously done by humans. A second is evident each time you use an ATM machine; this technology is basically an automated replacement for a human teller.

Another way to deal with job simplification problems, **job rotation** gives workers more variety by periodically shifting them between jobs. Also, **job enlargement** increases task variety by combining into one job two or more tasks that were previously assigned to separate workers. It is sometimes called *horizontal loading*, which simply means making a job bigger by allowing the worker to do tasks from earlier and later stages in the workflow.

Job Enrichment

Frederick Herzberg, whose two-factor theory of motivation was discussed earlier, not only questions the motivational value of job simplification, he also is critical of job enlargement and rotation. "Why," he asks, "should a worker become motivated when one or more meaningless tasks are added to previously existing ones, or when work assignments are rotated among equally meaningless tasks?" By contrast, he says: "If you want people to do a good job, give them a good job to do."[38] Herzberg believes this is best done through **job enrichment** that expands job content and increases *job depth*—the extent to which planning and controlling duties are performed by individual workers rather than the supervisor. Job enrichment is a form of *vertical loading*, which means increasing job depth and giving employees more responsibility for the way they carry out their tasks.

Job Characteristics Model

Management theory now takes job enrichment a step beyond Herzberg's approach. It adopts a contingency perspective that recognizes job enrichment may not be good for everyone. This thinking is evident in the job characteristics model developed by Hackman and Oldham and shown in Figure 16.6.[39] It focuses attention on the presence or absence of *five core job characteristics*:

1. *Skill variety*—the degree to which a job requires a variety of different activities to carry out the work and involves the use of a number of different skills and talents.

2. *Task identity*—the degree to which the job requires completion of a "whole" and identifiable piece of work, one that involves doing a job from beginning to end with a visible outcome.

Automation is the total mechanization of a job.

Job rotation increases task variety by periodically shifting workers between different jobs.

Job enlargement increases task variety by combining into one job two or more tasks previously done by separate workers.

Job enrichment increases job depth by adding work planning and evaluating duties normally performed by the supervisor.

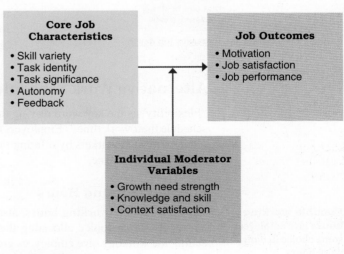

FIGURE 16.6

Job design essentials using the job characteristics model.

3. *Task significance*—the degree to which the job has a substantial impact on the lives or work of other people elsewhere in the organization, or in the external environment.

4. *Autonomy*—the degree to which the job gives the individual freedom, independence, and discretion in scheduling work and in choosing procedures for carrying it out.

5. *Feedback from the job itself*—the degree to which work activities required by the job result in the individual obtaining direct and clear information on his or her job performance.

A job that is high in the five core characteristics is considered enriched. But in true contingency fashion, an enriched job will not affect everyone in the same way. The figure indicates that people who respond most favorably to enriched jobs will have strong growth needs as described in Alderfer's ERG theory, appropriate job knowledge, skills, and abilities, and be otherwise satisfied with job context as discussed in Herzberg's two-factor theory. This creates a good person–job fit. When people without these characteristics are placed in enriched jobs, however, a poor person–job fit may cause their satisfaction and performance to fall instead of rise.

Improving Job Characteristics

For people and situations in which job enrichment is a good choice, Hackman and his colleagues recommend five ways to improve the core job characteristics. First, *combine tasks.*

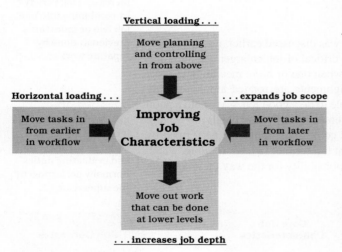

Expand job responsibilities by pulling a number of smaller tasks previously done by others into one larger job. Second, *form natural units of work.* Make sure that the tasks people perform are logically related to one another and provide a clear and meaningful task identity. Third, *establish client relationships.* Put people in contact with others who, as clients inside or outside the organization, benefit from their work. Fourth, *practice vertical loading*, which gives people authority to perform the planning and controlling previously done by supervisors. Fifth, *open feedback channels.* Provide opportunities for people both to receive performance feedback as they work and to learn how performance changes over time. In contrast to job enlargement and job rotation, which merely make jobs bigger horizontally by expanding job scope, the figure (left) shows that job enrichment expands job depth to make jobs vertically bigger as well.

Alternative Work Schedules

"Flexibility" is the key word driving the emergence of a range of alternative ways for people to schedule their work time.[40] Employers are finding that alternative work schedules help attract and retain motivated workers by offering them flexibility to deal with the complications of maintaining work–life balance.

Flexible Working Hours

Flexible working hours give employees some choice in daily work hours.

The term **flexible working hours**, also called *flextime*, describes any work schedule that gives employees some choice allocating their daily work hours. Flexible schedules for starting and ending the workday give employees greater autonomy while meeting their work responsibilities. Some may choose to come into work earlier and leave earlier while still completing a full workday; others may choose to start later and leave later. Flexible scheduling allows employees to

Research Brief

Generational Differences in Extrinsic and Intrinsic Work Values

Jean M. Twenge and her colleagues used a time-lag method to examine generational differences in work values among Baby Boomers (born between 1946 and 1964), Gen Xers (1965–1981), and Millennials (1982–1999). They did so by looking at 16,507 graduating high school seniors in 1976, 1991, and 2006.

The research studied how much each generation valued the outcomes of leisure (schedule flexibility and time off), extrinsic rewards (money and status), intrinsic rewards (interesting and challenging work and opportunities for growth), social rewards (making friends and contact with others), and altruistic rewards (helping others and contributing to society).

The findings shown in the box (right) support the popular notion that Millennials have a sense of entitlement. While they place a relatively high emphasis on money and status, they do not want to work harder to achieve these outcomes. Instead, they place a higher value on leisure and work–life balance than prior generations. Because leisure is so highly valued, companies might want to consider offering it through such things as flexible schedules, a compressed workweek, and increased vacation time as an incentive to attract members of the Millennial generation. Also, contrary to popular belief, Millennials do not place a higher value on either social or altruistic rewards than members of previous generations.

YOU BE THE RESEARCHER

Take a survey of your classmates and ask them to describe which aspects of work they value the most. How closely do your results match the findings of Twenge's study? Do you think these results would be different if you asked your parents and their colleagues?

Companies are currently experiencing a big change in the makeup of their workforce. Baby Boomers are starting to retire and companies are seeking to hire, develop, and retain a new generation of talent. What are some practical implications of this study's findings? What will companies and managers need to do in order to attract and get the best performance from members of the Millennial generation?

Summary of Study Findings

- Leisure is more important to Millennials than to Baby Boomers or Gen Xers.
- Millennials value extrinsic rewards more than Baby Boomers but less than Gen Xers.
- Millennials value intrinsic rewards less than Baby Boomers and Gen Xers.
- Social interactions at work (social rewards) are less important to Millennials than to Baby Boomers and Gen Xers.
- Altruistic rewards were equally valued across all generations.

handle personal and family needs such as medical appointments, home emergencies, and child care issues, as long as they get their work done. Reports indicate that flexible schedules reduce employee stress and diminish job turnover.[41] All top 100 companies in *Working Mother* magazine's list of best employers for working moms offer flexible scheduling.

Compressed Workweek

A **compressed workweek** is any work schedule that allows a full-time job to be completed in less than the standard five days of 8-hour shifts. The most common form is the "4–40," that is, accomplishing 40 hours of work in four 10-hour days. A key feature of the 4–40 schedule is that employees receive three consecutive days off from work each week. Many employees are on a four-day schedule at USAA, a diversified financial services company headquartered in San Antonio, Texas, listed among the 100 best companies to work for in America. Its advantages include improved employee morale, lower overtime costs, less absenteeism, and fewer days lost

A **compressed workweek** allows a full-time job to be completed in less than five days.

to sick leave, as well as lower costs of commuting.[42] Potential disadvantages of the compressed workweek include increased fatigue and family adjustment problems for individual employees, as well as scheduling problems for employers.

Job Sharing

Job sharing splits one job between two people.

Job sharing splits one full-time job between two or more persons. This can be done in a variety of ways, from half day to weekly or monthly sharing arrangements. Organizations benefit by employing talented people who are unable or unwilling to commit to a full-time job. A parent with young children, for example, might be unable to stay away from home for a full workday, but able to work half a day.

Telecommuting and Working from Home

Telecommuting involves working from home or outside the office at least part of the time.

It is increasingly popular for people to work by **telecommuting**, an arrangement that allows them to work from home or outside the office for at least a portion of scheduled time. It is facilitated by smart wireless devices that allow easy electronic links with customers and co-workers. New terms are even associated with telecommuting practices. We speak of *hoteling* when telecommuters come to the central office and use temporary office facilities. We also refer to *virtual offices* that include everything from an office at home to a mobile workspace in an automobile.

Although it would seem that telecommuting is in some ways a perfect fit with the modern workplace, the issues associated with it are far from straightforward. When asked what they like about this work arrangement, telecommuters report increased productivity, fewer distractions, less time spent commuting to and from work, and the freedom to schedule their own time. On the negative side, they may complain about working too much, difficulty separating work and personal life, and having less family time.[43] One telecommuter offers this advice: "You have to have self-discipline and pride in what you do, but you also have to have a boss that trusts you enough to get out of the way."[44]

From the employer's perspective, offering options to telecommute and work from home are ways of attracting and retaining talented workers who want this flexibility. But, a lack of face-to-face contact can also detract from the desired work culture. When Yahoo's CEO Marissa Meyer made a controversial decision to cut back on telecommuting, her justification was that people are "more collaborative and innovative when they're together."[45] What do you think? Is telecommuting a motivating cure all for stress and work-family conflicts? Or, is it a culture killer that reduces collaboration and productivity?

Contingency and Part-Time Work

Contingency workers are employed on a part-time and temporary basis to supplement a permanent workforce.

If there is one trend that has been reinforced by our tight economy, it's the use of more **contingency workers**, hired on a temporary and part-time basis to supplement the regular workforce.[46] You'll hear them called temps, freelancers, and contract hires. They provide just-in-time and as-needed work for employers who want to avoid the cost and responsibilities of hiring full-timers. One business analyst says the appeal for employers is that a temporary force is "easy to lay off, no severance; no company funded retirement plan; pay own health insurance; get zero sick days and no vacation."[47]

It is now possible to hire on a part-time basis every kind of personnel from executive support, such as a chief financial officer, to special expertise in areas like engineering, computer programming, and market research. Some worry that temporary employees lack the commitment of permanent workers, and thus may be less productive and provide lower product or service quality. Others argue that contingent employees frequently do just as good a job and offer cost savings of up to 30% over full-time workers.[48] But these cost advantages also are controversial. Contingency workers are generally paid less than their full-time counterparts, can experience stress and anxiety from their part-time and non-secure job status, and generally do not receive important benefits such as health care, life insurance, pension plans, and paid vacations, or even sick days!

Learning Check 4

TAKEAWAYQUESTION 4 **What is the link between job design and motivation?**

BE SURE YOU CAN • illustrate a job designed by simplification, rotation, and enlargement • list five core job characteristics • describe how an enriched job scores on these characteristics • describe advantages of the compressed workweek, flexible work hours, job sharing, and telecommuting • discuss the role of part-time contingency workers in the economy

Management Learning Review
Get Prepared for **Quizzes and Exams**

SUMMARY

TAKEAWAYQUESTION 1

How do individual needs influence motivation?

- Motivation predicts the level, direction, and persistence of effort expended at work; simply put, a highly motivated person works hard.
- Maslow's hierarchy of needs suggests a progression from lower-order physiological, safety, and social needs to higher-order esteem and self-actualization needs.
- Alderfer's ERG theory identifies existence, relatedness, and growth needs.
- Herzberg's two-factor theory describes the importance of both job content and job context to motivation and performance.
- McClelland's acquired needs theory identifies the needs for achievement, affiliation, and power, all of which may influence what a person desires from work.

FOR DISCUSSION How can team leaders meet the individual needs of members while still treating everyone fairly?

TAKEAWAYQUESTION 2

What are the process theories of motivation?

- Adams's equity theory recognizes that social comparisons take place when rewards are distributed in the workplace.
- People who feel inequitably treated are motivated to act in ways that reduce the sense of inequity; perceived negative inequity may result in someone working less hard in the future.
- The concept of equity sensitivity suggests that not all employees are equally concerned about being treated equitably and that not all employees respond to different types of inequity in the same way.
- Vroom's expectancy theory states that Motivation = Expectancy × Instrumentality × Valence.
- Locke's goal-setting theory emphasizes the motivational power of goals; task goals should be specific rather than ambiguous, difficult but achievable, and set with employees' participation.

- Bandura's self-efficacy theory indicates that when people believe they are capable of performing a task, they experience a sense of confidence and are more highly motivated to work hard at it.

FOR DISCUSSION What are the most common triggers of felt inequity in the workplace, and what can a manager do about them?

TAKEAWAYQUESTION 3

What role does reinforcement play in motivation?

- Reinforcement theory recognizes that human behavior is influenced by its environmental consequences.
- The law of effect states that behavior followed by a pleasant consequence is likely to be repeated; behavior followed by an unpleasant consequence is unlikely to be repeated.
- Reinforcement strategies used by managers include positive reinforcement, negative reinforcement, punishment, and extinction.
- Positive reinforcement works best when applied according to the laws of contingent and immediate reinforcement.

FOR DISCUSSION Can a manager or a parent rely solely on positive reinforcement strategies?

TAKEAWAYQUESTION 4

What is the link between job design and motivation?

- Job design is the process of creating or defining jobs by assigning specific work tasks to individuals and groups.
- Job simplification creates narrow and repetitive jobs composed of well-defined tasks with routine operations, such as typical assembly-line jobs.
- Job enlargement allows individuals to perform a broader range of simplified tasks; job rotation allows individuals to shift among different jobs with similar skill levels.

- The job characteristics model of job design analyzes jobs according to skill variety, task identity, task significance, autonomy, and feedback; a job high in these characteristics is considered enriched.
- Alternative work schedules make work hours more convenient and flexible to better fit workers' needs and personal responsibilities; options include the compressed workweek, flexible working hours, job sharing, telecommuting, and part-time work.

FOR DISCUSSION Should getting an enriched job be reward enough for job holders, or should they also get pay increases?

SELF-TEST 16

Multiple-Choice Questions

1. Lower-order needs in Maslow's hierarchy match well with _____ needs in ERG theory.
   (a) growth
   (b) affiliation
   (c) existence
   (d) achievement

2. When a team member shows strong ego needs in Maslow's hierarchy, the team leader should find that _____ will be motivating to him or her.
   (a) alternative work schedules
   (b) praise and recognition for job performance
   (c) social interactions with other team members
   (d) easy performance goals

3. A worker with a high need for _____ power in McClelland's theory tries to use power for the good of the organization.
   (a) position
   (b) expert
   (c) personal
   (d) social

4. In Herzberg's two-factor theory, base pay is considered a/an _____ factor.
   (a) valence
   (b) satisfier
   (c) equity
   (d) hygiene

5. Which of the following is a correct match?
   (a) McClelland—ERG theory
   (b) Skinner—reinforcement theory
   (c) Vroom—equity theory
   (d) Locke—expectancy theory

6. The expectancy theory of motivation says that motivation = expectancy × _____ × _____.
   (a) rewards, valence
   (b) instrumentality, valence
   (c) equity, instrumentality
   (d) rewards, valence

7. When someone has a high and positive "expectancy" in the expectancy theory of motivation, this means that the person _____.
   (a) believes he or she can meet performance expectations
   (b) highly values the rewards being offered
   (c) sees a link between high performance and available rewards
   (d) believes that rewards are equitable

8. In the _____ theory of motivation, someone who perceives herself under-rewarded relative to a co-worker might be expected to reduce his or her performance in the future.
   (a) ERG
   (b) acquired needs
   (c) two-factor
   (d) equity

9. In goal-setting theory, the goal of "doing a better job" would not be considered a good source of motivation because it fails the test of goal _____.
   (a) acceptance
   (b) specificity
   (c) challenge
   (d) commitment

10. The law of _____ states that behavior followed by a positive consequence is likely to be repeated, whereas behavior followed by an undesirable consequence is not likely to be repeated.
    (a) reinforcement
    (b) contingency
    (c) goal setting
    (d) effect

11. _____ is a positive reinforcement strategy that rewards successive approximations to a desirable behavior.
    (a) Extinction
    (b) Negative reinforcement
    (c) Shaping
    (d) Merit pay

12. B. F. Skinner would argue that "getting a paycheck on Friday" reinforces a person for coming to work on Friday, but it does not reinforce the person for having done an extraordinary job on Tuesday. This is because the Friday paycheck fails the law of _____ reinforcement.
    (a) negative
    (b) continuous
    (c) immediate
    (d) intermittent

13. When a job is redesigned to allow a person to do a whole unit of work from beginning to end, it becomes high on which core characteristic?
    (a) task identity
    (b) task significance
    (c) task autonomy
    (d) feedback

14. A typical compressed workweek schedule involves 40 hours of work done in _____ days.
    (a) 3
    (b) 4
    (c) 5
    (d) a flexible number of

15. A term often used to describe someone who is a long-term but part-time hire is _____ worker.
    (a) contingency
    (b) virtual
    (c) flexible
    (d) permatemp

Short-Response Questions

16. What preferences does a person with a high need for achievement bring to the workplace?

17. Why is participation important to goal-setting theory?

18. Where is the common ground in Maslow's, Alderfer's, and McClelland's views of human needs?

19. Why might an employer not want to offer employees the option of a compressed workweek schedule?

Essay Question

20. How can a manager combine the powers of goal setting and positive reinforcement to create a highly motivational work environment for workers with high needs for achievement?

Management Skills & Competencies Make yourself **valuable!**

Evaluate Career Situations

What Would You Do?

1. Paying the Going Rate

As the owner-manager of a small engineering company, you need to hire a replacement for a recently retired senior employee. The salaries you pay have always been a little below average, but it has never been an issue because you offer excellent benefits and a great work environment. The individual you want to hire has made it clear that she will not accept the job unless the offer is $5,000 more than you'd really like to pay, but it's also the competitive market rate. If you pay her the higher salary you'll risk alienating your current workforce. If you don't, you'll miss out on a great new hire. How can you best handle this dilemma?

2. Across-the-Board Raises

Because of a poor economy, your company has not been able to offer pay raises to employees for the past three years. This year, the salary budget has been increased by 5%. Your initial thought was to give everyone a 5% raise. Is this a good idea? How should you allocate salary increases in this situation?

3. Job Redesign for Better or for Worse?

As the manager of the university bookstore, you have come up with a plan to give part-time student workers more autonomy and control over their jobs. Your assistant manager believes this is a bad idea. She says that the student workers show no capacity for initiative or responsibility, and just want to do what they're told to do and get their weekly paychecks. She also predicts that both productivity and customer service will suffer under your plan. You think the student workers are bored and disengaged, but otherwise capable. What are you going to do and why?

Reflect on the Self-Assessment

Student Engagement Survey

Instructions

Use this scale to show the degree to which you agree with the following statements. Write your choices in the margin next to each question.[49]

1—No agreement; 2—Weak agreement; 3—Some agreement; 4—Considerable agreement; 5—Very strong agreement

1. I know what is expected of me in this course.

2. I have the resources and support I need to do my coursework correctly.

3. In this course, I have the opportunity to do what I do best all the time.

4. In the last week, I have received recognition or praise for doing good work in this course.

5. My instructor seems to care about me as a person.

6. There is someone in the course who encourages my development.

7. In this course, my opinions seem to count.

8. The mission/purpose of the course makes me feel my area of study is important.

9. Other students in the course are committed to doing quality work.

10. I have a good friend in the course.

11. In the last six class sessions, someone has talked to me about my progress in the course.

12. In this course, I have had opportunities to learn and grow.

Scoring

Score the instrument by adding up all your responses. A score of 0–24 suggests you are "actively disengaged" from the learning experience; a score of 25–47 suggests you are "moderately engaged"; a score of 48–60 indicates you are "actively engaged."

Interpretation

This instrument is a counterpart to a survey used by the Gallup Organization to measure the "engagement" of American workers. The Gallup results are surprising—indicating that up to 19% of U.S. workers are actively disengaged, with the annual lost productivity estimated at some $300 billion per year. One has to wonder: What are the costs of academic disengagement by students?

Contribute to the Class Exercise

Why We Work

Preparation

Read this "ancient story."[50]

In days of old, a wandering youth happened upon a group of men working in a quarry. Stopping by the first man, he said: "What are you doing?" The worker grimaced and groaned as he replied: "I am trying to shape this stone, and it is backbreaking work." Moving to the next man, the youth repeated the question. This man showed little emotion as he answered: "I am shaping a stone for a building." Moving to the third man, our traveler heard him singing as he worked. "What are you doing?" asked the youth. "I am helping to build a cathedral," the man proudly replied.

Instructions

In groups assigned by your instructor:

1. Discuss this short story.
2. Ask and answer the question: "What are the motivation and job design lessons of this ancient story?"
3. Discuss the question: How can managers help employees feel more inspired about what they are doing?
4. Have someone prepared to report and share the group's responses with the class as a whole.

Manage a Critical Incident

Great Worker Won't Take Vacation

Todd is a super hard worker and one of your team's top performers. He's also one of those workers who just won't take a vacation. Oh yes, he takes a day here and there. But each year he leaves as much as two weeks of vacation time on the table. You believe he would benefit from the occasional break, working happier and maybe more productively with some vacation time under his belt. His unwillingness to take time off is also a subject of conversation among his teammates. Their view is that he is starting to make them look and feel bad when they take the vacation time that they

earn. Some are starting to act a bit resentfully toward him, and you recently overheard this comment: "Take a little time off, Todd—for the good of the team, if not for yourself."

Questions

What can you do as the team leader to avoid having Todd's reluctance to take vacation turn into major team morale and working relationships problems? How might you motivate Todd to take more vacation time, without risking his high performance commitment and work ethic? How can you motivate his teammates to accept his behavior and be able to confidently continue with their own work styles?

Collaborate on the Team Activity

CEO Pay . . . Too High, or Just Right?

Question

What is happening in the area of executive compensation, and what do you think about it?

Instructions

1. Check the latest reports on CEO pay. Get the facts and prepare a brief report as if you were writing a short, informative article for *Fortune* magazine. The title of your article should be "Status Report: Where We Stand Today on CEO Pay."
2. Address the equity issue: Are CEOs paid too much, especially relative to the pay of average workers?
3. Address the pay-for-performance issue: Do corporate CEOs get paid for performance or for something else?
4. Gather some data: What do the researchers say? What do the business analysts say? What do the unions say? Find some examples to explain and defend your answers to these questions.
5. Address social responsibility issues: Is it "right" for CEOs to accept pay packages that reward them many times over what workers receive?
6. Take a position: Should a limit be set on CEO pay? If not, why not? If yes, what type of limit should be set? And who should set these limits—the government, company boards of directors, or someone else?

Analyze THE CaseStudy : UNITED PARCEL SERVICE : Delivering on Their Success

Go to **Management Cases for Critical Thinking** at the end of the book to find this case.

TEAMS AND TEAMWORK

KEY TAKEAWAYS

- Identify the ways teams contribute to organizations.
- Explain current trends in the use of teams in organizations.
- Describe the key processes through which teams work.
- Discuss the advantages and disadvantages of team decision making.

SKILLS MAKE YOU **VALUABLE**

- **EVALUATE** *Career Situations:*
  What Would You Do?
- **REFLECT** *On the Self-Assessment:*
  Team Leader Skills
- **CONTRIBUTE** *To the Class Exercise:*
  Work Team Dynamics
- **MANAGE** *A Critical Incident:*
  The Rejected Team Leader
- **COLLABORATE** *On the Team Activity:*
  Superstars on the Team
- **ANALYZE** *The Case Study:*
  Canon: A Picture of Teamwork

Surely you've experienced the highs and the lows of teams and teamwork—as a team contributor and as a team leader. Teams and teammates can be inspirational and they can be frustrating. They can accomplish great things or do very little of consequence. The more we know about teams, teamwork, and our personal tendencies toward team contributions, the better prepared we are to participate in today's team-driven organizations.

"Sticks in a bundle are hard to break"—*Kenyan proverb*

"Never doubt that a small group of thoughtful, determined people can change the world"—*Margaret Mead*, anthropologist

"Pick good people, use small teams and give them great tools so that they are very productive."—*Bill Gates,* businessman and philanthropist

"Gettin' good players is easy. Gettin' 'em to play together is the hard part"—*Casey Stengel*, Hall of Fame Major League baseball manager

From proverbs and societies to sports and business, the operation of teams and teamwork has been a consistent focal point of collective organization and is widely recognized as a critical tool for accomplishing great things.[1] Even so, just the words *group* and *team* elicit both positive and negative reactions in the minds of many people who have been involved—either as observers or participants—in these collectives. Although it is an embedded idiom in Western culture that "two heads are better than one," we also are warned by an idiom equally embedded in our culture that "too many cooks spoil the broth." A true skeptic of the kind of collective action implied by groups or teams can be heard to say: "A camel is a horse put together by a committee."

Teams have a great deal of performance potential but also are extremely complex in how they function. Teams can be a supercharged vehicle for the achievement of great successes, and they can also be the cause of equally monstrous failures.[2] More than a third of individuals participating in teams report dissatisfaction with teamwork. Less than half of team members report receiving training in team dynamics.[3] Still, many people prefer to work in teams than working independently. What is clear is that there is a great deal of variability in responses to—and the effectiveness of—teams in organizations today.

Teams in Organizations

TAKEAWAY 1   What are teams and how do they fit in organizations?

LEARN MORE | Teamwork pros • Teamwork cons • Meetings, meetings, meetings
ABOUT | Organizations as networks of groups

A **team** is a relatively small set of people with complementary skills who regularly interact with one another, working together interdependently to achieve shared goals.[4] **Teamwork** is the process of team members working together to accomplish these goals. Managers must be prepared to perform at least four important teamwork roles. A *team leader* serves as the appointed head of a team or a work unit. A *team member* serves as a contributing part of a project team. A *network facilitator* serves as the peer leader and networking hub for a special task force. A *coach or developer* serves as a team's advisor on ways to improve team processes and performance.

A fundamental difference between teams and groups is whether the goals or outcomes members are tasked with require that they work interdependently with one another or independently of one another. The **interdependence** that is characteristic of teams puts members in positions where they depend on each other to fulfill tasks and carry out work effectively.[5] Interdependence influences the way team members combine inputs such as ideas and efforts to create outcomes such as a completed task or project.[6] And when team members are interdependent, they tend to share information and communicate with one another more often, as well as act cooperatively and helpfully toward one another.[7]

> A **team** is a collection of people who regularly interact to pursue common goals.
>
> **Teamwork** is the process of people actively working together interdependently to accomplish common goals.
>
> **Interdependence** is the extent to which employees depend on other members of their team to carry out their work effectively.

Team leader

Team member

Network facilitator

Coach or Developer

Roles managers play in teams and teamwork

Teamwork Pros

Although working effectively with other members within a team can be hard work, the effort is worth it when the team meets anticipated performance expectations.[8] The real benefit of teams is their capacity to accomplish goals and performance expectations far greater than what's possible for individuals alone. This collective performance potential is called **synergy**, which is the creation of a whole that is greater than the sum of its individual parts.

Synergy pools the individual talents and efforts of a team's members to create extraordinary results through collective action. When Jens Voigt, one of the top racers on the Tour de France, was asked to describe a "perfect cyclist," for example, he created a composite of his nine-member team: "We take the time trial legs of Fabian Cancellara, the speed of Stuart O'Grady, the climbing

> **Synergy** is the creation of a whole greater than the sum of its individual parts.

capacity of our leaders and my attitude." His point in describing each of these individual's talents was that the tour is simply too hard for a single rider to win based on his own talents. Like so many other performance drivers in the workplace, the synergies made possible through effective teamwork represent a critical key to the success of teams.[9]

Just being a member of a team is often good for its members. The personal connections developed through membership can help employees to do their jobs better—getting help, making contacts, sharing ideas, responding to favors, and avoiding roadblocks. The personal relationships that develop among team members can help satisfy important needs that may be difficult to meet in regular work or personal settings, offering positive interpersonal interactions, a sense of security and belonging, and emotional support.[10]

> ### The Many Benefits of Teams
>
> - Performance gains through synergy
> - More resources for problem solving
> - Improved creativity and innovation
> - Improved decision-making quality
> - Greater member commitment to tasks
> - Increased member motivation
> - Increased need satisfaction of members

Teamwork Cons

Although teams have a great potential to increase the collective performance of members, what also is clear is that expectations and anticipated performance gains don't always materialize as intended when teams and teamwork are used. Problems with teams and members within teams can easily transform their great potential into frustration and failure.[11]

ethics > KNOW RIGHT FROM WRONG

> *The student complained that free riders were making it hard for her team to perform well.*

Social Loafing Is Hurting Team Performance

1. *Psychology study:* A German researcher asked people to pull on a rope as hard as they could. First, individuals pulled alone. Second, they pulled as part of a group. The results from this study showed that people pull harder when working alone than when working as part of a team. Such "social loafing" is the tendency for individuals to reduce their level of effort when working with others.

2. *Faculty office:* A student wants to speak with the instructor about his team's performance on the last project. There were four members, but two did almost all of the work. The other two largely disappeared, showing up only at the last minute to be part of the formal presentation. His point is that the team was disadvantaged because two free-riders were responsible for reduced performance capacity.

3. *Telephone call from the boss:* "John, I really need you to serve on this committee. Will you do it? Let me know tomorrow." In thinking about this, John ponders: I'm overloaded, but I don't want to turn down the boss. I'll accept but let the

committee members know about my situation. I'll be active in discussions and try to offer viewpoints and perspectives that are helpful. However, I'll let them know up front that I can't be a leader or volunteer for any extra work.

WHAT DO YOU THINK?

What are the ethical issues involved in team situations when some members sit back and let others do more of the work the entire team is responsible for doing? When you join a team, do all of the team's members have an ethical obligation to do a similar amount of work—why or why not? When it comes to John, does the fact that he intends to be honest with the other committee members make any difference? Isn't he still going to be a social loafer while earning credit from his boss for serving on the committee? Is his approach ethical—or should he simply decline to participate on the committee? What factors would make you more/less comfortable with another member not pulling their weight on the team?

Personality conflicts and work style differences can disrupt how well teams function. Unclear tasks, ambiguous agendas, and ill-defined problems and roles can cause teams to work too long on the wrong things. Sometimes team members start out motivated and then lose their motivation because teamwork takes too much time and effort away from other tasks, deadlines, and priorities. A lack of success also can hurt members' morale. It's also easy for members to lose motivation when the team is poorly organized and led, or when other members slack off.[12]

Social loafing is the tendency of some members to avoid responsibility by "free-riding" during group tasks.

Anyone who's had any extensive experience working in teams has encountered **social loafing**. This is the presence of "free-riders" who slack off because responsibility for various tasks is diffused in teams and others are present to do the work, picking up the slack.[13] Although social loafing can be very frustrating and can hurt team performance, there are things that team leaders or concerned team members can do when others don't do their work. The possibilities include making individual contributions more visible, rewarding individuals for their contributions, making task assignments more interesting, and keeping team sizes small so that free-riders are subject to more intense peer pressure and leader evaluation.[14]

Meetings, Meetings, Meetings

"We have the most ineffective meetings of any company," says a technology executive. "We just seem to meet and meet and meet, and we never seem to do anything," says another in the package delivery industry. "We realize our meetings are unproductive. A consulting firm is trying to help us, but we've got a long way to go," says a corporate manager.[15]

What do you think when someone says: "Let's have a meeting"? Are you ready and willing, or apprehensive and even upset to have to participate? We aren't always happy to get a request to add another meeting to our busy schedules. The problems described in the nearby box don't help.[16] You might even be able to add to the list from personal experience.

Seven Deadly Sins of Meetings

1. People arrive late, leave early, and don't take things seriously.
2. The meeting is too long, sometimes twice as long as necessary.
3. People don't stay on topic; they digress and are easily distracted.
4. The discussion lacks candor; people are unwilling to tell the truth.
5. The right information isn't available, so decisions are postponed.
6. Nothing happens when the meeting is over; no one puts decisions into action.
7. Things never get better; the same mistakes are made meeting after meeting.

Good meetings don't happen by accident. People have to work hard and work together to make meetings productive and rewarding. Face-to-face and virtual meetings are where lots of information is shared, decisions get made, and people gain understanding of the issues and of one another. They're important and necessary. This is why knowing more about teams and teamwork is so useful.

Organizations as Networks of Groups

A formal group is an officially recognized collective that is supported by the organization.

Formal groups are officially recognized and supported by the organization. They may be called departments (e.g., market research department), units (e.g., audit unit), groups (e.g., customer service group), or divisions (e.g., office products division), among other possibilities. These formal groups form interlocking networks that serve as the foundation of the organization's structure, and managers are key "linking pins" among them. Managers lead formal groups at one level while also serving as members of groups at the next higher level and in groups formed across functional areas.[17]

An informal group is unofficial and emerges from relationships and shared interests among members.

Informal groups also are present and important in all organizations. They emerge from natural or spontaneous relationships among members. Some informal groups are *interest groups* where workers join together to pursue a common cause, such as better working conditions. Some emerge as *friendship groups* that develop for a wide variety of personal reasons, including shared non-work interests and social connections. Others exist as *support groups*, in which members basically help one another to do their jobs or to cope with common problems.

Although people may sometimes use informal groups as a forum for airing dissatisfactions and spreading rumors, the social connections they offer can also play many positive roles in organizations. Tapping into relationships within informal groups can help speed workflow and "get things done" in ways not possible within the formal structure defined in an organizational chart. Members of informal groups can also satisfy needs that are otherwise left unmet in their formal work assignments. These include gaining friendship, security, support, and a sense of belongingness.

Learning Check 1

TAKEAWAYQUESTION **1 What are teams and how do they fit in organizations?**

BE SURE YOU CAN • define *team* and *teamwork* • explain why *interdependence* is a key characteristic of teams • identify four roles managers perform in teams • define *synergy* • explain teamwork pros and cons • discuss the implications of social loafing • explain the potential benefits of informal groups

Trends in the Use of Teams

TAKEAWAY 2   What are current trends in the use of teams?

LEARN MORE | Committees, project teams, and task forces • Cross-functional teams
ABOUT | Self-managing teams • Virtual teams • Team building

A trend toward greater empowerment in organizations today shows up as an emphasis on committees, project teams, task forces, cross-functional teams, and self-managing teams. Importantly, all of these different forms function in both face-to-face and virtual forms.

Committees, Project Teams, and Task Forces

A **committee** brings employees together outside of their daily job duties to work together for a specific purpose. A committee's agenda is typically narrow, focused, and ongoing. Organizations usually have a variety of permanent or standing committees dedicated to a wide variety of issues, such as diversity, quality, and product development. Committees are led by a designated head or chairperson, who is held accountable for the committee's performance.

Project teams or **task forces** bring people together to work on common problems, but on a temporary rather than permanent basis. The goals and task assignments are specific and completion deadlines are clear. Creativity and innovation may be part of the agenda. Project teams, for example, can be formed to develop a new advertising campaign, redesign an office layout, or streamline a work process.[18]

Cross-Functional Teams

Many organizations make use of **cross-functional teams** that pull together members from across different functional units to work on common goals. These teams help reduce the **functional chimneys problem** by eliminating "walls" that can otherwise limit communication and cooperation among employees from different departments and functions. Target CEO Gregg Steinhafel,

A **committee** is designated to work on a special task on a continuing basis.

A **project team** or **task force** is convened for a specific purpose and disbands when its task is completed.

A **cross-functional team** operates with members who come from different functional units of an organization.

The **functional chimneys problem** is a lack of communication across functions.

for example, says that his firm uses cross-functional teams from "merchandising, marketing, design, communications, presentation, supply chain and stores" to create and bring to customers new limited-edition fashions.[19]

Self-Managing Teams

> Members of a **self-managing work team** have the authority to make decisions about how they share and complete their work.

Traditional work teams consisting of first-level supervisors and their immediate subordinates are increasingly being replaced in a growing number of organizations with **self-managing work teams**. As shown in Figure 17.1, these teams operate with a high degree of task interdependence, authority to make many decisions about how they work, and collective responsibility for results.[20] The expected advantages from self-managed teams are better performance, reduced costs, and high levels of morale.

Multitasking is a key feature of all self-managing teams, whose members each have the skills to perform several different jobs. Within a team, the emphasis is always on participation. Self-managing teams operate with members sharing tasks and taking collective responsibility for management functions traditionally performed by supervisors. The "self-management" responsibilities include planning and scheduling work, training members in various tasks, distributing tasks, meeting performance goals, ensuring high quality, and solving day-to-day operating problems. In some self-managing teams, members have the authority to "hire" and "fire" other members. Typical characteristics of self-managing teams include:

> Characteristics of ▶ self-managing teams

- Members are held collectively accountable for performance results.
- Members have discretion in distributing tasks within the team.
- Members have discretion in scheduling work within the team.
- Members are able to perform more than one job on the team.
- Members train one another to develop multiple job skills.
- Members evaluate one another's performance contributions.
- Members are responsible for the total quality of team products.

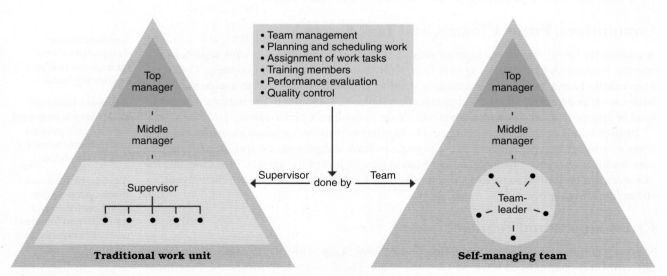

FIGURE 17.1
Organizational and management implications of self-managing work teams.

analysis > MAKE DATA YOUR FRIEND

> *Meetings are frequent, but many say the ones they attend are ineffective.*

Unproductive Meetings Are Major Time Wasters

A survey of some 38,000 workers around the world links low productivity with bad meetings, poor communication, and unclear goals.

- 69% of meetings attended are considered ineffective.

- 32% of workers complain about team communication.

- 31% complain about unclear objectives and priorities.

YOUR THOUGHTS?

Do the results from this survey match your own experiences with team meetings? Given the common complaints about meetings, what can a team leader do to improve them? Think about recent meetings you have attended. In what ways were the best meetings different from the worst meetings? Did your own behavior play a significant role in both of these cases? How do the interactions of team members influence the quality of these meetings? Why?

Virtual Teams

Scene: U.S.-based IT manager needs to meet with team members in Brazil, the Philippines, and Poland. Rather than pay for everyone to fly to a common location, he checks world time zones, sends an e-mail to schedule, and then turns on his tablet to join the other team members online at the scheduled time using Google FaceTime or Skype.

The constant emergence of new technologies is making virtual collaboration both easier and more common. At home, it may be Twitter, Linked In, or Instagram; at the office, it's likely to be a wide variety of online meeting resources. Members of **virtual teams**, also called **distributed teams**, work together through computer mediation rather than face to face.[21] They operate like other teams with respect to what gets done. In virtual teams, it's the way that things get done that is different. This difference has both potential advantages and disadvantages.[22]

In terms of potential advantages, virtual teams can save a significant amount of time and travel expense when members work in different locations. They also can be easily expanded to include more members as needed, and the discussions and shared information can be archived for later access. Virtual teams are usually quite efficient because members are less prone to stray off task and get sidetracked by interpersonal difficulties. A vice president for human resources at Marriott, for example, once called electronic meetings "the quietest, least stressful, most productive meetings you've ever had."[23]

The lack of face-to-face interaction in virtual teams also creates potential disadvantages. It limits the role of emotions and nonverbal cues in communication and often contributes to member relationships that are depersonalized.[24] "Human beings are social animals for whom building relationships matters a great deal," says one scholar. "Strip away the social side of teamwork and, very quickly, people feel isolated and unsupported."[25] The following guidelines can help keep the possible downsides of virtual teamwork to a minimum:[26]

- Select team members high in initiative and capable of self-starting.

- Select members who will join and engage the team with positive attitudes.

- Select members known for working hard to meet team goals.

- Begin with social messaging that allows members to exchange information about each other in order to personalize the process.

- Assign clear goals and roles so that members can focus while working alone and also know what others are doing.

*Members of a **virtual team** or **distributed team** work together and solve problems through computer-based interactions.*

◀ Guidelines for virtual teamwork

- Gather regular feedback from members about how they think the team is doing and how it might work more effectively.
- Provide regular feedback to team members about team accomplishments.

Team Building

Team building is a sequence of activities to analyze a team and make changes to improve its performance.

High-performance teams of all the types just described operate with characteristics like those shown in the box.[27] But real, effective teamwork and the great results teamwork can generate don't happen by accident.

Team building is a sequence of planned activities used to analyze the functioning of a team and make constructive, systematic changes in how it operates.[28] The process begins with developing awareness that a problem may be present or may develop within the team. Members then work together to gather data and fully understand the nature of the problem, make plans to correct it, implement the plans the team develops, and evaluate results from the plan. This whole process is repeated as difficulties or new problems are discovered within the team.

There are many ways to gather data for team building, including structured and unstructured interviews, survey questionnaires, and team meetings. Regardless of the method used to help understand what's happening, the basic principle of team building remains the same. It is a careful and collaborative assessment of all of the various aspects of the team, ranging from how members work together to the results they are able to achieve.

Characteristics of High-Performance Teams

- Clear and elevating goals
- Task-driven, results-oriented structure
- Competent, hard-working members
- Collaborative culture
- High standards of excellence
- External support and recognition
- Strong, principled leadership

Team building can be done with consulting assistance or under the direction of a manager. It can also be done in the workplace or take place at outside locations. A popular approach is to bring team members together in special outdoor settings where their capacities for teamwork are put to the test through unusual and physically demanding experiences, such as obstacle courses. There's lots of room for innovation in team building, with options including activities like scavenger hunts, work with charities, cooking schools, building and sculpting, and competitive activities.[29] Says one team-building trainer: "We throw clients into situations to try and bring out the traits of a good team."[30]

Learning Check 2

TAKEAWAYQUESTION **2 What are current trends in the use of teams?**

BE SURE YOU CAN • differentiate a committee from a task force • explain the benefits of cross-functional teams • discuss potential advantages and disadvantages of virtual teams • list the characteristics of self-managing work teams • explain how self-managing teams are changing organizations • describe the typical steps in team building

How Teams Work

TAKEAWAY 3   How do teams work?

LEARN MORE ABOUT | Team inputs • Stages of team development • Norms and cohesiveness | Task and maintenance roles • Communication networks

An **effective team** achieves high levels of task performance, membership satisfaction, and future viability.

An **effective team** does three things well—perform its tasks, satisfy its members, and remain viable for the future.[31] On the *task performance* side, a work team is expected to transform resource inputs (such as ideas, materials, and information) into product outputs (such as a report,

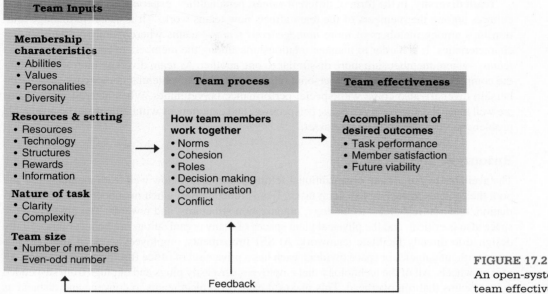

FIGURE 17.2
An open-systems model of
team effectiveness.

decision, service, or commodity). With respect to *member satisfaction,* members should take pleasure from both the team's performance accomplishments and their contributions toward making these happen. As to *future viability*, the team should have a social fabric and work climate that makes its members willing and able to work well together in the future, again and again as needed.

You sometimes hear top executives saying that team effectiveness comes from having "the right players in the right seats on the same bus, headed in the same direction."[32] The open-systems model in Figure 17.2 supports this view. It shows that a team's effectiveness is influenced by inputs—"right players in the right seats"—and by process—"on the same bus, headed in the same direction."[33] You can remember the implications of this figure by the following **Team Effectiveness Equation:**[34]

Team effectiveness = Quality of inputs + (Process gains − Process losses)

Team Effectiveness Equation Team effectiveness = Quality of inputs + (Process gains − Process losses).

Team Inputs

Among the important inputs that influence team effectiveness are membership characteristics, resources and setting, nature of the task, and team size.[35] You can think of these conditions as the drivers that prepare the team for action. A team with the right inputs has a greater chance of having a positive process and being effective.

Membership Characteristics

The right blend of member characteristics on a team is critical for success. Teams need members with the right abilities, or skill sets, to master and perform tasks well. Teams must also have members whose attitudes, values, and personalities are sufficiently compatible for everyone to work well together. How often, for example, have you read or heard about college sports teams where a lack of the right "chemistry" among talented players leads to subpar team performance? As one of the chapter opening quotes states: "Gettin' good players is easy. Gettin' 'em to play together is the hard part."[36]

Team diversity
represents the
differences in
values, personalities,
experiences,
demographics, and
cultures among
members.

Team diversity, in the form of different values, personalities, experiences, demographics, and cultures among the members of the team affects how teams work.[37] It is easier to manage relationships among members of more *homogeneous teams*—teams where members share similar characteristics. It is harder to manage relationships among the members of more *heterogeneous teams*—where members are more dissimilar to one another. As team diversity increases, so does the complexity of members' interpersonal relationships But the potential complications of membership diversity also come with special performance opportunities. When heterogeneous teams are well managed, the variety of ideas, perspectives, and experiences within them can be a valuable problem solving and performance asset.

Resources and Setting

The available resources and organizational setting can influence how well team members use and pool their talents to accomplish team tasks. Teams function best when members have good information, material resources, technology, organization structures, and rewards. The physical work space also is critical, and the physical plant spaces of many organizations are being architecturally designed to directly facilitate teamwork. At SEI Investments, employees work in a large, open space without cubicles or space dividers; each has a private set of office furniture and fixtures—all of it on wheels. All of the technology that employees use easily plugs and unplugs from suspended power beams that run overhead. This makes it easy for project teams to convene and disband as needed, and for people to meet and communicate during the ebb and flow of daily work.[38]

Nature of the Task

The nature of the tasks teams are responsible for not only sets standards for the talents needed by team members, it also affects how they work together. Clearly defined tasks are easier to deal with. Complex tasks require a lot more of members in terms of information sharing and coordinated action.[39] The next time you fly, check out the ground crews. You should notice some similarities between them and NASCAR pit crews. If you fly United Airlines, in fact, there's a chance that the members of the ramp crews have been through "Pit Crew U." United is among the many organizations sending employees to Pit Instruction & Training in Mooresville, North Carolina. At this facility, where NASCAR racing crews train, United's ramp workers learn to work intensely and under pressure while meeting the goals of teamwork, safety, and job preparedness. Teams participate in the training at the Mooresville facility to achieve better teamwork to reduce aircraft delays and service problems.[40]

Team Size

Team size affects how well team members work together, handle disagreements, and make decisions. Having an odd numbers of members, such as in juries, helps prevent "ties" when votes need to be taken. And importantly, the number of potential interactions among team members increases geometrically as teams get bigger. Large team size creates communication and relationship problems for members and leaders. It's also easier for individuals to hide and engage in social loafing in larger teams.

The general conclusions from social science research are that very small teams—four members or fewer—may be dominated by one or two strong characters. Six- to eight-member teams are probably best for creative problem solving because their members are better able to form trusting relationships and function more like families. When teams get larger than this, the added size and complexity can be difficult to manage.[41] Amazon.com's founder and CEO Jeff Bezos is a great fan of teams. But he also has a simple rule when it comes to sizing the firm's product development teams: No team should be larger than two pizzas can feed.[42] Have you ever been on a team that was too large? How did the members interact?

Stages of Team Development

Although having the right inputs is critical, it doesn't guarantee team effectiveness. **Team process** also plays an important role. This is the way that the members of a team actually work together as they transform inputs into output. Also called *group dynamics*, the process aspects of any group or team include how members develop norms and cohesiveness, share roles, make decisions, communicate with one another, and handle conflicts.[43] Importantly, teams experience different process challenges as they pass through the stages of team development—forming, storming, norming, performing, and adjourning.[44]

Team process is the way team members work together to accomplish tasks.

Forming Stage

The forming stage of team development involves the first entry of individual members into a team. This is a time of initial task orientation and interpersonal testing. When people first come together, they ask questions: "What can or does this team offer me?" "What will I be asked to contribute?" "Can my needs be met while my efforts serve the task needs of the team?"

In the forming stage, individuals begin to identify with other members and with the team itself. They are concerned about getting acquainted, establishing relationships, discovering what behavior is acceptable, and learning how others perceive the team's task. This may also be a time when some members rely on others who appear "powerful" or especially "knowledgeable." Such things as prior experience with team members in other contexts and personal impressions of organization culture, goals, and practices may affect emerging relationships between members. Difficulties in the forming stage tend to be greater in more culturally and demographically diverse teams.

Storming Stage

The storming stage is a period of high emotionality and can be the most difficult stage to pass through successfully. Tensions often emerge over tasks and interpersonal concerns. There may be periods of outright hostility and infighting. Coalitions or cliques may form around personalities or interests. Subgroups may form around fault-lines defined by areas of agreement and disagreement. Conflict also may develop as members compete to impose their preferences on other members and to become influential.

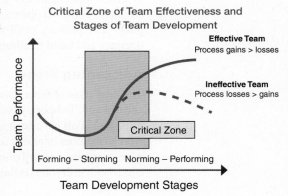

Critical Zone of Team Effectiveness and Stages of Team Development

Important changes occur in the storming stage as task agendas become clarified and members begin to understand one another's styles. Attention begins to shift toward obstacles that stand in the way of task accomplishment. Efforts are made to find ways to meet team goals while also satisfying members' individual needs. The storming stage is part of a "critical zone" in team development, where successes create long-term gains while failures create long-lasting problems.

Norming Stage

It is in the norming stage that team members begin to cooperate with one another. Shared rules of conduct emerge and the team develops a sense of leadership as each member starts to occupy and fulfill key roles. Interpersonal hostilities start to diminish and harmony is emphasized, but minority viewpoints may still be discouraged.

The norming stage is also part of the critical zone of team development. As members develop initial feelings of closeness, a division of labor, and shared expectations, this helps protect the team from disintegration. In fact, holding the team together may seem more important than accomplishing important tasks.

	Very poor			Very good	
1. Trust among members	1	2	3	4	5
2. Feedback mechanisms	1	2	3	4	5
3. Open communications	1	2	3	4	5
4. Approach to decisions	1	2	3	4	5
5. Leadership sharing	1	2	3	4	5
6. Acceptance of goals	1	2	3	4	5
7. Valuing diversity	1	2	3	4	5
8. Member cohesiveness	1	2	3	4	5
9. Support for each other	1	2	3	4	5
10. Performance norms	1	2	3	4	5

FIGURE 17.3
Criteria for assessing the maturity of a team.

Performing Stage

Teams in the performing stage are more mature, organized, and well-functioning. They score high on the criteria of team maturity shown in Figure 17.3.[45] Performing is a stage of integration in which team members are able to deal in creative ways with complex tasks and interpersonal conflicts. The team operates with a clear and stable structure, and members are motivated by team goals. The primary challenges in the performing stage are to continue to refine how the team operates and build relationships to keep everyone working well together as an integrated unit.

Adjourning Stage

The final stage of team development is adjourning, when team members prepare to achieve closure and disband. Temporary committees, task forces, and project teams should disband with a sense that important goals have been accomplished. This can be an emotional period after team members have worked together intensely for a period of time. Adjourning is a time when it is important to acknowledge everyone's contributions, praise them, and celebrate the team's success. A team ideally disbands with everyone feeling they would like to work with one another again in the future.

Norms and Cohesiveness

A norm is a behavioral expectation, rule, or standard to be followed by team members.

A **norm** is a behavioral expectation of team members.[46] It is a "rule" or "standard" that guides behavior. Typical team norms relate to such things as helpfulness, participation, timeliness, work quality, creativity and innovation. A team's performance norm is critical, as it defines the level of work effort and performance that members are expected to contribute. Work groups and teams with positive performance norms are more successful in accomplishing task objectives than are teams with negative performance norms.

Managing Team Norms

Team leaders should help and encourage members to develop positive norms. During the forming and storming stages of development, for example, norms relating to expected attendance and levels of commitment are important. By the time the performing stage is reached, norms relating to adaptability and change become relevant. Here are some things leaders can do to help their teams build positive norms:[47]

- Act as a positive role model.
- Reinforce desired behaviors with rewards.
- Control results by performance reviews and regular feedback.
- Train and orient new members to adopt desired behaviors.
- Recruit and select new members who exhibit desired behaviors.
- Hold regular meetings to discuss progress and ways of improving.
- Use team decision-making methods to reach agreement.

◀ How to build positive team norms

One normative issue of growing research interest is the extent to which members of teams display virtuousness and share a commitment to moral behavior. The work of scholar Kim Cameron, for example, discusses **team virtuousness** in respect to these five norms of moral behavior.[48] *Optimism*—Team members are expected to strive for success even when experiencing setbacks. *Forgiveness*—Team members are expected to forgive one another's mistakes and avoid assigning blame. *Trust*—Team members are expected to be courteous with one another and interact in respectful, trusting ways. *Compassion*—Team members are expected to help and support one another and to show kindness in difficult times. *Integrity*—Team members are expected to be honest in what they do and say while working together.

Team virtuousness indicates the extent to which members adopt norms that encourage shared commitments to moral behavior.

Managing Team Cohesiveness

Team members vary in their adherence to established group norms. Conformity to norms is largely determined by the strength of team **cohesiveness**, the degree to which members are attracted to and motivated to remain part of a team.[49] Members of teams that are highly cohesive value their membership and strive to maintain positive relationships with other team members. Because of this, they tend to conform to team norms. In the extreme, violation of a norm on a highly cohesive team can result in a member being expelled or socially ostracized.

Cohesiveness is the degree to which members are attracted to and motivated to remain part of a team.

Figure 17.4 shows the power of cohesiveness. The "best-case" scenario is a team with high cohesiveness and a high performance norm. Strong conformity to norms by members of "high-high" teams is likely to have a beneficial effect on team performance. Contrast this with the "worst-case" scenario of high cohesiveness and a low performance norm. Members of "high-low" teams conform to the low performance norm and restrict their work efforts in order to adhere to the norm.

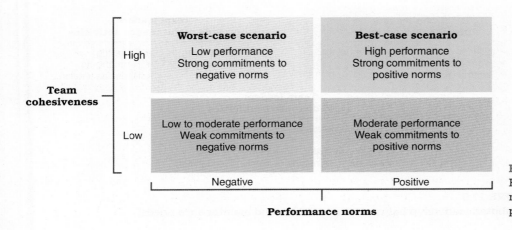

FIGURE 17.4
How cohesiveness and norms influence team performance.

We've already discussed ways to build positive norms. But, the implications of Figure 17.4 suggest that managers also must be good at building high levels of cohesiveness as well. This can be done in the following ways:

How to increase ▶
team cohesiveness

- Create agreement on team goals.
- Reward team rather than individual results.
- Increase membership homogeneity.
- Increase interactions among members.
- Decrease team size.
- Introduce competition with other teams.
- Provide physical isolation from other teams.

Task and Maintenance Roles

A **task activity** is an action taken by a team member that directly contributes to the team's performance purpose.

A **maintenance activity** is an action taken by a team member that supports the emotional life of the team.

Distributed leadership is when all members of a team contribute helpful task and maintenance behaviors.

Research on the social psychology of collectives such as groups and teams identifies two types of roles or activities that are essential if members are to work well together.[50] **Task activities** contribute directly to the team's performance purpose, while **maintenance activities** support the emotional life of the team as an ongoing social system.

Although the team leader or supervisor should give these activities special attention, the responsibility for task and maintenance activities also should be shared and distributed among all team members. Anyone can help lead a team by acting in ways that satisfy these needs. The concept of **distributed leadership** in teams makes every member continually responsible for both recognizing when task or maintenance activities are needed, and also taking actions to provide them.

Leading through task activities involves making an effort to define and solve problems, and to advance work activities toward performance results. Without the relevant task activities such as initiating agendas, sharing information, and others shown in Figure 17.5, teams have difficulty accomplishing their objectives. *Leading through maintenance activities*, by contrast, helps strengthen the team as a social system. When maintenance activities such as gatekeeping, encouraging others, and reducing tensions are performed, good interpersonal and working relationships are achieved, increasing the probability that the team will stay together over the longer term.

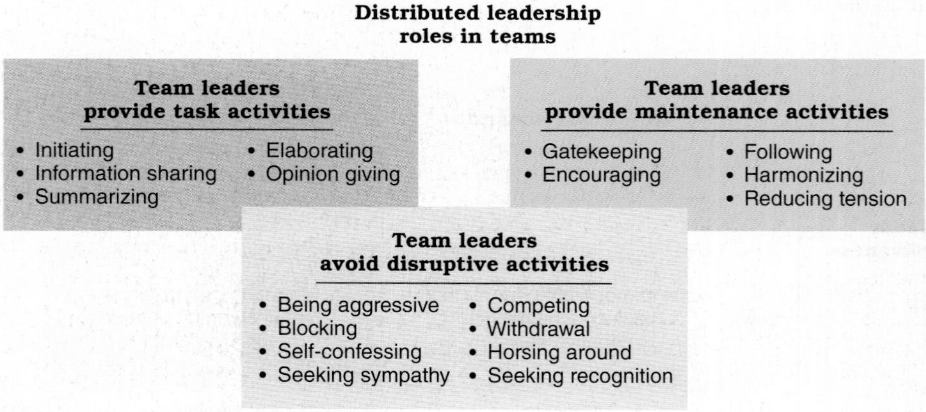

Distributed leadership roles in teams

Team leaders provide task activities	**Team leaders provide maintenance activities**
• Initiating • Elaborating • Information sharing • Opinion giving • Summarizing	• Gatekeeping • Following • Encouraging • Harmonizing • Reducing tension

Team leaders avoid disruptive activities

• Being aggressive	• Competing
• Blocking	• Withdrawal
• Self-confessing	• Horsing around
• Seeking sympathy	• Seeking recognition

FIGURE 17.5
Distributed leadership helps teams meet task and maintenance needs.

Both team task and maintenance activities stand in distinct contrast to the **disruptive activities** described in Figure 17.5. Activities such as showing incivility toward other members, withdrawing from discussions, and fooling around are self-serving and detract from, rather than enhance, team effectiveness. Unfortunately, very few teams are immune to dysfunctional behavior. Every team member shares in the responsibility for minimizing its occurrence.

Communication Networks

There is considerable research on the team interaction patterns and communication networks shown in Figure 17.6.[51] When team members must interact intensively and work closely together on complex tasks, this need is best met by a **decentralized communication network**. Sometimes called the *all-channel or star communication network*, this pattern of interaction is where all members communicate directly with one another. At other times team members can work on tasks independently, with the required work being divided among them. This creates a **centralized communication network**, sometimes called a *wheel or chain communication structure*. In this pattern of interaction, activities are coordinated and results pooled by a central point of control.

When teams are composed of subgroups experiencing issue-specific disagreements, such as a temporary debate over the best way to achieve a goal, the resulting interaction pattern often involves a **restricted communication network**. Here, polarized subgroups contest one another and may even engage in conflict. Communication between subgroups is limited and biased, with negative consequences for group process and effectiveness.

The best teams use each of these communication networks, but they use them in the right ways and at the right times. Centralized communication networks seem to work better on simple tasks.[52] These tasks lend themselves to more centralized control because they require little creativity, information processing, problem solving, or collaborative effort. The reverse is true for more complex tasks, for which interacting groups perform better. Decentralized communication networks support the more intense interactions and information sharing

Disruptive activities are self-serving behaviors that interfere with team effectiveness.

A **decentralized communication network** allows all members to communicate directly with one another.

In a **centralized communication network**, communication flows only between individual members and a hub, or center point.

In a **restricted communication network**, subgroups have limited communication with one another.

Pattern	Diagram	Characteristics
Interacting Group Decentralized communication network	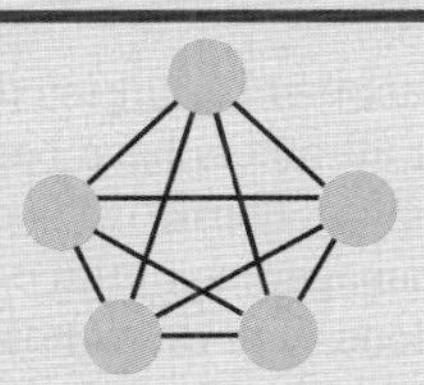	High interdependency around a common task Best at complex tasks
Co-acting Group Centralized communication network	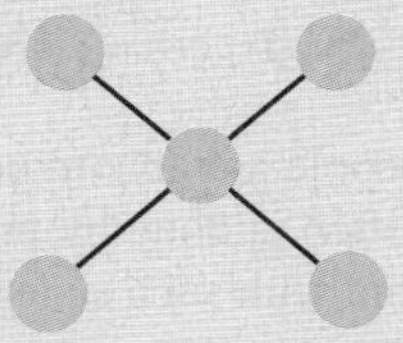	Independent individual efforts on behalf of common task Best at simple tasks
Counteracting Group Restricted communication network	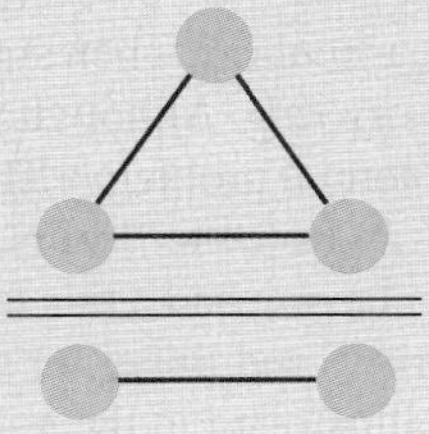	Subgroups in disagreement with one another Slow task accomplishment

FIGURE 17.6
Interaction patterns and communication networks in teams.

required to perform complicated tasks. Even conflicting groups can be useful. When teams get complacent, the conflict that emerges from them can be a source of creativity and critical evaluation. But when these subgroups stop communicating and helping one another, task accomplishment typically suffers—at least in the short term.

Learning Check 3

TAKEAWAYQUESTION **3 How do teams work?**

BE SURE YOU CAN • define team *effectiveness* • identify inputs that influence effectiveness • discuss how membership diversity influences team effectiveness • list five stages of group development • define *group norm* and list ways to build positive group norms • define *cohesiveness* and list ways to increase group cohesion • explain how norms and cohesiveness influence team performance • differentiate between task, maintenance, and disruptive activities • describe the use of decentralized and centralized communication networks

Decision Making in Teams

TAKEAWAY 4   How do teams make decisions?

LEARN MORE | Ways teams make decisions • Advantages and disadvantages of team decisions
ABOUT | Groupthink • Creative team decision making

Decision making is the process of making choices among alternative possible courses of action.

Decision making, the process of making choices among alternative possible courses of action, is one of the most important processes that occur in groups and teams. The best teams will use a variety of decision-making methods over time as they face different kinds of problems.[53] But as with other aspects of teamwork, decision making also can be challenging.[54] Edgar Schein, a respected scholar and consultant, says all this can be better understood when we recognize that teams use at least six methods to make decisions: lack of response, authority rule, minority rule, majority rule, consensus, and unanimity.[55]

Ways Teams Make Decisions

In *decision by lack of response*, one idea after another is suggested without any discussion taking place. When the team finally accepts an idea, all others have been bypassed by simple lack of response rather than by critical evaluation. The last alternative is chosen by default.

In *decision by authority rule*, the leader, manager, committee head, or other authority figure makes a decision for the team. This can be done with or without discussion and is very time-efficient. Whether the decision ultimately is good or bad, however, depends on whether the authority figure has the necessary information and expertise, and on how well this approach is accepted by other team members.

In *decision by minority rule*, two or three people are able to dominate or "railroad" the team into making a decision that they prefer. This often is done by providing a suggestion and then forcing quick agreement by challenging the team with such statements as "Does anyone object? No? Well, let's go ahead then."

One of the most common things teams do, particularly when signs of disagreement emerge, is to take a vote and arrive at a *decision by majority rule*. Although this is broadly consistent with the democratic political process, it has some potential problems. The very act of voting can create coalitions as some people become "winners" and others "losers." Those in the minority—the "losers"—may feel left out or discarded without having had a fair say. They may be unenthusiastic about implementing the decision of the "majority," and lingering resentments may impair future team effectiveness. Such possibilities are well illustrated in the political arena, where candidates

wisdom > LEARN FROM ROLE MODELS

> *If two pizzas aren't enough to feed a team, it's too big.*

Amazon's Jeff Bezos Feeds Innovation with Two-Pizza Teams

Ted S. Warren/AP Photos

Amazon.com's founder and CEO Jeff Bezos is one of America's top businesspersons and a technology visionary. He's also a great fan of teams. Bezos coined a simple rule when it comes to sizing the firm's product development teams: If two pizzas aren't enough to feed a team, it's too big.

Don't expect to spot a stereotyped corporate CEO in Jeff Bezos. His standard office attire is still blue jeans and a blue-collared shirt. But, this attire comes with a unique personality and a great business mind. If you go to Amazon.com and click on the "Gold Box" at the top, you'll be tuning in to Bezos's vision. It's a place for special deals, lasting only an hour and offering everything from a power tool to a new pair of shoes. If you join Amazon Prime and "1-Click" your way to free shipping and a hassle-free checkout, you're benefiting from his vision as well. And, of course, there's also the Kindle. Not only has it become Amazon's best-selling product ever, but it also made electronic books an everyday reality—one that competitors have been racing to take advantage of.

Amazon's innovations don't just come out of the blue. They're part and parcel of the management philosophy Bezos has instilled at the firm. And teams are a central ingredient in the innovation process. Bezos calls Amazon's small two-pizza teams "innovation engines," betting that they'll help fight creeping bureaucracy as the company grows larger and more complex.

FIND THE INSPIRATION

Is Bezos on to a great management lesson with his notion of the two-pizza team? What difference does team size make in your experience? Can you come up with an example of a team with over a dozen members that performed really well? If so, how can you explain its success? On the other hand, can a team be too small? What example can you give of a team that would have done better if it was just a little bigger?

receiving only small and controversial victory margins end up struggling against entrenched opposition from the losing party.

Teams often are encouraged to achieve *decision by consensus*. This is where full discussion leads to one alternative being favored by most members, and the other members agree to support it. When a consensus is reached, even those who may have opposed the decision know that their views have been heard by everyone involved. Consensus does not require unanimous support, but it does require that members be able to argue, engage in reasonable conflict, and still get along with and respect one another.[56] As pointed out in the box (right), true consensus occurs only when any dissenting members have been able to speak their mind and know they've been heard.[57]

How to Achieve Consensus

1. Don't argue blindly; consider others' reactions to your points.
2. Don't change your mind just to reach quick agreement.
3. Avoid conflict reduction by voting, coin tossing, or bargaining.
4. Keep everyone involved in the decision process.
5. Allow disagreements to surface so that issues can be deliberated over.
6. Don't focus on winning versus losing; seek acceptable alternatives.
7. Discuss assumptions, listen carefully, and encourage members' inputs.

A *decision by unanimity* may be the ideal state of affairs. "Unanimity" means that all team members agree on the course of action to be taken. This is a logically perfect method, but it also is extremely difficult to achieve in practice. One of the reasons that teams sometimes turn to authority decisions, majority voting, or even minority decisions is the difficulty of managing team processes to achieve consensus or unanimity.

Advantages and Disadvantages of Team Decisions

When teams take time to make decisions by consensus or unanimity, they gain special advantages over teams relying more on individual or minority decision methods.[58] The process of making a true team decision increases the availability of useful information, knowledge, and expertise. It expands the number of action alternatives teams examine, and helps to avoid bad decisions that emerge through tunnel vision and the consideration of only one or a few options. Team decisions also increase members' understanding and acceptance. This helps to build members' commitment to work hard to implement decisions the team has made together.

The potential disadvantages of team decision making trace largely to the difficulties with group processes. It can be hard to reach agreement when many people are trying to make a team decision. There may be social pressure to conform and even minority domination, where some members feel forced or "railroaded" into accepting a decision advocated by one vocal individual or small coalition. The time required to make team decisions also can sometimes be a real disadvantage. As more people are involved in the dialogue and discussion, decision making takes longer. This added time may be costly, even prohibitively so under certain circumstances.

Groupthink is a tendency for highly cohesive teams to lose their evaluative capabilities.

Groupthink

One of the potential downsides of team decision making is what psychologist Irving Janis called **groupthink**, the tendency for highly cohesive teams to lose their critical evaluative capabilities.[59]

Although it may seem counterintuitive, a high level of cohesiveness can be a disadvantage if strong feelings of team loyalty make it hard for members to criticize and evaluate one another's ideas and suggestions objectively.

Members of very cohesive teams may feel so strongly about the group that they won't say or do anything that might harm it. They end up publicly agreeing with actual or suggested courses of action about which they have serious private, unspoken doubts or objections. Groupthink occurs as the desire to hold the team together and avoid disagreements results in poor decisions.

Janis suggests that groupthink played a role in well-known historical disasters such as the lack of preparedness of U.S. naval forces for

---

Symptoms of Groupthink

Illusions of invulnerability—Members assume that the team is too good for criticism or is beyond attack.

Rationalizing unpleasant and disconfirming data—Members refuse to accept contradictory data or to thoroughly consider alternatives.

Belief in inherent group morality—Members act as though the group is inherently right and above reproach.

Stereotyping competitors as weak, evil, and stupid—Members refuse to look realistically at other groups.

Applying direct pressure to deviants to conform to group wishes—Members refuse to tolerate anyone who suggests the team may be wrong.

Self-censorship by members—Members refuse to communicate personal concerns to the whole team.

Illusions of unanimity—Members accept consensus prematurely, without testing its completeness.

Mind guarding—Members protect the team from hearing disturbing ideas or outside viewpoints.

the Japanese attack on Pearl Harbor, the Bay of Pigs invasion under President Kennedy, the many roads that led to the United States' difficulties in the Vietnam War, and the space shuttle *Challenger* explosion. But he also says that when the groupthink symptoms listed in the box (previous page) are spotted, managers and team leaders can prevent them from causing too much harm if they act proactively.

When you are leading or are part of a team heading toward groupthink, don't assume there's no way out. Janis noted, for example, that after suffering the Bay of Pigs fiasco, President Kennedy approached the Cuban missile crisis quite differently. He purposely did not attend some cabinet discussions and allowed the group to deliberate without him. His absence helped the cabinet members talk more openly and to be less inclined to try and say things that were consistent with his own thinking. When a decision was finally reached, the crisis was successfully resolved.

In addition to having the leader stay absent for some team discussions, Janis has other advice on how to get a team that is moving toward groupthink back on track. You can assign one member to act as a critical evaluator or "devil's advocate" during each meeting. Subgroups can be assigned to work on issues and then share their findings with the team as a whole. Outsiders can be brought in to observe and participate in team meetings and offer their advice and viewpoints on both team processes and tentative decisions. The team can also hold a "second chance" meeting after an initial decision is made to review, change, or even cancel the decision. With actions like these available, there's no reason to let groupthink lead a team down the wrong pathways.

Creativity in Team Decision Making

When team creativity is needed in special situations, managers shouldn't hesitate to use time-tested brainstorming and nominal group techniques. Both techniques can be used in face-to-face or in virtual team settings.

Classic **brainstorming** usually asks members to follow these strict guidelines. *Don't criticize each other*—withhold judging or evaluating ideas as they are being presented. *Welcome "freewheeling"*—the wilder or more radical the idea, the better. *Go for quantity*—the more ideas generated, the greater the likelihood that one or more will be outstanding. *Keep building on one another's ideas*—don't hesitate to piggyback and tweak one or more existing ideas into new forms.

> **Brainstorming** engages group members in an open, spontaneous discussion of problems and ideas.

At the Aloft Group, Inc., a small advertising firm in Newburyport, Massachusetts, President Matt Bowen says brainstorming works best if he specifies the goal—ideally in a sentence that he distributes a day or two ahead of the session. He limits the brainstorming session to an hour, and keeps the group small—ideally five to seven members. He allows no criticism—there is no such thing as a "bad" idea. He also encourages everyone to build on one another's ideas and is sure to follow up by implementing something from the brainstorming session.[60]

In situations where brainstorming won't work, such as in a situation prone to intense disagreement and interpersonal conflicts, an approach known as the **nominal group technique** can sometimes be useful.[61] It uses a highly structured meeting agenda that allows everyone to contribute ideas without the interference of evaluative comments by others. Participants are first asked to work alone and respond in writing with possible solutions to a stated problem. Ideas are then shared in round-robin fashion without any criticism or discussion, and all ideas are recorded as they are presented. Ideas are next discussed and clarified in another round-robin sequence, with no evaluative comments allowed. Finally, members individually and silently follow a written voting procedure that ranks all alternatives in priority order.

> The **nominal group technique** structures interaction among team members discussing problems and ideas.

Learning Check 4

TAKEAWAYQUESTION 4 **How do teams make decisions?**

BE SURE YOU CAN • illustrate how groups make decisions by authority rule, minority rule, majority rule, consensus, and unanimity • list advantages and disadvantages of group decision making • define *groupthink* and identify its symptoms • illustrate how brainstorming and the nominal group technique can improve creativity in team decision making

Management Learning Review
Get Prepared for **Quizzes and Exams**

SUMMARY

TAKEAWAYQUESTION 1

What are teams and how do they fit in organizations?

- A team is a collection of people working together interdependently to accomplish a common goal.
- Teams help organizations perform through synergy—the creation of a whole that is greater than the sum of its parts.
- Teams help satisfy important needs for their members by providing sources of job support and social satisfactions.
- Social loafing and other problems can limit the performance of teams.
- Organizations operate as networks of formal and informal teams and groups.

FOR DISCUSSION Why do people often tolerate social loafers at work?

TAKEAWAYQUESTION 2

What are current trends in the use of teams?

- Committees and task forces are used to accomplish special tasks and projects.
- Cross-functional teams bring members together from different departments and help improve lateral relations and integration in organizations.
- New developments in information technology are making virtual teams commonplace at work, but virtual teams also pose special management challenges.
- Self-managing teams are changing organizations, as team members perform many tasks previously done by their supervisors.
- Team building engages members in a process of assessment and action planning to improve teamwork and future performance.

FOR DISCUSSION What are some of the things that virtual teams probably can't do as well as face-to-face teams?

TAKEAWAYQUESTION 3

How do teams work?

- An effective team achieves high levels of task performance, member satisfaction, and team viability.

- Important team inputs include the organizational setting, nature of the task, size, and membership characteristics.
- A team matures through various stages of development, including forming, storming, norming, performing, and adjourning.
- Norms are the standards or rules of conduct that influence team members' behavior; cohesion is the attractiveness of the team to its members.
- In highly cohesive teams, members tend to conform to norms; the best situation is a team with positive performance norms and high cohesiveness.
- Distributed leadership occurs as members share in meeting a team's task and maintenance needs.
- Effective teams make use of alternative communication structures, such as centralized and decentralized networks, to best complete tasks with distinct communication requirements.

FOR DISCUSSION What can be done if a team gets trapped in the storming stage of group development?

TAKEAWAYQUESTION 4

How do teams make decisions?

- Teams can make decisions by lack of response, authority rule, minority rule, majority rule, consensus, and unanimity.
- Although group decisions often make more information available for problem solving and generate more understanding and commitment, they are slower than individual decisions and may involve social pressures to conform.
- Groupthink is the tendency for members of highly cohesive teams to lose their critical evaluative capabilities and make poor decisions.
- Techniques for improving creativity in teams include brainstorming and the nominal group technique.

FOR DISCUSSION Is it possible that groupthink doesn't only occur when groups are highly cohesive, but also when they are pre-cohesive?

SELF-TEST 17

Multiple-Choice Questions

1. When a group of people is able to achieve more than what its members could by working individually, this is called _____.
   (a) social loafing
   (b) consensus
   (c) viability
   (d) synergy

2. One of the recommended strategies for dealing with a group member who engages in social loafing is to _____.
   (a) redefine tasks to make individual contributions more visible
   (b) ask another member to encourage this person to work harder
   (c) give the person extra rewards and hope he or she will feel guilty
   (d) just forget about it

3. In an organization operating with self-managing teams, the traditional role of _____ is replaced by the role of team leader.
   (a) chief executive officer
   (b) first-line supervisor
   (c) middle manager
   (d) general manager

4. An effective team is defined as one that achieves high levels of task performance, member satisfaction, and _____.
   (a) resource efficiency
   (b) future viability
   (c) consensus
   (d) creativity

5. In the open-systems model of teams, the _____ is an important input factor.
   (a) communication network
   (b) decision-making method
   (c) performance norm
   (d) set of membership characteristics

6. The team effectiveness equation states the following: Team effectiveness = Quality of inputs + (_____ − Process losses).
   (a) Process gains
   (b) Leadership impact
   (c) Membership ability
   (d) Problem complexity

7. A basic rule of team dynamics states that the greater the _____ in a team, the greater the conformity to norms.
   (a) membership diversity
   (b) cohesiveness
   (c) task structure
   (d) competition among members

8. Members of a team tend to start to get coordinated and comfortable with one another in the _____ stage of team development.
   (a) forming
   (b) norming
   (c) performing
   (d) adjourning

9. One way for a manager to build positive norms within a team is to _____.
   (a) act as a positive role model
   (b) increase group size
   (c) introduce groupthink
   (d) isolate the team

10. To increase the cohesiveness of a group, a manager would be best off _____.
    (a) starting competition with other groups
    (b) increasing the group size
    (c) acting as a positive role model
    (d) introducing a new member

11. Groupthink is most likely to occur in teams that are _____.
    (a) large in size
    (b) diverse in membership
    (c) high-performing
    (d) highly cohesive

12. A team member who does a good job at summarizing discussion, offering new ideas, and clarifying points made by others is providing leadership by contributing _____ activities to the group process.
    (a) required
    (b) task
    (c) disruptive
    (d) maintenance

13. A _____ decision is one in which all members agree on the course of action to be taken.
    (a) consensus
    (b) unanimous
    (c) majority
    (d) nominal

14. A team performing very creative and unstructured tasks is most likely to succeed using _____.
    (a) a decentralized communication network
    (b) decisions by majority rule
    (c) decisions by minority rule
    (d) more task than maintenance activities

15. Which of the following approaches can help groups achieve creativity in situations where lots of interpersonal conflicts are likely to occur?
    (a) nominal group technique
    (b) minority rule
    (c) consensus
    (d) brainstorming

Short-Response Questions

16. How can a manager improve team effectiveness by modifying inputs?

17. What is the relationship among a team's cohesiveness, performance norms, and performance results?

18. How would a manager know that a team is suffering from groupthink (give two symptoms), and what could the manager do about it (give two responses)?

19. What makes a self-managing team different from a traditional work group?

EssayQuestion

20. Marcos Martinez has just been appointed manager of a production team operating the 11 p.m. to 7 a.m. shift in a large manufacturing firm. An experienced manager, Marcos is pleased that the team members really like and get along well with one another, but they also appear to be restricting their task outputs to the minimum acceptable levels. What could Marcos do to improve things in this situation, and why should he do them?

Management Skills & Competencies Make yourself **valuable!**

Evaluate Career Situations

What Would You Do?

1. New Task Force

It's time for the first meeting of the task force that you have been assigned to lead. This is a big opportunity, since it's the first time your supervisor has given you this level of responsibility. There are seven members of the task force, all of whom are your peers and co-workers. The task is to develop a proposal for increased use of flexible work schedules and telecommuting in the organization. What will your agenda be for the first meeting, and what opening statement will you make?

2. Declining Performance

You've been concerned for quite some time about a drop in the performance of your work team. Although everyone seems to like one another, the "numbers" in terms of measured daily performance are on the decline. It's time to act. What will you look at, and why, to determine where and how steps might be taken to improve the effectiveness of the work team?

3. Groupthink Possibilities

The members of the executive compensation committee that you are chairing show a high level of cohesiveness. It's obvious that they enjoy being part of the committee and are proud to be on the board of directors. But the committee is about to approve extraordinarily high bonuses for the CEO and five other senior executives. This is occurring at a time when executive pay is getting a lot of criticism from the press, unions, and the public at large. What can you do to make sure groupthink isn't causing this committee to potentially make a bad decision? What clues might you use to determine whether groupthink is having an influence on what is taking place?

Reflect on the Self-Assessment

Team Leader Skills

Instructions

Consider your experience in groups and work teams while completing the following inventory. Rate yourself on each item using the following scale (circle the number that applies).[62]

1 = Almost never   2 = Seldom
3 = Sometimes   4 = Usually
5 = Almost always

Question: "How do I behave in team leadership situations?"

1 2 3 4 5   **1.** Facilitate communications with and among team members between team meetings.

1 2 3 4 5   **2.** Provide feedback/coaching to individual team members on their performance.

1 2 3 4 5   **3.** Encourage creative and "out-of-the-box" thinking.

1 2 3 4 5   **4.** Continue to clarify stakeholder needs/expectations.

1 2 3 4 5   **5.** Keep team members' responsibilities and activities focused within the team's objectives and goals.

1 2 3 4 5   **6.** Organize and run effective and productive team meetings.

1 2 3 4 5   **7.** Demonstrate integrity and personal commitment.

1 2 3 4 5   **8.** Have excellent persuasive and influencing skills.

1 2 3 4 5   **9.** Respect and leverage the team's cross-functional diversity.

1 2 3 4 5   **10.** Recognize and reward individual contributions to team performance.

1 2 3 4 5   **11.** Use the appropriate decision-making style for specific issues.

1 2 3 4 5   **12.** Facilitate and encourage border management with the team's key stakeholders.

1 2 3 4 5   **13.** Ensure that the team meets its commitments.

1 2 3 4 5   **14.** Bring team issues and problems to the team's attention and focus on constructive problem solving.

1 2 3 4 5   **15.** Provide a clear vision and direction for the team.

Self-Assessment Scoring

The inventory measures seven dimensions of team leadership. Add your scores for the items listed next to each dimension below to get an indication of your potential strengths and weaknesses.

1, 9   Building the Team

2, 10 Developing People

3, 11 Team Problem Solving and Decision Making

4, 12 Stakeholder Relations

5, 13 Team Performance

6, 14 Team Process

7, 8, 15 Providing Personal Leadership

Interpretation

The higher your score, the more confident you are on the particular skill and leadership capability. Consider giving this inventory to people who have worked with you in teams and have them rate you. Compare the results to your self-assessment. Also, remember it is doubtful that any one team leader is capable of exhibiting all of the skills listed. More and more, organizations are emphasizing teams that blend a variety of skills, rather than depending on the vision of the single, heroic leader figure. As long as the necessary leadership skills are represented within the membership of the team, it is more likely that the team will be healthy and achieve a high level of performance. Of course, the more skills you bring with you to team leadership situations, the better the team is likely to perform.

Contribute to the Class Exercise

Work Team Dynamics

Preparation

Think about your class work group, a work group you are involved in for another course, or any other group suggested by your instructor. Use this scale to indicate how often each of the following statements accurately reflects your experience in the group.[63]

1   All the time   2   Very often

3   Sometimes   4   Never happens

1. My ideas get a fair hearing.

2. I am encouraged to give innovative ideas and take risks.

3. Diverse opinions within the group are encouraged.

4. I have all the responsibility I want.

5. There is a lot of favoritism shown in the group.

6. Members trust one another to do their assigned work.

7. The group sets high standards of performance excellence.

8. People share and change jobs a lot in the group.

9. You can make mistakes and learn from them in this group.

10. This group has good operating rules.

Instructions

Form teams as assigned by your instructor. Ideally, this will be the group you have just rated. Have all members share their ratings, and then make one overall rating for the team as a whole. Circle the items for which there are the biggest differences of opinion. Discuss those items and try to determine what accounts for these differences. In general, the better a team scores on this instrument, the higher its creative potential. Make a list of the five most important things members believe they can do to help the team perform better. Nominate a spokesperson to summarize your discussion for the class as a whole.

Manage a Critical Incident

The Rejected Team Leader

You have been a team leader at a big-box electronics store for three years, and the team you supervise is great. Everyone is hard working, gets along really well, comes in early, stays late, helps one another, and gets the job done. The members go out together after work and are good friends with each other and with you. A week ago, your team was assigned exclusive responsibility for designing and setting up the upcoming product display for tablets and other mobile devices in an entire section of the store. Crystal—one of your team members—was especially excited about the project. She has been taking online courses at the local technical college and wants to move into advertising design as a career. Because the team works so well together, you had expected the whole process to go smoothly with a bunch of great display formats figured out for you to choose from. But by the end of the week, you'd only gotten one proposal from the team, and it wasn't very good. You talked to each team member individually. They all stood behind the design the team had submitted. They got mad at you for suggesting that they come up with another design, and wouldn't even listen to you. They wouldn't tell you how they came up with the design, how they figured things out, or share any information with you at all. Even though you are the supervisor, you are also a friend, so it was hard when they reacted in such a hostile way to your feedback—particularly in light of the looming deadline.

Questions

What is happening in this team? These employees know and trust you, but you can't even get them to talk to you about what's happening—why? What can you do to get through the wall they've put around themselves? Why have you been shut out of the team in this way? What does it mean for the project and how you handle the team moving forward?

Collaborate on the Team Activity

Superstars on the Team

During a period of reflection following a down cycle for his teams, Sasho Cirovski, head coach of the two-time NCAA Division I University of Maryland men's soccer team, came to a realization. "I was recruiting talent," he said. "I wasn't doing a very good job of recruiting leaders." With a change of strategy, his teams moved back to top-ranked national competition.

Question

What do you do with a "superstar" on your team?

Instructions

1. Everywhere you look—in entertainment, in sports, and in business—a lot of attention goes to the superstars. What is the record of teams and groups with superstars? Do they really outperform the rest?

2. What is the real impact of a superstar's presence on a team or in the workplace? What do they add? What do they cost? Consider the potential cost of having a superstar on a team within the equation: Benefits = Cost—Value. What is the bottom line of having a superstar on the team?

3. Interview the athletic coaches on your campus. Ask them the previous questions about superstars. Compare and contrast their answers. Interview players from various teams, and ask them the same questions.

4. Develop a set of guidelines for creating team effectiveness in a situation where a superstar is present. Be thorough and practical.

Analyze THE CASE Study : CANON
A Picture of Teamwork

Go to *Management Cases for Critical Thinking* at the end of the book to find this case.

COMMUNICATION, CONFLICT, AND NEGOTIATION

KEY TAKEAWAYS

- Describe the elements in the communication process.

- Identify ways to improve the effectiveness of communication.

- Discuss how conflict can be functional and managed successfully.

- Explain ways to negotiate successfully and avoid negotiation pitfalls.

SKILLS MAKE YOU **VALUABLE**

- **EVALUATE** *Career Situations:* What Would You Do?

- **REFLECT** *On the Self-Assessment:* Conflict Management Strategies

- **CONTRIBUTE** *To the Class Exercise:* Feedback Sensitivities

- **MANAGE** *A Critical Incident:* Headphones on in the Office

- **COLLABORATE** *On the Team Activity:* How Words Count

- **ANALYZE** *The Case Study:* Twitter: Rewriting (or Killing) Communication

A lot of what we accomplish in life and at work depends on our abilities to communicate well and collaborate with others. Recruiters prize job candidates with strong communication skills who can achieve positive impact through their writing and presentations, and in teamwork and interpersonal settings. The ability to communicate and collaborate also includes conflict and negotiation situations. How well we handle them often makes the difference between success and failure when multiple interests are at play.

Whether you work at the top of an organization—building support for strategies and goals, or in teams at other levels—interacting with teammates and co-workers to support their efforts and your own, your career toolkit must include the abilities to achieve positive impact through communication and collaboration. They are foundations for **social capital**, the capacity to attract support and help from others in order to get things done. Whereas intellectual capital comes from what you know, social capital comes from the people you know and how well you relate to them. It's something all managers need, and it's all about communication, connections, and relationships. Pam Alexander, former CEO of Ogilvy Public Relations Worldwide, says: "Relationships are the most powerful form of media. Ideas will only get you so far these days. Count on personal relationships to carry you further."[1]

Social capital is a capacity to get things done with the support and help of others.

The Communication Process

TAKEAWAY 1   What is the communication process?

LEARN MORE | Effective communication • Persuasion and credibility in communication
ABOUT | Communication barriers • Cross-cultural communication

Communication
is the process of
sending and receiving
symbols with meanings
attached.

Figure 18.1 describes **communication** as an interpersonal process of sending and receiving symbols with messages attached to them. This process can be understood as a series of questions: "Who?" (*sender*) "says what?" (*message*) "in what ways?" (*channel*) "to whom?" (*receiver*) "with what result?" (*meaning*). It is through this process that people build and use social capital, exchange and share information, lead and inspire followers, and influence one another's attitudes, behaviors, and understandings.

It is important to respect and understand the communication process as the glue that binds together the four functions of planning, organizing, leading, and controlling.[2] *Planning* is accomplished and plans are shared through the communication of information. *Organizing* identifies and structures communication links among people and positions. *Leading* uses communication to achieve positive influence over organization members and stakeholders. *Controlling* relies on communication to process information to measure performance results.

Effective Communication

In **effective
communication** the
intended meaning is
fully understood by the
receiver.

**Efficient communi-
cation** occurs at
minimum cost.

Most of us probably think we're pretty good at communicating. However, this sense of confidence can cause a significant problem in the communication process: We take our abilities for granted and end up disappointed when things go wrong. Getting things to "go right" requires alertness to issues of "effectiveness" and "efficiency" in the ways we communicate. **Effective communication** occurs when the sender's message is fully understood by the receiver. **Efficient communication** occurs at minimum cost in terms of resources expended. It's great when our communications are both effective and efficient. But, trade offs between the two are common.

An efficient communication may not be effective. We are often too busy or too lazy to invest enough time to make sure that communication is effective. Instead, we shoot for efficiency. Picture your instructor taking the time to communicate individually with each student about this chapter. It would be virtually impossible and certainly very costly in terms of the instructor's time. This is why managers, co-workers, and even family members often communicate with others by leaving voice mail and sending texts and messages rather than visiting face to face. These choices are efficient but not always effective ways of communicating. Although an e-mail note sent to several people on a distribution list may save the sender's time, not all receivers might interpret the message in the same way.

By the same token, an effective communication may not be efficient. If a team leader visits each team member individually to explain new procedures, this may guarantee that everyone truly understands the change. But, it also requires a lot of the leader's time. And rightly or wrongly, saving time may be our top priority.

FIGURE 18.1
The interactive two-way
process of interpersonal
communication.

Persuasion and Credibility in Communication

Communication is not only about sharing information or being "heard." It's about the intent of one party to influence or motivate the other in a desired way. **Persuasive communication** results in a recipient agreeing with or supporting the message being presented.[3] Managers, for example, get things done by drawing on social capital in their relationships with peers, teammates, co-workers, and bosses. Their success often comes about more through convincing than by order giving. Scholar and consultant Jay Conger says that without credibility there is little chance that persuasion can be successful.[4] He describes **credible communication** as that which is based on trust, respect, and integrity in the eyes of others.

Credibility is gained through expertise, when you are knowledgeable about the issue in question or have a successful track record in dealing with similar issues in the past. In a hiring situation where you are trying to persuade team members to select candidate A rather than B, for example, you must be able to defend your reasons for this choice. And, it will always be better if your past recommendations turned out to be good for the team.

Credibility is also gained through relationships, when you work well and get along with the people to be persuaded. In a hiring situation where you want to persuade your boss to provide a special bonus package to attract top job candidates, for example, having a good relationship with your boss can add credibility to your request. This is social capital again: It is always easier to get someone to do what you want if that person likes you.

> **Persuasive communication** presents a message in a manner that causes the other person to support it.
>
> **Credible communication** earns trust, respect, and integrity in the eyes of others.

Communication Barriers

Scene: A Japanese executive used an interpreter when meeting with representatives of the firm's American joint venture partner. *Result:* About 20% of his intended meaning was lost in the exchange between himself and the interpreter, while another 20% was lost between the interpreter and the Americans.[5]

Noise, as shown in Figure 18.2, is anything that interferes with the effectiveness of the communication process. And, this isn't just a cross-cultural issue. Do you recognize its potential in everyday conversations, such as the nearby text messages exchanged between a high-tech millennial and her low-tech baby boomer manager? The differences show a clash of generational cultures and the challenges of communicating across these boundaries. Common sources of noise include information filtering, poor choice of channels, poor written or oral expression, failure to recognize nonverbal signals, and physical distractions.

> **Noise** is anything that interferes with the effectiveness of communication.

Millennial to Baby Boomer

• sry abt mtg b rdy nxt 1

Baby Boomer to Millennial

• Missed you at important meeting. Don't forget next one. Stop by to discuss.

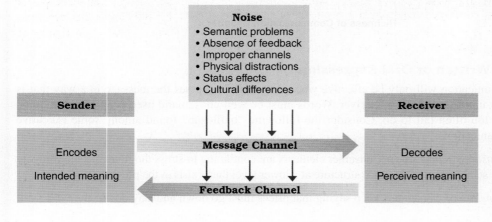

FIGURE 18.2
Downsides of noise, shown as anything that interferes with the effectiveness of the communication process.

Information Filtering

Information filtering is the intentional distortion of information to make it appear more favorable to the recipient.

"Criticize my boss? I don't have the right to." "I'd get fired." "It's her company, not mine." These comments display tendencies toward **information filtering**—the intentional distortion of information to make it appear favorable to the recipient. Management author and consultant Tom Peters calls it "Management Enemy Number 1." He even goes so far as to say that "once you become a boss you will never hear the unadulterated truth again."[6]

The problem with information filtering is that someone tells the boss only what they think he or she wants to hear. Whether the reason is career protection, fear of retribution for bringing bad news, unwillingness to identify personal mistakes, or just a general desire to please, the end result is the same. The higher level gets biased and inaccurate information from below and ends up making bad decisions. It's a continuing challenge for managers to fight this problem, and the larger the organization, the bigger the problem seems to get. Leadership consultant Deborah J. Cornwall says: "There's a tendency for people in large, hierarchical organizations to tell the boss what he wants to hear." During Congressional hearings on the General Motors ignition switch recall scandal, CEO Mary Barra confirms this view in her comment: "I cannot tell you why it took years for the safety defect to be announced in that program." Former Ford global vice president Martin Zimmerman says: "You get blindsided when things deteriorate. You want to know about mistakes."[7]

Poor Choice of Channels

A **communication channel** is the pathway through which a message moves from sender to receiver.

A **communication channel** is the pathway or medium through which a message is conveyed from sender to receiver. Good communicators choose the right channel or combination of channels to accomplish their intended purpose.[8]

Written channels—paper or electronic—are most acceptable for simple messages that are easy to convey, and for those that require quick and extensive dissemination to a wide audience. They also are useful when it is important to document information or directives. But, it's important to remember that these messages are largely impersonal and one-way interactions with only limited opportunity for feedback from recipients. *Spoken channels*—face-to-face or electronic—work best for complex and difficult messages and where immediate feedback to the sender is valuable. They are more personal and more likely to be perceived by the receiver as supportive or inspirational.

Low Richness
- Impersonal
- One-way
- Fast

| Postings, e-bulletins, reports | Memos, letters | E-mail, blogs, podcasts, voice-mail | Telephone, instant messaging | Face-to-face meetings, online conferences |

High Richness
- Personal
- Two-way
- Slow

Richness of Communication Channel

Poor Written or Oral Expression

Communication will only be effective when the sender expresses the message in a way that is clearly understood by the receiver. Words must be well chosen and used properly, something we all too often fail to do. Consider the following "bafflegab" found among some executive communications.[9]

A business report said: "Consumer elements are continuing to stress the fundamental necessity of a stabilization of the price structure at a lower level than exists at the present time."

Translation: Consumers keep saying that prices must go down and stay down.

A manager said: "Substantial economies were affected in this division by increasing the time interval between distributions of data-eliciting forms to business entities."

Translation: The division saved money by sending out fewer questionnaires.

A university president said: "We have strived to be as transparent as possible about the strategic alliance plans within the confines of our . . . closed negotiations."

Translation: The negotiations were confidential.

Failure to Recognize Nonverbal Signals

Nonverbal communication takes place through gestures, facial expressions, body posture, eye contact, and the use of interpersonal space. Research shows that up to 55% of a message's impact may come through nonverbal communication.[10] A lack of gestures and other nonverbal signals is one of the weaknesses of voice mail, texts, and other electronic communications. It's hard for things like clickable emoticons to make up for their absence.

Think of how nonverbal signals play out in your own communications.[11] Sometimes our body language "talks" even as we maintain silence. And when we do speak, our body may "say" different things than our words actually convey. This is called a **mixed message**—where words communicate one message while actions and body language communicate something else. Watch how people behave in a meeting. A person who feels under attack may move back in a chair or lean away from the presumed antagonist, even while expressing verbal agreement. All of this may be done quite unconsciously, but the mixed message will be picked up by those tuned in to nonverbal signals.

Nonverbal communication takes place through gestures and body language.

A mixed message results when words communicate one message while actions, body language, or appearance communicate something else.

Overloads and Distractions

Overloads and distractions caused by the availability and abundance of electronic communications and social media can make it hard to communicate well. McKinsey reports that professionals are spending 28% of their time dealing with e-mail, while the Radicati Group reports that the average business person deals with 108 e-mails per day.[12] Scholar Gloria Mark's research found that people check their e-mail inboxes as many as 74 times per day, causing her to say "It's really out of control."[13] Couple this information with everyday personal experience—e-mails, messages, and chats pretty much follow us wherever we go 24/7. They coexist simultaneously on our computer screens and smart devices, and they compete with one another, social media, and video streams for our attention. Our effectiveness in attending to this ever-present and shifting mix of electronic communications is often compromised by the size and stress of overwhelming demands.

Even a scheduled meeting may be compromised by overloads and distractions in the form of telephone interruptions, texts, e-mails, drop-in visitors, and lack of privacy. Consider the following exchange between George and his manager.[14]

> Okay, George, let's hear your problem [phone rings, manager answers it and promises caller to deliver a report "just as soon as I can get it done"]. Uh, now, where were we—oh, you're having a problem with your technician. She's . . . [manager's assistant brings in some papers that need his immediate signature] . . . you say she's overstressed lately, wants to leave. I tell you what, George, why don't you [phone beeps a reminder, boss looks and realizes he has a lunch meeting] . . . uh, take a stab at handling it yourself. I've got to go now [starts texting].

It's obvious that this manager was not effective in communicating with George, even if he really wanted to. But, errors like these can be easily avoided by anyone sincerely interested in communicating face to face with someone. At a minimum, adequate time should be set aside and arrangements made for privacy. The likelihood of interruptions such as the telephone, drop-in visitors, and electronic messages should be anticipated and then avoided by good planning and the discipline to stay focused on the visitor rather than on devices.

Cross-Cultural Communication

After taking over as the CEO of the Dutch publisher Wolters Kluwer, Nancy McKinstry initiated major changes in strategy and operations—cutting staff, restructuring divisions, and investing in new business areas. She was the first American to head the firm, and she described herself as "aggressive" when first meeting with her management team. After learning her use of that word wasn't well received by Europeans, she switched to "decisive." McKinstry says: "I was coming across as too harsh, too much of a results-driven American to the people I needed to get on board."[15]

Communicating across cultures requires lots of sensitivity, awareness, and the ability to quickly learn local rights and wrongs. The most difficult situation is when you don't speak the local language, or when one or both of the people trying to communicate are weak in a shared second language. Advertising messages are notorious for getting lost in translation. A Pepsi ad in Taiwan that was intended to say "The Pepsi Generation" came out as "Pepsi will bring your ancestors back from the dead." A KFC ad in China that was intended to say "finger lickin' good" came out as "eat your fingers off."[16]

Ethnocentrism is the tendency to consider one's culture superior to any and all others.

Ethnocentrism is a major enemy of effective cross-cultural communication. This is the tendency to consider one's culture superior to other cultures. It hurts communication in at least three major ways. First, it may lead to poor listening. Second, it may cause someone to address or speak with others in ways that alienate them. Third, it may lead to the use of inappropriate stereotypes.[17]

One of the ways ethnocentrism shows up is as a failure to respect cultural differences in nonverbal communication.[18] The American "thumbs-up" sign is an insult in Ghana and Australia; signaling "OK" with thumb and forefinger circled together is not okay in parts of Europe. Waving "hello" with an open palm is an insult in West Africa, suggesting the other person has five fathers.[19]

Learning Check 1

TAKEAWAYQUESTION 1 **What is the communication process?**

BE SURE YOU CAN • describe the communication process and identify its key components • differentiate between effective and efficient communication • explain the role of credibility in persuasive communication • list the common sources of noise that limit effective communication • explain how mixed messages interfere with communication • explain how ethnocentrism affects cross-cultural communication

Improving Collaboration through Communication

TAKEAWAY 2   How can we improve collaboration through communication?

LEARN MORE ABOUT | Transparency and openness • Use of electronic media • Active listening Constructive feedback • Space design

Effective communication is essential as people work together in teams and organizations. The better the communication, the more likely it is that collaboration will be successful. Pathways toward better communication are found in such things as attention to transparency and openness, good use of electronic media, active listening practices, focusing on constructive feedback, and appropriate space design.

Transparency and Openness

At HCL Industries, a large technology outsourcing firm, former CEO and currently Senior Advisor to HCL Vineet Nayar believes that one of his most important tasks as CEO was to create transparency so that a "culture of trust" exists within the firm. Transparency at HCL means that the firm's financial information is fully posted on the internal Web. "We put all the dirty linen on the table," Nayar says. Transparency also means that the results of 360-degree feedback reviews for HCL's 3,800 managers get posted as well, including Nayar's own reviews. When managers present plans to the top management team, Nayar insists that they also get posted so that everyone can read them and offer comments. His intent was to stimulate what he calls a company-wide process of "massive collaborative learning." This ensures that by the time a plan gets approved, it's most likely to be a good one.[20]

Communication transparency involves being honest in sharing accurate and complete information about the organization and workplace affairs. A lack of communication transparency is evident when managers try to hide information and restrict access to it by organizational members. High communication transparency, such as that just illustrated in the HCL case, is evident when managers openly share information throughout an organization.

The term **open book management** describes a form of communication transparency where employees are provided with essential financial information about their companies. At Bailard, Inc., a private investment firm, this openness extends to salaries. If you want to know what others are making at the firm, all you need to do is ask the chief financial officer. The firm's co-founder and CEO, Thomas Bailard, believes open book management is a good way to defeat office politics. "As a manager," he says, "if you know that your compensation decisions are essentially going to be public, you have to have pretty strong conviction about any decision you make."[21]

> **Communication transparency** involves openly sharing honest and complete information about the organization and workplace affairs.

> **Open book management** is where managers provide employees with essential financial information about their companies.

analysis > MAKE DATA YOUR FRIEND

> *Only 3% of HR executives give "A" grades to their firms' performance measurement systems.*

Value of Performance Reviews Gets Increasing Scrutiny

Surveys show people aren't always pleased with the way managers in their organizations do performance reviews. Some are so concerned that they suggest dropping them altogether. Check these survey findings:

- Only 30% of HR executives believed that employees trust their employer's performance measurement system.
- 60% of HR executives give their performance management systems "C" grades or worse.
- Top concerns of HR executives are that managers aren't willing to face employees and give constructive feedback, and employees don't have a clear understanding of what rates as good and bad performance.

- 1% of firms are completely doing away with performance reviews and shifting to regular one-on-one meetings where performance is discussed.

YOUR THOUGHTS?

Performance review is often a hot topic. The buzzwords are "merit pay" and "performance accountability." But is it really possible to have a performance measurement system that is respected by managers and workers alike? Do the data reported here fit with your own experiences? What are their implications for management practice? Will we soon see a dramatic increase in the number of employers who shift away from formal annual reviews and replace them with something less formal and more timely?

As the prior examples suggest, the benefits of communication transparency start with better decision making. When people are well informed, they can be expected to make good decisions that serve the best interests of the organization. But, the benefits of transparency also extend into the realm of motivation and engagement. When people are trusted with information, they also can be expected to feel more loyal and show more engagement as organizational members.

Use of Electronic Media

Are you part of the Twitter community, post to Facebook, a frequent messager on WhatsApp or Line, or generally a heavy user of your smart mobile devices? Technology hasn't just changed how we communicate. It has created a social media revolution—one that can be a performance asset or detriment in the world of work.[22]

To begin, we may be getting so familiar with writing online shorthand that we use it in the wrong places. Sending a message like "Thnx for the IView! I Wd Lv to Wrk 4 U!! ;)" isn't the follow-up most employers like to receive from job candidates. When Tory Johnson, founder and CEO of Women for Hire, Inc., received a thank-you note by e-mail from an intern candidate, it included "hiya," "thanx," three exclamation points, and two emoticons. She says: "That e-mail just ruined it for me."[23] Textspeak and emoticons may be the norm in social networks, but their use can be inappropriate in work settings.

Privacy also is a concern in any form of electronic communication.[24] When Facebook's CEO, Mark Zuckerberg, says privacy is "no longer a social norm," it's time to take the issue seriously. An American Management Association survey of 304 U.S. companies found that 66% monitor Internet connections; 43% store and review computer files and monitor e-mail; 45% monitor telephone time and numbers dialed; and 30% have fired employees for misuse of the Internet.[25] When it comes to Web browsing and using social media at work, the best advice comes down to this: Find out the employer's policy and follow it. Don't ever assume that you have electronic privacy; chances are the employer is checking or can easily check on you.[26]

Guidelines for Active Listening

1. *Listen for message content:* Try to hear exactly what content is being conveyed in the message.
2. *Listen for feelings:* Try to identify how the source feels about the content in the message.
3. *Respond to feelings:* Let the source know that her or his feelings are being recognized.
4. *Note all cues:* Be sensitive to nonverbal and verbal messages; be alert for mixed messages.
5. *Paraphrase and restate:* State back to the source what you think you are hearing.

Electronic grapevines use electronic media to pass messages and information among members of social networks.

The **electronic grapevine** that passes messages and information among members of social networks is now a fact of life. Electronic messages—both accurate and inaccurate—fly with great speed around our world. The YouTube grapevine stung Domino's Pizza executives when a posted video showed two employees doing nasty things to sandwiches. It was soon viewed over a million times. By the time the video was pulled (by one of its authors who apologized for "faking"), Domino's faced a crisis in customer confidence. The CEO finally created a Twitter account and posted a YouTube video message to present the company's own view of the story.[27]

Active Listening

Whether trying to communicate electronically or face to face, managers must be very good at listening. When people "talk," they are trying to communicate something. That "something" may or may not be what they are actually saying.

Active listening is the process of taking action to help someone say exactly what he or she really means or wants to communicate.[28] It involves being sincere and trying to find out the full meaning of what is being expressed. It also involves being disciplined in controlling emotions and withholding premature evaluations or interpretations. Different responses to the following two questions contrast how a "passive" listener and an "active" listener might act in real workplace conversations.[29]

Question 1: "Don't you think employees should be promoted on the basis of seniority?" *Passive listener's response:* "No, I don't!" *Active listener's response:* "It seems to you that they should, I take it?"

Question 2: "What does the supervisor expect us to do about these out-of-date computers?" *Passive listener's response:* "Do the best you can, I guess." *Active listener's response:* "You're pretty frustrated with those machines, aren't you?"

> **Active listening** helps the source of a message say what he or she really means.

Constructive Feedback

The process of telling other people how you feel about something they did or said, or about the situation in general, is called **feedback**. It occurs in the normal give-and-take of working relationships, and in more formal performance review sessions.

The art of giving feedback is an indispensable skill, particularly for managers who must regularly give feedback to other people. When poorly done, feedback can be threatening to the recipient and cause resentment. Properly handled feedback—even performance criticism—can be listened to, accepted, and used to good advantage by the receiver.[30] Consider someone who comes late to meetings. Feedback from the meeting chair might be *evaluative*—"You are unreliable and always late for everything." It might be *interpretive*—"You're coming late to meetings; you might be spreading yourself too thin and have trouble meeting your obligations." It might also be *descriptive*—"You were 30 minutes late for today's meeting and missed a lot of the context for our discussion."[31]

> **Feedback** is the process of telling someone else how you feel about something that person did or said.

Feedback is most useful and constructive, rather than harmful, when it offers real benefits to the receiver and doesn't just satisfy some personal need of the sender. A supervisor who berates a computer programmer for errors, for example, may actually be angry about failing to give clear instructions in the first place. Some thoughts on becoming a better receiver of critical feedback are shown in the box.[32] Advice on becoming a better giver of constructive feedback includes the following tips:[33]

- Give feedback directly and with real feeling, based on trust between you and the receiver.

- Make sure that feedback is specific rather than general; use good, clear, and preferably recent examples to make your points.

- Give feedback at a time when the receiver seems most willing or able to accept it.

> ### Don'ts and Do's for Handling Criticism
> *Don't* get mad or cry.
> *Do* say: "Let me give this some thought and we can talk later."
> *Don't* be defensive or deny things.
> *Do* say: "I'm surprised. Can you give me some examples?"
> *Don't* blame others.
> *Do* say: "That wasn't my impression. How did you come to see it that way?"

- Make sure the feedback is valid; limit it to issues the receiver can be expected to address.

- Give feedback in small doses; never give more than the receiver can handle at any particular time.

Space Design

Proxemics involves the use of space in communication.

Proxemics is the study of how we use space.[34] And, space counts in communication. The distance between people conveys varying intentions in terms of intimacy, openness, and status in interpersonal communications. Even the physical layout of an office or room is a form of nonverbal communication. Think about it. Offices with chairs available for side-by-side seating convey different messages than offices where the manager's chair sits behind the desk and those for visitors sit facing it in front.

Organizations today are being run with the premise that the better people communicate with one another, the better the organization will perform. We live in an increasingly connected world, and the same levels of connectedness are sought in the workplace. Google, for example, thrives and depends on high levels of innovation. So, the company's new headquarters is designed to make it easy for employees to have casual, not just formal, communications. "We want it to be easy [for] Googlers to bump into one another," says a spokeswoman.[35]

Part of the push toward greater connectedness and more casual conversations is found in what might be called the demise of the office cubicle. It's been popular for quite awhile to design office spaces with small cubicles for individual workers and larger meeting rooms for meetings. The new trend is toward smaller teams, less formal meetings, and more frequent casual interaction. Architects and office supply firms are responding with designs that eliminate or open up cubicles by giving them shorter walls or no walls at all. They are also creating lots of small office "nests" of six to eight co-workers and "focus rooms" where a few people can huddle up while exchanging ideas, working on a project, or just having a chat. Martha Clarkson heads Microsoft's global workplace strategy. She says it's based on a post-cubicle model because "Work is really getting done in smaller teams."[36]

Learning Check 2

TAKEAWAYQUESTION 2 **How can we improve collaboration through communication?**

BE SURE YOU CAN • explain how transparency and openness improves communication • explain how interactive management and practices like structured meetings can improve upward communication • discuss possible uses of electronic media by managers • define *active listening* and list active listening rules • illustrate the guidelines for constructive feedback • explain how space design influences communication

Managing Conflict

Conflict is a disagreement over issues of substance and/or an emotional antagonism.

TAKEAWAY 3   How can we deal positively with conflict?

LEARN MORE ABOUT | Functional and dysfunctional conflict • Conflict resolution
Conflict management styles • Structural approaches to conflict management

Conflict occurs as disagreements on substantive or emotional issues.[37] These disagreements can be overt and openly expressed, or covert and hidden behind false surface harmony and political intrigue. The ability to deal with conflicts is a critical communication and collaboration skill in the social settings of teams and organizations. Managers and team leaders become ineffective and lose credibility when they deny or hide from conflicts, or pass conflict situations on for others to handle as the "bad cops."[38]

Substantive conflict involves disagreements over goals, resources, rewards, policies, procedures, and job assignments.

Emotional conflict results from feelings of anger, distrust, dislike, fear, and resentment, as well as from personality clashes.

Substantive conflicts involve disagreements over such things as goals and tasks, allocation of resources, distribution of rewards, policies and procedures, and job assignments. **Emotional conflicts** result from feelings of anger, distrust, dislike, fear, and resentment, as well as from personality clashes and relationship problems. Both forms of conflict can cause difficulties. But, they can also stimulate creativity and high performance.

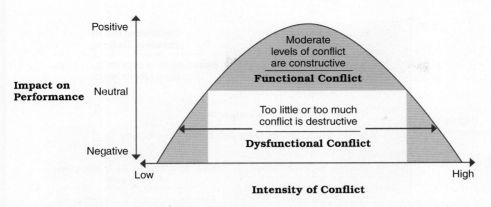

FIGURE 18.3
The relationship between
conflict and performance.

Functional and Dysfunctional Conflict

The inverted "U" curve depicted in Figure 18.3 shows that conflict of moderate intensity can be good for performance. This **functional conflict**, or constructive conflict, moves people toward greater work efforts, cooperation, and creativity. It helps teams achieve their goals and avoid making poor decisions because of groupthink. **Dysfunctional conflict**, or destructive conflict, harms performance, relationships, and even individual well-being. It occurs when there is either too much or too little conflict. Too much conflict is distracting and overwhelming. Too little conflict promotes groupthink, complacency, and the loss of a high-performance edge.

Functional conflict is constructive and helps task performance.

Dysfunctional conflict is destructive and hurts task performance.

Causes of Conflict

A number of drivers can cause or set the stage for conflict. *Role ambiguities* in the form of unclear job expectations and other task uncertainties increase the likelihood for people to work at cross-purposes. *Resource scarcities* cause conflict when people have to share or compete for them. *Task interdependencies* breed conflict when people depend on others to perform well in order to perform well themselves.

Competing objectives also are opportunities for conflict. When goals are poorly set or reward systems are poorly designed, individuals and groups may come into conflict by working to one another's disadvantage. Structural differentiation breeds conflict. Differences in organization structures and in the characteristics of the people staffing them may foster conflict because of incompatible approaches toward work. And, unresolved prior conflicts tend to erupt in later conflicts. Unless a conflict is fully resolved, it may remain latent only to emerge again in the future.

Conflict Resolution

When conflicts do occur, they can be "resolved" in the sense that the causes are corrected, or "suppressed" in that the causes remain but the conflict behaviors are controlled. Suppressed conflicts tend to fester and recur at a later time. They postpone issues and problems that may be best addressed immediately, and the suppression itself can be a source of personal stress.[39] True **conflict resolution** eliminates the underlying causes of conflict and reduces the potential for similar conflicts in the future.

Conflict resolution is the removal of the substantive and emotional reasons for a conflict.

Conflict Management Styles

People tend to respond to interpersonal conflict through different combinations of cooperative and assertive behaviors.[40] *Cooperativeness* is the desire to satisfy another party's needs

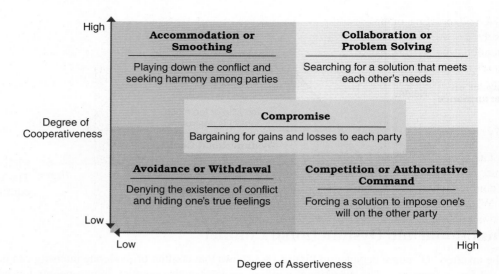

FIGURE 18.4
Alternative conflict management styles.

and concerns. *Assertiveness* is the desire to satisfy one's own needs and concerns. Figure 18.4 shows five interpersonal styles of conflict management resulting from combinations of these two tendencies.[41]

- **Avoidance** or *withdrawal*—being uncooperative and unassertive, downplaying disagreement, withdrawing from the situation, and/or staying neutral at all costs.

- **Accommodation** or *smoothing*—being cooperative but unassertive, letting the wishes of others rule, smoothing over or overlooking differences to maintain harmony.

- **Competition** or *authoritative command*—being uncooperative but assertive, working against the wishes of the other party, engaging in win–lose competition, and/or forcing through the exercise of authority.

- **Compromise**—being moderately cooperative and assertive, bargaining for "acceptable" solutions in which each party wins a bit and loses a bit.

- **Collaboration** or *problem solving*—being cooperative and assertive, trying to fully satisfy everyone's concerns by working through differences, finding and solving problems so that everyone gains.

The avoiding and accommodating styles often create **lose–lose conflict**.[42] No one achieves their true desires, and the underlying reasons for conflict remain. Although the conflict appears settled or may even disappear temporarily, it tends to recur in the future. Avoidance pretends that conflict doesn't really exist. Everyone withdraws and hopes it will simply go away. Accommodation plays down differences and highlights areas of agreement. Peaceful coexistence is the goal, but the real essence of a conflict may be ignored.

Competing and compromising styles tend to create **win–lose conflict** where each party strives to gain at the other's expense. Because win–lose methods don't address the root causes of conflict, future conflicts of the same or a similar nature are likely to reoccur. In competition, one party wins because superior skill or outright domination allows his or her desires to be forced on the other. An example is authoritative command where a supervisor simply dictates a solution to subordinates. Compromise occurs when trade-offs are made such that each party to the conflict gives up and gains something. But because each party loses something, antecedents for future conflicts are established.

Avoidance, or withdrawal, pretends that a conflict doesn't really exist.

Accommodation, or smoothing, plays down differences and highlights similarities to reduce conflict.

Competition, or authoritative command, uses force, superior skill, or domination to "win" a conflict.

Compromise occurs when each party to the conflict gives up something of value to the other.

Collaboration, or problem solving, involves working through conflict differences and solving problems so everyone wins.

In **lose–lose conflict**, no one achieves their true desires, and the underlying reasons for conflict remain.

In **win–lose conflict**, one party achieves its desires, and the other party does not.

A collaborating or problem-solving style is a form of **win–win conflict** where issues get resolved to everyone's benefit. Parties to the conflict recognize that something is wrong and needs attention, and they confront the issues head on. Win–win outcomes eliminate the underlying causes of the conflict because all matters and concerns are raised and discussed openly. But, this approach also takes more time because it involves efforts in information collection and analysis of one another's positions.

> In **win–win conflict** the conflict is resolved to everyone's benefit.

Structural Approaches to Conflict Management

Not all conflict can be resolved at the interpersonal level. Think about it. Aren't there likely to be times when personalities and emotions prove irreconcilable? In such cases, a structural approach to conflict management often can help.[43]

When conflict traces back to a resource issue, the structural solution is to *make more resources available*. Although costly and not always possible, this is a straightforward way to resolve resource-driven conflicts. When people are stuck in conflict and just can't seem to appreciate one another's points of view, *appealing to higher-level goals* can sometimes focus their attention on mutually desirable outcomes. In a student team where members are arguing over content choices for a PowerPoint presentation, for example, it might help to remind everyone that the goal is to get an "A" from the instructor. An appeal to higher goals offers a common frame of reference for analyzing differences and reconciling disagreements.

It may be necessary to *change the people*. There are times when

> ### Structural Ways to Manage Conflict
>
> - Make resources available.
> - Appeal to higher goals.
> - Change the people.
> - Change the environment.
> - Use integrating devices.
> - Provide training.
> - Change reward systems.

a manager may need to replace or transfer one or more of the conflicting parties to eliminate conflict. When the people can't be changed, they may have to be separated by *altering the physical environment*. Sometimes it is possible to rearrange facilities, work space, or workflows to physically separate conflicting parties and decrease opportunities for contact with one another. Organizations also can use *integrating devices* to help manage conflicts between groups. These approaches include assigning people to formal liaison roles, convening special task forces, setting up cross-functional teams, and even switching to the matrix form of organization.

By *changing reward systems*, it is sometimes possible to reduce conflicts that arise when people feel they have to compete with one another for attention, pay, and other rewards. An example is shifting pay bonuses, or even student project grades, to the group level. Using this approach allows individuals to benefit in direct proportion to how well the team performs as a whole. This is a way of reinforcing teamwork and reducing the tendencies of team members to compete with one another. Last, people who get good *training in interpersonal skills* are better prepared to communicate and work effectively in conflict-prone situations. When employers list criteria for recruiting new college graduates, such "soft" or "people" skills are often right at the top of that list. You can't succeed in today's horizontal and team-oriented organizations if you can't work well with other people, even when disagreements are inevitable.

Learning Check 3

TAKEAWAYQUESTION 3 **How can we deal positively with conflict?**

BE SURE YOU CAN differentiate substantive and emotional conflict • differentiate functional and dysfunctional conflict • explain the common causes of conflict • define *conflict resolution* • explain the conflict management styles of avoidance, accommodation, competition, compromise, and collaboration • discuss lose–lose, win–lose, and win–win conflicts • list the structural approaches to conflict management

Managing Negotiation

Negotiation is the process of making joint decisions when the parties involved have different preferences.

Substance goals in negotiation are concerned with outcomes.

Relationship goals in negotiation are concerned with the ways people work together.

Effective negotiation resolves issues of substance while maintaining a positive process.

TAKEAWAY 4   How can we negotiate successful agreements?

LEARN MORE ABOUT | Negotiation goals and approaches • Gaining agreement
Negotiation pitfalls • Third-party dispute resolution

Situation: Your employer offers you a promotion, but the pay raise being offered is disappointing.

Situation: You have enough money to send one person for training from your department, but two really want to go.

Situation: Your team members are having a "cook-out" on Saturday afternoon and want you to attend, but your husband wants you to go with him to visit his mother in a neighboring town.

Situation: Someone on your sales team has to fly to Texas to meet an important client; you've made the last two trips out of town and don't want to go; another member of the team hasn't been out of town in a long time and "owes" you a favor.

These are examples of the many work situations that lead to **negotiation**—the process of making joint decisions when the parties involved have different preferences. Stated a bit differently, negotiation is a way of reaching agreement. People negotiate over job assignments, work schedules, work locations, and salaries.[44] Any and all negotiations are ripe for conflict. And, like the salary negotiation described in the box, they are a stiff test of anyone's communication and collaboration skills.[45]

"Ins" and "Outs" of Negotiating Salaries

- *Prepare, prepare, prepare*—Do the research beforehand and find out what others make for a similar position inside and outside the organization, including everything from salary to benefits, bonuses, incentives, and job perks.

- *Document and communicate*—Identify and communicate your performance value; put forth a set of accomplishments that show how you have saved or made money and created value in your present job or for a past employer.

- *Identify critical skills and attributes*—Make a list of your strengths and link each of these with potential contributions to the new employer; show how *you* offer talents and personal attributes of immediate value to the work team.

- *Advocate and ask*—Be your own best advocate; the rule in salary negotiation is "Don't ask, don't get." But don't ask too soon; your boss or interviewer should be the first to bring up salary.

- *Stay focused on the goal*—Your goal is to achieve as much as you can in the negotiation; this means not only doing well at the moment but also getting better positioned for future gains.

- *View things from the other side*—Test your requests against the employer's point of view; ask if you are being reasonable, convincing, and fair; ask how the boss could explain to higher levels and to your peers a decision to grant your request.

- *Don't overreact to bad news*—Never "quit on the spot" if you don't get what you want; be willing to search for and consider alternative job offers.

Negotiation Goals and Approaches

Two important goals should be considered in any negotiation. **Substance goals** are concerned with negotiation outcomes. They are tied to content issues. **Relationship goals** are concerned with negotiation processes. They are tied to the ways in which people work together while negotiating and how they (and any constituencies they represent) will be able to work together again in the future.

Effective negotiation occurs when issues of substance are resolved and working relationships among the negotiating parties are maintained or even improved. The three criteria of effective negotiation are: (1) *Quality*—negotiating a "wise" agreement that is truly satisfactory to all sides. (2) *Cost*—negotiating efficiently, using a minimum of resources and time. (3) *Harmony*—negotiating in a way that fosters, rather than inhibits, good relationships.[46]

Gaining Agreements

In **distributive negotiation**, each party makes claims for certain preferred outcomes.[47] This emphasis on substance can become self-centered and competitive, with all parties thinking the only way for them to gain is for others to lose. Relationships often get sacrificed as process breaks down in these win–lose situations.

In **principled negotiation**, sometimes called **integrative negotiation**, the orientation is win–win. The goal is to achieve a final agreement based on the merits of each party's claims. No one should lose in a principled negotiation, and positive relationships should be maintained in the process. Four pathways or rules for gaining such integrated agreements are set forth by Roger Fisher and William Ury in their book *Getting to Yes*:[48]

1. Separate the people from the problem.
2. Focus on interests, not on positions.
3. Generate many alternatives before deciding what to do.
4. Insist that results be based on some objective standard.

The attitudinal foundations of principled negotiation involve each party's willingness to trust, share information, and ask reasonable questions. The information foundations involve both parties knowing what is important to them and finding out what is important to the other party.

Attitudes and information both come into play during classic two-party labor–management negotiations over a new contract and salary increase.[49] Look at Figure 18.5 and consider the situation from the labor union's perspective. The union negotiator has told her management counterpart that the union wants a new wage of $15.00 per hour. This expressed preference is the union's initial offer. However, she also has in mind a minimum reservation point of $13.25 per hour. This is the lowest wage she is willing to accept for the union. Now look at it from the perspective of the management negotiator. His initial offer is $12.75 per hour. But his maximum reservation point, the highest wage he is prepared to eventually offer the union, is $13.75 per hour.

The **bargaining zone** in a negotiation is defined as the space between one party's minimum reservation point and the other party's maximum reservation point. In this case it lies between $13.25 per hour and $13.75 per hour. It is a "positive" zone since the reservation points of the two parties overlap. If the union's minimum reservation point was greater than management's maximum reservation point, say $14 per hour, there would be no room for bargaining. A key task for any negotiator is to discover the other party's reservation point. It is difficult to negotiate effectively until this is known and each party realizes that there is a positive bargaining zone.

Negotiation Pitfalls

The negotiation process is admittedly complex, and negotiators must guard against common pitfalls. The first is the *myth of the "fixed pie."* This involves acting on the distributive win–lose assumption that in order for you to gain, the other person must give something up. This fails to recognize the

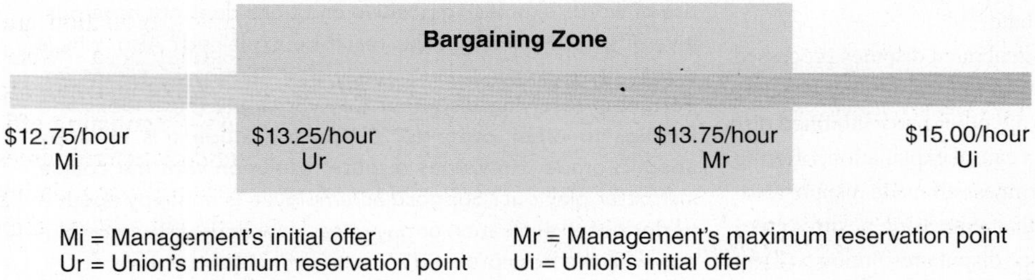

Distributive negotiation focuses on win–lose claims made by each party for certain preferred outcomes.

Principled negotiation or **integrative negotiation** uses a "win–win" orientation to reach solutions acceptable to each party.

◄ Rules for gaining integrated agreements

A bargaining zone is the space between one party's minimum reservation point and the other party's maximum reservation point.

Bargaining Zone

| $12.75/hour | $13.25/hour | $13.75/hour | $15.00/hour |
| Mi | Ur | Mr | Ui |

Mi = Management's initial offer
Ur = Union's minimum reservation point
Mr = Management's maximum reservation point
Ui = Union's initial offer

FIGURE 18.5
The bargaining zone in classic two-party negotiation.

integrative assumption that the "pie" can sometimes be expanded or utilized to everyone's advantage. A second negotiation error is *nonrational escalation of conflict*. The negotiator gets locked into previously stated "demands" and allows personal needs for "ego" and "saving face" to inflate the perceived importance of satisfying them.

A third negotiating error is *overconfidence and ignoring the other's needs*. The negotiator becomes overconfident, believes his or her position is the only correct one, and fails to consider the needs of the other party. The fourth error is *too much "telling" and too little "hearing."* The "telling" error occurs when parties to a negotiation don't really make themselves understood to each other. The "hearing" error occurs when they fail to listen well enough to understand what the other party is saying.[50]

Another potential negotiation pitfall in our age of globalization is *premature cultural comfort*. This occurs when a negotiator is too quick to assume that he or she understands the intentions, positions, and meanings of a negotiator from a different culture. A negotiator from a low-context culture, for example, is used to getting information through direct questions and answers. But this style might lead to difficulties if used with negotiators from a high-context

Research Brief

Words Affect Outcomes in Online Dispute Resolution

The National Consumer League reports that 41% of participants in online trading had problems, often associated with late deliveries. A study of online dispute resolution among eBay buyers and sellers found that using words that "give face" were more likely than words that "attack face" to result in settlement. Jeanne Brett, Mara Olekalns, Ray Friedman, Nathan Goates, Cameron Anderson, and Cara Cherry Lisco studied real disputes being addressed through Square Trade, an online dispute resolution service to which eBay refers unhappy customers. A "dispute" was defined as a form of conflict in which one party to a transaction makes a claim that the other party rejects.

The researchers adopted what they call a "language-based" approach using "face theory," essentially arguing that how participants use language to give and attack the face of the other party will have a major impact on results. For example, in filing a claim, an unhappy buyer might use polite words that preserve the positive self-image, or face, of the seller, or the buyer might use negative words that attack this sense of face. Examples of negative words are "agitated, angry, apprehensive, despise, disgusted, frustrated, furious, and hate."

This study examined 386 eBay-generated disputes processed through Square Trade. Results showed that expressing negative emotions and giving commands to the other party inhibited dispute resolution, whereas providing a causal explanation, offering suggestions, and communicating firmness all made dispute resolution more likely. The hypothesis that expressing positive emotions would increase the likelihood of dispute resolution was not

Online Dispute Resolution

Dispute resolution less likely when	Dispute resolution more likely when
• Negative emotions are expressed • Commands are issued	• Causal explanations given • Suggestions are offered • Communications are firm

supported. The study also showed that the longer a dispute played out, the less likely it was to be resolved.

In terms of practical implications, the researchers say: "Watch your language: Avoid attacking the other's face either by showing your anger toward them, or by expressing contempt. Avoid signaling weakness, and be firm in your claim. Provide causal accounts that take responsibility and give face."

YOU BE THE RESEARCHER

Why is it that using words that express negative emotions seems to have adverse effects on dispute resolution, but the use of words expressing positive emotions does not have positive effects? How might this result be explained? Also, why is it that using words that communicate "firmness" seems important in resolving disputes? Can you apply these ideas and findings to other contexts? Suppose a student is unhappy about a grade. How does dispute resolution with the course instructor play out? Suppose an employee is unhappy about a performance evaluation or pay raise. How does dispute resolution with the boss proceed?

culture. Their tendencies may be to communicate indirectly with non-declarative language, nonverbal signals, and avoidance of hard-and-fast position statements.[51]

It is important to avoid the *trap of ethical misconduct.* The motivation to negotiate unethically sometimes arises from pure greed and undue emphasis on the profit motive. This may be experienced as a desire to "get just a bit more" or to "get as much as you can" from a negotiation. The motivation to behave unethically also may result from a sense of competition. This is a desire to "win" a negotiation just for the sake of winning it, or because of the misguided belief that someone else must "lose" in order for you to gain.

When unethical behavior occurs in negotiation, the persons involved may try to explain it away with inappropriate rationalizing: "It was really unavoidable." "Oh, it's harmless." "The results justify the means." "It's really quite fair and appropriate."[52] These and other excuses for questionable behavior are morally unacceptable. Their use also runs the risk that any short-run gains will be offset by long-run losses. Unethical negotiators risk being viewed with distrust, disrespect, and dislike, and even the risk of being targeted for revenge in future negotiations.

> ### Beware of Negotiation Pitfalls
> - Myth of fixed pie
> - Escalation of conflict
> - Overconfidence
> - Too much telling
> - Too little hearing
> - Cultural miscues
> - Unethical behavior

insight > LEARN ABOUT YOURSELF

> **>** *Recruiters give communication and networking skills high priority when screening candidates for college internships and first jobs.*

Collaboration Begins with Communication and Networking

Recruiters give **communication and networking** skills high priority when screening candidates for college internships and first jobs. They're looking for candidates who can communicate well both orally and in writing, and network well with others for collaboration and teamwork. They also want people who gain social capital through communication and networking so that they can handle conflicts and negotiate successfully. But if you're like many of us, there's work to be done to master these challenges.

The American Management Association found that workers rated their bosses only slightly above average on transforming ideas into words, being credible, listening and asking questions, and giving written and oral presentations. More than three-quarters of university professors rated incoming high school graduates as only "fair" or "poor" in writing clearly, and in spelling and use of grammar. When it comes to decorum or just plain old "good manners," a *BusinessWeek* survey reported that 38% of women complain about "sexual innuendo, wisecracks and taunts" at work.

Social networking is very popular on the college campus and among young professionals, as everyone wants to be linked in. The same skills transfer to the workplace. A good networker acts as a *hub*—connected with others; *gatekeeper*—moving information to and from others; and *pulse-taker*—staying abreast of what is happening.

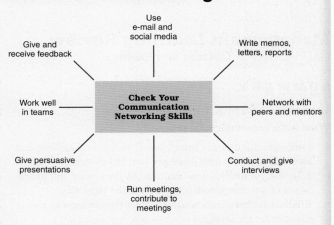

GET TO KNOW YOURSELF BETTER

Can you convince a recruiter that you are ready to run effective meetings? . . . write informative reports? . . . deliver persuasive presentations? . . . conduct job interviews? . . . use e-mail and social media well? network well with peers and mentors? . . . keep conflicts constructive and negotiations positive? Where does social capital rank on your own list of personal strengths? Ask friends, co-workers, and family members to rate your communication and networking skills. Turn these ratings into a personal development "To Do" list that you can share with your instructor.

Third-Party Dispute Resolution

In mediation, a neutral party tries to help conflicting parties improve communication to resolve their dispute.

Even with the best of intentions, it may not always be possible to achieve integrative agreements. When disputes reach a point of impasse, third-party assistance with dispute resolution can be useful. **Mediation** involves a neutral third party who tries to improve communication between negotiating parties and keep them focused on relevant issues. The mediator does not issue a ruling or make a decision, but can take an active role in discussions. This may include making suggestions in an attempt to move the parties toward agreement.

In arbitration, a neutral third party issues a binding decision to resolve a dispute.

Arbitration, such as salary arbitration in professional sports, is a stronger form of dispute resolution. It involves a neutral third party, the arbitrator, who acts as a "judge" and issues a binding decision. This usually includes a formal hearing in which the arbitrator listens to both sides and reviews all facets of the case before making a ruling that all parties are required to follow.

An ombudsperson is designated by the organization to listen to complaints and disputes in an attempt to resolve them.

Some organizations provide for a process called *alternative dispute resolution*. This approach uses mediation or arbitration, but does so only after direct attempts to negotiate agreements between conflicting parties have failed. A designated **ombudsperson** who listens to complaints and disputes often plays a key role in this process.

Learning Check 4

TAKEAWAYQUESTION 4   **How can we negotiate successful agreements?**

BE SURE YOU CAN • differentiate between distributive and principled negotiation • list four rules of principled negotiation • define *bargaining zone* and use this term to illustrate a labor–management wage negotiation • describe the potential pitfalls in negotiation • differentiate between mediation and arbitration

Management Learning Review
Get Prepared for **Quizzes and Exams**

SUMMARY

TAKEAWAYQUESTION 1

What is the communication process?

* Communication is the interpersonal process of sending and receiving symbols with messages attached to them.
* Effective communication occurs when the sender and the receiver of a message both interpret it in the same way.
* Efficient communication occurs when the message is sent at low cost for the sender.
* Persuasive communication results in the recipient acting as intended by the sender; credibility earned by expertise and good relationships is essential to persuasive communication.
* Noise is anything that interferes with the effectiveness of communication; common examples are poor utilization of channels, poor written or oral expression, physical distractions, and status effects.

FOR DISCUSSION When, if ever, is it okay to sacrifice effectiveness in order to gain efficiency in communication?

TAKEAWAYQUESTION 2

How can we improve collaboration through communication?

* Transparency in the sense that information conveyed to others is honest, credible, and fully disclosed is an important way to improve communication in the workplace.
* Interactive management through structured meetings, use of electronic media, and advisory councils can improve upward communication.
* Active listening, through reflecting back and paraphrasing, can help overcome barriers and improve communication.
* Constructive feedback is specific, direct, well-timed, and limited to things the receiver can change.
* Office architecture and space designs can be used to improve communication in organizations.
* Proper choice of channels and use of information technology can improve communication in organizations.
* Greater cross-cultural awareness and sensitivity are important if we are to overcome the negative influences of ethnocentrism on communication.

FOR DISCUSSION Which of the rules of active listening do people most often break?

TAKEAWAY QUESTION 3

How can we deal positively with conflict?

- Conflict occurs as disagreements over substantive or emotional issues.
- Moderate levels of conflict are functional for performance and creativity; too little or too much conflict becomes dysfunctional.
- Conflict may be managed through structural approaches that involve changing people, goals, resources, or work arrangements.
- Personal conflict management styles include avoidance, accommodation, compromise, competition, and collaboration.
- True conflict resolution involves problem solving through a win–win collaborative approach.

FOR DISCUSSION When can it be better to avoid conflict rather than to engage in it?

TAKEAWAY QUESTION 4

How can we negotiate successful agreements?

- Negotiation is the process of making decisions in situations in which participants have different preferences.
- Substance goals concerned with outcomes and relationship goals concerned with processes are both important in successful negotiation.
- Effective negotiation occurs when issues of substance are resolved while the process maintains good working relationships.
- Distributive negotiation emphasizes win–lose outcomes; integrative negotiation emphasizes win–win outcomes.
- Common negotiation pitfalls include the myth of the fixed pie, overconfidence, too much telling and too little hearing, and ethical misconduct.
- Mediation and arbitration are structured approaches to third-party dispute resolution.

FOR DISCUSSION How can you successfully negotiate with someone who is trapped in the "myth of the fixed pie"?

SELF-TEST 18

Multiple-Choice Questions

1. When the intended meaning of the sender and the interpreted meaning of the receiver are the same, a communication is _____.
   (a) effective
   (b) persuasive
   (c) selective
   (d) efficient

2. The use of paraphrasing and reflecting back what someone else says in communication is characteristic of _____.
   (a) mixed messages
   (b) active listening
   (c) projection
   (d) lose–lose conflict

3. Which is the best example of a supervisor making feedback descriptive rather than evaluative?
   (a) You are a slacker.
   (b) You are not responsible.
   (c) You cause me lots of problems.
   (d) You have been late to work three days this month.

4. When interacting with an angry co-worker who is complaining about a work problem, a manager skilled at active listening would most likely try to _____.
   (a) suggest that the conversation be held at a better time
   (b) point out that the conversation would be better held at another location
   (c) express displeasure in agreement with the co-worker's complaint
   (d) rephrase the co-worker's complaint to encourage him to say more

5. When a manager uses e-mail to send a message that is better delivered face to face, the communication process suffers from _____.
   (a) semantic problems
   (b) a poor choice of communication channels
   (c) physical distractions
   (d) information overload

6. If a visitor to a foreign culture makes gestures commonly used at home even after learning that they are offensive to locals, the visitor can be described as _____.
   (a) a passive listener
   (b) ethnocentric
   (c) more efficient than effective
   (d) an active listener

7. In order to be consistently persuasive when communicating with others in the workplace, a manager should build credibility by _____.
   (a) making sure rewards for compliance are clear
   (b) making sure penalties for noncompliance are clear
   (c) making sure they know who is the boss
   (d) making sure good relationships have been established

8. A manager who understands the importance of proxemics in communication would be likely to _____.
   (a) avoid sending mixed messages
   (b) arrange work spaces so as to encourage interaction
   (c) be very careful in the choice of written and spoken words
   (d) make frequent use of e-mail messages to keep people well informed

9. A conflict is most likely to be functional and have a positive impact on performance when it is _____.
   (a) based on emotions
   (b) resolved by arbitration
   (c) caused by resource scarcities
   (d) of moderate intensity

10. An appeal to super ordinate goals is an example of a/an _____ approach to conflict management.
    (a) avoidance   (c) dysfunctional
    (b) structural   (d) self-serving

11. The conflict management style with the greatest potential for true conflict resolution involves _____.
    (a) compromise   (c) smoothing
    (b) competition   (d) collaboration

12. When a person is highly cooperative but not very assertive in approaching conflict, the conflict management style is referred to as _____.
    (a) avoidance   (c) smoothing
    (b) authoritative   (d) collaboration

13. The three criteria of an effective negotiation are quality, cost, and _____.
    (a) harmony   (c) efficiency
    (b) timeliness   (d) effectiveness

14. In classic two-party negotiation, the difference between one party's minimum reservation point and the other party's maximum reservation point is known as the _____.
    (a) critical choice   (c) myth of the fixed pie
    (b) arena of indifference (d) bargaining zone

15. The first rule of thumb for gaining integrative agreements in negotiations is to _____.
    (a) separate the people from the problems
    (b) focus on positions
    (c) deal with a minimum number of alternatives
    (d) avoid setting standards for measuring outcomes

Short-Response Questions

16. Briefly describe how a manager would behave as an active listener when communicating with subordinates.

17. Explain the relationship between conflict intensity and performance.

18. How do tendencies toward assertiveness and cooperativeness in conflict management result in win–lose, lose–lose, and win–win outcomes?

19. What is the difference between substance and relationship goals in negotiation?

Essay Question

20. After being promoted to store manager for a new branch of a large department store chain, Kathryn was concerned about communication in the store. Six department heads reported directly to her, and 50 full-time and part-time sales associates reported to them. Given this structure, Kathryn worried about staying informed about all store operations, not just those coming to her attention as the senior manager. What steps might Kathryn take to establish and maintain an effective system of upward communication in this store?

Management Skills & Competencies Make yourself **valuable!**

Evaluate Career Situations

What Would You Do?

1. **Work versus Family**
   Your boss just sent a text message that he wants you at a meeting starting at 3 p.m. Your daughter is performing in a program at her elementary school at 2:45 p.m., and she expects you to attend. You're out of the office making previously scheduled sales calls that put you close to the school in the early afternoon. The office is all the way across town, and going there will mean you can't get back to the school in time to see your daughter's performance. Do you call your boss, text him, or send him an e-mail? What exactly will you say?

2. **Bearer of Bad News**
   The restaurant you own is hit hard by a bad economy. Customer count is down. So is the average dinner bill. You have a staff of 12, but it's obvious that you have to cut back so that the payroll covers no more than 8. One of the servers has just told you that a regular customer is tweeting that the restaurant is going to close its doors after the weekend. The staff is "buzzing" about the news and customers are asking questions. How do you deal with this situation?

3. **Can't Get Along**
   Two of your co-workers are constantly bickering. They just can't seem to get along, and it's starting to affect the rest of the

team—including you. Their bickering seems to have something to do with a difference in wages. One has been there a long time while the other is relatively new. But, the newcomer earns more than the veteran. The other team members think it's time to take the problem to the team leader, and they have asked you to do it. You're willing, but want to give the team leader not just the message but also a suggested plan of action. What will it be?

Reflect on the Self-Assessment

Conflict Management Strategies

Instructions

Think of how you behave in conflict situations in which your wishes differ from those of others. In the space to the left, rate each of the following statements on a scale of "1" = "not at all" to "5" = "very much." *When I have a conflict at work, school, or in my personal life, I do the following:*[53]

____ **1.** I give in to the wishes of the other party.

____ **2.** I try to realize a middle-of-the-road solution.

____ **3.** I push my own point of view.

____ **4.** I examine issues until I find a solution that really satisfies me and the other party.

____ **5.** I avoid a confrontation about our differences.

____ **6.** I concur with the other party.

____ **7.** I emphasize that we have to find a compromise solution.

____ **8.** I search for gains.

____ **9.** I stand for my own and the other's goals.

___ **10.** I avoid differences of opinion as much as possible.

___ **11.** I try to accommodate the other party.

___ **12.** I insist we both give in a little.

___ **13.** I fight for a good outcome for myself.

___ **14.** I examine ideas from both sides to find a mutually optimal solution.

___ **15.** I try to make differences seem less severe.

___ **16.** I adapt to the other party's goals and interests.

___ **17.** I strive whenever possible toward a 50–50 compromise.

___ **18.** I do everything to win.

___ **19.** I work out a solution that serves my own as well as other's interests as much as possible.

___ **20.** I try to avoid a confrontation with the other person.

Scoring

Total your scores for items as follows:

Yielding tendency: 1 + 6 + 11 + 16 = _____.

Compromising tendency: 2 + 7 + 12 + 17 = _____.

Forcing tendency: 3 + 8 + 13 + 18 = _____.

Problem-solving tendency: 4 + 9 + 14 + 19 = _____.

Avoiding tendency: 5 + 10 + 15 + 20 = _____.

Interpretation

Each of the scores above approximates one of the conflict management styles discussed in the chapter. Look back to Figure 18.4 and make the matchups. Although each style is part of management, only collaboration or problem solving leads to true conflict resolution. You should consider any patterns that may be evident in your scores and think about how to best handle future conflict situations in which you become involved.

Contribute to the Class Exercise

Feedback Sensitivities

Preparation

Indicate the degree of discomfort you would feel in each situation below by circling the appropriate number:[54]

1. High discomfort **2.** Some discomfort **3.** Undecided **4.** Very little discomfort **5.** No discomfort

1 2 3 4 5 **1.** Telling an employee who is also a friend that she or he must stop coming to work late.

1 2 3 4 5 **2.** Talking to an employee about his or her performance on the job.

1 2 3 4 5 **3.** Asking an employee for comments about your rating of her or his performance.

1 2 3 4 5 **4.** Telling an employee who has problems in dealing with other employees that he or she should do something about it.

1 2 3 4 5 **5.** Responding to an employee who is upset over your rating of his or her performance.

1 2 3 4 5 **6.** Responding to an employee's becoming emotional and defensive when you tell her or him about mistakes on the job.

1 2 3 4 5 **7.** Giving a rating that indicates improvement is needed to an employee who has failed to meet minimum requirements of the job.

1 2 3 4 5 **8.** Letting a subordinate talk during an appraisal interview.

1 2 3 4 5 **9.** Having an employee challenge you to justify your evaluation during an appraisal interview.

1 2 3 4 5 **10.** Recommending that an employee be discharged.

1 2 3 4 5 **11.** Telling an employee that you are uncomfortable having to judge his or her performance.

1 2 3 4 5 **12.** Telling an employee that her or his performance can be improved.

1 2 3 4 5 **13.** Telling an employee that you will not tolerate his or her taking extended coffee breaks.

1 2 3 4 5 **14.** Telling an employee that you will not tolerate her or his making personal telephone calls on company time.

Instructions

Form three-person teams as assigned by your instructor. Identify the three behaviors with which each person indicates the most discomfort. Then each team member should practice performing these behaviors with another member, while the third member acts as an observer. Be direct, but try to perform the behavior in an appropriate way. Listen to feedback from the observer and try the behaviors again, perhaps with different members of the group practicing each behavior. When finished, discuss the overall exercise.

Manage a Critical Incident

Headphones on in the Office

Sean has just started a new job in your company, where everyone works in an open-plan office. He's just out of college and is happy and getting into his new responsibilities. A music lover, he has been wearing ear buds off and on during the day while working on the computer at his work station. Yesterday an older colleague came over and offered him some advice. "You should take off the headphones in the office," she said, "it's not the way we do things here. People are starting to say that you aren't a team player." Now Sean is relating the incident to you. His point is that headphones today are as common in some offices as they are on the streets. For him it's "just normal to listen to music while he works" and that "it keeps me relaxed so that I work better." But as a newcomer to the company and its corporate culture, Sean is perceived as sending out a nonverbal message when he puts the ear buds in: "Do not disturb!" Sean is looking at you and expecting a reply, probably one that takes his side of this situation.

Questions

What do you say, and why? Do you do more than speak with Sean about this situation, and what it might represent in terms of work expectations and the new generation of workers? If so, what will you do and why?

Collaborate on the Team Activity

How Words Count

Question

What words do people use in organizations that carry meanings that create unintended consequences for the speaker?

Research Directions

1. Brainstorm with others to make a list of words that you have used or heard used by people and that cause other persons to react or respond negatively and even with anger toward the person speaking them.

2. For each word on the list, write its "positive" meaning and "negative" meaning.

3. Choose two or three of the words that seem especially significant. Write role-plays that display speakers using each word in the positive sense in conversations and in which the words are interpreted positively by receivers.

4. For these same words, write role-plays that display speakers using each word conversationally with positive intentions but in which they are interpreted negatively by receivers.

5. Explain the factors that influence whether the same words are interpreted positively or negatively by receivers.

6. Draft a report that explains how people in organizations can avoid getting trapped unintentionally in problems caused by poor choice and/or use of words in their conversations.

Analyze THE CaseStudy : TWITTER
Rewriting (or Killing) Communication

Go to *Management Cases for Critical Thinking* at the end of the book to find this case.

MANAGEMENT CASES FOR CRITICAL THINKING

ManagementCases
for CriticalThinking

Learn to Master
Complex Situations

MCDONALD'S
Grilling Up an Empire

McDonald's has been a staple in the restaurant business for as long as most of us can remember. The story of how it came to be is one that epitomizes entrepreneurship as well as capitalism. It has achieved success around the globe, but not without overcoming a fair amount of challenges in its pursuit of the title "King of Fast Food." Today, McDonald's leads the global food service industry with more than 32,000 local restaurants serving more than 60 million customers in 117 countries each day. More than 75% of McDonald's restaurants around the world are owned and operated independently by local entrepreneurs.[1]

Humble Beginnings

In 1940 Dick and Mac McDonald opened McDonald's Bar-B-Que restaurant in San Bernardino, California, offering a large menu and delivery of your food right to your car. Then in 1948, Dick and Mac decided to close their location to complete some renovations. After three months, they reopened as a self-service, drive-in restaurant offering a 9-item menu, with the most popular item being their 15-cent hamburger. Then in 1954, Ray Kroc, who was working as a multimixer salesperson, visited the restaurant with the intention of increasing his sales of mixers to the restaurant. Ray was captivated by the operation and learnt that the McDonald brothers had a desire to franchise their operations. The next year, Kroc opened his first McDonald's in Des Plaines, Illinois. By 1959, McDonald's had expanded its operations to a total of 100 stores.[2]

McDonald's venture into international markets began in 1967 with restaurant openings in Canada and Puerto Rico. It continued to expand around the globe at an epic pace. In fact, the 5,000th McDonald's restaurant to be opened was in Kanagawa, Japan, in 1978, which further extended the global reach of this fast-food chain. By 1981, McDonald's had begun operations in Spain, Denmark, and the Philippines, and within two years, it had a physical presence in a total of 32 countries around the world. As a sign of the changing political climate between the United States and the Soviet Union, the first McDonald's restaurant in Moscow was opened on January 31, 1990. Entering the Soviet Union market, however, was not without difficulty. According to Tony Royle, ". . . establishing such a well-known US icon in the former Soviet bloc was not a straightforward matter. It took 14 years of difficult negotiations, by a highly persistent group of McDonald's managers . . ."[3]

As times and tastes have changed, so too has McDonald's, as evidenced in its offerings of premium coffee and Wi-Fi access to its customers.[4]

Responsible Management

Within a growing empire, McDonald's has had to address the management of its restaurants around the globe. The focus on responsible management has evolved from the early teachings of Ray Kroc who, in 1958, described the management of McDonald's in stating: "The basis for our entire business is that we are ethical, truthful and dependable. It takes time to build a reputation. We are not promoters. We are business people with a solid, permanent, constructive ethical program that will be in style years from now even more than it is today."[5] This emphasis on proper conduct starts at the top of the McDonald's organization and flows all the way through to every employee. McDonald's has established a code of conduct for their Board of Directors to insure they act in the best interests of the company, by asking them to agree that they will:

- Act in the best interests of, and fulfill their fiduciary obligations to, McDonald's shareholders;

- Act honestly, fairly, ethically and with integrity;

- Conduct themselves in a professional, courteous and respectful manner;

- Comply with all applicable laws, rules and regulations;

- Act in good faith, responsibly, with due care, competence and diligence, without allowing their independent judgment to be subordinated;

- Act in a manner to enhance and maintain the reputation of McDonald's;

- Disclose potential conflicts of interest that they may have regarding any matters that may come before the Board, and abstain from discussion and voting on any matter in which the Director has or may have a conflict of interest;

- Make available to and share with fellow Directors information as may be appropriate to ensure proper conduct and sound operation of McDonald's and its Board of Directors;

- Respect the confidentiality of information relating to the affairs of the Company acquired in the course of their service as Directors, except when authorized or legally required to disclose such information; and

- Not use confidential information acquired in the course of their service as Directors for their personal advantage.[6]

A code of conduct has also been established to apply to all employees of McDonald's in order to insure they act in a manner acceptable to the organization and that employees are committed to acting ethically in all of the business dealings impacting McDonald's. This commitment emanates through the values of McDonald's that focus on being ethical, truthful and dependable. Employees undergo regular training covering a variety of laws, regulations and company-specific policies. Internationally, this training includes discussions on McDonald's policy concerning the Foreign Corrupt Practices Act (FCPA). For international employees, McDonald's insures that there is compliance based on the local version of standards with regard to the FCPA supplement. McDonald's also takes a proactive approach to enforcing international company policies that deal with the prohibition of money laundering, bribery, and conducting business with terrorist groups.[7]

The Global Perspective

McDonald's has developed a successful strategy for operating their fast-food enterprise across the globe. This strategy has been one that is developed based on existing operations as well as the local cultures and customs that make each McDonald's relevant to the international markets in which it operates. McDonald's could not rely merely on its brand success in the United States and simply run their international locations as they had in the U.S. They needed to attune their brand to the needs and wants of the local customers in each of the markets they had entered. According to Eckhardt and Houston, ". . . a brand's image comes from the interplay between the culture surrounding it and a marketing campaign. If culture is in a state of flux, brand meaning can also fluctuate."[8] With this awareness about brands and brand development, McDonald's faced a challenge that needed some serious considerations in order to insure its chances of success in international markets. To improve their chances of success, McDonald's would need to understand the local cultures and develop a strategy that would match up with the expectations of the local customer base. Eckhardt and Houston summarized this challenge by stating their findings from a study of McDonald's in Shanghai, China: ". . . in rapidly changing societies, brands can take on disparate cultural values and may even be central to how these disparate cultural values (traditional or new) are evaluated. For marketers, it becomes a difficult task to control the image the brand has in the marketplace. Marketers need to be aware of the cultural and societal connotations the brand is taking on and the way these are changing or staying the same as norms of interacting are changing or staying the same."

McDonald's has embraced its international operations and the challenges that come as part of this expansion. Its menus and brand offerings are catered to needs of the local customers. The ideas for how to address these diverse tastes know no boundaries. According to Nation's Restaurant News, some of the international innovations include: ". . . the McCafe coffee and dessert concept, developed in Australia and popularized in Latin America; a new line of toasted deli sandwiches, recently rolled out in Canada; home delivery in Egypt, Turkey, Hong Kong, and throughout Southeast Asia; and new unit designs from the chain's European Design Studio. There are also new playland concepts. McDonaldlandia in Mexico features an area for physical play as well as Nintendo video game stations. In France, the Ronald Gym Club offers a variety of physical activity areas for kids, including basketball, dance and judo stations."[9] Obviously, McDonald's is up to the challenge of meeting the local desires of its international operations, and it is not afraid to try some very unique approaches to its product offerings.

Looking Ahead

So, what does the future hold for McDonald's? Based on its past experiences, the future is looking bright. On the international front, there continues to be solid growth. McDonald's 2009 Annual Report states: "In 2009, global comparable sales increased 3.8 percent, fueled by solid gains in the United States (+2.6 percent), Europe (+5.2 percent), Asia/Pacific, Middle East and Africa (+3.4 percent), Latin America (+5.3 percent) and Canada (+5.8 percent). Earnings per share for the year increased 9 percent to $4.11 (13 percent in constant currencies), while consolidated operating income increased 6 percent (10 percent in constant currencies)."[10] The management personnel of McDonald's are no doubt interested in seeing these increases continue and only time will tell if they have the type of management talent necessary to ensure its continued success.

Discussion Questions

1. **Discussion** Describe some of the management challenges McDonald's has likely faced in its expansion internationally.

2. **Discussion** What types of managerial levels do you think exist within the McDonald's corporation? How would these levels interact to accomplish the goals of the organization?

3. **Problem Solving** How will McDonald's be able to develop managerial skills and competencies necessary to continue their success in the future?

4. **Further Research** Review McDonald's international operations currently in existence. How do you feel what they have learned so far will assist them in further international expansion?

CASE 2

ZARA INTERNATIONAL
Fashion at the Speed of Light

In this world of "hot today, gauche tomorrow," no company does fast fashion better than Zara International. Shoppers in a growing number of countries—86 at last count—are fans of Zara's knack for bringing the latest styles from sketchbook to clothing rack at lightning speed and reasonable prices.[1]

In Fast Fashion, Moments Matter

Zara's parent company Inditex is known for year-on-year strong sales gains. Low prices and a rapid response to fashion trends have pushed it into the top ranks of global clothing vendors. The chain specializes in lightning-quick turnarounds of the latest designer trends at prices tailored to the young—about $27 an item.[2] Louis Vuitton fashion director Daniel Piette has described Zara as "possibly the most innovative and devastating retailer in the world."[3]

Inditex shortens the time from order to arrival using a complex system of just-in-time production and inventory management that keeps Zara ahead of the competition. Their distribution centers can have items in European stores within 24 hours of order receipt, and in American and Asian stores in under 48 hours.[4] "They're a fantastic case study in terms of how they manage to get product to their stores so quick," said Stacey Cartwright, executive vice president and CFO of Burberry Group PLC. "We are mindful of their techniques."[5]

The firm carefully controls design, production, distribution, and retail sales to optimize the flow of goods, without having to share profits with wholesalers or intermediary partners. Customers win with access to new fashions while they're still fresh off the runway.[6] Twice a week Zara's finished garments are shipped to physical distribution centers that all simultaneously distribute products to stores worldwide. These small production batches help the company avoid the risk of oversupply. Because batches always contain new products, Zara's stores perpetually energize their inventories.[7] Most clothing lines are not replenished. Instead they are replaced with new designs to create scarcity value—shoppers cannot be sure that designs in stores one day will be available the next day.

Store managers track sales data with handheld devices. They can reorder hot items in less than an hour. Zara always knows what's selling and what's not. When a look doesn't pan out, designers promptly put together new products. New arrivals are rushed to store sales floors still on the black plastic hangers used in shipping. Shoppers who are in the know recognize these designs as the newest of the new; soon after, any items left over are rotated to Zara's standard wood hangers.[8]

Inside and out, Zara's stores are designed to strengthen the brand. Inditex considers this to be very important because that is where shoppers ultimately decide which fashions make the cut. In a faux shopping street in the basement of the company's headquarters, stylists craft and photograph eye-catching layouts that are e-mailed every two weeks to store managers for replication.[9]

Zara stores sit on some of the glitziest shopping streets—including New York's Fifth Avenue, near the flagship stores of leading international fashion brands—which make its reasonable prices stand out. It's all part of the strategy. "Inditex gives people the most up-to-date fashion at accessible prices, so it is a real alternative to high-end fashion lines," said Luca Solca, senior research analyst with Sanford C. Bernstein in London. That is good news for Zara as many shoppers trade down from higher priced chains.[10]

A Single Fashion Culture

The Inditex group began in 1963 when Amancio Ortega Gaona, chairman and founder of Inditex, got his start in textile manufacturing.[11] After a period of growth, he assimilated Zara into a new holding company, Industria de Diseño Textil.[12] Inditex has a tried-and-true strategy for entering new markets: start with a handful of stores and gain a critical mass of customers. Generally, Zara is the first Inditex chain to break ground in new countries, paving the way for the group's other brands, including Pull and Bear, Massimo Dutti, and Bershka.[13]

Inditex farms out much of its garment production to specialist companies, located on the Iberian Peninsula, which it supplies with its own fabrics. Although some pieces and fabrics are purchased in Asia—many of them not dyed or only partly finished—the company manufactures about half of its clothing in its hometown of La Coruña, Spain.[14] Inditex CEO Pablo Isla believes in cutting expenses wherever and whenever possible. Zara spends just 0.3% of sales on ads, making the 3–4% typically spent by rivals seem excessive in comparison. Isla disdains markdowns and sales as well.[15]

H&M, one of Zara's top competitors, uses a slightly different strategy. Around one-quarter of its stock is made up of fast-fashion items that are designed in-house and farmed out to independent factories. As at Zara, these items move quickly through the stores and are replaced often by fresh designs. But H&M also keeps a large inventory of basic, everyday items sourced from inexpensive Asian factories.[16]

Fast Fashion on the Move

Inditex launched its Zara online store in the United States by offering free 2–3 day shipping and free returns in the model of uber-successful e-retailer Zappos.[17] A Zara iPhone app has been downloaded by more prospective clients in the United States than in any other market, according to chief executive Pablo Isla—more than a million users in just three months. But, when will Inditex's rapid expansion bring undue pressure to its business? The rising number of overseas stores increases cost and complexity and could strain operations.[18] Is Zara expanding too quickly—opening about 400 stores per year?[19] Will its existing logistics system carry it into another decade of intense growth? Can fast-fashion win the long-term retailing race?

Discussion Questions

1. **Discussion** In what ways are elements of the classical and behavioral management approaches evident in how things are done at Zara International? How can systems concepts and contingency thinking explain the success of some of Zara's distinctive practices?

2. **Discussion** Zara's logistics system and management practices can handle the current pace of growth, but they will need updating at some point in the future. How could quantitative management approaches and data analytics help Zara executives plan for the next generation of its logistics and management approaches?

3. **Problem Solving** As a consultant chosen by Zara to assist with the expansion of its U.S. stores, you have been asked to propose how evidence-based management might help the firm smooth its way to success with an American workforce. What areas will you suggest be looked at for evidence-based decision making, and why?

4. **Further Research** Gather the latest information on competitive trends in the apparel industry, and on Zara's latest actions and innovations. Is the firm continuing to do well? Are other retailers getting just as proficient with the fast-fashion model? Is Zara adapting and innovating in ways needed to stay abreast of both its major competition and the pressures of a changing global economy? Is this firm still providing worthy management benchmarks for other firms to follow?

....

CASE 3

DELTA
Flying High by Managing Effectively

Delta Air Lines has experienced a great deal of adversity and success throughout its corporate history. Managing such an immense global organization is quite an undertaking, one that must be handled appropriately in order to insure the company's success.

Delta has encountered many situations where its management practices were put to the test. It has also experienced a great deal of conflict in managing the resource-intensive firm in an ethical and socially responsible manner. Faced with these challenges, Delta has had to make the necessary modifications within its management team in order to meet the societal expectations of how such a large organization should operate.

Taking Flight

Headquartered in Atlanta, Georgia, Delta has grown to a position of dominance within the airline industry. It was founded in 1928 in Monroe, Louisiana, and has since developed into one of the largest airlines in the world. In fact, its largest hub in Atlanta, Georgia, handles approximately 1,000 departures every day to over 200 destinations.

As a global force, Delta serves 65 different countries with 107 international destinations. With over 80,000 employees and more than US$35 billion in revenue, there are many challenges as well as opportunities in managing the organization. In many ways, the growth that it experienced has prepared it for the position it holds today.

In 1947, Delta completed a successful merger with Northwest that enabled it to create the Great Circle route to Asia, adding services to Tokyo, Seoul, Shanghai, and Manila. Then, in 1953, another key merger—this time with Chicago and Southern Airlines—provided it with the chance to service South America and the Caribbean. These mergers propelled Delta to new heights in the airline industry, as it could provide customers access to many more desired locations. By 1978, Delta was able to offer their first transatlantic flights from Atlanta to London-Gatwick.

All of this tremendous growth was not without its challenges, however, and in 1982, Delta suffered significant financial losses. Employees raised US$30 million via payroll deductions in order to buy the company's first Boeing 767, aptly named "The Spirit of Delta". This action speaks volumes about the level of commitment that the employees and management team had towards Delta's operations.

Continued growth ensued with the acquisition of Pan American World Airways in 1991, making Delta the largest U.S. airline across the Atlantic Ocean. Then in 2008, Delta and Northwest merged, creating a combined force with key operations in every region of the world. After the monumental merger with Northwest, Delta increased its presence in Australia by partnering with Virgin Australia, and has also achieved the first nonstop trans-Pacific service in three decades to Haneda Airport in Tokyo.[1]

Managing Ethically

Being such a large organization, Delta has had significant opportunities as well as challenges concerning the manner in which its operations were managed. There were also many constituents in the organization that have a vested interest in making sure that Delta operated with a high degree of ethical and social standards. One such challenge was when it had to work hard to emerge from a bankruptcy in 2007, and after it emerged from the financial disaster, Gerald Grinstein, then Delta's chief executive officer, stated:

> This is an exciting day for everyone at Delta. Achieving a turnaround of this magnitude in little more than 19 months would not have been possible without the hard work and dedication of Delta people worldwide; and the leadership, the vision, and the flawless execution of our plan by our outstanding management team.[2]

This was a pivotal point in the history of Delta Airlines, and speaks volumes of its management style—how it approaches such difficult situations with the determination and will to succeed. Many organizations have faced similar situations but were not able to achieve Delta's level of success. The fact that the merger with Northwest occurred the year after Delta's emergence from bankruptcy displays the resolve that the management team at Delta possessed.

In addition to managing its affairs in an ethical manner, Delta also has the responsibility to act in a manner that respects the environment where it runs its business. Operating a large fleet in the airline industry comes with the stigma of creating a very negative impact on the environment due to pollution and other harmful impacts of operating globally. According to Helen Howes, Delta's managing director for Safety, Health and Environment,

> We continue to 'raise the bar' with respect to external reporting but recognize that there is still more to be done. This year's report adds more information about employee programs and gives a more complete description of our greenhouse gas emissions as well as actions Delta and its employees are taking to reduce those emissions.

Significant accomplishments in its 2011 report included:

- Participating in natural disaster relief efforts, including raising more than US$1 million worth of combined aid for Japan after its earthquake.

- Rewarding the efforts of Delta employees by distributing more than US$324 million in Profit Sharing and Shared Rewards for 2011.

- Joining the Business Environmental Leadership Council for the prestigious Center for Climate and Energy Solutions, as the sole airline among 35 large companies discussing ways to find affordable and responsible energy.

- Continuing a tradition of support for a wide variety of charitable organizations, including the Breast Cancer Research Foundation, Habitat for Humanity, the American Red Cross and The Nature Conservancy.

- Promoting efforts to reduce greenhouse gases, by retiring older and less fuel-efficient aircraft from the fleet and by improving greenhouse gas emissions reporting.

- Earning recognition as top airline in the *Business Travel News* annual survey and *Travel Weekly's* readers' choice as Airline of the Year.[3]

Responding to the societal concerns over its business operations is obviously a top priority for Delta, and the work it has done demonstrates its commitment to and understanding of this social responsibility.

What the Future Holds for Delta

Achieving success at Delta has come with significant challenges, and by meeting these challenges head on, Delta has become a leader in the airline industry. The hard work and dedication is recognized by other organizations, validating the work that is being done at Delta. It has been voted "Airline of the Year" by the readers of *Travel Weekly* magazine and "Top Tech-Friendly U.S. Airline" by *PCWorld* magazine (for its innovation in technology); it has also won the Business Travel News Annual Airline Survey.[4] In addition to these fine accolades, Delta was ranked *Fortune* magazine's most admired airline worldwide in 2011.[5]

The airline industry is marked by a competitive environment that is unlike any other industry. Delta will need to continue meeting the needs of its customers and stakeholders in order to remain a top player in this industry. According to its 2011 10-K filing,

> The airline industry is highly competitive, marked by significant competition with respect to routes, fares, schedules (both timing and frequency), services, products, customer service and frequent flyer programs. The industry is going through a period of transformation through consolidation, both domestically and internationally, and changes in international alliances.[6]

Such a long and storied history has prepared Delta for greatness in the future. With its ability to build on the management successes and learn from challenges, Delta may remain a leader in the airline industry for many years to come.

Discussion Questions

1. **Discussion** How important is a solid ethical foundation for a company like Delta?

2. **Discussion** Create your own definition of ethics. How could your definition assist in the practical application of ethics in a business like Delta?

3. **Problem Solving** In an industry that is so competitive, do you feel ethical behavior becomes more or less important for firms to be successful? Why?

4. **Further Research** Research three other airlines and find what they have done to address their social responsibility as an airline. How does this compare to the stance taken by Delta?

CASE 4

YAHOO!
Cultivating the Right Corporate Culture

Yahoo! is a unique organization with a very interesting history. From its humble beginnings on the campus of Stanford University, it has grown into a global multimedia powerhouse. This tremendous growth has not come without considerable challenges to the company's livelihood, as well as changes in its management strategy. The manner in which these challenges were met speaks volumes about the way in which Yahoo! is structured and its ability to face challenges. In a dominant and volatile industry, only time will tell if Yahoo! is able to survive and thrive in such a competitive environment.

Searching for Success

In 1994, David Filo and Jerry Yang were in the midst of pursuing their doctoral degrees at Stanford University. They both shared a common desire to manage their personal interests on the Internet. Through this common desire for organizing information, Yahoo! was born, and it has since blossomed into an organization that today employs more than 13,700 people in 25 countries, provinces, and territories. The focus of the company is to allow its consumers to stay plugged in to whatever interests them, and yet be able to discover new interests they didn't even know existed. Yahoo!'s company profile states its mission as follows:

> Our vision is to deliver your world, your way. We do that by using technology, insights, and intuition to create deeply personal digital experiences that keep more than half a billion people connected to what matters the most to them—across devices, on every continent, in more than 30 languages. And we connect advertisers to the consumers who matter to them most—the ones who will build their businesses—through our unique combination of Science + Art + Scale.[1]

Yahoo! attempts to fulfill this mission by providing a variety of products and services centered around the three main areas that make up its primary categories of business: Communications and Communities; Search and Marketplaces; and Media. It also launched a strategic initiative in 2011 to analyze alternatives available to them that would enable a return to increased growth and innovation.[2] As with any company conducting such analyses, taking a close look at its external environment as well as the internal organization culture will yield crucial information on its operations. This would also assist Yahoo! in formulating new objectives that would enable it to return to its former glory.

A View from Without

The external environment in which Yahoo! competes is one that is riddled with intense competition and incredibly rapid changes. The industry is fueled by a consumer base that is very demanding—one that is often quick to change and adapt to new forms of innovation that better fit their unique needs. In order to be successful in such an environment, Yahoo! must find ways to be relevant to this demographic and meet the needs of these discriminating consumers. Ultimately, its success will be dependent on having a management team in place that can identify these opportunities and then develop and execute plans that will position Yahoo! strongly in meeting these demands.

Yahoo!'s interactions with the external environment have been displayed in many different scenarios. One such recent example is seen in its evaluation of its stake in Yahoo! Japan. Then chief executive officer, Scott Thompson, stated on a post-earning call on April 17, 2012:

> While we also plan to continue exploring alternatives to unlock the value of our Yahoo! Japan stake for shareholders, any transaction has to be at a value that makes sense for Yahoo! and its shareholders. We currently have a valuation gap with respect to the Yahoo! Japan stake that we have not been able to bridge.[3]

Yahoo! has also come under fire for the manner in which it addressed its growth opportunities, as well as the formulation of strategies to return to its former growth and compete more. According to Eric Savitz of Forbes.com:

> Yahoo! can't chop its way back to growth. And it isn't enough to simply maintain the vast number of users for properties like Yahoo! Finance, Sports, News and Mail. They need to innovate. While the company in recent years has been casting around for ways to redefine itself, it has fumbled key opportunities.[4]

A final example of Yahoo!'s interaction with its external environment was posed by Felix Gillette of Bloomberg Businessweek:

> The issue isn't the viability of display ads but whether Yahoo can stay in the game. From 2009 to 2011, the company's share of the market fell from 15.4 percent to 10.8 percent, according to EMarketer. The drop was largely due to the growth of Facebook (its display revenue in the U.S. more than tripled, from an estimated $518 million in 2009 to $1.7 billion in 2011, according to EMarketer) and Google's YouTube ($435 million to $1.7 billion over the same period).[5]

Through these three examples, it is evident that Yahoo! has some work to do in tackling challenges in its external market so that it can be more adept at meeting the needs of its consumers and stakeholders. One of the ways in which Yahoo! can do this is by examining the leadership within its corporation.

A View from Within

When looking at corporations such as Yahoo!, it is often necessary to examine the leadership within the organizations in determining whether the leader has the capability to fulfill the obligations of his or her role. The organizational culture of a company is often a determining factor in whether it will be able to achieve its goals. In the last few years, Yahoo!'s organizational culture has experienced significant turmoil. In January 2009, Yahoo!'s cofounder and longtime CEO, Jerry Yang, was replaced by Carol Bartz. From day one of the new CEO's tenure with Yahoo!, there had been high expectations and a strong desire to turn the company around to its former glory. However, Bartz's tenure with Yahoo! ended in September 2011, nearly two years later, without producing the type of results that were expected. The move to terminate Bartz was met with criticism, especially considering there was no successor in place when this decision was made.[6]

The next change in Yahoo!'s evolving organizational hierarchy occurred in January 2012, when Scott Thompson took over as CEO. The move was met with optimism and raised hopes of revitalizing the slumping media giant. In fact, Ken Fuchs, a Yahoo! executive in charge of the Yahoo! Sports operation, said of their new CEO:

> I've been at big companies my whole life, and there's always transition. Scott Thompson has incredible experience with the customer. He's bringing in an innovative culture and [has said] serving the customer is a priority. That aligns perfectly with what we're trying to do.[7]

On the surface it appeared Yahoo! was moving in the right direction and had a person at the helm who could move it towards its goals. However, Thompson's tenure with Yahoo! was a short one as news broke concerning his academic qualifications—it was discovered that Thompson had falsely listed his college degree, and after four short months on the job, he was fired.

Following that latest CEO exit, Yahoo! decided to promote Ross Levinsohn to the role of Interim CEO. Levinsohn had actually been considered for taking over the CEO position when the board decided on Scott Thompson.[8] With such a lot of changes and controversy in such a short span of time, it will be interesting to see how Yahoo!'s corporate leadership responds. In addition, these developments will definitely have an impact on the organizational culture within Yahoo!, and Levinsohn will be faced with the monumental challenge of rallying employees to unite, and together continue in the mission to meet the needs of consumers and stakeholders and return to its former success.

Discussion Questions

1. **Discussion** If you were an employee of Yahoo!, how might you respond to the recent changes within the CEO position? How might this impact your job?

2. **Discussion** How would these leadership changes and controversies impact the overall culture within Yahoo!?

3. **Problem Solving** If you were an executive at Yahoo! with many employees reporting to you, how would you explain these changes and ease their fears about the future of Yahoo! leadership?

4. **Further research** Look up other news releases concerning inappropriate activity of corporate CEOs. How was the inappropriate activity handled? How did this impact the organizational culture of the company?

HEWLETT-PACKARD
Managing on a Global Scale

Hewlett-Packard (HP) is a global organization that has experienced tremendous success in the technology sector. This success was achieved through a broad product offering as well as a clear focus on innovation, so that it could remain competitive in such a dynamic industry. It has triumphed in significant challenges throughout its tenure in this tumultuous market by focusing on its management of such an enormous organization. This style of management has a direct correlation to its success within the technology industry. Without the proper management staff and direction in place, HP could have turned out quite differently from its current form and position of prominence. The level of management to which HP has grown is not without controversy or challenges. To meet these challenges, HP developed key processes to prepare its staff to manage issues that crop up, and ultimately overcome barriers that lie in its path to continued success.

Computing a Path to Success

Hewlett-Packard was founded in 1939 by Stanford University classmates Bill Hewlett and Dave Packard. The order of their names in the corporate identity was decided by the flip of a coin. Its first product, built in a garage, was an audio oscillator used by sound engineers as an electronic test instrument.[1] By 1940, it had moved out of the garage and into its first leased space. Then, in 1942, HP began construction of its first corporate-owned building, designed with an open floor plan with an environment for creativity within the workspace of their eight employees. By 1951, HP had grown to 215 employees and was earning over US$5.5 million in revenues.

In 1957, HP introduced a stock option plan for all employees who had at least six months of service with the company. It also introduced its corporate objectives focused on empowerment and decentralized decision making, breaking away from the traditional top-down management style employed by most other companies. The year 1963 brought to fruition HP's first joint venture in the Asian market—Yokogawa-Hewlett-Packard (YHP) in Tokyo. Then in 1966, the HP lab was created, with a clear focus on developing new ideas. In the same year, HP's first computer was created, and then expanded upon over the next two years, to bring about the first "personal computer"—a desktop scientific calculator that could process information at a rate 10 times the speed of most machines at the time.

HP continued its dramatic growth, and by 1975, its revenues outside of the U.S. had exceeded those within the U.S. In fact, by 1981, HP products were available in China with the opening of the China Hewlett-Packard Representative office in Beijing. Throughout the 1980s, HP continued to expand its product offerings, introducing the first mass-market printer as well as the portable personal computer. The year 1998 brought about HP's first Personal Digital Assistant, which marked the precursor to its cellular phone designs. In 2002, HP merged with Compaq, creating a new entity that served more than a billion customers in 162 countries. HP continued its success with the acquisition of Electronic Data Systems in 2008, 3Com in 2009, and Palm, Inc. in 2010.[2] The future looks bright for HP as long as its management is up to the task of managing the challenges and opportunities that lie ahead.

Global Management

Creating a successful company such as HP does not come without a great deal of hard work and dedication on the part of those managing the operations. *Forbes* magazine ranked HP #67 on its Global 2000 list.[3] This distinguished achievement required a great deal of commitment from all levels of management at HP. With this recognition comes a great deal of responsibility to effectively manage its nearly 350,000 employees. Operating such a large organization is no small feat and must be done carefully if it is to remain successful.

A company that has purely a domestic reach will not encounter the same level of opportunities and challenges that a global firm does. There are many more considerations involved when you step outside of your home borders and enter other countries with your product offering. This is especially true with a firm such as HP. Part of this global reach struggle is illustrated in HP's move into India in 1988—this operation was under the leadership of Mr. Suresh Rajpal, and he described the process as follows:

> . . . the making of an excellent organization consists of two very important aspects—employee satisfaction and customer satisfaction. Traditionally the literature has pointed out very strongly towards customer satisfaction. However in HP it has been a belief that customer satisfaction is not possible without employee satisfaction.[4]

Therefore, in order to achieve success on a global scale, you must have the proper staff in place to handle the global challenge. Your employees are going to look towards the corporate management for support and direction to guide the work being done within the organization. This is an area in which HP has been applauded as well. According to Thomas Smith of BusinessWeekOnline, HP is viewed positively:

> Other aspects of corporate governance that we view as constructive are a compensation committee made up of independent outside directors, a board approved succession plan for the CEO position, and a lack of 'related party' transactions by directors.[5]

Developing Your Management

Having the right employees in the right jobs is not something that happens by chance. It takes a considerable amount of forethought to determine how best to run an organization. When it comes to an organization the size of HP, this process is further complicated. This is precisely why it was vitally important that management at the company received the proper training, and that HP also devised a corporate direction for developing its talent within the organization.

One initiative at HP to prepare for the future and insure it had the proper staff in place was the creation of the Business Excellence program. Created as a way to develop management members that HP needed to take them into the future, the program is described as follows:

> The curriculum evolved out of the needs of the business subgroups. Data was obtained from leadership team meetings; interviews; and complete surveys by support function financial leaders, the marketing department, HR, and employees. Course participants learn about company and business sector strategy, financial management, operational inspection, and the regional and business unit priorities. Managers also gain knowledge about how to leverage training solutions and how to deliver all constituencies of business.[6]

Through the Business Excellence program, HP could develop the staff necessary to effectively manage and grow its business in the future.

Another management area of importance to HP was that of technological innovation. HP exists in a very competitive and dynamic industry, and it does not rest on its past successes—it is always seeking new and improved ways to meet the needs of its customers. Research was conducted, using HP as a case study, to determine what contributed to the rate of innovation within such an organization, and from their research, Rio Rivas and David Gobeli concluded:

> A review of multiple programs in Hewlett-Packard revealed that the top enablers of innovation are highly skilled people, a helping culture, management support, using checkpoints to provide facts and interdisciplinary people working together.[7]

It is abundantly clear that this research speaks directly to the value of the employees and of the management that contributed to the success or failure of their innovations, and the rates at which these innovations occur.

The future holds a tremendous amount of opportunity for HP, and time will be the proving ground to see whether or not HP is up to the challenge. To best prepare for this exciting future, HP will need to insure it has the requisite employees and management in place to achieve the goals that have been set. Meg Whitman, president and CEO of HP, summarized HP's plans to address its management needs in saying:

> We also are investing in our people to attract, retain, and develop the best talent in the industry. We need the right people in the right jobs at the right time to meet customer needs and deliver results.[8]

Discussion Questions

1. **Discussion** What challenges do you foresee for HP as it manages such a large global workforce?

2. **Discussion** How does operating within a technology sector of business impact how HP manages its staff in order to be competitive within this industry?

3. **Problem Solving** How does the size of HP assist it in attracting and retaining the best management from around the world?

4. **Further research** Research the tenure of Carly Fiorina as the CEO of HP. How was her time with HP reflective of the success and failures of the organization as a whole? Do you feel her management style was a good fit for HP? Why or why not?

CASE 6

LENOVO
Tapping the Entrepreneurial Spirit

Chapter 6 provided us with many examples of individuals exhibiting the entrepreneurial spirit by launching a business based upon an idea which they formulated and acted upon. However, does this same type of spirit exist in larger organizations that are trying to maintain their market share while meeting the needs of their customers? The same characteristics that are displayed in the individuals that take on their start-up business are found in employees working for some of the largest organizations in the world. One of these examples is Lenovo, which has seen its fair share of changes and opportunities within its market. In order to survive in such a volatile market, Lenovo needs to formulate strategies that embody many entrepreneurial characteristics discussed in Chapter 6.

Constantly Evolving

With only US$25,000 in 1984, the Chinese Academy of Sciences funded the New Technology Developer, Inc. and the initial groundwork for what would later become Lenovo was launched. This creation came on the heels of IBM's introduction of its first personal computer in 1981. This market was in store for many changes as producers reacted to the swift changes and increasingly dynamic technology advances that would require firms to be agile and responsive to the needs of its customers. By 1988, Legend was established in Hong Kong as the next version of the New Technology Developer, Inc. company. Then, in 1990, Legend launched its very first personal computer (PC) as the company shifted to the role of producer and seller of its own branded computer products. In 1995, Legend entered the server market by expanding on its product offering. Next, in 1996, Legend introduced its first laptop while at the same time becoming the market share leader in China for the first time. These were some very interesting times and change was definitely a constant. After only eight years in production, the millionth Legend PC was produced in 1998. This type of product growth typified the massive expansion that was occurring within the computer market. In fact, by 1999, Legend had become the top PC supplier to the Asia-Pacific region, thus strengthening its presence in the area. The following year, in 2000, Legend became a constituent stock of Hong Kong's Hang Seng Index. In 2002, Legend created a supercomputer called DeepComp 1800 which was China's fastest computer for civilian use and was ranked 43rd in the listing of the Top 500 fastest computers in the world. 2003 brought another change as the "Lenovo" logo was introduced in preparation for overseas expansion of its products. 2004 brought another milestone in which Lenovo and IBM entered into an agreement allowing Lenovo to acquire IBM's Personal Computing Division. Once the acquisition was completed in 2005, Lenovo became the third largest personal computer company in the world. In 2006, Lenovo supported the computing needs of the 2006 Olympic Winter Games in Torino, Italy, by supplying 5,000 desktop PCs, 350 servers and 1,000 notebook computers. In 2008, Lenovo began its entrance into the worldwide PC market with the introduction

of its Idea brand and again met the needs of another Olympic Games event at the Beijing Olympic Games, the largest sporting event in history. 2010 brought with it the introduction of LePhone, Lenovo's first smartphone in the market. In 2011, Lenovo expanded its global reach by entering into a joint venture with NEC which gave rise to the largest PC company in Japan. In the same year, Lenovo also acquired Medion which was based in Germany and significantly increased its presence in West Europe. By 2013, Lenovo had earned the distinction of becoming the world's largest PC company and third largest smartphone company, as well as occupying position 329 in the Fortune 500.[1] Such a rapid and evolving growth pattern is not surprising within such an industry. However, in order to be successful, companies need to be able to adapt and encourage an entrepreneurial spirit within its employees.

Building a Culture of Entrepreneurship

It is easy to see by the rapid growth and constant change experienced by Lenovo throughout its history that being entrepreneurial is of the utmost importance to its overall success. However, building such a culture within a corporation of more than 54,000 employees operating in more than 60 countries, and with customers in more than 160 countries, is no easy task.[2] Procedures need to be in place in order for such a culture to be cultivated and maintained. Lenovo has taken the steps to ensure this entrepreneurial culture exists and flourishes within the entire organization.

So, how does a company of such magnitude create and maintain a culture in which innovation and entrepreneurial spirit are encouraged and rewarded? It definitely takes commitment and a desire to achieve the highest levels of creativity within the products and services offered to its customers. Lenovo identifies this type of commitment to innovation as one of its core values. According to Lenovo, this core value of innovation is at the heart of everything it does as an organization:

> Lenovo owns the greatest track record for innovation in the PC industry, consistently winning awards and receiving rave reviews. Lenovo remains committed to innovation and will continue to leverage our history of technological breakthroughs into new product categories that drive future growth. Innovation is how Lenovo achieves competitive differentiation and drives new market opportunities, such as mobile Internet, digital home and cloud computing. Lenovo operates 46 world-class labs, including research centers in Yokohama, Japan; Beijing, Shanghai, Wuhan and Shenzhen, China; and Morrisville, North Carolina, U.S. The company is

rich in talent, employing more than 3,200 engineers, researchers and scientists. Lenovo's R&D teams have introduced many industry firsts supported by a track record of innovation—including more than 6,500 globally recognized patents and more than 100 major design awards. Acquisitions, collaboration with industry associations, and investments in research and development even in down cycles enable us to stay ahead of market trends and deliver a comprehensive portfolio of products.[3]

This level of commitment is an undertaking that must be fostered corporate-wide and applied in all realms of the company. With such a large company, this level of commitment becomes a driving force for its product development in order to satisfy the needs of its customers.

Corporate Wide Commitment

In order to successfully implement any plans across a company as large as Lenovo, a clear and concise plan needs to be in place to drive all of the operations across all areas in which the company operates. In theory, this type of planning sounds great. However, in application, this corporate-wide commitment often begins to wane. So, in order to develop a corporate culture that will be responsive to the mission of the organization and maintain this focus in all aspects of the organization, a company needs to have a driving force behind its operations. Lenovo exhibits this dedication to fostering a beneficial corporate culture in the following way:

> Our culture defines us . . . it's our DNA. We call it the Lenovo Way and it's the values we share and the business practices we deploy. It's how we address our day-to-day commitments. The Lenovo Way is embodied in the statement: We do what we say and we own what we do. That culture also drives how we work every day, utilizing what we call the 5 P's:

- We **PLAN** before we pledge.
- We **PERFORM** as we promise.
- We **PRIORITIZE** the company first.
- We **PRACTICE** improving every day.
- We **PIONEER** new ideas.[4]

With such a culture, Lenovo has the ability and opportunity to maintain its competitive edge by encouraging an environment in the company that is focused on achieving the best individual results that will lead to positive results corporate-wide. It is clear from Lenovo's statement regarding its culture that it is interested in achieving such a dynamic working environment. However, in order to experience actual success, there needs to be some indicators from within the organization that this commitment to culture is in practice from its executives. One way in which this culture and commitment can be displayed is from the highest levels within the organization. According to Yang Yuanqing, Lenovo's Chairman and CEO:

> Building on our global momentum, we have strengthened our position as the world's number 4 smartphone player and we are pleased with our progress. Even more, we are proud today that for the first time, Lenovo is the number 1 smartphone company in China, the world's largest smartphone market. To win, Lenovo is focused on continuing to bring innovation, quality and choice to customers in China and around the world.[5]

This is the type of top-down commitment that needs to be present in order to effectively foster a culture of innovation and entrepreneurial spirit corporate-wide. The actions or inactions of top level executives in the organization will trickle down to all other areas within the organization and create an environment that is based upon the actions of these executives. Such a culture will set the course for future development and innovation within the organization and ultimately determine how an organization will operate in the future. As stated by Yang Yuanqing, Chairman and Chief Executive Officer:

> We will continue to make our products more exciting, and more useful, for our customers. Lenovo continues to expand beyond its strong position in China, the world's largest smartphone market, adding dozens of new markets in Asia, Europe and the Americas.[6]

Discussion Questions

1. **Discussion** How does Lenovo exhibit the stages in the life cycle of an entrepreneurial firm?
2. **Discussion** How might the progression through this life cycle of an entrepreneurial firm be different between a small firm and one such as Lenovo?
3. **Problem Solving** Describe how Lenovo might incorporate the practice of First-mover Advantage as discussed in Chapter 6 within its highly competitive industry.
4. **Further Research** Trace another firm in the electronics industry and compare its entrepreneurial growth with that experienced by Lenovo. What did they do differently?

CASE 7

AMAZON
One E-Store to Rule Them All

Amazon.com has soared ahead of other online merchants. What the firm can't carry in its worldwide fulfillment centers, affiliated retailers distribute for it. CEO Jeff Bezos keeps introducing new products and services to keep customers glued to the Amazon site. What drives Bezos's decisions, and will his moves and investments pay off in the years to come?

The Rocket Takes Off

From its modest beginning in Jeff Bezos's garage in 1995 as an online bookstore, Amazon.com has quickly sprouted into the preeminent online retailer. Once Bezos saw that Amazon could outgrow its role as an immense book retailer, even its logo was updated to symbolize that Amazon.com sells almost anything you can think of— from A to Z. Hundreds of other companies also list their products on the Amazon Marketplace. Amazon profits from the additional exposure and sales and the brand thrives by keeping on the site customers who might otherwise shop elsewhere.

Amazon keeps changing as it grows. No one is ever sure what will come next. CEO Jeff Bezos keeps investing to make his company bigger, stronger, and harder to catch. Its millions of square feet of distribution fulfillment space keep growing domestically and around the globe. The firm's products and services are continuously upgraded and expanded. Just go to the website and check multiple versions of the Kindle Fire e-book reader, Prime Instant Video TV, and a variety of cloud computer services. A *New York Times* article says that "within a few years, Amazon's creative destruction of both traditional book publishing and retailing may be footnotes to the company's larger and more secretive goal: giving anyone on the planet access to an almost unimaginable amount of computing power through its cloud services."[1]

Priming the Competition

Time and time again, Amazon has squared off against retail competition. Its Amazon Prime, an annual subscription providing free two-day shipping, was a big hit and has pushed other online retailers in free shipping options and promotions. In taking on Apple, Amazon launched its music downloading service and then, in a move of digital one-upmanship,[2] bought top-shelf audiobook vendor Audible.com. The Amazon Kindle keeps revamping the publishing industry. Sales of Kindle e-books now outnumber those of hardcovers.[3]

Contrary to other iPad competitors, the Kindle Fire has sold well.[4] Now, there's Fire TV to compete with Apple TV.

Apple isn't the only company in Amazon's sights. It competes with the likes of Hulu and Netflix with Amazon Prime Instant Videos, a library of streaming movies and TV shows available at no extra cost to Amazon Prime customers.[5] Prime subscribers also can borrow books from the Kindle Owners' Lending Library.[6]

Beyond simply finding more and more products to sell, Bezos pushes continuous innovation that creates new levels of service to complement existing products. "We have to say, 'What kind of innovation can we layer on top of that that will be meaningful for our customers?'" he explains.[7]

Pressing Too Hard?

While it often feels as if Amazon can't lose, this isn't always the case. Some high-profile retailers have pulled their products from the Amazon Marketplace, including Target, The Gap, and Macy's. According to Neel Grover, CEO of Buy.com—another retailer who abandoned Amazon's ship—"We didn't want to give them information on products and sales that Amazon could potentially use against us."

Despite Amazon's success in so many new markets, some critics question whether Amazon.com, let alone the Internet, is the best place to make high-involvement purchases. Bezos is characteristically confident. "We sell a lot of high-ticket items," he counters. "We sell diamonds that cost thousands of dollars and $8,000 plasma TVs. There doesn't seem to be any resistance, and, in fact, those high-priced items are growing very rapidly as a percentage of our sales."[8]

Looking Ahead

Amazon's stock fluctuates in value and has a very high price-earnings ratio that financial analysts like to criticize. But Bezos believes that customer service and anticipating customers' needs, not the stock ticker, define the Amazon experience and its success. "I think one of the things people don't understand is we can build more shareholder value by lowering product prices than we can by trying to raise margins," he says. "It's a more patient approach, but we think it leads to a stronger, healthier company. It also serves customers much, much better."[9]

In two decades, Amazon.com has grown from a one-man operation into the global giant of commerce. By forging alliances to ensure that he has what customers want and making astute purchases, Jeff Bezos has made Amazon the go-to brand for online shopping. With its significant investments in new media and services, does the company risk spreading itself too thin? Will customers—individual and corporate—continue to flock to Amazon, the go-to company for their every need?

Discussion Questions

1. **Discussion** In what ways does Bezos's decisions to develop and deliver the Kindle, Kindle Fire, and Fire TV lines show systematic and intuitive thinking?

2. **Discussion** How do you describe the competitive risk in Amazon's environment as other retailers, including Walmart, strengthen their online offerings?

3. **Problem Solving** Amazon is continuously looking for new markets to exploit. As CEO Jeff Bezos addresses the strategic opportunity of streaming video, he calls on you for advice on gaining more customers from the younger generations. Amazon's presence and technology are well established, but Bezos sees a lot of untapped potential in this market. But what decision error and traps might cause him to make the wrong decisions regarding Amazon's future moves in this regard, and why? What can he do to best avoid these mistakes?

4. **Further Research** What are the latest initiatives coming out of Amazon? How do they stack up in relation to actual or potential competition? Is Bezos making the right decisions as he guides the firm through the ever-evolving challenges of today's cyber markets? Or, is he starting to lose touch as the company grows and his other personal interests take more time and attention?

CASE 8

AVAGO TECHNOLOGIES
Planning for the Speed of Business

There is an old adage that states: If you fail to plan, then plan to fail. This is a harsh reality for many firms in today's competitive business landscape. As we learned in Chapter 8, planning is a crucial component to the success of any business today. We can even argue that planning could reap rewards of a competitive advantage over our rivals. Planning is also crucial so that we are able to meet the diverse and demanding needs of our customers as well as prepare ourselves for whatever lies ahead. So, with so much riding on the success of our planning, we need to ask ourselves: what does effective planning look like? In order to understand the impact of planning on an organization, it is helpful to look at a real-world example of how to plan effectively to maximize the results of your organization.

Recognizing our Past to Plan for the Future

Avago Technologies is headquartered in San Jose, CA and Singapore and is the ninth largest semiconductor company in the world, not including memory products.[1] Avago was founded in 1961 as part of the Hewlett-Packard company and today boasts US$2,520 billion in net revenue. Avago became a publicly traded company on August 6, 2009, trading under the AVGO symbol on the NASDAQ stock exchange.[2] As a publicly traded company, it would still be considered relatively new. However, this newness did not diminish the need for effective planning and might even heighten the need to plan accordingly if it wished to survive in such a competitive market. Since its Initial Public Offering (IPO), Avago has been producing and distributing a wide array of products that are geared specifically towards the markets in which it serves.

As Avago has grown over the years, planning for its future has been at the forefront of its strategy. According to its corporate profile:

> Avago Technologies is a leading designer, developer and global supplier of a broad range of analog, digital, mixed signal and optoelectronics components and subsystems with a focus in III-V compound semiconductor design and processing. Backed by an extensive portfolio of intellectual property, Avago products serve four primary target markets: wireless communications, wired infrastructure, enterprise storage, and industrial and other. Applications for our products in these target markets include cellular phones and base stations, data networking, storage and telecommunications equipment, factory automation, power generation and alternative energy systems, and displays.[3]

The Avago corporate profile shows the breadth of its product offering. With such a diverse set of product responsibilities, it is clear the need for planning effectively is crucial. The competitive landscape within such industries requires the players in these markets to be on the cutting edge of product development and deployment so as not to fall behind the strides made by competing firms. The corporate make-up of Avago speaks of its ability to meet the requirements of these markets by employing approximately 4,800 employees worldwide. Of these 4,800 employees, 1,400 are involved with research and development, 2,600 focus on manufacturing, 500 perform sales and marketing duties while 300 conduct general and administrative functions. In terms of the geographic breakdown, 42% of employees are based in Asia, 52% reside in North America, and the remaining 6% operate in Europe.[4] As its corporate profile shows, Avago, is dedicated to the planning and implementation of products that will be successful within its markets. The majority of Avago's employees operate in the realms of research and development as well as manufacturing. The planning that goes along with these roles is a significant undertaking and is one in which careful consideration must be exerted.

Planning is a Risky Business

Risk is part of any planning process. How a company approaches the assessment of risk determines its ability to effectively plan for such risks. There are risks associated with nearly every activity in which a firm participates. There is a risk in producing a product that may or may not effectively match the requirements of its customers. There are design risks in developing products that may create difficulties in the processes used to manufacture the product. Risks can also be encountered within its research and development as the company works with significant amounts of data that will help it to plan for its future. If it is not careful, this data interpretation could be skewed by its own opinions and biases. There are also those risks that are associated with operating an organization across a global landscape. Its constituents around the globe are varied and the correct paths are needed to lead the company to success in meeting the demands of all constituents no matter where they are located geographically.

Avago Technologies is not immune to these risks and will need to address them accordingly as part of its planning process in order to achieve the objectives for which it strives. Recognizing the risks is often a difficult task for many firms as they attempt to articulate the risk and determine the ramifications these risks could impose on their overall operations. In Avago's 2013 10-K filing with the Securities and Exchange Commission, it pinpointed certain risks involved within its unique operations:

Risks Relating to Investments in Singapore Companies:

- It may be difficult to enforce a judgment of U.S. courts for civil liabilities under U.S. federal securities laws against us, our directors or officers in Singapore.

- We are incorporated in Singapore and our shareholders may have more difficulty in protecting their interest than they would as shareholders of a corporation incorporated in the United States, and we may have more difficulty attracting and retaining qualified board members and executives.

- For a limited period of time, our directors have general authority to allot and issue new ordinary shares on terms and conditions as may be determined by our board of directors in its sole discretion.[5]

Since Avago has dual corporate headquarters in San Jose, CA and Singapore, these risks are especially important and carry significant weight with its corporate planning. The international dimension of its organization influences its approach to planning strategically. Therefore, Avago's planning needs to consider these risks in order to make preparations for its future. Failing to consider the impact of such risks could lead to devastating results on Avago's ability to operate effectively across all facets of its organization in addition to meeting the needs of its customers around the globe.

Planning for the Future

When a company plans for its future, it is really trying to chart a course for future product developments that will keep it relevant within its industry. Many times this requires the company to look outside of its current organizational structure in order to satisfy future needs. Part of this external focus could include mergers and acquisitions that will strengthen the organization as a whole and prepare it for the future demands it will face. When companies decide to pursue a merger or acquisition, it is often sought out for the benefits that can be realized from the synergy created from the merger or acquisition.

Avago is no exception to this external search in planning for its future. In May 2014, Avago acquired LSI Corporation as part of its future planning strategy. According to the press release:

> The acquisition creates a highly diversified semiconductor market leader with approximately US$5 billion in projected annual revenues. Avago believes the acquisition of LSI positions Avago as a leader in the enterprise storage market. The acquisition also expands Avago's product offerings and brings system-level expertise in its wired infrastructure market. With increased scale and a diversified product portfolio across multiple, attractive end markets, the combined company is strongly positioned to capitalize on the growing opportunities created by the rapid growth in data center IP and mobile data traffic.[6]

Mergers and acquisitions are strategic in nature and are meant to provide the organization with benefits as a result of the combined company. However, when planning for these mergers and acquisitions, there is a significant amount of attention placed on exactly what will be gained from the combination and realizing not all components gained are needed as part of the planning strategy. Consequently, shortly after Avago's acquisition of LSI Corporation, it was announced that: ". . . *Seagate will acquire the assets of LSI's Accelerated Solutions Division ("ASD") and Flash Components Division*

("FCD") from Avago for $450 million in cash."[7] Later that year, another announcement was made concerning the newly acquired LSI Corporation: "*Avago Technologies Limited and Intel Corporation today announced the signing of a definitive agreement for Intel to acquire LSI's Axxia Networking Business and related assets for $650 million in cash.*"[8] The type of behavior exhibited by Avago in these acquisitions and the later spin-offs is an example of how to effectively plan mergers and acquisitions in order to gain the advantages desired while at the same time realizing not all aspects of these acquisitions will provide benefits to the organization as a whole. As an organization plans its future pursuits, strategy will play a crucial role and will guide the decisions made, just as evidenced in the Avago handling of the LSI Corporation acquisition.

Discussion Questions

1. **Discussion** How might the handling of the LSI Corporation acquisition by Avago represent an effective example of controlling as part of the planning process?

2. **Discussion** Why would avoiding the complacency trap be crucial for a firm like Avago considering the industry in which it operates?

3. **Problem Solving** What would you suggest to Avago to help it avoid the complacency trap in its planning?

4. **Further Research** Find other companies that have headquarters in Singapore and determine if they are recognizing the risks associated with operating in this particular country. Do you feel they are more or less prepared for the risks associated with doing business in Singapore? Explain.

CASE 9

BRITISH PETROLEUM
Getting Drilled about Their Operations

Drilling for oil around the globe is a lucrative albeit dangerous operation that comes with significant rewards and intense criticism. If this drilling process is done well, the company will be rewarded with sizeable profits from a nearly unquenchable demand for fuel. However, if the drilling encounters any problems, the company should expect the backlash to be severe and long-drawn. British Petroleum (BP) is in the business of oil drilling and throughout its history has witnessed the benefits and disadvantages of operating within such an industry. The story of BP is riddled with major successes and some significant disasters that have changed the manner in which BP does business around the globe.

The Story Begins

BP first discovered oil in 1908, after years of making significant investments and waiting patiently for something to materialize from their drilling efforts. The oil strike in 1908 was welcomed by the public who, upon learning of the oil drilling success, had lined up for the opportunity to purchase stock in the Anglo-Persian Oil Company, which would later become BP.[1] The buzz over this discovery spread quickly but could not keep the company from future problems. In fact, in 1914, the company nearly went bankrupt due to a lack of demand for its oil, but was saved by Winston Churchill's push to secure a British-owned source of oil for the Royal Navy.[2] During the 1920s and 1930s, the flood of automobiles across Europe and the United States drove up the demand for gasoline. This increase in demand was a welcome change for the industry and helped to fuel profits from drilling operations. Unfortunately, in 1939, Britain entered World War II and gasoline suddenly became a rationed commodity.[3]

Surviving during wartime gave BP the resolve it needed to continue in a post-war economy. In the years following the end of World War II, BP expanded its operations by making refinery investments in France, Germany, and Italy, as well as developing new marketing initiatives in Switzerland, Greece, Scandinavia, and the Netherlands. In the 1960s, BP was able to drill for oil successfully in the UK and Alaska but experienced little success in Malta, Australia, and Papua New Guinea.[4] The 1970s brought about long lines at service stations, outrageous fuel prices, and power outages. In addition, many Middle Eastern countries had decided to nationalize the oil-producing facilities located within their borders, severely limiting BP's oil production.[5]

As it moved into the twenty-first century, BP remained focused on oil exploration and refining. However, it was also aware of the changing economic and natural climate in which it existed, and had made efforts to explore alternative fuel sources and reduce the negative impact it was creating on the environment.[6]

Looking Out for the Environment

BP operates in a volatile industry that combines high risks with high rewards. In order to be successful, BP must operate within the confines of safety and environmental sustainability. It is responsible not only to those who have invested in BP but also to the natural environment it operates in and shares with its customers. To address the issue of sustainability and environmental responsibility, BP has developed policies and procedures necessary for managing its operations and the possible disasters resulting from its drilling operations. It is in BP's best interests to be prepared for the worst case scenario so as not to disrupt the delicate balance of the environments in which it carries out explorations.

BP's focus on sustainability and the general concern for the natural environment may have surprised many people. As early as 1997, there were indications that BP was taking this issue seriously and would work diligently to respect the environment in which it worked. This was when John Browne, BP group chief executive, gave a speech on climate change at Stanford, saying: "It would be unwise and potentially dangerous to ignore the mounting concern."[7] Browne realized that managing the problem of climate change would take the united effort of many organizations and that BP would definitely be a part of this process to protect the environment. BP's stance, according to its 2009 Sustainability Report was: "We are committed to the safety and development of our people and the communities and societies in which we operate. We aim for no accidents, no harm to people and no damage to the environment."[8] This was also evidenced as recently as March 2, 2010, during BP's Strategy Presentation in which Tony Hayward, group chief executive, commented: "Safety remains our number one priority and we can see clear progress. There has been a significant reduction in the frequency of recordable injuries and the number of major incidents related to integrity failures has fallen. At the same time we're reducing containment losses in our operations."[9] This stance that BP had taken on protecting the natural environment was about to be put to the test as it would be experiencing one of the worst disasters in its history.

A Disaster in the Gulf

On April 20, 2010, BP's Deepwater Horizon drilling rig exploded, killing 11 individuals on the platform and releasing massive amounts of oil into the Gulf of Mexico. It was reported that approximately 200,000–1,000,000 barrels of oil were flowing into the sea every day, compromising the wildlife that use the area as their habitat and crippling the fishing industry in the gulf.

The damage from this spill is difficult to predict due to the magnitude of this disaster. There are concerns for the immediate area, as well as areas that water may flow to, carrying with it the spilled oil. According to Héctor M. Guzman of the Smithsonian Tropical Research Institute in Panama, who had researched the effects from the 1986 oil spill off Panama: "Once the oil, because of high tides or high winds, gets into the coastal wetland, it gets trapped in the sediment, then for decades you continue to see oil coming back out."[10] Based on the severity of this oil disaster, it would appear BP has a long road ahead of it in terms of managing the impact of the spill and taking responsibility for cleaning up the affected area.

The fact the BP is an international corporation that had a disaster in another country's territory turned this situation into a completely different type of disaster. Not only would BP have to contend with backlash in the UK, but authorities in the United States may also hand it a harsher sentence. Daniel Gross describes this unique situation that BP now finds itself in: "Through international expansion and mergers with American firms, including Amoco, it has become progressively less **British**. On its website, BP, which operates in 100 countries on six continents, notes: 'The BP group is the largest oil and gas producer and one of the largest gasoline retailers in the United States.' But ever since oil began gushing from the Deepwater Horizon rig in the Gulf of Mexico, BP has become as **British** as Wimbledon, as foreign as football played with a round ball. As a result, it's possible the company will suffer harsher treatment at the hands of consumers and lawmakers."[11] The response from BP was obviously under the constant scrutiny of multiple stakeholders around the globe.

BP realized that it was in the midst of the largest disaster of this kind in recent history and that it would have to formulate a strategy to control its response and address the concerns of stakeholders in the vicinity of the spill as well as those in the global marketplace. In an effort to restore its reputation, BP took several approaches to demonstrate that it was responding to the disaster and that it was committed to making the situation right. It attacked this from multiple fronts including significant advertising on television as well as social media sites: Facebook, Twitter, and YouTube. It kept interested parties informed of the progress being made to address this disaster. It even made changes to its Facebook page in order to pass on news and updates to interested parties, such as posting real-time results of the amount of oil collected, and videos on the health dangers posed to cleanup workers, as well as congressional hearings on the spill.[12]

BP's response to the gulf disaster will undoubtedly be criticized for years to come as the residual effects of this oil spill continue to be felt in the future. It will obviously need to justify the decisions made during the disaster and its level of preparedness for such an event. This is not to say that BP cannot recover from this disaster and regain the position it once held in the marketplace. Giles Palmer, CEO of Brandwatch, a company measuring the online reputations of organizations, contends that BP's standing may have been damaged by its poor management of the crisis but the company can still regain some of the trust it has lost.[13] Time will tell how BP weathers this storm and whether or not it will be able to convince customers that it is looking out for their best interests and seeking ways to ensure the business operates in a socially responsible manner.

Discussion Questions

1. **Discussion** How does BP's response to the oil spill disaster in the Gulf of Mexico display the control processes at BP?

2. **Discussion** How important are these control processes for a company like BP? How would it have responded to this disaster if it lacked any form of control processes?

3. **Problem Solving** What may BP have learned from this disaster? How will this information assist it in future operations?

4. **Further Research** Research other oil spills that have occurred throughout history. How does the severity compare to the BP oil spill in the Gulf of Mexico? How did the companies responsible for those spills respond?

CASE 10

SONY CORPORATION
An Evolution of Technology

The electronics industry is marked by intense growth and nearly constant change. In order to survive in this industry, firms need to establish and maintain strategies that will allow them to cope with the changing nature of the industry while meeting the high expectations of its customers. Firms lacking such strategies will find themselves behind the learning curve and extremely inept at serving their customers or challenging competitors in the electronics industry. Sony Corporation is one such firm in this industry that has made significant strides in technological advancements and has formulated strategies to meet the needs of the industry more effectively than its competition. With product interests in audio, video, television, information and communication, semiconductors and electronic components, as well as amassing a worldwide staff of 167,900 and consolidated sales and operating revenue of 7,214,000 yen, Sony is definitely poised for success.[1]

A History of Technology

It all started in May of 1946 when Tokyo Tsushin Kogyo K.K. (Tokyo Telecommunications Engineering Corporation), also known as Totsuko, was established in Nihonbashi, Tokyo. They possessed a beginning capital amount of 190,000 yen to be used for research and the eventual manufacture of telecommunications and measuring equipment. During the 1950s, the world witnessed the invention of magnetic tape as well as the first tape recorder. This period also marked a change for the company as the decision was made to change its name to Sony Corporation. The 1960s brought about the invention of the world's first ever portable television, the launch of the Chromatron color television, and the establishment of Sony Corporation of America in the United States. Throughout the next decade, Sony experienced continued growth and its hard work was recognized in 1973, as the

recipient of the first Emmy award ever given to a Japanese company for its development of the Trinitron color television system. The 1980s saw expansion of the Sony name with the introduction of the world's first ever Compact Disc (CD) player, the compact design of the Handycam camcorder, and the acquisition of Columbia Pictures Entertainment, which was renamed Sony Pictures Entertainment in 1991. Sony Computer Entertainment was established in 1993 to a growing computer industry desperate for technological innovations. As Sony entered the new millennium, we witnessed advancements in cellular phone technology with the creation of Sony Ericsson Mobile Communications. The early twenty-first century has also been marked by advancements in video technology with the introduction of the high-capacity optical disc "Blu-ray". Technology is at the heart of everything that Sony is involved with, and its continued presence has made a significant impact on the electronics industry.[2]

An Intentional Focus on Strategy

Strategy depends on a variety of factors, and putting together an effective strategy is an insurmountable task for many firms. Sony has been successful as it has successfully planned for its future growth and survived in its existing industries based on solid and well-structured strategies. An astute knowledge of the strengths and weaknesses of your own company will be useful in crafting an appropriate strategy to ensure success in your target industries. Being aware of your competition is also an important characteristic of effective strategy, as evidenced by the differing views of Sony and Samsung when it came to outsourcing versus building televisions on their own. Sony had always believed in outsourcing production whereas Samsung held true to manufacturing their products internally. According to Yoon Boo Keun, president of Samsung's TV business: "Giving up manufacturing is tantamount to abandoning your brand." Sony, however, believes: "We would like to concentrate our resources on Sony-unique applications," according to spokeswoman Sue Tanaka.[3]

Sony has attacked the notion of strategy from several different fronts and has proven to be very flexible and open to alternatives to its strategy formulation in order to achieve the goals set. One of the methods Sony has used is the formation of strategic partnerships that allow it to capitalize on its own strengths, as well as the strengths of other firms, to achieve synergy through the joint venture. This strategy tactic was realized in the alliance of Sony and Google with regard to the cellular phone market. By working together on this joint project, both Sony and Google were able to realize benefits of the partnership that could have been difficult to achieve independently. According to Howard Stringer, chairman, president, and CEO of Sony Corporation: "The combination of Sony's industry-leading product design, engineering and development expertise with the flexibility and growth potential of Google's innovative, open-source Android platform will provide consumers with a world of new and exciting Internet user experiences. Through this alliance, Sony will deliver new levels of connectivity and Internet integration across our range of assets and product categories." On the Google side of the partnership, Eric Schmidt had this to share about their alliance with Sony: "We believe that open systems lead to more innovation, value and choice for consumers, which is why we are so proud to work with Sony to bring the power of the Android platform to more consumers around the world."[4]

Part of Sony's success lies in its reliance on quality personnel committed to the corporate goals of Sony Corporation. Its strategy regarding human resources is paramount to staying competitive in such an ever-changing market fueled by rapid technological developments and high expectations. Sony realizes the value of human capital and strives to maintain a professional working relationship with its employees to insure they feel a part of the bigger picture at Sony. One way in which this is addressed is through its stance on Employee-Management Communication. According to this human resources strategy, "Sony places a high priority on communication between management and individual employees. Since fiscal year 2005, Sony's CEO, Howard Stringer, has made a point of visiting Sony sites around the world to communicate directly with employees by holding town hall meetings and creating other opportunities for dialogue." The goal of these worldwide meetings is to help explain: ". . . structural reforms and other management policies directly to employees and seek their understanding thereof, as well as to gain feedback from the front lines and promote dialogue on technology, management and other themes, top executives continue to regularly visit sites throughout Japan. Top executives also communicate with Sony Group employees by posting messages on Sony's intranet and seek feedback, thereby facilitating the sharing of information and creating a sense of unity for the Sony Group as a whole."[5]

Sony realizes that even having face-to-face meetings at their facilities around the globe does not allow all of their employees an equitable manner in which to voice their concerns to management and feel as though they are being heard. Therefore, Sony has also implemented a series of Employee Opinion Surveys for employees in each of its regions. The results of these surveys are deployed in action plans targeted at providing more comfortable workplace environments for its employees. These surveys have addressed such issues as workplace culture in Japan; corporate strategy comprehension in North America; management evaluation in Europe; work-life balance in China; awareness of management policies in Latin America; and employee motivation in the Pan-Asian region.[6]

Keeping Up in the Technology Industry

Obviously Sony has been diligent in its pursuit of effective strategies that will enable it to be successful. However, this doesn't mean that it can rest on its past successes in this industry without constantly being aware of changes and opportunities within the marketplace. Sony consistently invests its resources in research and development in order to maintain a competitive edge in the marketplace. In fact, Sony looks not only to its existing products but also in new markets where it can advance its position.[7] Sony also realizes that it must contend with its existing competitors in order to persuade the consumer to choose its product over that of the competition. This strategy was displayed in its focus on the retail side of its distribution where consumers were often opting for a cheaper priced television in lieu of purchasing Sony's Bravia model. The company recognized that some consumers may be swayed at the point of purchase even when the Bravia concept was effectively displayed in its advertising prior to purchase.[8] In addition to this tactic on its television market, Sony developed another campaign meant to integrate its entertainment and electronics business under one campaign. The "make believe" campaign includes a television advertisement that: ". . . shows a boy taking a 'magical journey' through the Sony 'worlds' of products, music, film and games," and will also entail digital, outdoor, and print advertisements.[9]

Looking Ahead

As Sony looks toward the future, there are no doubt opportunities as well as threats to the company and the industry as a whole. It will need to hold true to its roots and purpose as described by Howard Stringer, chairman, CEO, and president of Sony Corporation: "At its core, our brand stands for quality, creativity and the magic that can happen when our many diverse employees come together for a common purpose. It also stands for integrity and ethical business practices—doing the right thing for our people, our communities and the environment. These qualities have been a fundamental part of our company since it was founded more than 60 years ago and continue to guide our activities today."[10] The future will definitely include some challenging times for Sony, to which Stringer offers the following guidance: "We must increase our speed to market with desirable and competitively priced products and services."[11]

Discussion Questions

1. **Discussion** How would you rate Sony's ability to create and deploy their strategies?

2. **Discussion** How does the industry in which Sony competes dictate the type of strategy it must implement in order to be successful?

3. **Problem Solving** How might Sony plan for the future in the electronics industry? What opportunities and threats do you see coming in Sony's future?

4. **Further Research** Research Sony's competitors and determine the advantages and disadvantages they possess compared to Sony. How might they deal with these disadvantages in order to be more competitive with Sony?

CASE 11

TOYOTA
Designing as Effective Structure

Organizational structure is important in any company and the manner in which it is developed and maintained displays the level of importance it carries in the success of an organization. Companies cannot perform their essential functions without a guiding structure that assists them in carrying out their day-to-day activities. Just as the physical structure of a house or building supports everything within it, a company's organizational structure is the binding component of everything it does as an organization. Therefore, the importance of crafting an organizational structure effectively is paramount to the success of the company. This is especially important as a company grows into a larger organization and takes on additional employees and added responsibilities. In order to accommodate the responsibilities of a large organization, a proper structure must already be in place in order to address these responsibilities directly. An example of effectively meeting the diverse responsibilities placed upon a firm is evidenced by Toyota which has grown into one of the largest automobile manufacturers in the world. Without an appropriate organizational structure, Toyota would not have been prepared to meet the challenges it faces on a daily basis.

Humble Beginnings

Toyota was officially founded on August 28, 1937 and has grown to over 338,000 employees worldwide in 2014.[1] This kind of growth does not happen accidentally and takes a concerted effort of all involved to achieve the level of success to which Toyota has become accustomed. Therefore, the need for appropriate organizational structure is imperative to Toyota and is displayed in its daily business dealings. In fact, in the early years of Toyota before its official founding,

there were "Toyoda Precepts" that were to guide all of its dealings. These precepts consisted of five tenets:

1. Be contributive to the development and welfare of the country by working together, regardless of position, in faithfully fulfilling your duties.

2. Be at the vanguard of the times through endless creativity, inquisitiveness and pursuit of improvement.

3. Be practical and avoid frivolity.

4. Be kind and generous, strive to create a warm, home-like atmosphere.

5. Be reverent, and show gratitude for things great and small in thought and deed.[2]

These tenets show the desire for Toyota, even in its infancy as a company, to operate with purpose to achieve its goals. These guiding principles are important in the development of an individual as well as being the premise for establishing the right type of organizational structure for what the Toyota company would become.

Changing of the Organizational Structure

As with any organizational structure, there often comes a time when the company realizes a change is needed. For Toyota, an example of this need to adjust its structure came in 2011 when faced with the challenges of a downturn in the economy and concerns about the quality of its products. Toyota needed to make some changes to its organizational structure. Operating under the premise of business as usual was no longer going to equip Toyota to meet the demands of its constituents. A change was needed and for a company of such magnitude, this would be no easy task.

On March 9, 2011, Toyota released its Global Vision:

1. Toyota will lead the way to the future of mobility, enriching lives around the world with the safest and most responsible ways of moving people.

2. Through our commitment to quality, constant innovation and respect for the planet, we aim to exceed expectations and be rewarded with a smile.

3. We will meet our challenging goals by engaging the talent and passion of people, who believe there is always a better way.[3]

Toyota's vision as laid out in these three components was a step in the direction of meeting the challenges it faced by setting a guiding framework from which the entire company should operate. The three components provided a summary of what needed to take place to achieve the goals Toyota had set for itself. This guiding framework for Toyota still needed additional clarification as to how the automobile giant planned on meeting this vision on a practical level in its daily operations. To this end, Toyota added its Visionary Management to help clarify the actions that would be taking place as part of its global vision:

Toyota employed a tree metaphor—focusing on "roots", "trunk" and "fruit"—in expressing the Toyota Global Vision.

Roots: Shared values

The roots of the tree are shared values. Those are the same basic values that people at Toyota have expressed over the years as the Toyoda Precepts, as the Toyota Guiding Principles, and as The Toyota Way. They are the spirit of conscientious manufacturing.

Fruit: Making great cars and contributing to host communities

The fruit yielded by the tree symbolize Toyota's progress in creating ever-better vehicles and contributing to economic and social vitality in Toyota's host communities. That progress will earn a welcome place for Toyota in communities around the world.

Trunk: Solid business

Business vitality is the trunk that supports Toyota's activities toward creating products that will win customer smiles. In Toyota's tree metaphor, solid business is the trunk of the tree. Through that trunk flows the nutrition for supple limbs, branches and leaves and for bounteous fruit.

Toyota's vision thus evokes a virtuous circle. The company will contribute to its host communities by making excellent automobiles. Earning a welcome place for Toyota in its host communities will support sound returns. And Toyota will reinvest those returns in creating ever-better vehicles for customers and will achieve sustainable growth.[3]

So, at this point in its organizational structure change, Toyota has proposed an overreaching global vision to guide the company as a whole and now, a more theoretical application of how the activities contained within the visionary management plan will assist it in carrying out its vision. In this way, Toyota is addressing its challenges by setting a course to follow in meeting the expectations of its constituents.

This final component was a change to the executive structure in place at Toyota to position it to accomplish its vision and display some practical applications of how this vision would be realized, which included the following principles:

1. To swiftly communicate the voices of our customers and information from the frontline operation level of each region to our executive levels.

2. To enable prompt management decisions based on information from frontline operations.

3. To enable us to continuously check whether our management decisions are acceptable by society.

   Change #1—Reducing the number of directors.
   Change #2—Reducing the decision-making layers.
   Change #3—Establishing executive general managers.
   Change #4—Building the structure and system where each region can initiate decisions close to its customers.
   Change #5—Establishment of a mechanism to listen to outside opinion more closely, and reflect them in our management.[3]

This final component placed the emphasis on those daily activities that could assist Toyota in achieving its vision and give its constituents a complete picture of how this global vision would play out in the day-to-day activities of Toyota. The vision laid out for Toyota is definitely going to present some challenges as these changes are implemented and begin to permeate all aspects of Toyota's business. Time will tell if Toyota is able to accomplish such a lofty vision by instituting the changes identified to create an environment in which this vision will be realized. This process has a long-term focus and is not a quick-fix solution to address Toyota's objectives as noted by Toyota's President Akio Toyoda in his President's Message from the 2013 Annual Report:

There is a growing sense that the business model set forth in the Toyota Global Vision is steadily becoming more robust. It is important, however, to remember that we have merely reached the next starting line and that every member of the Toyota Group needs to focus on ensuring true competitiveness—competitiveness that will support sustainable growth regardless of external factors. Ultimately, true competitiveness cannot be measured simply in terms of profit and loss, but rather represents a challenge that must be met on a groupwide basis.[4]

Discussion Questions

1. **Discussion** Why would Toyota need a formal structure to its organization?

2. **Discussion** What are the pros and cons of a formal structure in organizations?

3. **Problem Solving** How might Toyota benefit from the use of a Matrix Structure?

4. **Further Research** Research how Toyota is performing today. Do you feel it has overcome the negative connotation with regards to its product quality? Explain.

CASE 12

APPLE INC.
People and Design

Over a span of more than 30 years, Apple Computer has existed paradoxically as one of the greatest business successes and as a company that sometimes failed to realize its potential. Apple Inc. ignited the personal computer industry in the 1970s,[1] bringing such behemoths as IBM and Digital Equipment almost to their knees; stagnated when a series of CEOs missed opportunities; and rebounded tremendously with the return of its cofounder and former CEO, Steve Jobs. The firm represents a fascinating microcosm of business as it continues to leverage its strengths while reinventing itself.

Corporate History

The history of Apple Inc. is a history of passion, whether on the part of its founders, its employees, or its loyal users.[2] It started with a pair of Stevens who, from an early age, had an interest in electronics. Steven Wozniak and Steven Jobs initially put their skills to work at Hewlett Packard and Atari, respectively. But then Wozniak constructed his first personal computer—the Apple I—and, along with Jobs, created the Apple Computer on April 1, 1976. Right from the start, Apple exhibited an extreme emphasis on new and innovative styling in its computer offerings. Jobs took a personal interest in the development of new products, including the Lisa and the first, now legendary, Macintosh, or "Mac."

The passion that Apple is so famous for was clearly evident in the design of the Mac. Project teams worked around the clock to develop the machine and its operating system, Mac OS. The use of graphical icons to create simplified user commands was an immensely popular alternative to the command-line structure of DOS found on IBM's first PCs.

When Apple and IBM began to clash head on in the personal computer market, Jobs recognized the threat and realized that it was time for Apple to "grow up" and be run in a more businesslike fashion. In early 1983, he persuaded John Sculley, at that time president of Pepsi-Cola, to join Apple as president. The two men clashed almost from the start, with Sculley eventually ousting Jobs from the company.

The launch of the Mac reinvigorated Apple's sales. However, by the 1990s, IBM PCs and clones were saturating the personal computer market. Furthermore, Microsoft launched Windows 3.0, a greatly improved version of the Wintel operating system, for use on IBM PCs and clones. Although in 1991, Apple had contemplated licensing its Mac operating system to other computer manufacturers, which would enable it to run on Intel-based machines, the idea was nixed by then chief operating officer Michael Spindler in a move that would ultimately give Windows the nod to dominate the market.

Apple continued to rely on innovative design to remain competitive in the 1990s. It introduced the very popular PowerBook notebook computer line, as well as the unsuccessful Newton personal digital assistant. Sculley was forced out and replaced by Michael Spindler. After a difficult time in the mid-1990s, Spindler was replaced with Gil Amelio, the former president of National Semiconductor. This set the stage for one of the most famous returns in corporate history.

Jobs's Return

After leaving Apple, Steven Jobs started NeXT computer, which produced an advanced personal computer with a sleek, innovative design. However, the computer, which entered the market late in the game and required proprietary software, never gained a large following. Jobs then cofounded the Pixar computer-animation studio, which coproduced a number of movies with Walt Disney Studios, including *Toy Story, Monsters, Inc., Finding Nemo, Ratatouille,* and *Up.*[3] Cofounder Alvy Ray Smith says of Jobs, who was running the struggling Pixar: "We should have failed, but Steve just wouldn't let it go."[4]

In late 1996, Apple purchased NeXT, and Jobs returned to Apple in an unofficial capacity as advisor to the president. When Amelio resigned, Jobs accepted the role of "interim CEO" of Apple Computer and wasted no time in making his return felt. He announced an alliance with Apple's former rival, Microsoft. In exchange for $150 million in Apple stock, Microsoft and Apple would share a five-year patent cross-license for their graphical interface operating systems. He revoked licenses allowing the production of Mac clones and started offering Macs over the web through the Apple Store.

Apple's recent successes have included growing to command approximately 35% of operating profits in the computer market[5] and 66% of the market share for computers priced over $1,000.[6] Apple has also paid close attention to its international business by offering 36 country/language combinations of its Apple Store website. The focus on international markets has been a rewarding venture for Apple. According to its 10-Q filing ending March 27, 2010, Apple's primary business segments include the Americas, Europe, Japan, Asia-Pacific and Retail operations. The results of these operations in 2010 compared to the same time period in 2009 are as follows:[7]

- Americas (North & South America)—26% net sales increase

- Europe—63% net sales increase

- Japan—51% net sales increase

- Asia-Pacific—184% net sales increase

Based on these performance numbers, it is evident that Apple's international operations are a significant contributor to its overall sales growth.

Furthermore, Apple is committed to ensuring that its operations around the globe operate in a responsible manner. The Apple Supplier Code of Conduct addresses such issues as labor and human rights, health and safety, environmental impact, and ethics. This commitment is stated as: "Apple's suppliers commit, in all of their activities, to operate in full compliance with the laws, rules, and regulations of the countries in which they operate. This Supplier Code of Conduct goes further, drawing upon internationally recognized standards, in order to advance social and environmental responsibility."[8]

What Does the Future Hold?

Whenever critics argued that Apple should reinvent itself again, it did just that—and then some. It now sets standards with new corporate strategies, taking advantage of the explosion of personal electronic devices. In its first week, iTunes sold 1.5 million songs and captured 80% of the market share of legal music downloads. And now we're into new generation iPhones, wondering just what Apple will next bring to the market.

Casting an ominous shadow on the company was Steve Jobs' announcement in early 2009 of a six-month medical leave. While Jobs was on leave, chief operating officer Tim Cook handled Apple's day-to-day operations. Some analysts thought Jobs might transition into an advisory role and focus on products and strategy, and Cook would formally become CEO. Collins Stewart analyst Ashok Kumar said investors were reassured that Jobs would be back at the helm of the company he helped resuscitate over the past decade with successful products such as the iPod, iPhone, and iPad.[9]

For most companies, such information is not crucial because they are not as closely associated with one person. But Apple may be an exception. Because he helped found Apple,

Steve Jobs has been inextricably linked to the company and its brand.[10] A lot of concern was expressed over Apple's ability to stay on its creative course without Jobs at the helm. Well, as we all know, Jobs did come back, even though his health remained a concern. The stock markets greeted him with share price rises, and consumers eagerly awaited Apple's next new product announcements. The "Jobs effect" was positive and evident, and this is due to his unique reputation. In April 2010, the iPad was launched in the US and 300,000 units were sold on the first day.[11] The hype had begun four months earlier when Apple touted the iPad as a revolutionary device for browsing the web, reading and sending email, enjoying photos, watching videos, listening to music, playing games, reading e-books, and more. The iPad features a responsive, high-resolution touch-screen, which lets users physically interact with applications and content.[12] By the end of May 2010, Apple added the availability of the iPad to nine additional countries worldwide. Two things that you won't find, however, are Adobe's Flash Player or Google's advertisements, causing rifts, rivalries, and SEC involvement. Upon the announcement that the iPad would not support Adobe Flash, Apple's share price dropped 3%.[13]

On October 5, 2011, Steve Jobs passed away, leaving a tremendous void in the lives of many including, Apple Inc. The ability for another individual to fill this role within the corporate culture for Apple is a daunting task. Through this tragedy, Apple has been faced with an enormous amount of change, and the manner in which it deals with this change may define the organization's future, as well as its product offerings.

Discussion Questions

1. **Discussion** Apple sells stylish and functional computers as well as a variety of electronic devices, and it operates retail stores. Describe the forces for change that best help Apple keep its creative edge, and explain why.

2. **Discussion** In light of Steve Jobs' passing, do you feel Apple's board of directors will be expecting transformational change or incremental change, or both, at this point in time? Why? How will this change impact Apple's operations internationally?

3. **Problem Solving** Describe change strategies employed by Apple throughout its history. Consider its relationships with Microsoft and Adobe. What model of change leadership do you feel Steve Jobs embodied, and why?

4. **Further Research** Review what the analysts are presently saying about Apple. Make a list of all of the praises and criticisms—organize them by theme and put them in the priority that you would tackle them if you were taking over as Apple's new CEO. In what ways can the praises and criticisms be used to create a leadership agenda for positive change and continuous improvement?

COCA-COLA
Staying Focused on Talent

Coca-Cola is a company synonymous with excitement and long-running success. This success has not come easy for Coca-Cola, and the company has made decisions throughout its history that have influenced its level of success. None of this would be possible without the company ensuring that it had the appropriate employees in the right jobs to capitalize on their strengths and assist the company in reaching its goals. That said, the act of managing human resources at Coca-Cola needs some serious consideration and there are many opportunities to accomplish great things through the people it employs. Employing the right people is just the first step in the process of effectively managing the human resources element at Coca-Cola; developing their talent is also a primary area of concern.

The Story of Coca-Cola

Curiosity was at the foundation of John Pemberton's creation of the Coca-Cola formula in 1886. This creation grew from meager sales of nine glasses per day in its first year, to 1.4 billion beverages daily today. As Coca-Cola moved into the twentieth century, it experienced rapid growth in the U.S. and began operations internationally, entering markets in Canada, Puerto Rico, France, and Panama, to name a few. Throughout the 1900s, Coca-Cola pursued a strategy of being within "arms reach of desire" by expanding its operations around the globe. Coca-Cola has always depended on advertising to spread its message, from "I'd like to buy the world a Coke" to "Always Coca-Cola" campaigns.[1] Advertising alone, however, will not enable Coca-Cola to achieve its mission; it also needs to employ the right people in order to meet the goals of its "Roadmap," which is part of its 2020 Vision:

- To refresh the world . . .
- To inspire moments of optimism and happiness . . .
- To create value and make a difference.[2]

Talent Search

Coca-Cola has invested a significant amount of time and resources in its brand; it also paid considerable attention to the human resources department and efficient management of its employees. The corporate website states: "Our company is built around two core assets, its brands and its people. We want our people to take pride in their work and in building brands others love. After all, it's the combined talents, skills, knowledge, experience and passion of our people that make us who we are."[3] This intentional focus on

employing the right people in the right areas of responsibility is of paramount importance to ensuring continued success at Coca-Cola. However, this is not an easy task to accomplish, and attracting the best quality talent in the marketplace requires good planning and preparation. In fact, there are some who disagree with the manner in which talent is maintained at Coca-Cola, as executive recruiter Joe Goodwin states: "Coke is a great company with great brands…People tend to get caught up in the Coke bureaucracy and get dead-ended in their careers."[4]

So, how does Coca-Cola inspire nearly 100,000 employees to remain focused on working smart: acting with urgency, remaining responsive to change, having the courage to change course when needed, remaining constructively discontent, and working efficiently?[5] In order to receive this level of work from its employees, Coca-Cola must be focused on growing their talent from within. According to Stevens J. Sainte-Rose, Group HR director: "Our marketing talent was telling us that they felt that we spent more time buying talent to fill our roles as opposed to developing our talent."[6] This type of corporate culture would not have allowed Coca-Cola to grow and experience the kind of success they aspired to achieve. Changes would need to be made and a more refined focus on human resources would be necessary. Securing the best talent in the marketplace is futile unless it is also combined with the ability to grow this talent.

People Make the Difference

Emphasis on employees and their abilities has been a key concern for the success of Coca-Cola as stated by former chairman and CEO, Neville Isdell: " . . . there are people who know what needs to be done and are looking for leaders to allow them to perform."[7] It is people like these who have helped Coca-Cola achieve the position of owning " . . . 4 of the world's top 5 nonalcoholic sparkling beverage brands: Coca-Cola, Diet Coke, Sprite and Fanta."[8] The talent pool at Coca-Cola is one that requires careful attention in order to encourage and sustain growth both professionally and personally. The act of grooming talent at Coca-Cola is necessary due to the enormity of the business. In order to accomplish this, Coca-Cola needs to look for opportunities in which to find and develop talent from within the organization. Part of this process includes the creation of new talent in the organization. According to Karen Hendrix, director of learning and development at Coca-Cola North America: "We identify 10 to 12 next generation leaders, each with less than five years with the company and all typically less than 35 years old."[9] Taking such an interest in developing new talent demonstrates Coca-Cola's concern for sustaining the thriving operations of Coca-Cola well into the future.

Time will tell whether Coca-Cola will be able to develop its employees to meet the needs of its customers as well as achieve the goals set by the organization. Based on its past, it is safe to say that Coca-Cola will continue to invest in its people to grow the talent they already possess. In doing, so it will be better prepared, as Muhtar Kent, chairman of the Board of Directors and CEO, pledges to ". . . continue to capture a growing share of the projected $1 trillion market for nonalcoholic ready-to-drink beverages by 2020."[10] Without the appropriate personnel in place, this goal would be near impossible to achieve.

Discussion Questions

1. **Discussion** What do you feel Coca-Cola has to offer potential employees? How does this help Coca-Cola attract a quality workforce?

2. **Discussion** Why would Coca-Cola want to employ the use of external as well as internal recruitment of potential job candidates? Which do you feel would yield the best results, and why?

3. **Problem Solving** Which type of training would you suggest for Coca-Cola? Why would this training method be the best approach for a company in the beverage industry?

4. **Further Research** Research a competitor to Coca-Cola in your local area. How does this competitor compare to Coca-Cola?

CASE 14

SAMSUNG
Leading the Way in Technology

Leaders of the world's largest and most successful companies are as varied as the companies themselves. Developing the kind of leadership within these organizations that will achieve success takes a concerted effort from all parties within organization. As was evidenced in Chapter 14's material, leadership comes in many forms and can often be a complex topic to understand. However, leadership is a necessary component of every organization and taking the time to develop effective leaders should be of the utmost concern for organizations around the world. Planning for effective leadership is a process which takes a considerable amount of time and resources in order to achieve a level of leadership that can propel a company forward to reach its goals. Samsung is a prime example of a company that is taking the right steps in cultivating and developing its leaders to yield advantages across the industries in which it competes.

Building a Company to Lead

Samsung began as Samsung Electronics Industry Co., Ltd. on January 13, 1969, and launched its Initial Public Offering (IPO) on June 11, 1975.[1] In 1972, Samsung began the production of black-and-white televisions and by 1976, had already surpassed the one millionth black-and-white television produced. By 1979, Samsung had begun producing microwave ovens, followed in 1980 by the initial production of air conditioners. In 1983, Samsung entered the personal computer (PC) market. Then, in 1992, Samsung produced its very first mobile phone system. In 1998, Samsung introduced the world to the first digital television. Fast forward a few years and in 2004, Samsung had reached the mark of 20 million cellular phones sold in the U.S. As of 2013, Samsung was ranked eighth in Interbrand's 'Best Global Brands.'[2]

It becomes easy to recognize the need for effective leadership in a company that has experienced such explosive growth across so many different technological industries. Samsung had made amazing strides in each of the markets it entered and this success depended on having in place the right kind of leadership that guided Samsung to compete successfully in such a volatile and competitive market. With tremendous growth came a significant responsibility to maintain the momentum created by entering into such a wide variety of product industries. The leadership in place at Samsung has allowed this growth to be realized at an impressive rate. In fact, in 1993, the company had sales of $36 billion while employing 123,500 employees and in less than 20 years, had driven these numbers to $268.8 billion in sales with 425,000 employees in 2013.[3]

Developing a Leadership Framework

Cultivating a culture of leadership takes a significant amount of time and attention to achieve an effective leadership team. Without the proper framework in place, it will be difficult to create a culture of leadership in which employees feel they can lead in their daily work responsibilities. Samsung has crafted The Samsung Philosophy outlining the manner in which it aspires to operate:

> At Samsung, we follow a simple business philosophy: to devote our talent and technology to creating superior products and services that contribute to a better global society.
>
> Every day, our people bring this philosophy to life. Our leaders search for the brightest talent from around the world and give them the resources they need to be the best at what they do. The result is that all of our products—from memory chips that help businesses store vital knowledge to mobile phones that connect people across continents—have the power to enrich lives. And that's what making a better global society is all about.[4]

Providing leaders with the tools and resources they need to accomplish the objectives of the organization is of crucial importance in today's business climate. Samsung's approach to such a philosophy speaks loudly about its desire to develop and equip its leaders to be successful in all facets of the organization. Without these tools and the ability to apply these resources to daily operations, a company would have no direction, and thus, ineffective leadership would be a result.

Clearly, The Samsung Philosophy is the framework for creating and developing the leadership style necessary to keep the company at the cutting edge in its industries. In order for such a philosophy to be effective, there must be some practical application of the philosophy for the company's employees who are carrying out the daily operations of the company. Samsung has identified this application of their philosophy by expanding on this vision through its values statement regarding its people: "*Quite simply, a company is its people. At Samsung, we're dedicated to giving our people a wealth of opportunities to reach their full potential.*"[5] Thus, Samsung is providing its employees with the resources required to lead each of their particular areas of responsibility which will lead to more effective leadership in the organization.

Looking for Leadership

Having the proper framework for developing leadership is a great way to ensure your company is operating at a high level of effective leadership in order to achieve the goals set out for the organization. However, we need to consider how does a company attract such individuals to the firm in order to develop such leadership talent? The ability to attract the right caliber of individual is a concern for nearly every organization around the world. The ability to not only gain the interest of the best candidates but to obtain their agreement with your corporate culture of leadership is a key determining factor in the overall success of any company. Samsung is no exception to this need to attract the right individuals.

Samsung has stated its concern for its employees and the value that each individual can bring to the company as a whole. In fact, Samsung has publicized this desire to employ the best individuals in its Diversity Vision: "*Create the future by developing a diverse and inclusive culture that attracts and grows the world's top talent.*"[6] This type of statement reiterates Samsung's desire to have quality individuals operating in all facets of the organizational structure. The search to attract the right talent requires a desire to find those individuals that will provide the best fit for the organization

and vice versa. This desire is evidenced in Samsung's career postings site which states:

> At Samsung the key to our efforts is our people, whose talent, creativity and dedication is the foundation of our success. To compete in the global market, we focus on attracting the best talent and offer a corporate culture in which every person can excel.
>
> Samsung's philosophy is based on our strong determination for growth, perpetual innovation and good corporate citizenship. Our practices have proven successful—we are one of America's fastest growing companies and an acknowledged leader in the digital convergence revolution. As one of the largest companies in the world, the possibilities are truly endless.
>
> In our pursuit of excellence, Samsung is continuously looking for dynamic individuals. Become a part of Samsung and let your potential soar.[7]

Through this statement, it is clear Samsung takes on the task of acquiring the right caliber of individuals as a serious matter.

Leadership permeates all areas in which a company is involved. Ensuring the right management level leadership is in place can be a daunting task for many organizations. Samsung is no exception to the need for acquiring and developing leadership within its management ranks. The importance of this particular recruitment activity is clearly seen in its statement regarding Samsung Management:

> Samsung looks for creative and collaborative visionaries to run our companies. By attracting talented managers and evolving our organization's culture to support them, we foster innovative ideas that advance technology, produce new products and improve the everyday lives of our customers.[8]

From these statements concerning management level employees as well as every other employee in Samsung, it is evident that the company is committed to not only finding the right talent but also building into its existing staff the qualities necessary to achieve effective leadership.

Discussion Questions

1. **Discussion** How would the Personal Leadership Traits listed in Chapter 14 impact the business in which Samsung operates? Explain.

2. **Discussion** Why is effective leadership crucial in the industries in which Samsung operates?

3. **Problem Solving** How would you describe Samsung's leadership in terms of its "leading" ability? *(Figure 14.1: Leading: building the commitments and enthusiasm for people to apply their talents to help accomplish plans.)*

4. Further Research Research other firms in one of the industries in which Samsung competes. Do you find the same attention to its employees and leaders? What do you feel this says about Samsung and its competition in terms of leadership ability?

CASE 15

INTEL
Processing Individuals to Succeed

Intel has enjoyed significant success in the computer processor chip market, and its influence in this market is far-reaching. Operating within such a competitive and rapidly paced industry takes efficient planning to insure the right people are in the right place to lend themselves to the overall success of the firm.

Intel has invested a significant amount of resources into developing individual employees into successful members of their organization. However, accomplishing this task was definitely no small feat. A firm needs the requisite culture and organizational structure in order to achieve the level of success enjoyed by Intel. Individual employees possess a variety of different backgrounds, experiences, and personalities. Collaborating across these varied dimensions is crucial to insure that the best is ascertained from each and every employee. By paying attention to the individual differences and capitalizing on the strengths of each employee, considerable work can be accomplished, and this resulting synergy is invaluable to the employer.

Building Intel

Intel is comprised of 82,500 employees responsible for generating US$54 billion in net revenue.[1] Rising to this level of success did not happen overnight for Intel, but rather, has been the result of many years of dedicated work.

Intel was founded in 1968 by Bob Noyce and Gordon Moore after they left their jobs at Fairchild Semiconductor. Their combined knowledge and experience fueled the desire at Intel to produce products that could successfully meet the diverse needs of its target markets in the computer industry. Intel would later go public with the first sale of company stock in 1971. This same year also witnessed the birth of Intel's first microprocessor—the 4004—which launched a new era in integrated electronics.

Intel began its international manufacturing in 1972 with the opening of its plant in Malaysia. By 1979, Intel had made its debut on the Fortune 500 list at No. 486. After only 10 years in existence, Intel had amassed over 10,000 employees company-wide.

In the early 1980s, the high-tech industry was hit by a recession. Intel employees responded to this decline in the economic climate by agreeing to put in an extra 25% each week without additional pay in order to fast-track products to the market. This is an unabashed example of the devotion of Intel's employees to the corporate cause. When the personal computer industry started to advance in 1982 and demand became significant, Intel found itself in a position to capitalize on its innovations with the Intel 286 microprocessor, which was embedded in numerous PCs. Although the remainder of the 1980s saw yet another recession in the high-tech industry, Intel continued its development of innovative products.

By the early 1990s, Intel was recognized as the largest semiconductor supplier in the world. In 1994, it was reported that 85% of all desktop computers were running on Intel chips. Intel continued to make strides in product development and enhancements, and by the year 2000, it had set its sights on wireless technology. In 2003, Intel developed a single silicon chip that combined components of cellular phones and handheld computers, and a year later it received the distinguished honor of being ranked No. 46 among *Fortune* magazine's 100 Best Companies to Work For. By 2011, Intel had achieved its greatest earnings to date with its sixth consecutive quarter of record earnings.[2] Throughout its history, Intel has achieved phenomenal success with its innovative products and services, and the credit for this success goes to its employees.

Building a Company of Individuals

The incredible success story of Intel has been well-documented and discussed, and there is no doubt that these accomplishments are direct results of its employees' efforts. But we should also ask ourselves: "How was Intel able to develop such amazing talent and cultivate this talent to its advantage in the technology industry?" Intel had made concerted efforts to determine the ways in which it could capitalize on its human resource investments, so that it could obtain the best results from each individual employee. It was a significant undertaking for such a large organization to determine how best to capitalize on each employee's strengths and leverage his or her unique abilities and skills. Intel identified four areas that it felt had the greatest potential in leveraging its human resources functions for strategic value:

1. *Strategy:* strategy development and strategic alignment.

2. *Organization Design:* organization design and strategic workforce planning.

3. *Leading Change:* change management and leadership staff development.

4. *Organizational Assessment and Diagnosis:* applying systems-based thinking and tools to assess and diagnose organizational issues.[3]

Taking such an approach to its human resources strategy shows the level of interest Intel has for its workforce. It is clear that Intel is committed to the development and success of its workforce as this has a direct correlation to the success it enjoys as an organization.

Taking the time to analyze its workforce and strategize how this workforce could assist it in achieving its corporate goals is one example of how Intel displays its focus and commitment to the individual employee. To succeed in maximizing the potential of its human capital, it requires a significant amount of commitment towards providing the proper culture and resources in the organization that will encourage individual development and performance. When asked about the culture that exists at Intel and how this culture has evolved over the firm's history, Paul Otellini responded:

> "Instantaneous communication is the biggest change in my career. I can make a video that instantly goes to Intel's 80,000 employees. Information has become a competitive advantage. Speed of business is obviously faster. In a given year, 90% of the revenue Intel gets in December comes from products that weren't on the market in January. Another change is the work/life balance. Intel used to be a company of 8 a.m. check-ins and time cards. But now people can telecommute, take time out during the day."[4]

This type of culture is one that has to be built over time and requires significant attention to be successful. Once the appropriate culture is developed, however, the benefits can be far-reaching and can afford a firm the advantage of being better prepared for opportunities within its particular market. Currently, Intel is facing a daunting challenge as it attempts to meet the needs of a demanding smartphone market. Thus far, Intel has been behind the game in this market but it is poised to make a significant contribution to the technology driving these vital products. Acknowledging the desire for Intel to operate successfully in the smartphone market even as it is behind its competitors, Otellini states:

> "Intel has enough momentum in our core business and enough assets that we're going to do this right. And we're going to win in the long run."[5]

This forward-looking confidence would not be possible without the right individuals in place to support Intel's move into the smartphone market successfully. Despite the competition being a step ahead, there is still a remarkable focus and determination at Intel to achieve its goals of meeting the needs of the smartphone consumer and capturing a share of this market.

The behavior of individual employees within a firm truly does have a significant and lasting impact of the success of an organization. The development of these individuals is a matter that demands incredible focus and significant resources in order to operate successfully. Through the example of Intel, it is glaringly apparent that the individual development of human capital within a company should be done with proper planning and decisive execution. The development of individuals within a company does not happen overnight either, and must be developed on a continuous basis. Individuals are just that—individuals. No two employees have the same background and experience and, thus, they cannot be developed in the same way. It took a concerted effort on the part of Intel to develop each employee as an individual in order to achieve the level of success it desired. In its 2011 Annual Report, Jane E. Shaw, chairman of the board, stated:

> "In 2011, the company launched a comprehensive leadership development series targeted at advancing career development and retention of African American and Hispanic employees. The program provides coaching in business acumen, organizational leadership, strategic thinking, communication, and more. Through another new program, Extend Our Reach, a group of Intel's most senior women executives have become sponsors who mentor and advocate for other female employees, as part of the company's ongoing Global Women's Initiative aimed at attracting, developing, and retaining female employees."[6]

It is through such initiatives that Intel can continue to advance the capabilities of its employees and encourage each individual to contribute his or her unique abilities towards the advancement of Intel within the technology industry.

Discussion Questions

1. **Discussion** Imagine if you were an employee of Intel during the time when employees were asked to work 25% more without pay in order to continue the technological advancements of the organization. Would you agree with this request? Why or why not?

2. **Discussion** Explain what you see as the pros and cons of encouraging individuals to express themselves and their ideas in the workplace.

3. **Problem Solving** If you were a member of the executive team at Intel, how would you encourage individuality within the workplace? How would you personally display this focus on the individual from your executive position?

4. **Further Research** Investigate Intel's attempts at entering the smartphone market thus far. Based on its past experiences in this market, how likely is it for Intel to be successful in the smartphone market?

CASE 16

UNITED PARCEL SERVICE
Delivering on Their Success

United Parcel Service (UPS) is known around the globe as a leader in package delivery. They have achieved this position in the industry through years of dedication to their operations as well as a keen sense of the wants and needs of their customers. Over the past century, UPS has transformed the package shipping business and made great strides in transportation and logistics for businesses all over the world. As times and demand have changed, UPS has been ready for the task and willing to make the necessary changes to their business operations in order to meet the needs of their customers.

A History of Growth

UPS was founded in 1907 as a messenger service and today has developed into a $49.7 billion business.[1] UPS has not only become a leader in the package delivery industry, but has also created a clear focus on facilitating commerce around the globe. The transporting function for many businesses affords them the opportunity to reach new markets in which to sell their products. Without an efficient method of delivering their goods, these businesses would truly be at a loss in terms of market expansion.

UPS started as the American Messenger Company when, in 1907, Jim Casey borrowed $100 from a friend to begin his business venture. In 1919, the company name was changed to United Parcel Service and by the mid-1920s, UPS was making strides in terms of efficiencies by introducing the first conveyor belt system to handle their packages.[2] Throughout the early 1930s and into the 1950s, UPS continued to expand its operations across the United States. By 1975, it had become the first package delivery company to serve every address in the 48 contiguous United States; two years later, with the expansion of air service, UPS was able to reach all 50 states.[3] By 1981, UPS was able to purchase its first aircraft to aid in the delivery service. Then, in 1985, it began its international delivery operations by delivering to six European countries. 1988 witnessed a historic change in the operations of UPS—it was granted permission to operate its own aircraft, and thereby became an official airline company. Within the span of one year, UPS had expanded its operations to more than 175 countries around the globe.[4]

As UPS entered the 1990s, it witnessed significant changes to its operations, allowing it to become more efficient and experience impressive growth. In 1992, it added electronic package tracking to its service, and was delivering 11.5 million packages to more than one million customers in over 200 countries. As part of the worldwide growth in Internet-based companies and services, UPS launched its own website in 1994. Two years later in 1996, UPS added the ability to see real-time images of the receiver's signature as part of its electronic package tracking capabilities. As the 1990s came to a close, UPS sold 10% of its stock as part of its initial public offering in 1999.[5] During the start of the 2000s, UPS offered many services, including rate calculation and transit times to wireless devices for its customers. It also witnessed an increase in online tracking requests, setting a record of 6.5 million requests in a day.[6] UPS has continued to experience rapid growth and expansion as reflected in the 200-plus countries it now services, the 408,000 worldwide employees, and the 3.8 billion packages and documents delivered yearly.[7, 8]

Weathering the Financial Storm

UPS is not immune to changes in the economy, as witnessed in 2008 to 2010. Major changes to the business markets around the globe led to a significant decrease in the need for package delivery. Slumping sales for many businesses coupled with the closure of large numbers of companies placed UPS in a financial challenge to continue its operations efficiently and remain profitable. Since UPS depends on the successes of other businesses and their need to ship packages, a downturn for those businesses ultimately signals a downtown in business for UPS. According to Kathleen Kingsbury: "UPS has not escaped this recession unscathed. Revenue last year shrank by about $6 billion from 2008, forcing widespread belt-tightening. Just last month, despite the improved outlook, [Scott] Davis [UPS CEO] revealed a major restructuring that included 1,800 management and administrative layoffs. Two weeks later, on February 8, he announced plans to furlough at least 300 of the company's 2,800 pilots. These cuts come on the heels of a 4% reduction in UPS's 408,000-strong global workforce in 2009."[9]

UPS has positioned itself to withstand the recent economic downturn and continue to operate efficiently and at a profit. Although these times have tested UPS, it continues to pursue initiatives aimed at strengthening and sustaining its operations even when the economy threatens its business. Kurt Kuehn, chief financial officer for UPS, describes its ability to sustain operations during an economic downturn as: "It was really just a process of having every function and every business unit realize that they've got to find a way to manage their costs to whatever level the revenue is going to come in. Finance stepped up and took a strong leadership role and helped every business and every function begin to read and develop plans to stay afloat and be prudent during this big downturn."[10] In fact, in the midst of this economic downturn, UPS was still seeking opportunities to expand its operations, as evidenced in its 2009 joint venture with a Turkish partner to more effectively reach the markets in the Mediterranean republic.[11]

Staying Current with Changing Markets

UPS has witnessed many changes over its 100-plus year history. It is not immune to the changing nature of the economy in which it operates, and must attune itself to the demands of the market in order to remain a sustainable force in the distribution and logistics industry. One such change to its business operations deals with the issue of sustainability and the impact its operations have on the environment. As a shipper of documents and packages, there are obvious concerns about how its delivery methods are impacting the natural environment that UPS shares with its stakeholders. One such stakeholder that has concerns over the natural environment is its customers. To meet the needs of customers wanting to reduce the impact their shipments have on the natural environment, UPS has provided a carbon-neutral shipping option that allows the customer to offset the carbon emissions associated with their shipments for a small fee. To show its commitment to this program, " . . . UPS plans to match all offset purchases purchased in 2009–2010, up to $1 million."[12] Bob Stoffel, senior vice president in charge of UPS's sustainability program, states this need as: "Our customers wanted a convenient, cost-effective means to address climate change in a real and tangible way."[13]

UPS has also made strides to ensure sustainability in other facets of its business operations. Due to the immense size of UPS's operations, it is necessary to look at all areas in which it can improve its sustainability and limit the negative impact made on the natural environment. Some of the ways in which UPS has attempted to address these issues are: using alternative fuel vehicles, optimizing delivery routes, reducing the number of engines used in taxiing, as well as using a system to calculate the most efficient air routes.[14] UPS continues to seek ways to improve its sustainability efforts and respect the natural environment in which it operates. According to CEO Scott Davis: "UPS is the environmental leader in the U.S. package delivery industry because of our integrated network, most modern airfleet, and extensive use of the rails. Nonetheless, we have pledged to reduce our airline's carbon emissions by an additional 20 percent by 2020 for a cumulative total reduction of 42 percent since 1990. UPS received numerous recognitions in 2009 for our efforts to reduce our climate impact, for corporate support of public policy initiatives on climate change, and for comprehensiveness and transparency in reporting."[15] By focusing on its sustainability efforts, UPS is not only impacting its own operations but is also displaying a sincere interest in protecting the natural environment and providing its customers with an opportunity to do the same.

Discussion Questions

1. **Discussion** How does the intentional focus of UPS on sustaining the natural environment relate to goal setting for the entire UPS organization?

2. **Discussion** What do you feel is the motivation behind UPS and its attention to the natural environment in which it exists?

3. **Problem Solving** Why was UPS able to effectively manage its operations through such a significant downturn in the economy? Do you feel that other companies would fare as well as UPS? Why?

4. **Further Research** Research the expansion of UPS into a new country. What challenges did it face in establishing itself in this new market? How was UPS prepared to meet these challenges?

CASE 17

CANON
A Picture of Teamwork

Working as part of a team is a fundamental part of business around the world. The challenge for most organizations is in developing a culture in which these teams can function effectively to achieve the desired objectives. On the surface, this may seem like an easy task to complete as we find ourselves asking: Why wouldn't employees of the organization be interested in working as part of a team and achieving so much more than they could by merely working alone? However, the issue is way more complex and there are issues related to developing a solid plan for the utilization of teamwork that if not done correctly can become counterproductive. Organizations competing in today's business climate exert a considerable amount of time and resources to the development of effective teams. By doing so, they are able to capitalize on the combined efforts of the individuals that comprise the team and achieve greater results in the end.

A Long and Storied Past

The predecessor to Canon, Precision Optical Instruments Laboratory, was formed in 1933 with the goal of conducting research on quality cameras. The company changed its name to what we now know as Canon in 1947 while at the same time earning the privilege of having its cameras designated as priority exports from Japan. In 1949, Canon shares were listed on the Tokyo stock exchange for the first time as trading resumed in a postwar economy. By 1961, Canon had completed its main production facility in Toride, Japan. Then, in 1965, Canon, USA, Inc. was established. Business continued to grow, resulting in the setting up of Canon's first manufacturing plant outside of Japan in Taiwan in 1970. Canon also decided to enter the personal calculator market. In 1984, Canon entered into a joint agreement with China to begin production of copy machines in plants in Zhanjiang and Tianjin. In 1995, Canon achieved a first for any Japanese company when the company was certified under the BS7750 international environmental standard at its Ami and Ueno production facilities. By 2005, Canon had completed construction of its ground-breaking technology headquarters in Shimomaruko, Japan, and in the same year, agreed to collaborate with Microsoft on image processing technology.[1]

Today, Canon has evolved into a company of such magnitude and presence that it is difficult to find someone who has not had some kind of encounter with at least one of Canon's products. This global empire as of 2013 has amassed net sales of $35,537 million and a net income of $2,195 million, with 194,151 employees working in 257 consolidated subsidiaries.[2] Canon has been able to achieve a great deal of success while at the same time recognizing its roots and the foundation on which it was established. In fact, in September 2014, Canon was able to pay tribute to its past during the 80th anniversary celebration of its first 35mm focal-plane-shutter camera, the Kwanon, from which the current company name was derived.[3]

Supporting an Environment of Teamwork

While teamwork carries significant value to organizations, establishing effective teamwork presents an added responsibility. Organizations must be willing to not only recognize the need for teamwork but also be able to establish a foundation on which these teams can be created and nurtured to achieve the desired results for the organization. Canon's approach to establishing an environment in which teams

can not only be utilized but function effectively is rooted in its belief in the *San-ji* (Three Selfs) Spirit:

> The Three Selfs, the foundation of the company's guiding principles that has been passed down since Canon was founded, are self-motivation, self-management and self-awareness. For Canon, which strives to be a truly excellent global corporation while maintaining the legacy of its corporate DNA, the Three Selfs continue to serve as the company's most important guiding principles. The Three Selfs are:

- **Self-motivation** – Take the initiative and be proactive in all things.
- **Self-management** – Conduct oneself with responsibility and accountability.
- **Self-awareness** – Understand one's situation and role in all situations.[4]

This basic philosophy, which is approached from the perspective of the self, creates a foundation for Canon in which teams can be developed and nurtured in order to achieve their goals. Teams, after all, are comprised of individuals having varied backgrounds and experiences that will create a synergistic effect for the team as a whole. By placing such importance on the individuals employed by Canon, the company is essentially equipping each employee to utilize his skills and abilities within the framework of a team to yield positive results for the organization.

The use of teamwork is further encouraged across all areas of the organization through Canon's *Kyosei* philosophy:

> Canon's corporate philosophy is *kyosei*. It conveys our dedication to seeing all people, regardless of culture, customs, language or race, harmoniously living and working together in happiness into the future. Unfortunately, current factors related to economies, resources and the environment make realizing *kyosei* difficult. Canon strives to eliminate these factors through corporate activities rooted in *kyosei*. Truly global companies must foster good relations with customers and communities, as well as with governments, regions and the environment as part of their fulfillment of social responsibilities. For this reason, Canon's goal is to contribute to global prosperity and the well-being of mankind as we continue our efforts to bring the world closer to achieving *kyosei*.[5]

From its commitment to *Kyosei* and the *San-ji* (Three Selfs) Spirit, it is apparent that Canon has a genuine and vested interest in the development and use of teams in carrying out its daily operations. It is this framework that empowers Canon to put into place activities in which teams can be utilized successfully.

Teamwork in Practice

Establishing the foundation for fully functioning teams is a key component for effectively reaping the rewards from teamwork. This foundation needs to have some practical applications in order to fully gain all of the benefits associated with the use of teams. How companies choose to apply the idea of teamwork is just as varied as the organizations themselves. For Canon, an example of the application of teamwork is seen in the Canon Global Assignment Policy (C-GAP):

> This program fosters active international personnel exchanges, not only to other countries from Japan, but also from other countries to Japan, or from the United States to Asia, for example. The goal is to promote global business cooperation and the development of human resources capable of functioning at the global level.
>
> C-GAP is a global personnel policy shared by our Group companies, and personnel assignment regulations in each respective region are established based upon it. Combining these regulations allows us to share basic philosophies and structures, while providing for flexibility in dealing with the special characteristics of each region, such as laws and culture.[6]

Allowing Canon's employees to engage in this policy provides an opportunity to create a diverse set of team members possessing a variety of skills and abilities. By bringing together different individuals into the fabric of teams, Canon is able to pool together their skills and abilities to create cross-functional teams that benefit greatly from the diversity of individual perspectives.

Discussion Questions

1. **Discussion** What are your suggestions for Canon in dealing with the issue of Social Loafing that often accompanies the use of teams?
2. **Discussion** How is the Canon Global Assignment Policy (C-GAP) a good example of Cross-Functional Teams as described in the material from this Chapter 17?
3. **Problem Solving** Describe the pros and cons of Virtual Teams. Do you feel that Virtual Teams would be a good fit for a company like Canon? Explain.
4. **Further Research** Research the variety of activities organizations use to engage in team building. How do you feel these activities will foster a culture of teamwork? Which activities do you feel are more successful for team building and why?

CASE 18

TWITTER
Rewriting (or Killing) Communication

Twitter's 140-character text-based messages, or "Twitter-speak," permeate everyday life. But questions about its influence are being asked—by parents, relationship partners, teachers, and employers. Is Twitter reinventing social communication or just abbreviating it? Do tweets create meaningful conversations or dumb down our abilities to write and communicate effectively with one another?

Twitter was conceived on a playground slide during a burrito-fueled brainstorming session by employees of podcasting company Odeo. Co-founder Jack Dorsey, now Twitter's executive chairman, suggested the idea of using short, SMS-like messages to connect with a small group. "[W]e came across the word *twitter*, and it was just perfect," Dorsey says. "The definition was 'a short burst of inconsequential information' and 'chirps from birds.' And that's exactly what the product was."[1]

Dorsey, also CEO and founder of Square, a mobile payments company, developed a working prototype based on an instant messaging platform. It was first used internally by Odeo employees, but was refined and released to the public. Within three months and sensing the magnitude of the invention, Dorsey and other members of Odeo, including product strategist Evan Williams and creative director Biz Stone, acquired Odeo and picked up Twitter.com in the process.

A Channel with Capacity

Twitter has become a vehicle for communicating carefully crafted messages of self-promotion and branding by major companies, nonprofits, activist groups, politicians, actors, athletes, and musicians. Top Twitter topics or "trends" driving tweets include sports, politics, and music as well as natural disasters, human conflicts, and crises. According to an Internet study by Pew Research, Twitter usage is pervasive among technology early adopters and widespread among a range of demographic groups.[2]

Messages With(out) Meanings

Twitter's 140-character limit keeps messages terse and to the point. However, there's no guarantee they'll be pertinent or that each message will be meaningful. Market research firm Pear Analytics analyzed 2,000 U.S. and British tweets sent during daytime hours over two weeks and concluded that 40% of them represented "pointless babble."[3] While avid Twitter users may agree that not all tweets are gems, the service has found a place in digital culture. Social network researcher Danah Boyd has criticized Pear Analytics' results, pointing out that pointless babble could be better characterized as *social grooming*, where tweeters "want to know what the people around them are thinking and doing and feeling."[4]

Tweets Travel Faster

Twitter's low overhead translates into instantaneous broadcast communication. And for some users, that's part of the appeal. "Twitter lets me hear from a lot of people in a very short period of time," says tech evangelist Robert Scoble.[5] In addition, Twitter has become a de facto emergency broadcast network for breaking news. It is a means to transmit up-to-date information during disasters and other unfolding situations.[6] Real-time news, video clips, and images rapidly spread through the Twitterverse, often providing faster information than formal news media.[7]

More managers are using Twitter and it's becoming a linchpin for teams, whose leaders and members use it as a fast-channel way to send announcements about upcoming events, post rapid-response items, and share links that bear on what's happening within the organization. Twitter is also being used in educational settings as a way to promote student interactions with faculty and administration and with one another.

Impulse Leads to Apology

Twitter's quick and short messages are shortening the stages of communication—quick thoughts warrant a tweet. They're increasing the frequency of communication—more time efficient than a direct message or an e-mail. But, it's not uncommon for well-known tweeters to apologize and explain a tweet or two after it was misinterpreted. The immediacy of tweeting can make it impulsive communication—tweets are oh so easy to send out—and regret later!

Discussion Questions

1. **Discussion** What are the advantages and disadvantages of communicating via Twitter? Can a 140-character tweet really be effective? What guidelines would you recommend for maximizing the effectiveness of a tweet?

2. **Discussion** Choose a national brand or entertainment personality and discuss how the use of Twitter has helped to create a following and desired brand image. How about a college course? How could an instructor use Twitter to improve the classroom or online learning experience? Is Twitter more appropriate for the national brand and entertainment personality than for the college instructor? Why or why not?

3. **Problem Solving** You've been given a first assignment as the new summer intern in the office of a corporate CEO. The task is to analyze Twitter and make a presentation to the CEO and her executive team recommending whether or not it should be used for corporate purposes. What points will you make in the presentation to summarize its potential uses, possible downsides, and overall strategic value to the firm?

4. **Further Research** Research current developments with Twitter. What is presently happening with the firm? What are the financial and business analysts saying? Is Twitter still innovating, and if so, what new directions are evident? Is Twitter on a continued path of success, or is its 140-character appeal starting to fade? Who are Twitter's major competitors? Are they real threats, or not? Is the tweet here to stay, or will it soon be displaced by the next best leap forward in communication technology?

CASE ENDNOTES

Case 1: McDonald's

[1] Getting to Know US, http://www.aboutmcdonalds.com/mcd/our_company.html.

[2] McDonald's History, http://www.aboutmcdonalds.com/mcd/our_company/mcd_history.html.

[3] Tony Royle, "The Union Recognition Dispute at McDonald's Moscow Food-Processing Factory," *Industrial Relations Journal*, vol. 36, issue 4 (July 2005), pp. 318–332.

[4] McDonald's History, http://www.aboutmcdonalds.com/mcd/our_company/mcd_history.html.

[5] McDonald's Corporate Governance, http://www.aboutmcdonalds.com/mcd/investors/corporate_governance.html

[6] Code of Conduct for the Board of Directors, http://www.aboutmcdonalds.com/mcd/investors/corporate_governance/director_code_of_conduct.html.

[7] Standards of Business Conduct for Employees, http://www.aboutmcdonalds.com/mcd/investors/corporate_governance/standards_of_business_conduct.html.

[8] Giana M. Eckhardt and Michael J. Houston, "Cultural Paradoxes Reflected in Brand Meaning: McDonald's in Shanghai, China," *Journal of International Marketing*, vol. 10, issue 2 (Summer 2002), pp. 68–82.

[9] Studying McDonald's Abroad: Overseas branches merge regional preferences, corporate directives," *Nation's Restaurant News* (4 November 2005), pp. 52–125.

[10] McDonald's 2009 Annual Report.

Case 2: Zara International

[1] "Inditex: Who We Are: Concepts: Zara," Inditex website, accessed February 21, 2012, http://www.inditex.com/.

[2] Cecilie Rohwedder, "Zara Grows as Retail Rivals Struggle," *Wall Street Journal* (March 26, 2012).

[3] "Zara, a Spanish Success Story," CNN, June 15, 2001.

[4] Inditex Press Dossier, Inditex website, accessed March 14, 2010, http://www.inditex.com/.

[5] Cecilie Rohwedder and Keith Johnson, "Pace-setting Zara Seeks More Speed to Fight Its Rising Cheap-Chic Rivals," *Wall Street Journal* (February 20, 2008).

[6] "The Future of Fast Fashion," *The Economist* (June 16, 2005), accessed April 4, 2008, http://economist.com.

[7] Rachel Tiplady, "Zara: Taking the Lead in Fast-Fashion," *BusinessWeek* (April 4, 2006).

[8] Rohwedder and Johnson, op. cit.

[9] Ibid.

[10] "Zara Grows as Retail Rivals Struggle," *Wall Street Journal* (March 26, 2009).

[11] Inditex Press Dossier, op. cit.

[12] Ibid.

[13] Ibid.

[14] "Shining Examples," *The Economist* (June 17, 2006).

[15] "The Future of Fast-Fashion," op. cit.

[16] Inditex Press Dossier, op. cit.

[17] "Zara Launches Online Shopping in the USA," *College Fashion*, accessed February 23, 1012, http://www.collegefashion.net.

[18] "Zara Grows as Retail Rivals Struggle," *Wall Street Journal* (March 26, 2009).

[19] Susan Berfield and Manuel Baigorri, "Zara's Fast Fashion Edge," *Bloomberg BusinessWeek* (November 14, 2013), accessed May 19, 2014, http://businessweek.com.

Case 3: Delta

[1] Delta Air Lines, Inc., *Stats & Facts*. http://news.delta.com/index.php?s=18&cat=47

[2] Yvette Shields, "Judge OKs Delta Reorganization; Airline Set to Shed Bankrupt Status Monday," *The Bond Buyer*, vol. 360, issue 32616 (April 26, 2007), p. 30.

[3] "Delta Releases 2011 Corporate Responsibility Report," Delta Air Lines news release, May 25, 2012, PRNewswire.

[4] "Delta Air Lines (NYSE: DAL) today reported strong financial and operating performance for April 2012," Delta Air Lines news release, May 2, 2012, PRNewswire.

[5] "Delta Tops 2011 FORTUNE World's Most Admired Companies Airline Industry List," Delta Air Lines news release, March 3, 2011, PRNewswire.

[6] Delta Airlines 10-K filing, 2011.

Case 4: Yahoo!

[1] Yahoo! Inc., company information, http://pressroom.yahoo.net/pr/ycorp/overview.aspx

[2] Yahoo! 10-K, 2011.

[3] Eric Savits, "Yahoo Says Talks Continue With Alibaba; But Not Yahoo Japan," *Forbes.com*, April 17, 2012.

[4] Eric Savits, "Yahoo: Do They Have A Plan? Why One Analyst Is Skeptical," *Forbes.com*, April 18, 2012, p. 66.

[5] Felix Gillette, "Can Yahoo! Hang On in The Ad Market?" *Bloomberg Businessweek*, issue 4279 (May 14, 2012), pp. 40–42.

[6] Verne G. Kopytoff and Claire Cain Miller "Yahoo Board Fires Chief Executive," *NYTimes.com*, September 6, 2011.

[7] Ki Mae Heussner, "Yahoo's Fuchs: We're No. 1!" Adweek, vol. 53, issue 4 (Jan 30, 2012), p. 15.

[8] Julianne Pepitone, "Yahoo Confirms CEO is Out After Resume Scandal," CNNMoneyTech, May 14, 2012.

Case 5: Hewlett Packard

[1] Hewlett-Packard Development Company, HP History, http://www8.hp.com/us/en/hp-information/about-hp/history/history.html

[2] Hewlett-Packard Development Company, HP Timeline, http://www8.hp.com/us/en/hp-information/about-hp/history/hp-timeline/hp-timeline.html

[3] http://www.forbes.com/companies/hewlett-packard/

[4] Vinnie Jauhari, "Employee and Customer Management Processes for Profitability—The Case of Hewlett-Packard India," *Journal of Services Research*, vol. 1, issue 1 (April–September 2001), p. 149.

[5] Thomas Smith, "Why Hewlett-Packard Stock Looks Like Good Value," *BusinessWeek Online* (October 8, 2008), p.8.

[6] Hewlett-Packard, *T+D*, vol. 60, issue 10 (October 2006), p. 61.

[7] Rio Rivas and David H. Gobeli, "Accelerating Innovation at Hewlett-Packard," *Research Technology Management*, vol. 48, issue 1 (Jan/Feb 2005), pp. 32–39.

[8] Hewlett-Packard Development Company, *2011 Hewlett-Packard Annual Report*.

Case 6: Lenovo

[1] Lenovo company history, http://www.lenovo.com/lenovo/us/en/company-history.shtml.

[2] Lenovo company description, http://www.lenovo.com/lenovo/us/en/our-company.shtml.

[3] "Innovation: A Core Value," http://www.lenovo.com/lenovo/us/en/our-company.shtml.

[4] Lenovo corporate culture, http://www.lenovo.com/lenovo/us/en/our-culture.shtml.

[5] "Lenovo Statement on China Smartphone Rankings," press release, 10 August 2014.

[6] Lenovo Annual Report 2013/14.

Case 7: Amazon

[1] "2012 Earnings: Third Quarter Amazon.com," *New York Times* (August 28, 2012), nytimes.com (accessed June 9, 2012). (accessed 9/6/12).

[2] Thomas Ricker, "Amazon Adds Audible to Its Digital Empire," engadget.com (accessed May 28, 2008).

[3] Claire Cain Miller, "E-Books Top Hardcovers at Amazon," *New York Times* (July 19, 2010), nytimes.com (accessed February 29, 2012).

[4] Zach Epstein, "Amazon To Sell 6 Million Kindle Fire Tablets, 8 Million eReaders in Q4," *Boy Genius Report* (December 13, 2011), bgr.com (accessed February 29, 2012).

[5] "Amazon Prime Members Now Get Unlimited, Commercial-free, Instant Streaming of More Than 5,000 Movies and TV Shows at No Additional Cost," *Amazon Media Room*, posted February 22, 2011, phx.corporateir.net (accessed February 29, 2012).

[6] Jason Boog, "Kindle Owners' Lending Library Unveiled," *Galleycat*, mediabistro.com (accessed February 29, 2012).

[7] David Meerman Scott, "The Flip Side of Free," *eContent*, vol. 28, no. 10 (October 2005).

[8] Jeffrey Ressner, "10 Questions for Jeff Bezos," *Time*, vol. 166, issue 5 (August 1, 2005).

[9] "Amazon CEO Takes Long View." *USA Today*, July 6, 2005.

Case 8: Avago

[1] Avago company overview, August 2014.

[2] Avago company history, http://www.avagotech.com/pages/corporate/company_history/.

[3] Corporate profile, http://investors.avagotech.com/phoenix.zhtml?c=203541&p=irol-IRHome.

[4] 2013 Securities and Exchange Commission 10-K filing

[5] 2013 Securities and Exchange Commission 10-K filing

[6] "Avago Technologies Completes Acquisition of LSI Corporation," press release, May 6, 2014.

[7] "Seagate to Acquire LSI'S Flash Business from Avago," press release, May 29, 2014.

[8] "Avago Agrees to Sell LSI's Axxia Networking Business and Related Assets to Intel for $650 Million," press release, August 13, 2014.

Case 9: British Petroleum

[1] BP History (1901–1908: First oil), http://www.bp.com/sectiongenericarticle.do?categoryId=9014440&contentId=7027520.

[2] BP History (1909–1924: Early history), http://www.bp.com/sectiongenericarticle.do?categoryId=9014441&contentId=7027521.

[3] BP History (1925–1945: Through world war two), http://www.bp.com/sectiongenericarticle.do?categoryId=9014442&contentId=7027522.

[4] BP History (1946–1970: Post war), http://www.bp.com/sectiongenericarticle.do?categoryId=9014443&contentId=7027523.

[5] BP History (1971–1999: Late century), http://www.bp.com/sectiongenericarticle.do?categoryId=9014444&contentId=7027525.

[6] BP History (2000 & Beyond: New millennium), http://www.bp.com/sectiongenericarticle.do?categoryId=9014445&contentId=7027526.

[7] The environment: A Growing Concern, http://www.bp.com/sectiongenericarticle.do?categoryId=9014510&contentId=7027667.

[8] BP Sustainability Review, 2009.

[9] BP Strategy Presentation, March 2, 2010.

[10] David Biello, "Lasting Menace," *Scientific American*, vol. 303, issue 1 (July 2010), pp. 16–18.

[11] Daniel Gross, "Death on Our Shores," *Newsweek*, vol. 155/156, issue 26/1 (June 28, 2010), pp. 36–39.

[12] Brian Morrissey, "Beleaguered BP Is Getting Aggressive Via Social Media," *Brandweek*, vol. 51, issue 25 (June 21, 2010), p. 27.

[13] Andrew McCormick, "BP funds digital drive to promote oil-spill effort," *Marketing* (June 16, 2010), p. 5.

Case 10: Sony Corporation

[1] Sony Corporation info, http://www.sony.net/SonyInfo/CorporateInfo/.

[2] Sony Corporation: Corporate History, http://www.sony.net/SonyInfo/CorporateInfo/History/history.html#list6.

[3] Moon Ihlwan and Mariko Yasu, "Sony and Samsung's Strategic Split," *BusinessWeek* issue 4136 (January 18, 2010).

[4] "Sony and Google Establish Strategic Alliance to Deliver Compelling New Cloud-based Products and Services with the Android Platform," Sony Corporation press release, May 20, 2010.

[5] Employee-Management Communications, http://www.sony.net/SonyInfo/csr/employees/working/index.html.

[6] Employee Opinion Surveys, http://www.sony.net/SonyInfo/csr/employees/working/index.html.

[7] Sony Research and Development Strategies, http://www.sony.net/SonyInfo/IR/info/faq/qfhh7c000000ep8s-att/R_D.pdf.

[8] Alex Brownsell, "Sony plots retail experience focus," *Marketing* (February 18, 2009), p. 3.

[9] Fiona Ramsay, "Sony to roll out global 'make-believe' activity," *Marketing* (November 4, 2009), p. 3.

[10] Sony Corporate Social Responsibility Report 2009, http://www.sony.net/SonyInfo/csr/management/message/index.html.

[11] Sony Corporation 2010 Annual Report.

Case 11: Toyota

[1] http://www.toyota-global.com/company/profile/overview/.

[2] http://www.toyota-global.com/company/toyota_traditions/company/apr_2012.html.

[3] "Toyota Unveils Global Vision: Rewarded with a smile by exceeding your expectations", Toyota City, Japan, March 9, 2011.

[4] Toyota President's message, July 2013, http://www.toyota-global.com/investors/ir_library/annual/pdf/2013/p04.pdf.

Case 12: Apple Inc.

[1] Apple Inc. home page, http://www.apple.com.

[2] Ibid.

[3] Pixar home page, http://www.pixar.com.

[4] Peter Burrows, "The Improbable Heroes of Toontown," *BusinessWeek* (May 26, 2008), pp. 81–82.

[5] http://www.businessinsider.com/chart-of-the-day-revenue-vsoperating-profit-share-of-top-pc-vendors-2010-3.

[6] apple20.blogs.fortune.cnn.com/2008/05/19/report-applesmarket-share-of-pcs-over-1000-hits-66/.

[7] Apple 10-Q, Quarterly filing for period ended March 27, 2010.

[8] Apple Supplier Code of Conduct, p. 1.

[9] Burrows, op. cit.

[10] Brad Stone, "Apple's Chief Takes a Medical Leave."

[11] http://www.apple.com/pr/library/2010/04/05ipad.html.

[12] http://www.apple.com/pr/library/2010/01/27ipad.html.

[13] Ben Worthen and Yukari Iwatani Kane, "New iPad Puts Focus On Apple's Flash Feud: New iPad Puts Focus On Apple's Flash Feud," *The Wall Street Journal* (February 10, 2010).

Case 13: Coca-Cola

[1] Coca-Cola History, http://heritage.coca-cola.com/.

[2] Mission, Vision & Values, http://www.thecoca-colacompany.com/ourcompany/mission_vision_values.html.

[3] Working as a Global Team, http://www.thecoca-colacompany.com/ourcompany/meet_our_people.html.

[4] Dean Foust, "Where Headhunters Fear to Tread," *BusinessWeek*, issue 4146 (September 14, 2009), pp. 42–46.

[5] Mission, Vision & Values, http://www.thecoca-colacompany.com/ourcompany/mission_vision_values.html.

[6] "Caught by the Fizz," *People Management*, vol. 14, issue 16 (August 7, 2008), pp. 24–26.

[7] Adrienne Fox, "Refreshing a Beverage Company's Culture," *HRMagazine*, vol. 52, issue 11 (November 2007), pp. 58–60.

[8] Coca-Cola Company Fact Sheet, www.thecoca-colacompany.com.

[9] "Tips from the Top," *Training and Development*, March 2007.

[10] Coca-Cola 2009 Annual Review.

Case 14: Samsung

[1] Samsung Electronics Co., Ltd., Half Year Report, January 1, 2014–June 30, 2014.

[2] http://www.samsung.com/us/aboutsamsung/samsung_group/history/.

[3] Samsung Profile 2013.

[4] The Samsung Philosophy, http://www.samsung.com/us/aboutsamsung/samsung_group/values_and_philosophy/.

[5] Samsung values, http://www.samsung.com/us/aboutsamsung/samsung_group/values_and_philosophy/.

[6] http://www.samsung.com/us/aboutsamsung/sustainability/people/.

[7] http://www.samsung.com/us/aboutsamsung/careers/whysamsung/Careers_WhySAMSUNG.html.

[8] http://www.samsung.com/us/aboutsamsung/samsung_electronics/management/.

Case 15: Intel

[1] *Intel Company*, http://www.intel.com/content/www/us/en/company-overview/company-facts.html.

[2] *Intel Timeline: A History of Innovation*, http://www.intelcom/content/www/us/en/history/historic-timeline.html.

[3] L. K. Stepp, "Building an Internal Organization Design Capability at Intel," *People & Strategy*, vol. 24, issue 4 (2011), pp. 60–63.

[4] Rich Karlgaard, "Intel Inside: CEO Otellini on the Future," *Forbes*, vol. 187, issue 4 (March 14, 2011).

[5] Michal Lev-Ram, "Intel's (Latest) Mobile Comeback," *Fortune*, vol. 165, issue 3 (February 27, 2012).

[6] Intel Corporation. 2011 Annual Report.

Case 16: United Parcel Service

[1] About UPS, http://www.ups.com/content/us/en/about/index.html?WT.svl=Footer

[2] UPS Time Capsule (1907–1929), http://www.ups.com/content/us/en/about/history/1929.html?WT.svl=SubNav

[3] UPS Time Capsule (1930–1980), http://www.ups.com/content/us/en/about/history/1980.html?WT.svl=SubNav

[4] UPS Time Capsule (1981–1990), http://www.ups.com/content/us/en/about/history/1990.html?WT.svl=SubNav

[5] UPS Time Capsule (1991–1999), http://www.ups.com/content/us/en/about/history/1999.html?WT.svl=SubNav

[6] UPS Time Capsule (2000–2007), http://www.ups.com/content/us/en/about/history/2007.html?WT.svl=SubNav

[7] About UPS, http://www.ups.com/content/us/en/about/index.html?WT.svl=Footer

[8] Worldwide Facts, http://www.ups.com/content/us/en/about/facts/worldwide.html

[9] Kathleen Kingsbury, "Road to Recovery," *Time*, vol. 175, issue 9 (March 8, 2010), pp. G14–16.

[10] Susan Kelly, "Delivering the Goods in Bad Times," *Treasury & Risk* (May 2010), pp. 24–26.

[11] Avram Davis, "UPS Venture Will Expand Foothold," *Mergers & Acquisitions Report*, vol. 22, issue 27 (July 6, 2009), p. 1.

[12] "Spend Some Green to Go Green," *Industry Week/IW*, vol. 258, issue 12 (Dec 2009), p. 47.

[13] UPS Press Release, Carbon Neutral Shipping Extended Internationally: http://www.ups.com/pressroom/us/press_releases/press_release/Press+Releases/Current+Press+Releases/ci.Carbon+Neutral+Shipping+Extended+Internationally.syndication

[14] Roger Morton, "It's What's On Top That Counts," *Material Handling Management*, vol. 64, issue 7, pp. 26–28.

[15] UPS 2009 Annual Report.

Case 17: Canon

[1] http://www.canon.com/corporate/information/history/01.html.

[2] Canon by the Numbers, http://www.canon.com/corporate/pdf/Canon_Story_2014-2015_e.pdf.

[3] "Canon celebrates 80th anniversary of Kwanon, Company's first camera," press release, September 2, 2014.

[4] The *San-ji* (Three Selfs) Spirit, http://www.canon.com/corporate/vision/strategies.html.

[5] Corporate philosophy, http://www.canon.com/corporate/vision/philosophy.html.

[6] Canon Sustainability Report 2014, p. 81.

Case 18: Twitter

[1] Lauren Duggan, "Twitter to Surpass 500 Million Registered Users," *Media Bistro*, mediabistro.com (accessed January 15, 2013).

[2] Pew Research, "The Demographics of Twitter Users," mindjumpers.com (accessed 1/15/13); and Shea Bennet, "22% of Black Internet Users Are Active on Twitter (Compared to 16% of White)," mediabistro.com (accessed March 4, 2014).

[3] Ryan Kelly, "Twitter Study Reveals Interesting Results About Usage—40% Is Pointless Babble," pearanalytics.com (accessed February 26, 2014).

[4] Danah Boyd, "Twitter: 'Pointless Babble' or Peripheral Awareness + Social Grooming?" zephoria.org (accessed February 26, 2014).

[5] Alex Santoso, "10 Quickie Quotes about Twitter," netorama.com (accessed February 26, 2014).

[6] Jochan Embley, "Twitter Alerts: Service to Help During Emergencies, Natural Disasters Comes to the UK," independent.co.uk (accessed March 4, 2014).

[7] Jolie O'Dell, "How Egyptians Used Twitter During the January Crisis," mashable.com (accessed March 4, 2014).

SELF-TEST ANSWERS

Chapter 1

1. d **2.** c **3.** a **4.** b **5.** a **6.** a **7.** c **8.** a **9.** b **10.** b **11.** c
12. a **13.** b **14.** c **15.** c

16. Managers must value people and respect subordinates as mature, responsible, adult human beings. This is part of their ethical and social responsibility as persons to whom others report at work. The work setting should be organized and managed to respect the rights of people and their human dignity. Included among the expectations for ethical behavior would be actions to protect individual privacy, provide freedom from sexual harassment, and offer safe and healthy job conditions. Failure to do so is socially irresponsible. It may also cause productivity losses due to dissatisfaction and poor work commitments.

17. The manager is held accountable by her boss for performance results of her work unit. The manager must answer to her boss for unit performance. By the same token, the manager's subordinates must answer to her for their individual performance. They are accountable to her.

18. If the glass ceiling effect were to operate in a given situation, it would act as a hidden barrier to advancement beyond a certain level. Managers controlling promotions and advancement opportunities in the firm would not give them to African American candidates, regardless of their capabilities. Although the newly hired graduates might advance for a time, sooner or later their upward progress in the firm would be halted by this invisible barrier. Although unstated and perhaps even unrecognized as such by top management, this would be outright discrimination against the African Americans in this firm.

19. Globalization means that the countries and peoples of the world are increasingly interconnected and that business firms increasingly cross national boundaries in acquiring resources, getting work accomplished, and selling their products. This internationalization of work will affect most everyone in the new economy. People will be working with others from different countries, working in other countries, and certainly buying and using products and services produced in whole or in part in other countries. As countries become more interdependent economically, products are sold and resources purchased around the world, and business strategies increasingly target markets in more than one country.

20. One approach to this question is through the framework of essential management skills offered by Katz. At the first level of management, technical skills are important, and I would feel capable in this respect. However, I would expect to learn and refine these skills through my work experiences.

Human skills, the ability to work well with other people, will also be very important. Given the diversity anticipated for this team, I will need good human skills. Included here would be my emotional intelligence, or the ability to understand my emotions and those of others when I am interacting with them. I will also have a leadership responsibility to help others on the team develop and utilize these skills so that the team itself can function effectively.

Finally, I would expect opportunities to develop my conceptual or analytical skills in anticipation of higher-level appointments. In terms of personal development, I should recognize that the conceptual skills will increase in importance relative to the technical skills as I move upward in management responsibility. The fact that the members of the team will be diverse, with some of different demographic and cultural backgrounds from my own, will only increase the importance of my abilities in the human skills area.

It will be a challenge to embrace and value differences to create the best work experience for everyone and to fully value everyone's potential contributions to the audits we will be doing. Conceptually I will need to understand the differences and try to utilize them to solve problems faced by the team, but in human relationships I will need to excel at keeping the team spirit alive and keeping everyone committed to working well together over the life of our projects.

Chapter 2

1. c **2.** b **3.** d **4.** a **5.** a **6.** b **7.** a **8.** c **9.** a **10.** a **11.** c **12.** a **13.** d **14.** c **15.** b

16. Theory Y assumes that people are capable of taking responsibility and exercising self-direction and control in their work. The notion of self-fulfilling prophecies is that managers who hold these assumptions will act in ways that encourage workers to display these characteristics, thus confirming and reinforcing the original assumptions. The emphasis on greater participation and involvement in the modern workplace is an example of Theory Y assumptions in practice. Presumably, by valuing participation and involvement, managers will create self-fulfilling prophecies in which workers behave this way in response to being treated with respect. The result is a positive setting where everyone gains.

17. According to the deficit principle, a satisfied need is not a motivator of behavior. The social need will only motivate if it is not present, or in deficit. According to the progression principle, people move step-by-step up Maslow's hierarchy as they strive to satisfy needs. For example, once the social need is satisfied, the esteem need will be activated.

18. Contingency thinking takes an "if–then" approach to situations. It seeks to modify or adapt management approaches to fit the needs of each situation. An example would be to give more customer contact responsibility to workers who want to satisfy social needs at work, while giving more supervisory responsibilities to those who want to satisfy their esteem or ego needs.

19. The external environment is the source of the resources an organization needs to operate. In order to continue to obtain these resources, the organization must be successful in selling its goods and services to customers. If customer feedback is negative, the organization must make adjustments or risk losing the support needed to obtain important resources.

20. A bureaucracy operates with a strict hierarchy of authority, promotion based on competency and performance, formal rules and procedures, and written documentation. Enrique can do all of these things in his store, since the situation is probably quite stable and most work requirements are routine and predictable. However, bureaucracies are quite rigid and may deny employees the opportunity to make decisions on their own. Enrique must be careful to meet the needs of the workers and not to make the mistake—identified by Argyris—of failing to treat them as mature adults. While remaining well organized, the store manager should still be able to help workers meet higher-order esteem and self-fulfillment needs, as well as assume responsibility consistent with McGregor's Theory Y assumptions.

Chapter 3

1. b **2.** a **3.** d **4.** c **5.** c **6.** d **7.** b **8.** a **9.** b **10.** d **11.** c **12.** d **13.** b **14.** d **15.** c

16. The individualism view is that ethical behavior is that which best serves long-term interests. The justice view is that ethical behavior is fair and equitable in its treatment of people.

17. The rationalizations are believing that: (1) The behavior is not really illegal, (2) the behavior is really in everyone's best interests, (3) no one will find out, and (4) the organization will protect you.

18. The socioeconomic view of corporate social responsibility argues that investing in socially responsible behavior is in a firm's long-run best interest. It should be good for profits, it creates a positive public image, it helps avoid government regulation, it meets public expectations, and it is an ethical obligation. In contrast, the classical view of social responsibility is that the only obligation of the firm is to produce profits. This is what should drive executive decision making, and direct expenditures to pursue socially responsible activities are wasteful. The argument is that by pursuing profits the firm will do what society wants most in the long run because, if it doesn't, profits will suffer as customers abandon the firm and its products. The market, in other words, is the arbiter of what society wants.

19. Management scholar Archie Carroll describes the immoral, amoral, and moral manager this way: An immoral manager does bad things on purpose, choosing to behave unethically. The amoral manager does bad things sometimes, but this is not intentional or calculated; it happens because the amoral manager just doesn't incorporate ethics into his or her analysis of the situation. The moral manager, by contrast, always includes ethics as a criterion for evaluating his or her approach to decisions and situations. This manager strives to act ethically and considers ethical behavior a personal goal.

20. The manager could make a decision based on any one of the strategies. As an obstructionist, the manager may assume that Bangladesh needs the business and that it is a local matter as to who will be employed to make the gloves. As a defensive strategy, the manager may decide to require the supplier to meet the minimum employment requirements under Bangladeshi law. Both of these approaches represent cultural relativism. As an accommodation strategy, the manager may require that the supplier go beyond local laws and meet standards set by equivalent laws in the United States. A proactive strategy would involve the manager in trying to set an example by operating in Bangladesh only with suppliers who not only meet local standards, but also actively support the education of children in the communities in which they operate. These latter two approaches would be examples of universalism.

Chapter 4

1. a **2.** b **3.** b **4.** c **5.** b **6.** d **7.** a **8.** b **9.** c **10.** d **11.** d **12.** a **13.** c **14.** d **15.** b

16. When it comes to organizational stakeholders, the list should always begin with customers and suppliers to establish the output/input players in the value chain. Employees should be included as well as shareholders/investors to identify the interests of the "producers" and the "owners." Given the significance of sustainability, it is important to include society at large and future generations in the stakeholder map; it is also important to include the local communities in which the organization operates. Beyond these basic map components, the stakeholders for any given organization will include a broad mix of people, groups, and organizations from regulators to activist organizations to government agencies, and more.

17. To make "sustainability" part of any goal statement or objective for an organization, the basic definition should reflect the concept of sustainable development. That is, the organization should act in ways that while making use of the environment to produce things of value today the potential for that environment to meet the needs of future generations is also being protected and ideally being enhanced.

18. Product innovations affect what goods and services an organization offers to its customers. Process innovations affect how the organization goes about its daily work in producing goods and services. Business model innovations affect the way the organization makes money and adds value to society.

19. Reverse innovation means finding innovations in alternative settings such as emerging markets and moving them into uses in established markets. An example would be portable and low-cost medical diagnostic equipment developed in markets like India and China and then brought to the United States and sold there.

20. First of all it sounds like a good idea to have a Chief Sustainability Officer, or CSO, in order to focus attention on sustainability goals and also bring some point of accountability at the senior executive level for their accomplishment. In terms of the job description, I would argue that things like this would need to be reflected. First, there should be some acknowledgment of the "triple bottom line" of economic, social, and environmental performance. Second, there should be a clear focus on sustainable development in respect to moving the organization forward in ways that while making use of the environment and its resources, the capacity of the environment to nurture and serve future generations is also being protected. This sets the foundation for further priorities or objectives to be set in the areas of pushing for green management practices that support sustainability in all aspects of an organization's operations. And finally, there should be a responsibility to serve as the "champion" for sustainable innovations that advance the capability of the organization to be sustainable by green products, green processes, and even green business models.

Chapter 5

1. c **2.** c **3.** b **4.** d **5.** a **6.** a **7.** d **8.** c **9.** a **10.** d **11.** d **12.** a **13.** c **14.** c **15.** c

16. The relationship between a global corporation and a host country should be mutually beneficial. Sometimes, however, host countries complain that MNCs take unfair advantage of them and do not include them in the benefits of their international operations. The complaints against MNCs include taking excessive profits out of the host country, hiring the best local labor, not respecting local laws and customs, and dominating the local economy. Engaging in corrupt practices is another important concern.

17. The power-distance dimension of national culture reflects the degree to which members of a society accept status and authority inequalities. Since organizations are hierarchies with power varying from top to bottom, the way power differences are viewed from one setting to the next is an important management issue. Relations between managers and subordinates, or team leaders and team members, will be very different in high-power-distance cultures than in low-power-distance ones. The significance of these differences is most evident in international operations, when a manager from a high-power-distance culture has to perform in a low-power-distance one, or vice versa. In both cases, the cultural differences can cause problems as the manager deals with local workers.

18. A tight culture is one in which clear norms exist for social behavior and members know that deviance from these norms will not be tolerated. There are both norms and a high degree of conformity to those norms. In a loose culture the norms and social expectations are often general and ambiguous. Individuals tend to behave with independence and in recognition that deviation is generally tolerated.

19. For each region of the world you should identify a major economic theme, issue, or element. For example: Europe—the European Union should be discussed for its economic significance to member countries and to outsiders; the Americas—NAFTA should be discussed for its importance to Mexico, the United States, and Canada, and also for implications in political debates within these countries; Asia—the Asia-Pacific Economic Forum should be identified as a platform for growing regional economic cooperation among a very economically powerful group of countries, including China; Africa—the nonracial democracy in South Africa should be cited as an example of growing foreign investor interest in the countries of Africa.

20. Kim must recognize that the cultural differences between the United States and Japan may affect the success of group-oriented work practices such as quality circles and work teams. The United States was the most individualistic culture in Hofstede's study of national cultures; Japan is much more collectivist. Group practices such as the quality circle and teams are natural and consistent with the Japanese culture. When introduced into a more individualistic culture, these same practices might cause difficulties or require some time for workers to get used to them. At the very least, Kim should proceed with caution; discuss ideas for the new practices with the workers before making any changes; and then monitor the changes closely so that adjustments can be made to improve them as the workers gain familiarity with them and have suggestions of their own.

Chapter 6

1. c **2.** a **3.** b **4.** b **5.** b **6.** a **7.** d **8.** a **9.** d **10.** b **11.** a **12.** b **13.** c **14.** c **15.** d

16. Entrepreneurship is rich with diversity. It is an avenue for business entry and career success that is pursued by many women and members of minority groups. Data show that almost 40% of U.S. businesses are owned by women. Many report leaving other employment because they had limited opportunities. For them, entrepreneurship made available the opportunities for career success that they had lacked. Minority-owned businesses are one of the fastest-growing sectors, with the growth rates highest for Hispanic-owned, Asian-owned, and African American–owned businesses, in that order.

17. The three stages in the life cycle of an entrepreneurial firm are birth, breakthrough, and maturity. In the birth stage, the leader is challenged to get customers, establish a market, and find the money needed to keep the business going. In the breakthrough stage, the challenges shift to becoming and staying profitable, and managing growth. In the maturity stage, a leader is more focused on revising/maintaining a good business strategy and more generally managing the firm for continued success, and possibly for more future growth.

18. The limited partnership form of small business ownership consists of a general partner and one or more "limited partners." The general partner(s) play an active role in managing and operating the business; the limited partners do not. All contribute resources of some value to the partnership for the conduct of the business. The advantage of any partnership form is that the partners may share in profits, but their potential for losses is limited by the size of their original investments.

19. A venture capitalist, often a business, makes a living by investing in and taking large ownership interests in fledgling companies, with the goal of large financial gains eventually, when the company is sold. An angel investor is an individual who is willing to make a financial investment in return for some ownership in the new firm.

20. My friend is right—it takes a lot of forethought and planning to prepare the launch of a new business venture. In response to the question of how to ensure that I am really being customer-focused, I would ask and answer for myself the following questions. In all cases I would try to frame my business model so that the answers are realistic, but still push my business toward a strong customer orientation. The "customer" questions might include: "Who are my potential customers? What market niche am I shooting for? What do the customers in this market really want? How do these customers make purchase decisions? How much will it cost to produce and distribute my product/service to these customers? How much will it cost to attract and retain customers?" After preparing an overall executive summary, which includes a commitment to this customer orientation, I would address the following areas in writing up my initial business plan: a company description—mission, owners, and legal form—as well as an industry analysis, product and services description, marketing description and strategy, staffing model, financial projections with cash flows, and capital needs.

Chapter 7

1. c **2.** b **3.** c **4.** a **5.** a **6.** c **7.** c **8.** b **9.** a **10.** c **11.** b
12. c **13.** a **14.** b **15.** d

16. An optimizing decision is one that represents the absolute "best" choice of alternatives. It is selected from a set of all known alternatives. A satisficing decision selects the first alternative that offers a "satisfactory" choice, not necessarily the absolute best choice. It is selected from a limited or incomplete set of alternatives.

17. The ethics of a decision can be checked with the "spotlight" question: "How would you feel if your family found out?" "How would you feel if this were published in the local newspaper?" Also, one can test the decision by evaluating it on four criteria: (1) Utility—does it satisfy all stakeholders? (2) Rights—does it respect everyone's rights? (3) Justice—is it consistent with fairness and justice? (4) Caring—does it meet responsibilities for caring?

18. A manager using systematic thinking is going to approach problem solving in a logical and rational way. The tendency will be to proceed in a linear, step-by-step fashion, handling one issue at a time. A manager using intuitive thinking will be more spontaneous and open in problem solving. He or she may jump from one stage in the process to another and deal with many different issues simultaneously.

19. It almost seems contradictory to say that one can prepare for a crisis, but it is possible. The concept of crisis management is used to describe how managers and others prepare for unexpected high-impact events that threaten an organization's health and future. Crisis management involves both anticipating possible crises and preparing teams and plans ahead of time for how to handle them if they do occur. Many organizations today, for example, are developing crisis management plans to deal with terrorism and cyber attacks.

20. This is what I would say in the mentoring situation: continuing developments in information technology are changing the work setting for most employees. An important development for the traditional white-collar worker falls in the area of office automation—the use of computers and related technologies to facilitate everyday office work. In the "electronic office" of today and tomorrow, you should be prepared to work with and take full advantage of the following: smart workstations supported by desktop computers; voice messaging systems, whereby computers take dictation, answer the telephone, and relay messages; database and word processing systems that allow storage, access, and manipulation of data, as well as the preparation of reports; electronic mail systems that send mail and data from computer to computer; electronic bulletin boards for posting messages; and computer conferencing and videoconferencing that allow people to work with one another every day over distance. These are among the capabilities of the new workplace. To function effectively, you must be prepared not only to use these systems to full advantage, but also to stay abreast of new developments as they emerge in the market.

Chapter 8

1. d **2.** a **3.** a **4.** d **5.** b **6.** c **7.** a **8.** d **9.** a **10.** b **11.** a
12. c **13.** c **14.** d **15.** c

16. The five steps in the formal planning process are: (1) Define your objectives, (2) determine where you stand relative to objectives, (3) develop premises about future conditions, (4) identify and choose among action alternatives to accomplish objectives, and (5) implement action plans and evaluate results.

17. Benchmarking is the use of external standards to help evaluate one's own situation and develop ideas and directions for improvement. The bookstore owner/manager might visit other bookstores in other towns that are known for their success. By observing and studying the operations of those stores and then comparing her store to them, the owner/manager can develop plans for future action.

18. Planning helps improve focus for organizations and for individuals. Essential to the planning process is identifying your objectives and specifying exactly where it is you hope to get in the future. Having a clear sense of direction helps keep us on track by avoiding getting sidetracked on things that might not contribute to accomplishing our objectives. It also helps us to find discipline in stopping periodically to assess how well we are doing. With a clear objective, present progress can be realistically evaluated and efforts refocused on accomplishing the objective.

19. Very often plans fail because the people who make the plans aren't the same ones who must implement them. When people who will be implementing are allowed to participate in the planning process, at least two positive results may happen that help improve implementation: (1) Through involvement they better understand the final plans, and (2) through involvement they become more committed to making those plans work.

20. I would begin the speech by describing the importance of goal alignment as an integrated planning and control approach. I would also clarify that the key elements are objectives and participation. Any objectives should be clear, measurable, and time defined. In addition, these objectives should be set with the full involvement and participation of the employees; they should not be set by the manager and then told to the employees. That understood, I would describe how each business manager should jointly set objectives with each of his or her employees and jointly review progress toward their accomplishment. I would suggest that the employees should work on the required activities while staying in communication with their managers. The managers in turn should provide any needed support or assistance to their employees. This whole process could be formally recycled at least twice per year.

Chapter 9

1. a **2.** b **3.** d **4.** b **5.** b **6.** b **7.** d **8.** b **9.** b **10.** c **11.** a **12.** b **13.** c **14.** c **15.** c

16. The four steps in the control process are: (1) Establish objectives and standards, (2) measure actual performance, (3) compare actual performance with objectives and standards, and (4) take necessary action.

17. Feedforward control involves the careful selection of system inputs to ensure that outcomes are of the desired quality and up to all performance standards. In the case of a local bookstore, one of the major points of influence over performance and customer satisfaction is the relationship between the customers and the store's employees who serve them. Thus, a good example of feedforward control is exercising great care when the manager hires new employees and then trains them to work according to the store's expectations.

18. Douglas McGregor's concept of Theory Y involves the assumption that people can be trusted to exercise self-control in their work. This is the essence of internal control—people controlling their own work by taking personal responsibility for results. If managers approach work with McGregor's Theory Y assumptions, they will, according to him, promote more self-control—or internal control—by people at work.

19. The four questions to ask when developing a balanced scorecard for inclusion on an executive dashboard are: (1) *Financial Performance*—To improve financially, how should we appear to our shareholders? (2) *Customer Satisfaction*—To achieve our vision, how should we appear to our customers? (3) *Internal Process Improvement*—To satisfy our customers and shareholders, at what internal business processes should we excel? (4) *Innovation and Learning*—To achieve our vision, how will we sustain our ability to change and improve?

20. A very large number of activities are required to complete a new student center building on a college campus. Among them, one might expect the following to be core requirements: (1) land surveys and planning permissions from local government, (2) architect plans developed and approved, (3) major subcontractors hired, (4) site excavation completed, (5) building exterior completed, (6) building interior completed and furnishings installed. Use the figure from the chapter as a guide for developing your CPM/PERT diagram.

Chapter 10

1. a **2.** b **3.** c **4.** d **5.** b **6.** c **7.** a **8.** c **9.** b **10.** c **11.** a **12.** c **13.** d **14.** b **15.** a

16. A corporate strategy sets long-term direction for an enterprise as a whole. Functional strategies set directions so that business functions such as marketing and manufacturing support the overall corporate strategy.

17. A SWOT analysis is useful during strategic planning. It involves the analysis of organizational strengths and weaknesses, and of environmental opportunities and threats.

18. The focus strategy concentrates attention on a special market segment or niche. The differentiation strategy concentrates on building loyalty to a unique product or service.

19. Strategic leadership is the ability to create enthusiasm in people to participate in continuous change, performance enhancement, and the implementation of organizational strategies. The special qualities of the successful strategic leader include the ability to make trade-offs, create a sense of urgency, communicate the strategy, and engage others in continuous learning about the strategy and its performance responsibilities.

20. Porter's competitive strategy model involves the possible use of three alternative strategies: differentiation, cost leadership, and focus. In this situation, the larger department store seems better positioned to follow the cost leadership strategy. This means that Kim may want to consider the other two alternatives.

A differentiation strategy would involve trying to distinguish Kim's products from those of the larger store.

This might involve a "Made in America" theme, or an emphasis on leather, canvas, or some other type of clothing material. A focus strategy might specifically target college students and try to respond to their tastes and needs, rather than those of the larger community population. This might involve special orders and other types of individualized services for the college student market.

Chapter 11

1. b **2.** a **3.** b **4.** a **5.** a **6.** c **7.** d **8.** b **9.** b **10.** b **11.** c **12.** b **13.** b **14.** c **15.** b

16. The functional structure is prone to problems of internal coordination. One symptom may be that the different functional areas, such as marketing and manufacturing, are not working well together. This structure also is slow to respond to changing environmental trends and challenges. If the firm finds that its competitors are getting to market faster with new and better products, this is another potential indicator that the functional structure is not supporting operations properly.

17. A network structure often involves one organization "contracting out" aspects of its operations to other organizations that specialize in them. The example used in the text was of a company that contracted out its mailroom services. Through the formation of networks of contracts, the organization is reduced to a core of essential employees whose expertise is concentrated in the primary business areas. The contracts are monitored and maintained in the network to allow the overall operations of the organization to continue, even though they are not directly accomplished by full-time employees.

18. The term "contingency" is used in management to indicate that management strategies and practices should be tailored to fit the unique needs of specific situations. There is no universal solution that fits all problems and circumstances. Thus, in organizational design, contingency thinking must be used to identify and implement particular organizational points in time. What works well at one point in time may not work well at another, as the environment and other conditions change. For example, the more complex, variable, and uncertain the elements in the environment, the more difficult it is for the organization to operate. This situation calls for a more organic design. In a stable and more certain environment, the mechanistic design is appropriate, because operations are more routine and predictable.

19. Several options for answering this question are described in the chapter.

20. Faisal must first have confidence in the two engineers—he must trust them and respect their capabilities. Second, he must have confidence in himself, trusting his own judgment to give up some work and allow the others to do it. Third, he should follow the rules of effective delegation. These include being very clear on what must be accomplished by each engineer. Their responsibilities should be clearly understood. He must also give them the authority and resources to act in order to fulfill their responsibility, especially in relationship to the other engineers. He must also not forget his own final accountability for the results. He should remain in control and, through communication, make sure that work proceeds as planned.

Chapter 12

1. b **2.** a **3.** d **4.** a **5.** b **6.** a **7.** b **8.** b **9.** d **10.** c **11.** b **12.** c **13.** c **14.** d **15.** b

16. Core values indicate important beliefs that underlie organizational expectations about the behavior and contributions of members. Sample values for high-performance organizations might include expressed commitments to honesty and integrity, innovation, customer service, quality, and respect for people.

17. Subcultures are important in organizations because of the many aspects of diversity found in the workforce today. Although working in the same organization and sharing the same organizational culture, members differ in subculture affiliations based on such aspects as gender, age, sexual orientation, religious and ethnic differences, as well as with respect to occupational and functional affiliations. It is important to understand how subculture differences may influence working relationships. For example, a 40-year-old manager of 20-year-old workers must understand that the values and behaviors of the younger workforce may not be totally consistent with what she believes in, and vice versa.

18. Lewin's three phases of planned change and the relevant change leadership responsibilities are unfreezing—preparing a system for change; changing—moving or creating change in a system; and refreezing—stabilizing and reinforcing change once it has occurred. In addition, we might also talk about an additional or parallel phase of "improvising." This calls for change leadership that is good at gathering feedback, listening to resistance, and making constructive modifications as the change is in progress to smooth its implementation and ensure that what is implemented is a best fit for the circumstances and people involved.

19. Use of force-coercion as a strategy of planned change is limited by the likelihood of compliance being the major outcome. People comply with force only so long as it remains real, visible, and likely, but they have no personal commitment to the behavior. So, when the force goes away, so does the behavior. Also, a manager who relies on forcing people to get changes made is likely to be viewed negatively and suffer from additional negative halo effects in other work with them. Rational persuasion and shared power are likely to have a more long-lasting impact on behavior because employees respond to the change strategy by internalization of the value of the behavior being encouraged. Because of this commitment, the influence on their actions is more likely to be long-lasting rather than temporary as in the case of force-coercion.

20. I disagree with this statement, because a strong organizational or corporate culture can be a positive influence on any organization, large or small. Also, issues of diversity, inclusiveness, and multiculturalism apply as well. In fact, such things as a commitment to pluralism and respect for diversity should be part of the core values and distinguishing features of the culture of every organization. The woman working for the large company is mistaken in thinking that the concepts do not apply to her friend's small business. In fact, the friend—as owner and perhaps founder of the business—should be working hard to establish the values and other elements that will create a strong and continuing culture and respect for diversity. Employees of any organization should have core organizational values to serve as reference points for their attitudes and behavior. The rites and rituals of everyday organizational life also are important ways to recognize positive accomplishments and add meaning to the employment relationship. It may even be that the friend's roles as diversity leader and creator and sponsor of the corporate culture are magnified in the small business setting. As the owner and manager, she is visible every day to all employees. How she acts will have a great impact on any "culture."

Chapter 13

1. a **2.** c **3.** a **4.** d **5.** b **6.** d **7.** c **8.** d **9.** d **10.** b **11.** a **12.** b **13.** a **14.** d **15.** d

16. Internal recruitment deals with job candidates who already know the organization well. It also is a strong motivator because it communicates to everyone the opportunity to advance in the organization through hard work. External recruitment may allow the organization to obtain expertise not available internally. It also brings in employees with new and fresh viewpoints who are not biased by previous experience in the organization.

17. Orientation activities introduce a new employee to the organization and the work environment. This is a time when individuals may develop key attitudes and when performance expectations also will be established. Good orientation communicates positive attitudes and expectations and reinforces the desired organizational culture. It formally introduces the individual to important policies and procedures that everyone is expected to follow.

18. The graphic rating scale simply asks a supervisor to rate an employee on an established set of criteria, such as quantity of work or attitude toward work. This leaves a lot of room for subjectivity and debate. The behaviorally anchored rating scale asks the supervisor to rate the employee on specific behaviors that have been identified as positively or negatively affecting performance in a given job. This is a more specific appraisal approach and leaves less room for debate and disagreement.

19. Mentoring is when a senior and experienced individual adopts a newcomer or more junior person with the goal of helping him or her develop into a successful worker. The mentor may or may not be the individual's immediate supervisor. The mentor meets with the individual and discusses problems, shares advice, and generally supports the individual's attempts to grow and perform. Mentors also are considered to be very useful for persons newly appointed to management positions.

20. As Sy's supervisor, you face a difficult but perhaps expected human resource management problem. Not only is Sy influential as an informal leader, he also has considerable experience on the job and with the company. Even though he is experiencing performance problems using the new computer system, there is no indication that he doesn't want to work hard and continue to perform for the company. Although retirement is an option, Sy also may be transferred, promoted, or simply terminated. The last response seems unjustified and may cause legal problems. Transferring Sy, with his agreement, to another position could be a positive move; promoting Sy to a supervisory position in which his experience and networks would be useful is another possibility. The key in this situation seems to be moving Sy out so that a computer-literate person can take over the job, while continuing to utilize Sy in a job that better fits his talents. Transfer and/or promotion should be actively considered, both in his and in the company's interest.

Chapter 14

1. d **2.** d **3.** b **4.** b **5.** a **6.** a **7.** b **8.** d **9.** a **10.** b **11.** b **12.** a **13.** a **14.** c **15.** a

16. Position power is based on reward; coercion, or punishment; and legitimacy, or formal authority. Managers, however, need to have more power than that made available to them by the position alone. Thus, they have to develop personal power through expertise, reference, and information and networking. This personal power is essential in helping managers to get things done beyond the scope of their position power alone.

17. The leader-participation model suggests that leadership effectiveness is determined in part by how well managers or leaders handle the many different problem or decision situations that they face every day. Decisions can be made through individual or authority, consultative, or group-consensus approaches. No one of these decision methods is always the best; each is a good fit for certain types of situations. A good manager or leader is able to use each of these approaches and knows when each is the best approach to use in particular situations.

18. The three variables used in Fiedler's model to diagnose situational favorableness are: (1) position power—how much power the leader has in terms of rewards, punishments, and legitimacy; (2) leader–member relations—the quality of relationships between the leader and followers; and (3) task structure—the degree to which the task is either clear and well defined, or open-ended and more ambiguous.

19. Drucker says that good leaders have more than the "charisma" or "personality" being popularized in the concept of transformational leadership. He reminds us that good leaders work hard to accomplish some basic things in their everyday activities. These include: (1) establishing a clear sense of mission; (2) accepting leadership as a responsibility, not a rank; and (3) earning and keeping the respect of others.

20. In his new position, Marcel must understand that the transactional aspects of leadership are not sufficient to guarantee him long-term leadership effectiveness. He must move beyond the effective use of task-oriented and people-oriented behaviors and demonstrate through his personal qualities the capacity to inspire others. A charismatic leader develops a unique relationship with followers, in which they become enthusiastic, highly loyal, and high achievers. Marcel needs to work very hard to develop positive relationships with the team members. In those relationships he must emphasize high aspirations for performance accomplishments, enthusiasm, ethical behavior, integrity and honesty in all dealings, and a clear vision of the future. By working hard with this agenda and by allowing his personality to positively express itself in the team setting, Marcel should make continuous progress as an effective and a moral leader.

Chapter 15

1. c **2.** b **3.** d **4.** a **5.** c **6.** d **7.** b **8.** c **9.** a **10.** b **11.** d **12.** d **13.** c **14.** d **15.** c

16. A psychological contract is the individual's view of the inducements he or she expects to receive from the organization in return for his or her work contributions. The contract is healthy when the individual perceives that the inducements and contributions are fair and balanced.

17. Self-serving bias is the attribution tendency to blame the environment when things go wrong—"It's not my fault; 'they' caused all this mess." Fundamental attribution error is the tendency to blame others for problems that they have—"It's something wrong with 'you' that's causing the problem."

18. All the Big Five personality traits are relevant to the workplace. Consider the following basic examples. Extraversion suggests whether or not a person will reach out to relate and work well with others. Agreeableness suggests whether a person is open to the ideas of others and willing to go along with group decisions. Conscientiousness suggests whether or not someone can be depended on to meet commitments and perform agreed-on tasks. Emotional stability suggests whether someone will be relaxed and secure, or uptight and tense, in work situations. Openness to experience suggests whether or not someone will be open to new ideas or resistant to change.

19. The Type A personality is typical of people who bring stress on themselves by virtue of personal characteristics. These tend to be compulsive individuals who are uncomfortable waiting for things to happen, who try to do many things at once, and who generally move fast and have difficulty slowing down. Type A personalities can be stressful for both themselves and the people around them. Managers must be aware of Type A personality tendencies in their own behavior and among others with whom they work. Ideally, this awareness will help the manager take precautionary steps to best manage the stress caused by this personality type.

20. Scott needs to be careful. Although there is modest research support for the relationship between job satisfaction and performance, there is no guarantee that simply doing things to make his employees happier at work will cause them to be higher performers. Scott needs to take a broader perspective on this issue and his responsibilities as a manager. He should be interested in job satisfaction for his therapists and do everything he can to help them to experience it. But he should also be performance-oriented and should understand that performance is achieved through a combination of skills, support, and motivation. He should be helping the therapists to achieve and maintain high levels of job competency. He should also work with them to find out what obstacles they are facing and what support they need—things that perhaps he can deal with on their behalf. All of this relates as well to research that performance can be a source of job satisfaction. Finally, Scott should make sure that the therapists believe they are being properly rewarded for their work, because research shows that rewards have an influence on both job satisfaction and job performance.

Chapter 16

1. c **2.** b **3.** d **4.** d **5.** b **6.** b **7.** a **8.** d **9.** b **10.** d **11.** c **12.** c **13.** a **14.** b **15.** d

16. People high in need for achievement will prefer work settings and jobs in which they have (1) challenging but achievable goals, (2) individual responsibility, and (3) performance feedback.

17. Participation is important to goal-setting theory because, in general, people tend to be more committed to the accomplishment of goals they have helped set. When people participate in the setting of goals, they also understand them better. Participation in goal setting improves goal acceptance and understanding.

18. Maslow, McClelland, and Herzberg would likely find common agreement regarding a set of "higher order" needs. For Maslow these are self-actualization and ego; they correspond with Alderfer's growth needs, and with McClelland's needs for achievement and power. Maslow's social needs link up with relatedness needs in Alderfer's theory and the need for affiliation in McClelland's theory. Maslow's safety needs correspond to Alderfer's existence needs. Herzberg's "satisfier-factors" correspond to satisfactions of Maslow's higher needs, Alderfer's growth needs, and McClelland's need for achievement.

19. The compressed workweek or 4–40 schedule offers employees the advantage of a three-day weekend. However, it can cause problems for employers in terms of ensuring that operations are covered adequately during the normal five workdays of the week. Labor unions may resist, and the compressed workweek will entail more complicated work scheduling. In addition, some employees find that the schedule is tiring and can cause family adjustment problems.

20. It has already been pointed out in the answer to question 16 that a person with a high need for achievement likes moderately challenging goals and performance feedback. Participation of both managers and subordinates in goal setting offers an opportunity to choose goals to which the subordinate will respond, and which also will serve the organization. Further, through goal setting managers and individual subordinates can identify performance standards or targets. The manager can positively reinforce progress toward these targets. Such reinforcement can serve as an indicator of progress to someone with a high need for achievement, satisfying their desire for performance feedback.

Chapter 17

1. d **2.** a **3.** b **4.** b **5.** c **6.** a **7.** b **8.** b **9.** a **10.** a **11.** d **12.** b **13.** b **14.** a **15.** a

16. Input factors can have a major impact on group effectiveness. In order to best prepare a group to perform effectively, a manager should make sure that the right people are put in the group (maximize available talents and abilities), that these people are capable of working well together (membership characteristics should promote good relationships), that the tasks are clear, and that the group has the resources and environment needed to perform up to expectations.

17. A group's performance can be analyzed according to the interaction between cohesiveness and performance norms. In a highly cohesive group, members tend to conform to group norms. Thus, when the performance norm is positive and cohesion is high, we can expect everyone to work hard to support the norm—high performance is likely. By the same token, high cohesion and a low performance norm will yield the opposite result—low performance is likely. With other combinations of norms and cohesion, the performance results will be more mixed.

18. The textbook lists several symptoms of groupthink, along with various strategies for avoiding groupthink.

For example, a group whose members censor themselves from contributing "contrary" or "different" opinions and/or whose members keep talking about outsiders as "weak" or the "enemy" may be suffering from groupthink. This may be avoided or corrected, for example, by asking someone to be the "devil's advocate" for a meeting, and by inviting in an outside observer to help gather different viewpoints.

19. In a traditional work group, the manager or supervisor directs the group. In a self-managing team, the members of the team provide self-direction. They plan, organize, and evaluate their work, share tasks, and help one another develop skills; they may even make hiring decisions. A true self-managing team does not need the traditional "boss" or supervisor, because the team as a whole takes on traditional supervisory responsibilities.

20. Marcos is faced with a highly cohesive group whose members conform to a negative or low-performance norm. This is a difficult situation that is ideally resolved by changing the performance norm. In order to gain the group's commitment to a high-performance norm, Marcos should act as a positive role model for the norm. He must communicate the norm to the group clearly and positively and should not assume that everyone knows what he expects of them. He may also talk to the informal leader and gain his or her commitment to the norm. He might carefully reward high-performance behaviors within the group and may introduce new members with high-performance records and commitments. He might also hold group meetings in which performance standards and expectations are discussed, with an emphasis on committing to new high-performance directions. If his attempts to introduce a high-performance norm fail, Marcos may have to take steps to reduce group cohesiveness so that individual members can pursue higher-performance results without feeling bound by group pressures to restrict their performance.

Chapter 18

1. a **2.** b **3.** d **4.** d **5.** b **6.** b **7.** d **8.** b **9.** d **10.** b **11.** d **12.** c **13.** a **14.** d **15.** a

16. The manager's goal in active listening is to help the subordinate say what he or she really means. To do this, the manager should carefully listen for the content of what is being said, paraphrase or reflect back what the person appears to be saying, remain sensitive to nonverbal cues and feelings, and not be evaluative.

17. The relationship between conflict intensity and performance can be pictured as an inverted "U" curve. It shows that performance increases as conflict intensity increases from low to moderate levels. Conflict of moderate intensity creates the zone of constructive conflict, where its impact on performance is most positive. As conflict intensity moves into extreme levels, performance tends to decrease. This is the zone of destructive conflict. When conflict is too low, performance also may suffer.

18. Win–lose outcomes are likely when conflict is managed through high-assertiveness and low-cooperativeness styles. In this situation of competition, conflict is resolved by one person or group dominating another. Lose–lose outcomes occur when conflict is managed through avoidance (where nothing is resolved), and possibly when it is managed through compromise (where each party gives up something to the other). Win–win outcomes are associated mainly with problem solving and collaboration in conflict management, which result from high assertiveness and high cooperativeness.

19. In a negotiation, both substance and relationship goals are important. Substance goals relate to the content of the negotiation. A substance goal, for example, may relate to the final salary agreement between a job candidate and a prospective employer. Relationship goals relate to the quality of the interpersonal relationships among the negotiating parties. Relationship goals are important, because the negotiating parties most likely have to work together in the future. For example, if relationships are poor after a labor–management negotiation, the likelihood is that future problems will occur.

20. Kathryn can do a number of things to establish and maintain a system of upward communication for her department store branch. To begin, she should, as much as possible, try to establish a highly interactive style of management based on credibility and trust. Credibility is earned by building personal power through expertise and reference. In regard to credibility, she might set the tone for the department managers by practicing transparency and sharing information through open-book management. Once this pattern is established, trust will build between her and other store employees, and she should find that she learns a lot from interacting directly with them. Kathryn also should set up a formal communication structure, such as bimonthly store meetings, where she communicates store goals, results, and other issues to the staff and listens to them in return. An e-mail system where Kathryn and her staff can send messages would also be beneficial.

GLOSSARY

3 P's of organizational performance are profit, people, and planet.

360-degree appraisals include superiors, subordinates, peers, and even customers in the appraisal process.

A

Accommodation, or smoothing, plays down differences and highlights similarities to reduce conflict.

Accommodative strategy accepts social responsibility and tries to satisfy society's basic ethical expectations.

Accountability is the requirement to show performance results to a supervisor.

Active listening helps the source of a message say what he or she really means.

Adaptive organizations operate with a minimum of bureaucratic features and encourage worker empowerment and teamwork.

Administrators are managers in a public or nonprofit organization.

Affirmative action is an effort to give preference in employment to women and minority group members who have traditionally been underrepresented.

After-action review is a systematic assessment of lessons learned and results accomplished in a completed project.

Agenda setting develops action priorities for accomplishing goals and plans.

Agreeableness is being good-natured, cooperative, and trusting.

Amoral managers fail to consider the ethics of their behavior.

Analytical competency is the ability to evaluate and analyze information to make actual decisions and solve real problems.

Analytics involves systematic gathering and processing of data to make informed management decisions.

Anchoring and adjustment bias bases a decision on incremental adjustments from a prior decision point.

Angel investors are wealthy individuals willing to invest in a new venture in return for an equity stake.

Arbitration occurs when a neutral third party issues a binding decision to resolve a dispute.

Asia Pacific Economic Cooperation (APEC) links 21 countries to promote free trade and investment in the Pacific region.

Assessment centers examine how job candidates handle simulated work situations.

Attitude is a predisposition to act in a certain way.

Attribution is the process of explaining events.

Authentic leadership activates positive psychological states to achieve self-awareness and positive self-regulation.

Authoritarianism is the degree to which a person tends to defer to authority.

Authority decisions are made by the leader and then communicated to the group.

Authority-and-responsibility principle states that authority should equal responsibility when work is delegated.

Autocratic leaders act in a command-and-control fashion.

Automation is the total mechanization of a job.

Availability bias bases a decision on recent information or events.

Avoidance, or withdrawal, pretends that a conflict doesn't really exist.

B

Balance sheets show assets and liabilities at one point in time.

Balanced scorecards tally organizational performance in financial, customer service, internal process, and innovation and learning areas.

Bargaining zone refers to the space between one party's minimum reservation point and the other party's maximum reservation point.

Base compensation is a salary or hourly wage paid to an individual.

BCG Matrix analyzes business opportunities according to market growth rate and market share.

Behavioral decision model describes decision making with limited information and bounded rationality.

Behavioral interviews ask job applicants about past behaviors.

Behaviorally anchored rating scales use specific descriptions of actual behaviors to rate various levels of performance.

Benchmarking uses external and internal comparisons to plan for future improvements.

Benefit corporation, or B Corp, is a corporate form for businesses whose stated goals are to combine making a profit with benefiting society and the environment.

Best practices are things people and organizations do that lead to superior performance.

Biculturalism is when minority members display characteristics of majority cultures in order to succeed.

Big data exists in huge quantities and is difficult to process without sophisticated mathematical and computing techniques.

Big-C creativity occurs when extraordinary things are done by exceptional people.

Biodata methods collect certain biographical information that has been proven to correlate with good job performance.

Board of directors or board of trustees is a board whose members are supposed to make sure an organization is well run and managed in a lawful and ethical manner.

Bona fide occupational qualifications are employment criteria justified by the capacity to perform a job.

Bonus pay plans provide one-time payments based on performance accomplishments.

Bottom-up change is when change initiatives come from all levels in the organization.

Boundaryless organizations eliminate internal boundaries among subsystems and external boundaries with the external environment.

Bounded rationality describes making decisions within the constraints of limited information and alternatives.

Brainstorming engages group members in an open, spontaneous discussion of problems and ideas.

Breakeven analysis performs what-if calculations under different revenue and cost conditions.

Breakeven point occurs when revenues just equal costs.

Budgets are plans that commit resources to projects or activities.

Bullying is antisocial behavior that is intentionally aggressive, intimidating, demeaning, and/or abusive.

Bureaucracy is a rational and efficient form of organization founded on logic, order, and legitimate authority.

Bureaucratic control influences behavior through authority, policies, procedures, job descriptions, budgets, and day-to-day supervision.

Business incubators offer space, shared services, and advice to help get small businesses started.

Business intelligence taps information systems to extract and report data in organized ways that are helpful to decision makers.

Business model innovations result in ways for firms to make money.

Business models are plans for making a profit by generating revenues that are greater than costs.

Business plans describe the direction for a new business and the financing needed to operate it.

Business strategy identifies how a division or strategic business unit will compete in its product or service domain.

C

Centralization is the concentration of authority for most decisions at the top level of an organization.

Centralized communication networks are when communication flows only between individual members and a hub, or center point.

Certain environments offer complete information on possible action alternatives and their consequences.

Chains of command link all employees with successively higher levels of authority.

Change leaders take initiative in trying to change the behavior of another person or within a social system.

Changing is the phase where a planned change actually takes place.

Chapter 11 bankruptcy under U.S. law protects a firm from creditors while management reorganizes to restore solvency.

Charismatic leaders inspire followers in extraordinary ways.

Child labor is the employment of children for work otherwise done by adults.

Clan control influences behavior through norms and expectations set by the organizational culture.

Classic entrepreneurs are willing to pursue opportunities in situations others view as problems or threats.

Classical decision model means that decisions are made with complete information.

Classical view of CSR holds that business should focus on profits.

Co-opetition is the strategy of working with rivals on projects of mutual benefit.

Coaching occurs as an experienced employee offers performance advice to a less experienced co-worker.

Code of ethics is a formal statement of values and ethical standards.

Coercive power is the capacity to punish or withhold positive outcomes as a means of influencing other people.

Cognitive dissonance is discomfort felt when attitude and behavior are inconsistent.

Cognitive styles are shown by the ways individuals deal with information while making decisions.

Cohesiveness is the degree to which members are attracted to and motivated to remain part of a team.

Collaboration, or problem solving, involves working through conflict differences and solving problems so everyone wins.

Collective bargaining is the process of negotiating, administering, and interpreting a labor contract.

Commitment represents how hard you work to apply your talents and capabilities to important tasks.

Committees are designated to work on a special task on a continuing basis.

Communication channels are the pathways through which a message moves from sender to receiver.

Communication is the process of sending and receiving symbols with meanings attached.

Communication transparency involves openly sharing honest and complete information about the organization and workplace affairs.

Commutative justice is the degree to which an exchange or a transaction is fair to all parties.

Comparable worth holds that persons performing jobs of similar importance should be paid at comparable levels.

Comparative management studies how management practices differ among countries and cultures.

Competency represents your personal talents or job-related capabilities.

Competition, or authoritative command, uses force, superior skill, or domination to "win" a conflict.

Competitive advantage is something that an organization does extremely well, is difficult to copy, and that gives it an advantage over competitors in the marketplace.

Competitive advantage is the ability to do something so well that one outperforms competitors.

Complacency trap means being carried along by the flow of events.

Compressed workweeks allow a full-time job to be completed in less than five days.

Compromise occurs when each party to the conflict gives up something of value to the other.

Concentration growth occurs within the same business area.

Conceptual skill is the ability to think analytically to diagnose and solve complex problems.

Concurrent control focuses on what happens during the work process.

Confirmation error occurs when focusing only on information that confirms a decision already made.

Conflict is a disagreement over issues of substance and/or an emotional antagonism.

Conflict minerals are ones sourced in the Democratic Republic of Congo and surrounding region and whose sale finances armed groups that perpetuate violence.

Conflict resolution is the removal of the substantive and emotional reasons for a conflict.

Conscientiousness is being responsible, dependable, and careful.

Constructive stress or **eustress** is a positive stress outcome that can increase effort, stimulate creativity, and encourage diligence in one's work.

Consultative decisions are made by a leader after receiving information, advice, or opinions from group members.

Contingency planning identifies alternative courses of action to take when things go wrong.

Contingency thinking tries to match management practices with situational demands.

Contingency workers are employed on a part-time and temporary basis to supplement a permanent workforce.

Continuous improvement involves always searching for new ways to improve work quality and performance.

Continuous reinforcement rewards each time a desired behavior occurs.

Control equation: Need for Action = Desired Performance − Actual Performance.

Controlling is the process of measuring performance and taking action to ensure desired results.

Core competencies are special strengths that gives an organization a competitive advantage.

Core culture consists of the core values, or underlying assumptions and beliefs that shape and guide people's behaviors in an organization.

Core values are beliefs and values shared by organization members.

Corporate governance is the oversight of top management by a board of directors.

Corporate social responsibility is the obligation of an organization to serve the interests of multiple stakeholders, including society at large.

Corporate strategy sets long-term direction for the total enterprise.

Corporations are legal entities that exist separately from their owners.

Corruption involves illegal practices to further one's business interests.

Cost leadership strategy seeks to operate with low cost so that products can be sold at low prices.

Cost-benefit analysis involves comparing the costs and benefits of each potential course of action.

CPM/PERT is a combination of the critical path method and the program evaluation and review technique.

Creativity is the generation of a novel idea or unique approach that solves a problem or crafts an opportunity.

Credible communication earns trust, respect, and integrity in the eyes of others.

Crisis decisions occur when an unexpected problem arises that can lead to disaster if not resolved quickly and appropriately.

Critical path is the longest pathway in a CPM/PERT network.

Critical-incident technique keeps a log of employees' effective and ineffective job behaviors.

Cross-functional teams operate with members who come from different functional units of an organization.

Crowdfunding is when entrepreneurs starting new ventures go online to get startup financing from crowds of investors.

Cultural intelligence is the ability to adapt, adjust, and work well across cultures.

Cultural relativism suggests there is no one right way to behave; ethical behavior is determined by its cultural context.

Culture is a shared set of beliefs, values, and patterns of behavior common to a group of people.

Culture shock is the confusion and discomfort a person experiences when in an unfamiliar culture.

Customer structure groups together people and jobs that serve the same customers or clients.

D

Data are raw facts and observations.

Data mining is the process of analyzing data to produce useful information for decision makers.

Debt financing involves borrowing money that must be repaid over time, with interest.

Decentralization is the dispersion of authority to make decisions throughout all organization levels.

Decentralized communication networks allow all members to communicate directly with one another.

Decision making is the process of making choices among alternative possible courses of action.

Decision-making process begins with identification of a problem and ends with evaluation of results.

Decisions are choices among possible alternative courses of action.

Defensive strategy does the minimum legally required to display social responsibility.

Deficit principle states that a satisfied need does not motivate behavior.

Delegation is the process of distributing and entrusting work to others.

Demand legitimacy indicates the validity and legitimacy of a stakeholder's interest in the organization.

Democratic leaders emphasize both tasks and people.

Design thinking unlocks creativity in decision making through a process of experiencing, ideation, and prototyping.

Destructive stress or **strain** is a negative stress outcome that impairs the performance and well-being of an individual.

Differentiation strategy offers products that are unique and different from the competition.

Discrimination actively denies minority members the full benefits of organizational membership.

Disruptive activities are self-serving behaviors that interfere with team effectiveness.

Disruptive innovation creates products or services that become so widely used that they largely replace prior practices and competitors.

Distributed leadership is when all members of a team contribute helpful task and maintenance behaviors.

Distributive justice focuses on whether or not outcomes are distributed fairly.

Distributive negotiation focuses on win–lose claims made by each party for certain preferred outcomes.

Diversification growth occurs by acquisition of or investment in new and different business areas.

Divestiture sells off parts of the organization to refocus attention on core business areas.

Divisional structure groups together people working on the same product, in the same area, with similar customers, or on the same processes.

Downsizing strategy decreases the size of operations.

Dysfunctional conflict is destructive and hurts task performance.

E

Early retirement incentive programs offer workers financial incentives to retire early.

Ecological fallacy assumes that a generalized cultural value applies equally well to all members of the culture.

Economic order quantity method places new orders when inventory levels fall to predetermined points.

Effective communication means that the intended meaning is fully understood by the receiver.

Effective managers help others achieve high performance and satisfaction at work.

Effective negotiation resolves issues of substance while maintaining a positive process.

Effective teams achieve high levels of task performance, membership satisfaction, and future viability.

Efficient communication occurs at minimum cost.

Electronic grapevines use electronic media to pass messages and information among members of social networks.

Emotional intelligence is the ability to manage our emotions in social relationships.

Emotional stability is being relaxed, secure, and unworried.

Emotions are strong feelings directed toward someone or something.

Employee assistance programs help employees cope with personal stresses and problems.

Employee benefits are nonmonetary forms of compensation such as health insurance and retirement plans.

Employee engagement is a strong positive feeling about one's job and the organization.

Employee stock ownership plans (ESOPs) help employees purchase stock in their employing companies.

Employee value propositions are packages of opportunities and rewards that make diverse and talented people want to belong to and work hard for the organization.

Employment-at-will means that employees can be terminated at any time for any reason.

Empowerment allows others to make decisions and exercise discretion in their work.

Entrepreneurship is risk-taking behavior that results in new opportunities.

Environmental capital or natural capital is the supply of natural resources—atmosphere, land, water, and minerals—that sustains life and produces goods and services for society.

Environmental uncertainty is a lack of information regarding what exists in the environment and what developments may occur.

Equal employment opportunity is the requirement that employment decisions be made without regard to sex, race, color, ethnicity, national origin, able-bodiedness, or religion.

Equity financing involves exchanging ownership shares for outside investment monies.

Equity sensitivity reflects that people have different preferences for equity and react differently to perceptions of inequity.

Escalating commitment is the continuation of a course of action even though it is not working.

Ethical behavior is "good" or "right" in the context of a governing moral code.

Ethical dilemmas are situations that offer potential benefit or gain and that may also be considered unethical.

Ethical framework is a personal rule or strategy for making ethical decisions.

Ethical imperialism is an attempt to impose one's ethical standards on other cultures.

Ethics establish standards of good or bad, or right or wrong, in one's conduct.

Ethics intensity or **issue intensity** indicates the degree to which an issue or a situation is recognized to pose important ethical challenges.

Ethics self-governance is making sure day-to-day performance is achieved ethically and in socially responsible ways.

Ethics training seeks to help people understand the ethical aspects of decision making and to incorporate high ethical standards into their daily behavior.

Ethnic subcultures or **national subcultures** form among people who work together and have roots in the same ethnic community or nationality.

Ethnocentrism is the tendency to consider one's culture superior to others.

Euro is the common European currency.

European Union is a political and economic alliance of European countries.

Evidence-based management involves making decisions based on hard facts about what really works.

Executive dashboards visually display graphs, charts, and scorecards of key performance indicators and information on a real-time basis.

Existence needs are desires for physical well-being.

Expectancy is a person's belief that working hard will result in high task performance.

Expert power is the capacity to influence others' because of specialized knowledge.

Exporting involves local products being sold abroad to foreign customers.

External recruitment seeks job applicants from outside the organization.

Extinction discourages behavior by making the removal of a desirable consequence contingent on its occurrence.

Extraversion is being outgoing, sociable, and assertive.

F

Family business feuds occur when family members have major disagreements over how the business should be run.

Family businesses are owned and controlled by members of a family.

Family-friendly benefits help employees achieve better work–life balance.

Feedback control takes place after an action is completed.

Feedback is the process of telling someone else how you feel about something that person did or said.

Feedforward control ensures that directions and resources are right before the work begins.

First-mover advantage comes from being first to exploit a niche or enter a market.

Flat structures have wide spans of control and few hierarchical levels.

Flexible benefits programs allow employees to choose from a range of benefit options.

Flexible working hours give employees some choice in daily work hours.

Focus strategy concentrates on serving a unique market segment better than anyone else.

Focused cost leadership strategy seeks the lowest costs of operations within a special market segment.

Focused differentiation strategy offers a unique product to a special market segment.

Followership is the act of joining with a leader to accomplish tasks and goals.

Force-coercion strategy pursues change through formal authority and/ or the use of rewards or punishments.

Forecasting attempts to predict the future.

Foreign Corrupt Practices Act (FCPA) makes it illegal for U.S. firms and their representatives to engage in corrupt practices overseas.

Foreign subsidiary is a local operation completely owned by a foreign firm.

Formal groups are officially recognized collectives that are supported by the organization.

Formal structure is the official structure of the organization.

Framing error is trying to solve a problem in the context in which it is perceived.

Franchise is when one business owner sells to another the right to operate the same business in another location.

Free-agent economy means that people change jobs more often, and many work on independent contracts with a shifting mix of employers.

Frustration-regression principle states that an already satisfied need can become reactivated when a higher-level need is blocked.

Functional chimneys or **functional silos problem** is a lack of communication, coordination, and problem solving across functions.

Functional conflict is constructive and helps task performance.

Functional managers are responsible for one area, such as finance, marketing, production, personnel, accounting, or sales.

Functional plans indicate how different operations within the organization will help advance the overall strategy.

Functional strategy guides activities within one specific area of operations.

Functional structure groups together people with similar skills who perform similar tasks.

Fundamental attribution error overestimates internal factors and underestimates external factors driving individual behavior.

G

Gain-sharing plans allow employees to share in cost savings or productivity gains realized by their efforts.

Gantt charts graphically display the scheduling of tasks required to complete a project.

Gender similarities hypothesis holds that males and females have similar psychological properties.

Gender subcultures form among persons who share gender identities and display common patterns of behavior.

General environment consists of economic, legal-political, socio-cultural, technological, and natural environment conditions in which the organization operates.

General managers are responsible for complex, multifunctional units.

Generational cohorts consist of people born within a few years of one another and who experience somewhat similar life events during their formative years.

Generational subcultures form among persons who work together and share similar ages, such as millennials and baby boomers.

Geographical structure groups together people and jobs performed in the same location.

Glass ceiling effect is an invisible barrier limiting career advancement of women and minorities.

Global corporations are multinational enterprises (MNEs) or multinational corporations (MNCs) that conduct commercial transactions across national boundaries.

Global economy means that resources, markets, and competition are worldwide in scope.

Global management involves managing business and organizations with interests in more than one country.

Global managers are culturally aware and informed on international affairs.

Global sourcing means that materials or services are purchased around the world for local use.

Global strategic alliances are partnerships in which foreign and domestic firms share resources and knowledge for mutual gains.

Globalization gaps occur when large multinational corporations and industrialized nations gain disproportionately from the benefits of globalization.

Globalization is the worldwide interdependence of resource flows, product markets, and business competition.

Globalization strategy adopts standardized products and advertising for use worldwide.

Graphic rating scales use a checklist of traits or characteristics to evaluate performance.

Greenfield ventures are foreign subsidiaries built from the ground up by the foreign owner.

Group or team decisions are made by team members.

Groupthink is a tendency for highly cohesive teams to lose their evaluative capabilities.

Growth needs are desires for personal growth and development.

Growth strategy involves expansion of the organization's current operations.

H

Halo effect occurs when one attribute is used to develop an overall impression of a person or situation.

Hawthorne effect is the tendency of persons singled out for special attention to perform as expected.

Heuristics are strategies for simplifying decision making.

Hierarchy of goals or **hierarchy of objectives** means that lower-level goals and objectives support accomplishment of higher-level goals and objectives.

High-context cultures rely on nonverbal and situational cues as well as on spoken or written words in communication.

Higher-order needs are esteem and self-actualization needs in Maslow's hierarchy.

Human capital is the economic value of people with job-relevant knowledge, skills, abilities, ideas, energies, and commitments.

Human relations leaders emphasize people over task.

Human resource management is a process of attracting, developing, and maintaining a talented workforce.

Human resource planning analyzes staffing needs and identifies actions to fill those needs.

Human skill or interpersonal skill is the ability to work well in cooperation with other people.

Hygiene factor is found in the job context, such as working conditions, interpersonal relations, organizational policies, and compensation.

I

Immoral managers choose to behave unethically.

Importing involves the selling in domestic markets of products acquired abroad.

Impression management is the systematic attempt to influence how others perceive us.

Improvisational change makes continual adjustments as changes are being implemented.

Incivility is antisocial behavior in the forms of disrespectful acts, social exclusion, and use of hurtful language.

Income statements show profits or losses at one point in time.

Incremental change bends and adjusts existing ways to improve performance.

Independent contractors are hired as needed and are not part of the organization's permanent workforce.

Individualism view holds that ethical behavior advances long-term self-interests.

Individualism–collectivism is the degree to which a society emphasizes individuals and their self-interests.

Informal groups are unofficial and emerge from relationships and shared interests among members.

Informal structure is the set of social networks found in unofficial relationships among the members of an organization.

Information and networking power is the ability to influence others through access to information and contacts with other people.

Information competency is the ability to locate, gather, and organize information for use in decision making.

Information filtering is the intentional distortion of information to make it appear more favorable to the recipient.

Information is data made useful for decision making.

Initial public offerings, or IPOs, are an initial selling of shares of stock to the public at large.

Innovation is the process of taking a new idea and putting it into practice.

Input standards measure work efforts that go into a performance task.

Insourcing is job creation through foreign direct investment.

Instrumental values are preferences regarding the means to desired ends.

Instrumentality is a person's belief that various outcomes will occur as a result of task performance.

Integrity is acting with honesty, credibility, and consistency in putting values into action.

Intellectual capital is the collective brainpower or shared knowledge of a workforce.

Interactional justice is the degree to which others are treated with dignity and respect.

Interactive leaders are strong communicators and act in democratic and participative ways with followers.

Intercultural competencies are skills and personal characteristics that help

us be successful in cross-cultural situations.

Interdependence is the extent to which employees depend on other members of their team to carry out their work effectively.

Intermittent reinforcement rewards behavior only periodically.

Internal recruitment seeks job applicants from inside the organization.

International businesses conduct for-profit transactions of goods and services across national boundaries.

Internet censorship is the deliberate blockage and denial of public access to information posted on the Internet.

Intuitive thinking approaches problems in a flexible and spontaneous fashion.

Inventory control ensures that inventory is only big enough to meet immediate needs.

ISO certification indicates conformance with a rigorous set of international quality standards.

Issue urgency indicates the extent to which a stakeholder's concerns need immediate attention.

J

Job analysis studies exactly what is done in a job, and why.

Job burnout is a feeling of physical and mental exhaustion from work stress.

Job descriptions detail the duties and responsibilities of a job holder.

Job design is arranging work tasks for individuals and groups.

Job discrimination occurs when someone is denied a job or work assignment for reasons that are not job relevant.

Job enlargement increases task variety by combining into one job two or more tasks previously done by separate workers.

Job enrichment increases job depth by adding work planning and evaluating duties normally performed by the supervisor.

Job involvement is the extent to which an individual feels dedicated to a job.

Job migration occurs when firms shift jobs from a home country to foreign ones.

Job rotation increases task variety by periodically shifting workers between different jobs.

Job satisfaction is the degree to which an individual feels positive or negative about a job.

Job sharing splits one job between two people.

Job simplification employs people in clearly defined and specialized tasks with narrow job scope.

Job specifications list the qualifications required of a job holder.

Joint ventures operate in a foreign country through co-ownership by foreign and local partners.

Just-in-time scheduling (JIT) routes materials to workstations just in time for use.

Justice view holds that ethical behavior treats people impartially and fairly.

K

Knowledge workers are people whose mindsare a critical asset to their employers.

L

Labor contracts are formal agreements between a union and an employer about the terms of work for union members.

Labor unions are organizations that deal with employers on the workers' collective behalf.

Lack-of-participation error is failure to involve in a decision the persons whose support is needed to implement it.

Laissez-faire leaders have a "do the best you can and don't bother me" attitude.

Law of contingent reinforcement states that a reward should only be given when a desired behavior occurs.

Law of effect states that behavior followed by pleasant consequences is likely to be repeated; behavior followed by unpleasant consequences is not.

Law of immediate reinforcement states that a reward should be given as soon as possible after a desired behavior occurs.

Leadership double bind means that women get criticized for displaying stereotypical male leadership characteristics and also for displaying stereotypical female leadership characteristics.

Leadership is the process of inspiring others to work hard to accomplish important tasks.

Leadership style is a recurring pattern of behaviors exhibited by a leader.

Leading is the process of arousing enthusiasm and inspiring efforts to achieve goals.

Leaking pipeline problem is where glass ceilings and other obstacles cause qualified and high-performing women to drop out of upward career paths.

Lean startups use resources such as open-source software while containing costs, staying small, and keeping operations as simple as possible.

Learning goals set targets to create the knowledge and skills required for performance.

Learning is a change in behavior that results from experience.

Least-preferred co-worker scale, LPC, is used in Fiedler's contingency model to measure leadership style.

Legitimate power is the capacity to influence others by virtue of formal authority, or the rights of office.

Leniency is the tendency to give employees a higher performance rating than they deserve.

Licensing agreement is where a local firm pays a fee to a foreign firm for rights to make or sell its products.

Lifelong learning is continuous learning from daily experiences.

Limited liability corporation (LLC) is a hybrid business form combining the advantages of the sole proprietorship, partnership, and corporation.

Line managers directly contribute to producing the organization's goods or services.

Liquidation is where a business closes and sells its assets to pay creditors.

Little-C creativity occurs when average people come up with unique ways to deal with daily events and situations.

Locus of control is the extent to which one believes that what happens is within one's control.

Long-term plans typically look three or more years into the future.

Loose cultures have relaxed social norms and allows conformity by members to vary a good deal.

Lose–lose conflict occurs when no one achieves their true desires, and the underlying reasons for conflict remain.

Low-context cultures emphasize communication via spoken or written words.

Lower-order needs are physiological, safety, and social needs in Maslow's hierarchy.

M

Machiavellianism describes the extent to which someone is emotionally detached and manipulative.

Maintenance activities are actions taken by a team member that support the emotional life of the team.

Management by exception focuses attention on substantial differences between actual and desired performance.

Management development is training to improve knowledge and skills in the management process.

Management information systems collect, organize, and distribute data for use in decision making.

Management process is planning, organizing, leading, and controlling the use of resources to accomplish performance goals.

Managers are people who support, activate, and are responsible for the work of others.

Managing diversity is a leadership approach that creates an organizational culture that respects diversity and supports multiculturalism.

Market control is essentially the influence of market competition on the behavior of organizations and their members.

Masculinity–femininity is the degree to which a society values assertiveness and materialism.

Matrix structure combines the functional and divisional approaches to create permanent cross-functional project teams.

Mechanistic design is centralized, with many rules and procedures, a clear-cut division of labor, narrow spans of control, and formal coordination.

Mediation a neutral party tries to help conflicting parties improve communication to resolve their dispute.

Mentoring assigns new hires and early-career employees as protégés to more senior employees.

Merit pay awards pay increases in proportion to performance contributions.

Middle managers oversee the work of large departments or divisions.

Mission statements express the organization's reason for existence in society.

Mixed messages result when words communicate one message while actions, body language, or appearance communicate something else.

Mompreneurs pursue business opportunities they spot as mothers.

Monochronic cultures are where people tend to do one thing at a time.

Mood contagion is the spillover of one's positive or negative moods to others.

Moods are generalized positive and negative feelings or states of mind.

Moral absolutism suggests ethical standards apply universally across all cultures.

Moral leadership is always "good" and "right" by ethical standards.

Moral managers make ethical behavior a personal goal.

Moral overconfidence is an overly positive view of one's strength of character.

Moral rights view holds that ethical behavior respects and protects fundamental rights.

Most favored nation status gives a trading partner most favorable treatment for imports and exports.

Motion study is the science of reducing a task to its basic physical motions.

Multicultural organizations have a culture with core values that respect diversity and support multiculturalism.

Multiculturalism in organizations involves inclusiveness, pluralism, and respect for diversity.

Multidimensional thinking is an ability to address many problems at once.

Multidomestic strategy customizes products and advertising to best fit local needs.

Multiperson comparison compares one person's performance with that of others.

N

NAFTA is the North American Free Trade Agreement linking Canada, the United States, and Mexico in an economic alliance.

Necessity-based entrepreneurship takes place because other employment options don't exist.

Need for achievement is the desire to do something better, to solve problems, or to master complex tasks.

Need for affiliation is the desire to establish and maintain good relations with people.

Need for power is the desire to control, influence, or be responsible for other people.

Needs are physiological or psychological deficiencies that a person feels compelled to satisfy.

Negative reinforcement strengthens behavior by making the avoidance of an undesirable consequence contingent on its occurrence.

Negotiation is the process of making joint decisions when the parties involved have different preferences.

Network structure uses information technologies to link with networks of outside suppliers and service contractors.

Networking is the process of creating positive relationships with people who can help advance agendas.

Noise is anything that interferes with the effectiveness of communication.

Nominal group technique structures interaction among team members discussing problems and ideas.

Nonprogrammed decisions apply a specific solution crafted for a unique problem.

Nontariff barriers to trade discourage imports in nontax ways such as quotas and government import restrictions.

Nonverbal communication takes place through gestures and body language.

Norms are behavioral expectations, rules, or standards to be followed by team members.

O

Objectives and **goals** are specific results that one wishes to achieve.

Observable culture is visible in the way members behave, and in the stories, heroes, rituals, and symbols that are part of daily organizational life.

Obstructionist strategy tries to avoid and resist pressures for social responsibility.

Occupational and functional subcultures form among persons who share the same skills and work responsibilities.

Offshoring is the outsourcing of jobs to foreign locations.

Ombudsperson is a designated neutral third party who listens to complaints and disputes in an attempt to resolve them.

Onboarding or **orientation** familiarizes new hires with the organization's mission and culture, their jobs and co-workers, and performance expectations.

Open book management is where managers provide employees with essential financial information about their companies.

Open systems interact with their environment and transform resource inputs into outputs.

Openness to experience is being curious, receptive to new ideas, and imaginative.

Operant conditioning is the control of behavior by manipulating its consequences.

Operating objectives are specific results that organizations try to accomplish.

Operational plans identify short-term activities to implement strategic plans.

Optimizing decisions choose the alternative giving the absolute best solution to a problem.

Organic design is decentralized, with fewer rules and procedures, open divisions of labor, wide spans of control, and more personal coordination.

Organization is a collection of people working together to achieve a common purpose.

Organization charts describe the arrangement of work positions within an organization.

Organization structure is a system of tasks, reporting relationships, and communication linkages.

Organizational behavior is the study of individuals and groups in organizations.

Organizational citizenship behavior is a willingness to "go beyond the call of duty" or "go the extra mile" in one's work.

Organizational commitment is the loyalty an individual feels toward the organization.

Organizational culture is the system of shared beliefs and values that guides behavior in organizations.

Organizational design is the process of creating structures that accomplish mission and objectives.

Organizational subcultures or **co-cultures** consist of members who share similar beliefs and values based on their work, personal characteristics, or social identities.

Organizing is the process of defining and assigning tasks, allocating resources, and providing resource support.

Outcome goals set targets for actual performance results.

Output standards measure performance results in terms of quantity, quality, cost, or time.

Over-reward inequity (positive inequity) is when an individual perceives that rewards received are more than what is fair for work inputs.

P

Pareto Principle states that 80% of consequences come from 20% of causes.

Participatory planning includes the persons who will be affected by plans and/or those who will implement them.

Partnership is when two or more people agree to contribute resources to start and operate a business together.

Perception is the process through which people receive, organize, and interpret information from the environment.

Performance assessment or review is the process of formally evaluating performance and providing feedback to a job holder.

Performance coaching provides frequent and developmental feedback for how a worker can improve job performance.

Performance effectiveness is an output measure of task or goal accomplishment.

Performance efficiency is an input measure of resource cost associated with goal accomplishment.

Performance management systems set standards, assess results, and plan for performance improvements.

Performance opportunities are situations that offer the chance for a better future if the right steps are taken.

Performance threats are situations in which something is obviously wrong or has the potential to go wrong.

Permatemps are workers who are employed in a temporary status for an extended period of time.

Person–job fit is the extent to which an individual's knowledge, skills, experiences and personal characteristics are consistent with the requirements of their work.

Person–organization fit is the extent to which an individual's values, interests, and behavior are consistent with the culture of the organization.

Personal wellness is the pursuit of one's full potential through a personal health-promotion program.

Personality is the profile of characteristics making a person unique from others.

Persuasive communication presents a message in a manner that causes the other person to support it.

Planning is the process of setting goals and objectives and making plans to accomplish them.

Plans are statements of intended means for accomplishing objectives.

Policies are standing plans that communicate broad guidelines for decisions and action.

Political risk is the potential loss in value of a foreign investment due to instability and political changes in the host country.

Political-risk analysis tries to forecast political disruptions that can threaten the value of a foreign investment.

Polychronic cultures are where time is used to accomplish many different things at once.

Positive reinforcement strengthens behavior by making a desirable consequence contingent on its occurrence.

Power is the ability to get others to do something you want done or to make things happen the way you want.

Power distance is the degree to which a society accepts unequal distribution of power.

Prejudice is the display of negative, irrational attitudes toward members of diverse populations.

Principled negotiation or **integrative negotiation** uses a "win–win" orientation to reach solutions acceptable to each party.

Proactive strategy actively pursues social responsibility by taking discretionary actions to make things better in the future.

Problem avoiders ignore information indicating a performance opportunity or threat.

Problem seekers constantly process information looking for problems to solve, even before they occur.

Problem solvers try to solve problems when they occur.

Problem solving involves identifying and taking action to resolve problems.

Procedural justice is concerned that policies and rules are fairly applied.

Procedures are rules describing actions that are to be taken in specific situations.

Process innovations result in better ways of doing things.

Process structure groups jobs and activities that are part of the same processes.

Product innovations result in new or improved goods or services.

Product structure groups together people and jobs focused on a single product or service.

Productivity is the quantity and quality of work performance, with resource utilization considered.

Profit-sharing plans distribute to employees a proportion of net profits earned by the organization.

Programmed decisions apply a solution from past experience to a routine problem.

Progression principle states that a need isn't activated until the next lower-level need is satisfied.

Projects are one-time activities with many component tasks that must be completed in proper order and according to budget.

Project management is the responsibility for overall planning, supervision, and control of projects.

Project teams or **task forces** are convened for a specific purpose and disband when their task is completed.

Projection is the assignment of personal attributes to other individuals.

Protectionism is a call for tariffs and favorable treatments to protect domestic firms from foreign competition.

Proxemics is the study of how people use space to communicate.

Psychological contract is the set of individual expectations about the employment relationship.

Punishment discourages behavior by making an unpleasant consequence contingent on its occurrence.

Q

Quality of work life is the overall quality of human experiences in the workplace.

R

Rational persuasion strategy pursues change through empirical data and rational argument.

Realistic job previews provide job candidates with all pertinent information about a job and an organization, both positive and negative.

Recency bias overemphasizes the most recent behaviors when evaluating individuals' performance.

Recruitment is a set of activities designed to attract a talented pool of job applicants.

Referent power is the capacity to influence other people because of their desire to identify personally with you.

Refreezing is the phase at which change is stabilized.

Regional economic alliances link member countries in agreements to work together for economic gains.

Relatedness needs are desires for good interpersonal relationships.

Relationship goals in negotiation are concerned with the ways people work together.

Reliability means that a selection device repeatedly gives consistent results.

Representativeness bias bases a decision on similarity to other situations.

Reshoring is the movement of jobs from foreign locations back to domestic ones.

Restricted communication networks are those in which subgroups have limited communication with one another.

Retrenchment, restructuring, and turnaround strategies pursue radical changes to solve problems.

Reverse innovation is launched from lower organizational levels and diverse locations, including emerging markets.

Reverse mentoring is when younger employees mentor seniors to improve their technology skills.

Reward power is the capacity to offer something of value as a means of influencing other people.

Risk environments lack complete information but offer "probabilities" of the likely outcomes for possible action alternatives.

S

Satisficing decisions are the choice of the first satisfactory alternative that comes to one's attention.

Satisfier factors are found in job content, such as challenging and exciting work, recognition, responsibility, advancement opportunities, or personal growth.

Scenario planning identifies alternative future scenarios and makes plans to deal with each.

Scientific management emphasizes careful selection and training of workers and supervisory support.

Selection is choosing individuals to hire from a pool of qualified job applicants.

Selective perception is the tendency to define problems from one's own point of view.

Self-control is internal control that occurs through self-management and self-discipline in fulfilling work and personal responsibilities.

Self-efficacy is a person's belief that she or he is capable of performing a task.

Self-enhancement bias is the tendency to view oneself as more capable, intelligent, and ethical than others.

Self-fulfilling prophecy occurs when a person acts in ways that confirm another's expectations.

Self-management is the ability to understand oneself, exercise initiative, accept responsibility, and learn from experience.

Self-managing work team members have the authority to make decisions about how they share and complete their work.

Self-monitoring is the degree to which someone is able to adjust behavior in response to external factors.

Self-serving bias explains personal success by internal causes and personal failures by external causes.

Serial entrepreneurs start and run businesses and nonprofits over and over again, moving from one interest and opportunity to the next.

Servant leadership is follower-centered and committed to helping others in their work.

Sexual harassment is behavior of a sexual nature that affects a person's employment situation.

Shamrock organizations operate with a core group of full-time long-term workers supported by others who work on contracts and part-time.

Shaping is positive reinforcement of successive approximations to the desired behavior.

Shared power strategy pursues change by participation in assessing change needs, values, and goals.

Shared value view of CSR sees economic progress for a firm and social progress for society as fundamentally interconnected.

Short-term plans typically cover one year or less.

Situational interviews ask job applicants how they would react in specific situations.

Skill is the ability to translate knowledge into action that results in desired performance.

Small Business Development Centers founded with support from the U.S. Small Business Administration provide advice to new and existing small businesses.

Small businesses have fewer than 500 employees, are independently owned and operated, and do not dominate their industry.

Social business innovation finds ways to use business models to address important social problems.

Social capital is a capacity to get things done with the support and help of others.

Social enterprises have a social mission to help make lives better for underserved populations.

Social entrepreneurship is a unique form of ethical entrepreneurship that seeks novel ways to solve pressing social problems.

Social loafing is the tendency of some members to avoid responsibility by "free-riding" during group tasks.

Social network analysis or **sociometrics** identifies the informal structures and their embedded social relationships that are active in an organization.

Social networking is the use of dedicated websites and applications to connect people having similar interests.

Social recruiting is where employers browse social media sites looking for prospective job candidates.

Social responsibility audits measure an organization's performance in various areas of social responsibility.

Socialization is the onboarding process through which new members learn the culture of an organization.

Socioeconomic view of CSR holds that business should focus on broader social welfare as well as profits.

Sole proprietorship is when an individual pursues business for a profit.

Southern Africa Development Community (SADC) links 14 countries of southern Africa in trade and economic development efforts.

Span of control is the number of subordinates directly reporting to a manager.

Specific environment, or **task environment,** includes the people and groups with whom an organization interacts.

Spotlight questions test the ethics of a decision by exposing it to scrutiny through the eyes of family, community members, and ethical role models.

Staff managers use special technical expertise to advise and support line workers.

Staff positions provide technical expertise for other parts of the organization.

Stakeholder power refers to the capacity of the stakeholder to positively or negatively affect the operations of the organization.

Stakeholders are the persons, groups, and other organizations that are directly affected by the behavior of the organization and that hold a stake in its performance.

Startups are new and temporary ventures that are trying to discover a profitable business model for future success.

Stereotypes occur when attributes commonly associated with a group are assigned to an individual.

Stewardship means taking personal responsibility to always respect and protect the interests of organizational stakeholders, including society at large.

Stock options give the right to purchase shares at a fixed price in the future.

Strategic alliance is a cooperation agreement with another organization to jointly pursue activities of mutual interest.

Strategic analysis is the process of analyzing the organization, the environment, and the organization's competitive position and current strategies.

Strategic control makes sure strategies are well implemented and that poor strategies are scrapped or modified.

Strategic human resource management mobilizes human capital to implement organizational strategies.

Strategic intent focuses and applies organizational energies on a unifying and compelling goal.

Strategic leadership inspires people to continuously change, refine, and improve strategies and their implementation.

Strategic management is the process of formulating and implementing strategies.

Strategic opportunism focuses on long-term objectives while being flexible in dealing with short-term problems.

Strategic plans identify long-term directions for the organization.

Strategy is a comprehensive plan guiding resource allocation to achieve long-term organization goals.

Strategy formulation is the process of crafting strategies to guide the allocation of resources.

Strategy implementation is the process of putting strategies into action.

Stress is a state of tension caused by extraordinary demands, constraints, or opportunities.

Stressors are anything that causes tension.

Stretch goals are performance targets that one must work extra hard and stretch to reach.

Strong organizational cultures are clear, well defined, and widely shared among members.

Structured problems are straightforward and clear with respect to information needs.

Substance goals in negotiation are concerned with outcomes.

Substantive conflict involves disagreements over goals, resources, rewards, policies, procedures, and job assignments.

Substitutes for leadership are factors in the work setting that direct work efforts without the involvement of a leader.

Subsystem is a smaller component of a larger system.

Succession plans describe how the leadership transition and related financial matters will be handled.

Succession problem means the issue of who will run the business when the current head leaves.

Sustainability means acting in ways that support a high quality of life for present and future generations.

Sustainable businesses operate in ways that meet the needs of customers while protecting or advancing the well-being of our natural environment.

Sustainable competitive advantage is the ability to outperform rivals in ways that are difficult or costly to imitate.

Sustainable development uses environmental resources to support societal needs today while also preserving and protecting them for future generations.

Sustainable innovations or **green innovations** help reduce an organization's negative impact and enhance its positive impact on the natural environment.

Sweatshops employ workers at very low wages for long hours in poor working conditions.

SWOT analysis examines organizational strengths and weaknesses and environmental opportunities and threats.

Symbolic leaders use language to communicate core values, and their actions are consistent with core values and the organizational culture.

Synergy is the creation of a whole greater than the sum of its individual parts.

System is a collection of interrelated parts working together for a purpose.

Systematic thinking approaches problems in a rational and analytical fashion.

T

Tactical plans help to implement all or parts of a strategic plan.

Tall structures have narrow spans of control and many hierarchical levels.

Tariffs are taxes governments levy on imports from abroad.

Task activity is an action taken by a team member that directly contributes to the team's performance purpose.

Tax inversion is where a U.S.-based MNC buys a firm in a low-tax country in order to shield foreign earnings from U.S. taxes.

Team building is a sequence of activities to analyze a team and make changes to improve its performance.

Team diversity represents the differences in values, personalities, experiences, demographics, and cultures among members.

Team Effectiveness Equation: Team effectiveness = Quality of inputs + (Process gains − Process losses).

Teams are collections of people who regularly interact to pursue common goals.

Team leaders report to middle managers and supervise non-managerial workers.

Team process is the way team members work together to accomplish tasks.

Team structure uses permanent and temporary cross-functional teams to improve lateral relations.

Team virtuousness indicates the extent to which members adopt norms that encourage shared commitments to moral behavior.

Teamwork is the process of people actively working together interdependently to accomplish common goals.

Tech IQ is the ability to use technology and to stay updated as technology continues to evolve.

Technical skill is the ability to use expertise to perform a task with proficiency.

Technological competency is the ability to understand new technologies and to use them to their best advantage.

Technology personality reflects levels of social media use and how media are used to connect to others.

Telecommuting involves using IT to work at home or outside the office.

Terminal values are preferences about desired end states.

Termination is the involuntary dismissal of an employee.

Theory X assumes people dislike work, lack ambition, act irresponsibly, and prefer to be led.

Theory Y assumes people are willing to work, like responsibility, and are self-directed and creative.

Tight cultures have rigid social norms expects members to conform with them.

Time orientation is the degree to which a society emphasizes short-term or long-term goals.

Top managers guide the performance of the organization as a whole or of one of its major parts.

Top-down change occurs when the change initiatives come from senior management.

Total quality management is an organization-wide commitment to continuous improvement, product quality, and customer needs.

Traditional recruitment focuses on selling the job and organization to applicants.

Training provides learning opportunities to acquire and improve job-related skills.

Transformational change results in a major and comprehensive redirection of the organization.

Transformational leadership is inspirational and arouses extraordinary effort and performance.

Transnational corporations are global corporations or MNEs that operate worldwide on a borderless basis.

Transnational strategy seeks efficiencies of global operations with attention to local markets.

Triple bottom line evaluates organizational performance on economic, social, and environmental criteria.

Turnaround strategy tries to fix specific performance problems.

Type A personality is a person oriented toward extreme achievement, impatience, and perfectionism.

U

Uncertain environments lack so much information that it is difficult to assign probabilities to the likely outcomes of alternatives.

Uncertainty avoidance is the degree to which a society tolerates risk and uncertainty.

Under-reward inequity (negative inequity) is when an individual perceives that rewards received are less than what is fair for work inputs.

Unfreezing is the phase during which a situation is prepared for change.

Unintended consequences are unanticipated positive or negative side effects that result from a decision.

Unstructured interviews are those in which the interviewer does not work from a formal and pre-established list of questions that is asked of all interviewees.

Unstructured problems have ambiguities and information deficiencies.

Upside-down pyramid view of organizations shows customers at the top being served by workers who are supported by managers.

Utilitarian view holds that ethical behavior delivers the greatest good to the most people.

V

Valence is the value a person assigns to work-related outcomes.

Validity means that scores on a selection device have a demonstrated correlation with future job performance.

Values are broad beliefs about what is appropriate behavior.

Value-based management actively develops, communicates, and enacts shared values.

Venture capitalists make large investments in new ventures in return for an equity stake in the business.

Vertical integration growth occurs by acquiring upstream suppliers or downstream distributors.

Virtual organizations use mobile IT to engage a shifting network of strategic alliances.

Virtual teams or **distributed teams** work together and solve problems through computer-based interactions.

Virtuous circles occur when socially responsible behavior improves financial performance, which leads to more responsible behavior in the future.

Vision clarifies the purpose of the organization and expresses what it hopes to be in the future.

Visionary leadership brings to the situation a clear sense of the future and an understanding of how to get there.

W

Whistleblowers expose the misdeeds of others in organizations.

Win–lose conflict is where one party achieves its desires, and the other party does not.

Win–win conflict is where the conflict is resolved to everyone's benefit.

Withdrawal behaviors occur as temporary absenteeism and actual job turnover.

Work processes are groups of related tasks that collectively create a valuable work product.

Work sampling is when applicants are evaluated while performing actual work tasks.

Work–life balance involves balancing career demands with personal and family needs.

Workforce diversity describes workers' differences in terms of gender, race, age, ethnicity, religion, sexual orientation, and able-bodiedness.

Workplace privacy is the right to privacy while at work.

Workplace rage is showing aggressive behavior toward co-workers or the work setting.

Workplace spirituality creates meaning and shared community among organizational members.

World 3.0 is a world where nations balance cooperation in the global economy with national identities and interests.

World Trade Organization member nations agree to negotiate and resolve disputes about tariffs and trade restrictions.

Wrongful discharge is a doctrine giving workers legal protections against discriminatory firings.

X, Y, Z

Zero-based budgets allocate resources as if each budget were brand new.

ENDNOTES

Chapter 1

Endnotes

[1] James O'Toole and Edward E. Lawler III, *The New American Workplace* (New York: Palgrave Macmillan, 2006).

[2] Quote from Philip Delves Broughton, "A Compelling Vision of a Dystopian Future for Workers and How to Avoid it," *Financial Times*, Kindle Edition (May 19, 2011). See also Lynda Gratton, *The Shift: The Future of Work Is Already Here* (London: HarperCollins UK, 2011).

[3] Thomas A. Stewart, *Intellectual Capital: The Wealth of Organizations* (New York: Bantam, 1998).

[4] Charles O'Reilly III and Jeffrey Pfeffer, *Hidden Value: How Great Companies Achieve Extraordinary Results with Ordinary People* (Boston: Harvard Business School Press, 2000), p. 2.

[5] Dave Ulrich, "Intellectual Capital = Competency + Commitment," *Harvard Business Review* (Winter 1998), pp. 15–26.

[6] See Peter F. Drucker, *The Changing World of the Executive* (New York: T.T. Times Books, 1982); *The Profession of Management* (Cambridge, MA: Harvard Business School Press, 1997); and Francis Horibe, *Managing Knowledge Workers: New Skills and Attitudes to Unlock the Intellectual Capital in Your Organization* (New York: Wiley, 1999).

[7] Daniel Pink, *A Whole New Mind: Moving from the Information Age to the Conceptual Age* (New York: Riverhead Books, 2005).

[8] Gary Hamel, "Gary Hamel Sees More Options . . . Fewer Grand Visions," *Wall Street Journal*, Special Advertising Section (October 6, 2009), p. Akl16.

[9] See Kenichi Ohmae's books *The Borderless World: Power and Strategy in the Interlinked Economy* (New York: Harper, 1989); *The End of the Nation State* (New York: Free Press, 1996); *The Invisible Continent: Four Strategic Imperatives of the New Economy* (New York: Harper, 1999); and *The Next Global Stage: Challenges and Opportunities in Our Borderless World* (Philadelphia: Wharton School Publishing, 2006).

[10] Information from Micheline Maynard, "A Lifeline Not Made in the USA," *New York Times* (October 18, 2009), nytimes.com (accessed April 15, 2010).

[11] See Joseph E. Stiglitz, *Globalization and Its Discontents* (New York: W.W. Norton, 2003); and Joseph E. Stiglitz, *Making Globalization Work* (New York: W.W. Norton, 2007).

[12] Michael E. Porter, *The Competitive Advantage of Nations: With a New Introduction* (New York: Free Press, 1998).

[13] See, for example, John Bussey, "Buck Up America: China Is Getting Too Expensive," *Wall Street Journal* (October 7, 2011), pp. B1, B2.

[14] "Intel's Ambitions Bloom in Arizona Desert," *Financial Times,* Kindle Edition (January 23, 2012).

[15] Esmé E. Deprez, "Madoff Sentenced to Maximum 150 Years," *Bloomberg BusinessWeek* (June 29, 2009), *BusinessWeek.com* (accessed April 15, 2010).

[16] For discussions of ethics in business and management, see Linda K. Trevino and Katherine A. Nelson, *Managing Business Ethics,* 4th ed. (Hoboken, NJ: John Wiley & Sons, 2010); and Richard DeGeorge, *Business Ethics,* 7th ed. (Englewood Cliffs, NJ: Prentice-Hall, 2009).

[17] Daniel Akst, "Room at the Top for Improvement," *Wall Street Journal* (October 26, 2004), p. D8; and Herb Baum and Tammy King, *The Transparent Leader* (New York: Collins, 2005).

[18] "The Responsible Economy: You Are Part of It," patagonia.com (accessed December 10, 2013).

[19] Workforce 2000, *Work and Workers for the 21st Century* (Indianapolis, IN: Towers Perrin/Hudson Institute, 1987); Richard W. Judy and Carol D'Amico (eds.), *Work and Workers for the 21st Century* (Indianapolis, IN: Hudson Institute, 1997). See also Richard D. Bucher, *Diversity Consciousness: Opening Our Minds to People, Cultures, and Opportunities* (Upper Saddle River, NJ: Prentice-Hall, 2000); R. Roosevelt Thomas, "From Affirmative Action to Affirming Diversity," *Harvard Business Review* (March–April 1990), pp. 107–17; and *Beyond Race and Gender: Unleashing the Power of Your Total Workforce by Managing Diversity* (New York: AMACOM, 1992).

[20] June Dronholz, "Hispanics Gain in Census," *Wall Street Journal* (May 10, 2006), p. A6; Phillip Toledano, "Demographics: The Population Hourglass," *Fast Company* (March 2006), p. 56; June Kronholz, "Racial Identity's Gray Area," *Wall Street Journal* (June 12, 2008), p. A10; "We're Getting Old," *Wall Street Journal* (March 26, 2009), p. D2; Les Christie, "Hispanic Population Boom Fuels Rising U.S. Diversity," *CNNMoney*, cnn.com; Betsy Towner, "The New Face of 501 America," *AARP Bulletin* (June 2009), p. 31; Kelly Evans, "Recession Drives More Women in the Workforce," *Wall Street Journal* (November 12, 2009), p. A21; and "Minority Report: U.S. Sees Surge in Asian, Hispanic Populations," *Wall Street Journal* (May 28–29, 2011), p. A3.

[21] Information from "Women and Work: We Did It!" *The Economist* (December 31, 2009); Joann S. Lublin, "Female Directors: Why So Few?" *Wall Street Journal* (December 27, 2011), p. B5; and Ben Waber, "Gender Bias by the Numbers," *Bloomberg BusinessWeek* (February 3–9, 2014), pp. 8, 9.

[22] "The Glass Precipice: Why Female Bosses Fail more often than Male Ones," *The Economist*, Kindle Edition (May 6, 2014).

[23] Sylvia Ann Hewitt, "Cracking the Code That Stalls Multicultural Professionals," *HBR Blog Network* (January 22, 2014), blogs.hbr.org/2014/01.

[24] Information from "Racism in Hiring Remains, Study Says," *Columbus Dispatch* (January 17, 2003), p. B2; Waber, op cit.

[25] Ashleigh Shelby Rosette, Geoffrey J. Leonardelli, and Katherine W. Phillips, "The White Standard: Racial Bias in Leader Categorization," *Journal of Applied Psychology,* vol. 93 (2008), pp. 758–77. See also, "Race Influences How Leaders Are Assessed," *Wall Street Journal* (January 3, 2012), p. B7.

[26] Survey data reported in Sue Shellenbarger, "New Workplace Equalizer: Ambition," *Wall Street Journal* (March 26, 2009), p. D5.

[27] Waber, op cit.

[28] Judith B. Rosener, "Women Make Good Managers. So What?" *BusinessWeek* (December 11, 2000), p. 24.

[29] See Leslie Kwoh, "Firms Hail New Chief (of Diversity)," *Wall Street Journal* (January 5, 2012), p. B10.

[30] Charles Handy, *The Age of Unreason* (Cambridge, MA: Harvard Business School Press, 1990); also see Charles Handy, *A Business Guru's Portfolio Life* (New York: AMACOM, 2008); and *Myself and Other Important Matters* (New York: AMACOM, 2008).

[31] See Peter Coy, Michelle Conlin, and Moira Herbst, "The Disposable Worker," *Bloomberg BusinessWeek* (January 18, 2010), pp. 33–39.

[32] See Gareille Monaghan, "Don't Get a Job, Get a Portfolio Career," *Sunday Times* (April 26, 2009), p. 15.

[33] Tom Peters, "The New Wired World of Work," *BusinessWeek* (August 28, 2000), pp. 172–73.

[34] Quotes from "IBM vs. the Carnegie Corporation: Making the World Work Better," *The Economist*, Kindle Edition (June 9, 2011); and "Corporate Responsibility at IBM: A Foreword by IBM's Chairman," ibm.com/ibm/responsibility/letter.shtml (accessed October 3, 2011).

[35] Quote from Stephen Moore, "The Conscience of a Capitalist," *Wall Street Journal* (October 3–4, 2009), p. A11; see also wholefoods.com/company.

[36] For an overview of organizations and organization theory, see W. Richard Scott, *Organizations: Rational, Natural and Open Systems*, 4th ed. (Englewood Cliffs, NJ: Prentice-Hall, 1998).

[37] Information from Paul F. Nunes, Geoffrey Godbey, and H. James Wilson, "Bet the Clock," *Wall Street Journal* (October 26, 2009), p. R6; and Steve Hamm, "The King of the Cloud," *Bloomberg BusinessWeek* (November 30, 2009), p. 77.

[38] Includes ideas from Jay A. Conger, *Winning 'em Over: A New Model for Managing in the Age of Persuasion* (New York: Simon & Schuster, 1998), pp. 180–81; Stewart D. Friedman, Perry Christensen, and Jessica DeGroot, "Work and Life: The End of the Zero-Sum Game," *Harvard Business Review* (November–December 1998), pp. 119–29; Chris Argyris, "Empowerment: The Emperor's New Clothes," *Harvard Business Review* (May–June 1998), pp. 98–105; and John A. Byrne, "Management by Web," *BusinessWeek* (August 28, 2000), pp. 84–98. See also emerging reports such as O'Toole and Lawler, op. cit.; Jon Nicholson and Amanda Nairn, *The Manager of the 21st Century: 2020 Vision* (Sydney: Boston Consulting Group, 2008); and Jeffrey Pfeffer, "Building Sustainable Organizations: The Human Factor," *Academy of Management Perspectives,* vol. 24 (February 2010), pp. 34–45.

[39] Jeffrey Pfeffer and John F. Veiga, "Putting People First for Organizational Success," *Academy of Management Executive*, vol. 13 (May 1999), pp. 37–48; and Jeffrey Pfeffer, *The Human Equation: Building Profits by Putting People First* (Boston: Harvard Business School Press, 1998).

[40] Henry Mintzberg, "The Manager's Job: Folklore and Fact," *Harvard Business Review*, vol. 53 (July–August 1975), p. 61. See also his book, *The Nature of Managerial Work* (New York: Harper-Row, 1973: HarperCollins, 1997).

[41] For an example of research on corporate boards, see Marta Geletkanycz and Brian Boyd, "CEO Outside Directorships and Firm Performance: A Reconciliation of Agency and Embeddedness Views," *Academy of Management Journal*, vol. 54 (April 2011), pp. 335–52.

[42] Ellen Byron, "P&G's Lafley Sees CEOs as Link to World," *Wall Street Journal* (March 23, 2009), p. B6; and Stefan Stern, "What Exactly Are Chief Executives For?" *Financial Times* (May 15, 2009).

[43] For a perspective on the first-level manager's job, see Leonard A. Schlesinger and Janice A. Klein, "The First-Line Supervisor: Past, Present and Future," in Jay W. Lorsch (ed.), *Handbook of Organizational Behavior,* pp. 370–82 (Englewood Cliffs, NJ: Prentice-Hall, 1987).

[44] Pfeffer, op. cit.

[45] George Anders, "Overseeing More Employees—With Fewer Managers," *Wall Street Journal* (March 24, 2008), p. B6.

[46] This running example is developed from information from "Accountants Have Lives, Too, You Know," *BusinessWeek* (February 23, 1998), pp. 88–90; Silvia Ann Hewlett and Carolyn Buck Luce, "Off-Ramps and On-Ramps: Keeping Talented Women on the Road to Success," *Harvard Business Review* (March 2005), reprint 9491; and the Ernst-Young website, ey.com.

[47] Mintzberg (1973/1997), op. cit., p. 30.

[48] See Mintzberg (1973/1997), op. cit., Henry Mintzberg, "Covert Leadership: The Art of Managing Professionals," *Harvard Business Review* (November–December 1998), pp. 140–47; and Jonathan Gosling and Henry Mintzberg, "The Five Minds of a Manager," *Harvard Business Review* (November 2003), pp. 1–9.

[49] For research on managerial work, see Morgan W. McCall Jr., Ann M. Morrison, and Robert L. Hannan, *Studies of Managerial Work: Results and Methods. Technical Report #9* (Greensboro, NC: Center for Creative Leadership, 1978),

pp. 7–9. See also John P. Kotter, "What Effective General Managers Really Do," *Harvard Business Review* (November–December 1982), pp. 156–57.

[50] Mintzberg (1973/1997), op. cit., p. 60.

[51] Scene based on Kotter, op. cit., p. 164. See also his book *The General Managers* (New York: Free Press, 1986); and David Barry, Catherine Durnell Crampton, and Stephen J. Carroll, "Navigating the Garbage Can: How Agendas Help Managers Cope with Job Realities," *Academy of Management Executive*, vol. 2 (May 1997), pp. 43–56.

[52] "Business Schools Get Low Marks from CEOs," *Wall Street Journal* (March 19, 2014), p. B7.

[53] Robert L. Katz, "Skills of an Effective Administrator," *Harvard Business Review* (September–October 1974), p. 94.

[54] Ibid.

[55] See, for example, Melissa Korn and Joe Light, "On the Lesson Plan: Feelings," *Wall Street Journal* (May 5, 2011), p. B6; and Alina Dizik, "Women Embrace the Skills and Strategies for a Corporate Life," *Financial Times* (September 12, 2011), p. 12.

[56] See Daniel Goleman's books, *Emotional Intelligence* (New York: Bantam, 1995) and *Working with Emotional Intelligence* (New York: Bantam, 1998); and his articles "What Makes a Leader," *Harvard Business Review* (November–December 1998), pp. 93–102, and "Leadership That Makes a Difference," *Harvard Business Review* (March–April 2000), pp. 79–90; quote from p. 80.

[57] See Daniel Goleman, Richard Boyatzis, and Annie McKee, *Primal Leadership: Realizing the Power of Emotional Intelligence* (Boston: Harvard Business School Press, 2002).

[58] "Business Schools Get Low Marks from CEOs," op cit. See also Richard E. Boyatzis, "Competencies in the 21st Century," *Journal of Management Development*, vol. 27, no. 1 (2008), pp. 5–12; and Richard Boyatzis (Guest Editor), "Competencies in the EU," *Journal of Management Development*, vol. 28 (2009), special issue.

[59] Quote from Tony Wagner, *The Global Achievement Gap: Why Even our Best Schools Don't Teach the New Survival Skills our Children Need and What We Can Do About It* (New York: Basic Books, 2008), pp. 14–17.

[60] Suggested by and some items included from *Outcome Measurement Project, Phase I and Phase II Reports* (St. Louis: American Assembly of Collegiate Schools of Business, 1986).

Feature Notes

Analysis: Information from Kate Taylor, "Why Millennials Are Ending the 9 to 5," *FORBESWOMAN* (August 23, 2013), forbes.com (accessed September 9, 2013); Mandy Dorn and Michele Vana, "Younger Managers Rise in the Ranks," *EY Building a Better Working World,* ey.com (accessed December 9, 2013).

Research Brief: References from Robert J. House, P. J. Hanges, Mansour Javidan, P. Dorfman, and V. Gupta (eds.), *Culture, Leadership and Organizations: The GLOBE Study of 62 Societies* (Thousand Oaks, CA: Sage Publications, 2004); Mansour Javidan, Peter W. Dorfman, Mary Sully de Luque, and

Robert J. House, *Academy of Management Perspective*, vol. 20 (2006), pp. 67–90.

Wisdom: Information and quotes from Ellen McGurt, "Fresh Copy," *Fast Company* (December 2011/January 2012), news. xerox.com (accessed August 25, 2012); "Game Changer in Business and Tech: Ursula Burns," *Huffington Post* (November 1, 2011), huffingtonpost.com; and Carol Hymowitz, "Ursula Burns, CEO, Xerox," *Bloomberg BusinessWeek* (August 12–25, 2013), pp. 57–58.

Chapter 2

Endnotes

[1] A thorough review and critique of the history of management thought, including management in ancient civilizations, is provided by Daniel A. Wren, *The Evolution of Management Thought*, 4th ed. (New York: Wiley, 1993).

[2] Pauline Graham, *Mary Parker Follett—Prophet of Management: A Celebration of Writings from the 1920s* (Boston: Harvard Business School Press, 1995).

[3] For a timeline of 20th-century management ideas, see "75 Years of Management Ideas and Practices: 1922–1997," *Harvard Business Review*, supplement (September–October 1997).

[4] For a sample of this work, see Henry L. Gantt, *Industrial Leadership* (Easton, MD: Hive, 1921, Hive edition published in 1974); Henry C. Metcalfe and Lyndall Urwick (eds.), *Dynamic Administration: The Collected Papers of Mary Parker Follett* (New York: Harper-Brothers, 1940); James D. Mooney, *The Principles of Administration,* rev. ed. (New York: Harper-Brothers, 1947); Lyndall Urwick, *The Elements of Administration* (New York: Harper-Brothers, 1943); and *The Golden Book of Management* (London: N. Neame, 1956).

[5] Frederick W. Taylor, *The Principles of Scientific Management* (New York: W.W. Norton, 1967), originally published by Harper-Brothers in 1911. See also the biography, Robert Kanigel, *The One Best Way* (New York: Viking, 1997).

[6] For criticisms of Taylor and his work, see Charles W. Wrege and Amedeo G. Perroni, "Taylor's Pig-Tale: A Historical Analysis of Frederick W. Taylor's Pig Iron Experiments," *Academy of Management Journal*, vol. 17 (March 1974), pp. 6–27; Charles W. Wrege and Richard M. Hodgetts, "Frederick W. Taylor's 1899 Pig Iron Observations: Examining Fact, Fiction and Lessons for the New Millennium," *Academy of Management Journal,* vol. 43 (2000), pp. 1283–91; and Jill Lepore, "Not So Fast," *The New Yorker* (October 12, 2009), newyorker.com.

[7] For a discussion of the contemporary significance of Taylor's work, see Edwin A. Lock, "The Ideas of Frederick W. Taylor: An Evaluation," *Academy of Management Review*, vol. 7 (1982), p. 14.

[8] Information from Raymund Flandez and Kelly K. Sports, "Tackling the Energy Monster," *Wall Street Journal* (June 16, 2008), p. R1; and Jennifer Levitz, "Delivery Drivers to Pick up Pace by Surrendering Keys," *Wall Street Journal*, Kindle Edition (September 16, 2011).

[9] Frank B. Gilbreth, *Motion Study* (New York: Van Nostrand, 1911).

[10] Information from Karl Taro Greenfield, "Taco Bell and the Golden Age of Drive Through," *BusinessWeek* (May 5, 2011), businessweek.com (accessed October 30, 2013).

[11] Available in English as *Henri Fayol, General and Industrial Administration* (London: Pitman, 1949); subsequent discussion is based on M. B. Brodie, *Fayol on Administration* (London: Pitman, 1949).

[12] A. M. Henderson and Talcott Parsons (eds. and trans.), *Max Weber: The Theory of Social Economic Organization* (New York: Free Press, 1947).

[13] Ibid., p. 337.

[14] For classic treatments of bureaucracy, see Alvin Gouldner, *Patterns of Industrial Bureaucracy* (New York: Free Press, 1954); and Robert K. Merton, *Social Theory and Social Structure* (New York: Free Press, 1957).

[15] "Highlights of GAO-10-455, a Report to Congressional Committees," United States Government Accountability Office (April 2010), gao.gov/assets/310/303039.pdf (accessed December 22, 2013).

[16] M. P. Follett, *Freedom and Coordination* (London: Management Publications Trust, 1949).

[17] Judith Garwood, "A Review of Dynamic Administration: The Collected Papers of Mary Parker Follett," *New Management,* vol. 2 (1984), pp. 61–62; eulogy from Richard C. Cabot, *Encyclopedia of Social Work,* vol. 15, "Follett, Mary Parker," p. 351.

[18] The Hawthorne studies are described in detail in F. J. Roethlisberger and William J. Dickson, *Management and the Worker* (Cambridge, MA: Harvard University Press, 1966), and G. Homans, *Fatigue of Workers* (New York: Reinhold, 1941). For an interview with three of the participants in the relay–assembly test–room studies, see R. G. Greenwood, A. A. Bolton, and R. A. Greenwood, "Hawthorne a Half Century Later: Relay Assembly Participants Remember," *Journal of Management,* vol. 9 (1983), pp. 217–31.

[19] The criticisms of the Hawthorne studies are detailed in Alex Carey, "The Hawthorne Studies: A Radical Criticism," *American Sociological Review,* vol. 32 (1967), pp. 403–16; H. M. Parsons, "What Happened at Hawthorne?" *Science,* vol. 183 (1974), pp. 922–32; and B. Rice, "The Hawthorne Defect: Persistence of a Flawed Theory," *Psychology Today,* vol. 16 (1982), pp. 70–74. See also Wren, op. cit.

[20] This discussion of Maslow's theory is based on Abraham H. Maslow, *Eupsychian Management* (Homewood, IL: Richard D. Irwin, 1965) and Abraham H. Maslow, *Motivation and Personality,* 2nd ed. (New York: Harper-Row, 1970).

[21] Douglas McGregor, *The Human Side of Enterprise* (New York: McGraw-Hill, 1960).

[22] This notion is also discussed in terms of the "pygmalion effect." See Dov Eden, *Pygmalion in Management* (Lexington, MA: Lexington Books, 1990), and Dov Eden, Dvorah Geller, and Abigail Gerwirtz, "Implanting Pygmalion Leadership Style through Workshop Training: Seven Field

Experiments," *Leadership Quarterly,* vol. 11, issue 2 (June 1, 2000), pp. 171–210.

[23] Gary Heil, Deborah F. Stevens, and Warren G. Bennis, *Douglas McGregor on Management: Revisiting the Human Side of Enterprise* (New York: Wiley, 2000).

[24] Chris Argyris, *Personality and Organization* (New York: Harper-Row, 1957).

[25] Stefan Stern, "Smarter Leaders Are Betting Big on Data," *Financial Times,* Kindle Edition (March 9, 2010). See also Thomas H. Davenport, Jeanne G. Harris, and Robert Morison, *Analytics at Work: Smarter Decisions, Better Results* (Cambridge, MA: Harvard Business Press, 2010).

[26] Scott Morrison, "Google Searches for Staffing Answers," *Wall Street Journal* (May 19, 2009), p. B1; and Dennis K. Berman, "So, What's Your Algorithm?" *Wall Street Journal* (January 4, 2012), pp. B1, B2.

[27] The ideas of Chester I. Bamard, *Functions of the Executive* (Cambridge, MA: Harvard University Press, 1938), and Ludwig von Bertalanffy, "The History and Status of General Systems Theory," *Academy of Management Journal,* vol. 15 (1972), pp. 407–26, contributed to the emergence of this systems perspective on organizations. The systems view is further developed by Daniel Katz and Robert L. Kahn in their classic book, *The Social Psychology of Organizations* (New York: Wiley, 1978). For an integrated systems view, see Lane Tracy, *The Living Organization* (New York: Quorum Books, 1994). For an overview, see W. Richard Scott, *Organizations: Rational, Natural, and Open Systems,* 4th ed. (Upper Saddle River, NJ: Prentice-Hall, 1998).

[28] For an overview, see Scott, op. cit., pp. 95–97.

[29] See, for example, the classic studies of Tom Burns and George M. Stalker, *The Management of Innovation* (London: Tavistock, 1961, and republished by Oxford University Press, London, 1994) and Paul R. Lawrence and Jay W. Lorsch, *Organizations and Environment* (Boston: Division of Research, Graduate School of Business Administration, Harvard University, 1967).

[30] W. Edwards Deming, *Quality, Productivity, and Competitive Position* (Cambridge, MA: MIT Press, 1982); and Rafael Aguay, *Dr. Deming: The American Who Taught the Japanese about Quality* (New York: Free Press, 1997).

[31] See Howard S. Gitlow and Shelly J. Gitlow, *The Deming Guide to Quality and Competitive Position* (Englewood Cliffs, NJ: Prentice-Hall, 1987).

[32] See Denise M. Rousseau, "On Organizational Behavior," *BizEd* (May/June, 2008), pp. 30–31; and David G. Allen, Phillip C. Bryant, and James A. Vardaman, "Retaining Talent: Replacing Misconceptions with Evidence-Based Strategies," *Academy of Management Perspectives,* vol. 24, no. 2 (May 1, 2010).

[33] See Bruce G. Resnick and Timothy L. Smunt, "From Good to Great to . . ." *Academy of Management Perspectives* (November 2008), pp. 6–12; and Bruce Niendorf and Kristine Beck, "Good to Great, or Just Good?" *Academy of Management Perspectives* (November 2008), pp. 13–20.

[34] Jeffrey Pfeffer and Robert I. Sutton, *Hard Facts, Dangerous Half-Truths, and Total Nonsense: Profiting from Evidence-Based Management* (Boston: Harvard Business School Press, 2006).

[35] Jeffrey Pfeffer and Robert I. Sutton, "Management Half-Truths and Nonsense," *California Management Review,* vol. 48, no. 3 (Spring 2006), pp. 77–100; and Jeffrey Pfeffer and Robert I. Sutton, "Evidence-Based Management," *Harvard Business Review* (January 2006), reprint R0601E.

[36] Rob B. Viner, David Denyer, and Denise M. Rousseau, "Evidence-Based Management: Concept Cleanup Time?" *Academy of Management Perspectives,* vol. 23 (November 2009), pp. 19–28. For the debate on the concept, see the exchange between ibid. and Trish Reay, Whitney Berta, and Melanie Kazman Kohn, "What's the Evidence on Evidence-Based Management?" *Academy of Management Perspectives,* vol. 23 (November 2009), pp. 5–18.

[37] Jeffrey Pfeffer, *The Human Equation: Building Profits by Putting People First* (Boston: Harvard Business School Press, 1998); and Charles O'Reilly III and Jeffrey Pfeffer, *Hidden Value: How Great Companies Achieve Extraordinary Results with Ordinary People* (Boston: Harvard Business School Press, 2000).

[38] Ibid

[39] Developed from Sara L. Rynes, Tamara L. Giluk, and Kenneth G. Brown, "The Very Separate Worlds of Academic and Practitioner Periodicals in Human Resource Management: Implications for Evidence-Based Management," *Academy of Management Journal,* vol. 50 (October 2008), p. 986; and David G. Allen, Phillip C. Bryant, and James M. Vardaman, "Retaining Talent: Replacing Misconceptions with Evidence-Based Strategies," *Academy of Management Perspectives,* vol. 24 (May 2010).

Feature Notes

Ethics: Information from Spencer E. Ante and Lauren Weber, "Memo to Workers: The Boss Is Watching," *Wall Street Journal* (October 23, 2013), pp. B1, B6; and Spencer E. Ante and Lauren Weber, "With Little on Law Books, Employers Have Latitude in Monitoring Workers," *Wall Street Journal* (October 23, 2013), p. B6.

Insight: See David A. Kolb, *Experiential Learning: Experience as the Source of Learning and Development* (Englewood Cliffs, NJ: Prentice-Hall, 1984); and David A. Kolb, "Experiential Learning Theory and the Learning Style Inventory," *The Academy of Management Review*, vol. 6 (1981), pp. 289–96.

Wisdom: Information from "Chapter 2," *Kellogg* (Winter 2004), p. 6; David Pilling, "Establishing Libraries to Help Children Gain a Love of Books," *Financial Times* (December 8, 2009); *Leaving Microsoft to Change the World* (New York: HarperCollins), 2006; and David Pilling, "Establishing Libraries to Help Gain a Love of Books," *Financial Times,* Kindle Edition (December 8, 2009).

Chapter 3

Endnotes

Quotes are from Sarbanes-Oxley Essential Information, sox-online.com (accessed June 10, 2014); and "Company Ordered to Pay $1.9 Million to Former CFO for Sarbanes Oxley Act Violations," employerbrief.com/2013/10/company-ordered-to-pay-1-9-million-to-former-cfo-for-sarbanes-oxley-act-violations/, \o employerbrief.com (accessed June 10, 2014).

[1] Christopher M. Matthews, "Judge Wants Toyota Probe to Delve into Employees," *Wall Street Journal* (March 21, 2014), p. B3.

[2] Desmond Tutu, "Do More Than Win," *Fortune* (December 30, 1991), p. 59.

[3] For an overview, see Linda K. Trevino and Katherine A. Nelson, *Managing Business Ethics*, 3rd ed. (New York: Wiley, 2003).

[4] M. J. O'Fallon and K. D. Butterfield, "A Review of the Empirical Ethical Decision-Making Literature: 1996–2003," *Journal of Business Ethics,* vol. 59 (2005), pp. 375–413; and S. J. Vitell and E. R. Hidalgo, "The Impact of Corporate Ethical Values and Enforcement of Ethical Codes on the Perceived Importance of Ethics in Business: A Comparison of U.S. and Spanish Managers," *Journal of Business Ethics,* vol. 64 (2006), pp. 31–43.

[5] D. Lyons, *Ethics and the Rule of Law* (Cambridge, UK: Cambridge University Press, 1984).

[6] See, for example, James Oliver Horton and Lois E. Horton, *Slavery and the Making of America* (New York: Oxford University Press, 2004).

[7] Trevino and Nelson, op. cit.

[8] Milton Rokeach, *The Nature of Human Values* (New York: Free Press, 1973). See also W. C. Frederick and J. Weber, "The Values of Corporate Executives and Their Critics: An Empirical Description and Normative Implications," in W. C. Frederick and L. E. Preston (eds.), *Business Ethics: Research Issues and Empirical Studies* (Greenwich, CT: JAI Press, 1990).

[9] Philip Delves Broughton, "MBA Students Sway Integrity for Plagiarism," *Financial Times* (May 19, 2008), p. 13.

[10] Case reported in Michelle Conlin, "Cheating—Or Postmodern Learning?" *BusinessWeek* (May 14, 2007), p. 42.

[11] See Gerald F. Cavanagh, Dennis J. Moberg, and Manuel Velasquez, "The Ethics of Organizational Politics," *Academy of Management Review,* vol. 6 (1981), pp. 363–74; Justin G. Locknecker, Joseph A. McKinney, and Carlos W. Moore, "Egoism and Independence: Entrepreneurial Ethics," *Organizational Dynamics* (Winter 1988), pp. 64–72; and Justin G. Locknecker, Joseph A. McKinney, and Carlos W. Moore, "The Generation Gap in Business Ethics," *Business Horizons* (September–October 1989), pp. 9–14.

[12] Raymond L. Hilgert, "What Ever Happened to Ethics in Business and in Business Schools?" *The Diary of Alpha Kappa Psi* (April 1989), pp. 4–8.

[13] The Universal Declaration of Human Rights was adopted by General Assembly resolution 217 A (III), December 10, 1948, in the United Nations. See un.org/Overview/rights.html.

[14] Jerald Greenburg, "Organizational Justice: Yesterday, Today, and Tomorrow," *Journal of Management*, vol. 16 (1990), pp. 399–432; and Mary A. Konovsky, "Understanding Procedural Justice and Its Impact on Business Organizations," *Journal of Management*, vol. 26 (2000), pp. 489–511.

[15] For a review, see Russell Cropanzano, David E. Bown, and Stephen W. Gilliland, "The Management of Organizational Justice," *Academy of Management Perspectives* (November 2007), pp. 34–48.

[16] Interactional justice is described by Robert J. Bies, "The Predicament of Injustice: The Management of Moral Outrage," in L. L. Cummings and B. M. Staw (eds.), *Research in Organizational Behavior*, vol. 9 (Greenwich, CT: JAI Press, 1987), pp. 289–319. The example is from Carol T. Kulik and Robert L. Holbrook, "Demographics in Service Encounters: Effects of Racial and Gender Congruence on Perceived Fairness," *Social Justice Research*, vol. 13 (2000), pp. 375–402.

[17] M. Fortin and M. R. Fellenz, "Hypocrisies of Fairness: Towards a More Reflexive Ethical Base in Organizational Justice Research and Practice," *Journal of Business Ethics,* vol. 78 (2008), pp. 415–33; and W. Sadurski, "Social Justice and Legal Justice," *Law and Philosophy,* vol. 3 (1984), pp. 329–54.

[18] Robert D. Haas, "Ethics—A Global Business Challenge," *Vital Speeches of the Day* (June 1, 1996), pp. 506–9.

[19] This discussion is based on Thomas Donaldson, "Values in Tension: Ethics Away from Home," *Harvard Business Review*, vol. 74 (September–October 1996), pp. 48–62.

[20] Thomas Donaldson and Thomas W. Dunfee, "Towards a Unified Conception of Business Ethics: Integrative Social Contracts Theory," *Academy of Management Review*, vol. 19 (1994), pp. 252–85.

[21] Donaldson, op. cit.

[22] Reported in Barbara Ley Toffler, "Tough Choices: Managers Talk Ethics," *New Management*, vol. 4 (1987), pp. 34–39. See also Barbara Ley Toffler, *Tough Choices: Managers Talk Ethics* (New York: Wiley, 1986).

[23] See, for example, Steven N. Brenner and Earl A. Mollander, "Is the Ethics of Business Changing?" *Harvard Business Review*, vol. 55 (January–February 1977).

[24] Survey results from Del Jones, "48% of Workers Admit to Unethical or Illegal Acts," *USA Today* (April 4, 1997), p. A1.

[25] For a discussion of similar approaches, see Denis Collins, *Business Ethics: How to Design and Manage Ethical Organizations* (Hoboken, NJ: John Wiley & Sons, 2012), pp. 146–47.

[26] Reported in Adam Smith, "Wall Street's Outrageous Fortunes," *Esquire* (April 1987), p. 73. See also Long Wang and J. Keith Murnighan, "On Greed," *The Academy of Management Annals*, vol. 5 (2011), pp. 279–316.

[27] Lawrence Kohlberg, *The Psychology of Moral Development: The Nature and Validity of Moral Stages* (*Essays in Moral Development*, Volume 2) (New York: HarperCollins, 1984). See also the discussion by Linda K. Trevino, "Moral Reasoning and Business Ethics: Implications for Research, Education, and Management," *Journal of Business Ethics*, vol. 11 (1992), pp. 445–59.

[28] See Thomas M. Jones, "Ethical Decision Making by Individuals in Organizations: An Issue Contingent Model," *Academy of Management Review*, vol. 16 (1991), pp. 366–95; Sara Morris and Robert A. McDonald, "The Role of Moral Intensity in Moral Judgments: An Empirical Investigation," *Journal of Business Ethics*, vol. 14, issue 9 (1995), pp. 715–26; and Tim Barnett, "Dimensions of Moral Intensity and Ethical Decision Making: An Empirical Study," *Journal of Applied Social Psychology*, vol. 31 (2001), pp. 1038–57.

[29] David M. Mayer, Samir Nurmohamed, Linda Klebe Treviño, Debra L. Shapiro, and Marshall Schminke, "Encouraging Employees to Report Unethical Behavior Internally: It Takes a Village," *Organizational Behavior and Human Decision Processes*, vol. 121 (2013), pp. 89–103.

[30] Information on this case from William M. Carley, "Antitrust Chief Says CEOs Should Tape All Phone Calls to Each Other," *Wall Street Journal* (February 15, 1983), p. 23; "American Air, Chief End Antitrust Suit, Agree Not to Discuss Fares with Rivals," *Wall Street Journal* (July 15, 1985), p. 4; "American Airlines Loses Its Pilot," *The Economist* (April 18, 1998), p. 58.

[31] Situations from Alison Damast and Erin Zlomek, "Top B-School Stories of 2011," *Bloomberg BusinessWeek* (December 28, 2011), *BusinessWeek*.com; and Joe Palazzolo and Emily Glazer, "Grand Jury Gets Evidence," *Wall Street Journal* (February 13, 2012), pp. A1, A2.

[32] Saul W. Gellerman, "Why 'Good' Managers Make Bad Ethical Choices," *Harvard Business Review*, vol. 64 (July–August 1986), pp. 85–90.

[33] See Spencer E. Ante and Don Clark, "H-P Settles Bribery Case," *Wall Street Journal* (April 10, 2014), p. B1; and Jeff Bennett, "GM Recall Probe Heats Up," *Wall Street Journal* (March 6, 2014), p. B1

[34] Archie B. Carroll, "In Search of the Moral Manager," *Business Horizons* (March/April 2001), pp. 7–15.

[35] Kohlberg, op. cit.

[36] Alan L. Otten, "Ethics on the Job: Companies Alert Employees to Potential Dilemmas," *Wall Street Journal* (July 14, 1986), p. 17; and "The Business Ethics Debate," *Newsweek* (May 25, 1987), p. 36.

[37] Information from corporate website, gapinc.com/communitysourcing/vendor_conduct.htm.

[38] See "Whistle-Blowers on Trial," *BusinessWeek* (March 24, 1997), pp. 172–78, and "NLRB Judge Rules for Massachusetts Nurses in Whistle-Blowing Case," *American Nurse* (January–February 1998), p. 7.

[39] For a review of whistleblowing, see Marcia P. Micelli and Janet P. Near, *Blowing the Whistle* (Lexington, MA:

Lexington Books, 1992); see also Micelli and Near, "Whistleblowing: Reaping the Benefits," *Academy of Management Executive*, vol. 8 (August 1994), pp. 65–72; and M. J. Gundlach, S. C. Douglas, and M. J. Martinko, "The Decision to Blow the Whistle: A Social Information Processing Framework," *Academy of Management Review*, vol. 28, no. 1 (2003), pp. 107–23.

[40] "A Tip for Whistleblowers: Don't," *Wall Street Journal* (May 31, 2007), p. B6.

[41] Mayer, et al., op cit.

[42] Information from Ethics Resource Center, "Major Survey of America's Workers Finds Substantial Improvements in Ethics," ethics.org/releases/nr_20030521_nbes.html.

[43] James A. Waters, "Catch 20.5: Mortality as an Organizational Phenomenon," *Organizational Dynamics*, vol. 6 (Spring 1978), pp. 3–15.

[44] See Thomas Donaldson and Lee Preston, "The Stakeholder Theory of the Corporation," *Academy of Management Review*, vol. 20 (January 1995), pp. 65–91.

[45] Michael E. Porter and Mark R. Kramer, "Strategy & Society: The Link between Competitive Advantage and Corporate Social Responsibility," *Harvard Business Review* (December 2006), Reprint R0612D.

[46] R. K. Bradley, R. Agle, and D. J. Wood, "Toward a Theory of Stakeholder Identification and Salience: Defining the Principle of Who and What Really Counts," *Academy of Management Review*, vol. 22 (1997), pp. 853–86.

[47] Kara Scannell, "NY Regulator Targets Individuals Behind Corporate Wrongdoing," *Financial Times*, Kindle Edition (March 10, 2014).

[48] Definition from pgsupplier.com/en/current-suppliers/environmental-sustainability-scorecard.shtml (accessed May 5, 2014).

[49] Alfred A. Marcus and Adam R. Fremeth, "Green Management Matters Regardless," *Academy of Management Perspectives*, vol. 23 (August 2009), pp. 17–26.

[50] Jeffrey Pfeffer, "Building Sustainable Organizations: The Human Factor," *Academy of Management Perspectives*, vol. 24 (February 2010), pp. 34–45.

[51] Joe Biesecker, "What Today's College Graduates Want: It's Not All about Paychecks," *Central Penn Business Journal* (August 10, 2007); and Sarah E. Needleman, "The Latest Office Perk: Getting Paid to Volunteer," *Wall Street Journal* (April 29, 2008), p. D1.

[52] Ibid. Biesecker.

[53] The historical framework of this discussion is developed from Keith Davis, "The Case for and against Business Assumption of Social Responsibility," *Academy of Management Journal* (June 1973), pp. 312–22; Keith Davis and William Frederick, *Business and Society: Management: Public Policy, Ethics*, 5th ed. (New York: McGraw-Hill, 1984). The debate is also discussed by Makower, op. cit., pp. 28–33. For further perspective on this debate, see, for example, Marcus and Fremeth, op cit., and Donald S. Siegel, "Green Management Matters Only if It Yields More Green: An Economic/Strategic Perspective,"

Academy of Management Perspectives, vol. 23 (August 2009), pp. 5–16.

[54] The Friedman quotation is from Milton Friedman, *Capitalism and Freedom* (Chicago: University of Chicago Press, 1962). See also Henry G. Manne, "Milton Friedman Was Right," *Wall Street Journal* (November 24, 2006), p. A12.

[55] For more on this line of thinking, see Aneel Kamari, "The Case against Corporate Social Responsibility," *Wall Street Journal* (August 23, 2010), wsj.com.

[56] The Samuelson quotation is from Paul A. Samuelson, "Love That Corporation," *Mountain Bell Magazine* (Spring 1971). Both are cited in Davis, op. cit.

[57] Michael E. Porter and Mark R. Kramer, "Shared Value: How to Reinvent Capitalism and Unleash a Wave of Innovation and Growth," *Harvard Business Review* (January–February, 2011), pp. 62–77.

[58] Ibid., p. 64.

[59] See Makower, op. cit. (1994), pp. 71–75; Sandra A. Waddock and Samuel B. Graves, "The Corporate Social Performance—Financial Performance Link," *Strategic Management Journal* (1997), pp. 303–19; Michael E. Porter and Mark R. Kramer, "Strategy-Society: The Link between Competitive Advantage and Corporate Social Responsibility," *Harvard Business Review* (December 2006), pp. 78–92.

[60] Information and quotes from Mara Lemos-Stein, "Talking about Waste with P&G," *Wall Street Journal* (September 13, 2011), p. R8; and "Benefits Flow as Top People Join the Battle," *Financial Times*, Kindle Edition (June 23, 2011); and nestle.com/csv/ruraldevelopment/responsiblesourcing (retrieved February 18, 2012); and "How to Create a Green Supply Chain," *Financial Times*, Kindle Edition (November 11, 2010).

[61] Ioannis Ioannou and George Serafeim, "The Consequences of Mandatory Corporate Sustainability Reporting," *HBS Working Paper No. 11-100*, Harvard Business School (March 2011).

[62] The "compliance–conviction" distinction is attributed to Mark Goyder in Martin Waller, "Much Corporate Responsibility Is Box-Ticking," *The Times Business* (July 8, 2003), p. 21. See also Archie B. Carroll, "A Three-Dimensional Model of Corporate Performance," *Academy of Management Review*, vol. 4 (1979), pp. 497–505.

[63] Elizabeth Gatewood and Archie B. Carroll, "The Anatomy of Corporate Social Response," *Business Horizons*, vol. 24 (September–October 1981), pp. 9–16; and Mark S. Schwartz and Archie B. Carroll, "Corporate Social Responsibility: A Three Domain Approach," *Business Ethics Quarterly*, vol. 13 (2003), pp. 503–30.

[64] Judith Burns, "Everything You Wanted to Know about Corporate Governance . . . But Didn't Know How to Ask," *Wall Street Journal* (October 27, 2003), pp. R1, R7.

[65] Sarbanes-Oxley Essential Information, sox-online.com (accessed June 10, 2014); and "Company Ordered to Pay $1.9 Million to Former CFO for Sarbanes Oxley Act Violations," employerbrief.com (accessed June 10, 2014).

Feature Notes

Analysis: Manager Behavior: Information from Deloitte LLP, "Leadership Counts: 2007 Deloitte & Touche USA Ethics & Workplace Survey Results," *Kiplinger Business Resource Center* (June 2007), kiplinger.com.

Ethics: Information and quotes from Eric Spitznagel, "Rise Up, Interns," *Bloomberg BusinessWeek* (June 24–30, 2013), p. 78.

Insight: For more on individual character and tensions of expediency, see Charles R. Stoner and Jason S. Stoner, *Building Leaders: Paving the Path for Emerging Leaders* (New York: Routledge, 2013), Chapter 2. For more on hyper-competitiveness, see R. M. Ryckman, M. Hammer, L. M. Kaczor, and J. A. Gold, "Construction of a Hypercompetitive Attitude Scale," *Journal of Personality Assessment,* vol. 55 (1990), pp. 630–39.

Chapter 4

Endnotes

[1] Quotes from Chris Isidore and Katy Lobosco, "GM CEO Barra 'I am Deeply Sorry'," *CNN Money* (April 1, 2014), cnnmoney.com (accessed May 20, 2014); and Jeff Plungis and Tim Higgins, "GM to Pay Record $35 Million Fine Over Handling of Recall," *Bloomberg News* (May 16, 2014), Bloomberg.com (accessed May 20, 2014).

[2] Paul Lienert and Marilyn Thompson, "GM Didn't Fix Deadly Ignition Switch Because It Would Have Cost $1 Per Car," *Reuters* (April 2, 2014), huffingtonpost.com (accessed May 20, 2014); and Michael A. Fletcher, "GM Fined $35 million in Ignition-Switch Safety Case," *Washington Post* (May 16, 2014), washingtonpost.com (accessed May 20, 2014).

[3] Fletcher, op cit.

[4] See, for example, Ellen Byron, "P&G Tweaks Its Products as U.S. Shoppers Trade Down," *Wall Street Journal* (September 13, 2011), pp. 14–15; and Conor Dougherty, "Young Men Suffer Worst as Economy Staggers," *Wall Street Journal* (November 7, 2011), pp. B1, B2.

[5] "The Trade Deficit," *The Economist*, Kindle Edition (January 4, 2014).

[6] See Kris Maher and Bob Tita, "Caterpillar Joins 'Onshoring' Trend," *Wall Street Journal* (March 10, 2010), pp. B1, B7.

[7] Information from John Letzing and Ian Sherr, "HTC Sues Apple via Google," *Wall Street Journal* (September 9–11, 2011), p. 22; Ian Sherr and Jessica & Vascellaro, "Apple Hits Samsung Phone," *Wall Street Journal* (February 13, 2012), p. B1; and John Letzing, "Yahoo Threatens Suit vs. Facebook," *Wall Street Journal* (February 29, 2012) p. B5.

[8] Charles Forelle, "EU Fines Microsoft $1.35 Billion," *Wall Street Journal* (February 28, 2008), p. B2.

[9] Audrey Wozniak, "Apple Pays $60 Million for iPad Name in China," *ABC News Blogs,* abcnews.go.com (accessed May 20, 2014).

[10] Ibid; and Ben Worthen and Siobhan Gorman, "Google Prepares to Stop Censoring in China," *Wall Street Journal* (March 12, 2010), p. B1.

[11] See "It's Time for a Breakthrough," Special Advertising Section, *Bloomberg BusinessWeek* (July 4–10, 2011), pp. S1–S9; and Miriam Jordan, "White-Minority Wealth Gulf Widens," *Wall Street Journal*, Kindle Edition (July 26, 2011).

[12] See Jean M. Twenge, Stacy M. Campbell, Brian J. Hoffman, and Charles E. Lance, "Generational Difference in Work Values: Leisure and Extrinsic Values Increasing, Social and Intrinsic Values Decreasing," *Journal of Management Online First* (March 1, 2010), jom.sagepub.com.

[13] See, for example, Sharon Jayson, " 'iGeneration' Has No Off Switch," *USA Today* (February 10, 2010), pp. D1, D2.

[14] Roger Lowenstein, "Is Any CEO Worth $189,000 per Hour?" *Bloomberg BusinessWeek* (February 20–26, 2012), pp. 8, 5; Anne Baxter, "Public College Presidents Get Big Paychecks," *Marketplace Education* (May 18, 2014), marketplace.org (accessed May 20, 2014).

[15] Venessa Wong, "CEO-Worker Pay Gap," *Bloomberg BusinessWeek* (April 18, 2014), bloomberg.com (accessed May 201, 2014).

[16] See Cara Pring, "100 More Social Media Statistics, 2012," thesocialskinny.com (accessed February 28, 2012).

[17] Information from Martin Giles, "Online Social Networks Are Changing the Way People Communicate," *The Economist*, Kindle Edition (February 4, 2010).

[18] Bobby White, "The New Workplace Rules: No Video-Watching," *Wall Street Journal* (March 4, 2008), pp. B1, B3.

[19] Reported in "Surprising Attitudes toward Texting," *BizEd* (May–June, 2011), p. 72.

[20] See for example, Andy Pasztor, "Pilots Cited in July Jet Crash," *Wall Street Journal* (December 9, 2013), p. A3.

[21] See, for example, Martin Fackler, "Large Zone Near Japanese Reactors to Be Off Limits," *New York Times* (August 22, 2011), nytimes.com.

[22] See Thomas L. Freedman, "Efficiency Must be the Wave of the Future," *The Columbus Dispatch* (March 6, 2012), p. A9.

[23] See ibid.; Bradfield Moody and Bianca Nogrady, *The Sixty Wave: How to Succeed in a Resource Limited World* (Sydney: Random House Australia, 2012); and Andrew Bolger, "Bond Markets Join the Green Revolution," *Financial Times* (May 20, 2014), ft.com (accessed May 20, 2014).

[24] "Selling Green," *The Wall Street Journal* (March 26, 2012), p. R8; and Emily Gosden, "BP Warns Gulf Spill Costs Will Exceed $42.4bn as Compensation Costs Rise," *The Telegraph* (July 30, 2013), telegraph.co.uk (accessed May 20, 2014).

[25] See Thomas Donaldson and Lee Preston, "The Stakeholder Theory of the Corporation," *Academy of Management Review*, vol. 20 (January 1995), pp. 65–91.

[26] See Michael E. Porter, *Competitive Strategy: Techniques for Analyzing Industries and Competitors* (New York: Free Press, 1980); and *Competitive Advantage: Creating and Sustaining Superior Performance* (New York: Free Press, 1986);

see also Richard A. D'Aveni, *Hyper-Competition: Managing the Dynamics of Strategic Maneuvering* (New York: Free Press, 1994).

[27] Michael E. Porter, "Strategy and the Internet," *Harvard Business Review*, vol. 79, no. 3 (March 2001).

[28] James D. Thompson, *Organizations in Action* (New York: McGraw-Hill, 1967); and Robert B. Duncan, "Characteristics of Organizational Environments and Perceived Environmental Uncertainty," *Administrative Science Quarterly*, vol. 17 (1972), pp. 313–27. For a discussion of the implications of uncertainty, see Hugh Courtney, Jane Kirkland, and Patrick Viguerie, "Strategy under Uncertainty," *Harvard Business Review* (November–December 1997), pp. 67–79.

[29] Tom Peters, *The Circle of Innovation* (New York: Knopf, 1997).

[30] See, for example, Muhammad Yunus, *Creating a World without Poverty: Social Business and the Future of Capitalism* (New York: Public Affairs, 2008). Note that abuses of microcredit lending have been publicized in the press, and both the microfinance industry as a whole and the Grameen Bank in particular have been criticized by the Bangladesh government. Muhammad Yunus published his own criticism of the industry and defense of the Grameen Bank model in "Sacrificing Microcredit for Megaprofits," *New York Times* (January 14, 2011), nytimes.com. A Norwegian documentary that aired criticisms of how Yunus and Grameen Bank handled funds has largely been refuted, but Yunus continues to be criticized by the Bangladesh government.

[31] Gary Hamel, *Leading the Revolution: How to Thrive in Turbulent Times* (Boston: Harvard Business School Press, 2002).

[32] "The Joys and Perils of 'Reverse Innovation,'" *BusinessWeek* (October 5, 2009), p. 12; "How to Compete in a World Turned Upside Down," *Financial Times*, Kindle Edition (October 6, 2009).

[33] See Clay Christensen, *The Innovator's Dilemma: When New Technologies Cause Great Firms to Fail,* Reprint Edition (New York: Harper Paperbacks, 2011); and Clay Christensen, Jeff Dyer, and Hal Gregersen, *The Innovator's DNA: Mastering the Five Skills of Disruptive Innovators* (Cambridge, MA: Harvard Business Press, 2011).

[34] wbcsd.org.

[35] Economics—Creating Environmental Capital," *Wall Street Journal* (March 8, 2010), p. R1.

[36] "Indra Nooyi of PepsiCo," View from the Top, *Financial Times* (February 1, 2010), ft.com (accessed March 11, 2010).

[37] Marcus and Fremeth, op. cit.

[38] Definition from sustainablebusiness.com.

[39] See Sarah Murray, "Companies Ensure Efforts Are Not Beyond Description," *Financial Times*, Kindle Edition (June 23, 2011).

[40] David Cooperrider, "Sustainable Innovation," *BizEd* (July/August, 2008), pp. 32–38.

[41] Examples from "The Eco Advantage: The Pioneers," *Inc.* (November 1, 2006), inc.com.

[42] Information from *Bloomberg BusinessWeek* (June 6–12, 2011), pp. 70–74.

[43] "Clean-Tech Companies: Ranking the Top Venture-Backed Firms," *Wall Street Journal* (March 8, 2010), p. R4.

[44] Jeffrey Pfeffer, "Building Sustainable Organizations: The Human Factor," *Academy of Management Perspectives,* vol. 24 (February 2010), pp. 34–45.

[45] Quotes from ibid.

[46] Information and quote from Syed Zain Al-Mahmood, Christina Passareiello, and Preetika Rana, "The Global Garment Trail: From Bangladesh to a Mall Near You," *Wall Street Journal* (May 4–5, 2013), pp. A1, A11.

[47] Based on S. Budner, "Intolerance of Ambiguity as a Personality Variable," *Journal of Personality,* vol. 30, no. 1 (1962), pp. 29–50.

Feature Notes

Analysis: Information from Colleen McCain Nelson, "Poll: Most Women See Bias in the Workplace," *Wall Street Journal* (April 12, 2013), p. A5; Brenda Cronin, "Women's Wage Gap Stays Stuck in Place," *Wall Street Journal* (September 18, 2013), p. A3; Jonathan House, "Record Number of Women in the Workplace," *Wall Street Journal* (November 18, 2013), p. A4; and Hope Yen, "Pay Gap Thins for Young Women," *The Columbus Dispatch* (December 11, 2013), p. D3.

Research brief: Jean M. Twenge, Stacy M. Campbell, Brian J. Hoffman, and Charles E. Lance, "Generational Difference in Work Values: Leisure and Extrinsic Values Increasing, Social and Intrinsic Values Decreasing," *Journal of Management Online First* (March 1, 2010), www.jom.sagepub.com.

Wisdom: Information and quotes from Jessica Hodgson, "Selling and Software," *Wall Street Journal* (December 17, 2009), p. A25; Steve Hamm, "The King of the Cloud," *BusinessWeek* (November 30, 2009), p. 77, and "Charlie Rose Talks to Marc Benioff," *Bloomberg BusinessWeek* (December 5–11, 2011), p. 52. See also Marc Benioff, *Behind the Cloud: The Untold Story of How Salesforce.com Went from Idea to Billion-Dollar Company and Revolutionized an Industry* (San Francisco: Jossey-Bass, 2009); and salesforce.com.

Chapter 5

Endnotes

[1] John Aidan Byrne, "IBM now employs more workers in India than US," *New York Post* (October 5, 2013), nypost.com (accessed May 22, 2014).

[2] See, for example, Dan Gearino, "Made in This Hemisphere," *Columbus Dispatch* (January 11, 2010), pp. A10, A11; and David Welch, "One Man, One Car, One World," *Bloomberg BusinessWeek* (January 25, 2010), pp. 48–49.

[3] "Boeing: Faster, Faster, Faster," *The Economist,* Kindle Edition (January 29, 2012).

[4] See, for example, Kenichi Ohmae's books, *The Borderless World: Power and Strategy in the Interlinked Economy* (New York: Harper, 1989); *The End of the Nation State* (New York: Free Press, 1996); and *The Next Global Stage: Challenges and Opportunities in Our Borderless World* (Philadelphia: Wharton School Publishing, 2006). See also Thomas L. Friedman, *Hot, Flat, and Crowded: Why We Need a Green Revolution—and How It Can Renew America* (New York: Farrar, Straus and Giroux, 2008).

[5] Pankaj Ghemawat, *World 3.0: Global Prosperity and How to Achieve It* (Cambridge, MA: Harvard Business Press, 2011).

[6] Pietra Rivoli, *The Travels of a T-Shirt in the Global Economy*, 2nd ed. (Hoboken, NJ: John Wiley & Sons, 2009).

[7] Rosabeth Moss Kanter, *World Class: Thinking Locally in the Global Economy* (New York: Simon and Schuster, 1995), preface.

[8] Information from Mark Niquette, "Honda's 'Bold Move' Paid Off," *Columbus Dispatch* (November 16, 2002), pp. C1, C2; and "Marysville Auto Plant," ohio.honda.com.

[9] Information from Mei Fong, "Chinese Refrigerator Maker Finds U.S. Chilly," *Wall Street Journal* (March 18, 2008), pp. B1, B2.

[10] Quote from John A. Byrne, "Visionary vs. Visionary," *BusinessWeek* (August 28, 2000), p. 210.

[11] Information from newbalance.com/corporate; and "Nike Strategy Leaves It Room to Run," *Wall Street Journal* (March 16, 2010), p. C10.

[12] Steve Hamm, "Into Africa: Capitalism from the Ground Up," *BusinessWeek* (May 4, 2009), pp. 60–61.

[13] See "U. S. R&D Jobs Shift to Asia," *Wall Street Journal* (January 18, 2012), p. B2; and "Thomas L. Friedman, 'Made in the World,'" *New York Times* (January 28, 2012), nytimes.com.

[14] David Murphy, "A Foxconn Breakdown: Its Strengths, Strangeness, and Scrutiny," *PC Magazine* (January 22, 2012), pcmag.com.

[15] Jessica E. Vascellaro and Own Fletcher, "Apple Navigates China Maze," *Wall Street Journal* (January 14–15, 2012), pp. B1, B2.

[16] Information and quote from "More Than a Third of Large Manufacturers Are Considering Reshoring from China to the U.S.," Boston Consulting Group press release, bcg.com (April 20, 2012), (accessed May 5, 2013); "A Revolution in the Making, *Wall Street Journal* (June 11, 2013), pp. R1, R2; and Don Lee, "After Long Exodus, Companies Returning to U.S.," *Arizona Daily Star* (May 25, 2014), p. D7.

[17] Information from Michael A. Fletcher, "Ohio Profits from Exports," *Columbus Dispatch* (December 30, 2007), p. B3.

[18] "Survey: Intellectual Property Theft Now Accounts for 31 Percent of Global Counterfeiting," Gieschen Consultancy, February 25, 2005.

[19] Information from "Not Exactly Counterfeit," *Fortune* (April 26, 2006), money.cnn.com/magazines/fortune.

[20] James K. Jackson, "Outsourcing and Insourcing Jobs in the U.S. Economy: Based on Foreign Direct Investment Data," *Congressional Research Office* (June 21, 2013).

[21] Criteria for choosing joint venture partners developed from Anthony J. F. O'Reilly, "Establishing Successful Joint Ventures in Developing Nations: A CEO's Perspective," *Columbia Journal of World Business* (Spring 1988), pp. 65–71; and "Best Practices for Global Competitiveness," *Fortune* (March 30, 1998), pp. S1–S3, special advertising section.

[22] See James T. Areddy, "Danone Pulls Out of Disputed China Venture," *Wall Street Journal* (October 1, 2009), p. B1.

[23] Karby Leggett, "U.S. Auto Makers Find Promise—and Peril—in China," *Wall Street Journal* (June 19, 2003), p. B1; "Did Spark Spark a Copycat?" *BusinessWeek* (February 7, 2005), p. 64; and "New Height, New Growth," news release (July 28, 2011), cheryinternational.com.

[24] "Best Practices for Global Competitiveness," *Fortune* (March 30, 1998), pp. S1–S3, special advertising.

[25] Information from Sam Schechner and Vanessa Mock, "Google's Settlement in Europe Under Pressure," *Wall Street Journal* (May 24-25, 2014), p. B3.

[26] "Starbucks Wins Trademark Case," *The Economic Times,* Bangalore (January 3, 2006), p. 8.

[27] Information and quote from "Multinational Groups Shrug off Mexican Drugs Violence," *Financial Times*, Kindle Edition (July 30, 2011).

[28] wto.org (accessed March 25, 2008).

[29] Information and quotes from Dexter Roberts, "Closing for Business?" *Bloomberg BusinessWeek* (April 5, 2010), pp. 32–37.

[30] Information and quote from "WTO Takes Up U.S. Complaint against China Patent Regime," *AFP* (September 7, 2007), afp.com (accessed March 25, 2008).

[31] Pete Engardio, Geri Smith, and Jane Sasseen, "Refighting NAFTA," *BusinessWeek* (March 31, 2008), pp. 55–59.

[32] "NAFTA at 20 Ready to Take Off Again," *The Economist*, Kindle Edition (January 4, 2014).

[33] *The Economist* is a good weekly source of information on Africa; and "Embracing Africa," *BusinessWeek* (December 18, 2006), p. 101.

[34] See Robert Farzad, "Can Greed Save Africa?" *BusinessWeek* (December 10, 2007), pp. 46–54; "The Big Bounce," *Bloomberg BusinessWeek* (May 17–23, 2010), pp. 48–57; and Will Connors and Sarah Childress, "Africa's Local Champions Begin to Spread Out," *Wall Street Journal* (May 26, 2010), p. B8.

[35] See, for example, Patrick McGroarty, "Middle Class in Africa Set to Boom, but Risks Remain," *Wall Street Journal* (October 13, 2011), p. A17; and "U.S. Firms in Africa Hustle to Catch Up," *Wall Street Journal* (June 6, 2011), p. A16.

[36] sadc.int/about_sadc/vision.php.

[37] Data from "The Big Mac Index: Currency Comparisons to Go," *The Economist* (January 23, 2014), economist.com.

[38] See Peter F. Drucker, "The Global Economy and the Nation-State," *Foreign Affairs*, vol. 76 (September–October 1997), pp. 159–71.

[39] "Flags of Incovenience," *The Economist* (May 16, 2014), Kindle Edition; and "Flags of Incovenience," economist.com (accessed May 25, 2014).

[40] Friedman, op. cit. (2012).

[41] Information from Steve Hamm, "IBM vs. TATA: Which Is More American?" *BusinessWeek* (May 5, 2008), p. 28; and Greg Farrell, "McDonald's Continues to Rely on European Restaurants for Growth," *Financial Times,* Kindle Edition (April 20, 2010).

[42] "Sweden vs. Exxon," *Bloomberg BusinessWeek* (March 5–11, 2012), p. 91.

[43] Michael Mandel, "Multinationals: Are They Good for America?" *BusinessWeek* (February 28, 2008), BusinessWeek.com; and Deutsch Welle, "Globalization Widens Wealth Gap as Advanced Economies Outpace Developing World," *DW Top Stories* (March 214, 2014), dw.de (accessed May 22, 2014).

[44] Developed from R. Hall Mason, "Conflicts between Host Countries and Multinational Enterprise," *California Management Review*, vol. 17 (1974), pp. 6, 7.

[45] Mandel, op. cit.; Engardio, op. cit.

[46] See "The Paradox of Bangladesh," *Bloomberg BusinessWeek* (May 13–19, 2013), pp. A1–A4.

[47] Thomas Donaldson, "Values in Tension: Ethics Away from Home," *Harvard Business Review*, vol. 74 (September–October 1996), pp. 48–62.

[48] See transparency.org. See also Blake E. Ashforth, Dennis A. Gioia, Sandra L. Robinson, and Linda K. Trevino, "Special Topic Forum on Corruption," *Academy of Management Review*, vol. 33 (July 2008), p. 6701.

[49] Transparency International, "Corruption Perceptions Index 2009," transparency.org (accessed April 23, 2010).

[50] Carol Matlack, "The Peril and Promise of Investing in Russia," *BusinessWeek* (October 5, 2009), pp. 48–51.

[51] See Dionne Searcey, "U.S. Cracks Down on Corporate Bribes," *Wall Street Journal* (May 26, 2009), pp. A1, A4.

[52] John Bussey, "The Rule of Law Finds Its Way Abroad, However Painfully," *Wall Street Journal* (June 24, 2011), pp. B1, B2.

[53] International Labour Organization, *Facts on Child Labor 2010* (Geneva, Switzerland: April 1, 2010).

[54] See, for example, Jason Dean and Ting-I Tsai, "Suicides Spark Inquiries," *Wall Street Journal* (May 27, 2010), pp. B1, B7.

[55] Juliette Garside, "Underage Labour Discovered in Apple's Supply Chain," *The Guardian* (January 25, 2013), theguardian.com (accessed December 27, 2013).

[56] "The Paradox of Bangladesh," op. cit.

[57] Shelly Banjo, "Wal-Mart Toughens Supplier Policies," *Wall Street Journal* (January 22, 2013), pp. B1, B7; and Shelly Banjo, "Wal-Mart Audits Reveal Bangladesh Safety Woes," *Wall Street Journal* (November 18, 2013), p. B3.

[58] See definition in Ernst & Young, *Conflict Minerals: What you need to know about the new disclosure and reporting requirements and how Ernst & Young can help*, ey.com (accessed May 25, 2014).

[59] Emily Chasan and Joel Schectman, "War and the Supply Chain," *Wall Street Journal* (May 20, 2014), p. B8; and Don Ford, "Intel Files First Audited Conflict Minerals Report," *Wall Street Journal* (May 22, 2014), blogs.wsj.com: (accessed May 25, 2014).

[60] Chasan and Schectman, op. cit.

[61] Ibid.; and Ford, op. cit.

[62] Examples reported in Neil Chesanow, *The World-Class Executive* (New York: Rawson Associates, 1985).

[63] For alternative definitions of culture, see Martin J. Gannon, *Paradoxes of Culture and Globalization* (Thousand Oaks, CA: Sage, 2008), Chapter 2.

[64] P. Christopher Earley and Elaine Mosakowski, "Toward Cultural Intelligence: Turning Cultural Differences into Workplace Advantage," *Academy of Management Executive*, vol. 18 (2004), pp. 151–57.

[65] For a good overview of the practical issues, see Lewis, op. cit.; and Martin J. Gannon, *Understanding Global Cultures* (Thousand Oaks, CA: Sage, 1994).

[66] Developed from Jacob Eisenberg, Hyun-Jung Lee, Frank Brük, Barbara Brenner, Marie-Therese Claes, Jacek Mironski, and Roger Bell, "Can Business Schools Make Students Culturally Competent? Effects of Cross-Cultural Management Courses on Cultural Intelligence," *Academy of Management Learning & Education*, vol. 12 (2013), pp. 603–21.

[67] Edward T. Hall, *The Silent Language* (New York: Anchor Books, 1959).

[68] Edward T. Hall, *Beyond Culture* (New York: Doubleday, 1976).

[69] Edward T. Hall, *The Hidden Dimension* (New York: Anchor Books, 1969) and *Hidden Differences* (New York: Doubleday, 1990).

[70] Ibid.

[71] Michele J. Gelfand, Lisa H. Nishii, and Jana L. Raver, "On the Nature and Importance of Cultural Tightness-Looseness," *Journal of Applied Psychology*, vol. 91 (2006), pp. 1225–44.

[72] Michele J. Gelfand and 42 co-authors, "Differences between Tight and Loose Cultures: A 33 Nation Study," *Science*, vol. 332 (May 2011), pp. 1100–04.

[73] Geert Hofstede, *Culture's Consequences* (Beverly Hills, CA: Sage, 1984), and *Culture's Consequences: Comparing Values, Behaviors, Institutions and Organizations across Nations*, 2nd ed. (Thousand Oaks, CA: Sage, 2001). See also Michael H. Hoppe, "An Interview with Geert Hofstede," *Academy of Management Executive*, vol. 18 (2004), pp. 75–79.

[74] Geert Hofstede and Michael H. Bond, "The Confucius Connection: From Cultural Roots to Economic Growth," *Organizational Dynamics*, vol. 16 (1988), pp. 4–21.

[75] See Geert Hofstede, *Culture and Organizations: Software of the Mind* (London: McGraw-Hill, 1991).

[76] For another perspective, see Harry Triandis and M. Gelfand, "Convergent Measurement of Horizontal and Vertical Collectivism," *Journal of Personality & Social Psychology*, vol. 74 (1998), pp. 118–28.

[77] This dimension is explained more thoroughly by Geert Hofstede et al., *Masculinity and Femininity: The Taboo Dimension of National Cultures* (Thousand Oaks, CA: Sage, 1998).

[78] Information for "Stay Informed" from "The Conundrum of the Glass Ceiling," *The Economist* (July 23, 2005), p. 634, and "Japan's Diversity Problem," *Wall Street Journal* (October 24, 2005), pp. B1, B5.

[79] See Hofstede and Bond, op. cit.

[80] See, for example, Nancy Adler and Allison Gundersen, *International Dimensions of Organizational Behavior*, 5th ed. (New York: Thomson South-Western, 2008).

[81] For additional cultural models and research, see Fons Trompenaars, *Riding the Waves of Culture: Understanding Cultural Diversity in Business* (London: Nicholas Brealey, 1993); Harry C. Triandis, *Culture and Social Behavior* (New York: McGraw-Hill, 1994); Steven H. Schwartz, "A Theory of Cultural Values and Some Implications for Work," *Applied Psychology: An International Review*, vol. 48 (1999), pp. 23–47; and Martin J. Gannon, *Understanding Global Cultures*, 3rd ed. (Thousand Oaks, CA: Sage, 2004). See also research known as Project GLOBE: Robert J. House, Paul J. Hanges, Mansour Javidan, Peter W. Dorfman, and Vipin Gupta (eds.), *Culture, Leadership and Organizations: The GLOBE Study of 62 Societies* (Thousand Oaks, CA: Sage, 2004). Further issues on Project GLOBE are developed in George B. Graen, "In the Eye of the Beholder: Cross-Cultural Lessons in Leadership from Project GLOBE: A Response Viewed from the Third Culture Bonding (TCB) Model of Cross-Cultural Leadership," *Academy of Management Perspectives*, vol. 20 (November 2006), pp. 95–101, and Robert J. House, Mansour Javidan, Peter W. Dorfman, and Mary Sully de Luque, "A Failure of Scholarship: Response to George Graen's Critique of GLOBE," *Academy of Management Perspectives*, vol. 20 (November 2006), pp. 102–14.

[82] See, for example, Rosalie L. Tung and Alain Verbeke, "Beyond Hofstede and GLOBE: Improving the Quality of Cross-Cultural Research," *Journal of International Business Studies*, vol. 41 (2010), pp. 1259–74.

[83] Geert Hofstede, "Motivation, Leadership, and Organization: Do American Theories Apply Abroad?" *Organizational Dynamics* (1980), p. 43; Geert Hofstede, "The Cultural Relativity of Organizational Practices," *Journal of International Business Studies* (Fall 1983), pp. 75–89. See also Hofstede's "Cultural Constraints in Management Theories," *Academy of Management Review*, vol. 7 (1993), pp. 81–94.

[84] Discussion based on Allan Bird, Mark Mendenhall, Michael J. Stevens, and Gary Oddou, "Defining the Content Domain of Intercultural Competence for Global Leaders," *Journal of Managerial Psychology*, vol. 25 (2010), pp. 810–28.

[85] Geert Hofstede, "A Reply to Goodstein and Hunt," *Organizational Dynamics,* vol. 10 (Summer 1981), p. 68.

[86] Developed from "Is Your Company Really Global?" *BusinessWeek* (December 1, 1997).

[87] Based on Martin J. Gannon, *Understanding Global Cultures* (Thousand Oaks, CA: Sage, 1994), Chapter 16: "American Football."

Feature Notes

Ethics: Information from Information from Raul Burgoa, "Bolivia Seizes Control of Oil and Gas Fields," *Bangkok Post* (May 3, 2006), p. B5.

Insight: Quote from Richard D. Lewis, *The Cultural Imperative: Global Trends in the 21st Century* (Yarmouth, ME: Intercultural Press, 2002).

Research Brief: Margaret A. Shaffer, David A. Harrison, Hal Gregersen, J. Steward Black, and Lori A. Ferzandi, "You Can Take It with You: Individual Differences and Expatriate Effectiveness," *Journal of Applied Psychology*, vol. 91 (2006), pp. 109–125.

Chapter 6

Endnotes

[1] Information from Gwen Moran, "How Military Veterans Are Finding Success in Small Business," *Entrepreneur* (February 20, 2012), entrepreneur.com (accessed January 11, 2013). See also, Ian Mount, "Open for Business," *USAA Magazine* (Summer 2012), pp. 20–24.

[2] Information and quotes for these examples from Alison Damasi, "No Job? Create One," *Bloomberg BusinessWeek* (March 22 & 29, 2010), p. 89; Laura Lorber, "Older Entrepreneurs Target Peers," *Wall Street Journal* (February 16, 2010), p. B6; and Dale Buss, "The Mothers of Invention," *Wall Street Journal* (February 8, 2010), p. R7.

[3] Information from "Women Business Owners Receive First-Ever Micro Loans Via the Internet," *Business Wire* (August 9, 2000); Jim Hopkins, "Non-Profit Loan Group Takes Risks on Women in Business," *USA Today* (August 9, 2000), p. 2B; and "Women's Group Grants First Loans to Entrepreneurs," *Columbus Dispatch* (August 10, 2000), p. B2.

[4] Quote from "Working for Somebody Else Never Amounted to Anything—Wayne Huizenga," youngentrepreneur.com (accessed January 22, 2010).

[5] Information and quote from Chuck Green, "When Entrepreneurs Don't Take No for an Answer," *Wall Street Journal* (April 29, 2013), p. R5.

[6] Speech at the Lloyd Greif Center for Entrepreneurial Studies, Marshall School of Business, University of Southern California, 1996.

[7] Information and quotes from the corporate websites; Entrepreneur's Hall of Fame at 1tbn.com/halloffame.html; "Disruptor of the Day: Caterina Fake—Because She Had a Flickr of a Hunch about an Etsy," *Daily Disruption* (January 31, 2012), dailydisruption.com; Zack O'Malley Greenburg, "Jay-Z's Business Commandments" (March 16, 2011), forbes.com; and "Shawn 'Jay Z' Carter," www.BlackEntrepreneurProfile.com (accessed March 8, 2012); hunch.com. See also Anita Roddick, *Business As Unusual: My Entrepreneurial Journey, Profits with Principles* (West Sussex, England: Anita Roddick Books, 2005).

[8] Quote from http://foundercollective.com/founders-Caterina-Fake.

[9] Quote from Earl G. Graves, *How to Succeed in Business without Being White* (New York: HarperCollins Publishers, 1998).

[10] Elmer-Dewitt, Philip, "Anita the Agitator," *Time* (January 25, 1993), pp. 52–55.

[11] Quote from Jake Brown, *Jay Z and the Roc-A-Fella Records Dynasty* (Phoenix: Amber Books, 2005), p. 30.

[12] Examples from "America's Best Young Entrepreneurs 2008," *BusinessWeek* (September 8, 2009), businessweek.com.

[13] For the top-selling franchises, see "Top 10 Franchises for 2009," *Entrepreneur Magazine* (January 2009), entrepreneur.com.

[14] This list is developed from Timmons, op. cit., pp. 47–48; and Hisrich and Peters, op. cit., pp. 67–70.

[15] For a review and discussion of the entrepreneurial mind, see Jeffry A. Timmons, *New Venture Creation: Entrepreneurship for the 21st Century* (New York: Irwin/McGraw-Hill, 1999), pp. 219–25; and "Can Entrepreneurship Be Taught?" *Wall Street Journal* (March 19, 2012), p. R4.

[16] See the review by Robert D. Hisrich and Michael P. Peters, *Entrepreneurship*, 4th ed. (New York: Irwin/McGraw-Hill, 1998), pp. 67–70; and Paulette Thomas, "Entrepreneurs' Biggest Problems and How They Solve Them," *Wall Street Journal Reports* (March 17, 2003), pp. R1, R2.

[17] Based on research summarized by Hisrich and Peters, op. cit., pp. 70–74.

[18] Timothy Butler and James Waldroop, "Job Sculpting: The Art of Retaining Your Best People," *Harvard Business Review* (September–October 1999), pp. 144–52.

[19] Information from Jim Hopkins, "Serial Entrepreneur Strikes Again at Age 70," *USA Today* (August 15, 2000).

[20] Quote from anitaroddick.com/aboutanita.php (accessed April 24, 2010).

[21] Data from *Paths to Entrepreneurship: New Directions for Women in Business* (New York: Catalyst, 1998), as summarized on the National Foundation for Women Business Owners website, nfwbo.org/key.html.

[22] National Foundation for Women Business Owners, *Women Business Owners of Color: Challenges and Accomplishments* (1998).

[23] Data from "New Census Data Reinforces the Economic Power of Women-Owned Businesses in the U.S. Says NAWBO," National Association of Women Business Owners press release, (July 15, 2010); and Mark D. Wolfe, "Women-Owned Businesses: America's New Job Creation Engine," *Forbes* (January 12, 2010), forbes.com.

[24] Leah Yomtovian, "The Funding Landscape for Minority Entrepreneurs," ideacrossing.org (February 16, 2011); and mbda.gov.

[25] "Wanted: More Black Entrepreneurs," *Bloomberg BusinessWeek* (January 23–29, 2012), pp. 4–16.

[26] Information and quote from Rieva Lesonsky, "Women Owned Businesses Have Come a Long Way But It's Not Far Enough," *Small Business Trends* (October 12, 2011), smallbiztrends.com.

[27] David Bornstein, *How to Change the World: Social Entrepreneurs and the Power of New Ideas* (Oxford, UK: Oxford University Press, 2004).

[28] Sharon Shinn, "Profit and Purpose," *BizEd* (May–June, 2011), pp. 24–31.

[29] "The 10 Best Social Enterprises of 2009," *Fast Company* (December 1, 2009), fastcompany.com/magazine (accessed April 24, 2010); and Dan Simmons, "Keepod: Can a $7 Stick Provide Billions Computer Access?" *BBC* (May 9, 2014), bbc.com (accessed May 9, 2014).

[30] Examples are from Byrnes and "Growing Green Business," *Northwestern* (Winter 2007), p. 19; Byrnes, op. cit.; and Regina McEnery, "Cancer Patients Getting the White-Glove Treatment," *Columbus Dispatch* (March 1, 2008).

[31] "Advocacy: The Voice of Small Business," *SBA Office of Advocacy* (September 2012), sba.gov/advocacy.

[32] U.S. Small Business Administration website, sba.gov/advocacy/7495/8420 (accessed October 21, 2011); Carl Bialik, "Sizing Up the Small-Business Jobs Machine," *Wall Street Journal* (October 15–16, 2011), p. A2, "Job Creators No More," *Bloomberg BusinessWeek* (February 10–16, 2014), p. 18; and "Advocacy: The Voice of Small Business," op. cit.

[33] Angus Loten, "Firms Face Hurdles Overseas," *Wall Street Journal*, Kindle Edition (August 25, 2011); and Rhonda Colvin, "The Cost of Expanding Overseas," *Wall Street Journal* (February 27, 2014), p. B6.

[34] Charles Kenny, "Small Isn't Beautiful," *Bloomberg BusinessWeek* (October 3–9, 2011), pp. 10–11.

[35] Information reported in "The Rewards," *Inc. State of Small Business* (May 20–21, 2001), pp. 50–51.

[36] Information from Sue Shellenbarger, "Plumbing for Joy? Be Your Own Boss," *Wall Street Journal* (September 16, 2009), pp. D1, D2.

[37] Information and quotes from Steve Lohr, "The Rise of the Fleet-Footed Start-Up," *New York Times* (April 23, 2010), nytimes.com.

[38] Ibid.

[39] See U.S. Small Business Administration website, sba.gov.

[40] George Gendron, "The Failure Myth," *Inc.* (January 2001), p. 13.

[41] Discussion based on "The Life Cycle of Entrepreneurial Firms," in Ricky Griffin (ed.), *Management*, 6th ed. (New York: Houghton Mifflin, 1999), pp. 309–10; and Neil C. Churchill and Virginia L. Lewis, "The Five Stages of Small Business Growth," *Harvard Business Review* (May–June 1993), pp. 30–50.

[42] Information and quotes from Tracy Turner, "Smooth Transition: Three Sisters Take over Family's Velvet Ice Cream Business," *Columbus Dispatch* (September 25, 2009), pp. A12, A13.

[43] Data reported by The Family Firm Institute, ffi.org/looking/factsfb.html.

[44] Conversation from the case "Am I My Uncle's Keeper?" by Paul I. Karofsky (Northeastern University Center for Family Business) and published at fambiz.com.

[45] *Survey of Small and Mid-Sized Businesses: Trends for 2000* (Arthur Andersen, 2000).

[46] Ibid.

[47] Anne Field, "Business Incubators Are Growing Up," *BusinessWeek* (November 16, 2009), p. 76.

[48] See sba.gov/aboutsba. For a discussion on the pros and cons on the SBA, see "Should the Small Business Administration Be Abolished?" *Wall Street Journal* (March 19, 2012), p. R2.

[49] Developed from William S. Sahlman, "How to Write a Great Business Plan," *Harvard Business Review* (July–August 1997), pp. 98–108.

[50] Marcia H. Pounds, "Business Plan Sets Course for Growth," *Columbus Dispatch* (March 16, 1998), p. 9; see also the firm's website, calcustoms.com.

[51] Information from Colleen DeBaise, "Why You Need a Business Plan," *Wall Street Journal* (September 27, 2009), wsj.com.

[52] Standard components of business plans are described in many text sources such as Linda Pinson and Jerry Jinnett, *Anatomy of a Business Plan: A Step-by-Step Guide to Starting Smart, Building the Business, and Securing Your Company's Future*, 4th ed. (Dearborn Trade, 1999); and on websites such as americanexpress.com/us/small-business, businesstown.com, and BizplanIt.com.

[53] Angus Loten, "With New Law, Profits Take a Back Seat," *Wall Street Journal* (January 19, 2012), wsj.com (accessed November 24, 2012); Mark Underberg, "Benefit Corporations vs. 'Regular' Corporations: A Harmful Dichotomy" (June 18, 2012), businessethics.com (accessed November 24, 2012); and Angus Loten, "Can Firms Aim to Do Good If It Hurts Profits?" *Wall Street Journal* (April 11, 2013), p. B6.

[54] As of this writing, the B Corp is legal in 12 states and is being considered in 20 others. For an update, see Certified B Corporation: bcorporation.net.

[55] "You've Come a Long Way Baby," *BusinessWeek Frontier* (July 10, 2000).

[56] "Charley Rose Talks to . . . Yancy Strickler," *Bloomberg BusinessWeek* (March 20, 2014), p. 46.

[57] See kickstarter.com, angel.com, and Spencer E. Ante and Evelyun M. Rustli, "Breaking Down the Walls for New Angel Investors," *Wall Street Journal* (October 9, 2013), p. B1, B2.

[58] See Jean Eaglesham, "Crowdfunding Efforts Draw Suspicion," *Wall Street Journal* (January 18, 2013), p. C1.

[59] See for example, Javier Espinoza, "The New Rules of Capital," *Wall Street Journal* (September 30, 2013), p. R3.

[60] Information from "Should Equity-Based Crowd Funding Be Legal?" *Wall Street Journal* (March 19, 2012), p. R3; Angus Loten, "Avoiding the Equity Crowd Funding," *Wall Street Journal* (March 29, 2012), wsj/com; and Ruth Simon and Angus Loten, "Frustration Rises Over Crowdfunding Rules," *Wall Street Journal* (May 1, 2014), p. B3.

[61] Adapted from Norman M. Scarborough and Thomas W. Zimmerer, *Effective Small Business Management*, 3rd ed. (Columbus, OH: Merrill, 1991), pp. 26–27. Used by permission.

Feature Notes

Ethics: Information from Jessica Shambora, "The Story Behind the World's Hottest Shoemaker," *Financial Times,* Kindle Edition (March 21, 2010), toms.com; John Tozzi, "The Ben & Jerry's Law: Principles before Profit," *Bloomberg BusinessWeek* (April 26–May 2, 2010), pp. 69, 70; and Blake Mycoskie, "Why Is Giving Back Good for Business?" *Spirit* (January, 2014), p. 51.

Insight: See also Stephen Covey, "How to Succeed in Today's Workplace," *USA Weekend* (August 29–31, 1997), pp. 4–5.

Wisdom: Information and quotes from Susan Berfield, "A Startup's New Prescription for Eyewear," *Bloomberg BusinessWeek* (July 4–10, 2011), pp. 49–51; and warbyparker.com.

Chapter 7

Endnotes

[1] Information and quotes from "Last Miner Out Hailed as a Shift Boss Who Kept Group Alive," news:blog.cnn.com (October 14, 2010): and Eva Bergara, "Chilean Miners Honored in Ceremony, Football Game," news.yahoo.com (October 25, 2010).

[2] For a good discussion, see Michael S. Hopkins, Steve LaValle, and Fred Balboni. "10 Insights: A First Look at the New Intelligent Enterprise Survey on Winning with Data." *Sloan Management Review*, vol. 52 (Fall 2010), pp. 22–27.

[3] "UPS Says Auto Routes Will Transform Delivery," *Wall Street Journal* (October 31, 2013), p. B5.

[4] Elizabeth Dwoskin, "Data Mining Thanks to Twitter," *Wall Street Journal* (October 7, 2013), pp. B1, B8.

[5] Brad Stone, "The Secrets of Bezos: How Amazon Became the Everything Store," *Bloomberg BusinessWeek*, businessweek.com (accessed October 10, 2013).

[6] Information from Karen Berman and Joe Knight, "What Your Employees Don't Know Will Hurt You," *Wall Street Journal* (February 27, 2012), p. R4.

[7] Information on executive dashboards and quote from Jessica Tennyman, "Dashboards Make the Corporate Drive Easier," *Financial Times*, Kindle Edition (March 21, 2012).

[8] Noel M. Tichy and Warren G. Bennis, "Judgment: How Winning Leaders Make Great Calls," *BusinessWeek* (November 19, 2007), pp. 68–72.

[9] Henry Mintzberg, *The Nature of Managerial Work* (New York: Harper Collins, 1997).

[10] Information from "What's the Quickest Way to Board a Plane?" *CNNGo*, cnn.com (September 2, 2011).

[11] For a good discussion, see Watson H. Agor, *Intuition in Organizations: Leading and Managing Productively* (Newbury Park, CA: Sage, 1989); Herbert A. Simon, "Making Management Decisions: The Role of Intuition and Emotion," *Academy of Management Executive*, vol. 1 (1987), pp. 57–64; Orlando Behling and Norman L. Eckel, "Making Sense Out of Intuition," *Academy of Management Executive*, vol. 5 (1991), pp. 46–54.

[12] See, for example, William Duggan, *Strategic Intuition: The Creative Spark in Human Achievement* (New York: Columbia Business School, 2007).

[13] Alan Deutschman, "Inside the Mind of Jeff Bezos," *Fast Company*, Issue 85 (August 2004), fastcompany.com.

[14] See Susan Berfield, "The Limits of Going with Your Gut," *BusinessWeek* (December 21, 2009), p. 90. See also Michael J. Mauboussin, *Think Twice: Harnessing the Power of Counterintuition* (Boston: Harvard Business, 2009).

[15] Daniel J. Isenberg, "How Senior Managers Think," *Harvard Business Review*, vol. 62 (November–December 1984), pp. 81–90.

[16] Daniel J. Isenberg, "The Tactics of Strategic Opportunism," *Harvard Business Review*, vol. 65 (March–April 1987), pp. 92–97.

[17] Quote from Susan Carey, "Pilot 'in Shock' as He Landed Jet in River," *Wall Street Journal* (February 9, 2009), p. A6.

[18] Based on Carl Jung's typology as described in Donald Bowen, "Learning and Problem-Solving: You're Never Too Jung," in Donald D. Bowen, Roy J. Lewicki, Donald T. Hall, and Francine S. Hall, eds., *Experiences in Management and Organizational Behavior*, 4th ed. (New York: Wiley, 1997), pp. 7–13; and John W. Slocum Jr., "Cognitive Style in Learning and Problem Solving," ibid., pp. 349–53.

[19] Developed from Anna Muoio, "Where There's Smoke It Helps to Have a Smoke Jumper," *Fast Company*, vol. 33, p. 290.

[20] For scholarly reviews, see Dean Tjosvold, "Effects of Crisis Orientation on Managers' Approach to Controversy in Decision Making," *Academy of Management-Journal*, vol. 27 (1984), pp. 130–38; and Jan I. Mitroff, Paul Shrivastava, and Firdaus E. Udwadia, "Effective Crisis Management," *Academy of Management Executive*, vol. 1 (1987), pp. 283–92.

[21] Information and quotes from Jeff Kingston. "A Crisis Made in Japan." *Wall Street Journal* (February 6–7, 2010), pp. W1, W2; Kate Linebaugh, Dionne Searcey, and Norihiko Shirouzu. "Secretive Culture Led Toyota Astray." *Wall Street Journal* (February 10, 2010), pp. A1, A16; and Richard Fedlow, "Toyota Was in Denial, How About You?" *Bloomberg BusinessWeek* (April 19, 2010), p. 76.

[22] Richard Fedlow, "Toyota Was in Denial, How About You?" *Bloomberg BusinessWeek* (April 19, 2010), p. 76.

[23] Information from Paul Farhi, "Behind Domino's Mea Culpa Ad Campaign," *Washington Post* (January 13, 2010): washingtonpost.com (accessed June 5, 2010); and J. Patrick Doyle, "Hard Choices," *Bloomberg BusinessWeek* (May 3–9, 2010), p. 84.

[24] Information and quotes from Terry Kosdrosky and John D. Stoll, "GM Puts Electric-Car Testing on Fast Track to 2010," *Wall Street Journal* (April 4, 2008), p. B2.

[25] See George P. Huber, *Managerial Decision Making* (Glenview, IL: Scott, Foresman, 1975). For a comparison, see the steps in Xerox's problem-solving process as described in David A. Garvin. "Building a Learning Organization," *Harvard Business Review* (July–August 1993), pp. 78–91; and the Josephson model for ethical decision making described at josephsoninstitute.org.

[26] Peter F. Drucker, *Innovation and Entrepreneurship: Practice and Principles* (New York: Harper Row, 1985).

[27] Information from Julie Jargon and Eric Morath, "As Wage Debate Rages, Owners Shuffle Costs," *Wall Street Journal* (April 9, 2014), pp. B1, B4.

[28] For a sample of Simon's work, see Herbert A. Simon, *Administrative Behavior* (New York: Free Press, 1947); James G. March and Herbert A. Simon, *Organizations* (New York: Wiley, 1958); Herbert A. Simon, *The New Science of Management Decision* (New York: Harper, 1960).

[29] Developed from conversations with Dr. Alma Acevedo of the University of Puerto Rico at Rio Piedras, and her articles "Of Fallacies and Curricula: A Case of Business Ethics," *Teaching Business Ethics*, vol. 5 (2001), pp. 157–70; and "Business Ethics: An Introduction," Working Paper (2009).

[30] See the discussion by Denis Collins, *Business Ethics: How to Design and Manage Ethical Organizations* (Hoboken, NJ: John Wiley & Sons, 2012), p. 158.

[31] Based on Gerald F. Cavanagh, *American Business Values,* 4th ed. (Upper Saddle River, NJ: Prentice-Hall, 1998).

[32] Josephson, op. cit.

[33] Damel Kahneman. *Thinking Fast and Slow* (New York: Farrar, Straus & Giroux. 2011).

[34] Example from Roger Lowenstein. "Better Think Twice," *Bloomberg BusinessWeek* (October 31, November 6, 2011), pp. 98–99. This article is a review of Daniel Kahneman, op cit. (2011).

[35] Daniel Kahneman and Amos Tversky, "Psychology of Preferences," *Scientific American*, vol. 246 (1982), pp. 161–73; and Kahneman, op cit., 2011.

[36] This presentation is based on the discussion in Max H. Bazerman, *Judgment in Managerial Decision Making*, 6th ed. (Hoboken, NJ: Wiley, 2005).

[37] Barry M. Staw, "The Escalation of Commitment to a Course of Action," *Academy of Management Review*, vol. 6 (1981), pp. 577–87; and Barry M. Staw and Jerry Ross, "Knowing When to Pull the Plug," *Harvard Business Review*, vol. 65 (March–April 1987), pp. 68–74.

[38] For a review of research on escalating commitment, see Dustin J. Sleesman, Donald E. Conlon, Gerry McNamara, and Jonathan E. Miles, "Cleaning Up the Big Muddy: A Meta-Analytic Review of the Determinants of Escalation of Commitment," *Academy of Management Journal*, vol. 55 (2012), pp. 541–562.

[39] Example from Dayton Fandray, "Assumed Innocent: Hidden and Unexamined Assumptions Can Ruin Your Day," *Continental. com/Magazine* (December 2007), p. 100.

[40] See, for example, Roger von Oech's books *A Whack on the Side of the Head* (New York: Warner Books, 1983) and *A Kick in the Seat of the Pants* (New York: Harper & Row, 1986); John Lehrer, "How to Be Creative," *Wall Street Journal* (March 10–11, 2012), pp. C1, C2; and John Lehrer, *Imagine: How Creativity Works* (New York; Houghton Mifflin Harcourt, 2012).

[41] For discussions of Big-C creativity and Little-C creativity, see James C. Kaufman and Ronald A. Beghetto, "Beyond Big and Little: The Four C Model of Creativity," *Review of General Psychology,* Vol. 13 (2009), pp. 1–12. My thanks go to Dr. Erin R. Flvegge of Southeastern Missouri State University for bringing this useful distinction to my attention.

[42] Carolyn T. Geer. "Innovation 101." *Wall Street Journal* (October 17, 2011). p. R5.

[43] Teresa M. Amabile, "Motivating Creativity in Organizations," *California Management Review*, vol. 40 (Fall 1997), pp. 39–58.

[44] See Jeff Dyer, Hal Gregersen, and Clayton M. Christensen. *The Innovator's DNA: Mastering the Five Skills of Disruptive Innovators* (Cambridge, MA: Harvard Business Press 2011).

[45] Developed from discussions by Edward De Bono, *Lateral Thinking: Creativity Step-by-Step* (New York: HarperCollins, 1970); John S. Dacey and Kathleen H. Lennon, *Understanding Creativity* (San Francisco: Jossey-Bass, 1998); and Bettina von Stamm, *Managing Innovation, Design & Creativity* (Chichester, England: Wiley, 2003).

[46] Josephson, op. cit.

[47] Information from Stephen H. Wildstrom, "Video iPod, I Love You," *BusinessWeek* (November 7, 2005), p. 20; "Voices of Innovation," *BusinessWeek* (December 12, 2005), p. 22.

[48] Developed from Donald Bowen, "Learning and Problem-Solving: You're Never Too Jung," in Donald D. Bowen, Roy J. Lewicki, Donald T. Hall, and Francine S. Hall (eds.), Experiences in Management and Organizational Behavior, 4th ed. (New York: Wiley, 1997), pp. 7–13; and John W. Slocum Jr., "Cognitive Style in Learning and Problem Solving," ibid., pp. 349–53.

[49] Adapted from "Lost at Sea: A Consensus-Seeking Task," in the 1975 Handbook for Group Facilitators. Used with permission of University Associates, Inc.

[50] See "Asking for a Raise? Avoid Round Numbers," *Wall Street Journal* (May 29, 2013), p. B10.

Feature Notes

Analysis: Information and quotes from Michael S. Hopkins, Steve LaValle, and Fred Balboni, "10 Insights: First Look at the New Intelligent Enterprise Survey on Winning with Data" and Nina Kruschwitz and Rebecca Shockley, "10 Data Points: Information and Analytics at Work," *Sloan Management Review*, vol. 52 (Fall 2010), pp. 22–27 and pp. 28–31; and Melissa Korn and Shara Tibken, "Business Schools Plan Leap into Data," *Wall Street Journal*, Kindle edition (August 4, 2010).

Insight: Quotes from Situation from Carol Hymowitz, "Middle Managers Are Unsung Heroes on Corporate Stage," *Wall Street Journal* (September 19, 2005), p. B1; and Ram Charan, "Six Personality Traits of a Leader," career-advice.monster.com/leadership-skills (retrieved August 6, 2008).

Research Brief: Marc Street and Vera L. Street, "The Effects of Escalating Commitment on Ethical Decision Making," Journal of Business Ethics, vol. 64 (2006), pp. 343–56.

Chapter 8

Endnotes

[1] "What are the Top Five Risks the World Faces in 2014?" *K@W* (January 17, 2014): knowledge.wharton.upennn.edu (accessed January 22, 2014).

[2] Eaton Corporation Annual Report, 1985.

[3] Paul Ingrassia, "The Right Stuff," *Wall Street Journal* (April 18, 2005), p. D5.

[4] Quote from Stephen Covey and Roger Merrill, "New Ways to Get Organized at Work," *USA Weekend* (February 6–8, 1998), p. 18. Books by Stephen R. Covey include *The 7 Habits of Highly Effective People: Powerful Lessons in Personal Change* (New York: Fireside, 1990); and Stephen R. Covey and Sandra Merrill Covey, *The 7 Habits of Highly Effective Families: Building a Beautiful Family Culture in a Turbulent World* (New York: Golden Books, 1996).

[5] See Stanley Thune and Robert House, "Where Long-Range Planning Pays Off," *Business Horizons*, vol. 13 (1970), pp. 81–87. For a critical review of the literature, see Milton Leontiades and Ahmet Teel, "Planning Perceptions and Planning Results," *Strategic Management Journal*, vol. 1 (1980), pp. 65–75; and J. Scott Armstrong. "The Value of Formal Planning for Strategic Decisions," *Strategic Management Journal*, vol. 3 (1982), pp. 197–211. For special attention to the small business setting, see Richard B. Robinson Jr., John A. Pearce II, George S. Vozikis, and Timothy S. Mescon, "The Relationship between Stage of Development and Small Firm Planning and Performance," *Journal of Small Business Management*, vol. 22 (1984), pp. 45–52; and Christopher Orphen, "The Effects of Long-Range Planning on Small Business Performance: A Further Examination," *Journal of Small Business Management*, vol. 23 (1985), pp. 16–23. For an empirical study of large corporations, see Vasudevan Ramanujam and N. Venkataraman, "Planning and Performance: A New Look at an Old Question," *Business Horizons*, vol. 30 (1987), pp. 19–25.

[6] "McDonald's Tech Turnaround," *Harvard Business Review* (November 2004), p. 128.

[7] Information from Carol Hymowitz, "Packed Calendars Rule Over Executives," *Wall Street Journal* (June 16, 2008), p. B1.

[8] Quote from *BusinessWeek* (August 8, 1994), pp. 78–86.

[9] See William Oncken Jr. and Donald L. Wass, "Management Time: Who's Got the Monkey?" *Harvard Business Review*, vol. 52 (September–October 1974), pp. 75–80, and featured as an HBR classic, *Harvard Business Review* (November–December 1999).

[10] Dick Levin, *The Executive's Illustrated Primer of Long Range Planning* (Englewood Cliffs, NJ: Prentice-Hall, 1981).

[11] See Elliot Jaques, *The Form of Time* (New York: Russak-Co., 1982). For an executive commentary on his research, see Walter Kiechel III, "How Executives Think," *Fortune* (December 21, 1987), pp. 139–44.

[12] Information from "Avoiding a Time Bomb: Sexual Harassment," *BusinessWeek*, Enterprise issue (October 13, 1997), pp. ENT20–21.

[13] For a thorough review of forecasting, see J. Scott Armstrong, *Long-Range Forecasting*, 2nd ed. (New York: Wiley, 1985).

[14] Information and following quotes from Guy Chazan and Neil King. "BP's Preparedness for Major Crisis Is Questioned." *Wall Street Journal* (May 10, 2010), p. A6, and Ben Casselman and Guy Chazan. "Disaster Plans Lacing at Deep Rigs," *Wall Street Journal*. (May 18, 2010), p. A1.

[15] The scenario-planning approach is described in Peter Schwartz, *The Art of the Long View* (New York: Doubleday/Currency, 1991).

[16] The scenario-planning approach is described in Peter Schwartz. *The Art of Long View* (New York: Doubleday/Currency, 1991); and Arie de Geus, *The Living Company. Habits for Survival in a Turbulent Business Environment* (Boston: Harvard Business School Press. 1997).

[17] See, for example, Robert C. Camp, *Business Process Benchmarking* (Milwaukee: ASQ Quality Press 1994); Michael J. Spendolini, *The Benchmarking Book* (New York: AMACOM, 1992); and Christopher E. Bogan and Michael J. English, *Benchmarking for Best Practices: Winning through Innovative Adaptation* (New York: McGraw-Hill, 1994).

[18] David Kiley, "One Ford for the Whole World," *BusinessWeek* (June 15, 2009), pp. 58–59.

[19] Rachel Tiplady, "Taking the Lead in Fast-Fashion," *BusinessWeek Online* (August 29, 2006); and Cecile Rohwedder and Keith Johnson, "Pace-Setting Zara Seeks More Speed to Fight Its Rising Cheap-Chic Rivals," *Wall Street Journal* (February 20, 2008), pp. B1, B6.

[20] Quote from Kenneth Roman, "The Man Who Sharpened Gillette," *Wall Street Journal* (September 5, 2007), p. D8.

[21] Stephanie Banchero, "Columbus, Ohio, School District Hit By Cheating Allegations," *Wall Street Journal* (January 28, 2014), wsj.com (accessed June 10, 2014).

[22] Tom Cohen, "Audit: More Than 120,000 Veterans Waiting or Never Got Care," *CNN* (June 9, 2014), cnn.com (accessed June 10, 2014).

[23] Lisa D. Ordóñez, Maurice E. Schweitzer, Adam D. Galinsky, and Max H. Bazerman, "Goals Gone Wild: How Goals Systematically Harm Individuals and Organizations," *Academy of Management Perspectives*, vol. 23 (2009), pp. 6–16; and Edwin A. Locke and Gary P. Latham, "Has Goal Setting Gone Wild, or Have Its Attackers Abandoned Good Scholarship?" *Academy of Management Perspectives*, vol. 23 (2009), pp. 17–23.

[24] Quotes from Cohen, op. cit.

[25] See David T. Welsh and Lisa D. Ordóñez, "The Dark Side of Consecutive High Performance Goals: Linking Goal Setting, Depletion, and Unethical Behavior," *Organizational Behavior and Human Decision Processes*, vol. 123 (2014), pp. 79–89; and Gary P. Latham and Gerard Seijts, "Learning Goals or Performance Goals: Is It the Journey or the Destination?" *Ivey Business Journal* (May/June, 2006), iveybusinessjournal.com (accessed June 10, 2014).

[26] Latham and Seijts, op cit.

[27] See Dale D. McConkey, *How to Manage by Results*, 3rd ed. (New York: AMACOM, 1976); Stephen J. Carroll Jr. and Henry J. Tosi Jr., *Management by Objectives: Applications and Research* (New York: Macmillan, 1973); and Anthony P. Raia, *Managing by Objectives* (Glenview, IL: Scott, Foresman, 1974). See also Steven Kerr, "Overcoming the Dysfunctions of MBO," *Management by Objectives*, vol. 5, no. 1 (1976).

[28] The work on goal-setting theory is well summarized in Edwin A. Locke and Gary P. Latham, *Goal Setting: A Motivational Technique That Works!* (Englewood Cliffs, NJ: Prentice Hall, 1984). See also Edwin A. Locke, Kenneth N.

Shaw, Lisa A. Saari, and Gary P. Latham, "Goal Setting and Task Performance 1969–1980," *Psychological Bulletin*, vol. 90 (1981), pp. 125–52; Mark E. Tubbs, "Goal Setting: A Meta-Analytic Examination of the Empirical Evidence," *Journal of Applied Psychology*, vol. 71 (1986), pp. 474–83; and Terence R. Mitchell, Kenneth R. Thompson, and Jane George-Falvy, "Goal Setting: Theory and Practice," Chapter 9 in Cary L. Cooper and Edwin A. Locke, eds., *Industrial and Organizational Psychology: Linking Theory with Practice* (Malden, MA: Blackwell Business, 2000), pp. 211–49.

[29] See Lauren Weber, "Why Dads Don't Take Paternity Leave," *Wall Street Journal* (June 13, 2013), pp. B1, B7.

Feature Notes

Ethics: Information from "Trial and Error," *Forbes* (June 19, 2006), pp. 128–30; Drake Bennett, "Measures of Success," *Boston Globe Online* (July 2, 2006); William Easterly, "Measuring How and Why Aid Works—Or Doesn't," *Wall Street Journal* (April 30–May 1, 2011), p. C5.

Research Brief: Michael C. Mankins and Richard Steele, "Stop Making Plans; Start Mak-ing Decisions," Harvard Business Review (January 2006), reprint R0601F.

Wisdom: Information and quotes from Information and quotes from the Associated Press, "Oprah Opens School for Girls in S. Africa," "Lavish Leadership Academy Aims to Give Impoverished Chance to Succeed," MSNBC.com (January 2, 2007); "Oprah Winfrey Leadership Academy for Girls—South Africa Celebrates Its Official Opening," oprah.com/about; Jed Dreben, "Oprah Winfrey: 'I Don't Regret' Opening School," people.com (December 12, 2007); and "Gibson Foundation Builds Relationship with Oprah Winfrey Leadership Academy to Support Music Education," news release (April 14, 2009), gibson.com (accessed January 26, 2010).

Chapter 9

Endnotes

[1] Information from "Is Nike's Flyknit the Swoosh of the future?" *Bloomberg Business Week* (March 19–25, 2012), pp. 31, 32.

[2] Ben Popken, "Target estimates breach affected up to 110 million," *NBC News* (January 10, 2014), nbcnews.com (accessed January 14, 2014).

[3] "The Renewal Factor: Friendly Fact, Congenial Controls," *BusinessWeek* (September 14, 1987), p. 105.

[4] Rob Cross and Lloyd Baird, "Technology Is Not Enough: Improving Performance by Building Institutional Memory," *Sloan Management Review* (Spring 2000), p. 73.

[5] Based on discussion by Harold Koontz and Cyril O'Donnell, *Essentials of Management* (New York: McGraw-Hill, 1974), pp. 362–65; see also Cross and Baird, op. cit.

[6] See John F. Love, *McDonald's: Behind the Arches* (New York: Bantam Books, 1986); Ray Kroc and Robert Anderson, *Grinding It Out: The Making of McDonald's* (New York: St. Martin's Press, 1990).

[7] Information and quote from Gregg Segal, "Hyundai Smokes the Competition," *Financial Times* (January 5, 2010).

[8] This distinction is made in William G. Ouchi, "Markets, Bureaucracies and Clans," *Administrative Science Quarterly*, vol. 25 (1980), pp. 129–41.

[9] Douglas McGregor, *The Human Side of Enterprise* (New York: McGraw-Hill, 1960).

[10] See Sue Shellenbarger, "If You Need to Work Better, Maybe Try Working Less," *Wall Street Journal* (September 23, 2009), p. D1.

[11] For an overview, see soxlaw.com

[12] Gregory J. Millman, "For Compliance Chiefs, Who's the Boss?" *Wall Street Journal* (January 14, 2014), p. B7.

[13] See for example, Ram Charan, Dennis Carey, and Michael Useem, *The New Decision Makers* (Cambridge, MA: Harvard Business School Press, 2013).

[14] Martin LaMonica, "Wal-Mart Readies Long-Term Move into Solar Power," CNET News.com (January 3, 2007).

[15] Emily Chasan, "72% Share of S&O 500 Companies that Published Sustainability Reports Last Year," *Wall Street Journal* (June 10, 2014), p. B8.

[16] Rhymer Rigby, "Giving 100% Effort is Too Much," *Financial Times*, Kindle Edition (March 17, 2014).

[17] Information from Leon E. Wynter, "Allstate Rates Managers on Handling Diversity," *Wall Street Journal* (October 1, 1997), p. B1.

[18] Information from Kathryn Kranhold, "U.S. Firms Raise Ethics Focus," *Wall Street Journal* (November 28, 2005), p. B4.

[19] Example from George Anders, "Management Guru Turns Focus to Orchestras, Hospitals," *Wall Street Journal* (November 21, 2005), pp. B1, B5.

[20] Information from Raju Narisetti, "For IBM, a Groundbreaking Sales Chief," *Wall Street Journal* (January 19, 1998), pp. B1, B5.

[21] Information from Karen Carney, "Successful Performance Measurement: A Checklist," *Harvard Management Update* (No. U9911B), 1999.

[22] Robert S. Kaplan and David P. Norton, "The Balanced Scorecard: Measures That Drive Performance," *Harvard Business Review* (July–August 2005); see also Robert S. Kaplan and David P. Norton, *The Balanced Scorecard* (Cambridge, MA: Harvard Business School Press, 1996).

[23] Julian P. Rotter, "External Control and Internal Control," *Psychology Today* (June, 1971). p. 42. Used by permission.

[24] Developed from Roy J. Lewicki, Donald D. Bowen, Douglas T. Hall, and Francine S. Hall, *Experiences in Management and Organizational Behavior,* 4th ed. (New York: Wiley, 1997), pp. 195–97.

Feature Notes

Analysis: Information and quotes from Rachel Emma Silverman, "Here's Why You Won't Finish This Article," *Wall Street Journal* (December 12, 2012), pp. B1, B6.

Ethics: Amaol Sharma, "Google Pulls Some Content in India," *Wall Street Journal* (February 7, 2012), p. B3; Richard Waters, "Twitter, Darling of Political Activists, Bows to Business Reality on Censorship," *Financial Times*, Kindle Edition (January 29, 2012); Rachel McArthy, "Twitter Censorship' Raises Concerns from Press Freedom Group," (January 27, 2012), journalism.com.uk (accessed March 12, 2012); Alison Maitland, "Skype Says Text Messages Censored by Partner in China," *Financial Times* (April 19, 2006), p. 15; and "Web Firms Criticized Over China," CNN.com (July 20, 2006).

Insight: Information from Beth Howard, "The Secrets of Resilient People," *AARP* (November–December 2009), pp. 26, 37; Resiliency Quick Test developed from "How Resilient Are You?" *AARP* (November–December 2009), p. 37.

Chapter 10

Endnotes

[1] Information and quote from Walter Mossberg, "Changing the Economics of Education," *Wall Street Journal* (June 4, 2012), p. R8; and Douglas Belkin, "What Role Will Large Online Courses Play in the Future of Higher Education?" *Wall Street Journal* (May 12, 2014), p. R3.

[2] Information and quotes from Marcia Stepanek, "How Fast Is Net Fast?" *Business Week E-Biz* (November 1, 1999), pp. EB52–54.

[3] Keith H. Hammonds, "Michael Porter's Big Ideas," *Fast Company* (March 2001), pp. 150–56.

[4] See, for example, Walter Kiechel III, *The Lords of Strategy* (Cambridge, MA: Harvard Business Press, 2010).

[5] Michael E. Porter, *Competitive Strategy: Techniques for Analyzing Industries and Competitors* (New York: Free Press, 1980).

[6] Geoffrey A. Fowler and Nick Wingfield, "Apple's Showman Takes the Stage," *Wall Street Journal* (March 3, 2011), p. B1.

[7] See Daisuke Wakarayashi, "Apple Engineer Recalls iPhone's Birth," *Wall Street Journal* (March 26, 2014), pp. B1, B3.

[8] See Porter, op. cit.; Michael E. Porter, *Competitive Advantage: Creating and Sustaining Superior Performance* (New York: Free Press, 1986); and Richard A. D'Aveni, *Hyper-Competition: Managing the Dynamics of Strategic Maneuvering* (New York: Free Press, 1994).

[9] facebook.com/facebook/info (accessed June 13, 2014).

[10] "Inside Facebook's Mobile Strategy," mashable.com (accessed June 13, 2014).

[11] Gary Hamel and C. K. Prahalad, "Strategic Intent." *Harvard Business Review* (May–June 1989), pp. 63–76.

[12] Brad Stone and Graeme Mitchell, "Facebook's Next Decade," *Bloomberg BusinessWeek* (January 30, 2014), pp. 44–49.

[13] Join Us in the Common Threads Partnership," patagonia.com/us/commonthreads (accessed January 19, 2014).

[14] Headline examples from Nathan Ingraham, "Google," *The Verge* (January 3, 2014), theverge.com, accessed January 17, 2014; Juhana Rossi, "Rovio's 'Angry Birds' Flies Free," *Wall Street Journal* (January 3, 2014), p. B5; and Peter Marsh, "Virtual Maker of Chips Conjures Up Real Advances," *Financial Times* (August 24, 2011), p. 16.

[15] See reviews.cnet.com/suv/2015-porsche-macan-suv/4505-10868_7-35831777.html.

[16] Marsh, op cit.

[17] For research support, see Daniel H. Gray, "Uses and Misuses of Strategic Planning," *Harvard Business Review*, vol. 64 (January–February 1986), pp. 89–97.

[18] Peter F. Drucker, *Management: Tasks, Responsibilities, Practices* (New York: Harper-Row, 1973), p. 122.

[19] Peter F. Drucker, "Five Questions," *Executive Excellence* (November 6, 1994), pp. 6–7.

[20] See Laura Nash. "Mission Statements—Mirrors and Windows," *Harvard Business Review* (March–April 1988), pp. 155–56; James C. Collins and Jerry I. Porras, "Building Your Company's Vision," *Harvard Business Review* (September–October 1996), pp. 65–77; and James C. Collins and Jerry I. Porras, *Built to Last: Successful Habits of Visionary Companies* (New York: Harper Business, 1997).

[21] Gary Hamel, *Leading the Revolution* (Boston: Harvard Business School Press, 2000), pp. 72–73.

[22] Values quote from patagonia.com/web/us/patagonia.go?assetid53351.

[23] patagonia.com/web/us/patagonia.go?assetid52047&ln524.

[24] Steve Hamm, "A Passion for the Plan," *BusinessWeek* (August 21/28, 2006), pp. 92–94; quote in box from "Yvon Chouinard: Patagonia's Founder Turned His Passion into Profit," *Spirit* (August, 2008), p. 40.

[25] "Our Reason for Being," patagonia.com/us (accessed January 19, 2014).

[26] Terrence E. Deal and Allen A. Kennedy, *Corporate Cultures: The Rites and Rituals of Corporate Life* (Reading, MA: Addison-Wesley, 1982), p. 22. For more on organizational culture see Edgar H. Schein, *Organizational Culture and Leadership*, 2nd ed. (San Francisco: Jossey-Bass, 1997).

[27] "Jobs," patagonia.com/us (accessed January 19, 2014).

[28] Peter F. Drucker's views on organizational objectives are expressed in his classic books *The Practice of Management* (New York: Harper-Row, 1954) and *Management: Tasks, Responsibilities, Practices* (New York: Harper-Row, 1973). For a more recent commentary, see his article "Management: The Problems of Success," *Academy of Management Executive*, vol. 1 (1987), pp. 13–19.

[29] Hamm, op. cit., 2006.

[30] C. K. Prahalad and Gary Hamel, "The Core Competencies of the Corporation," *Harvard Business Review* (May–June 1990), pp. 79–91.

[31] See D'Aveni, op. cit.

[32] For a discussion of Michael Porter's approach to strategic planning, see his books *Competitive Strategy* and *Competitive Advantage* and his article "What Is Strategy?" *Harvard Business Review* (November–December 1996), pp. 61–78; and Richard M. Hodgetts's interview, "A Conversation with Michael E. Porter. A Significant Extension toward Operational Improvement and Positioning," *Organizational Dynamics* (Summer 1999), pp. 24–33.

[33] See, for example, "Deals: Google's Shopping List," *Bloomberg BusinessWeek* (January 20–26, 2014), p. 32.

[34] See Gerald B. Allan, "A Note on the Boston Consulting Group Concept of Competitive Analysis and Corporate Strategy," Harvard Business School, Intercollegiate Case Clearing House, ICCH9-175-175 (Boston: Harvard Business School, June 1976).

[35] Richard G. Hammermesh, "Making Planning Strategic," *Harvard Business Review,* vol. 64 (July/August 1986), pp. 115–20; and Richard G. Hammermesh, *Making Strategy Work* (New York: Wiley, 1986).

[36] The four grand strategies were described by William F. Glueck, in *Business Policy: Strategy Formulation and Management Action* (New York: McGraw-Hill, 1976).

[37] Information from Vauhini Vara, "Facebook CEO Seeks Help as Site Suffers Growing Pains," *Wall Street Journal* (March 5, 2008), pp. A1, A14.

[38] *See* "Fast-Food Giant Plans to Increase Capital Spending," *Wall Street Journal* (October 11, 2011), p. B4.

[39] Information and quote from Rajesh Mahapatra, "Tata Group Catapults into Global Marketplace," *Columbus Dispatch* (April 3, 2008), pp. C1, C9.

[40] Liam Denning, "Vertical Integration Isn't Just for Christmas," *Wall Street Journal* (December 30, 2009), p. C12.

[41] See William McKinley, Carol M. Sanchez, and A. G. Schick, "Organizational Downsizing: Constraining, Cloning, Learning," *Academy of Management Executive*, vol. 9 (August 1995), pp. 32–44.

[42] Spencer E. Ante, "H-P Buys Time for Turnaround," *Wall Street Journal* (May 29, 2014), p. B5.

[43] Kim S. Cameron, Sara J. Freeman, and A. K. Mishra, "Best Practices in White-Collar Downsizing: Managing Contradictions," *Academy of Management Executive*, vol. 4 (August 1991), pp. 57–73.

[44] Information and quote from Steven Musil and Jonathan E. Skillings, "Sold! eBay Jettisons Skype in $2 Billion Deal," *CNET News* (September 1, 2009), news.cnet.com (accessed April 25, 2010).

[45] Amir Efrat and John Letzing, "Yahoo, Facebook in Patent Row," *Wall Street Journal* (March 13, 2012), p. B9.

[46] This strategy classification is found in R. Duane Ireland and Michael A. Hitt, "Achieving and Maintaining Strategic Competitiveness in the 21st Century," *Academy of Management Executive*, vol. 13 (1999), pp. 43–57; the attitudes are from a discussion by Howard V. Perlmutter, "The Tortuous Evolution of the Multinational Corporation," *Columbia Journal of World Business*, vol. 4 (January–February 1969). See also Pankaj Ghemawat, "Managing Differences," *Harvard Business Review* (March 2007), Reprint R0703C.

[47] Adam M. Brandenburger and Barry J. Nalebuff, *Co-Opetition: A Revolutionary Mindset That Combines Competition and Cooperation* (New York: Bantam, 1996).

[48] See Jack Ewing: "2 Carmakers Prefer to Take Cooperation One Step at a Time," *International Herald Tribune* (September 15, 2011), p. 16.

[49] For a discussion of Michael Porter's approach to strategic planning, see his books *Competitive Strategy and Competitive Advantage,* and his article, "What Is Strategy?" *Harvard Business Review* (November/December, 1996), pp. 61–78; and Hodgetts, op. cit.

[50] Information from polo.com.

[51] Porter, op. cit. (1996).

[52] See Eric Bellman and Deniel Michaels, "In Asia, Budget Flights Multiply," *Wall Street Journal* (February 27, 2012), p. B5.

[53] patagonia.com/web/us/patagonia.go?assetid53351.

[54] For research support, see Daniel H. Gray, "Uses and Misuses of Strategic Planning," *Harvard Business Review*, vol. 64 (January–February 1986), pp. 89–97.

[55] See Judith Burns, "Everything You Wanted to Know about Corporate Governance . . . but Didn't Know How to Ask," *Wall Street Journal* (October 27, 2003), pp. R1, R7.

[56] Ram Charan, Dennis Carey, and Michael Useem, *The New Decision Makers* (Cambridge, MA: Harvard Business School Press, 2013).

[57] Paul Ingrassia, "The Auto Makers Are Already Bankrupt," *Wall Street Journal* (November 21, 2008), p. A23.

[58] Ireland and Hitt, op. cit.

[59] Hodgetts, op. cit.

[60] *AIM Survey* (El Paso, TX: ENFP Enterprises, 1989), Copyright ©1989 by Weston H. Agor. Used by permission.

[61] Suggested by an exercise in John F. Veiga and John N. Yanouzas, *The Dynamics of Organization Theory: Gaining a Macro Perspective* (St. Paul, MN: West, 1979), pp. 69–71.

Feature Notes

Analysis: Information from Daniel Costello, "The Drought Is Over (At Least for CEOs)," *The New York Times* (April 9, 2011), nytimes.com (accessed May 3, 2011); Joann S. Lublin, "CEO Pay in 2010 Jumped 11%," *Wall Street Journal* (May 9, 2011), p. 81; and AFL-CIO, "2011 CEO Paywatch," aflcio.org.

Ethics: Information and quotes from "Life and Death at the iPad Factory," *Bloomberg BusinessWeek* (June 7–13, 2010), pp. 35–36; and John Bussey, "Measuring the Human Cost of an iPad Made in China," *Wall Street Journal* (June 3, 2011), pp. B1, B2.

Research Brief: Richard A. Vernardi, Susan M. Bosco, and Katie M. Vassill, "Does Female Representation on Boards of Directors Associate with Fortune's, '100 Best Companies to Work For' List?" Business and Society, vol. 45 (June 2006), pp. 235–48.

Chapter 11

Endnotes

[1] Henry Mintzberg and Ludo Van der Heyden, "Organigraphs: Drawing How Companies Really Work," *Harvard Business Review* (September–October 1999), pp. 87–94.

[2] The classic work is Alfred D. Chandler, *Strategy and Structure* (Cambridge, MA: MIT Press, 1962).

[3] See Alfred D. Chandler, Jr., "Origins of the Organization Chart," *Harvard Business Review* (March–April 1988), pp. 156–57.

[4] Information from Jena McGregor, "The Office Chart That Really Counts," *BusinessWeek* (February 27, 2006), pp. 48–49.

[5] For a good description see Ben Waber, "Gender Bias by the Numbers," *Bloomberg BusinessWeek* (February 3–9, 2014), pp. 8, 9.

[6] See David Krackhardt and Jeffrey R. Hanson, "Informal Networks: The Company Behind the Chart," *Harvard Business Review* (July–August 1993), pp. 104–11.

[7] Waber, op cit.; and Rachel Feintzeig, "The Boss's Next Demand: Make Lots of Friends," *Wall Street Journal* (February 12, 2014), pp. B1, B6.

[8] Ibid.

[9] Information from Dana Mattioli, "Job Fears Make Offices All Ears," *Wall Street Journal* (January 20, 2009), www.wsj.com.

[10] See Kenneth Noble, "A Clash of Styles: Japanese Companies in the U.S.," *New York Times* (January 25, 1988), p. 7.

[11] For a discussion of departmentalization, see H. I. Ansoff and R. G. Bradenburg, "A Language for Organization Design," *Management Science*, vol. 17 (August 1971), pp. B705–31.

[12] "A Question of Management," *Wall Street Journal* (June 2, 2009), p. R4.

[13] Quote from Jeff Bennett and Mike Ramsey, "GM Takes Blame, Vows Culture Shift," *Wall Street Journal* (June 6, 2014), pp. A1, A2.

[14] "Organization Structure: The Basic Conformations," in Mariann Jelinek, Joseph A. Litterer, and Raymond E. Miles, eds., *Organizations by Design: Theory and Practice* (Plano, TX: Business Publications, 1981), pp. 293–302; Henry Mintzberg, "The Structuring of Organizations," in James Brian Quinn, Henry Mintzberg, and Robert M. James, eds., *The Strategy Process: Concepts, Contexts, and Cases* (Englewood Cliffs, NJ: Prentice-Hall, 1988), pp. 276–304.

[15] Norihiko Shirouzu, "Toyota Plans a Major Overhaul in U.S.," *Wall Street Journal* (April 10, 2009), p. B3.

[16] Information and quotes from "Management Shake-Up to Create 'Leaner Structure'," *Financial Times* (June 11, 2009).

[17] Information Mae Anderson, "Procter & Gamble to Have Four Divisions," *The Columbus Dispatch* (June 6, 2013), p. D4.

[18] The focus on process is described in Michael Hammer, *Beyond Reengineering* (New York: Harper Business, 1996).

[19] Excellent reviews of matrix concepts are found in Stanley M. Davis and Paul R. Lawrence, *Matrix* (Reading, MA: Addison-Wesley, 1977); Paul R. Lawrence, Harvey F. Kolodny,

and Stanley M. Davis, "The Human Side of the Matrix," *Organizational Dynamics*, vol. 6 (1977), pp. 43–61; and Harvey F. Kolodny, "Evolution to a Matrix Organization," *Academy of Management Review*, vol. 4 (1979), pp. 543–53.

[20] Developed from Frank Ostroff, *The Horizontal Organization: What the Organization of the Future Looks Like and How It Delivers Value to Customers* (New York: Oxford University Press, 1999).

[21] Quote from Andrew Hill, "Is Radical Innovation a Thing of the Past?" *Financial Times,* Kindle edition (September 27, 2011).

[22] Susan Albers Mohrman, Susan G. Cohen, and Allan M. Mohrman Jr., *Designing Team-Based Organizations* (San Francisco: Jossey-Bass, 1996).

[23] See Glenn M. Parker, *Cross-Functional Teams* (San Francisco: Jossey-Bass, 1995).

[24] See the discussion by Jay R. Galbraith, "Designing the Networked Organization: Leveraging Size and Competencies," in Susan Albers Mohrman, Jay R. Galbraith, Edward E. Lawler III, and associates, *Tomorrow's Organizations: Crafting Winning Strategies in a Dynamic World* (San Francisco: Jossey-Bass, 1998), pp. 76–102. See also Rupert F. Chisholm, *Developing Network Organizations: Learning from Practice and Theory* (Reading, MA: Addison-Wesley, 1998).

[25] See the discussion by Michael S. Malone, *The Future Arrived Yesterday: The Rise of the Protean Corporation and What It Means for You* (New York: Crown Books, 2009).

[26] See, for example, Dawn Wotapka, "School Wants to Get Out of Campus Housing," *Wall Street Journal* (December 13, 2011), p. B6.

[27] See Jerome Barthelemy, "The Seven Deadly Sins of Outsourcing," *Academy of Management Executive*, vol. 17 (2003), pp. 87–98.

[28] See Ron Ashkenas, Dave Ulrich, Todd Jick, and Steve Kerr, *The Boundaryless Organization: Breaking the Chains of Organizational Structure* (San Francisco: Jossey-Bass, 1996).

[29] Information from "Scott Livengood and the Tasty Tale of Krispy Kreme," *BizEd* (May–June 2003), pp. 16–20.

[30] Information from John A. Byrne, "Management by Web," *BusinessWeek* (August 28, 2000), pp. 84–97; see the collection of articles by Cary L. Cooper and Denise M. Rousseau, eds., *The Virtual Organization: Vol. 6, Trends in Organizational Behavior* (New York: Wiley, 2000).

[31] For a classic work, see Jay R. Galbraith, *Organizational Design* (Reading, MA: Addison-Wesley, 1977).

[32] This framework is based on Harold J. Leavitt, "Applied Organizational Change in Industry," in James G. March, *Handbook of Organizations* (New York: Rand McNally, 1965), pp. 1144–70; and Edward E. Lawler III, *From the Ground Up: Six Principles for the New Logic Corporation* (San Francisco: Jossey-Bass, 1996), pp. 44–50.

[33] Max Weber, *The Theory of Social and Economic Organization*, A. M. Henderson, trans., and H. T. Parsons (New York: Free Press, 1947).

[34] Ibid.

[35] For classic treatments of bureaucracy, see Alvin Gouldner, *Patterns of Industrial Bureaucracy* (New York: Free Press, 1954); and Robert K. Merton, *Social Theory and Social Structure* (New York: Free Press, 1957).

[36] Tom Burns and George M. Stalker, *The Management of Innovation* (London: Tavistock, 1961; republished by Oxford University Press, London, 1994). See also Paul R. Lawrence and Jay W. Lorsch, *Organizations and Environment* (Boston: Division of Research, Graduate School of Business Administration, Harvard University, 1967).

[37] See Henry Mintzberg, *Structure in Fives: Designing Effective Organizations* (Englewood Cliffs, NJ: Prentice-Hall, 1983).

[38] See Rosabeth Moss Kanter, *The Changing Masters* (New York: Simon & Schuster, 1983). Quotation from Rosabeth Moss Kanter and John D. Buck, "Reorganizing Part of Honeywell: From Strategy to Structure," *Organizational Dynamics*, vol. 13 (Winter 1985), p. 6.

[39] See, for example, Jay R. Galbraith, Edward E. Lawler III, and associates, *Organizing for the Future* (San Francisco: Jossey-Bass, 1993); and Mohrman, Galbraith, Lawler, and associates, *Tomorrow's Organizations*.

[40] nucor.com/aboutus.htm

[41] David Van Fleet, "Span of Management Research and Issues," *Academy of Management Journal*, vol. 26 (1983), pp. 546–52.

[42] Jeffrey Pfeffer and John F. Veiga, "Putting People First for Organizational Success," *Academy of Management Executive*, vol. 13, No. 2 (1999), pp. 37–48.

[43] Information and quote from Juhana Rossi and Sven Grundberg, "Angry Birds Maker Rovio Aims for Next Level," *Wall Street Journal* (May 7, 2014), p. B6.

[44] Burns and Stalker, op. cit.

[45] Questionnaire adapted from L. Steinmetz and R. Todd*, First Line Management*, 4th ed. (Homewood, IL: BPI/Irwin, 1986), pp. 64–67. Used by permission.

Features Notes

Analysis: Information and quote from "Bosses Overestimate Their Managing Skills," *Wall Street Journal* (November 1, 2010), p. B10.

Chapter 12

Endnotes

[1] See the discussion of Anthropologie in William C. Taylor and Polly LaBarre, *Mavericks at Work: Why the Most Original Minds in Business Win* (New York: William Morrow, 2006).

[2] Edgar H. Schein, "Organizational Culture," *American Psychologist*, vol. 45 (1990), pp. 109–19. See also *Schein's Organizational Culture and Leadership*, 2nd ed. (San Francisco: Jossey-Bass, 1997) and *The Corporate Culture Survival Guide* (San Francisco: Jossey-Bass, 1999).

[3] James Collins and Jerry Porras, *Built to Last* (New York: HarperBusiness, 1994).

[4] Information and quotes from Christopher Palmeri, "Now for Sale, the Zappos Culture," *BusinessWeek* (January 11, 2010), p. 57. See also Tony Hsieh, *Delivering Happiness! A Path to Profits, Passion, and Purpose* (New York: BusinessPlus, 2010).

[5] Jena McGregor, "Zappos' Secret: It's an Open Book," *BusinessWeek* (March 23–30, 2009), p. 62.

[6] For an overview see Mark G. Ehrhart, Benjamin Schneider, and William H. Macey, *Organizational Climate and Culture: An Introduction to Theory, Research, and Practice* (New York: Routledge, 2014).

[7] This framework is described by Kim S. Cameron & Robert E. Quinn, *Diagnosing and Changing Organizational Culture: Based on the Competing Values Framework* (Reading, MA: Addison-Wesley, 1999).

[8] Information from "Workplace Cultures Come in Four Kinds," *Wall Street Journal* (February 7, 2012), p. B6.

[9] Jena McGregor, "Zappos' Secret: It's an Open Book," *Business Week* (March 23 & 30, 2009), p. 62.

[10] James Collins and Jerry Porras, *Built to Last* (New York: Harper Business, 1994).

[11] Schein, op. cit. (1997); Terrence E. Deal and Alan A. Kennedy, *Corporate Cultures: The Rites and Rituals of Corporate Life* (Reading, MA: Addison-Wesley, 1982); and Ralph Kilmann, *Beyond the Quick Fix* (San Francisco: Jossey-Bass, 1984).

[12] Jeff Bennett and Mike Ramsey, "GM Takes Blame, Vows Culture Shift," *Wall Street Journal* (June 6, 2014), pp. A1, A2.

[13] John P. Wanous, *Organizational Entry*, 2nd ed. (New York: Addison-Wesley, 1992).

[14] Scott Madison Patton, *Service Quality, Disney Style* (Lake Buena Vista, FL: Disney Institute, 1997).

[15] This is a simplified model developed from Schein, op. cit. (1997).

[16] Schein, op. cit. (1997); Terrence E. Deal and Alan A. Kennedy, *Corporate Cultures: The Rites and Rituals of Corporate Life* (Reading, MA: Addison-Wesley, 1982); Ralph Kilmann, *Beyond the Quick Fix* (San Francisco: Jossey-Bass, 1984).

[17] James C. Collins and Jerry I. Porras, "Building Your Company's Vision," *Harvard Business Review* (September–October 1996), pp. 65–77.

[18] See corporate websites for Whole Foods, Under Armour, Tesla, and Honest Tea.

[19] Tom's of Maine example is from Jenny C. McCune, "Making Lemonade," *Management Review* (June 1997), pp. 49–53.

[20] See, for example, Lee G. Bolman and Terrence E. Deal, *Reframing Organizations: Artistry, Choice, and Leadership*, 4th ed. (San Francisco: Jossey-Bass, 2008).

[21] See Robert A. Giacalone and Carol L. Jurkiewicz (eds.), *Handbook of Workplace Spirituality and Organizational Performance* (Armonk, NY: M. E. Sharpe, 2005).

[22] McCune, op. cit.

[23] "Bias Against Gay Workers," *Bloomberg BusinessWeek* (September 23–29, 2013), p. 31.

[24] R. Roosevelt Thomas Jr., *Beyond Race and Gender* (New York: AMACOM, 1992), p. 10. See also R. Roosevelt Thomas Jr., "From 'Affirmative Action' to 'Affirming Diversity,'" *Harvard Business Review* (November–December 1990), pp. 107–17; R. Roosevelt Thomas Jr., with Marjorie I. Woodruff, *Building a House for Diversity* (New York: AMACOM, 1999).

[25] Taylor Cox Jr., *Cultural Diversity in Organizations* (San Francisco: Berrett Koehler, 1994).

[26] Thomas, op cit.

[27] Survey reported in "The Most Inclusive Workplaces Generate the Most Loyal Employees," *Gallup Management Journal* (December 2001), retrieved from gmj.gallup.com/press_room/release.asp?i=117.

[28] Data reported in Laura Petrecca. "Number of Female 'Fortune' 500 CEOs at Record High." *USA Today* (October 26, 2011), usa.com.

[29] Thomas Kochan, Katerina Bezrukova, Robin Ely, Susan Jackson, Aparna Joshi, Karen Jehn, Jonathan Leonard, David Levine, and David Thomas, "The Effects of Diversity on Business Performance: Report of the Diversity Research Network," reported in *SHRM Foundation Research Findings*, retrieved from shrm.org/foundation/findings.asp. Full article published in *Human Resource Management* (2003).

[30] Information from "Demographics: The Young and the Restful," *Harvard Business Review* (November 2004), p. 25.

[31] See, for example, Richard Donkin, "Caught Somewhere between the Ys and the Boomers," *Financial Times*, Kindle Edition (December 31, 2009).

[32] "Many U.S. Employees Have Negative Attitudes to Their Jobs, Employers and Top Managers." *The Harris Poll #38* (May 6, 2005), available from harrisinteractive.com; and "U.S. Job Satisfaction Keeps Falling," *The Conference Board Reports Today* (February 25, 2005; retrieved from conference-board.org).

[33] Mayo Clinic, "Workplace Generation Gap: Understand Differences Among Colleagues" (July 6, 2005), retrieved from cnn.com/HEALTH/library/WL/00045.html.

[34] Barbara Benedict Bunker, "Appreciating Diversity and Modifying Organizational Cultures: Men and Women at Work," Chapter 5 in Suresh Srivastava and David L. Cooperrider, *Appreciative Management and Leadership* (San Francisco: Jossey-Bass, 1990).

[35] See Gary N. Powell, *Women-Men in Management* (Thousand Oaks, CA: Sage, 1993), and Cliff Cheng (ed.), *Masculinities in Organizations* (Thousand Oaks, CA: Sage, 1996). For added background, see also Sally Helgesen, *Everyday Revolutionaries: Working Women and the Transformation of American Life* (New York: Doubleday, 1998).

[36] See Ben Waber, "Gender Bias by the Numbers," *Bloomberg BusinessWeek* (February 3–9, 2014), pp. 8–9.

[37] See Joseph A. Raelin, *Clash of Cultures* (Cambridge, MA: Harvard Business School Press, 1986).

[38] "Statistical Overview of Women in the Workplace," *Catalyst Knowledge Center*, catalyst.org (December 10, 2013): accessed

January 24, 2014; "Women CEOs of the Fortune 1000 List," *Catalyst Knowledge Center*, catalyst.org (January 15, 2014): accessed January 24, 2014; and Joann S. Lublin and Theo Francis, "Women Gain Board Seats—Abroad," *Wall Street Journal* (February 5, 2014), p. B6.

[39] Laurie Landro, "Of Women and Working," *Wall Street Journal*, online edition (December 5, 2009); and Sue Shellenbarger, "The XX Factor: What's Holding Women Back?" *Wall Street Journal* (May 7, 2012), pp. B7–B12 .

[40] Waber, op cit.; and *Damned or Doomed—Catalyst Study on Gender Stereotyping at Work Uncovers Double-Bind Dilemmas for Women,* Knowledge Center, Catalyst.org (July 15, 2007).

[41] "Bias Cases by Workers Increase 9%," *Wall Street Journal* (March 6, 2008), p. D6.

[42] Sue Shellenbarger, "More Women Pursue Claims of Pregnancy Discrimination," *Wall Street Journal* (March 27, 2008), p. D1; and Rob Walker, "Sex vs. Ethics." *Fast Company* (June 2008), pp. 73–78.

[43] Study cited in Waber, op cit.

[44] Walker, op cit. (2008).

[45] Thomas, op. cit. (1992); and Shellenbarger, op. cit. (2012).

[46] Ibid.

[47] For a review of scholarly work on organizational change, see Arthur G. Bedian, "Organizational Change: A Review of Theory and Research," *Journal of Management,* vol. 25 (1999), pp. 293–315; and W. Warner Burke, *Organizational Change: Theory and Practice,* 2nd ed. (Thousand Oaks, CA: Sage, 2008).

[48] Quote from Pilita Clark, "Delayed, Not Cancelled," *Financial Times* (December 19, 2009).

[49] Adam Auriemma, "Chiefs at Big Firms Often Last to Know," *Wall Street Journal* (April 3, 2014), pp. B1, B2.

[50] For a review of data on change failures see Bernard Burnes, "Introduction: Why Does Change Fail, and What Can We Do About It?" *Journal of Change Management*, vol. 11, No. 4 (2011), pp. 445–50; and Mark Hughes, "Do 70 Per Cent of All Organizational Change Initiatives Fail?" *Journal of Change Management*, Vol. 11, No. 4 (2011), pp. 451–64.

[51] Jack and Suzy Welch, "Finding Innovation Where It Lives," *BusinessWeek* (April 21, 2008), p. 84.

[52] This is based on Rosabeth Moss Kanter's "Innovation Pyramid," *BusinessWeek* (March 2007), p. IN 3.

[53] For a discussion of alternative types of change, see David A. Nadler and Michael L. Tushman, *Strategic Organizational Design* (Glenview, IL: Scott, Foresman, 1988); Kotter, op. cit.; and W. Warner Burke, *Organization Change* (Thousand Oaks, CA: Sage, 2002).

[54] Based on John P. Kotter, "Leading Change: Why Transformation Efforts Fail," *Harvard Business Review* (March–April 1995), pp. 59–67.

[55] Kurt Lewin. "Group Decision and Social Change," in G. E. Swanson, T. M. Newcomb, and E. L. Hartley (eds.), *Readings in Social Psychology* (New York: Holt, Rinehart, 1952), pp. 459–73.

[56] See Wanda J. Orlikowski and J. Debra Hofman, "An Improvisational Model for Change Management: The Case of
Groupware Technologies," *Sloan Management Review* (Winter 1997), pp. 11–21.

[57] Ibid.

[58] This discussion is based on Robert Chin and Kenneth D. Benne, "General Strategies for Effecting Changes in Human Systems," in Warren G. Bennis, Kenneth D. Benne, Robert Chin, and Kenneth E. Corey (eds.), *The Planning of Change*, 3rd ed. (New York: Holt, Rinehart, 1969), pp. 22–45.

[59] The change agent descriptions here and following are developed from an exercise reported in J. William Pfeiffer and John E. Jones, *A Handbook of Structured Experiences for Human Relations Training*, vol. 2 (La Jolla, CA: University Associates, 1973).

[60] Information from Mike Schneider, "Disney Teaching Excess Magic of Customer Service." *Columbus Dispatch* (December 17, 2000), p. G9.

[61] Teresa M. Amabile, "How to Kill Creativity," *Harvard Business Review* (September–October 1998), pp. 77–87.

[62] For an overview see Jeffrey D. Ford, Laurie W. Ford, and Angelo D'Amoto, "Resistance to Change: The Rest of the Story," *Academy of Management Review*, vol. 33, no. 2 (2008), pp. 362–77; and Jeffrey D. Ford and Laurie W. Ford, "Decoding Resistance to Change," *Harvard Business Review* (April 2009), pp. 99–103.

[63] These checkpoints are developed from Everett M. Rogers, *Communication of Innovations*, 3rd ed. (New York: Free Press, 1993).

[64] John P. Kotter and Leonard A. Schlesinger, "Choosing Strategies for Change," *Harvard Business Review*, vol. 57 (March–April 1979), pp. 109–12. Example from *Fortune* (December 1991), pp. 56–62; additional information from corporate website toro.com.

[65] Based on an instrument developed by W. Warner Burke. Used by permission.

Feature Notes

Analysis: Information and quote from "Bosses Overestimate Their Managing Skills," *Wall Street Journal* (November 1, 2010), p. B10.

Research Brief: Harry Sminia and Antonie Van Nistelrooij, "Strategic Management and Organizational Development: Planned Change in a Public Sector Organization," *Journal of Change Management*, vol. 6 (March 2006), pp. 99–113.

Chapter 13

Endnotes

[1] Jeffrey Pfeffer, *The Human Equation: Building Profits by Putting People First* (Boston: Harvard University Press, 1998), p. 292.

[2] Quote from William Bridges, "The End of the Job," *Fortune* (September 19, 1994), p. 68. Edward E. Lawler III, "The HR Department: *Give It More Respect*," (March 10, 2008), p. R8.

[3] *Dictionary of Business Management* (New York: Oxford University Press, 2006).

[4] T. Sekiguchi, "Person–Organization Fit and Person–Job Fit in Employee Selection: A Review of the Literature," *Osaka Keidai Ronshu*, vol. 54, no. 6 (2004), p. 179.

[5] Information from "New Face at Facebook Hopes to Map Out a Road to Growth," *Wall Street Journal* (April 15, 2008), pp. B1, B5.

[6] James N. Baron and David M. Kreps, *Strategic Human Resources: Framework for General Managers* (New York: Wiley, 1999).

[7] Julie Jargon and Douglas Belkin, "Starbucks to Subsidize Online Degrees," *Wall Street Journal* (June 16, 2013), p. B3.

[8] For a discussion of affirmative action, see R. Roosevelt Thomas Jr., "From 'Affirmative Action' to 'Affirming Diversity,'" *Harvard Business Review* (November–December 1990), pp. 107–17.

[9] See the discussion by David A. DeCenzo and Stephen P. Robbins, *Human Resource Management*, 6th ed. (New York: Wiley, 1999), pp. 66–68 and 81–83.

[10] Ibid., pp. 77–79.

[11] Information from the U.S. Department of Labor, retrieved from dol.gov/whd/fmla/index.htm.

[12] "A Bill: Bias Against Gay Workers," *Bloomberg BusinessWeek* (September 23–September 29, 2013), p. 32.

[13] "Employment Non-Discrimination Act: H.R. 1755; S. 815," *Human Rights Campaign* (November 7, 2013): hrc.org (accessed February 8, 2014).

[14] Quote from Mark Lifscher, "Rising use of 'perma-temp' workers is stirring up a legislative fight," *Los Angeles Times* (May 7, 2014), latimes.com (accessed June 19, 2014).

[15] Ibid.

[16] Elizabeth Dwoskin, "Give me Back my Privacy," *Wall Street Journal* (March 24, 2014), pp. R1, R2.

[17] See Frederick S. Lane, *The Naked Employee: How Technology Is Compromising Workplace Privacy* (New York: AMACOM, 2003).

[18] Quote from George Myers, "Bookshelf," *Columbus Dispatch* (June 9, 2003), p. E6.

[19] See Ernest McCormick, "Job and Task Analysis," in Marvin Dunnette (ed.), *Handbook of Industrial and Organizational Psychology* (Chicago: Rand McNally, 1976), pp. 651–96.

[20] Adam Auriemma, "Zappos Zaps Job Postings, Seeks Hires on Social Media," *Wall Street Journal* (May 27, 2014), p. B5.

[21] See John P. Wanous, *Organizational Entry: Recruitment, Selection, and Socialization of Newcomers* (Reading, MA: Addison-Wesley, 1980), pp. 34–44.

[22] Information and quotes from William Poundstone, "How to Ace a Google Interview," *Wall Street Journal* (December 24–25, 2012), pp. C1, C2.

[23] Oddball and common interview questions can be found at glassdoor.com. These examples are from Darrell Smith, "Interview Curveballs," *The Seattle Times* (February 2, 2014), p. F1.

[24] Theresa Feathers, *Three Major Selection and Assessment Techniques, Their Popularity in Industry and Their Predictive Validity*, December 2000.

[25] See Michael A. D. McDaniel, Deborah L. Whetzel, Frank L. Schmidt, and Steven Maurer, "The Validity of Employment Interviews: A Comprehensive Review and Meta-analysis," *Journal of Applied Psychology,* vol. 79, no. 4 (August 1994), pp. 599–616.

[26] Information from "Biodata: The Measure of an Applicant?" *New York Law Journal* (May 21, 2007).

[27] Information from "Google Answer to Filling Jobs Is an Algorithm," *New York Times* (January 3, 2007).

[28] For a scholarly review, see John Van Maanen and Edgar H. Schein, "Toward a Theory of Socialization," in Barry M. Staw (ed.), *Research in Organizational Behavior*, vol. 1 (Greenwich, CT: JAI Press, 1979), pp. 209–64; for a practitioner's view, see Richard Pascale, "Fitting New Employees into the Company Culture," *Fortune* (May 28, 1984), pp. 28–42.

[29] Caitlin Huston, "How to Win Talent War: Spend Time Launching the New Hire," *Wall Street Journal* (January 16, 2014), p. B5.

[30] This involves the social information processing concept as discussed in Gerald R. Salancik and Jeffrey Pfeffer, "A Social Information Processing Approach to Job Attitudes and Task Design," *Administrative Science Quarterly*, vol. 23 (June 1978), pp. 224–53.

[31] Alan Fowler, "How to Decide on Training Methods," *People Management*, vol. 25 (1995), pp. 36–38.

[32] Gouri Shukla, "Job Rotation and How It Works," April 27, 2005, retrieved from rediff.com/money/2005/apr/27spec1.htm.

[33] Sue Shellenbarger, "Tech-Impaired? Pair Up with a Younger Worker," *Wall Street Journal* (May 28, 2014), p. D3.

[34] See Larry L. Cummings and Donald P. Schwab, *Performance in Organizations: Determinants and Appraisal* (Glenview, IL: Scott, Foresman, 1973).

[35] Claire Suddath, "You Get a 'D+' in Teamwork," *Bloomberg BusinessWeek* (November 7, 2013), p. 91.

[36] Ibid.

[37] Dick Grote, "Performance Appraisal Reappraised," *Harvard Business Review Best Practice* (1999), Reprint F00105.

[38] See Gary P. Latham, Joan Almost, Sara Mann, and Celia Moore, "New Developments in Performance Management," *Organizational Dynamics*, vol. 34, no. 1 (2005), pp. 77–87.

[39] See Jeffrey S. Kane, John H. Bernardin, Peter Villanova, and Joseph Peyrefitte, "Stability of Rater Leniency: Three Studies," *Academy of Management Journal*, vol. 38, no. 4 (1995), pp. 1036–51.

[40] See Edward E. Lawler III, "Reward Practices and Performance Management System Effectiveness," *Organizational Dynamics*, vol. 32, no. 4 (November 2003), pp. 396–404.

[41] Information from Ilana DeBare, "360 Degrees of Evaluation—More Companies Turn to Full-Circle Job Reviews," *San Francisco Chronicle* (May 5, 1997).

[42] Latham, op. cit.

[43] Timothy Butler and James Waldroop, "Job Sculpting: The Art of Retaining Your Best People," *Harvard Business Review* (September–October 1999), pp. 144–52.

[44] Information from "What Are the Most Effective Retention Tools?" *Fortune* (October 9, 2000), p. S7.

[45] See Betty Friedan, *Beyond Gender: The New Politics of Work and the Family* (Washington, DC: Woodrow Wilson Center Press, 1997); and James A. Levine, *Working Fathers: New Strategies for Balancing Work and Family* (Reading, MA: Addison-Wesley, 1997).

[46] Study reported in Ann Belser, "Employers Using Less-Costly Ways to Retain Workers," *Columbus Dispatch* (June 1, 2008), p. D3.

[47] Information from *Working Mother* (workingmother.com/best-companies/2011-working-mother-100-best-companies).

[48] "Should Companies Offer Sabbaticals?," *CNNMoney* (retrieved January 3, 2011, from management.fortune.cnn.com/2011/01/03/should-companies-offer-sabbaticals).

[49] "Vacation Policies Are Here to Stay," *CNNMoney* (retrieved February 1, 2011, from money.cnn.com/2011/01/31/news/companies/no_vacation_policies.fortune/index.htm).

[50] A good overview of trends and issues is found in the special section on "Employee Benefits," *Wall Street Journal* (April 22, 2008), pp. A11–A17.

[51] "What Is the Typical Cost of Benefits per Employee?" *eHow.com* (retrieved June 29, 2011, from ehow.com/info_8663999_typical-cost-benefits-per-employee.html#ixzz1kRAYVptc).

[52] See Kaja Whitehouse, "More Companies Offer Packages Pay Plans to Performance," *Wall Street Journal* (December 13, 2005), p. B6.

[53] Ibid.

[54] Information from Susan Pulliam, "The New Dot-Com Mantra: 'Just Pay Me in Cash, Please,'" *Wall Street Journal* (November 28, 2000), p. C1.

[55] Information from Andrew Blackman, "You're the Boss," *Wall Street Journal* (April 11, 2005), p. R5.

[56] Information from intel.com and "Stock Ownership for Everyone," Hewitt Associates (November 27, 2000).

[57] Quote from Jeffrey Sparshott, "Workplace Benefits Get Focus," *Wall Street Journal* (June 24, 2014), p. A6.

[58] Angus Loten and Sarah E. Needleman, "Laws on Paid Sick Leave Divide Businesses," *Wall Street Journal* (February 6, 2014), p. B5.

[59] For reviews see Richard B. Freeman and James L. Medoff, *What Do Unions Do?* (New York: Basic Books, 1984); Charles C. Heckscher, *The New Unionism* (New York: Basic Books, 1988); and Barry T. Hirsch, *Labor Unions and the Economic Performance of Firms* (Kalamazoo, MI: W. E. Upjohn Institute for Employment Research, 1991).

[60] Ibid.

[61] See thinkprogress.org/politics/2011/03/05/148930/top-five-things-unions.

[62] Data on union membership trends from huffingtonpost.com/2013/01/23.

[63] Developed in part from Robert E. Quinn, Sue R. Faerman, Michael P. Thompson, and Michael R. McGrath, *Becoming a Master Manager: A Contemporary Framework* (New York: Wiley, 1990), p. 187. Used by permission.

[64] Developed from Eugene Owens, "Upward Appraisal: An Exercise in Subordinate's Critique of Superior's Performance," *Exchange: The Organizational Behavior Teaching Journal*, vol. 3 (1978), pp. 41–42.

Feature Notes

Analysis: Information from Jenny Marlar, "Underemployed Report Spending 36% Less Than Employed," *Gallup.com*, February 23, 2010 (retrieved December 8, 2011), gallup.com/poll/125639/gallup-daily-workforce.aspx; Jordan Weissman, "44% of Young College Grads Are Underemployed (and That's Good News)," *The Atlantic*, theatlantic.com

Wisdom: Information from zappos.com; mahalo.com/tony-hsieh; Tony Hsieh, *Delivering Happiness: A Path to Profits, Passion, and Purpose* (New York: BusinessPlus, 2010); interview of Tony Hsieh by Victoria Brown on May 27, 2010 (retrieved from bigthink.com/ideas/20673); and Brad Stone, "What Starts Up in Vegas Stays in Vegas," *Bloomberg BusinessWeek* (February 6–12, 2012), pp. 37–39.

Chapter 14

Endnotes

[1] Quote from Marshall Loeb, "Where Leaders Come From," *Fortune* (September 19, 1994), pp. 241–42. For additional thoughts, see Warren Bennis, *Why Leaders Can't Lead* (San Francisco: Jossey-Bass, 1996).

[2] Barry Z. Posner, "On Leadership," *BizEd* (May–June 2008), pp. 26–27.

[3] Tom Peters, "Rule #3: Leadership Is Confusing as Hell," *Fast Company* (March 2001), pp. 124–40.

[4] See Jean Lipman-Blumen, *Connective Leadership: Managing in a Changing World* (New York: Oxford University Press, 1996), pp. 3–11.

[5] Abraham Zaleznick, "Leaders and Managers: Are They Different?" *Harvard Business Review* (May–June 1977), pp. 67–78.

[6] Rosabeth Moss Kanter, "Power Failure in Management Circuits," *Harvard Business Review* (July–August 1979), pp. 65–75.

[7] For a good managerial discussion of power, see David C. McClelland and David H. Burnham, "Power Is the Great Motivator," *Harvard Business Review* (March–April 1976), pp. 100–10.

[8] The classic treatment of these power bases is John R. P. French Jr. and Bertram Raven, "The Bases of Social Power," in Darwin Cartwright, ed., *Group Dynamics: Research and Theory* (Evanston, IL: Row, Peterson, 1962), pp. 607–13. For managerial applications of this basic framework, see Gary Yukl and Tom Taber, "The Effective Use of Managerial Power," *Personnel*, vol. 60 (1983), pp. 37–49; and Robert C. Benfari, Harry E. Wilkinson, and Charles D. Orth, "The Effective Use of Power," *Business Horizons*, vol. 29 (1986), pp. 12–16; Gary A. Yukl, *Leadership in Organizations*, 4th ed. (Englewood Cliffs, NJ: Prentice-Hall, 1998) includes "information" as a separate, but related, power source.

[9] See Rob Cross, "A Smarter Way to Network," *Harvard Business Review*, vol. 89 (July–August, 2011), pp. 149–153; and Rachel Feintzeig, "The Boss's Next Demand: Make a Lot of Friends," *Wall Street Journal* (February 14, 2014), pp. B1, B6.

[10] James M. Kouzes and Barry Z. Posner, "The Leadership Challenge," *Success* (April 1988), p. 68. See also their books *Credibility: How Leaders Gain and Lose It; Why People Demand It* (San Francisco: Jossey-Bass, 1996); *Encouraging the Heart: A Leader's Guide to Rewarding and Recognizing Others* (San Francisco: Jossey-Bass, 1999); and *The Leadership Challenge: How to Get Extraordinary Things Done in Organizations*, 3rd ed. (San Francisco: Jossey-Bass, 2002).

[11] Burt Nanus, *Visionary Leadership: Creating a Compelling Sense of Vision for Your Organization* (San Francisco: Jossey-Bass, 1992).

[12] Lorraine Monroe, "Leadership Is about Making Vision Happen—What I Call 'Vision Acts,'" *Fast Company* (March 2001), p. 98; School Leadership Academy website, lorrainemonroe.com.

[13] Quote from Andy Serwer, "Game Changers: Legendary Basketball Coach John Wooden and Starbucks' Howard Schultz Talk about a Common Interest—Leadership," *Fortune* (August 11, 2008): cnnmoney.com.

[14] Robert K. Greenleaf and Larry C. Spears, *The Power of Servant Leadership: Essays* (San Francisco: Berrett-Koehler, 1996), p. 78.

[15] Monroe, op. cit., p. 98; School Leadership Academy website, www.lorrainemonroe.com.

[16] Loeb, op. cit.

[17] A classic work is Greenleaf and Spears, op. cit.

[18] Jay A. Conger, "Leadership: The Art of Empowering Others," *Academy of Management Executive*, vol. 3 (1989), pp. 17–24.

[19] See Shamir Boas, Pillai Rajnandini, Michelle C. Bligh, and Mary Uhl-Bien (Eds.), *Follower-Centered Perspectives on Leadership: A Tribute to the Memory of James R. Meindl* (Pittsburgh: Information Age Publishing, 2006).

[20] Mary Uhl-Bien and Rajnandini Pillai, "The Romance of Leadership and the Social Construction of Followership," pp. 187–209, in Boas, et al., op cit.

[21] See the discussion in Mary Uhl-Bien, John R. Schermerhorn, Jr., and Richard N. Osborn, *Organizational Behavior*, 13th Edition (Hoboken, NJ: John Wiley & Sons, 2014), pp. 291–92.

[22] The early work on leader traits is well represented in Ralph M. Stogdill, "Personal Factors Associated with Leadership: A Survey of the Literature," *Journal of Psychology*, vol. 25 (1948), pp. 35–71. See also Edwin E. Ghiselli, *Explorations in Management Talent* (Santa Monica, CA: Goodyear, 1971); and Shirley A. Kirkpatrick and Edwin A. Locke, "Leadership: Do Traits Really Matter?" *Academy of Management Executive* (1991), pp. 48–60.

[23] See also John W. Gardner's article, "The Context and Attributes of Leadership," *New Management*, vol. 5 (1988),

pp. 18–22; John P. Kotter, *The Leadership Factor* (New York: Free Press, 1988); and Bernard M. Bass, *Stogdill's Handbook of Leadership* (New York: Free Press, 1990).

[24] Kirkpatrick and Locke, op. cit., 1991.

[25] This work traces back to classic studies by Kurt Lewin and his associates at the University of Iowa. See, for example, K. Lewin and R. Lippitt, "An Experimental Approach to the Study of Autocracy and Democracy: A Preliminary Note," *Sociometry*, vol. 1 (1938), pp. 292–300; K. Lewin, "Field Theory and Experiment in Social Psychology: Concepts and Methods," *American Journal of Sociology*, vol. 44 (1939), pp. 886–96; and K. Lewin, R. Lippitt, and R. K. White, "Patterns of Aggressive Behavior in Experimentally Created Social Climates," *Journal of Social Psychology*, vol. 10 (1939), pp. 271–301.

[26] The original research from the Ohio State studies is described in R. M. Stogdill and A. E. Coons, eds., *Leader Behavior: Its Description and Measurement*, Research Monograph No. 88 (Columbus: Ohio State University Bureau of Business Research, 1951); see also Chester A. Schreisham, Claudia C. Cogliser, and Linda L. Neider, "Is It 'Trustworthy'? A Multiple-Levels-of-Analysis Reexamination of an Ohio State Leadership Study with Implications for Future Research," *Leadership Quarterly*, vol. 2 (Summer 1995), pp. 111–45. For the University of Michigan studies, see Robert Kahn and Daniel Katz, "Leadership Practices in Relation to Productivity and Morale," in Dorwin Cartwright and Alvin Alexander, eds., *Group Dynamics: Research and Theory*, 3rd ed. (New York: Harper-Row, 1968).

[27] See Bass, op. cit., 1990.

[28] Robert R. Blake and Jane Srygley Mouton, *The New Managerial Grid III* (Houston: Gulf Publishing, 1985).

[29] See Lewin and Lippitt, op. cit., 1938.

[30] For a good discussion of this theory, see Fred E. Fiedler, Martin M. Chemers, and Linda Mahar, *The Leadership Match Concept* (New York: Wiley, 1978); Fiedler's current contingency research with the cognitive resource theory is summarized in Fred E. Fiedler and Joseph E. Garcia, *New Approaches to Effective Leadership* (New York: Wiley, 1987).

[31] See Pino Audia, "A New B-School Specialty: Self-Awareness," Forbes.com (December 4, 2009).

[32] Paul Hersey and Kenneth H. Blanchard, *Management and Organizational Behavior* (Englewood Cliffs, NJ: Prentice-Hall, 1988). For an interview with Paul Hersey on the origins of the model, see John R. Schermerhorn Jr., "Situational Leadership: Conversations with Paul Hersey," *Mid-American Journal of Business* (Fall 1997), pp. 5–12.

[33] See Claude L. Graeff, "The Situational Leadership Theory: A Critical View," *Academy of Management Review*, vol. 8 (1983), pp. 285–91; and Carmen F. Fernandez and Robert P. Vecchio, "Situational Leadership Theory Revisited: A Test of an Across-Jobs Perspective," *Leadership Quarterly*, vol. 8 (Summer 1997), pp. 67–84.

[34] See, for example, Robert J. House, "A Path–Goal Theory of Leader Effectiveness," *Administrative Sciences Quarterly*, vol. 16 (1971), pp. 321–38; Robert J. House and Terrence R. Mitchell,

"Path–Goal Theory of Leadership," *Journal of Contemporary Business* (Autumn 1974), pp. 81–97. The path–goal theory is reviewed by Bass, op. cit. A supportive review of research is offered in Julie Indvik, "Path–Goal Theory of Leadership: A Meta-Analysis," in John A. Pearce II and Richard B. Robinson Jr., eds., *Academy of Management Best Paper Proceedings* (1986), pp. 189–92. The theory is reviewed and updated in Robert J. House, "Path–Goal Theory of Leadership: Lessons, Legacy and a Reformulated Theory," *Leadership Quarterly*, vol. 7 (Autumn 1996), pp. 323–52.

[35] See the discussions of path–goal theory in Bernard M. Bass, "Leadership: Good, Better, Best," *Organizational Dynamics* (Winter 1985), pp. 26–40.

[36] See Steven Kerr and John Jermier, "Substitutes for Leadership: Their Meaning and Measurement," *Organizational Behavior and Human Performance*, vol. 22 (1978), pp. 375–403; Jon P. Howell and Peter W. Dorfman, "Leadership and Substitutes for Leadership Among Professional and Nonprofessional Workers," *Journal of Applied Behavioral Science*, vol. 22 (1986), pp. 29–46.

[37] An early presentation of the theory is F. Dansereau Jr., G. Graen, and W. J. Haga, "A Vertical Dyad Linkage Approach to Leadership Within Formal Organizations: A Longitudinal Investigation of the Role-Making Process," *Organizational Behavior and Human Performance*, vol. 13, pp. 46–78.

[38] This discussion is based on Yukl, op. cit., pp. 117–22.

[39] Ibid.

[40] Victor H. Vroom and Arthur G. Jago, *The New Leadership: Managing Participation in Organizations* (Englewood Cliffs, NJ: Prentice-Hall, 1988). This is based on earlier work by Victor H. Vroom, "A New Look in Managerial Decision-Making," *Organizational Dynamics* (Spring 1973), pp. 66–80; and Victor H. Vroom and Phillip Yetton, *Leadership and Decision-Making* (Pittsburgh: University of Pittsburgh Press, 1973).

[41] Vroom and Jago, op. cit.

[42] For a review, see Yukl, op. cit.

[43] See the discussion by Victor H. Vroom, "Leadership and the Decision-Making Process," *Organizational Dynamics*, vol. 28 (2000), pp. 82–94.

[44] Among the popular books addressing this point of view are Warren Bennis and Burt Nanus, *Leaders: The Strategies for Taking Charge* (New York: Harper Business 1997); Max DePree, *Leadership Is an Art* (New York: Doubleday, 1989); and Kouzes and Posner, op. cit. (2002).

[45] These terms are from James MacGregor Burns, *Leadership* (New York: Harper & Row, 1978), and further developed by Bernard Bass, *Leadership and Performance Beyond Expectations* (New York: Free Press, 1985), and Bernard M. Bass, "Leadership: Good, Better, Best," *Organizational Dynamics* (Winter 1985), pp. 26–40. See also Bernard M. Bass, "Does the Transactional-Transformational Leadership Paradigm Transcend Organizational and National Boundaries?" *American Psychologist*, vol. 52 (February 1997), pp. 130–39.

[46] Daniel Goleman, "Leadership That Gets Results," *Harvard Business Review* (March/April 2000), pp. 78–90. See also his books *Emotional Intelligence* (New York: Bantam Books, 1995) and *Working with Emotional Intelligence* (New York: Bantam Books, 1998).

[47] Daniel Goleman, Annie McKee, and Richard E. Boyatzis, *Primal Leadership: Realizing the Power of Emotional Intelligence* (Boston: Harvard Business School Press, 2002), p. 3.

[48] Daniel Goleman, "What Makes a Leader?" *Harvard Business Review* (November–December 1998), pp. 93–102.

[49] Goleman, op. cit., 1998.

[50] Information from "Women and Men, Work, and Power," *Fast Company*, issue 13 (1998), p. 71.

[51] Jane Shibley Hyde, "The Gender Similarities—Hypothesis," *American Psychologist*, vol. 60, no. 6 (2005), pp. 581–92.

[52] A. H. Eagley, S. J. Daran, and M. G. Makhijani, "Gender and the Effectiveness of Leaders: A Meta-Analysis," *Psychological Bulletin*, vol. 117 (1995), pp. 125–45.

[53] Research on gender issues in leadership is reported in Sally Helgesen, *The Female Advantage: Women's Ways of Leadership* (New York: Doubleday, 1990); Judith B. Rosener, "Ways Women Lead," *Harvard Business Review* (November–December 1990), pp. 119–25; and Alice H. Eagley, Steven J. Karau, and Blair T. Johnson, "Gender and Leadership Style Among School Principals: A Meta Analysis," *Administrative Science Quarterly*, vol. 27 (1992), pp. 76–102; Jean Lipman-Blumen, *Connective Leadership: Managing in a Changing World* (New York: Oxford University Press, 1996); Alice H. Eagley, Mary C. Johannesen-Smith, and Marloes L. van Engen, "Transformational, Transactional and Laissez-Faire Leadership: A Meta-Analysis of Women and Men," *Psychological Bulletin*, vol. 124, no. 4 (2003), pp. 569–91; and Carol Hymowitz, "Too Many Women Fall for Stereotypes of Selves, Study Says," *Wall Street Journal* (October 24, 2005), p. B.1.

[54] Ibid.

[55] See Alice Eagley and Linda L. Cari, "Women and the Labyrinth of Leadership," *Harvard Business Review* (September, 2007), Reprint 0709C.

[56] Quote from "As Leaders, Women Rule," BusinessWeek (November 2, 2000), pp. 75–84. Rosabeth Moss Kanter is the author of Men and Women of the Corporation, 2nd ed. (New York: Basic Books, 1993).

[57] Eagley et al., op. cit.; Hymowitz, op. cit.; Rosener, op. cit.; Vroom, op. cit.; Herminia Ibarra and Otilia Obodaru, "Women and the Vision Thing," *Harvard Business Review* (January, 2009): Reprint R0901E.

[58] Ibarra and Obodaru, op. cit.

[59] Rosener, op. cit.

[60] For debate on whether some transformational leadership qualities tend to be associated more with female than male leaders, see "Debate: Ways Women and Men Lead," *Harvard Business Review* (January–February 1991), pp. 150–60.

[61] See Herminia Ibarra and Morten T. Hansen, "Are You a Collaborative Leader?" *Harvard Business Review*, Vol. 89 (July–August, 2011), pp. 68–74.

[62] Hyde, op. cit.; Hymowitz, op. cit.

[63] Julie Bennett, "Women Get a Boost Up that Tall Leadership Ladder," *Wall Street Journal* (June 10, 2008), p. D6.

[64] Based on the discussion by John W. Dienhart and Terry Thomas, "Ethical Leadership: A Primer on Ethical Responsibility," in John R. Schermerhorn, Jr., *Management*, 7th ed. (New York: Wiley, 2003).

[65] "Many U.S. Employees Have Negative Attitudes to Their Jobs, Employers, and Top Managers," *Harris Poll #38* (May 6, 2005), harrisinteractive.com.

[66] "The Stat," *Business Week* (September 12, 2005), p. 16.

[67] See Nitin Nohria, "The Big Question: What Should We Teach Our Business Leaders?" *Bloomberg BusinessWeek* (November 14–20, 2011), p. 68.

[68] Ibid.

[69] Fred Luthans and Bruce Avolio, "Authentic Leadership: A Positive Development Approach," in K. S. Cameron, J. E. Dutton, and R. E. Quinn, eds., *Positive Organizational Scholarship* (San Francisco: Berrett-Koehler, 2003), pp. 241–58.

[70] See Doug May, Adrian Chan, Timothy Hodges, and Bruce Avolio, "Developing the Moral Component of Authentic Leadership," *Organizational Dynamics*, vol. 32 (2003), pp. 247–60; and William L. Gardner, Claudia C. Cogliser, Kelly M. Davis, and Matthew P. Dickens, "Authentic Leadership: A Review of the Literature and Research Agenda," *Leadership Quarterly*, vol. 22 (2011), pp. 1120–1145.

[71] See Arménio Rego, Filipa Sousa, Carla Marques, and Miguel Pina e Cunha, "Authentic Leadership Promoting Employee's Capital and Creativity," *Journal of Business Research,* vol. 65 (2012), pp. 429–37.

[72] Peter F. Drucker, "Leadership: More Doing than Dash," *Wall Street Journal* (January 6, 1988), p. 16. For a compendium of writings on leadership, sponsored by the Drucker Foundation, see Frances Hesselbein, Marshall Goldsmith, and Richard Beckhard, *Leader of the Future* (San Francisco: Jossey-Bass, 1997).

[73] Quote from ibid.

[74] Ibid.

[75] Fred E. Fiedler and Martin M. Chemers, *Improving Leadership Effectiveness: The Leader Match Concept,* 2nd ed. (New York: Wiley, 1984). Used by permission.

Feature Notes

Insight: List developed from S. Bartholomew Craig and Gigrid B. Qustafson, "Perceived Leader Integrity Scale: An Instrument for Assessing Employee Perceptions of Leader Integrity," *Leadership Quarterly*, vol. 9 (1998), pp. 127–45.

Research Brief: Joyce E. Bono and Remus Ilies, "Charisma, Positive Emotions and Mood Contagion," Leadership Quarterly, vol. 17 (2006), pp. 317–34.

Wisdom: Information and quotes from Lorraine Monroe, "Leadership Is about Making Vision Happen—What I Call 'Vision Acts,'" *Fast Company* (March 2001), p. 98; Lorraine Monroe Leadership Institute website, lorrainemonroe.com. See also, Lorraine Monroe, *Nothing's Impossible: Leadership Lessons from Inside and Outside the Classroom* (New York:

PublicAffairs Books, 1999), and *The Monroe Doctrine: An ABC Guide to What Great Bosses Do* (New York: PublicAffairs Books, 2003).

Chapter 15

Endnotes

[1] Max DePree, "An Old Pro's Wisdom: It Begins with a Belief in People," *New York Times* (September 10, 1989), p. F2; Max DePree, *Leadership Is an Art* (New York: Doubleday, 1989); David Woodruff, "Herman Miller: How Green Is My Factory," *BusinessWeek* (September 16, 1991), pp. 54–56; and Max DePree, *Leadership Jazz* (New York: Doubleday, 1992); quote from depree.org/html/maxdepree.html.

[2] See 9to5.org.

[3] This example is reported in *Esquire* (December 1986), p. 243. Emphasis is added to the quotation. *Note:* Nussbaum became director of the Labor Department's Women's Bureau during the Clinton administration and subsequently moved to the AFL–CIO as head of the Women's Bureau.

[4] See 9to5.org.

[5] See H. R. Schiffman, *Sensation and Perception: An Integrated Approach*, 3d ed. (New York: Wiley, 1990).

[6] John P. Kotter, "The Psychological Contract: Managing the Joining Up Process," *California Management Review*, vol. 15 (Spring 1973), pp. 91–99; Denise Rousseau, ed., *Psychological Contracts in Organizations* (San Francisco: Jossey-Bass, 1995); Denise Rousseau, "Changing the Deal While Keeping the People," *Academy of Management Executive*, vol. 10 (1996), pp. 50–59; and Denise Rousseau and Rene Schalk, eds., *Psychological Contracts in Employment: Cross-Cultural Perspectives* (San Francisco: Jossey-Bass, 2000).

[7] For reviews see E. L. Jones, ed., *Attribution: Perceiving the Causes of Behavior* (Morristown, NJ: General Learning Press, 1972); John H. Harvey and Gifford Weary, "Current Issues in Attribution Theory and Research," *Annual Review of Psychology*, vol. 35 (1984), pp. 427–59; and Paul Harvey, Kristen Madison, Mark Martinko, R. Russell Crook, and Tamara A. Crook, "Attribution Theory in the Organizational Sciences: The Road Traveled and the Path Ahead," *The Academy of Management Perspectives*, vol. 28, No. 2 (2014), pp. 128–46.

[8] These examples are from Natasha Josefowitz, *Paths to Power* (Reading, MA: Addison-Wesley, 1980), p. 60. For more on gender issues, see Gray N. Powell, ed., *Handbook of Gender and Work* (Thousand Oaks, CA: Sage, 1999).

[9] "Tales from Trailing Husbands," *Financial Times*, Kindle Edition (June 11, 2013).

[10] Information from "Misconceptions about Women in the Global Arena Keep Their Numbers Low," Catalyst Study: catalystwomen.org/home.html.

[11] The classic work is Dewitt C. Dearborn and Herbert A. Simon, "Selective Perception: A Note on the Departmental Identification of Executives," *Sociometry*, vol. 21 (1958),

pp. 140–44. See also J. P. Walsh, "Selectivity and Selective Perception: Belief Structures and Information Processing," *Academy of Management Journal*, vol. 24 (1988), pp. 453–70.

[12] Alexandra Wolfe, "Richard Branson," *Wall Street Journal* (November 2–3, 2014), p. C11.

[13] Quotation from Sheila O'Flanagan, "Underestimate Casual Dressers at Your Peril," *Irish Times* (July 22, 2005). See also Christina Binkley, "How to Pull Off 'CEO Casual,'" *Wall Street Journal* (August 7, 2008), pp. D1–D8.

[14] See William L. Gardner and Mark J. Martinko, "Impression Management in Organizations," *Journal of Management* (June 1988), p. 332.

[15] Sandy Wayne and Robert Liden, "Effects of Impression Management on Performance Ratings," *Academy of Management Journal* (February 2005), pp. 232–52.

[16] See M. R. Barrick and M. K. Mount, "The Big Five Personality Dimensions and Job Performance: A Meta-Analysis," *Personnel Psychology*, vol. 44 (1991), pp. 1–26.

[17] Ibid.

[18] For a good summary see Stephen P. Robbins and Timothy A. Judge, *Organizational Behavior*, 12th ed. (Upper Saddle River, NJ: Prentice-Hall), 2007, p. 112.

[19] Carl G. Jung, *Psychological Types*, H. G. Baynes trans. (Princeton, NJ: Princeton University Press, 1971).

[20] I. Briggs-Myers, *Introduction to Type* (Palo Alto, CA: Consulting Psychologists Press, 1980).

[21] See, for example, William L. Gardner and Mark J. Martinko, "Using the Myers-Briggs Type Indicator to Study Managers: A Literature Review and Research Agenda," *Journal of Management*, vol. 22 (1996), pp. 45–83; Naomi L. Quenk, *Essentials of Myers-Briggs Type Indicator Assessment* (New York: Wiley, 2000).

[22] See businessnewsdaily.com/3557-technology-personality-types.html.

[23] See the discussion in John R. Schermerhorn, Jr., James G. Hunt, Richard N. Osborn, and Mary Uhl-Blen, *Organizational Behavior*, 11th Edition (Hoboken, NJ: John Wiley & Sons, 2010), pp. 31–37.

[24] J. B. Rotter, "Generalized Expectancies for Internal versus External Control of Reinforcement," *Psychological Monographs*, vol. 80 (1966), pp. 1–28; see also Thomas W. Ng, Kelly L. Sorensen, and Lillian T. Eby, "Cocos of Control at Work: A Meta-Analysis," *Journal of Organizational Behavior* (2006).

[25] T. W. Adorno, E. Frenkel-Brunswick, D. J. Levinson, and R. N. Sanford, *The Authoritarian Personality* (New York: Harper-Row, 1950).

[26] Niccolo Machiavelli, *The Prince,* trans. George Bull (Middlesex, UK: Penguin, 1961).

[27] Richard Christie and Florence L. Geis, *Studies in Machiavellianism* (New York: Academic Press, 1970).

[28] See M. Snyder, *Public Appearances/Private Realities: The Psychology of Self-Monitoring* (New York: Freeman, 1987).

[29] The classic work is Meyer Friedman and Ray Roseman, *Type A Behavior and Your Heart* (New York: Knopf, 1974).

[30] Information and quote from Joann S. Lublin, "How One Black Woman Lands Her Top Jobs: Risks and Networking," *Wall Street Journal* (March 4, 2003), p. B1.

[31] Martin Fishbein and Icek Ajzen, *Belief, Attitude, Intention and Behavior: An Introduction to Theory and Research* (Reading, MA: Addison-Wesley, 1973).

[32] See Leon Festinger, *A Theory of Cognitive Dissonance* (Palo Alto, CA: Stanford University Press, 1957).

[33] Timothy A. Judge and Allan H. Church, "Job Satisfaction: Research and Practice," Chapter 7 in Cary L. Cooper and Edwin A. Locke, eds., *Industrial and Organizational Psychology: Linking Theory with Practice* (Malden, MA: Blackwell Business, 2000); and Timothy A. Judge, "Promote Job Satisfaction through Mental Challenge," Chapter 6 in Edwin A. Locke, ed., *The Blackwell Handbook of Organizational Behavior* (Malden, MA: Blackwell, 2004).

[34] See ibid; Timothy A. Judge, "Promote Job Satisfaction through Mental Challenge," Chapter 6 in Edwin A. Locke, ed., *The Blackwell Handbook of Organizational Behavior* (Malden, MA: Blackwell, 2004); "U.S. Employees More Dissatisfied with Their Jobs," *Associated Press* (February 28, 2005), retrieved from msnbc.com; "U.S. Job Satisfaction Keeps Falling, The Conference Board Reports Today," The Conference Board (February 28, 2005), retrieved from conference-board. org; "Americans' Job Satisfaction Falls to Record Low," *USA Today* (January 5, 2010), usatoday.com (accessed March 27, 2012); and Rich Morin, "Why It's Great to Be the Boss," *Pew Research Social & Demographic Trends* (January 9, 2014): pewsocialtrends.org (accessed April 3, 2014).

[35] work.com/blog/2011/03/only-45-satisfied-with-their-jobs; and Matt Sedensky, "Not Happy with Work: Wait until You're 50 or Older," *Associated Press* (October 27, 2013), suntimes.com (accessed October 28, 2013).

[36] Data reported in Jeannine Aversa, "Happy Workers Harder to Find," *Columbus Dispatch* (January 5, 2010), pp. A1, A4. Data from "U.S. Job Satisfaction the Lowest in Two Decades," press release, The Conference Board (January 5, 2010): conference-board.org (accessed January 6, 2010); "Americans' Job Satisfaction Falls to Record Lows," op. cit.

[37] Judge and Church, op. cit., 2000; Judge, op. cit., 2004.

[38] Reported in "When Loyalty Erodes, So Do Profits," *BusinessWeek* (August 13, 2001), p. 8.

[39] Data reported in "When Loyalty Erodes, So Do Profits," *BusinessWeek* (August 13, 2001), p. 8.

[40] Tony DiRomualdo, "The High Cost of Employee Disengagement" (July 7, 2004), wistechnology.com.

[41] See "The Things They Do for Love," *Harvard Business Review* (December 2004), pp. 19–20.

[42] See, for example, Joshua Brustein, "Fix this Workplace: Jim Harter, Chief Scientist, Workplace Management and Well-being, Gallup," *Bloomberg BusinessWeek* (December 18, 2013), p. 84.

[43] Information from Sue Shellenbarger, "Employers Are Finding It Doesn't Cost Much to Make a Staff Happy," *Wall Street Journal* (November 19, 1997), p. B1. See also "Job Satisfaction on the Decline," The Conference Board (July 2002).

[44] See Mark C. Bolino and William H. Turnley, "Going the Extra Mile: Cultivating and Managing Employee Citizenship Behavior," *Academy of Management Executive*, vol. 17 (August 2003), pp. 60–67.

[45] Dennis W. Organ, *Organizational Citizenship Behavior: The Good Soldier Syndrome* (Lexington, MA: Lexington Books, 1988).

[46] Christine Porath and Christine Pearson, "The Price of Incivility: Lack of Respect Hurts Morale and the Bottom Line," *Harvard Business Review*, vol. 91 (January–February, 2013), pp. 114–21.

[47] See Sandra L. Robinson and Rebecca J. Bennett, "A Typology of Deviant Workplace Behaviors: A Multidimensional Scaling Study," *Academy of Management Journal* 38 (1995), pp. 555–72; Reeshad S. Dalal, "A Meta-Analysis of the Relationship Among Organizational Citizenship Behavior and Counterproductive Work Behavior," *Journal of Applied Psychology* 90 (2005), pp. 1241–55; and HealthForceOntario, *Bullying in the Workplace: A Handbook for the Workplace* (Toronto: Ontario Safety Association for Community and Health Care, 2009).

[48] Katia Hetter, "And the Most Satisfying Airline is. . . ," *CNN* (May 15, 2013), cnn.com (accessed May 16, 2013).

[49] These relationships are discussed in Charles N. Greene, "The Satisfaction-Performance Controversy," *Business Horizons*, vol. 15 (1982), p. 31. Michelle T. Iaffaldano and Paul M. Muchinsky, "Job Satisfaction and Job Performance: A Meta-Analysis," *Psychological Bulletin*, vol. 97 (1985), pp. 251–73; Judge, op. cit., 2004; and Michael Riketta, "The Causal Relation between Job Attitudes and Performance: A Meta-Analysis of Panel Studies," *Journal of Applied Psychology*, vol. 93, no. 2 (March, 2008), pp. 472–81.

[50] This discussion follows conclusions in Judge, op. cit., 2004.

[51] Incident reported in Jon Ostrower, "Pressure Mounts on Boeing's Top Salesman," *Wall Street Journal* (October 9, 2013), p. B10.

[52] Daniel Goleman, "Leadership That Gets Results," *Harvard Business Review* (March–April 2000), pp. 78–90. See also his books *Emotional Intelligence* (New York: Bantam Books, 1995) and *Working with Emotional Intelligence* (New York: Bantam Books, 1998).

[53] Goleman, op. cit., 1998.

[54] See Robert G. Lord, Richard J. Klimoski, and Ruth Knafer (eds.), *Emotions in the Workplace; Understanding the Structure and Role of Emotions in Organizational Behavior* (San Francisco: Jossey–Bass, 2002); and Roy L. Payne and Cary L. Cooper (eds.), *Emotions at Work: Theory Research and Applications for Management* (Chichester, UK: Wiley, 2004); and Daniel Goleman and Richard Boyatzis, "Social Intelligence and the Biology of Leadership," *Harvard Business Review* (September 2008), Reprint R0809E.

[55] Joyce E. Bono and Remus Ilies, "Charisma, Positive Emotions and Mood Contagion," *Leadership Quarterly*, vol. 17 (2006), pp. 317–34; and Goleman and Boyatzis, op. cit.

[56] Bono and Ilies, op. cit.

[57] Information on the emotional contagion study and quote from Inga Kiderra, "Facebook Feelings Are Contagious, Study Shows," UC San Diego News Center (March 12, 2014), ucsdnews.ucsd.edu (accessed June 19, 2014). See also Robert Lee Hotz, "Emotions Spread Online, Study Finds," *Wall Street Journal* (March 13, 2014), p. A3; and Lorenzo Coviello, Yunkyu Sohn, Adam D. I. Kramer, Cameron Marlow, Massimo Franceschetti, Nicholas A. Christakis, James H. Fowler, "Detecting Emotional Contagion in Massive Social Networks," *PLoS One* (March 12, 2014); plosone.org (accessed June 19, 2014). *Research Ethics Note:* Research on emotional contagion using experimentally manipulated Facebook posts—see Adam D. I. Kramer, Jamie E. Guillory, and Jeffrey T. Hancock, "Experimental Evidence of Massive-scale Emotional Contagion through Social Networks," *Proceedings of the National Academy of Sciences of the United States of America*, vol. 111, no. 24 (June 2, 2014): pp. 8788–90, pnas.org (accessed July 9, 2014)—has been criticized for privacy intrusions and lack of protection of human subjects in research, Facebook's internal review process for research using its vast databases has also been criticized for inadequacy. A statement by the journal that published the Kramer, et al., research said it was "a matter of concern that the collection of the data by Facebook may have involved practices that were not fully consistent with the principles of obtaining informed consent and allowing participants to opt out." See "Science Journal says Facebook Experiment 'a Concern,'" phys.org. (July 3, 2014), phys.org/news/2014-07.

[58] See "Charm Offensive: Why America's CEOs Are So Eager to Be Loved," *BusinessWeek* (June 26, 2006), *BusinessWeek*.com (accessed September 20, 2008).

[59] See Sue Shellenbarger, "Work & Family Mailbox," *Wall Street Journal* (April 9, 2014), p. D3.

[60] See Arthur P. Brief, Randall S. Schuler, and Mary Van Sell, *Managing Job Stress* (Boston: Little, Brown, 1981), pp. 7, 8; and James Campbell Quick and Cary L. Cooper, *Stress and Strain* (Oxford: Health Press, 2003).

[61] Data from Michael Mandel, "The Real Reasons You're Working So Hard," *BusinessWeek* (October 3, 2005), pp. 60–70; "Many U.S. Employees Have Negative Attitudes to Their Jobs, Employers and Top Managers," The Harris Poll #38 (May 6, 2005), harrisinteractive.com.

[62] Data from Sue Shellenbarger, "If You Need to Work Better, Maybe Try Working Less," *Wall Street Journal* (September 23, 2009), p. D1.

[63] Sue Shellenbarger, "Do We Work More or Not? Either Way, We Feel Frazzled," *Wall Street Journal* (July 30, 1997), p. B1.

[64] Michael Mandel, "The Real Reasons You're Working So Hard," *BusinessWeek* (October 3, 2005), pp. 60–70; "Many U.S. Employees Have Negative Attitudes to Their Jobs, Employers and Top Managers," The Harris Poll #38 (May 6, 2005), harrisinteractive.com.

[65] Carol Hymowitz, "Impossible Expectations and Unfulfilling Work Stress Managers, Too," *Wall Street Journal* (January 16, 2001), p. B1.

[66] See Steve M. Jex, *Stress and Job Performance* (San Francisco: Jossey-Bass, 1998).

[67] Quick and Cooper, op cit.

[68] See Daniel C. Ganster and Larry Murphy, "Workplace Interventions to Prevent Stress-Related Illness: Lessons from Research and Practice," Chapter 2 in Cooper and Locke (eds.), op. cit., 2000; Long working hours linked to high blood pressure," Gn.com/2006/Health (accessed August 29, 2006).

[69] See "workplace violence" discussed by Richard V. Denenberg and Mark Braverman, *The Violence-Prone Workplace* (Ithaca, NY: Cornell University Press, 1999).

[70] Ganster, Danielle C., Fusilier, Marcelline R., and Bronston T. Mayes, "Role of Social Support in the Experience of Stress at Work," *Journal of Applied Psychology*, vol. 71(1986), pp. 102–10.

[71] Allison Linn, "Workaholic Americans Don't Take All their Vacation Days," cnbc.com (accessed April 3, 2014).

[72] Information and quote from Shellenbarger, op. cit., 2009.

[73] Jan de Jonge, J., Ellen Spoor, Sabine Sonnentag, Christian Dormann, and Marieke van den Tooren, "Take a Break?! Off-Job Recovery, Job Demands, and Job Resources as Predictors of Health, Active Learning, and Creativity," *European Journal of Work and Organizational Psychology*, vol. 21 (2012), pp. 321–48.

[74] From Richard D. Lennox and Raymond N. Wolfe "Revision of the Self-Monitoring Scale," *Journal of Personality and Social Psychology*, vol. 46 (1984), pp. 1349–64. Used by permission.

[75] Adapted from Roy J. Lewicki, Donald D. Bowen, Douglas T. Hall, and Francine S. Hall, "What Do You Value in Work?" *Experiences in Management and Organizational Behavior*, 3rd ed. (New York: Wiley, 1988), pp. 23–26. Used by permission.

Feature Notes

Insight: References and quotes from Ram Charan, *Know-How: The 8 Skills that Separate People Who Perform from Those That Don't* (New York: Crown Business, 2007); and Ram Charan, "Six Personality Traits of a Leader," career-advice.monster.com (accessed August 6, 2008). See also Joyce Hogan and Brent Holland, "Using Theory to Evaluate Personality and Job-performance Relations: A Socio-analytic Perspective," *Journal of Applied Psychology,* vol. 88 (2003), pp. 100–112.

Research Brief: Joseph C. Rode, Marne L. Arthaud-Day, Christine H. Mooney, Janet P. Near, Timothy T. Baldwin, William H. Bommer, and Robert S. Rubin, "Life Satisfaction and Student Performance," Academy of Management Learning & Education, vol. 4 (2005), pp. 421–33.

Wisdom: Information from Leigh Buchanan, "Life Lessons," *Inc.*, inc.com/magazine (accessed June 6, 2006). "A Fortune Coined from Cheerfulness Entrepreneurship," *Financial Times* (May 20, 2009); and lifeisgood.com/about.

Chapter 16

Endnotes

[1] Information from Melinda Beck, "If at First You Don't Succeed, You're in Excellent Company," *Wall Street Journal* (April 29, 2008), p. D1.

[2] Data from Joshua Brustein, "Fix this Workplace," *Bloomberg BusinessWeek* (December 13, 2013), p. 84; Jerry Krueger and Emily Killham, "At Work, Feeling Good Matters," *Gallup Management Journal* (December 8, 2005), gmj.gallup.com; and Ellen Wulfhorst, "Morale Is Low, Say Quarter of Employers in Poll," *Reuters Bulletin* (November 17, 2009), reuters.com; and Julie Ray, "Gallup's Top 10 World News Findings of 2013," *Gallup World* (December 27, 2013), gallup.com (accessed June 19, 2014).

[3] See Paul Glader, "Firms Move Gingerly to Remove Salary Cuts," *Wall Street Journal* (March 1, 2010), pp. B, B7.

[4] See Abraham H. Maslow, *Eupsychian Management* (Homewood, IL: Richard D. Irwin, 1965); Abraham H. Maslow, *Motivation and Personality*, 2nd ed. (New York: Harper-Row, 1970). For a research perspective, see Mahmoud A. Wahba and Lawrence G. Bridwell, "Maslow Reconsidered: A Review of Research on the Need Hierarchy," *Organizational Behavior and Human Performance*, vol. 16 (1976), pp. 212–40.

[5] See Clayton P. Alderfer, *Existence, Relatedness, and Growth* (New York: Free Press, 1972).

[6] The two-factor theory is in Frederick Herzberg, Bernard Mausner, and Barbara Block Synderman, *The Motivation to Work*, 2nd ed. (New York: Wiley, 1967); Frederick Herzberg, "One More Time: How Do You Motivate Employees?" *Harvard Business Review* (January–February 1968), pp. 53–62, and reprinted as an HBR classic (September–October 1987), pp. 109–20.

[7] Critical reviews are provided by Robert J. House and Lawrence A. Wigdor, "Herzberg's Dual-Factor Theory of Job Satisfaction and Motivation: A Review of the Evidence and a Criticism," *Personnel Psychology*, vol. 20 (Winter 1967), pp. 369–89; Steven Kerr, Anne Harlan, and Ralph Stogdill, "Preference for Motivator and Hygiene Factors in a Hypothetical Interview Situation," *Personnel Psychology*, vol. 27 (Winter 1974), pp. 109–24.

[8] Frederick Herzberg, "Workers' Needs: The Same Around the World," *Industry Week* (September 21, 1987), pp. 29–32.

[9] For a collection of McClelland's work, see David C. McClelland, *The Achieving Society* (New York: Van Nostrand, 1961); "Business Drive and National Achievement," *Harvard Business Review*, vol. 40 (July–August 1962), pp. 99–112; David C. McClelland and David H. Burnham, "Power Is the Great Motivator," *Harvard Business Review* (March–April 1976), pp. 100–10; David C. McClelland, *Human Motivation* (Glenview, IL: Scott, Foresman, 1985); David C. McClelland and Richard E. Boyatsis, "The Leadership Motive Pattern and Long-Term Success in Management," *Journal of Applied Psychology*, vol. 67 (1982), pp. 737–43.

[10] Information from money.cnn.com/2011/04/19/news/economy/ceo_pay/index.htm; aflcio.org/corporatewatch/paywatch; and "S&P 500 CEOs Make 354 Times More Than Their Average Workers: AFL-CIO," *HuffPost Business* (April 15, 2013), huffingtonpost.com (accessed June 19, 2014).

[11] See, for example, J. Stacy Adams, "Toward an Understanding of Inequity," *Journal of Abnormal and Social Psychology*, vol. 67 (1963), pp. 422–36; J. Stacy Adams, "Inequity in Social Exchange," in L. Berkowitz (ed.), *Advances in Experimental Social Psychology*, vol. 2 (New York: Academic Press, 1965), pp. 267–300.

[12] See, for example, J. W. Harder, "Play for Pay: Effects of Inequity in a Pay-for-Performance Context," *Administrative Science Quarterly*, vol. 37 (1992), pp. 321–35.

[13] L. A. Clark, D. A. Foote, W. R. Clark, and J. L. Lewis, "Equity Sensitivity: A Triadic Measure and Outcome/Input Perspectives." *Journal of Managerial Issues,* vol. 22, no. 3 (2010), pp. 286–305; R. C. Huseman, J. D. Hatfield, and E.W. Miles, "A New Perspective on Equity Theory: The Equity Sensitivity Construct," *Academy of Management Review,* vol. 12, no. 2, pp. 222–34.

[14] Victor H. Vroom, *Work and Motivation* (New York: Wiley, 1964; republished by Jossey-Bass, 1994).

[15] Ibid.

[16] Information and quotes from "The Boss: Goal by Goal," *New York Times* (August 31, 2008), p. 10.

[17] The work on goal-setting theory is well summarized in Edwin A. Locke and Gary P. Latham, *Goal Setting: A Motivational Technique That Works!* (Englewood Cliffs, NJ: Prentice Hall, 1984). See also Edwin A. Locke, Kenneth N. Shaw, Lisa A. Saari, and Gary P. Latham, "Goal Setting and Task Performance 1969–1980," *Psychological Bulletin*, vol. 90 (1981), pp. 125–52; Mark E. Tubbs, "Goal Setting: A Meta-Analytic Examination of the Empirical Evidence," *Journal of Applied Psychology*, vol. 71 (1986), pp. 474–83; Gary P. Latham and Edwin A. Locke, "Self-Regulation through Goal Setting," *Organizational Behavior and Human Decision Processes*, vol. 50 (1991), pp. 212–47; and Terence R. Mitchell, Kenneth R. Thompson, and Jane George-Falvy, "Goal Setting: Theory and Practice," Chapter 9 in Cary L. Cooper and Edwin A. Locke (eds.), *Industrial and Organizational Psychology: Linking Theory with Practice* (Malden, MA: Blackwell Business, 2000), pp. 211–49.

[18] Lisa D. Ordóñez, Maurice E. Schweitzer, Adam D. Galinsky, and Max H. Bazerman, "Goals Gone Wild: How Goals Systematically Harm Individuals and Organizations," *Academy of Management Perspectives*, vol. 23 (2009), pp. 6–16; and Edwin A. Locke and Gary P. Latham, "Has Goal Setting Gone Wild, or Have Its Attackers Abandoned Good Scholarship?" *Academy of Management Perspectives*, vol. 23 (2009), pp. 17–23.

[19] "Pressured Schedulers Masked Wait Times, According to VA Audit," *Arizona Daily Star* (May 31, 2014), p. A3; and Tom Cohen, "Audit: More Than 120,000 Veterans Waiting or Never Got Care," *CNN* (June 9, 2014), cnn.com (accessed June 10, 2014).

[20] Quotes from Cohen, op cit.

[21] Richard Simon, "Lawmakers Attack VA's 'Culture' of Bonuses," *The Columbus Dispatch* (June 21, 2014), p. A6.

[22] See David T. Welsh and Lisa D. Ordóñez, "The Dark Side of Consecutive High Performance Goals: Linking Goal Setting, Depletion, and Unethical Behavior," *Organizational Behavior and Human Decision Processes*, vol. 123 (2014), pp. 79-89; and Gary P. Latham and Gerard Seijts, "Learning Goals or Performance Goals: Is It the Journey or the Destination?" *Ivey Business Journal* (May/June, 2006), iveybusinessjournal.com (accessed June 10, 2014).

[23] Latham and Seijts, op cit.

[24] Albert Bandura, *Social Learning Theory* (Englewood Cliffs, NJ: Prentice-Hall, 1977); and Albert Bandura, *Self-Efficacy: The Exercise of Control* (New York: W. H. Freeman, 1997).

[25] Quote from des.emory.edu/mfp/self-efficacy.html.

[26] Beck, op. cit.

[27] Bandura, op. cit., 1977 and 1997.

[28] E. L. Thorndike, *Animal Intelligence* (New York: Macmillan, 1911), p. 244.

[29] See B. F. Skinner, *Walden Two* (New York: Macmillan, 1948); *Science and Human Behavior* (New York: Macmillan, 1953); *Contingencies of Reinforcement* (New York: Appleton-Century-Crofts, 1969).

[30] Fred Luthans and Robert Kreitner, *Organizational Behavior Modification* (Glenview, IL: Scott, Foresman, 1975); and Fred Luthans and Robert Kreitner, *Organizational Behavior Modification and Beyond* (Glenview, IL: Scott, Foresman, 1985); see also Fred Luthans and Alexander D. Stajkovic, "Reinforce for Performance: The Need to Go Beyond Pay and Even Rewards," *Academy of Management Executive*, vol. 13 (1999), pp. 49–57.

[31] Knowledge@Wharton, "The Importance of Being Richard Branson," Wharton School Publishing (June 3, 2005), whartonsp.com.

[32] Information and quote from Frederik Broden, "Motivate Without Spending Millions," *Fortune*, Kindle edition (April 13, 2010). See also David Novak, *The Education of an Accidental CEO: Lessons Learned from the Trailer Park to the Corner Office* (New York: Crown Business, 2007); and D. Novak, *Taking People with You: The Only Way to Make BIG Things Happen* (New York: Portfolio Penguin, 2012).

[33] See Luthans and Kreitner, op. cit.

[34] Ibid.

[35] For a review, see Arne L. Kalleberg, "The Mismatched Worker: When People Don't Fit their Jobs," *Academy of Management Perspectives* (February 2008), pp. 24–40.

[36] See Frederick W. Taylor, *The Principles of Scientific Management* (New York: W.W. Norton, 1967), originally published by Harper-Brothers in 1911; and Robert Kanigel, *The One Best Way* (New York: Viking, 1997).

[37] Greg R. Oldham and J. Richard Hackman, "Not What It Was and Not What It Will Be: The Future of Job Design Research," *Journal of Organizational Behavior*, vol. 31 (2010), pp. 463–79.

[38] See Frederick Herzberg, Bernard Mausner, and Barbara Block Synderman, *The Motivation to Work*, 2nd ed. (New York:

Wiley, 1967). The quotation is from Frederick Herzberg, "One More Time: How Do You Motivate Employees?" *Harvard Business Review* (January–February 1968), pp. 53–62, and reprinted as an HBR Classic in September–October 1987, pp. 109–20.

[39] For a complete description of the core characteristics model, see J. Richard Hackman and Greg R. Oldham, *Work Redesign* (Reading, MA: Addison-Wesley, 1980). See also, Oldham and Hackman, op. cit. (2010).

[40] See Allen R. Cohen and Herman Gadon, *Alternative Work Schedules: Integrating Individual and Organizational Needs* (Reading, MA: Addison-Wesley, 1978), p. 125; Simcha Ronen and Sophia B. Primps, "The Compressed Work Week as Organizational Change: Behavioral and Attitudinal Outcomes," *Academy of Management Review*, vol. 6 (1981), pp. 61–74.

[41] Sue Shellenbarger, "What Makes a Company a Great Place to Work," *Wall Street Journal* (October 4, 2007), p. D1.

[42] Information from Lesli Hicks, "Workers, Employers Praise Their Four-Day Workweek," *Columbus Dispatch* (August 22, 1994), p. 6; and Mary Williams Walsh, "Luring the Best in an Unsettled Time," *New York Times* (January 30, 2001), nytimes.com.

[43] For a review, see Wayne F. Cascio, "Managing a Virtual Workplace," *Academy of Management Executive*, vol. 14 (2000), pp. 81–90.

[44] Quote from Phil Porter, "Telecommuting Mom Is Part of a National Trend," *Columbus Dispatch* (November 29, 2000), pp. H1, H2.

[45] Christopher Tkaczyk, "Marissa Mayer Breaks Her Silence on Yahoo's Telecommuting Policy," tech.fortune.cnn.com/2013/04/19/marissa-mayer-telecommuting/.

[46] Kris Maher, "Slack U.S. Demand Spurs Cut in Work Hours," *Wall Street Journal* (January 8, 2008), *Career Journal*, p. 29.

[47] Quotes from Sudeep Reddy, "Wary Companies Rely on Temporary Workers," *Wall Street Journal* (March 6–7, 2010), p. A4.

[48] Michael Orey, "They're Employees, No, They're Not," *BusinessWeek* (November 16, 2009), pp. 73–74.

[49] This survey was developed from a set of "Gallup Engagement Questions" presented in John Thackray, "Feedback for Real," *Gallup Management Journal* (March 15, 2001), gmj.gallup.com (accessed June 5, 2003); data reported from James K. Harter, "The Cost of Disengaged Workers," *Gallup Poll* (March 13, 2001).

[50] Developed from Brian Dumaine, "Why Do We Work?" *Fortune* (December 26, 1994), pp. 196–204.

Feature Notes

Ethics: Information on this situation from Jared Sandberg, "Why You May Regret Looking at Papers Left on the Office Copier," *Wall Street Journal* (June 20, 2006), p. B1.

Research Brief: Jean M. Twenge, Stacy M. Campbell, Brian J. Hoffman, and Charles E. Lance, "Generational Differences in Work Values: Leisure and Extrinsic Values Increasing, Social and Intrinsic Values Decreasing," *Journal of Management*, vol. 36, no. 5 (September 2010), pp. 1117–42.

Wisdom: Information from "HopeLab Video Games for Health," Fast Company (December, 2008/ January, 2009), p. 116; "Zamzee works! Research, Iteration and Positive New Results," (September 24, 2012), blog.hopelab.org; and hopelab.org.

Chapter 17

Endnotes

[1] Chambers quote from Charles O'Reilly III and Jeffrey Pfeffer, *Hidden Value: How Great Companies Achieve Extraordinary Results through Ordinary People* (Boston: Harvard Business School Publishing, 2000), p. 4; other quotes from quotegarden.com.

[2] For a discussion, see Jon R. Katzenbach and Douglas K. Smith, *The Wisdom of Teams: Creating the High Performance Organization* (Boston: Harvard Business School Press, 1993).

[3] Lynda C. McDermott, Nolan Brawley, and William A. Waite, *World-Class Teams: Working across Borders* (New York: Wiley, 1998), p. 5; "White Collar Workers Shoulder Together—Like It or Not," *BusinessWeek* (April 28, 2008), p. 58.

[4] Katzenbach and Smith, op. cit.

[5] See, for example, Ruth Wageman, "Interdependence and Group Effectiveness," *Administrative Science Quarterly*, vol. 40 (1995), pp. 145–80; and Martin Lundin, "Explaining Cooperation: How Resource Interdependence, Goal Congruence, and Trust Affect Joint Actions In Policy Implementation," *Journal of Public Administration Research and Theory*, vol. 17, pp. 651–72.

[6] See, for example, James D. Thompson, *Organizations in Action: Social Science Bases of Administrative Theory* (New York: McGraw-Hill, 1967); Andrew H. Van de Ven and Diane L. Ferry, *Measuring and Assessing Organizations* (New York: Wiley, 1980); and Richard A. Guzzo and Gregory P. Shea, "Groups as Human Resources," pp. 323–56 in Gerald. R. Ferris and Ken M. Rowlands (eds.), *Research in Personnel and Human Resources Management*, vol. 5 (Greenwich, CT: JAI Press, 1989).

[7] See, for example, David W. Johnson, "Communication in Conflict Situations: A Critical Review of the Research," *International Journal of Group Tensions*, vol. 3 (1973), pp. 46–67; Jone L. Pearce and Hal B. Gregersen, "Task Interdependence and Extra-Role Behavior: A Test of the Mediating Effects of Felt Responsibility," *Journal of Applied Psychology*, vol. 76 (1991), pp. 838–44; Moses N. Kiggundu, "Task Interdependence and Job Design: Test of a Theory." *Organizational Behavior and Human Performance*, vol. 31 (1983), pp. 145–72; and Marvin E. Shaw, *Group Dynamics: The Psychology of Small Group Behavior* (New York: Harper, 1961).

[8] See, for example, Edward E. Lawler III, Susan Albers Mohrman, and Gerald E. Ledford, Jr., *Employee Involvement and Total Quality Management: Practices and Results in Fortune 100 Companies* (San Francisco: Jossey-Bass, 1992); and Susan A. Mohrman, Susan A. Cohen, and Monty A. Mohrman, *Designing Team-based Organizations: New Forms for Knowledge Work* (San Francisco: Jossey-Bass, 1995).

[9] Joe Lindsey, "Nine Riders, and Nearly as Many Jobs," *Wall Street Journal* (July 9, 2008), online.wsj.com.

[10] Harold J. Leavitt, "Suppose We Took Groups More Seriously," in Eugene L. Cass and Frederick G. Zimmer (eds.), *Man and Work in Society* (New York: Van Nostrand Reinhold, 1975), pp. 67–77.

[11] Shaw, op cit.; Harold J. Leavitt, "Suppose We Took Groups More Seriously," in Eugene L. Cass and Frederick G. Zimmer (eds.), *Man and Work in Society* (New York: Van Nostrand Reinhold, 1975), pp. 67–77.

[12] For insights on how to conduct effective meetings, see Mary A. De Vries, *How to Run a Meeting* (New York: Penguin, 1994).

[13] A classic work is Bib Latané, Kipling Williams, and Stephen Harkins, "Many Hands Make Light the Work: The Causes and Consequences of Social Loafing," *Journal of Personality and Social Psychology*, vol. 37 (1978), pp. 822–32.

[14] John M. George, "Extrinsic and Intrinsic Origins of Perceived Social Loafing in Organizations," *Academy of Management Journal* (March 1992), pp. 191–202; and W. Jack Duncan, "Why Some People Loaf in Groups While Others Loaf Alone," *Academy of Management Executive*, vol. 8 (1994), pp. 79–80.

[15] Survey reported in "Meetings among Top Ten Time Wasters," *San Francisco Business Times* (April 7, 2003), bizjournals.com/.

[16] Developed from Eric Matson, "The Seven Sins of Deadly Meetings," *Fast Company* (April/May 1996).

[17] The "linking pin" concept is introduced in Rensis Likert, *New Patterns of Management* (New York: McGraw-Hill, 1962).

[18] See Susan D. Van Raalte, "Preparing the Task Force to Get Good Results," *S.A.M. Advanced Management Journal*, vol. 47 (Winter 1982), pp. 11–16; Walter Kiechel III, "The Art of the Corporate Task Force," *Fortune* (January 28, 1991), pp. 104–6.

[19] Matt Golosinski, "With Teamwork, Gregg Steinhafel Hits the Bulls Eye at Target," *Kellogg* (Summer 2007), p. 32.

[20] See, for example, Paul S. Goodman, Rukmini Devadas, and Terri L. Griffith Hughson, "Groups and Productivity: Analyzing the Effectiveness of Self-Managing Teams," Chapter 11 in John R. Campbell and Richard J. Campbell (eds.), *Productivity in Organizations* (San Francisco: Jossey-Bass, 1988); Jack Orsbrun, Linda Moran, Ed Musslewhite, and John H. Zenger, with Craig Perrin, *Self-Directed Work Teams: The New American Challenge* (Homewood, IL: Business One Irwin, 1990); and Dale E. Yeatts and Cloyd Hyten, *High Performing Self-Managed Work Teams* (Thousand Oaks, CA: Sage, 1997).

[21] Greg R. Oldham and J. Richard Hackman, "Not What It Was and Not What It Will Be: The Future of Job Design Research," *Journal of Organizational Behavior*, vol. 31 (2010), pp. 463–79.

[22] See Wayne F. Cascio, "Managing a Virtual Workplace," *Academy of Management Executive*, vol. 14 (2000), pp. 81–90; Sheila Simsarian Webber, "Virtual Teams: A Meta-Analysis," shrm.org/foundation/findings.asp; Stacie A. Furst, Martha Reeves, Benson Rosen, and Richard S. Blackburn, "Managing the Life Cycle of Virtual Teams," *Academy of Management*

Executive, vol. 18 (2004), pp. 6–20; and J. Richard Hackman and Nancy Katz, "Group Behavior and Performance," Chapter 32 (pp. 1208–51) in Susan T. Fiske, Daniel T. Gilbert, and Gardner Lindzey (eds.), *Handbook of Social Psychology*, 5th ed. (Hoboken, NJ: John Wiley & Sons, 2010).

[23] R. Brent Gallupe and William H. Cooper, "Brainstorming Electronically," *Sloan Management Review* (Winter 1997), pp. 11–21.

[24] Cascio, op. cit.; Hackman and Katz, op. cit.

[25] Quote from Chris Tosic, "Tactics for Remote Teamwork," *Financial Times*, Kindle Edition (February 14, 2010).

[26] See ibid.; Cascio, op. cit.; Furst et al., op. cit.

[27] Edgar Schein, *Process Consultation* (Reading, MA: Addison-Wesley, 1988), pp. 69–75.

[28] A good overview is William D. Dyer, *Team-Building* (Reading, MA: Addison-Wesley, 1977).

[29] Toddi Gutner, "Team Building—but Fun," *Wall Street Journal* (April 28, 2014), p. R4.

[30] Dennis Berman, "Zap! Pow! Splat!" *BusinessWeek*, Enterprise issue (February 9, 1998), p. ENT22.

[31] For a discussion of effectiveness in the context of top management teams, see Edward E. Lawler III, David Finegold, and Jay A. Conger, "Corporate Boards: Developing Effectiveness at the Top," pp. 23–50 in Susan Albers Mohrman, Jay R. Galbraith, and Edward E. Lawler III, *Tomorrow's Organization: Crafting Winning Capabilities in a Dynamic World* (San Francisco: Jossey-Bass, 1998).

[32] Quote from Alex Markels, "Money & Business," *U.S. News Online* (October 22, 2006).

[33] Mathew A. Cronin, Laurie R. Weingart, and Gergana Todorova, "Dynamics in Groups: Are We There Yet?" *Academy of Management Annals*, vol. 5 (June 2011), pp. 571–612.

[34] For a review of research on group effectiveness, see J. Richard Hackman, "The Design of Work Teams," in Jay W. Lorsch (ed.), *Handbook of Organizational Behavior* (Englewood Cliffs, NJ: Prentice-Hall, 1987), pp. 315–42; and J. Richard Hackman, Ruth Wageman, Thomas M. Ruddy, and Charles L. Ray, "Team Effectiveness in Theory and Practice," Chapter 5 in Cary L. Cooper and Edwin A. Locke (eds.), *Industrial and Organizational Psychology: Linking Theory with Practice* (Malden, MA: Blackwell, 2000).

[35] Ibid.; Lawler et al., op. cit., 1998; Linda Hill and Michel J. Anteby, "Analyzing Work Groups," *Harvard Business School*, 9-407-032 (August 2007).

[36] Casey Stengel, quotegarden.com.

[37] See for example, Warren Watson. "Cultural Diversity's Impact on Interaction Process and Performance," *Academy of Management Journal*, vol. 16 (1993); Christopher Earley and Elaine Mosakowski, "Creating Hybrid Team Structures: An Empirical Test of Transnational Team Functioning," *Academy of Management Journal*, vol. 5 (February 2000), pp. 26–49; Eric Kearney, Diether Gebert, and Sven C. Voilpel, "When and How Diversity Benefits Teams: The Importance of Team Members' Need for Cognition," *Academy of Management Journal*, vol. 52 (2009), pp. 582–98; and Aparna Joshi and Hyuntak Roh, "The

Role of Context in Work Team Diversity Research: A Meta-Analytic Approach," *Academy of Management Journal,* vol. 52 (2009), pp. 599–628.

[38] Example from "Designed for Interaction," *Fortune* (January 8, 2001), p. 150.

[39] See, for example, Lynda Gratton and Tamara J. Erickson, "Eight Ways to Build Collaborative Teams," *Harvard Business Review*, Reprint R0711F (November 2007).

[40] Information from Susan Carey, "Racing to Improve," *Wall Street Journal* (March 24, 2006), pp. B1, B6.

[41] See, for example, "She Wants to Make Offices More like Jail," *Wall Street Journal* (April 2, 2014), P. B7; and George Bradt, "Why You Should Adopt Google's Nested Approach to Office Layouts," *Forbes* (June 17, 2014), forbes.com (accessed June 21, 2014).

[42] Robert D. Hof. "Amazon's Risky Bet," *BusinessWeek* (November 13, 2006), p. 52.

[43] Shaw, op. cit.; and Cronin, Weingart, and Todorova, op. cit.

[44] J. Steven Heinen and Eugene Jacobson, "A Model of Task Group Development in Complex Organizations and a Strategy of Implementation," *Academy of Management Review*, vol. 1 (1976), pp. 98–111; Bruce W. Tuckman, "Developmental Sequence in Small Groups," *Psychological Bulletin*, vol. 63 (1965), pp. 384–99; and Bruce W. Tuckman and Mary Ann C. Jensen, "Stages of Small-Group Development Revisited," *Group Organization Studies*, vol. 2 (1977), pp. 419–27.

[45] See, for example, Schein, op. cit.; and Linda C. McDermott, Nolan Brawley, and William A. Waite, *World-Class Teams: Working across Borders* (New York: Wiley, 1998).

[46] For a good discussion, see Robert F. Allen and Saul Pilnick, "Confronting the Shadow Organization: How to Detect and Defeat Negative Norms," *Organizational Dynamics* (Spring 1973), pp. 13–16.

[47] See Schein, op. cit., pp. 76–79.

[48] See Kim S. Cameron and Bradley Winn, "Virtuousness in Organizations," pp. 231–45 in Kim S. Cameron and Gretchen M. Spreitzer (eds.), *The Oxford Handbook of Positive Organizational Scholarship* (Oxford: Oxford University Press, 2012).

[49] Ibid.; Shaw, op. cit.

[50] A classic work in this area is K. Benne and P. Sheets, "Functional Roles of Group Members," *Journal of Social Issues*, vol. 2 (1948), pp. 42–47; see also Likert, op. cit., pp. 166–69; Schein, op. cit., pp. 49–56.

[51] Based on John R. Schermerhorn Jr., James G. Hunt, and Richard N. Osborn, *Organizational Behavior*, 9th ed. (New York: Wiley, 2005).

[52] Research on communication networks is found in Alex Bavelas, "Communication Patterns in Task-Oriented Groups," *Journal of the Acoustical Society of America*, vol. 22 (1950), pp. 725–30; Shaw, op. cit.

[53] See Victor H. Vroom and Arthur G. Jago, *The New Leadership: Managing Participation in Organizations* (Englewood Cliffs, NJ: Prentice-Hall, 1988); Victor H. Vroom, "A New Look in Managerial Decision-Making," *Organizational Dynamics* (Spring 1973), pp. 66–80; and Victor H. Vroom and

Phillip Yetton, *Leadership and Decision-Making* (Pittsburgh: University of Pittsburgh Press, 1973).

[54] Norman F. Maier, "Assets and Liabilities in Group Problem Solving," *Psychological Review*, vol. 74 (1967), pp. 239–49.

[55] Schein, op. cit.

[56] See Kathleen M. Eisenhardt, Jean L. Kahwajy, and L. J. Bourgeois III, "How Management Teams Can Have a Good Fight," *Harvard Business Review* (July–August 1997), pp. 77–85.

[57] Consensus box developed from a classic article by Jay Hall, "Decisions, Decisions, Decisions," *Psychology Today* (November 1971), pp. 55–56.

[58] See Maier, op. cit.

[59] See Irving L. Janis, "Groupthink," *Psychology Today* (November 1971), pp. 43–46; *Victims of Groupthink*, 2nd ed. (Boston: Houghton Mifflin, 1982).

[60] Information from Kelly K. Spors, "Productive Brainstorms Take the Right Mix of Elements," *Wall Street Journal* (July 28, 2008), wsj.online.com.

[61] André L. Delbecq, Andrew H. Van de Ven, and David H. Gustafson, *Group Techniques for Program Planning* (Homewood, IL: Scott Foresman, 1975).

[62] Developed from Lynda McDermott, Nolan Brawley, and William Waite, *World-Class Teams: Working across Borders* (New York: Wiley, 1998).

[63] Adapted from William Dyer, *Team Building*, 2nd ed. (Reading, MA: Addison-Wesley, 1987), pp. 123–25.

Feature Notes

Analysis: Survey data reported in "Two Wasted Days at Work," *CNNMoney.com* (March 16, 2005), cnnmoney.com.

Ethics: See Bib Latané, Kipling Williams, and Stephen Harkins, "Many Hands Make Light the Work: The Causes and Consequences of Social Loafing," *Journal of Personality and Social Psychology*, vol. 37 (1978), pp. 822–32; and W. Jack Duncan, "Why Some People Loaf in Groups and Others Loaf Alone," *Academy of Management Executive*, vol. 8 (1994), pp. 79–80.

Wisdom: Information and quotes from Robert D. Hof, "Amazon's Risky Bet," *BusinessWeek* (November 13, 2006), p. 52; Jon Neale, "Jeff Bezos," *Business Wings* (February 16, 2007), businesswings.com.uk; Alan Deutschman, "Inside the Mind of Jeff Bezos," *Fast Company* (December 19, 2007): fastcompany.com.

Chapter 18

Endnotes

[1] See Henry Mintzberg, *The Nature of Managerial Work* (New York: Harper & Row, 1973 and Harper-Collins, 1997); John P. Kotter, "What Effective General Managers Really Do," *Harvard Business Review,* vol. 60 (November–December 1982), pp. 156–57; and *The General Managers* (New York Macmillan, 1986).

[2] "Relationships Are the Most Powerful Form of Media," *Fast Company* (March 2001), p. 100.

[3] Jay A. Conger, *Winning 'Em Over: A New Model for Managing in the Age of Persuasion* (New York: Simon & Schuster, 1998), pp. 24–79.

[4] Ibid.

[5] *BusinessWeek* (February 10, 1992), pp. 102–8.

[6] Tom Peters and Nancy Austin, *A Passion for Excellence* (New York: Random House, 1985); and "Epigrams and Insights from the Original Modern Guru," *Financial Times,* Kindle Edition (March 4, 2010). See also Tom Peters, *The Little Big Things: 163 Ways to Pursue EXCELLENCE* (New York: HarperStudio, 2010).

[7] Quotes from Adam Auriemma, "Chiefs at Big Firms Often Last to Know," *Wall Street Journal* (April 3, 2014), pp. B1, B2.

[8] See Robert H. Lengel and Richard L. Daft, "The Selection of Communication Media as an Executive Skill," *Academy of Management Executive*, vol. 2 (August 1988), pp. 225–32.

[9] University example from Melissa Korn, "Business School Copes with Deal Backlash," *Wall Street Journal* (January 29, 2014), p. B5.

[10] Martin J. Gannon, *Paradoxes of Culture and Globalization* (Los Angeles: Sage, 2008), p. 76.

[11] David McNeill, *Hand and Mind: What Gestures Reveal about Thought* (Chicago: University of Chicago Press, 1992).

[12] Information from "How to Cope with Email Overload," *Financial Times*, Kindle Edition (February 10, 2014).

[13] Rachel Feintzeig, "A Company without Email? Not So Fast," *Wall Street Journal* (June 18, 2014), p. B7.

[14] Adapted from Richard V. Farace, Peter R. Monge, and Hamish M. Russell, *Communicating and Organizing* (Reading, MA: Addison-Wesley, 1977), pp. 97–98.

[15] Information from Carol Hymowitz, "More American Chiefs Are Taking Top Posts at Overseas Concerns," *Wall Street Journal* (October 17, 2005), p. B1.

[16] Examples reported in Martin J. Gannon, *Paradoxes of Culture and Globalization* (Los Angeles: Sage Publications, 2008), p. 80.

[17] See Edward T. Hall, *The Silent Language* (New York: Doubleday, 1973).

[18] Gannon, op. cit.

[19] Information from Ben Brown, "Atlanta Out to Mind Its Manners," *USA Today* (March 14, 1996), p. 7.

[20] Information and quotes from Adam Bryant, "Creating Trust by Destroying Hierarchy," *The Global Edition of the New York Times* (February 15, 2010), p. 19.

[21] Information and quote from Kelly K. Spors, "Top Small Workplaces 2009," *Wall Street Journal* (September 28, 2009), pp. R1–R4.

[22] See, for example, John Freeman, *The Tyranny of E-mail* (New York: Scribner, 2009).

[23] Information and quotes from Sarah E. Needleman, "Thnx for the IView! I Wud Luv to Work 4 U!!)," *Wall Street Journal Online* (July 31, 2008).

[24] For a review of legal aspects of e-mail privacy, see William P. Smith and Filiz Tabak, "Monitoring Employee E-mails: Is There Any Room for Privacy?" *Academy of Management Perspectives*, vol. 23 (November 2009), pp. 33–48.

[25] Information from American Management Association, "Electronic Monitoring & Surveillance Survey" (February 8, 2008), press.amanet.org/press-releases; and Liz Wolgemuth, "Why Web Surfing is a Nonproblem, *U.S. News & World Report* (August 22, 2008), usnews.com/blogs.

[26] "Tread: Rethinking the Workplace," *BusinessWeek* (September 25, 2006), p. IN.

[27] Stephanie Clifford, "Video Prank at Domino's Taints Brand," *New York Times* (April 16, 2009), nytimes.com; and Deborah Stead, "An Unwelcome Delivery," *BusinessWeek* (May 4, 2009), p. 15.

[28] This discussion is based on Carl R. Rogers and Richard E. Farson, "Active Listening" (Chicago: Industrial Relations Center of the University of Chicago, n.d.); see also Carl R. Rogers and Fritz J. Roethlisberger, "Barriers and Gateways to Communication," *Harvard Business Review* (November–December 2001), Reprint 91610.

[29] Ibid.

[30] A useful source of guidelines is John J. Gabarro and Linda A. Hill, "Managing Performance," Note 996022 (Boston: Harvard Business School Publishing, n.d.).

[31] Sue DeWine, *The Consultant's Craft* (Boston: Bedford/St. Martin's Press, 2001), pp. 307–14.

[32] Based on Sue Shellenbarger, "'It's Not My Fault!' Better Ways to Handle Criticism at Work," *Wall Street Journal* (June 8, 2014), pp. D1, D2.

[33] Developed from John Anderson, "Giving and Receiving Feedback," in Paul R. Lawrence, Louis B. Barnes, and Jay W. Lorsch, eds., *Organizational Behavior and Administration*, 3rd ed. (Homewood, IL: Richard D. Irwin, 1976), p. 109.

[34] A classic work on proxemics is Edward T. Hall's book, *The Hidden Dimension* (Garden City, NY: Doubleday, 1986).

[35] Information and quote from Rachel Emma Silverman, "When Water-Cooler Chats Aren't Enough," *Wall Street Journal* (May 1, 2013), p. B6.

[36] Information and quotes from Ben Kesling and James R. Hagerty, "Say Goodbye to the Office Cubicle," *Wall Street Journal* (April 3, 2013), pp. B1, 2.

[37] Richard E. Walton, *Interpersonal Peacemaking: Confrontations and Third-Party Consultation* (Reading, MA: Addison-Wesley, 1969), p. 2.

[38] See "The Managers Who Fear Conflict," *Financial Times*, Kindle Edition (June 5, 2014).

[39] Carole A. Townsley, "Resolving Conflict in Work Teams," *The Team Building Directory*, innovativeteambuilding.co.uk (accessed June 26, 2014).

[40] See Robert R. Blake and Jane Strygley Mouton, "The Fifth Achievement," *Journal of Applied Behavioral Science*, vol. 6 (1970), pp. 413–27; Alan C. Filley, *Interpersonal Conflict Resolution* (Glenview, IL: Scott, Foresman, 1975).

[41] See Kenneth W. Thomas, "Conflict and Conflict Management," in M. D. Dunnett, ed., *Handbook of Industrial and Organizational Behavior* (Chicago: Rand McNally, 1976), pp. 889–935.

[42] This and following discussion developed from Alan C. Filley, *Interpersonal Conflict Resolution* (Glenview, IL: Scott, Foresman, 1975).

[43] See also Walton, op. cit.

[44] See, for example, Robert Moskowitz, "How to Negotiate an Increase," worktree.com (retrieved March 8, 2007); Mark Gordon, "Negotiating What You're Worth," *Harvard Management Communication Letter*, vol. 2, no. 1 (Winter 2005); and Dona DeZube, "Salary Negotiation Know-How," monster.com (retrieved March 8, 2007).

[45] Portions of this treatment of negotiation originally adapted from John R. Schermerhorn, Jr., James G. Hunt, and Richard N. Osborn, *Managing Organizational Behavior*, 4th ed. (New York: Wiley, 1991), pp. 382–87. Used by permission.

[46] See Roger Fisher and William Ury, *Getting to Yes: Negotiating Agreement Without Giving In* (New York: Penguin, 1983); James A. Wall, Jr., *Negotiation: Theory and Practice* (Glenview, IL: Scott, Foresman, 1985); William L. Ury, Jeanne M. Brett, and Stephen B. Goldberg, *Getting Disputes Resolved* (San Francisco: Jossey-Bass, 1997).

[47] Fisher and Ury, op. cit.

[48] Fisher and Ury, op. cit.

[49] Developed from Max H. Bazerman, *Judgment in Managerial Decision Making*, 4th ed. (New York: Wiley, 1998), Chapter 7.

[50] Fisher and Ury, op. cit.

[51] "A Classes Grapher's Care," *Kellogg* (Summer 2006), p. 40.

[52] Roy J. Lewicki and Joseph A. Litterer, *Negotiation* (Homewood, IL: Irwin, 1985).

[53] This instrument is described in Carsten K. W. De Drew, Arne Evers, Bianca Beersma, Esther S. Kluwer, and Aukje Nauta, "A Theory-Based Measure of Conflict Management Strategies in the Workplace," *Journal of Organizational Behavior*, vol. 22 (2001), pp. 645–68. Used by permission.

[54] Feedback questionnaire is from Judith R. Gordon, *A Diagnostic Approach to Organizational Behavior*, 3rd ed. (Boston: Allyn & Bacon, 1991), p. 298. Used by permission.

Feature Notes

Analysis: Information from Joe Light, "Human-Resource Executives Say Reviews Are Off the Mark," *Wall Street Journal* (November 8, 2010), p. B8; and Rachel Emma Silverman, "Work Reviews Losing Steam," *Wall Street Journal* (December 19, 2011), p. B7.

Insight: Information from American Management Association, "The Passionate Organization Fast-Response Survey" (September 25–29, 2000) and organization website, amanct.org/aboutama/index.htm; data from "Is the Workplace Getting Raunchier?" *BusinessWeek* (March 17, 2008), p. 19; "Cultivating Personal Awareness," *BizEd* (May/June 2009), p. 26; and information from Scott Thurm, "Teamwork Raises Everyone's Game," *Wall Street Journal* (November 7, 2005), p. B7.

Research Brief: Dora C. Lau and J. Keith Murnighan, "Interactions within Groups and Subgroups: The Effects of Demographic Faultlines," *Academy of Management Journal*, vol. 48 (2005), pp. 645–59; "Demographic Diversity and Faultlines: The Compositional Dynamics of Organizational Groups," *Academy of Management Review*, vol. 23 (1998), pp. 325–40.

NAME INDEX

Organization Index

SUBJECT INDEX